A L W D

C I T A T I O N

M A N U A L

ALWD

CITATION

MANUAL

A PROFESSIONAL SYSTEM OF CITATION

Third Edition

Association of Legal Writing Directors
and
Darby Dickerson, Stetson University College of Law

ASPEN
PUBLISHERS

111 Eighth Avenue, New York, NY 10011
www.aspenpublishers.com

In memory of Appalachian School of Law's
Professor Thomas F. Blackwell,
Dean L. Anthony Sutin, and
student Angela Dales.

Aspen Publishers
Attn: Permissions
111 Eighth Avenue, 7th Floor
New York, NY 10011-5201

Printed in the United States of America

2 3 4 5 6 7 8 9 0

ISBN 0-7355-5571-0

Library of Congress Cataloging-in-Publication Data

ALWD citation manual : a professional system of citation / Association of Legal Writing Directors and Darby Dickerson. — 3rd ed.
        p. cm.
    Includes index.
    ISBN 0-7355-5571-0 (alk. paper)
    1. Citation of legal authorities—United States.   2. Annotations and citations (Law)—United States.   I. Title: Citation manual.   II. Dickerson, Darby, 1963-
    III. Association of Legal Writing Directors.

KF245.A45 2006
808'.027—dc22

                                                          2005030963

About Aspen Publishers

Aspen Publishers, headquartered in New York City, is a leading information provider for attorneys, business professionals, and law students. Written by preeminent authorities, our products consist of analytical and practical information covering both U.S. and international topics. We publish in the full range of formats, including updated manuals, books, periodicals, CDs, and online products.

Our proprietary content is complemented by 2,500 legal databases, containing over 11 million documents, available through our Loislaw division. Aspen Publishers also offers a wide range of topical legal and business databases linked to Loislaw's primary material. Our mission is to provide accurate, timely, and authoritative content in easily accessible formats, supported by unmatched customer care.

To order any Aspen Publishers title, go to *www.aspenpublishers.com* or call 1-800-638-8437.

To reinstate your manual update service, call 1-800-638-8437.

For more information on Loislaw products, go to *www.loislaw.com* or call 1-800-364-2512.

For Customer Care issues, e-mail *CustomerCare@aspenpublishers.com*; call 1-800-234-1660; or fax 1-800-901-9075.

Aspen Publishers
a Wolters Kluwer business

CONTENTS

PART 7   **APPENDICES**   **357**

ABOUT

THE AUTHORS

The Association of Legal Writing Directors is a learned society for professors who coordinate legal writing instruction in legal education. ALWD members teach at nearly all American law schools. ALWD is headquartered at the University of Michigan School of Law, 625 South State Street, Ann Arbor, MI 48109-1215.

Darby Dickerson is Vice President and Dean of Stetson University College of Law. From 1996 through 2004, she directed Stetson's Legal Research and Writing Program. She is a leading authority on American legal citation and has written in depth on the subject.

Copies of this book can be ordered from Aspen Publishers by calling 1-800-638-8437. Law school teachers should call 1-800-950-5259 for a complimentary copy.

PREFACE

The Association of Legal Writing Directors created the *ALWD Citation Manual* because lawyers, judges, law teachers, and law students need a citation manual that is easy to use, easy to teach from, and easy to learn from.

ALWD was fortunate to recruit for this purpose a leading authority on American legal citation, Dean Darby Dickerson of the Stetson University College of Law. Dean Dickerson has a thorough knowledge of the forms of legal citation used throughout the United States for the last century or more. And as a professional legal writing teacher, she writes in a style marked by clarity and conciseness.

In her work on the third edition, Dean Dickerson was guided by the same principles she was in writing the first two editions—that the *Manual* should be easy to use and have a clear style. Her work was informed by the insights of a number of people, including the ALWD Citation Manual Advisory Committee, which reviewed and offered detailed comments on the manuscript.

Every effort has gone into writing and printing the book in a format that is accessible as well as gentle on the eye. Among its attributes are flexibility where it facilitates good writing without hindering the easy identification and verification of the cited source, a single and consistent set of rules for all forms of legal writing, a set of rules that reflects a consensus in the legal profession about how citations should function, and an appendix that includes the court-mandated citation rules of every state. To keep the size of this edition manageable, some materials appear on the ALWD Web site, http://www.alwd.org. Those materials are cross-referenced in the *Manual*.

The goals for the third edition were to refine and clarify rules and to respond to users' inquiries. Below are some of the most notable changes in the third edition.

Rule 1 **(typeface)**	Information has been added in **Rule 1.1** and in **Sidebar 23.2** about how to use large and small capital letters as a typeface when submitting material to law journals and book publishers that require that typeface.

Rule 2 **(abbreviations)**	**Rule 2.3** now permits abbreviation of "U.S." in case citations that appear in textual sentences (**Rule 12.2(e)** was also revised to acknowledge this change).
Rule 3 **(capitalization)**	**Sidebar 3.1** provides a list of prepositions commonly used in titles. New **Rule 3.4** addresses capitalization rules for titles in French, German, and Spanish.
Rule 6 **(sections and** **paragraphs)**	An addition explains how to prevent confusion when citing both page numbers and section and paragraph numbers.
Rule 7 **(footnotes and** **endnotes)**	New **Rule 7.2** provides guidance about how to prevent confusion when citing both page numbers and footnote or endnote numbers. New **Rule 7.3** provides additional guidance about how to cite footnotes and endnotes when using the *id.* short citation format.
Rule 8 **(supplements)**	New **Rule 8.4** addresses citing material that appears in multiple supplements.
Rule 9 **(other** **subdivisions)**	An addition explains how to prevent confusion when citing both page numbers and other subdivisions, such as appendices and tables.
Rule 11 **(short citations)**	This rule has been clarified to explain when the term "at" is used in short citation formats.
Rule 12 **(cases)**	Additional guidance has been provided about how to cite bankruptcy cases. In addition, new sections of **Rule 12.2** explain how to cite popular case names and how to present cases with multiple decisions. **Rule 12.4** regarding which reporter or reporters to cite has been rewritten to clarify the rules presented in the first and second editions.
Rule 14 **(statutes)**	This rule now provides that titles of statutes should be presented in ordinary type, not italics. Although the *Manual* attempted to achieve uniformity by indicating that all titles should be presented in italics, it simply has not become common practice to italicize the titles of statutes and statute-like material; thus, we opted to reflect the format used by most practicing attorneys. In addition, **Sidebar 14.2** now indicates that the abbreviation "U.S.C." may be used in textual sentences. Finally, throughout the *Manual*, the term "LEXIS," when used to denote the publisher now known as LexisNexis, has been changed to "Lexis."

Rule 19 (federal administrative and executive materials)	Revised **Rule 19** provides additional guidance about how to cite Code of Federal Regulations sections that appear in electronic databases. It also clarifies how to cite proposed federal regulations. New **Rule 19.13** shows how to cite patents.
Rule 21 (citing sources)	**Rule 21** has been expanded to include rudimentary information about citing basic international, foreign, and intergovernmental sources.
Rule 22 (books and treatises)	New information was added about how to cite books with multiple publishers and books in a language other than English. Information and examples also have been provided about how to cite the Koran and the Talmud.
Rule 23 (periodicals)	New sections have been added about how to cite letters to the editor, cartoons and comic strips, and advertisements. **Rule 23** also now provides specific guidance about whether to italicize the comma when a title ends with quotation marks.
Rule 24 (A.L.R.)	New examples show the format for A.L.R.6th and A.L.R. Fed. 2d.
Rule 37 (unpublished material)	New **Rule 37.3** explains how to cite working papers, including material that appears on SSRN.
Rule 40 (World Wide Web)	New **Rule 40.3** explains how to cite weblogs.
Rule 44 (signals)	A clarification in **Rule 44.4** and **Rule 46.1** indicates that explanatory parentheticals should be used to assist readers and need not be included any time a signal is used.
Rule 45 (order of citation)	The list now includes foreign, international, and intergovernmental organizations, and clarifies where material from electronic sources should be inserted.
Rule 48 (altering quoted material)	New **Rule 48.3** addresses the relatively rare situation when an author needs to insert a footnote into the middle of a block quotation.
Appendices	All appendices now appear in the book. In both the first and second editions, portions of **Appendices 1, 2, 4,** and **5** appeared only on the ALWD Web site, and **Appendices 1A** and **8** appeared only on the Web site. **Appendix 2** now includes lists of subject matter abbreviations that can be used when preparing material for California and New York

courts and practitioners. In addition, country and region abbreviations have been added to **Appendix 3.**

In addition, the index has been expanded and examples throughout the *Manual* have been updated.

We appreciate input that will help us with the ongoing process of making the *Manual* as complete, accurate, and user-friendly as possible. If you find any errors or omissions in this *Manual*, or if you have suggested revisions, please notify Darby Dickerson at darby@law.stetson.edu, or at 1401 61st Street South, Gulfport, FL 33707.

The Association of Legal Writing Directors
November 2005

ACKNOWLEDGMENTS TO THE FIRST EDITION

I would like to thank and recognize the following people and organizations without whom the *ALWD Citation Manual* would not have become a reality:

The Association of Legal Writing Directors (ALWD), whose officers and directors conceived the idea of a new citation system and provided guidance and support throughout the process.

Members of the ALWD Citation Manual Advisory Committee who reviewed draft manuscripts and provided valuable input, support, and suggestions: Coleen Barger, Mary Beth Beazley, Maria Ciampi, Eric B. Easton, Ruth Ann McKinney, Craig T. Smith, Kathleen Elliott Vinson, Marilyn R. Walter, and Ursula H. Weigold.

Special thanks to the co-chairs of the ALWD Citation Manual Advisory Committee, Steven D. Jamar and Amy E. Sloan, to Richard K. Neumann, Jr., who served as a liaison between ALWD and the publisher and provided invaluable assistance and advice from the beginning of the project through the end, and to Jan Levine, who conceived the idea of the *Manual* and supported and contributed to it throughout the process.

The four presidents of ALWD who served during the pendency of this project and who helped facilitate its completion: Jan Levine, Katie McManus, Maureen Straub Kordesh, and Sue Liemer.

The other ALWD officers, including Molly Warner Lien, who supported and nurtured the project.

Henry T. Wihnyk: for participating in the initial stages of the project.

Joe Kimble and Christy B. Nisbett for providing insightful and detailed comments on a prior draft of the *Manual.*

The anonymous reviewers who provided helpful critiques of earlier drafts of the *Manual.*

The administration and faculty of Stetson University College of Law for providing generous financial support and ongoing encouragement for the project.

Professor Peter L. Fitzgerald for sharing his knowledge about international treaties and Internet sources.

The Stetson University College of Law Reference Librarians—Pamela Burdett, Dorothy Clark, Michael Dahn, Earlene Kuester, Madison Mosley, and Sally

Waters—for locating difficult-to-find material, processing many interlibrary loan requests, and serving as excellent sources of bibliographic information.

The Stetson University College of Law Faculty Support Services Department, headed by Connie P. Evans, for superb clerical services and moral support.

The following Stetson University College of Law students who provided top-notch research assistance: Robert Taylor Bowling, Christopher H. Burrows, Victoria L. Cecil, David F. Chalela, Julianne J. Flynn, Darren D. McClain, Ashkan Najafi, Nicole D. Quinn, Tyra Nicole Read, Jeffrey P. Rosato, and Debra A. Tuomey. Students Victoria J. Avalon, Danielle M. Bonett, Pamela H. Cazares, and Kevin M. Iurato deserve special recognition for their painstaking and detail-oriented work on several appendices and other portions of the *Manual*.

Aspen Law & Business for recognizing the value of this project and enhancing the quality of the manuscript. Within Aspen, I would like to specifically recognize Dan Mangan, Melody Davies, Ellen Greenblatt, Carol McGeehan, and Linda Richmond for their creativity, persistence, and hard work.

Finally, a special thanks to my husband, Michael P. Capozzi, for understanding why I have not been around much during the last year.

Darby Dickerson
Associate Dean, Professor of Law, and
Director, Legal Research and Writing
Stetson University College of Law
St. Petersburg, Florida

April 2000

ACKNOWLEDGMENTS TO THE SECOND EDITION

As with many projects, there are so many people to thank and such little space in which to express that thanks. Over the years, many individuals and organizations have contributed to the production and success of the *ALWD Citation Manual*. In addition to those recognized in the *Manual*'s first edition, I would like to thank the following for their assistance with the second edition:

The Association of Legal Writing Directors (ALWD), and its officers, directors, and members, who have supported this project from the beginning.

Specifically, I would like to thank the following ALWD presidents who have served since the first edition was published and while the second edition was being prepared: Sue Liemer, Pamela Lysaght, Nancy Schultz, and Amy Sloan.

The members of the *ALWD Citation Manual* Advisory Committee for the Second Edition, who provided invaluable input and guidance: Tracy L. Bach, Coleen Barger, Jan Levine, Tracy McGaugh, Judith Rosenbaum, Arnold I. Siegel, and Grace Tonner.

Richard K. Neumann, Jr. and Jan Levine, who conceived the idea of the *Manual* and have provided input, suggestions, and support since that time.

Members of the *ALWD Citation Manual* Adoption Committee for their work in spreading the word about the *Manual*. Special thanks goes to co-chairs Coleen Barger, Wayne Schiess, and Hether Macfarlane.

My former student and now colleague Brooke J. Bowman for her assistance with so many of the painstaking details.

The following current and former Stetson University College of Law students who provided excellent research assistance: Irene Bosco, Tracy Carpenter, Catherine Shannon Christie, Tanya Dentamaro, Dale Goerne (tax appendix), Moein Marashi, Susan St. John, Bridget Remington, and Natsha Wolfe.

Stetson University College of Law, for continued support and resources.

The anonymous reviewers of the new tax appendix.

The many law librarians and state reporters of decisions who took time to complete surveys regarding the *Manual*.

The many users who took the time to write with comments and changes. A special thanks goes to C. Edward Good for his comments.

The many research and writing professionals who took the time to write reviews of the first edition.

Aspen Publishers, for helping in so many ways to make the *Manual* a success. I would like to extend special thanks to Dan Mangan, Melody Davies, Carol McGeehan, Michael Gregory, Barbara Lasoff, and Paul Sobel for their hard work on this project.

Despite all of the help, all errors remain my own.

Darby Dickerson
Stetson University College of Law
Tampa Bay, Florida

November 2002

ACKNOWLEDGMENTS TO THE THIRD EDITION

To be a success, a project the magnitude of the *ALWD Citation Manual* requires the expertise and assistance of many people. As with the first two editions, I have many people to thank for helping to bring the third edition to fruition, including the following:

The Association of Legal Writing Directors (ALWD) and its officers, directors, and members for continuing to support this project.

The ALWD presidents who have served and supported the *Manual* since the second edition was printed: Jo Anne Durako, Brad Clary, and Kristin Gerdy.

The members of the *ALWD Citation Manual* Advisory Committee, who provided outstanding advice and guidance: Pam Armstrong, Brooke J. Bowman, Pamela Lysaght, Tracy McGaugh, Amy E. Sloan, Tracy Weissman, and Melissa H. Weresh.

The members of the *ALWD Citation Manual* Adoptions Committee who have generated many creative ideas over the years. A special thanks goes to Hether Macfarlane, who has chaired that committee for many years.

Molly Lien, for providing material on foreign and international citations for Rule 21.

My Stetson colleague Brooke J. Bowman, who helped to update several rules and appendices, and was a source of constant support and encouragement during this project.

My assistants Roxane Latoza and Vicky Baumann, for managing the office while I was locked away preparing this edition.

Stetson law students Paula Bentley, Sarah Lahlou-Amine, and Josephine Thomas for their assistance in updating rules and examples.

The Stetson reference librarians, and particularly Sally G. Waters, who helped to locate sources and materials for this edition.

Members and editors of the *Stetson Law Review* for passing along suggestions to help improve the *Manual.*

Stetson University and Stetson University College of Law for continued support and resources.

The many users who took the time to write with questions, ideas, and suggestions.

The research and writing professionals who took the time to write reviews of the first and second editions, and who showed confidence in the *Manual* by adopting it in their classes.

Aspen Publishers, for its continued efforts to make the *Manual* a success. I would like to extend special thanks to Carol McGeehan, Melody Davies, Barbara Lasoff, Laurel Ibey, Michael Gregory, and George Serafin for their help over the years and for their hard work on the third edition.

And, as usual, despite all of the help, all errors remain my own.

Darby Dickerson
Stetson University College of Law
Tampa Bay, Florida

November 2005

PART

INTRODUCTORY

MATERIAL

A   PURPOSE AND USE OF CITATIONS

In legal writing, a "citation" is a reference to a specific legal authority or other source. A legal citation contains various words, abbreviations, and numbers presented in a specific format that allows a reader to locate the cited material. The typical information in a citation includes the cited material's author, the name of the authority or source, information about where the pertinent information can be found within the source (such as a volume or page number), the publisher, and the date. **Rules 1** through **37** of this Manual explain and illustrate how to present this information for both primary and secondary authorities.

Legal citations serve many purposes. First, a citation should tell readers **where to find** the cited source. Readers often want to review the cited source, either to verify what the source says or to learn additional details from the source. Therefore, it is important that the citation provide all the information necessary to locate both the source and the exact reference. For this reason, each citation must be accurate.

Second, from reading the citation, readers should be able to determine information about the **weight and persuasiveness of that source.** For example, when reading a case citation in a brief, readers should be able to determine whether the court must follow this case. Readers also should be able to make other judgments about the cited authority, such as who the author is, the level of court deciding a specific case, how old the authority is, and whether the authority is still good law.

Third, a citation should convey the **type and degree of support** that it provides for a particular proposition. For example, one case might provide strong, direct support for a proposition, while another authority might contradict your statement. Readers should be able to discern this information from the citation, typically through the use of introductory signals (addressed in **Rule 44**).

In addition, attorneys use citations to **demonstrate that their positions are well researched and well supported.** Nearly all legal research is based on prior research. Readers expect to see that you have thoroughly researched a proposition and that you have referred to authorities that support your proposition. Citations allow you to document such research and support. On a related note, citations **give credit** to those who originated an idea that you are now presenting. Giving proper attribution to those whose thoughts, words, and ideas you use is an important concept in legal writing and legal citation.

B How to Use This Book

This book contains a single citation system that can be used to develop citations for any type of legal document. The book codifies the most commonly followed rules for legal citation. While no citation system can anticipate every source a writer might need or choose to cite, the system presented here provides rules and examples for the most frequently cited materials and guidelines for citing new or rarely encountered materials.

This book focuses primarily on sources of United States law and provides limited guidance regarding international and foreign sources, except for treaties binding on the United States. If you need to cite a legal source from a foreign country, consult ALWD & Molly Lien, *ALWD Citation Manual: International Sources* (Aspen Publishers forthcoming).

Overall Organization

This book is organized into seven parts:

(1) Part 1 contains introductory material, including information on local citation formats and on how your word processor may affect citations you write.

(2) Part 2, "Citation Basics," addresses key concepts you will use when citing most types of legal sources. You should read Part 2 before attempting to cite any particular source.

(3) Part 3 provides citation formats for print (as opposed to electronic) versions of various primary and secondary sources. Use these rules to determine how to cite a specific source, such as a case or legal periodical.

(4) Part 4 addresses electronic materials, including sources available on Lexis, Westlaw, and the Internet.

(5) Part 5, "Incorporating Citations into Documents," explains how to insert citations into various documents, such as memoranda or law review articles. It also addresses other important concepts you need to know when writing documents that contain legal citations, such as when and how to use introductory signals and how to use explanatory parentheticals.

(6) Part 6 discusses how to quote material and how to properly reflect alterations to and omissions from quoted material.

(7) Part 7 consists of various appendices, including one on court-specific formats and another that lists commonly used abbreviations. In addition, a full-text sample of a legal memorandum demonstrates how to insert citations into such documents.

Organization within Each Part of This Book

Each part of this book is further divided into rules, which may, in turn, have several subsections. Each rule provides detailed instructions about citing a particular source or using a particular concept. Examples illustrate key points and exceptions to general rules.

Rules about citing a particular source, such as a case, begin by identifying the components of the full citation, such as the case name and the date. The different components are separated by green circles (●). *A green circle (●) does not designate a space.* Instead, green triangles (▲) are used throughout to designate spaces. Green circles show where different components of a citation end. A component includes a comma that would not appear in a citation if the rest of that component were missing (for example, the comma before a pinpoint page). Those components that should be italicized appear in italics; those that should be enclosed in parentheses appear in parentheses. An example immediately follows the presentation of the components. The parts of the example are labeled with the corresponding component terms. The example below comes from **Rule 12** on cases.

Case name,● Reporter volume● Reporter abbreviation● Initial page● , Pinpoint page● (Court abbreviation● Date),● *Subsequent history designation,*● Subsequent history citation.

Example

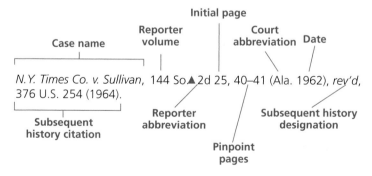

After the initial example, each component of the full citation is explained in detail, and additional examples are provided.

Rules 12 through **37** and **Rules 39** through **42** each begin with a section called "Fast Formats," which provides sample citations for the commonly cited materials within that category. Use these formats to check your own citations or to refresh your memory when you have not used a particular rule in some time.

Finally, throughout the book, you will encounter "Sidebars" presented on a gray background. These provide additional information on various concepts, caveats about common mistakes, and tips for citing particular sources.

Finding Tools

To understand the book's overall organization and to quickly locate rules on the major sources of law, use the table of contents in the front of the book. To find the rule covering a specific source or concept, use the detailed index in the back.

Caveats

You may read citations in other sources that are inconsistent with ALWD citation rules. For example, West Group and other legal publishers often follow their own unique citation formats. In addition, as noted below in section C, many courts have special citation rules that attorneys must follow when submitting documents to those courts. Finally, for many years, the most commonly used citation guide was *The Bluebook: A Uniform System of Citation.* When you find nonconforming citations, put them in ALWD citation format. The one exception to this rule applies when submitting a brief to a court that has its own local citation format (see listings in **Appendix 2**): Always follow a court's own citation rules, if any, when submitting a document to that court.

Footnotes Versus Endnotes

This book covers material contained in a document's footnotes. (An example of a document with footnotes is a law review article.) Although the word "footnote" is used in this book, the rules also apply to endnotes.

Footnotes and endnotes serve the same purpose: Both contain citations or additional text that supports, contradicts, or further explains material in the main text. The difference is in the location of the notes in relation to the main text. When notes appear at the bottom—or foot—of the page with the corresponding main text, they are called footnotes. When notes appear at the end of the paper or at the end of a chapter or section, they are called endnotes. Again, the same citation rules apply to both footnotes and endnotes.

Citing Sources Not Covered in This Book

Think of this book as a statute. In the absence of a rule exactly on point, use the most analogous rule. Remember, the primary goal of legal citation is to lead the interested reader to the cited source. By analogizing to the most similar format in the book, you stand the best chance of providing your readers with the information they need to find the source. Essential information about a source typically includes the name of its author, its title, the relevant page or other subdivision, its publisher, and its date of publication. For cases, also include the issuing court and any subsequent history. Do not spend hours agonizing over how to cite the source. Select a logical format and be consistent. Consistency is as important for clarity as is following a particular rule.

Sources for Additional Information

For additional guidance on matters of style, punctuation, capitalization, and special citation formats, consult the most recent editions of the *United States Government Printing Office Style Manual, The Chicago Manual of Style,* the *ALWD Citation Manual: International Sources* (forthcoming), or Bryan A. Garner, *The Redbook: A Manual on Legal Style.*

Citing This Book

Cite this book as ALWD & Darby Dickerson, *ALWD Citation Manual* (3d ed., Aspen Publishers 2006).

Web Site for Updates and Frequently Asked Questions

The rules in this book will not be changed arbitrarily. However, because types and formats of legal sources constantly evolve—and because no work is perfect—some clarifications, updates, and additions will be inevitable. To keep this edition current, any such changes will be posted on a Web site located at www.alwd.org. The information on this Web site is available for browsing and downloading at no charge.

C   LOCAL CITATION RULES

Many state and federal courts have adopted local citation rules that practitioners **must** follow when submitting documents to those courts. Therefore, if you are writing a court document, such as a brief, consult the entry in **Appendix 2** for your particular jurisdiction. If a particular source is not covered in **Appendix 2**, use the rules and formats in other sections of this book. If your court is included in **Appendix 2**, also check the current court rule or statute in a rule book or statutory code because rules and statutes change more frequently than this manual is updated. When using **Appendix 2**, you should consult only the entries for the court to which you are submitting the document; you will not use other courts' special citation formats.

Law students and new practitioners should be aware that local custom sometimes dictates that local rules also be used in other documents within that jurisdiction, such as interoffice memoranda. Determine whether such preferences apply before preparing documents containing citations. Some local customs—but not all—are included in **Appendix 2.**

For all other documents and purposes, use the rules in **Parts** 2 through 7 (other than **Appendix 2**).

D | HOW YOUR WORD PROCESSOR MAY AFFECT CITATIONS

How you format your word processor may affect the way citations look on the page. Below are some issues you should consider before preparing a document that contains citations.

Margin Justification

The "justification" function on your word processor will affect whether text at your left and right margins appears "straight" or "ragged." The justification choices typically are "full," "centered," "right-only," and "left-only." Full justification produces straight edges at both side margins. Centered justification produces ragged edges at both side margins. Right-only justification produces a straight right margin and a ragged left margin. Left-only justification produces the opposite: a straight left margin and a ragged right margin. The only two options appropriate for a legal paper are full justification and left-only justification. Below are examples of these two options.

Examples

Full justification

The cooperation requirement does allow for a "good cause" exception to cooperation, if it is determined to be in the best interests of the child. 42 U.S.C. § 654(4)(a)(1) (2000). The good cause exception works better in theory than in practice, however, as documentation of prior domestic violence, not a well-founded fear of future violence, is required. Jacqueline M. Fontana, *Cooperation and Good Cause: Greater Sanctions and the Failure to Account for Domestic Violence*, 15 Wis. Women's L.J. 367, 383 (2000).

Left-only justification

The cooperation requirement does allow for a "good cause" exception to cooperation, if it is determined to be in the best interests of the child. 42 U.S.C. § 654(4)(a)(1)

(2000). The good cause exception works better in theory than in practice, however, as documentation of prior domestic violence, not a well-founded fear of future violence, is required. Jacqueline M. Fontana, *Cooperation and Good Cause: Greater Sanctions and the Failure to Account for Domestic Violence*, 15 Wis. Women's L.J. 367, 383 (2000).

The margin justification you select for your document may affect the spacing within citations. To avoid a possible spacing problem, first determine whether your word-processing program distorts spacing when you justify the margins on both sides of the page (called "full justification" in most programs). If the program does not distort spacing, use full justification because it creates a more professional look.

If the program does distort spacing, consider whether readers will prefer a fully justified page, with whatever spacing distortion your software creates, or a page that is justified only on the left margin, with undistorted citation spacing. The trade-off for perfect spacing in a left-justified document is that left-only justification leaves the right edge of the text ragged.

When deciding which justification setting to use, consider the sensibilities of your readers. If you are submitting an article for publication in a law review, you might opt for perfect spacing because law review editors care a great deal about perfect citation format. If you are submitting a brief to a court or a memo to a senior partner, you might opt for full justification because judges and partners often appreciate an eye-friendly page.

Default Settings and Quick Correct Features

Some word-processing programs come preloaded with default features that may affect citations. Below are some settings about which you should be aware.

Periods and automatic spacing

The default settings in some word-processing programs automatically place one or two spaces after each period, regardless of whether the period ends the sentence. Such formatting does not conform to the citation rules in this book. Accordingly, reformat your word processor so that it does not automatically insert spaces after each period. In current word-processing programs, you can correct this problem by pulling down the "Tools" menu bar and then selecting an item called "QuickCorrect" in WordPerfect or "AutoCorrect" in Word.

Example of problem: N. E. 2d
Correct citation: N.E.2d

Automatic capitalization

Some word-processing programs default to a setting that automatically capitalizes the first letter after a period. This setting can also cause problems. In current word-processing programs, you can correct this problem by pulling down the "Tools" menu bar and then selecting an item called "QuickCorrect" in WordPerfect or "AutoCorrect" in Word.

Example of problem: *Johnson Steel Corp. V. Smith,*
Correct citation: *Johnson Steel Corp. v. Smith,*

Automatic ordinal superscript

As explained in **Rule 4.3,** ordinals are numbers that denote a series. "First," "second," and "third" are ordinals. In legal citation, ordinal contractions, such as 1st, 4th, and 5th, are used quite frequently. Some word-processing programs automatically place the letter portion of the ordinal contraction in superscript, above other text. While this is not a serious problem and superscripted ordinals are not prohibited by this citation manual, superscripted ordinals will look incorrect to many readers. Also, some readers will be distracted if some ordinals are presented in superscript and others are not. Thus, the best policy is to disable this default setting by consulting the "Tools" menu bar, as described above.

Example of problem: (5th Cir. 2003)
Preferred citation: (5th Cir. 2003)

Automatic replacement of words and symbols

Some word-processing programs will automatically change one word, term, or symbol into another. In legal citation, the most problematic changes are those converting (c) to © and (r) to ®. Again, you can avoid this problem by disabling the default setting by consulting the "Tools" menu bar, as described above.

Example of problem: Rule 26©
Correct citation: Rule 26(c)

Automatic hyperlinks

Some word-processing programs automatically insert a hyperlink when you type a URL (Uniform Resource Locator, which is an Internet "address"). The hyperlink typically appears as an underline; in addition, the entire address is presented in a color, such as blue. Although having hyperlinks in a document can be helpful, in some types of legal writing, such as in law review articles, they are not necessary and should be removed. To remove hyperlinks, you may either delete them as you type or disable the default setting that inserts them automatically. Consult the "Tools" menu bar to disable the function.

Example of problem: http://www.findlaw.com
Preferred citation: http://www.findlaw.com

CITATION BASICS

1.0   **TYPEFACE FOR CITATIONS**

1.1   **Typeface Choices**

Most material in legal citations should be presented in ordinary type. Another type convention, *italics*, is used for specific elements of citations (**Rule 1.3**). Italics may be represented with *slanted type* or with <u>underlining</u>.

Once you decide how to present italicized material, use that choice consistently. Do not use italics for some types of material and underline other types of material.

If you choose to denote italics by using an underline, underline spaces within a component, but do not underline spaces between components of the citation. Note that while periods typically are parts of the component (and usually are underlined), commas typically are not parts of the component (and usually are not underlined).

Please note that some law journals and book publishers that do not follow the *ALWD Citation Manual* strictly also use a third typeface convention, LARGE AND SMALL CAPITAL LETTERS. If you are working with a journal or publisher that requires you to use this convention, please consult **Sidebar 23.2** for explanations and examples.

Examples (using an underline to reflect italics)

<u>Hofstee v. Dow</u>, 36 P.3d 1073, 1076 (Wash. App. Div. 3 2001).

<u>See</u> <u>Warrick v. Cheatham County Hwy. Dept.</u>, 60 S.W.3d 815, 819 (Tenn. 2001).

<u>See e.g.</u> <u>Warrick v. Cheatham County Hwy. Dept.</u>, 60 S.W.3d 815, 819 (Tenn. 2001).

Incorrect: <u>See Warrick v. Cheatham County Hwy. Dept.,</u>
(The space between "See" and the case name should not be underlined and the comma at the end should not be underlined)

See <u>Warrick v. Cheatham County Hwy. Dept.,</u>
(Do not mix italics and underlining within a paper)

1.2   **When to Use Ordinary Type in Citations**

Ordinary type consists of uppercase and lowercase letters without any enhancement. Use ordinary type for everything not listed in **Rule 1.3**.

1.3   **When to Use Italics in Citations**

Italicize only the following material:

(1)   Introductory signals (such as *see*; **Rule 44**).

(2)   Internal cross-references (such as *supra* and *infra*; **Rule 10**).

(3)   Case names (in both full citation format and short citation format; **Rules 12.2(a)** and **12.21**).

(4) Phrases indicating subsequent or prior history (such as *aff'd*; **Rules 12.8** and **12.9**).

(5) Titles of most documents (for example, **Rules 15.7(c)**, **22.1(b)**, and **23.1(b)**).

(6) Topics or titles in legal encyclopedia entries (**Rule 26.1(c)**).

(7) Names of Internet sites (**Rule 40.1(b)**).

(8) The short forms *id.* and *supra* (**Rule 11**).

1.4   Typeface for Punctuation in Citations

Italicize punctuation when it is located within other italicized material in the citation. Do not italicize a comma that follows a case name, title, or other italicized material. The same rule holds true if you use underlining to represent italics. Underline punctuation located within other underlined material, but do not underline a comma that follows a case name, title, or other underlined material (N.Y. Times Co. v. Sullivan,). The sample memorandum in **Appendix 6** uses underlining.

Examples (italicized and underlined periods appear in bold green and are circled)

Landgraf v. USI Film Prods., 968 F.2d 427 (5th Cir. 1992), *aff'd*, 511 U.S. 244 (1994).

See id⊙

See id⊙

1.5   Possessive Endings of Italicized Material

Do not italicize or underline the possessive ending of a publication name, case name, or other similar italicized or underlined material.

Examples

Smith's impact on how police officers conduct automobile searches will be significant.

In 2001, Ralph J. Rohner wrote an essay celebrating the *Catholic University Law Review*'s fiftieth anniversary.

1.6   Italicized Material within Italicized Material

When words or phrases within italicized or underlined material would themselves have been italicized or underlined under another rule in this *Manual*, such as a case name in a book title, change those words or phrases to ordinary type.

Examples

Aaron Ponzo, Student Author, *Title II of the Americans with Disabilities Act Is a Valid Exercise of Congress' Power to Abrogate State Sovereign Immunity:* Tennessee v. Lane, 43 Duq. L. Rev. 317 (2005).

Robert Batey, *Kenneth Starr—Among Others—Should Have (Re)Read* Measure for Measure, 26 Okla. City U. L. Rev. 261, 298 (2001).

1.7 Italics to Show Emphasis

It is permissible to use italics or underlining to show emphasis; however, this stylistic convention should not be overused.

Example

J.K. Corporation will suffer *substantial* harm if the injunction is not granted.

1.8 Italicizing Foreign Words

It is permissible to italicize or underline foreign words that have not been incorporated into normal English. Below is a short list of commonly used foreign words and abbreviations that have been incorporated into normal English and thus should **not** be italicized or underlined in writing unless they appear as part of a citation that requires italics or underlining, such as the title of a law review article or case name (**Rule 1.3**). To determine whether to italicize or underline other words, consult the most current version of *Black's Law Dictionary*.

Selected words that ordinarily should not be italicized in legal writing

ad hoc	habeas corpus
amicus curiae	i.e.,
certiorari	in personam
de facto	in rem
de jure	inter alia
de novo	passim
dicta, dictum	prima facie
e.g.,	quantum meruit
en banc	quid pro quo
et al.	res gestae
et seq.	res ipsa loquitur
etc.	res judicata

2.0 | **ABBREVIATIONS**

2.1 Use

2.1(a)

Abbreviations are used in legal citations for common sources, such as legal periodicals, case names, and court names, and for some other less common items that are identified throughout this book. Tables of standard abbreviations are included in **Appendices 3, 4,** and **5.** Do not abbreviate words not listed in this book, unless required by local court rule.

2.1(b)

On occasion, the same abbreviation may be used for different words. For example, "J." sometimes stands for "Journal," "Judge," or "Justice," depending on the context.

2.2 Spacing for Abbreviations

2.2(a)

Generally do not insert a space between consecutive single capital letters. However, you may insert a space between consecutive capital letters if the space would help avoid confusion. For example, if one party in a case is Northern Railroad, you may use N.▲R.R. instead of N.R.R. to avoid confusion.

2.2(b)

When abbreviating the name of a legal periodical, set the institutional or geographic abbreviation off from other parts of the abbreviation. Thus, insert one space before and after a group of consecutive capital letters that denotes a geographic or institutional entity.

2.2(c)

Insert one space between any two abbreviations when **either** is not a single capital letter.

2.2(d)

When an abbreviated word is combined with a word that is not abbreviated, insert one space on each side of the word that is not abbreviated.

2.2(e)

For purposes of this rule, treat an ordinal contraction, such as 2d or 5th, as a single capital letter. Ordinals are defined and discussed in **Rule 4.3**.

2.2(f)

For purposes of this rule, do not treat a section symbol (§), paragraph symbol (¶), or ampersand (&) as a single capital letter; always place one space on each side of these symbols.

Examples (spaces are denoted by ▲)

Abbreviation	Explanation
S.D.N.Y.	The abbreviation consists of four consecutive single capital letters. Thus, do not insert any spaces. (**Rule 2.2(a)**)
N.E.2d	The abbreviation consists of two consecutive single capital letters and an ordinal, which is treated like a single capital letter. Thus, do not insert any spaces. (**Rules 2.2(a)** and **2.2(e)**)
B.U.▲L.▲Rev.	Do not insert a space between "B." and "U." because they are consecutive single capital letters. (**Rule 2.2(a)**) Insert one space between "U." and "L." to offset the institutional abbreviation, "B.U." for "Boston University" in this periodical name. (**Rule 2.2(b)**) Insert one space between "L." and "Rev." because "Rev." is not a single capital letter. (**Rule 2.2(c)**)
F.▲Supp.	Insert one space between "F." and "Supp." because "Supp." is not a single capital letter. (**Rule 2.2(c)**)
J.▲Air▲L.▲&▲Com.	Insert one space on each side of "Air" because the word is not abbreviated. (**Rule 2.2(d)**) Insert one space on each side of "&" because an ampersand is not treated as a single capital letter. (**Rule 2.2(f)**)

2.3 Authorities Referred to in Textual Sentences

Do not abbreviate the name of an authority used as an integral part of a textual sentence. Consult **Rule 12.2(q)** regarding case names that begin with "The."

Example

Correct: In *Los Angeles Memorial Coliseum Commission v. National Football League*, the NFL was concerned about stability and tried to prevent the Oakland Raiders from leaving Oakland for Los Angeles.

Incorrect: In *L.A. Meml. Coliseum Commn. v. Natl. Football League*, the NFL was concerned about stability and tried to prevent the Oakland Raiders from leaving Oakland for Los Angeles.

However, in case names, you may abbreviate commonly used acronyms (see **Rule 12.2(e)(4)**) and the following words: and (&), Association (Assn.), Brothers (Bros.), Company (Co.), Corporation (Corp.), Incorporated (Inc.), Limited (Ltd.), Number (No.), and United States (U.S.).

Correct: In *Mark Twain Kansas City Bank v. Kroh Bros. Development Co.*, the Court concluded that the transaction at issue violated the terms of the trust agreement. 829 P.2d 907, 914 (Kan. 1992).

Consult **Sidebars 13.1** and **14.2** for additional guidance about using constitutions and statutes in textual sentences.

3.0 | **SPELLING AND CAPITALIZATION**

3.1 Words in Titles

3.1(a)

When presenting the title of a source, such as the title of a book or law review article, retain the spelling in the original source, but change capitalization to conform to **Rule 3.1(b)**.

3.1(b)

In titles, capitalize the initial letter in the following words:

(1) The first word in the title.

(2) The first word in any subtitle.

(3) The first word after a colon or dash.

(4) All other words except articles (such as "a" and "the"), prepositions (such as "of," "to," and "under"), the word "to" when used as part of an infinitive (such as "to go"), and coordinating conjunctions (such as "and," "but," "or," "nor," and "for").

Examples

Nicole B. Casarez, *Examining the Evidence: Post-verdict Interviews and the Jury System*, 25 Hastings Commun. & Ent. L.J. 499 (2003).

Kelly McMurry, *Illinois High Court to Rule Whether Consumer Fraud Law Applies to Lawyers*, 34 Tr. 80 (Aug. 1998).

3.1(c)

(1) When one or more words are joined by a hyphen, always capitalize the first letter of the first word. Except as noted in subsections **(2)** and **(3)** below, also capitalize the first letter of the first word after the hyphen.

Examples

Secret Keeper or Tattletale: Incursions upon the Attorney-Client Privilege

Abridging the Freedom of Non-English Speech

Twenty-Five Years of the Fordham International Law Journal

(2) If a word following the hyphen is an article, preposition, or conjunction, do not capitalize that word.

SIDEBAR 3.1

COMMON PREPOSITIONS IN TITLES

Unless a preposition appears as the first word of a title or subtitle, it should not be capitalized. Below is a list of commonly used prepositions. Please note that this list is not exhaustive. If you are not certain whether a word is a preposition, you should consult a dictionary, especially since these same words can function as adverbs and other parts of speech.

about	by	outside
above	down	over
across	during	since
after	except	through
against	for	throughout
around	from	till
at	in	to
before	inside	toward
behind	into	under
below	like	until
beneath	near	up
beside	of	upon
besides	off	versus
between	on	with
beyond	out	without

Examples

The Knock-Down, Drag-Out Battle over Government Regulation of Television Violence

Duties and Responsibilities of the Guardian on a Day-to-Day Basis

(3) If the word before the hyphen is a prefix *and* the word after the hyphen is something other than a proper noun or proper adjective, do not capitalize the word that follows the hyphen.

Examples

Frozen Pre-embryos and the Right to Change One's Mind

The Accordion of the Thirteenth Amendment: Quasi-persons and the Right of Self-interest

From the Pre-Bakke Cases to the Post-Adarand Decisions: The Evolution of Supreme Court Decisions on Race and Remedies

3.2 General Rules

3.2(a) Professional titles and titles of honor or respect

(1) Capitalize professional titles and titles of honor or respect that immediately precede a person's name. Also capitalize titles of honor or respect that immediately follow a person's name, or substitute for a person's name, provided that the title identifies a head or assistant head of state, a head or assistant head of an existing or proposed national governmental unit, a diplomatic title, or a ruler or prince.

Examples

Title precedes name

General Colin Powell
Professor Peter F. Lake
Pope Benedict XVI

President John Quincy Adams
Crown Princess Masako
Dr. Welby

Title follows name

Diana, Princess of Wales

Orin Smith, president of Starbucks

Title substitutes for name

the Vice President
the Chargé d'Affaires

Clerk of the Supreme Court

(2) Capitalize titles even if a title refers to more than one name (e.g., Mayors Giuliani and Bloomberg).

(3) Capitalize titles presented in the second person (e.g., Your Honor, Your Majesty, Madam Secretary).

3.2(b) Organization names

Capitalize the full names of organized bodies, and their shortened forms.

Examples

U.S. Congress
Department of Labor

the Congress
the Department

3.2(c) Proper nouns

Capitalize proper nouns; proper nouns include the names of people and places, trademarks, titles of books, statutes, articles, and artistic works. Also capitalize the short form of proper nouns.

Examples

University of Michigan	the University
Gulf of Tonkin Resolution	the Resolution

3.2(d) Adjectives formed from proper nouns

Capitalize adjectives derived from words that exist only as proper nouns (e.g., American, German, Orwellian). However, when a word does not exist exclusively as a proper noun, do not capitalize the adjective (e.g., congressional, constitutional, presidential).

3.2(e) Holidays, events, and epochs

Capitalize the names of holidays, epochs, and historical, cultural, economic, and political events.

Examples

Fourth of July	Labor Day	Boston Tea Party
Battle of Gettysburg	the Renaissance	Dark Ages
Lyndon Johnson's New Deal	Kentucky Derby	Great Depression

3.2(f) Numerical designations

Unless it is part of a proper name, do not capitalize numerical designations.

Examples

twenty-first century	Fourth Republic

3.2(g) Midword capitalizations

Use midword capitalization if used by the company or product at issue (e.g., HarperCollins).

3.2(h) Defined terms

Once a word is defined in a document, it becomes a proper noun and thus should be capitalized.

Example

Jackson Elementary School (Buyer) agrees to purchase five hundred half-pint cartons of milk each week from SmartDairy, Inc. (Seller). Buyer will pay Seller within thirty days of receiving an invoice from Seller.

3.3 Capitalizing Specific Words

Capitalize the following words according to the specific listed rules. For words
not listed, use the general rules listed above or consult the most recent edition
of *The Redbook: A Manual on Legal Style*, the *United States Government Printing
Office Style Manual*, or *The Chicago Manual of Style*.

Act: Capitalize only when (a) referring to a specific act or (b) as a substitute for a specific act.

Examples

Americans with Disabilities Act

Act (as a later reference to an act referred to earlier in the text, such as the Americans with Disabilities Act)

Board: Capitalize only when (a) part of a proper name or (b) part of a governmental board.

Examples

Civil Aeronautics Board, General Electric Board

The board of directors for Meade Corporation met last week.

Circuit: Capitalize only when used with a circuit number.

Examples

Eleventh Circuit

The circuit court held . . . .

Code: Capitalize only when referring to a specific code.

Examples

United States Code, Internal Revenue Code

Many states have codes that address . . . .

Commission: Capitalize only when (a) part of a proper name or (b) part of a governmental commission.

Examples

Warren Commission, Federal Trade Commission

According to the ABA commission, some version of the rules has been adopted by forty-two states and the District of Columbia.

| Committee, Subcommittee: | Capitalize only when (a) part of a proper name or (b) part of a governmental committee. |

Examples

Senate Appropriations Committee, Immigration Subcommittee of the Senate Judiciary Committee

Both bills were blocked or defeated in committee.

| Commonwealth: | Capitalize only when (a) part of the full title of a state or federation of states, (b) used as a substitute for a specific state or federation of states, or (c) referring to a state or federation of states as a governmental actor or party to litigation. |

Examples

Commonwealth of Virginia

Jamaica, like Scotland, is part of the Commonwealth . . . .

The Commonwealth argued that the defendant should not be released . . . .

As a commonwealth develops politically, it often develops economically as well.

| Congressional: | Capitalize only when the word it modifies is capitalized. |

Examples

Congressional Medal of Honor

congressional hearings

| Constitution: | Capitalize only when (a) naming any constitution in full or (b) when referring to the United States Constitution. Also capitalize parts of the United States Constitution. |

Examples

Texas Constitution, First Amendment, Equal Protection Clause

| Court: | Capitalize only when: (a) naming the court in full; (b) referring to the highest court in any jurisdiction, once it has been identified by full name (such as "the Ohio Supreme Court"), |

whether it is the United States Supreme Court or the highest court in a state; or (c) referring to the Court to whom the document (such as a brief) is submitted. Do not capitalize "court" when referring to any other court by partial name or to lower courts in general.

Examples

Ohio Supreme Court

the Court (when referring to the United States Supreme Court or to a state supreme court that previously has been identified)

This Court should rule . . . . (within a brief)

federal courts

The trial court found that . . . .

Defendant: Capitalize only when submitting a document to a court (such as a brief) and that document refers to a party in the pending case.

Examples

The Defendant filed a counterclaim . . . . (referring to a litigant in the case in which the court document is submitted)

In *Smith*, the defendant . . . .

Department: Capitalize only when (a) part of a proper name or (b) part of a governmental department.

Examples

Department of Agriculture, Harvard University Department of Economics

The local police department holds an annual safety day for children.

Federal: Capitalize only when the word it modifies is capitalized.

Examples

Federal Aviation Administration

federal government

Judge, Justice:	Capitalize only when (a) giving the name of a specific judge or justice or (b) referring to a Justice of the United States Supreme Court.

Examples

Judge Susan C. Bucklew, Judge Fitzwater, Justice Ruth Bader Ginsburg, Magistrate Judge Mary S. Scriven

the Justice (when referring to a United States Supreme Court Justice)

Defense counsel argued that the judge did not instruct the jury properly.

Nation:	Capitalize only when used (a) as part of a proper name or (b) as a synonym for the United States.

Examples

United Nations, Cherokee Nation

Throughout the Nation, ...

other nations have expanded trade . . . .

National:	Capitalize only when the word it modifies is capitalized.

Examples

National Guard

national government

Plaintiff:	Capitalize only when submitting a document to a court (such as a brief) and that document refers to a party in the pending case.

Examples

The Plaintiff in this case . . . . (referring to a litigant in the case in which the court document is submitted)

In *Smith*, the plaintiff . . . .

President:	Capitalize only when the word (a) immediately precedes a person's name or (b) immediately follows a person's name or substitutes for a person's name, provided that the title identifies a head or assistant head of state.

Examples

President of the United States, President Eisenhower

The President gave his State of the Union address last night.

Frederick J. Krebs, president of the American Corporate Counsel Association

A public university president ordered a tenured professor to change a student's grade . . . .

State: Capitalize only when (a) part of the full title of a state or federation of states, (b) when used as a substitute for a specific state, or (c) when referring to a state as a governmental actor or party to litigation.

Examples

State of Nebraska, Organization of American States

The State passed legislation . . . .

The State argued that the defendant should not be released . . . .

3.4 Capitalization in Selected Non-English Languages

3.4(a) French

In titles, capitalize the initial letter of the following words: (1) the first word in the title; (2) if the first word is an article or other determiner, the first noun and any adjective that precedes it; and (3) important nouns. Do not capitalize the following words unless they start a title or subtitle: (1) the subject pronoun *je*, (2) the names of months and days of the week, (3) the names of languages, (4) adjectives derived from proper nouns, (5) titles preceding personal names, and (6) the names of places such as "street" and "mountain."

Example

A Simple Heart   *Un Coeur simple*

3.4(b) German

In titles, capitalize the initial letter of the first word and of all subsequent nouns. The following terms are not capitalized unless they start a title or subtitle:

(1) the subject pronoun *ich*; (2) the names of languages and days of weeks used as adjectives, adverbs, or complements of prepositions; and (3) adjectives and adverbs formed from proper nouns.

Example

Harry Potter and the Prisoner   Harry Potter und der Gefangene von Azkaban
of Azkaban

3.4(c) Spanish

In titles, capitalize only the initial letter of the first word and the initial letter of any proper nouns.

Example

One Hundred Years of Solitude   Cien años de soledad

3.5   Other Capitalization and Spelling Rules

For other capitalization and spelling rules, consult the most recent edition of the *United States Government Printing Office Style Manual, The Chicago Manual of Style,* or *The Redbook: A Manual of Legal Style.*

4.0 NUMBERS

4.1 Numbers in Citations

Present numbers within citations as numerals, unless the number appears in a title. In titles, copy the number as presented in the original, as noted in **Rule 3.1(a).**

Examples

Citations

Maxwell sued under 42 U.S.C. § 1983, claiming that the school district violated his constitutional rights.

Federal Rule of Civil Procedure 26(e) requires parties to supplement certain disclosures and discovery responses.

Titles

Ten Principles to Aid the Quest for Peace in the Middle East

10 Hard-Earned Lessons about Life and Law

4.2 Numbers in Textual Material

4.2(a) Words or numerals

Unless otherwise noted below, you may designate numbers with numerals (such as 19 or 234) or words (such as thirty-five or one hundred). *Whichever numbering method you select, be consistent.*

In law, the convention is to spell out zero to ninety-nine and to use numerals for higher numbers, such as 117 or 398. One exception is that lawyers typically spell out round numbers, such as hundred, thousand, and million.

In many non-legal settings, the trend is to spell out zero through nine and to use numerals for higher numbers, such as 10, 15, and 25.

4.2(b) Numbers that begin a sentence

Always spell out a number that begins a sentence.

Examples

Nineteen ninety-eight began with many significant legal events.

Two hundred ninety-five students attended the seminar.

Title 42 U.S.C. § 1983 permits lawsuits for damages for "the deprivation of any rights, privileges, or immunities secured by the Constitution and laws."

4.2(c) Numbers in a series and numbers in proximity

(1)   If one item in a series should be presented as a numeral, present all items as numerals.

Example

Dexter O'Conner was sentenced to 5, 10, and 110 years for his various crimes.

(2)   Even if numbers are not strictly in a series, typically present numbers that denote the same type of thing in a consistent format.

Example

Only 5 of 357 delegates voted on the measure.

4.2(d) Arabic rather than Roman numerals

When using numerals, typically use Arabic numerals (1, 2, 3) and not Roman numerals (I, II, i, ii).

4.2(e) Decimals, ratios, and time

Use a numeral when the number contains a decimal point (8.3), colon (4:1), or time abbreviation (4:30 p.m.).

4.2(f) Numbers and symbols

Use a numeral with a dollar, percentage, degree, or similar symbol. Do not insert a space between the symbol and numeral.

Instead of using numerals and symbols, you may spell out the phrase. Most lawyers prefer that a symbol not be used if the number should be spelled out (e.g., seven percent, as opposed to 7%). See **Rule 4.2(a)** regarding when to spell out numbers and when to use numerals.

Examples

$27.50	**or**	twenty-seven dollars and fifty cents
9%	**or**	nine percent
60"	**or**	sixty inches
104°	**or**	one hundred four degrees

4.2(g) Fractions

Typically spell out fractions. However, when a fraction appears with a whole number, you may use words or numerals. If using numerals, do not insert a space between the whole number and the fraction.

Example

Mr. Stanford's will provided that his daughter Marie receive three-fourths of his estate.

Dr. Suarez purchased 58¾ shares of stock in the limited liability professional corporation.

4.2(h) Commas in numerals

(1) As a general rule, when using numerals, insert commas between the third and fourth digits, the sixth and seventh digits, and so on.

Examples

1,000   10,000   100,000   1,000,000

(2) Do not place commas within page, paragraph, or section numbers unless the cited source uses commas.

Examples

On page 1704, the author stated . . . .

13 F.3d 1477

Comma in original page number: 69 Fed. Reg. 12,057

(3) Do not insert commas in numbers when the classification system does not include commas. Examples include docket numbers, Internet and other databases, product serial numbers, road numbers, room numbers, social security numbers, street addresses, telephone numbers, and years.

Examples

Address: 1600 Pennsylvania Avenue
Social security number: 247-89-4717
Database: 2005 WL 447189 (S.D.N.Y. Feb. 24, 2005)

4.2(i) Additional information about numbers

For additional information on numbers, consult the most recent edition of the *United States Government Printing Office Style Manual, The Chicago Manual of Style,* or *The Redbook: A Manual on Legal Style.*

4.3 Ordinal Numbers

4.3(a) Definitions

An ordinal is any number used to designate position in a series. "First," "second," and "third" are ordinal numbers. An ordinal contraction is a way to designate ordinals using numerals and letters (for example, 1st, 4th). Ordinals should not be presented in superscript format. Remember that some word-processing programs automatically superscript some ordinals. For example, 1st will become 1st; however, 2d will not become 2^d because 2d is a legal convention. Consult **Part 1(D)** for information about how to disable the automatic superscript function.

4.3(b)

(1) Ordinal contractions appear in many citations. For example, ordinal contractions are used in certain court abbreviations (such as 11th Cir.) and to designate series of publications (such as Am. Jur. 2d and F.3d).

(2) For ordinals in citations, use the contractions below as guidelines.

First:	1st	**Fourth:**	4th
Second:	2d	**Twenty-second:**	22d
Third:	3d	**Forty-third:**	43d

(3) Ordinal contractions used in other contexts may differ from this format by including additional letters, such as "2nd" for "2d" or "3rd" for "3d." These longer contractions should not be used in legal citations.

(4) In legal writing, do not use an ordinal to denote a date.

Examples

Correct:	June 17, 2005	**Incorrect:**	June 17th, 2005
	June 17		June 17th

4.3(c) Punctuation

Do not place a period after the ordinal contraction.

Example

Correct:	3d	**Incorrect:**	3d.

5.0   PAGE NUMBERS

5.1   Initial Pages

5.1(a) Definition

The "initial page" is the page on which a particular source begins.

5.1(b) Use

(1) When citing a source that has page numbers and is contained within a larger source, always include the initial page number.

Examples of a case and law review article (the initial page appears in green)

Archer v. Warner, 538 U.S. **314** (2003).

Mary Beth Beazley & Linda H. Edwards, *The Process and the Product: A Bibliography of Scholarship about Legal Scholarship*, 49 Mercer L. Rev. **741** (1998).

(2) When citing a freestanding source—a source consisting of a single document—do not include the initial page number unless specifically referring to material on that page.

Example of a treatise

William A. Fischel, *Regulatory Takings: Law, Economics, and Politics* (Harv. U. Press 1995).

(3) Do not use the abbreviations "p." and "pp." when referring to pages in a citation.

5.2   Pinpoint Pages

5.2(a) Definition

The term "pinpoint page" refers to the page on which a quotation or other relevant passage appears. It is sometimes called a "jump citation" or "jump page."

Example (the pinpoint pages appear in green)

Brunelle v. Town of S. Kingstown, 700 A.2d 1075, **1080–1083** (R.I. 1997).

5.2(b) Use

(1) When quoting specific material from a source divided into pages, always include a pinpoint page reference that provides the exact location of cited material.

Example (the pinpoint page appears in green)

Branch Rickey, who helped build the Dodgers, commented that "[a] baseball club in any city in America is a quasi-public institution, and in Brooklyn, the Dodgers were public without the quasi." Geoffrey C. Ward & Ken Burns, *Baseball: An Illustrated History* **348** (Alfred A. Knopf, Inc. 1994).

(2) Even when not quoting specific material, include a pinpoint page reference that provides the exact location of the cited material. For example, when referring to the holding in a case, cite the page or pages on which the holding appears.

Example (the pinpoint page appears in green)

The Court held that a regulation is a taking when the landowner is left with no economically beneficial use of the land. *Lucas v. S.C. Coastal Council*, 505 U.S. 1003, **1019** (1992).

(3) If a pinpoint page might be confused with the title, insert ", at" before the pinpoint page. A pinpoint page number might be confused with a title if the title ends with a numeral.

Example (the pinpoint pages appear in green)

During that period, a lynch mob mentality prevailed. Philip J. Ethington, *The Public City: The Political Construction of Urban Life in San Francisco, 1850–1900*, at **104–105** (Cambridge U. Press 1994).

(4) If the pinpoint page is also the initial page, repeat the initial page number.

Example (the pinpoint page appears in green)

"Although not an entirely new development, franchise relocation is occurring more frequently in professional sports . . . ." Robert Taylor Bowling, Student Author, *Sports Aggravated: The Fan's Guide to the Franchise Relocation Problem in Professional Sports*, 28 Stetson L. Rev. 645, **645** (1999).

(5) On the rare occasion when a citation refers to the entire source, no pinpoint page is required.

SIDEBAR 5.1

IMPORTANCE OF USING PINPOINT REFERENCES

The importance of including pinpoint references whenever possible cannot be overstated. If you do not refer readers to specific pages or other subdivisions where the referenced material appears, readers will be frustrated. Moreover, if a judge or judicial law clerk cannot locate support for your position, you may lose credibility with the court, or the court may discount your position. Accordingly, always spend the extra time it takes to insert the pinpoint reference.

5.3 Citing Consecutive Pages

5.3(a)

When citing material on consecutive pages (sometimes called a "page span"), give the inclusive page numbers, separated by a hyphen, an en dash, or the word "to." Consult **Sidebar 5.2** for additional information on the use of hyphens, en dashes, and "to" in citations.

5.3(b)

When citing a span of pages, numbers can be presented in two ways: by retaining all digits on both sides of the span or by dropping repetitious digits. If the second format is used, retain two digits on the right-hand side of the span. Be consistent, whatever style you choose.

Examples

Correct:	12–13	**Incorrect:**	12–3
Correct:	103–107 **or** 103–07	**Incorrect:**	103–7
Correct:	1230–1234 **or** 1230–34	**Incorrect:**	1230–4

5.4 Citing Scattered Pages

When citing multiple pages that are not consecutive, separate the page numbers by a comma and one space. Do not include an ampersand (&) or the word "and" before the final page number.

Example

Correct: 5, 14, 26 **Incorrect:** 5, 14 & 26 **and** 5, 14, and 26

SIDEBAR 5.2

USING HYPHENS, EN DASHES, AND "TO" FOR SPANS

A span of pages or other subdivisions may be denoted by a hyphen (-), an en dash (–), or the word "to."

In typed material, such as a memorandum or brief, most people use a hyphen to denote a span. A hyphen is made by striking the hyphen key once. On most keyboards, the hyphen key is located two keys to the left of the backspace key.

In typeset material, such as books and law reviews, most people use an en dash to denote a span. To insert an en dash using WordPerfect, press Ctrl-W, which will display the symbol box. Select "Typographical symbols." The en dash is symbol 4,33. To insert an en dash using Word, pull down the "Insert" menu bar. Select "Symbol," and then "Special Characters." Highlight the en dash and press "Insert."

The word "to" is typically used when a hyphen or an en dash would create ambiguity or cause confusion. For example, the page numbering in some legal materials, such as treatises and looseleaf services, includes a hyphen as part of the number (example: 53-01, 53-02). Accordingly, using a hyphen or an en dash to denote the span would be confusing (53-01–53-02). In this situation, using "to" is the only way to avoid confusion. Thus, the span would appear as 53-01 to 53-02.

5.5 Passim

Although most attorneys and judges prefer to use specific pinpoint references, "passim" may be used to indicate that a particular point appears in many places; "passim" can be used as a pinpoint reference. "Passim" also can be used in the table of authorities in a brief.

Example

For a discussion of the criticism and a defense of Judge Arnold's conclusions, see Polly J. Price, *Precedent and Judicial Power after the Founding*, 42 B.C. L. Rev. 81, passim (2001).

Table of authorities entry   *Page(s)*

Sutton v. United Airlines, Inc., 527 U.S. 471 (1999). . . . . passim

6.0   CITING SECTIONS AND PARAGRAPHS

6.1   General Rules

6.1(a)

If a source is divided either by sections or by paragraphs, cite the relevant subdivisions. Insert one space before and after the section (§) or paragraph (¶) symbol. Consult **Sidebar 6.1** for instructions on how to physically insert section and paragraph symbols into your paper.

Examples

28 U.S.C. § 1332 (2000).

Model Code Prof. Resp. preamble ¶ 1 (ABA 1980).

6.1(b)

(1) If the source is divided by sections or paragraphs **and** pages, refer to both in the citation unless citing the entire section or paragraph. Insert the section or paragraph first. Then insert the page number on which the material appears.

Examples

Robert B. Reich, *Secession of the Successful*, 141 N.Y. Times § 6, 16 (Jan. 20, 1991).

Julian Conrad Juergensmeyer & Thomas E. Roberts, *Land Use Planning and Control Law* § 10.4, 425 (West 1998).

John E. Nowak & Ronald D. Rotunda, *Constitutional Law* § 17.3, 1427, § 17.4, 1438 (7th ed., West 2004).

(2) If a reader might be confused about which number is the paragraph or section number and which is the page number, you may insert ", at" before the page number. Confusion might occur if the paragraph or section number is similar or close to the page number.

Examples

§ 3, at 4, § 4, at 12

¶ 6.1, at 6

6.2   Spacing

Insert a space between the section symbol (§) or paragraph symbol (¶) and the following number or letter.

Examples (the symbol ▲ denotes a space)

Correct: §▲1332   **Incorrect:**   §1332
Correct: ¶▲A   **Incorrect:**   ¶A

6.3   Unnumbered Paragraphs

6.3(a)

If a document contains indented, but unnumbered, paragraphs and is not divided by another method, cite paragraphs as if they were numbered, but enclose the paragraph symbol and paragraph number or letter in brackets to show readers that you added the information.

Example

Declaration of Independence [¶ 2] (1776).

6.3(b)

If a document contains other designated subdivisions, such as pages, do not refer to unnumbered paragraphs.

SIDEBAR 6.1

INSERTING THE SYMBOLS FOR SECTIONS AND PARAGRAPHS

Because section and paragraph symbols are used frequently in legal citation, it is important that you learn how to insert these symbols into your paper.

If using WordPerfect, press Ctrl-W, which will display the symbol box. Select "Typographical symbols." The paragraph symbol is symbol 4,5; the section symbol is symbol 4,6. Select the desired symbol, and hit "Insert" or "Insert and Close."

If using Word, pull down the "Insert" menu bar. Select "Symbol" and then "Special Characters"; highlight either "Section" or "Paragraph," and press "Insert."

6.4   Subsections and Subparagraphs

6.4(a)

Include the smallest subdivision possible when citing a section or paragraph.

6.4(b)

To denote subsections, use the punctuation the original source uses to separate sections from subsections.

6.4(c)

If the source does not contain any separating punctuation, place the subdivisions in parentheses. Do not insert a space between the main section and the subdivision.

Examples

Fed. R. Civ. P. 26(a)(1)(D).

28 U.S.C. § 2284(b)(2) (2000).

6.5   Distinguishing Sections from Subsections

Section designations sometimes include letters as well as numbers (for example, "2000e-2"). Because these letters do not refer to subsections, do not use separating punctuation.

Example

Correct: 42 U.S.C. § 2000e-2(a) (2000).
Incorrect: 42 U.S.C. § 2000(e)(2)(a) (2000).

6.6   Citing Consecutive Sections or Paragraphs

6.6(a)

When citing consecutive sections or paragraphs, include both the first and the last sections or paragraphs of the span cited. Separate the first and last sections or paragraphs with a hyphen, an en dash, or the word "to." Consult **Sidebar** 5.2 for additional information.

Examples

§§ 1–55   ¶¶ 73–107

6.6(b)

Use two consecutive section symbols (§§) or two consecutive paragraph symbols (¶¶) to denote any quantity of multiple sections or paragraphs.

Examples

§§ 1961–1965   ¶¶ 33(a)–104(c)

6.6(c)

Retain all digits or letters on either side of the span.

Example

Correct: §§ 1961–1965   **Incorrect:**   §§ 1961–65

6.6(d) Et seq.

"Et seq." means "and the following ones." Although some attorneys use "et seq." to denote a span of statutory sections, it is better to provide the reader with the actual span. Accordingly, the use of "et seq." is not encouraged.

Examples

Correct: 15 U.S.C. §§ 2301–2310 (2000).
Incorrect: 15 U.S.C. §§ 2301 et seq. (2000).

6.7   Citing Scattered Sections or Paragraphs

6.7(a)

When citing multiple sections or paragraphs that are not consecutive, separate each section or paragraph with a comma and one space.

6.7(b)

Use two consecutive section symbols (§§) or two consecutive paragraph symbols (¶¶) to denote any number of multiple sections or paragraphs.

6.7(c)

Do not include an ampersand (&) or the word "and" before the final section or paragraph.

Examples

§§ 1961, 1963, 1965   ¶¶ 47(c), 58(m), 107(a)

6.8 Citing Consecutive Subdivisions within a Single Section or Paragraph

When citing multiple subsections or subparagraphs that fall within a single section or paragraph, follow **Rule 6.6,** but use only one section symbol (§) or one paragraph symbol (¶).

Examples (the symbol ▲ denotes a space)

Correct

§▲22(a)–(c)

¶▲3601(a)–(c)

¶▲3601(a)▲to▲(c)

Incorrect	Problem
¶¶▲3601(a)–(c)	two paragraph symbols used
¶▲3601(a)–01(c)	repetitious digits dropped
¶3601(a)–(c)	no space after paragraph symbol

6.9 Citing Scattered Subdivisions within a Single Section or Paragraph

When citing multiple, scattered subdivisions within a single section or paragraph, separate the subdivisions by a comma and one space. Follow **Rule 6.7,** but use only one section symbol (§) or one paragraph symbol (¶).

Examples

§ 1961(a), (c), (e)   ¶ 47(c), (m)

6.10 Citing Multiple Subdivisions within Multiple Sections or Paragraphs

When citing multiple subdivisions within multiple sections or paragraphs, use **Rules 6.6** and **6.7** as guidelines.

Examples

§§ 107(a)–110(b)   (consecutive)

§§ 357(a)(1) to 423(c)(3)   (consecutive)

¶¶ 33(b)(7), 33(c)(5), 34(h)(1)   (scattered)

6.11   Referring to Sections and Paragraphs in Textual Material

When referring to a specific section or paragraph in textual material, you may either use the symbol (§ or ¶) or spell out the words ("section" or "paragraph"). However, do not begin a sentence with a symbol.

Examples (all correct)

The police officers sought immunity under § 1983.

The police officers sought immunity under section 1983.

Section 1983 might provide a possible defense for police officers charged with conducting an illegal search.

7.0 CITING FOOTNOTES AND ENDNOTES

7.1 General Rules

When citing a footnote or an endnote, include the page on which the note begins (even if the note spans multiple pages) and provide the note number. Abbreviate one note as "n." and multiple notes as "nn." Insert one space between this abbreviation and the note number or numbers. When citing multiple notes, use **Rules 6.6** through **6.10** as guides.

Examples

Single footnote

Suzanna Sherry, *Hard Cases Make Good Judges*, 3 Nw. U. L. Rev. 3, 7 n. 12 (2004).

Charles W. Wolfram, *Modern Legal Ethics* § 9.4.5, 541 n. 10 (student ed., West 1986).

Multiple, consecutive notes on a single page

Suzanna Sherry, *Hard Cases Make Good Judges*, 3 Nw. U. L. Rev. 3, 7 nn. 12–16 (2004).

Charles W. Wolfram, *Modern Legal Ethics* § 9.4.5, 541 nn. 10 to 13 (student ed., West 1986).

Scattered notes on a single page

Suzanna Sherry, *Hard Cases Make Good Judges*, 3 Nw. U. L. Rev. 3, 7 nn. 12, 15 (2004).

Charles W. Wolfram, *Modern Legal Ethics* § 9.4.5, 541 nn. 10, 13 (student ed., West 1986).

Multiple, consecutive notes on different pages

Suzanna Sherry, *Hard Cases Make Good Judges*, 3 Nw. U. L. Rev. 3, 7 n. 16 to 9 n. 31 (2004).

Charles W. Wolfram, *Modern Legal Ethics* § 9.4.5, 541 n. 10 to 542 n. 13 (student ed., West 1986).

Scattered notes on different pages

Suzanna Sherry, *Hard Cases Make Good Judges*, 3 Nw. U. L. Rev. 3, 7 n. 12, 8 n. 20 (2004).

Charles W. Wolfram, *Modern Legal Ethics* § 9.4.5, 541 n. 10, 542 n. 14 (student ed., West 1986).

7.2 Preventing Confusion

You may sometimes need to deviate from the general rules to ensure that the reader is not confused about which numbers refer to pages and which refer to endnotes or footnotes. For example, confusion may result if you use the general rules to cite footnotes 60 and 62 on page 50 of an article, and material on page 70 of that same article. The citation under the general rules would appear as follows: 50 nn. 60, 62, 70. In this citation, the reader likely would think "70" referred to a footnote.

One way to resolve this dilemma is to use two separate citations. For example, to cite consecutive notes 2 through 5 on page 16 of the Berman article, and to cite material on page 18 of the same article, follow the example below.

Example

Harold J. Berman, *The Historical Foundations of Law*, 54 Emory L.J. 13, 16 nn. 2–5 (2005); *id.* at 18.

7.3   Footnotes and Endnotes in Short Citations

Short citation formats are discussed generally in **Rule 11** and are discussed specifically within the rules that address particular sources. One point of confusion is how to cite footnotes or endnotes when the *id.* short citation is used. Below are two methods, both of which are correct. Under the first alternative, footnote 6 includes the repeated pinpoint page, while footnote 6 in the second alternative does not. The second alternative is technically more accurate under **Rule 11.3(b)(1)**, but many writers prefer the first alternative. Once you select an alternative, use it consistently throughout the paper you are writing.

First Alternative

[5]Harold J. Berman, *The Historical Foundations of Law*, 54 Emory L.J. 13, 16 nn. 2–5 (2005).

[6]*Id.* at 16 n. 4.

[7]*Id.* at 18 n. 7.

Second Alternative

[5]Harold J. Berman, *The Historical Foundations of Law*, 54 Emory L.J. 13, 16 nn. 2–5 (2005).

[6]*Id.* at n. 4.

[7]*Id.* at 18 n. 7.

8.0 | **SUPPLEMENTS**

8.1 Citing Material Found Only in a Supplement

If the cited material appears only in a supplement, such as a pocket part, provide just the date of the supplement. "Cited material" means that part of the source to which you want to refer readers. Before the date, inform readers that you are citing a supplement by using the abbreviation "Supp." Insert one space between the abbreviation "Supp." and the date. If the supplement is revised or has another designation, such as a number, include that information as well.

Examples

18 U.S.C. § 1965 (Supp. 2004).

42 U.S.C. § 3796hh (Supp. I 2001).

Geoffrey C. Hazard, Jr. & W. William Hodes, *The Law of Lawyering* vol. 2, § 31.2 (3d ed., Aspen Publishers Supp. 2004).

18 Pa. Consol. Stat. Ann. § 3122.1 (West Rev. Supp. 1998).

8.2 Citing Material Found Only in the Main Volume

Even for sources with supplements, provide only the date of the main volume if the cited material appears only there. Typically use the date on the copyright page of the main volume; when citing U.S.C., use the date on the spine.

Examples

18 U.S.C. § 1965 (2000).

Geoffrey C. Hazard, Jr. & W. William Hodes, *The Law of Lawyering* vol. 2, § 31.2 (3d ed., Aspen Publishers 2001).

8.3 Citing Material in Both the Main Volume and a Supplement

If the cited material appears in both the main volume and a supplement, provide both dates. Give the date of the main volume followed by the date of the supplement. Separate the two dates with an ampersand (&), and place one space on either side of the ampersand. Use the abbreviation "Supp." before the date of the supplement.

Examples

18 U.S.C. § 1965 (2000 & Supp. 2004).

Geoffrey C. Hazard, Jr. & W. William Hodes, *The Law of Lawyering* vol. 2, § 31.2 (3d ed., Aspen Publishers 2001 & Supp. 2004).

8.4   Citing Material in Multiple Supplements

If material appears in multiple supplements, cite the supplements in chronological order.

Examples

Citing multiple supplements, different years: 17 U.S.C. § 512 (Supps. IV 1999 & V 2000).

Citing multiple supplements, same year: 17 U.S.C. § 512(d)(1)–(3) (Supps. IV & V 1994).

Citing main volume and multiple supplements: 29 U.S.C. §§ 201–219 (1988 & Supps. I 1989, II 1990, III 1991, IV 1992, V 1993).

Citing only supplements to second edition: Peter W. Low & John C. Jeffries, Jr., *Civil Rights Actions: Section 1983 and Related Statutes* (2d ed., Found. Press Supps. 1994 & 1996).

Citing second edition main volume and supplements: Phillip E. Areeda & Herbert Hovenkamp, *Antitrust Law* (2d ed., Aspen Publishers 2002 & Supps. 2002, 2003).

GRAPHICAL MATERIAL, APPENDICES, AND OTHER SUBDIVISIONS

9.1 Citing Graphical Material

When citing graphical material, such as tables, charts, figures, graphs, and illustrations, include the following material:

(1) The page number on which the graphical material begins, followed by one space;

(2) The abbreviation from **Appendix 3**(C) for the particular type of graphical material cited, followed by one space; and

(3) The number, letter, or other designation for the graphical material, if any. Analogize to **Rules 6.6** through **6.10** when citing multiple graphics.

Examples

Gary L. Blasi, *What Lawyers Know: Lawyering Expertise, Cognitive Science, and the Functions of Theory*, 45 J. Leg. Educ. 313, 370 fig. 4 (1995).

Bryan A. Garner, *The Winning Brief* 413 chart (2d ed., Oxford U. Press 2004).

Other examples

Type of graphic	Citation
Table in a law review article	1950, 1954 tbl.
Illustration in a book	52 illus. 1
Multiple charts in a book (consecutive)	743 charts 3–5

9.2 Citing Appendices

9.2(a) Citing an entire appendix

(1) When citing an entire appendix, place the abbreviation "app." after the largest subdivision to which the appendix is attached. For example, if an appendix is attached to a law review article, provide the initial page of the law review article and then designate the appendix. If the appendix is attached to a particular section of a book, provide the section number, and then refer to the appendix.

(2) Insert a comma and one space before "app."

(3) If the appendix has a designation, such as a number or letter, place that designation after the abbreviation "app."; insert one space between "app." and the number.

(4) As noted in **Appendix 3**, the abbreviation for multiple appendices is "apps." For multiple appendices, analogize to **Rules 6.6** through **6.10** concerning sections and paragraphs.

Examples

M.H. Sam Jacobson, *Providing Academic Support without an Academic Support Environment*, 3 Leg. Writing 241, app. B (1997).

20 C.F.R. subpt. P, app. 1 (2005).

Other examples

Multiple consecutive appendices: apps. 1–3
Multiple scattered appendices: apps. 1, 5, 8

9.2(b) Citing material within an appendix

When citing specific material within an appendix, place a comma and one space after the appendix designation; then insert the pinpoint reference.

Examples

M.H. Sam Jacobson, *Providing Academic Support without an Academic Support Environment*, 3 Leg. Writing 241, app. B, 261–263 (1997).

20 C.F.R. subpt. P, app. 1, § 9.04(A) (2005).

9.3 Citing Other Subdivisions

When citing a subdivision not specifically described in **Rules 5** through **9.2**, use the most similar subdivision as an analogy. Also consult **Appendix 3(C)** for the proper abbreviation.

Examples

Chapter: Philip C. Kissam, *The Discipline of Law Schools* ch. 3 (Carolina Academic Press 2003).

Comment: Model R. Prof. Conduct 7.3 cmt. 5 (ABA 2004).

Historical note: Fla. Stat. Ann. § 316.237 hist. n. (West 1999).

9.4 Preventing Confusion

You may sometimes need to deviate from the general rules to ensure that the reader is not confused about which numbers refer to pages, sections, and paragraphs, and which refer to graphical material. In such instances, analogize to the solutions presented in **Rules 6.1(b)(2)** and **7.2**.

10.0 INTERNAL CROSS-REFERENCES

10.1 Definition

Internal cross-references refer readers to other parts of the document you are writing. They do not refer readers to outside sources, such as cases or statutes. Internal cross-references are found most commonly in documents written with footnotes or endnotes.

10.2 Material That May Be Cross-Referenced

10.2(a)

You may cross-reference text, footnotes, appendices, or any other internal material that might help readers or help you avoid repeating the point.

10.2(b)

You may **not** use an **internal** cross-reference to cite outside sources, such as cases and statutes, that you have used in your paper. Instead, use an appropriate short citation. Short citations are addressed in **Rule 11.2.**

Incorrect example (cross-referencing a case)

[17]*Johnson Mfg. Co., supra* n. 3.

10.3 *Supra* and *Infra*

10.3(a) *Supra*

To refer to material that appears earlier in your paper, use *supra,* which means "above."

Example

[62]*Supra* n. 5.

10.3(b) *Infra*

To refer to material that will appear later in the paper, use *infra,* which means "below."

Example

63*Infra* n. 112.

10.3(c) Typeface

Italicize or underline *supra* and *infra*.

10.4   Format for Internal Cross-References

10.4(a) Be specific

Provide the most specific reference possible, which often means using a footnote number for readers to find the exact text to which you are referring.

10.4(b) Where reference appears

When the cross-reference appears in a citation, use the abbreviation for the subdivision, such as "n." for note. When the cross-reference appears in a textual sentence, spell out the words.

10.4(c) Explanatory parenthetical

If the accompanying text or citation does not adequately identify the subject of the reference, add an explanatory parenthetical to the cross-reference. Consult **Rule 46** for additional information on explanatory parentheticals.

Examples

Cross-references to material in one or more footnotes or endnotes

17*Supra* n. 5 (providing the text of Federal Rule of Civil Procedure 37(b)).

34*Supra* nn. 20–31 (discussing the history of the Supreme Court's decisions on attorney advertising).

72For a discussion of the attorney-client privilege in the corporate context, consult *infra* notes 91–95. ["Notes" is not abbreviated here because it appears in a textual sentence, not a citation.]

Cross-references to material in text

47*Infra* pt. A(1) (discussing proper deposition objections).

58For additional information on Federal Rule of Evidence 403, review the text accompanying *supra* note 53.

Cross-references to material in both text and notes

[96]For examples of the most common errors in drafting partnership agreements, review *supra* notes 47–58 and accompanying text.

[101]*Infra* n. 218 and accompanying text (discussing Justice Scalia's dissent).

Cross-references to other material within the paper

[39]For a more complete description of each state's kidnapping statute, see *infra* appendix 3.

[75]*Supra* tbl. 5 (listing settlement rates for civil cases in each federal district court).

SIDEBAR 10.1

THE TWO USES OF *SUPRA*

In legal citation, the word *"supra"* has two distinct functions. As noted in **Rule 10.3(a)**, *supra* is sometimes used as an internal cross-reference. But as explained in **Rule 11.4**, *supra* also can be used as a short citation for certain types of sources. Although the formats are somewhat different, both uses lead readers to information that appears earlier in the paper.

INTRODUCTION TO FULL AND SHORT CITATION FORMATS

11.1 Full Citation Format

11.1(a) Definition

A full citation includes each component required for that particular source and gives readers sufficient information to locate that source in a library or an online database.

11.1(b) Components of a full citation

Each specific source will require slightly different components. Subject to special forms developed in **Rules** 12 through **42,** the types of information typically provided in a full citation include the author's name; the title or name of the source; the volume, if any; the page, section, or other subdivision within which the referenced material is located within the source; the publisher; and the date.

11.1(c) Use

(1) Use a full citation the first time a source is cited in the paper.

(2) Some attorneys and judges prefer that a source be cited in full only once in the paper. Others prefer that full citations be used more frequently—such as each time the writer reaches a new major section of the paper. Either preference is permissible.

11.2 Short Citation Format

11.2(a) Definition

A short citation is used only after an authority has been cited once in full citation format. A short citation typically omits some of the required full citation components but still provides enough information for readers to identify and locate the source.

11.2(b) Use

(1) Short citations are used to save space in a paper. In addition, they are less disruptive to the flow of text than are full citations.

(2) Use a short citation when (a) the reader will not be confused about which source is being referenced, and (b) the reader will not have trouble locating the full citation quickly. Thus, in a short legal document, you may need only one full citation for a particular source and then may use short citations in each instance thereafter. In longer legal documents, you may need a full citation each time you start a new section.

(3) Throughout this book, you will be introduced to several variations of short citations. The types of short citation that can be used will vary depending on (a) whether the paper you are preparing is one with citations embedded within the text or one with footnotes, (b) where the short citation appears in relation to the full citation, and (c) the type of source cited.

(4) In this book, each rule for a specific source contains information on both the full and short citation formats. Accordingly, consult the rule for the particular source you are citing for in-depth information on appropriate uses and formats.

11.3   *Id.* as a Short Citation

11.3(a) Definition

"*Id.*" is the abbreviation for "*idem*," which means "the same."

11.3(b) Use

(1) Except when used in a parallel citation (**Rule 12.21(f)**), *id.* replaces as much of the immediately preceding citation as is identical with the current one.

(2) *Id.* may be used as a short citation for any source except appellate records (**Rule 29.6**) and internal cross-references (**Rule 10**).

(3) If *id.* is appropriate, use *id.* as the preferred short citation.

SIDEBAR 11.1

ID. VERSUS *IBID.*

Id. is used in legal citations the same way *ibid.* is used in nonlegal citation systems.

(4) *Id.* may be used only in the following circumstances:

    (a) **In papers without footnotes,** use *id.* only when referring to the immediately preceding authority.

Example

Full citation for first case

Id., alone, is correct because this citation is also to page 784 of *Johnson.*

Full citation for second case

Id. is proper because it refers to *R.R.;* since the material is from page 791, not page 796, add the new page number.

Id. is not appropriate because the preceding case is *R.R.;* thus, you must use another short citation format.

Some states have enforced surrogacy agreements. For example, the California Supreme Court held that surrogacy contracts do not violate the policies governing the termination of parental rights. *Johnson v. Calvert,* 851 P.2d 776, 784 (Cal. 1993). The Court reached this ruling because the contract was based on services, not the termination of parental rights. *Id.* Other states, however, have refused to enforce surrogacy agreements. The Massachusetts Supreme Court, for example, held that a contract in which the birth mother receives payment for her services is not enforceable if the payment is used to influence her decision to relinquish custody. *R.R. v. M.H.,* 689 N.E.2d 790, 796 (Mass. 1998). In *R.R.,* the surrogate was artificially inseminated with the intended father's sperm. *Id.* at 791. The contract indicated that the surrogate would receive $10,000 for delivering the child. The Court refused to enforce the contract because the payment vitiated the surrogate's intent. *Id.* at 796.

The California Court gave several public policy reasons why surrogacy contracts should be enforced. *Johnson,* 851 P.2d at 784.

    (b) **In papers with footnotes,** use *id.* only when referring to (1) the immediately preceding authority within the same footnote or (2) the immediately preceding authority in the preceding footnote. For a clear reference to material in the preceding footnote, that footnote must contain only one source. If the preceding footnote contains multiple sources, do not use *id.*

Examples

Refers to *Nollan* at page 834

Refers to *Nollan* at page 835

Refers to *Richardson* at page 1157

Id. is not appropriate because note 23 concerns *Nollan,* not *Richardson.*

[18]*Nollan v. Cal. Coastal Commn.,* 483 U.S. 825, 834 (1987).

[19]*Id.*

[20]*See id.* at 835.

[21]*Richardson v. City of Honolulu,* 124 F.3d 1150, 1155–1160 (9th Cir. 1997).

[22]*Id.* at 1157.

[23]*Nollan,* 438 U.S. at 834.

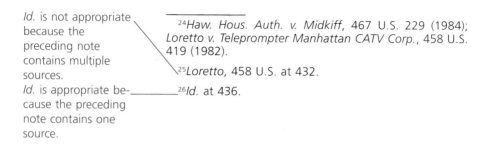

Id. is not appropriate because the preceding note contains multiple sources.

Id. is appropriate because the preceding note contains one source.

²⁴*Haw. Hous. Auth. v. Midkiff*, 467 U.S. 229 (1984); *Loretto v. Teleprompter Manhattan CATV Corp.*, 458 U.S. 419 (1982).

²⁵*Loretto*, 458 U.S. at 432.

²⁶*Id.* at 436.

11.3(c) Typeface

Italicize *id.* If you use underlining to represent italics, underline the period in *id.* (id.).

11.3(d) Capitalization

When *id.* begins a sentence, capitalize the "i." When *id.* does not start a sentence, use a lowercase "i."

Examples

¹⁸*Nollan v. Cal. Coastal Commn.*, 483 U.S. 825, 834 (1987).

¹⁹*Id.*

²⁰*See id.* at 835.

11.3(e) *Id.* used with pinpoint references

When *id.* is used with a pinpoint reference, include "at" before the pinpoint page, section, paragraph, or other division.

Examples

Page number: *Id.* at 321.
Section number: *Id.* at § 14.3.
Paragraph number: *Id.* at ¶ 6-6.
Other reference: *Id.* at app. 1.

11.3(f) Referring to shorter works within a collection

When citing a shorter work in a collection, use *id.* to refer to the shorter work, not to the collection. For books, also consult **Rules 22.1(l)**, **22.1(m)**, and **22.3**.

Examples

Correct

⁴⁵Stanley D. Robinson, *Antitrust Developments: 1973*, in *Antitrust in Transition* vol. 1, 1, 7 (Milton Handler ed., Transnatl. Juris Publications 1991).

⁴⁶*Id.* at 3.

Incorrect

⁴⁵Stanley D. Robinson, *Antitrust Developments: 1973*, in *Antitrust in Transition* vol. 1, 1, 7 (Milton Handler ed., Transnatl. Juris Publications 1991).

⁴⁶Michael Malina, *The Antitrust Jurisprudence in the Second Circuit*, in *id.* at 817.

11.3(g)   Intervening sources

Sources included in an explanatory parenthetical (**Rule 46**), a subsequent history designation (**Rule 12.8**), or a prior history designation (**Rule 12.9**) are not considered intervening sources for purposes of determining when *id.* can be used. The following examples reflect the correct use of *id.* This rule also applies to documents without footnotes, such as memos and briefs.

Examples

¹⁰⁰*Haw. Hous. Auth. v. Midkiff*, 467 U.S. 229, 241 (1984) (quoting *U.S. v. Gettysburg Elec. Ry.*, 160 U.S. 668, 680 (1896)).

¹⁰¹*Id.* at 242.

¹⁰²634 N.Y.S.2d 740 (App. Div. 2d Dept. 1995), *aff'd*, 679 N.E.2d 1035 (N.Y. 1997).

¹⁰³*Id.* at 741.

11.4   *Supra* as a Short Citation

11.4(a)   Definition

The term "*supra*," which means "above," can be used to develop a short citation that cross-references the full citation. This use of *supra* is different from that described in **Rule 10.3**. Consult **Sidebar 10.1** for additional information on the different uses of *supra*.

11.4(b)   Use

(1)   As with any short citation, use *supra* only after the source has been cited once in full format.

(2)   Although a source cited in full format for the first time in an explanatory parenthetical may be used as a full citation for purposes of this rule, the writer should evaluate whether readers will be able to easily find the full citation when it is part of a parenthetical. If the writer determines that readers should be able to find the full citation format easily, the *supra* short form may be used. Alternatively, the writer may choose to cite the source again in full format, and use the short form thereafter.

(3) Do not use *supra* if *id.* is appropriate.

(4) The *supra* citation format cannot be used for all sources. *Supra* most typically is used for sources cited by author name, such as books, law review articles, and Web sites. Do **not** use *supra* as a short citation for the following sources: cases, statutes, session laws, ordinances, legislative materials (other than hearings), constitutions, and administrative regulations.

(5) If the source is not listed in the "not" portion of **Rule 11.4(b)(4)**, *supra* is appropriate. For additional information on using the *supra* format for a particular source, consult the "short citation format" rule for the source you are citing.

11.4(c) Format

Use the following format for a *supra* short citation for documents with footnotes. Retain the word "at" even if the pinpoint reference is a section or paragraph number.

Author's last name (or, if not available, *Title*),•*supra* n.▲Note number,•at Pinpoint reference.

Examples

---

[3]Debra Baker, *How Safe Is Your 'Burb?* 85 ABA J. 50, 51–52 (Sept. 1999).

•   •   •

[14]Baker, *supra* n. 3, at 55.

11.4(d) "Hereinafter" and *supra*

(1) Use

    (a) "Hereinafter" can be used in limited circumstances to shorten a *supra* citation or to shorten a long title that must be used in the short citation format.

Examples

---

[21]*Terrorism: Victims' Access to Terrorist Assets: Hearing before the Senate Committee on the Judiciary,* 106th Cong. 17 (1999) [hereinafter *Terrorism Hearing*].

•   •   •

[24]*Terrorism Hearing, supra* n. 21, at 17–18.

(b) Use "hereinafter" in **only** the following circumstances:

★ When the cited source has no author and the title is long.

Examples

---

[143]*Settlement Reached in Case Arising from Electrocution of Worker When Crane Struck Power Line,* 10 Verdicts, Settles. & Tactics 215 (June 1990) [hereinafter *Power Line Settlement*].

• • •

[147]*Power Line Settlement, supra* n. 143, at 215.

★ When the full citation appears in a footnote that contains at least two authorities by the **same** author.

Examples

---

[5]Lani Guinier, *Lessons and Challenges of Becoming Gentlemen,* 24 N.Y.U. Rev. L. & Soc. Change 1, 11 (1998) [hereinafter Guinier, *Lessons*]; Lani Guinier, *Reframing the Affirmative Action Debate,* 86 Ky. L.J. 505, 517–518 (1997–1998) [hereinafter Guinier, *Reframing Debate*].

• • •

[18]Guinier, *Lessons, supra* n. 5, at 12–15.

[19]*Id.* at 13, 17.

[20]Guinier, *Reframing Debate, supra* n. 5, at 520.

★ When the regular shortened form would confuse the reader, or when the "hereinafter" format would help readers identify the source more readily. However, be careful not to overuse the "hereinafter" format.

Examples

---

[191]Santa Clara U., *Santa Clara Law Review, Candidate Cite-Checking Handbook 2004–2005,* http://www.scu.edu/law/client/pdf/lawreview_cite-checking.pdf (accessed July 17, 2005) [hereinafter *Santa Clara Handbook*].

• • •

[200]*Santa Clara Handbook, supra* n. 191.

---

[39]Fla. Legis., Off. of Prog. Policy Analysis & Govt. Accountability, *Private Prison Review* 2 (Rpt. No. 99-33 Feb. 2000) (available at http://www.oppaga.state.fl.us/reports/crime/r99-33s.html) [hereinafter *Florida Study*].

• • •

[46]*Florida Study, supra* n. 39, at 4.

★ As described in **Rule 22.2(b).**

(2) Format

(a) The "hereinafter" designation appears in brackets ([ ]) at the end of the first full citation to the authority. Insert one space between the full citation and the "hereinafter" designation. (No punctuation should intervene.) Within the brackets, insert the word "hereinafter," one space, and the shortened form of the title you have selected.

(b) The word "hereinafter" should appear in ordinary type.

(c) Present the information following "hereinafter" in the same typeface as the material would appear in the full citation.

(d) If you are using "hereinafter" because the title is long, either use the first few words of the full title, or use a shortened form that conveys the subject matter of the source. See the *Power Line Settlement* examples in **Rule 11.4(d)(1)(b).**

(e) If you are using "hereinafter" to avoid ambiguity, use the author's last name and a shortened version of the title. See the Lani Guinier examples above in **Rule 11.4(d)(1)(b).**

(f) Place the hereinafter information before any explanatory parenthetical.

Example

Insert one space before the "hereinafter" bracket.

Insert the "hereinafter" designation before the explanatory parenthetical.

Do not need "hereinafter" because the author is different.

[78]Laurence H. Tribe, *American Constitutional Law* ch. 5 (3d ed., Found. Press 2000) [hereinafter Tribe, *American Constitutional Law*]; Laurence H. Tribe, *Constitutional Choices* 30 (Harv. U. Press 1985) [hereinafter Tribe, *Choices*] (discussing the need to interpret the words of a statute as written); Laurence H. Tribe & Michael C. Dorf, *On Reading the Constitution* (Harv. U. Press 1991).

CITING SPECIFIC

PRINT SOURCES

FAST FORMATS

CASES

United States Supreme Court	*Tenn. v. Lane*, 541 U.S. 509 (2004).
United States Court of Appeals	*Knology, Inc. v. Insight Commun. Co.*, 393 F.3d 656 (6th Cir. 2004).
	Morris v. Diaz, 119 Fed. Appx. 316 (2d Cir. 2004) (unpublished).
United States District Court	*Stratton v. Marsh*, 71 F. Supp. 2d 475 (E.D. Pa. 1999).
	Dukes v. Wal-Mart Stores, Inc., 222 F.R.D. 137 (N.D. Cal. 2004).
State supreme court (not using local rule)	*Fletcher Hill, Inc. v. Crosbie*, 872 A.2d 292 (VT. 2005).
State appellate court (not using local rule)	*Dunston v. Miss. Dept. Marine Resources*, 892 So. 2d 837 (Miss. App. 2005).
Parallel citation	*Jackson v. Greger*, 160 Ohio App. 3d 258, 826 N.E.2d 900 (2d Dist. 2005).
Electronic citation	*Jackson v. Mich. St. U.*, 2005 WL 1652195 (Mich. App. July 14, 2005).
Dissenting opinion	*Meister v. Safety Kleen*, 987 S.W.2d 749, 751 (Ark. App. Divs. II & III 1999) (Hart, Neal & Meads, JJ., dissenting).
Short citations	*Id.* at 838. 892 So. 2d at 838. *Dunston*, 892 So. 2d at 838.

12.0   CASES

12.1 Full Citation Format

A full citation for a case may contain as many as nine components. However, some citations will contain fewer components.

Case name,●Reporter volume●Reporter abbreviation●Initial page●, Pinpoint page●(Court abbreviation●Date),●*Subsequent history designation,*●Subsequent history citation [if any].

Example

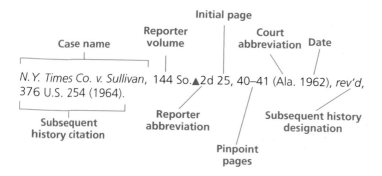

12.2   Case Name

12.2(a) Typeface and punctuation

Italicize or underline the case name. Do not italicize or underline the comma that follows the case name.

12.2(b) Case cited

(1) Consolidated actions

If the caption lists two or more cases, cite only the case first listed.

Example

Caption (as it appears in a reporter or an online database)

The New York Times Company v. L.B. Sullivan
Ralph B. Abernathy et al. v. L.B. Sullivan

  Correct name: *N.Y. Times Co. v. Sullivan*

(2) Two names for one case

If one case has two different names, use the one listed first. For additional information on bankruptcy cases, which often have two names, see **Rule 12.2(o)(2)**.

Example

Caption

In re Trans World Airlines, Incorporated

Interface Group-Nevada, Incorporated v. Trans World Airlines, Incorporated

Correct name: *In re Trans World Airlines, Inc.*

SIDEBAR 12.1

DISTINGUISHING CASE NAMES FROM PARTY NAMES

In a textual sentence, use italics or underlining to refer to the case name, but use regular type to refer to the name of the person.

Case name

In *Smith*, the jury rendered a verdict in favor of the prosecution.

Person

Smith was convicted for larceny.

12.2(c) Parties cited

(1) Cite only the first-listed party on each side of the case. Also include the first-listed relator, if any. Consult **Rule 12.2(n)** for information on relators.

(2) Do not use *"et al.," "et ux.,"* or other terms to denote omitted parties.

(3) If a party has been otherwise named, do not include any party's designation, such as plaintiff, defendant, appellant, appellee, petitioner, respondent, intervenor, administrator, executor, licensee, or trustee.

(4) Place a *"v."* between the parties' names if that is done in the caption.

Examples

Caption

Floyzell Jones et al., Plaintiffs and Appellants v. KMart Corporation et al., Defendants and Appellees

Correct name: Jones v. KMart Corp.

Caption

United States ex rel. David Hancock, Plaintiff, and Relator v. Charles F. Regan, Jr., William A. Gordon, Harold J. Neems, Robert H. Thomas, Howard Peffer, Harry C. Burgess, Francis S. Blake, John F. Welch, Mayer, Brown & Platt, an Illinois partnership, and General Electric Company, a corporation, Defendants

Correct name: U.S. ex rel. Hancock v. Regan

12.2(d) Individual as party

(1) Use only the individual's surname (last name). Retain all parts of the surname, even if it is hyphenated or contains more than one word. If you are unsure about what part of an individual party's name to include as the surname, consult the index of the reporter in which the case appears. Do not use **Appendix 3** to abbreviate an individual's name, even if the name appears in **Appendix 3.**

Examples

Caption

Vivian C. Smith-Gregg v. Department of Interior

Correct name: Smith-Gregg v. Dept. of Int.

Caption

Herbert H. Becker v. Ellen M. Von Nardroff

Correct name: Becker v. Von Nardroff

(2) In some cultures, the family name comes first, and in others there are two family names, one for each parent. Retain names that follow a family name. Thus, if the name is entirely in a language in which the family name comes first, such as Chinese, Korean, or Vietnamese, retain the full name. For Spanish and Portuguese names, include the family name and all following names. For additional information on names, consult the most recent edition of *The Chicago Manual of Style.*

Examples

Caption

Kang Joo Kwan v. United States

>   ***Correct name:*** *Kang Joo Kwan v. U.S.*

Caption

Juan Manuel Ortiz Alvear v. United States

>   ***Correct name:*** *Ortiz Alvear v. U.S.*

Caption

Pedro Luis Rodriguez y Paz v. National Products Company

>   ***Correct name:*** *Rodriguez y Paz v. Natl. Prods. Co.*

(3) If a party is designated only by initials (usually to preserve anonymity), retain all initials as the name. If a party's last name is reduced to a single initial (usually to preserve anonymity), use both the first name and the initial that represents the surname.

Examples

J.M. v. Webster County Bd. of Educ.

Nancy P. v. D'Amato

12.2(e) Organization as party

(1) Include the organization's full name, but omit abbreviations such as "d/b/a" ("doing business as") and words that follow such abbreviations. As noted in **Rule 12.2(q),** typically omit "The" when it appears as the first word in a party's name.

Examples

Caption

Taylor Equipment, Inc., dba Midcon Equipment Company v. John Deere Company

>   ***Correct name:*** *Taylor Equip., Inc. v. John Deere Co.*

Caption

James R. Richardson v. The State-Record Company, Inc.

>   ***Correct name:*** *Richardson v. State-Record Co.*

(2) If the organization name includes the name of an individual, include the full name, not just the surname.

67

Example

Caption

William Lloyd, Inc. v. Walter Hrab

>   *Correct name:*   *William Lloyd, Inc. v. Hrab*

(3)   When a case name appears in a citation clause or sentence (**Rule 43**), you **may** abbreviate any word in the party's name included in **Appendix 3**. When you abbreviate one word in a case name, you should abbreviate all words listed in **Appendix 3**. However, if an abbreviation would cause confusion, do not use it even if the word appears in **Appendix 3**. Using this rationale—except for state names—do not abbreviate a name that consists only of one word. Do not abbreviate words not listed in **Appendix 3**, even if the source cited, such as a reporter, abbreviates those words.

Example when abbreviating words might cause confusion

Caption

Walter Flagg v. Northern Pacific Transportation Company

>   *Confusing abbreviation:*   *Flagg v. N.P. Transp. Co.*

>   *Better abbreviations:*   *Flagg v. N. Pacific Transp. Co. or*
>   *Flagg v. Northern P. Transp. Co.*

(4)   As noted in **Rule 2.3**, if the case name appears in text, it is traditional to spell out virtually all words in the name. However, the following words need not be spelled out: and (&), Association (Assn.), Brothers (Bros.), Company (Co.), Corporation (Corp.), Incorporated (Inc.), Limited (Ltd.), Number (No.), and United States (U.S.). See **Rule 12.2(g)** regarding "United States as party."

(5)   You **may** shorten long organization names (more than five words) in a sensible way by eliminating some words from the end of the name. You also **may** omit geographical terms that are not essential parts of the organization name, and prepositions and articles that are not needed for clarity.

Examples

Caption

Hallison H. Young v. Motor City Apartments Limited Dividend Housing Association No. 1 and No. 2

>   *Correct name:*   *Young v. Motor City Apts.*

Caption

Sci-Tel Associates v. Michigan National Bank, Village of Franklin

> ***Correct name:*** *Sci-Tel Assocs. v. Mich. Natl. Bank*

(6) When there is no danger of confusion, commonly known initials **may** be substituted for a party's complete name. Do not insert periods between the initials. Examples include ACLU, NAACP, and MADD.

(7) When a name includes two business designations, delete the second business designation. Business designations are Assn., Co., Corp., F.S.B., Inc., L.L.C., LLP, LP, Ltd., N.A., P.A., P.C., R.R., Ry., and S.A.

Example

Caption

Morgan and Company, Inc. v. Olin Corporation, Inc.

> ***Correct name:*** *Morgan & Co. v. Olin Corp.*

12.2(f) Union as party

Cite only the local unit. Otherwise, follow **Rule 12.2(e)** for organizations.

Example

Caption

Teamsters Brewery & Soft Drink Workers Local Union 896, International Brotherhood of Teamsters, AFL–CIO v. Anheuser-Busch, Inc., et al.

> ***Correct name:*** *Teamsters Brewery & Soft Drink Workers Loc. Union 896 v. Anheuser-Busch, Inc.*

12.2(g) United States as party

Cite as U.S. Omit "of America."

Examples

Browne v. U.S.   *U.S. v. Rouse*

12.2(h) State or commonwealth as party

When a U.S. state is a party to a case, indicate its name differently according to whether the case is decided by a court of that same state or by another court.

(1)   When citing a decision of that state's court, retain only "State," "Common-wealth," or "People," depending on how the caption of the case reads. For example, if an Iowa court decides a case that involves the State of Iowa, use only "State" as the party name. For clarity, do not abbreviate "State" or "Commonwealth" in this situation.

Example

Caption

Commonwealth of Massachusetts v. Armand R. Therrien, 703 N.E.2d 1175 (Mass. 1998)

> *Correct citation:*   *Commonwealth v. Therrien*, 703 N.E.2d 1175 (Mass. 1998).

(2)   If the case is decided by another state's court or by a federal court, use only the state's name or abbreviation from **Appendix 3.** For example, if a federal district court decides a case involving the State of New York, use "N.Y." as the party name.

Example

Caption

Dennis L. Blackhawk v. Commonwealth of Pennsylvania, et al., 381 F.3d 202 (3d Cir. 2004)

> *Correct citation:*   *Blackhawk v. Pa.*, 381 F.3d 202 (3d Cir. 2004).

12.2(i)   Cities and municipalities as parties

Retain the full names of cities and other municipalities. You may omit larger geographical references.

Example

Caption

Charlie D. Love v. Town of Lake Providence, Louisiana, et al.

> *Correct name:*   *Love v. Town of Lake Providence*

12.2(j)   Commissioner of Internal Revenue as party

Cite as Commr.

Example

Matteson v. Commr.

12.2(k) Individual government official as party

Follow **Rule** 12.2(**d**) regarding individuals as parties. Omit the individual's title or office.

Example

Caption

Einar R. Petersen v. Elizabeth Dole, Secretary of Labor

> ***Correct name:*** *Petersen v. Dole*

12.2(l) Other governmental parties

For other governmental parties, such as agencies and departments, follow **Rule** 12.2(**e**) for organizations. When there is no danger of confusion, commonly known initials, such as FAA, NLRB, OSHA, and SEC, may be substituted for a party's complete name.

Examples

Caption

M. Lorene Pyle, Petitioner v. Department of Public Welfare, Respondent

> ***Correct name:*** *Pyle v. Dept. of Pub. Welfare*

SIDEBAR 12.2

PUBLIC OFFICIAL NAMED AS A PARTY

When a federal public official is a party to an action in his or her official capacity and the official leaves office during the pendency of the case, the name of the case will change to that of the successor. Fed. R. Civ. P. 25(d).

For example, when Lloyd Bentsen became Secretary of the Treasury, he was substituted for Nicholas Brady, the former Treasury Secretary, on all pending cases in which Brady had been sued in an official capacity. Thus, *Fulani v. Brady*, 809 F. Supp. 1112 (S.D.N.Y. 1993), was affirmed on appeal *sub nom. Fulani v. Bentsen*, 35 F.3d 49 (2d Cir. 1994). (Consult **Rule** 12.10(**b**) about when to use "**sub nom.**")

Many state rules of civil procedure contain similar provisions about substituting public officials.

Caption

Paul A. Bilzerian v. Securities and Exchange Commission

Correct name: *Bilzerian v. SEC*

12.2(m) Property as party

Include only the first-listed piece of real or personal property. For addresses, use the street address. You may omit larger geographical designations.

Examples

Caption

United States of America v. 5307 West 90th Street, Oak Lawn, Illinois, and Gary Taylor

Correct name: *U.S. v. 5307 W. 90th St.*

Caption

United States of America v. One 1969 Plymouth Fury Automobile, Serial No. PM43G9D199088

Correct name: *U.S. v. One 1969 Plymouth Fury*

12.2(n) Relator as party

(1)   A relator is a party who sues on behalf of another interested person or entity. For example, a guardian may sue on behalf of a ward, or a government may sue on behalf of a private citizen.

(2)   Put the relator's name in front of the procedural phrase "*ex rel.*" and the interested person or entity after "*ex rel.*" "*Ex rel.*" is defined in **Sidebar 12.3.** If the caption contains multiple relators or interested persons, include only the first-listed relator or interested person per side.

Examples

Caption

Ronald F. Petronella, Commissioner of Labor, ex rel. Glenn Maiorano et al. v. Venture Partners, Ltd., et al.

Correct name: *Petronella ex rel. Maiorano v. Venture Partners, Ltd.*

Caption

United States of America, ex rel. Gary R. Eitel v. Roy D. Reagan et al.

Correct name: *U.S. ex rel. Eitel v. Reagan*

12.2(o) Procedural phrases in case names

(1) Include *"in re," "ex parte,"* and *"ex rel."* when these procedural phrases, or related phrases, appear in case names. These terms are defined in **Sidebar 12.3**. Also consult **Sidebar 12.3** to determine when to replace other terms, such as "in the matter of," with the listed terms.

(2) Bankruptcy cases often have two names, one adversary (one party v. another party) and one nonadversary (typically starting with *"In re"*). If a bankruptcy case has two names, use the adversary name, even if it is not listed first. Although not required, it is permissible to also include the nonadversary name in parentheses following the adversary name. Do not italicize or underline the parentheses around the nonadversary case name. If the case has only one name, use just that name; do not attempt to create a second name for the case.

Example

Caption

In re Frank Lamont Swain and Esther Marie Swain, Debtors

Frank Lamont Swain and Esther Marie Swain, Plaintiffs-Appellants v. Dredging, Inc., d/b/a Scott's Concrete and Jane Ellen Martin, Defendants-Appellees

> **Correct citation:** *Swain v. Dredging, Inc.*, 325 B.R. 264 (Bankr. App. 8th Cir. 2005).

> **Permissible citation:** *Swain v. Dredging, Inc. (In re Swain)*, 325 B.R. 264 (Bankr. App. 8th Cir. 2005).

(3) Omit all procedural phrases except the first.

(4) "Estate of" and "will of" are not treated as procedural phrases and should be included in the case name.

(5) Present procedural phrases in italics, as you would the rest of the case name.

Examples

Caption

Ex parte Caterpillar, Inc. (Re T.A. Hall v. Thompson Tractor Company, Inc., and Caterpillar, Inc.)

> **Correct name:** *Ex parte Caterpillar, Inc.*

Caption

In the Matter of the Estate of Edith B. Allen

> *Correct name:*   *In re Est. of Allen*

Caption

Matter of Attorney Janese B. Crosgrove

> *Correct name:*   *In re Crosgrove*

12.2(p)   Geographical locations

Retain only the first geographical location in a party's name.

Example

Caption

Alexander Leon v. Superior Court of California, Los Angeles County

> *Correct name:*   *Leon v. Super. Ct. of Cal.*

12.2(q)   "The" as first word of a party's name

Omit "the" if it is the first word in a party's name except (1) when it is part of an object in an in rem action, (2) when referring to an established popular name, and (3) when referring to "The King" or "The Queen" as a party.

Examples

Caption (example of general rule)

The New Yorker Magazine, Inc. v. Lawrence E. Gerosa

> *Correct name:*   *New Yorker Mag., Inc. v. Gerosa*

Caption (in rem)

Callaway Ice & Fuel Co., Inc. v. The Rutheline, her engines, tackle, furniture, apparel, etc.

> *Correct name:*   *Callaway Ice & Fuel Co. v. The Rutheline*

Caption (established popular name)

The Civil Rights Cases

> *Correct name:*   *The Civil Rights Cases*

Caption (English case)

Barry Victor Randall v. The Queen

> *Correct name:*   *Randall v. The Queen*

EXPLANATION OF COMMONLY USED PROCEDURAL PHRASES

In re

"*In re*" means "regarding." It is the usual method of labeling a proceeding with no adversarial parties, but with some res, such as a bankrupt's estate or a proposed public project. "*In re*" is used to replace phrases such as "in the matter of," "matter of," "petition of," and "application of."

Ex parte

"*Ex parte*" means "from or on behalf of only one side to a lawsuit." It is the usual method of labeling an action made by, for, or on behalf of one party, often without notice to or contest by the other side. For example, an ex parte divorce hearing is one in which only one spouse participates and the other does not appear.

Ex rel.

"*Ex rel.*" is the abbreviation for "*ex relatione*," which means "upon relation or information." It is the usual method of labeling an action instituted by one person on behalf of another. In citations, "*ex rel.*" is used to replace phrases such as "on the relation of," "for the use of," and "on behalf of."

12.2(r) Popular case names

Sometimes, a case or group of cases becomes well known by a popular name, as opposed to the formal name that appears in the reporter. The popular name may either be substituted for the formal name that appears in the reporter or may be added parenthetically after the formal name. Do not italicize or underline the parentheses around the popular case name.

Examples

Correct citation: *Slaughter-House Cases*, 83 U.S. 36 (1872).

Correct citation: *Butchers' Benv. Assn. of New Orleans v. Crescent City Live-Stock Landing & Slaughter-House Co.* (*Slaughter-House Cases*), 83 U.S. 36 (1872).

12.2(s) Cases with multiple decisions

Sometimes, when multiple decisions have been issued in a single case, it may help readers to provide an identifier for each decision. The identifier is typically the short case name followed by a Roman numeral. The identifier may be embedded within nonitalicized or nonunderlined parentheses following the formal case name or may be included in a "hereinafter" construction after the date parenthetical. Whichever format you select, use the same format throughout the paper you are writing. The identifier also may be used in textual sentences.

Examples

U.S. v. Singleton (*Singleton II*), 165 F.3d 1297 (10th Cir. 1999).

U.S. v. Singleton, 165 F.3d 1297 (10th Cir. 1999) [hereinafter *Singleton II*].

In *Singleton II*, the court held . . . .

12.3   Reporter Volume

After the case name, include the volume number of the cited reporter. Insert one space before and after the volume number.

12.4   Reporter Abbreviation

12.4(a) Placement

(1)   After the volume number, include the abbreviation for the reporter in which the case appears. **Chart 12.1** contains abbreviations for many commonly used reporters. Other abbreviations are listed in **Appendix 1**.

(2)   For any reporter series other than the first, include the series number as part of the reporter abbreviation. To denote the series, use an ordinal contraction (**Rule 4.3**).

Examples

P., P.2d, P.3d

F. Supp., F. Supp. 2d

(3)   Insert one space after the reporter abbreviation

12.4(b) General rules regarding which reporter or reporters to cite

(1)   Case citations in court documents

     (a)   **State courts:** When submitting a document, such as a brief, to a state court, conform all case citations to the local rules of that court, if

---

CHART 12.1

COMMON REPORTER ABBREVIATIONS

(The symbol ▲ denotes a space.)

Reporter	Abbreviation
United States Reports	U.S.
Supreme Court Reporter	S.▲Ct.
United States Supreme Court Reports, Lawyers' Edition	L.▲Ed., L.▲Ed.▲2d
Federal Reporter	F., F.2d, F.3d
Federal Appendix	Fed.▲Appx.
Federal Supplement	F.▲Supp., F.▲Supp.▲2d
Federal Rules Decisions	F.R.D.
Bankruptcy Reporter	B.R.
Atlantic Reporter	A., A.2d
California Reporter	Cal.▲Rptr., Cal.▲Rptr.▲2d, Cal.▲Rptr.▲3d
New York Supplement	N.Y.S., N.Y.S.2d
North Eastern Reporter	N.E., N.E.2d
North Western Reporter	N.W., N.W.2d
Pacific Reporter	P., P.2d, P.3d
South Eastern Reporter	S.E., S.E.2d
South Western Reporter	S.W., S.W.2d, S.W.3d
Southern Reporter	So., So.▲2d

Note: West Group typically starts a new reporter series when the prior series reaches volume 999. To date, West has not permitted a series of reporters to reach volume 1000.

---

any. Local rules for state courts that have them are reprinted in **Appendix 2.** If a state court requires the citation of both official and unofficial reporters (a "parallel citation"), and does not provide a specific format within its own rules, use **Rule 12.4(d)** for guidance. If the court does not have local rules, cite only one source, most typically the West regional reporter, as described in **Rule 12.4(b)(2).**

(b) **Federal courts:** When submitting a document, such as a brief, to a federal court, conform all case citations to the local rules of that court, if any. Local rules for federal courts that have them are reprinted in **Appendix 2.** If the court does not have local rules, cite only one source, most typically the West regional reporter, as described in **Rule 12.4(b)(2).**

(2) Case citations in other documents

    (a) When citing cases in noncourt documents, such as office memoranda and law review articles, cite only one source, in the following order of preference:

- A West reporter (regional reporters for state cases and the appropriate reporter, such as F.3d or F. Supp. 2d, for federal cases; see **Rule 12.4(c)** regarding United States Supreme Court cases).
- Another print reporter in which the case appears (for example, an offset reporter such as N.Y.S.2d or an official reporter such as Ohio App. 3d);
- An online source (see **Rule 39** for examples, including citations to LexisNexis and Westlaw databases and **Rule 40** for other Internet citations);
- A looseleaf reporter (see **Rule 28** for examples);
- Any other source in which the case appears (for example, a legal newspaper).

    (b) **California Reporter and New York Supplement**
When citing a case that appears in both North Eastern Reporter and New York Supplement, cite the North Eastern Reporter, unless there is a strong local preference to the contrary (as there is in New York).

      When citing a case that appears in both the Pacific Reporter and the California Reporter, cite the Pacific Reporter, unless there is a strong local preference (as there is in California).

      Thus, when preparing noncourt documents for California or New York attorneys, it often is best to cite Cal. Rptr. and N.Y.S., respectively, instead of the West regional reporter.

12.4(c) Reporter for United States Supreme Court cases

(1) Unless required by local rule (see **Appendix 2**), typically cite only one source, in the following order of preference:

- United States Reports;
- Supreme Court Reporter;
- United States Supreme Court Reports, Lawyers' Edition;
- United States Law Week;
- An online source (such as LexisNexis, Westlaw, or the Internet);
- Any other source.

Example

Brown v. Bd. of Educ., 349 U.S. 294 (1955).

(2) Many attorneys prefer to include a parallel citation that includes the United States Reports, the Supreme Court Reporter, and sometimes the Lawyers' Edition—in that order. Although not preferred, this citation format is permitted.

Example of alternate format

Brown v. Bd. of Educ., 349 U.S. 294, 75 S. Ct. 753, 99 L. Ed. 1083 (1955).

(3) Do not cite named reporters, such as Dallas or Cranch, because United States Reports now subsumes those reporters. For additional information on named reporters, consult **Sidebar 12.4.**

Example

Correct: *Marbury v. Madison*, 5 U.S. 137 (1803).
Incorrect: *Marbury v. Madison*, 1 Cranch 137 (1803).
                  Marbury v. Madison, 5 U.S. (1 Cranch) 137 (1803).

12.4(d) Parallel citations and court reporters

(1) Definition

A parallel citation is a citation that lists two or more sources that have published the same cited authority. For example, the following citation contains a parallel citation to a case that appears in both Nevada Reports and Pacific Reporter, Second Series. Consult **Sidebar 12.5** for information on how to locate parallel citations.

Example

Dow Chem. Co. v. Mahlum, 114 Nev. 1468, 970 P.2d 98 (1998).

(2) Use

Use parallel citations only when required by local rule or custom, or if they will be particularly helpful to the reader. A parallel citation "will be particularly helpful to the reader" if the writer knows that the reader may have only the official set of reporters available in his or her office. Consult **Appendix 2** to determine whether a particular court requires parallel citations. If the court does not have local rules, follow **Rule 12(b)(1). Appendix 2** also refers to some local customs; however, the best way to determine local custom is to speak with

---

SIDEBAR 12.4

EARLY SUPREME COURT REPORTERS

The first 90 volumes of United States Reports originally were named for the individuals (the "reporters") who compiled the cases for publication. Although you should not cite the named reporter, you will find several sources that do. Therefore, use this chart only for purposes of conversion.

Reporter and Abbreviation	U.S. Volumes	Years
Dallas (Dall.)	1–4	1789–1800
Cranch (Cranch)	5–13	1801–1815
Wheaton (Wheat.)	14–25	1816–1827
Peters (Pet.)	26–41	1828–1842
Howard (How.)	42–65	1843–1860
Black (Black)	66–67	1861–1862
Wallace (Wal.)	68–90	1863–1874

The first 107 volumes of United States Reports (through the 1882 term) generally do not provide the exact date of the decision. The United States Supreme Court's official Web site, http://www.supremecourtus .gov, now provides the exact date for each decision issued during this period. When you visit the Court's Web site, select "Opinions" and then "Dates of Early Supreme Court Decisions."

---

attorneys and judges who practice in the jurisdiction and to consult local research guides, such as *Illinois Legal Research* (Carolina Academic Press 2003) by Professor Mark E. Wojcik, or *Oregon Legal Research* (Carolina Academic Press 2003) by Professor Suzanne Rowe.

(3) Format for parallel citations

(a) Cite official reporters before unofficial reporters. Consult **Appendix 1** to determine which reporters are official and which are unofficial.

(b) If there are two official reporters, place the government-published reporter before the commercially published reporter. This rule typically means that the West regional reporter, which is an official reporter in some states, will be cited last.

SIDEBAR 12.5

LOCATING PARALLEL CITATIONS

Not every case will have a parallel citation because the opinion may appear in only one source. However, if a court's opinions are published in more than one source and you must include a parallel citation, below are several easy ways to locate the parallel citation. To use these methods, you need to know only one citation for the case.

★ The first page of the West unofficial reporter typically provides the parallel citation to the official reporter.
★ The first page of some official reporters prints the unofficial citation.
★ Cases retrieved on LexisNexis and Westlaw typically reprint the official reporter citation on the first page of the case.
★ Shepard's on LexisNexis and Westlaw's KeyCite provide parallel citations.
★ Shepard's citators include parallel citations for cases that have them. In Shepard's, parallel citations are enclosed in parentheses and are located at the top of the list of entries.
★ Many digests provide parallel citations.

In addition, it often is not necessary to consult both versions of the case to determine internal pagination. Instead, some reporters embed the pagination for the parallel reporter within the text of the case.

For example, opinions in permanent versions of the Supreme Court Reporter and the Lawyers' Edition include references that allow you to determine how the case is paginated in United States Reports. In the Supreme Court Reporter, the United States Reports page numbers are located throughout the opinion and appear as subscript numbers (example: $\perp_{188}$). In the Lawyers' Edition, United States Reports numbers appear in bolded superscript and are enclosed in brackets (example: [513 U.S. 1304]).

(c) Except as required in **Rule 12.4(c)** for United States Supreme Court cases, if there are two unofficial reporters, place the West reporter last.

(d) If both unofficial reporters are published by West, place the regional reporter last.

(e) If a court uses neutral parallel citations, also consult **Rule 12.16(b)**.

(f) Separate each citation with a comma and one space.

(g)   Eliminate all or part of the court abbreviation if the name of any cited reporter clearly indicates which court decided the case. Consult **Rule 12.6(e)** for additional explanation and examples.

Examples

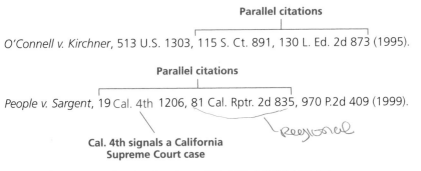

Parallel citations

O'Connell v. Kirchner, 513 U.S. 1303, 115 S. Ct. 891, 130 L. Ed. 2d 873 (1995).

Parallel citations

People v. Sargent, 19 Cal. 4th 1206, 81 Cal. Rptr. 2d 835, 970 P.2d 409 (1999).

Regional

Cal. 4th signals a California
Supreme Court case

Ainsworth v. Perreault, 254 Ga. App. 470, 563 S.E.2d 135 (2002).

In re Estate of Netherton, 62 Ill. App. 3d 55, 57–58, 378 N.E.2d 800, 802 (3d Dist. 1978).

Argonaut Ins. Co. v. Safway Steel Prods., Inc., 355 Ill. App. 3d 1, 290 Ill. Dec. 797, 822 N.E.2d 79 (1st Dist. 2004).

People v. Glanda, 18 A.D.3d 956, 794 N.Y.S.2d 712 (3d Dept. 2005).

12.5   Page Numbers

12.5(a)   Initial page numbers

After the reporter abbreviation, include the initial page number, which is the page on which the case begins. For more information on pages, consult **Rule 5**.

12.5(b)   Pinpoint references

If referring to specific pages within the case, also include the relevant pinpoint references, as described more fully in **Rule 5.2**.

12.5(c)   Pinpoint references and parallel citations

(1)   When using parallel citations (**Rule 12.4(d)**), provide pinpoint references for at least the West reporter.

(2)   Other pinpoint references are optional. It is best, however, to include pinpoint references for each source to which readers would have ready access. In practice, you may anticipate that readers have ready access to West's National Reporter System and to official reporters for the state in which they work.

(3) Consult **Sidebar 12.5** for information on locating pinpoint references for parallel citations.

12.5(d) Dissenting and concurring opinions

Give the initial page on which the case begins, not the page on which the dissenting or concurring opinion begins. Then include pinpoint references to the pages that contain the cited material. See **Rule 12.11(a)** for additional information about dissenting and concurring opinions.

Examples of different page numbers

Initial page only: *In re Estate of Hewitt*, 721 A.2d 1082 (Pa. 1998).

Pinpoint reference: *In re Estate of Hewitt*, 721 A.2d 1082, 1085–1086 (Pa. 1998).

Parallel citation with *In re Estate of Hewitt*, 554 Pa. 486, 493, 721 A.2d 1082,
pinpoint references: 1085 (1998).

Dissenting opinion: *In re Estate of Hewitt*, 721 A.2d 1082, 1089 (Pa. 1998) (Catille, J., dissenting).

12.6   Court Abbreviation

12.6(a) General rules

(1) Include the abbreviation for the court that decided the case. **Appendices 1** and **4** list court abbreviations.

(2) Except as noted in **Rule 12.6(d)** for United States Supreme Court cases and **Rule 12.6(e)** for some parallel citations, the court abbreviation should appear in a parenthetical that also includes the date.

Example

Thomas v. N.W. Natl. Ins. Co., 973 P.2d 804 (Mont. 1998).

(3) Insert the opening parenthesis before the court abbreviation and insert one space after the court abbreviation.

(4) Do not include state designations when citing United States Courts of Appeals cases.

Example

Correct: *Howard v. Wal-Mart Stores, Inc.*, 160 F.3d 358 (7th Cir. 1998).
Incorrect: *Howard v. Wal-Mart Stores, Inc.*, 160 F.3d 358 (7th Cir. Ill. 1998).

12.6(b) Counties, departments, districts, and divisions

(1) Except as noted in **Rule 12.6(c)**, when citing a federal case, do not include information about divisions.

Examples

Correct: *Lipford v. Carnival Corp.*, 346 F. Supp. 2d 1276 (S.D. Fla. 2004).
Incorrect: *Lipford v. Carnival Corp.*, 346 F. Supp. 2d 1276 (S.D. Fla. Miami Div. 2004)..

Correct: *Fireman's Fund Mortg. Corp. v. Zollicoffer*, 719 F. Supp. 650 (N.D. Ill. 1989).
Incorrect: *Fireman's Fund Mortg. Corp. v. Zollicoffer*, 719 F. Supp. 650 (N.D. Ill. E. Div. 1989).

(2) When citing a state case, include available information about counties, departments, districts, or divisions (see **Appendix 1**) to inform readers whether the case is binding within a certain jurisdiction or to reflect the weight of the case. The ALWD Web site, http://www.alwd.org, contains **Chart 12.7**, State Appellate Court Divisions, which shows each state and whether and how its appellate court is divided. If there are multiple subdivisions, include only the largest. Present the county, department, district, or division information in the order and numerical style used by the particular court; thus, "First District" would become "1st Dist.," "Division 2" would become "Div. 2," and Department III would become "Dept. III." Include the county, department, district, or division information after the court abbreviation but before the date.

Examples

Deere v. State, 59 Ark. App. 174, 954 S.W.2d 943 (Div. III 1997).

Griffin v. Paul, 901 So. 2d 1034 (Fla. 2d Dist. App. 2005).

Breaux v. Auto Zone, Inc., 787 So. 2d 322 (La. App. 1st Cir. 2000).

Dearlove v. Genzyme Transgenics Corp., 70 Pa. D. & C. 4th 314 (Common Pleas Phila. Co. 2004).

12.6(c) Fifth Circuit split

(1) History

On October 1, 1981, the former United States Court of Appeals for the Fifth Circuit was divided to create the current Fifth and Eleventh Circuits.

(2) Binding precedent in the Eleventh Circuit

Former Fifth Circuit cases decided before October 1, 1981, are binding precedent in the Eleventh Circuit unless overruled by the Eleventh Circuit sitting en banc.

In addition, decisions of Unit B of the former Fifth Circuit and en banc decisions of the former Fifth Circuit handed down after September 30, 1981, are binding on the Eleventh Circuit unless overruled by the Eleventh Circuit sitting en banc. Unit A en banc decisions and Unit A panel decisions decided after September 30, 1981, are only persuasive precedent in the Eleventh Circuit.

(3) Binding precedent in the Fifth Circuit

Decisions of the former Fifth Circuit, regardless of date and unit, are binding on the new Fifth Circuit.

(4) Citation format

(a) For any former Fifth Circuit case, insert "Unit A" or "Unit B" after "5th Cir." whenever possible.

(b) For en banc decisions of the former Fifth Circuit decided after September 30, 1981, use "Former 5th Cir." as the court abbreviation.

Examples

Gullatte v. Potts, 654 F.2d 1007 (5th Cir. Unit B 1981).

Wilkinson v. D.M. Weatherly Co., 655 F.2d 47 (5th Cir. Unit A 1981).

U.S. v. Martino, 681 F.2d 952 (Former 5th Cir. 1981) (en banc).

12.6(d) United States Supreme Court

For United States Supreme Court decisions, do not include the court abbreviation in the date parenthetical unless citing United States Law Week (U.S.L.W.).

Examples

Correct: *Penry v. Lynaugh*, 492 U.S. 302 (1989).
Incorrect: *Penry v. Lynaugh*, 492 U.S. 302 (U.S. 1989).

Correct: *Kelo v. City of New London*, 73 U.S.L.W. 4552 (U.S. June 23, 2005).
Incorrect: *Kelo v. City of New London*, 73 U.S.L.W. 4552 (2005).

12.6(e) Parallel citations and court abbreviations

As noted in **Rule 12.4(d)(3)**, eliminate all or part of the court abbreviation in the date parenthetical if the name of any cited reporter clearly indicates which court decided the case.

Examples

Ascuittio v. Farricielli, 244 Conn. 692, 711 A.2d 708 (1998).

    The court abbreviation "Conn." for Connecticut Supreme Court has been eliminated from the date parenthetical because the abbreviation for the official reporter, "Conn." for Connecticut Reports, clearly indicates that the Connecticut Supreme Court decided the case.

People v. Carroll, 300 A.D.2d 911, 753 N.Y.S.2d 148 (3d Dept. 2002).

    The abbreviation "N.Y." for "New York" and the abbreviation "App. Div." for "Appellate Division" have been eliminated from the court abbreviations because the official reporter, A.D.2d, which stands for Appellate Division, Second Series, and the abbreviation for the West reporter, New York Supplement, Second Series, together indicate that the New York Appellate Division decided the case. However, the abbreviation "3d Dept." for "Third Department" must be included because that departmental information is required and cannot be gleaned from the reporter abbreviations. Important note: Individuals preparing documents for New York courts always should consult the local rules of court (**Appendix 2**).

    For additional guidance, see the parallel citation examples accompanying **Rule 12.6(b)**.

12.7   Date

12.7(a)   General rule

After the court abbreviation, if any, include the date on which the case was decided. Insert a closing parenthesis after the date.

12.7(b)   Dates for cases in reporters

Include only the year in which the case was decided.

Examples

Estate of Zimmerman v. S.E. Pa. Transp. Auth., 168 F.3d 680 (3d Cir. 1999).

Pittman v. Stevens, 613 S.E.2d 378 (S.C. 2005).

12.7(c)   Dates for cases in other sources

For unpublished cases and cases available only in online or looseleaf format, provide the exact date (month-day-year) of the decision to help readers locate the case. When providing the exact date, abbreviate the month according to **Appendix 3**.

Examples

Allen v. Adams, 2004 U.S. Dist. LEXIS 6313 (W.D. Tex. Mar. 30, 2004).

Klein v. Salvi, 2004 WL 596109 (S.D.N.Y. Mar. 30, 2004).

M.T. McBrian, Inc. v. Liebert Corp., 38 Fed. R. Serv. 3d 1294 (N.D. Ill. Nov. 20, 1996).

12.8   Subsequent History

Include subsequent history if the action is listed in **Rule 12.8(a)**. Also indicate when a judgment in a cited case has been overruled.

12.8(a)   Actions to include

Include the following actions, and any other actions with similar effect. Do not italicize or underline the comma that precedes or follows the history designation.

(1)   Affirmed (, *aff'd,*).

(2)   Affirmed on other grounds (, *aff'd on other grounds,*).

(3)   Affirmed in part, reversed in part (, *aff'd in part and rev'd in part,*).

(4)   Appeal denied (, *appeal denied,*) if the cited case—not the denial—was decided within the last two years or if the denial is particularly important to the discussion. Consult **Sidebar 12.6** for a discussion of what is considered "particularly important."

(5)   Appeal dismissed (, *appeal dismissed,*) if the cited case—not the dismissal—was decided within the last two years.

(6)   Appeal filed (, *appeal filed,*). Do not include *"appeal filed"* information after the higher court decides the case.

(7)   Certiorari denied (, *cert. denied,*) if the cited case—not the denial of certiorari—was decided within the last two years or if the denial is particularly important to the discussion. Consult **Sidebar 12.6** for additional information on denials of certiorari.

(8)   Certiorari dismissed (, *cert. dismissed,*) if the cited case—not the dismissal—was decided within the last two years.

(9)   Certiorari granted (, *cert. granted,*). Do not include *"cert. granted"* information after the higher court decides the case.

SIDEBAR 12.6

INFORMATION ABOUT DENIALS OF CERTIORARI

A writ of certiorari is a device used by courts of last resort, such as the United States Supreme Court, that have discretion to select the cases they want to hear. If the party who lost in the court below seeks review in a court that has discretion to hear the appeal, that party files a "Petition for Writ of Certiorari." If the court grants the petition, it will hear the appeal. If the court denies the petition, it will not hear the appeal.

Precedential Value

Denials of certiorari—abbreviated *"cert. denied"* in citations—carry no precedential value and do not indicate that the higher court agreed with the lower court's decision. Accordingly, denials of certiorari typically should not be included as subsequent history. However, because denials inform readers that the lower court's decision has become final, the information should be included if the cited lower-court decision is two years old or less. Two years was selected because that is the time within which most cases are resolved on appeal.

"Particularly Important"

The denial also should be included if the case is particularly important to the discussion in your paper. A denial of certiorari is important if the case is the focus of the discussion. It also is important when the higher court issues an opinion explaining why a petition for certiorari was denied or when a judge issues a dissenting opinion concerning the denial of certiorari.

Be careful not to copy *"cert. denied"* information from other sources, as they may not follow **Rule 12.8.**

---

(10) Certifying question to (, *certifying question to,*).

(11) Enforced (, *enforced,*).

(12) Mandamus denied (, *mandamus denied,*).

(13) Modified (, *modified,*).

(14) Overruled (, *overruled,*).

(15) Petition for certiorari filed (, *petition for cert. filed,*). Do not include this information after the higher court decides the case.

(16) Reversed (, *rev'd,*).

(17) Reversed in part on other grounds (, *rev'd in part on other grounds,*).

(18) Reversed in part and affirmed in part (, *rev'd in part and aff'd in part,*).

(19) Superseded (, *superseded,*).

(20) Vacated (, *vacated,*).

(21) Withdrawn (, *withdrawn,*).

12.8(b) Actions to exclude

Do not include information concerning remands, rehearings, or rehearings en banc, unless the history is particularly relevant (defined in **Sidebar 12.6**) to the purpose for which the case is cited.

12.8(c) Placement and format of subsequent history

(1) Include appropriate subsequent history as defined in Rules **12.8(a)** and **(b) whenever** citing the lower court case in full. Never attach subsequent history to a short citation.

(2) Insert the history designation after the court and date parenthetical. Italicize the history designation but not the comma preceding or following the designation.

(3) After the history designation, include all required components of the higher court case, but typically exclude the case name. If the case name changed on appeal, follow **Rule 12.10(b)**. "Overruled" is one exception to this general principle because two separate cases are involved.

(4) When citing a decision with multiple decisions in the same year, include the year for each cited decision. If you will be referring to the multiple decisions several times in your paper, consider using **Rule 12.2(s)**.

(5) If the history is not separately reported but is denoted only on the face of a lower court opinion, include only the court abbreviation and exact date (month-day-year) in a parenthetical that follows the history designation.

Examples

Am. Natl. Fire Ins. Co. v. B & L Trucking & Constr. Co., 920 P.2d 192 (Wash. App. Div. 2 1996), *aff'd*, 951 P.2d 250 (Wash. 1998).

Bowers v. Hardwick, 478 U.S. 186, 195–196 (1986), *overruled*, *Lawrence v. Tex.*, 539 U.S. 558 (2003).

Crockett v. Essex, 9 S.W.3d 561 (Ark. App. Divs. II & III 2000), *rev'd*, 19 S.W.3d 585 (Ark. 2000).

History not separately printed

Mellies v. Dearborn, 558 S.E.2d 460 (Ga. App. 2001), *cert. denied*, (Ga. Apr. 15, 2002).

12.9   Prior History

12.9(a) Use

(1)   It is never mandatory to include prior history.

(2)   Use prior history sparingly.

(3)   Include prior history only when it is significant to a point addressed in your paper. For example, if you are writing about a supreme court opinion and include a discussion about what happened in the lower courts, you might use a prior history citation.

12.9(b) Format

(1)   Attach prior history after a full citation. Do not attach prior history to a short citation.

(2)   Most subsequent history designations in **Rule 12.8(a)** can be converted to prior history designations by replacing the "-ed" suffix with an "-ing" suffix. Examples: affirming (, *aff'g*), reversing (, *rev'g*), and vacating (, *vacating*).

(3)   Insert prior history in the same manner as subsequent history (**Rule 12.8(c)**).

Example

Snyder v. U.S. Fid. & Guar. Co., 70 Cal. Rptr. 2d 498 (App. 1st Dist. 1997), *vacating* 68 Cal. Rptr. 2d 396 (App. 1st Dist. 1997).

12.10 Additional Rules Concerning Subsequent and Prior History

12.10(a) Explanation of history

You may include an explanation for the disposition. Examples include *vacating as moot, appeal dismissed per stipulation, rev'd without opinion,* and *aff'd by an equally divided court.*

12.10(b) Case name changed on appeal

(1) When the case name is changed on appeal, provide the new case name as part of the history **except** when (a) the parties' names are merely reversed or (b) certiorari has been denied under a different name.

(2) Use the italicized abbreviation *"sub nom."* to denote the name change. *"Sub nom."* is short for *"sub nomine,"* which means "under the name."

(3) Insert *sub nom.* directly after the history designation and drop the comma that normally would follow the designation. Insert one space between *sub nom.* and the changed case name, followed by the rest of the subsequent history case components.

Examples

Subsequent history

McHenry v. Fla. Bar, 808 F. Supp. 1543 (M.D. Fla. 1992), *aff'd*, 21 F.3d 1038 (11th Cir. 1994), *rev'd sub nom. Fla. Bar v. Went For It, Inc.*, 515 U.S. 618 (1995).

Prior history

Fla. Bar v. Went For It, Inc., 515 U.S. 618 (1995), *rev'g sub nom. McHenry v. Fla. Bar*, 21 F.3d 1038 (11th Cir. 1994).

12.10(c) Order of multiple histories

(1) If the history itself has history, attach the additional history with another history term. See the subsequent history example in **Rule 12.10(b)**.

(2) If citing both prior and subsequent histories, provide the prior history first. Include the italicized word *"and"* before the subsequent history.

Example

McHenry v. Fla. Bar, 21 F.3d 1038 (11th Cir. 1994), *aff'g* 808 F. Supp. 1543 (M.D. Fla. 1992), *and rev'd sub nom. Fla. Bar v. Went For It, Inc.*, 515 U.S. 618 (1995).

12.10(d) Multiple decisions by a single court

Connect multiple decisions by a single court with the italicized word "*and.*"

Example

Shell Oil Co. v. Meyer, 684 N.E.2d 504 (Ind. App. 4th Dist. 1997), *vacated*, 698 N.E.2d 1183 (Ind. 1998), *and aff'd in part and vacated in part*, 705 N.E.2d 962 (Ind. 1998).

12.10(e) Relation to parenthetical information

Follow **Rule 46** regarding placement of parenthetical information. Thus, if the parenthetical concerns the lower court case, it should follow the lower court case. If the parenthetical concerns the higher court case, it should follow the higher court case.

Examples

Parenthetical relates to lower court case

Mapp v. Ohio, 166 N.E.2d 387 (Ohio 1960) (holding that contraband obtained by an unlawful search is admissible evidence), *rev'd*, 347 U.S. 643 (1961).

Parenthetical relates to higher court case

Mapp v. Ohio, 166 N.E.2d 387 (Ohio 1960), *rev'd*, 347 U.S. 643 (1961) (holding that evidence obtained by an unconstitutional search is not admissible).

12.10(f) No effect on order of authorities

As explained in **Rule 45.3(d)**, subsequent history is a "tagalong" to the cited case and thus does not affect the order of authorities within a signal.

12.10(g) No effect on use of *id.*

As explained in **Rule 11.3(f)**, prior and subsequent histories are not intervening sources and thus do not prohibit the use of *id.*

12.11   Parenthetical Information

12.11(a) Dissenting, concurring, and plurality opinions

(1)   In a separate parenthetical, identify any opinion, such as a dissenting opinion, concurring opinion, or plurality opinion, that does not constitute the majority opinion.

(2)   This type of parenthetical should follow both full citations and short citations.

(3)   Follow the formatting instructions in **Rule 46.3.**

(4)   For plurality opinions, simply include "plurality" in the parenthetical.

(5)   For dissents and concurrences, include the last name and title abbreviation of any judge who participated in the minority decision. List the names in the order they appear on the decision. **Chart 12.2** lists common title abbreviations for judges and other judicial officials. After the judge's title and abbreviation, indicate the type of opinion.

Example

Meister v. Safety Kleen, 987 S.W.2d 749, 751 (Ark. App. Divs. II & III 1999) (Hart, Neal & Meads, JJ., dissenting).

Other examples

(O'Connor, Ginsburg & Breyer, JJ., dissenting in part and concurring in part).

(Rehnquist, C.J. & Thomas, J., concurring in parts I–III, and dissenting from parts IV–VII).

(6)   When alternating between citations to different opinions within the same case, include a designating parenthetical each time you switch opinions. As illustrated below, if using *id.* to refer to the same opinion within the case, the parenthetical need not be repeated with the *id.* citation.

Examples

[59]*Id.* at 381 (Souter, J., concurring).

[60]*Id.*

[61]*Id.* at 387 (Scalia, J., dissenting).

[62]*Id.* at 382 (Souter, J., concurring).

[63]*Id.* at 369 (majority).

[64]*Id.* at 371.

[65]*Id.* at 389 (Scalia, J., dissenting).

CHART 12.2

ABBREVIATIONS FOR TITLES OF JUDGES AND OTHER JUDICIAL OFFICIALS

Administrative Law Judge	A.L.J.
Arbitrator	Arb.
Chief Judge, Chief Justice	C.J.
Commissioner	Commr.
Judge, Justice	J.
Judges, Justices	JJ.
Magistrate, Magistrate Judge	Mag.
Mediator	Med.
President	Pres.

12.11(b) Weight of authority

You may parenthetically provide information about the weight of the case. Examples include whether the opinion is an en banc decision or a per curiam opinion; the split among the judges who decided the case; whether the cited proposition is dictum as opposed to a holding; and whether a disposition is without an opinion, which is called a memorandum opinion and is abbreviated "mem."

Examples

Ellis v. Anderson Tully Co., 727 So. 2d 716 (Miss. 1998) (en banc).

Brown v. Mentz Founds., Inc., 126 S.W.3d 770 (Mo. App. E. Dist. 2004) (mem.).

Aguilar v. Felton, 473 U.S. 402 (1985) (affirming 5–4).

12.11(c) Explanatory parentheticals

It is often helpful to provide an explanatory parenthetical that summarizes the holding, provides a pertinent quotation, or explains the relevance of the cited case. Consult **Rule 46** for additional information about explanatory parentheticals.

12.12 Cases Published Only on LexisNexis or Westlaw

12.12(a) Format

(1) When a case is published only on LexisNexis or Westlaw, include the case name as required by **Rule 12.2**; the database identifier, which typically includes the year, the name of the database (either LEXIS or WL), and a unique document number; and a parenthetical that includes the court abbreviation and exact date (month-day-year).

(2) If the database identifier clearly indicates which court decided the case, all or part of the court abbreviation may be eliminated. The database identifier clearly indicates which court decided the case if the database abbreviation is identical to the court abbreviation listed in **Appendix 1.**

Examples

Goodyear Tire & Rubber Co. v. Moore, 2005 WL 1611323 (Va. App. July 12, 2005).

Boedeker v. Larson, 2004 Va. App. LEXIS 596 (Dec. 7, 2004).

12.12(b) Pinpoint references

To provide a pinpoint reference, insert the word "at" after the database identifier. Then insert one asterisk (for a single page) or two asterisks (for multiple pages) and the page number or numbers.

Examples

Am. Online, Inc. v. IMS, 1998 U.S. Dist. LEXIS 20645 at *5 (E.D. Va. Dec. 30, 1998).

Am. Online, Inc. v. IMS, 1998 U.S. Dist. LEXIS 20645 at **5–9 (E.D. Va. Dec. 30, 1998).

12.12(c) Parallel citations

Do not include a parallel citation to LexisNexis or Westlaw when the case is available in a reporter. LexisNexis and Westlaw, through their "get a document" and "find" functions, permit users to easily access the case using the reporter information.

12.13   Cases Not Yet Reported

If a case will be printed in a reporter but the volume and page numbers are not yet available, use the rules for reported cases, except (a) replace both the volume number and the page number with three underlined spaces, (b) include a parallel citation to Westlaw or LexisNexis when available, and (c) use the exact date (month-day-year).

Example

People v. Carter, ___ N.W.2d ___, 2005 WL 473932 (Mich. App. Mar. 1, 2005).

12.14 Table Cases and Federal Appendix Cases

12.14(a) Cases in reporter tables

If only the disposition of a case is listed in a reporter table, use the format for published cases. However, insert one space and "(table)" after the citation. If the entire opinion, as opposed to the disposition, is on LexisNexis or Westlaw, insert "(table)" after the initial page number and include the database identifier.

Examples

If opinion is not available online

U.S. v. Maden, 173 F.3d 865 (10th Cir. 1999) (table).

If opinion is available online

U.S. v. Maden, 173 F.3d 865 (table), 1999 WL 261014 (10th Cir. 1999).

12.14(b) Cases in Federal Appendix

(1) Background

On September 1, 2001, West began publishing a reporter called Federal Appendix; cases in this reporter date from January 1, 2001. Federal Appendix contains **unpublished cases** from all federal courts of appeals except the Third Circuit, Fifth Circuit, and Eleventh Circuit. (West does not receive unpublished opinions from these three courts.) An "unpublished case" is a term of art that means that the case was not selected by the court for official publication. The general rule is that unpublished cases cannot serve as binding precedent; indeed, many courts prohibit attorneys from citing unpublished cases (**Sidebar 12.7**). Cases that appear in Federal Appendix do not lose their "unpublished" status; thus, attorneys should consult the controlling rules before citing a case that appears in Federal Appendix.

(2) Format

Cite Federal Appendix cases using the format for United States Court of Appeals cases, but add a separate parenthetical noting that the case has been designated as "unpublished." Abbreviate "Federal Appendix" as "Fed. Appx.," which is the abbreviation selected by West.

Example

Scarborough v. Morgan, 21 Fed. Appx. 279, 280 (6th Cir. 2001) (unpublished).

12.15 Cases on the Internet

12.15(a) Use

Do not cite the Internet if the case is available in a reporter, an online database such as Westlaw or LexisNexis, or a looseleaf service.

12.15(b) Format

If it is necessary to cite a case published on the Internet, provide the case name as required by **Rule 12.2.** Then either (1) use the neutral format in **Rule 12.16** or (2) insert the Uniform Resource Locator (URL) and a parenthetical with the court abbreviation and exact date (month-day-year). For additional information on citing Internet sources, consult **Rule 40.**

Example using URL

John's Heating Serv. v. Lamb, http://touchngo.com/sp/html/sp-5572.htm (Alaska May 10, 2002).

12.15(c) Pinpoint reference

It may not be possible to provide pinpoint references for court decisions found on the Internet. Some courts, however, number each paragraph of the opinion or include page numbers within the posted opinion. When possible, include a pinpoint reference using the formats below.

Examples

Page number

In re Vt. Verde Antique Intl., Inc., http://dol.state.vt.us/gopher_root3/supct/current/2001-116.op, at 4 (Vt. Sept. 6, 2002).

Paragraph number

Savage v. Savage, http://www.sdbar.org/opinions/2003/April/2003_046.htm, at ¶ 10 (S.D. Apr. 23, 2003).

12.16   Neutral Citations

12.16(a) Definition

Neutral citations are ones that do not refer to a particular vendor's source (such as West Group's regional reporters) or to a particular type of source (such as a reporter, a CD-ROM, or an Internet site).

12.16(b) Use

Use neutral citations when required by local rule. Consult **Appendix 2** to determine whether a particular court requires neutral citations. If a court does not require neutral citations, you may still include a neutral citation as a parallel citation as explained in **Rule 12.16(c)**.

12.16(c) Format

To include a neutral citation, use either the format adopted by the court to which you are submitting the document or the following format:

Case name,•Year of decision•Court abbreviation•Opinion number,•Citation to reporter or online source.

Examples

North Dakota Supreme Court local format

Johnson v. Traynor, 1998 ND 115, 579 N.W.2d 184.

ALWD format with reporter citation

Johnson v. Traynor, 1998 N.D. 115, 579 N.W.2d 184.

ALWD format with online citation

State v. Robinson, 1999 Me. 86, 1999 WL 353072 (June 3, 1999).

12.17   Cases Published Only in a Looseleaf Service

Follow **Rule 28**.

12.18   Unreported Cases

12.18(a) Format

When a case is unreported and is available only in a separately paginated slip opinion, include the following components:

Case name,•Docket number•(Court abbreviation•Exact date of disposition).

Example

Operator Serv. Co. v. Croteau, No. CL961672Al (Fla. 15th Cir. Aug. 5, 1996).

12.18(b) Pinpoint reference

To include a pinpoint reference, insert the following after the docket number: a comma, the phrase "slip op. at" and the cited page or pages.

Example

Operator Serv. Co. v. Croteau, No. CL961672Al, slip op. at 2 (Fla. 15th Cir. Aug. 5, 1996).

12.18(c) Date other than disposition

If the date included is not the date of disposition, indicate the significance immediately before the date.

Example

Woods v. Wyeth Labs. Inc., No. 94-1493 (W.D. Pa. filed Sept. 1, 1994).

12.19 Early Federal Circuit Cases

When citing cases from the old federal circuits, which were abolished on June 1, 1912, follow the format for current United States Court of Appeals cases, but alter the court abbreviation to include "C.C." instead of "Cir."

Example

Combs v. Hodge, 6 F. Cas. 194 (C.C.D.C. 1857), *rev'd*, 62 U.S. 397 (1858).

12.20 Court Documents, Transcripts, and Records

Insert the title of the document as identified on its cover or first page, followed by a pinpoint reference and a citation to the case to which it relates. Abbreviate words in the title according to **Appendix 3**. Present the title in ordinary type.

Consult **Rule 29** to cite practitioner documents (such as pleadings, motions, and affidavits), transcripts, and records in documents submitted in the same case as the cited materials.

SIDEBAR 12.7

COURT RULES PROHIBITING OR LIMITING CITATION OF UNREPORTED CASES IN BRIEFS

Since the 1970s, an increasing number of court decisions are not published in reporters. Even though cases designated "unpublished" by the court do not appear in reporters, they may be available online or through other sources.

Before citing an opinion designated "unpublished," check the controlling local court rules. Different courts have differing rules on whether litigants can cite "unpublished" cases. Even if "unpublished" cases can be cited, some courts limit the precedential value these cases carry.

Three court rules concerning the citation of unpublished cases in briefs or other documents submitted to the court are listed below. **These are only samples; always consult the rules for the particular court in which you are practicing.**

★ **Iowa Court of Appeals:** "An unpublished opinion of the Iowa appellate courts or of any other appellate court may be cited in a brief; however, unpublished opinions shall not constitute controlling legal authority. A copy of the unpublished opinion shall be attached to the brief and shall be accompanied by a certification that counsel has conducted a diligent search for, and fully disclosed, any subsequent disposition of the unpublished opinion. For purposes of these rules, an 'unpublished' opinion means an opinion the text of which is not included or designated for inclusion in the National Reporter System. When citing an unpublished appellate opinion, a party shall include, when available, an electronic citation indicating where the opinion may be readily accessed on line." Iowa R. App. P. 6.14.

★ **United States Court of Appeals for the First Circuit:** "Unpublished opinions may be cited only in related cases. Only published opinions may be cited otherwise." 1st Cir. R. 36(b)(2).

★ **United States Court of Appeals for the Eleventh Circuit:** "Unpublished opinions are not considered binding precedent. They may be cited as persuasive authority, provided that a copy of the unpublished opinion is attached to or incorporated within the brief, petition, motion or response in which such citation is made." 11th Cir. R. 36-2.

SIDEBAR 12.7 (CONTINUED)

For background on these and other "no citation" rules, see Charles E. Carpenter, *The No-Citation Rule for Unpublished Opinions: Do the Ends of Expediency for Overloaded Appellate Courts Justify the Means of Secrecy?* 50 S.C. L. Rev. 235 (1998), and Melissa H. Weresh, *The Unpublished, Non-Precedential Decision: An Uncomfortable Legality?* 3 J. App. Prac. & Process 169 (2001).

Example

Br. of Petr. at 33, *Camps Newfound/Owatonna, Inc. v. Town of Harrison*, 520 U.S. 564 (1997).

12.21   Short Citation Format

12.21(a) *Id.* as the preferred short citation

If *id.* is appropriate, use it as the preferred short citation. Consult **Rules 11.2** and **11.3** for additional information on *id.* and other forms of short citations. If *id.* is not appropriate, use one of the short forms described in **Rules 12.21(b)** through **12.21(f)**.

Examples

Document without footnotes

A divided Court later held that in personam jurisdiction over a defendant based on in-state service of process was valid when the defendant had no minimum contacts with the forum. *Burnham v. Super. Ct. Cal.*, 495 U.S. 604, 628 (1990). In dicta, Justice Scalia's majority opinion reasoned that when a person or property was located in the forum, personal jurisdiction was valid without considering the minimum contacts standard. *Id.* at 609. Justice Brennan's concurring opinion, however, followed the earlier line of decisions and applied the minimum contacts standard, while arriving at the same decision. *Id.* at 628 (Brennan, J., concurring).

Document with footnotes

A divided Court later held that in personam jurisdiction over a defendant based on in-state service of process was valid when the defendant had no minimum contacts with the forum.[23] In dicta, Justice Scalia's majority opinion reasoned that when a person or property was located in the forum, personal jurisdiction was valid without considering the minimum contacts standard.[24]

---

[23]*Burnham v. Super. Ct. Cal.*, 495 U.S. 604, 628 (1990).

[24]*Id.* at 609.

12.21(b) Short citation format when the case name, or part of the case name, is *not* included in the textual sentence

(1) When all or part of the cited case's name does not appear in the textual sentence, typically use the following format. You may omit the party's name if the case is being discussed throughout the section or paragraph and there is no danger that the reader will be confused.

Example of the general rule

The Whistleblowers' Protection Act "seeks to protect the integrity of the law by removing barriers to employee efforts to report violations of the law." *Melchi v. Burns Intl. Sec. Servs., Inc.*, 597 F. Supp. 575, 581 (E.D. Mich. 1984). The Act prevents employers from retaliating against employees who report possible violations of the law. *Chandler v. Dowell Schlumberger, Inc.*, 572 N.W.2d 210, 211 (Mich. 1998). However, the Act does not protect employees who make reports in bad faith. *Melchi*, 597 F. Supp. at 583.

Example

Full citation: *Seel v. Van Der Veur*, 971 P.2d 924 (Utah 1998).
Short citation: *Seel*, 971 P.2d at 924.

(2) When making only a general reference to the case, as opposed to citing a particular page, use the same format but eliminate "at." Use this format *only* when citing to the case as a whole; use a pinpoint page whenever possible. For the page reference, include the initial page.

Example

Correct: *Seel*, 971 P.2d 924.
Incorrect: *Seel*, at 924.

(3) When selecting which party's name to retain, typically use the first party's name unless using that party's name would cause confusion. For example, using the first party's name would cause confusion if you cited several cases in which the first party's name was Smith. Using the first party's name would also cause confusion if the first party is a government or geographical designation, such as United States, Massachusetts, or People.

(4) If it would cause confusion to use the first party's name, use the second party's name.

Example

Full citation: *U.S. v. Chairse*, 18 F. Supp. 2d 1021 (D. Minn. 1998).
Short citation: *Chairse*, 18 F. Supp. 2d at 1024.

(5) If the name is particularly long, include only that amount necessary for the reader to understand which case is being cited. **Rule 12.2(e)(5)** describes when and how an organizational party's name may be shortened in a full citation.

Example

Full citation: *Sportsman Store of Lake Charles, Inc. v. Sonitrol Security Sys. of Calcasieu, Inc.*, 725 So. 2d 74 (La. App. 3d Dist. 1998), *rev'd*, 748 So. 2d 417 (La. 1999).
Short citation: *Sportsman Store*, 725 So. 2d at 82–83.

12.21(c) Short citation format when the case name, or part of the case name, *is* included in the textual sentence

(1) In general, use the following components:

Volume number•Reporter abbreviation•at•Pinpoint reference.

Examples

Document without footnotes

The decision in *International Shoe* specifically addressed minimum contacts relating to in personam jurisdiction. 326 U.S. at 316.

Document with footnotes

The decision in *International Shoe* specifically addressed minimum contacts relating to in personam jurisdiction.[17]

---

[17]326 U.S. at 316.

(2) When making only a general reference to the case, as opposed to citing a particular page, use the same format but eliminate "at." As noted in **Rule 12.21(b)(2)**, use general references sparingly. For the page reference, include the initial page. Alternatively, if the cited case has been cited in full format within the same general discussion, the case may be referred to in text by one party's name without further citation.

Examples

International Shoe also addresses minimum contacts. 326 U.S. 310.

   or

International Shoe also addresses minimum contacts.

12.21(d) Short citation formats for online cases

When *id.* is not appropriate, use **Rules 12.21(b)** and **12.21(c)**, but replace the reporter volume and reporter abbreviation with the database identifier. Use one asterisk to denote a single pinpoint page and two asterisks to denote multiple pinpoint pages.

Examples

Case name not included in the textual sentence

Full citation: *White v. C.J. Coakley Co.*, 1999 Va. App. LEXIS 261 (May 4, 1999).
Short citation: *White*, 1999 Va. App. LEXIS 261 at *3.

Case name included in the textual sentence

Full citation: *Young v. Apfel*, 1999 WL 325026 (N.D. Ind. May 19, 1999).
Short citation: 1999 WL 325026 at **4–5.

12.21(e) Short citation formats for unpublished cases

When *id.* is not appropriate, follow **Rules 12.21(b)** and **12.21(c)** regarding case names. Then include "slip op. at" and the pinpoint reference.

Example

Full citation: *Operator Serv. Co. v. Croteau*, No. CL961672AI, slip op. at 2 (Fla. 15th Cir. Aug. 5, 1996).

Short citation (case name not included in the textual sentence): *Operator Serv. Co.*, slip op. at 1.

Short citation (case name included in the textual sentence): Slip op. at 1.

12.21(f) Short citation formats for parallel citations

(1) When the full citation includes parallel citations, *id.* is not an appropriate short citation. *Id.* is not appropriate because *id.* refers to a single source and a parallel citation refers to two or more reporters. However, unless a local court rule provides otherwise, *id.* may be used to refer to the first source in the parallel citation.

Example

Full citation: *Dow Chem. Co. v. Mahlum*, 114 Nev. 1468, 970 P.2d 98 (1998).
Short citation: *Id.* at 1469, 970 P.2d at 99.

(2) Use the rules regarding case names in **12.21(b)** and **12.21(c)**.

(3) Unless a local court rule requires otherwise, select **one** of the following short citation formats, which are listed in order of preference. When possible, provide pinpoint references for each cited reporter. Always provide a pinpoint citation for at least the West reporter.

Examples (assume a local rule requires a parallel citation)

Full citation: *O'Connell v. Kirchner*, 513 U.S. 1303, 115 S. Ct. 891, 130 L. Ed. 2d 873 (1995).
Short citation option one: *O'Connell*, 513 U.S. at 1304.
Short citation option two: *Id.* at 1304, 115 S. Ct. at 892, 130 L. Ed. 2d at 875.

Full citation: *Abel v. Fox*, 247 Ill. App. 3d 811, 221 Ill. Dec. 129, 654 N.E.2d 591 (4th Dist. 1995).
Short citation option one: *Abel*, 654 N.E.2d at 592.
Short citation option two: *Id.* at 812, 221 Ill. Dec. at 129, 654 N.E.2d at 592.

CONSTITUTIONS

Full citation format for U.S. Constitution (provision currently in force)	U.S. Const. art. IV, § 5(b).
Full citation format for U.S. Constitution (provision not currently in force)	U.S. Const. amend. XVIII (repealed 1933 by U.S. Const. amend. XXI).
Full citation format for state constitutions (provisions currently in force)	Conn. Const. art. XIII, § 1. N.J. Const. art. I, ¶ 9.
Full citation format for state constitutions (provisions not currently in force)	Cal. Const. art. XVII (repealed 1949 by Cal. Const. art. XXI).
Short citation format (any constitution)	*Id.* *Id.* at amend. V.

13.0 CONSTITUTIONS

13.1 Which Source to Cite

Unless citing a constitution for a historical purpose, cite the constitution currently in force.

13.2 Full Citation Format for Constitutions Currently in Force

A full citation to a constitution currently in force contains two components.

Name of constitution•Pinpoint reference.

Example

Name of constitution

U.S. Const. amend. XIV, § 2.

Pinpoint reference

13.2(a) Name of constitution

For the name of the constitution, use the appropriate jurisdictional abbreviation in **Appendix 3**, followed by one space and the abbreviation "Const."

Examples (the symbol ▲ denotes a space)

Ala.▲Const.▲art.▲IV,▲§▲88.

Conn.▲Const.▲art.▲XIII,▲§▲1.

N.J.▲Const.▲art.▲I,▲¶▲9.

13.2(b) Pinpoint reference

After the name of the constitution, include the relevant pinpoint reference. Be as specific as possible, including all sections and subsections. Use the subdivision abbreviations in **Appendix 3(C)**.

Examples

U.S. Const. art. I.

U.S. Const. amend. XIV, § 2.

U.S. Const. art. I, § 9, cl. 2.

U.S. Const. preamble.

Ohio Const. art. IV, § 5(b).

Utah Const. art. VIII, § 4.

13.2(c) Date

Do not include the date for a constitutional provision currently in force.

13.2(d) Other information

You may parenthetically include information about amendments or other information that would assist readers.

Example

Iowa Const. art. 2, § 1 (amended 1868).

13.3 Full Citation Format for Constitutions No Longer in Force

If citing a constitutional provision that is no longer in force, such as a provision that has been repealed or superseded, use the citation format for current constitutions, but explain in a parenthetical why the provision is no longer in force, and include the year in which it lost effect. You may include the year in which the repealed or superseded provision was enacted.

Examples

U.S. Const. amend. XVIII (repealed 1933 by U.S. Const. amend. XXI).

Cal. Const. art. XXV (repealed 1949 by Cal. Const. art. XXVII).

La. Const. art. I, § 6 (1921) (superseded 1974 by La. Const. art. I, § 22).

Or. Const. art. II, § 6 (repealed 1927).

13.4 Short Citation Format

When appropriate, use *id.* as a short-form citation for constitutional provisions (whether current or no longer in force). Consult **Rule 11.3** for additional information on *id.* Do not use any other citation format. In other words, if *id.* is not appropriate, repeat the full citation.

Example

Full citation: U.S. Const. art. I, § 10, cl. 3.
Short citation: *Id.* at art. VI, cl. 2.

SIDEBAR 13.1

REFERRING TO CONSTITUTIONS IN TEXT

When referring to a constitutional provision in a textual sentence, do not use the citation format. Instead, spell out the provision. See **Rule 6.11** for additional information.

Example

Article IX, section 1 of the Florida Constitution provides that "[a]dequate provision shall be made by law for a uniform system of free public schools."

STATUTORY CODES, SESSION LAWS, AND SLIP LAWS

Full citation format for United States Code	19 U.S.C. § 2411 (2000).
Full citation format for United States Code Annotated (citing a supplement)	18 U.S.C.A. § 2441 (West Supp. 2004).
Full citation format for United States Code Service (citing main volume and a supplement)	18 U.S.C.S. § 2241 (Law. Coop. 1991 & Lexis Supp. 2005).
Full citation format for state statute *(consult Appendix 1 for each state's format)*	Ga. Code Ann. § 9-9-17 (2004). Okla. Stat. tit. 5, § 11 (2004).
Statutes available on electronic database	Del. Code Ann. tit. 13, § 101(a), (d) (Westlaw current through 2005 1st Reg. Sess.).
Short citation formats for federal and state statutes	*Id.* 19 U.S.C. § 2411. Ga. Code Ann. § 17-10-30. § 17-10-30.
Federal session law	Pub. L. No. 109-2, 119 Stat. 12 (2005).
State session law *(consult Appendix 1 for each state's format)*	1985 N.J. Laws 308.
Federal slip law	Pub. L. No. 108-173, § 1201 (Dec. 8, 2003), 2003 U.S.C.C.A.N. (117 Stat.) 2066, 2469.
State slip law	Ill. Pub. Act. No. 94-4, § 5 (June 1, 2005) (available in Westlaw at 2005 Ill. Legis. Serv. P.A. 94-4).

14.0 STATUTORY CODES, SESSION LAWS, AND SLIP LAWS

14.1 Which Source to Cite

14.1(a)

When possible, cite a statute in a code rather than in a session law.

14.1(b)

When two codes contain the same statute, usually cite the official code. Official codes are identified in **Appendix 1.** You may cite the print or online version of the code.

14.1(c)

If the official code is not readily available or does not yet contain the cited statute, cite an unofficial code. You may cite the print or online version of the unofficial code.

14.1(d)

If the statute does not appear in an official or unofficial code, cite the session law. You also may cite a session law if you want readers to review the statute in the form enacted by the legislature.

14.1(e)

If the statute is not in a code or in a session law, cite a slip law.

14.2 Full Citation, Print Format for Federal Statutes Currently in Force

A full citation to a federal statute currently in force typically has five or six components, depending on whether the code is official or unofficial.

Title number•Code abbreviation•Section symbol•Section number•(Publisher [unofficial only]•Date).

111

Example

Title number
Section symbol
Date
18 U.S.C. § 1965 (2000).
Section number
Code abbreviation

14.2(a) Title number

(1) Federal statutes are grouped by subject matter. Each subject matter is called a "title" and is given a number. The title number can be found on the spine and front cover of a code volume.

(2) Start the citation with the title number. Insert one space after the title number.

14.2(b) Code abbreviation

(1) After the title, insert the abbreviation for the code.

(2) The official code for federal statutes is United States Code, which is abbreviated "U.S.C." The two unofficial codes are United States Code Annotated, which is abbreviated "U.S.C.A.," and United States Code Service, which is abbreviated "U.S.C.S."

(3) If citing material within the Internal Revenue Code, the abbreviation "I.R.C." may be substituted for "U.S.C." When using the "I.R.C." abbreviation, omit the title number. See **Appendix 7(A)** for additional information on I.R.C.

Examples

28 U.S.C. § 1679 (2000).

42 U.S.C.A. § 1997e(a) (West 2005).

8 U.S.C.S. § 1103(a)(1) (Lexis 2005).

I.R.C. § 104 (2000).

14.2(c) Section symbol

Insert one section symbol (§) when citing a single section. Insert two section symbols (§§) when citing multiple sections. Insert one space after the last section symbol. Consult **Sidebar 6.1** for instructions on how to insert a section symbol into your paper.

14.2(d) Section number

(1) After the section symbol or symbols, include the specific section number or numbers you are citing. Be as specific as possible. Consult **Rule 6.4** for more detailed rules on citing sections.

Examples (the symbol ▲ represents a space):

Single section:	18▲U.S.C.▲§▲1965▲(2000).
Multiple, consecutive sections:	18▲U.S.C.▲§§▲1961–1965▲(2000).
Multiple, consecutive subsections:	18▲U.S.C.▲§▲1961(a)–(d)▲(2000).
Multiple, nonconsecutive sections:	18▲U.S.C.▲§§▲1961,▲1965▲(2000).
Multiple, nonconsecutive subsections:	18▲U.S.C.▲§▲1961(a),▲(f)▲(2000).

(2) To cite material in an appendix, use the format in the example.

Examples

46 U.S.C. app. § 1279e(d)(1)(B) (2000).

18 U.S.C. app. §§ 1–16 (2000).

(3) Include any reference to a note or similar information after the section number. You may use a parenthetical to identify which of several named notes is being cited.

Examples

28 U.S.C. § 1350 n. (2000).

50 U.S.C. § 1701 n. (2000) (Assistance to Sudan).

28 U.S.C. § 1359 hist. nn. (2000).

14.2(e) Publisher

(1) Do not include a publisher for U.S.C.

(2) Within the parenthetical that contains the date, insert "West" as the publisher for U.S.C.A. and "Lexis" as the publisher for U.S.C.S. Insert one space after the publisher's name.

14.2(f) Date

(1) Include the year in which the particular volume you are using was published. Use the date on the spine of the volume, on the copyright page, or on the title page—in that order of preference. See **Sidebar 14.1** regarding the date of U.S.C. Enclose the year in parentheses.

(2) You may need to provide the date for the main volume, a supplement, or both. For information on which date to include, consult **Rule 8**.

Examples

Cited material appears only in the main volume

18 U.S.C. § 1965 (2000).

18 U.S.C.A. § 1965 (West 2005).

18 U.S.C.S. § 1965 (Lexis 2005).

Cited material appears only in a supplement

18 U.S.C. § 1965 (Supp. 2002).

16 U.S.C.A. § 6202 (West Supp. 2005).

20 U.S.C.S. § 1232h(b) (Lexis Supp. 2005).

Cited material appears in both the main volume and a supplement

18 U.S.C. § 1965 (2000 & Supp. 2002).

16 U.S.C.A. § 6202 (West 2000 & Supp. 2005).

20 U.S.C.S. § 3473 (Lexis 1997 & Supp. 2005).

SIDEBAR 14.1

DATE OF UNITED STATES CODE

A new edition of the United States Code is prepared every six years. The most recent edition is the 2000 edition. Use the 2000 version unless you are doing historical research. Use the 2000 date even if the copyright page contains another date. The next series will be dated 2006, but it typically takes a year or so for the government to issue the new set.

Volumes of the United States Code Annotated and the United States Code Service are issued only as required for updating; thus, different volumes of these codes will have different dates. When citing these codes, use the date on the copyright page.

14.2(g) Name of act

You may include the name of the act. If included, insert the name, in ordinary type, before the title number. Separate the name from the title number with a comma and one space. Capitalize words in the title using **Rule 3**.

Example

Americans with Disabilities Act of 1990, 42 U.S.C. §§ 12101–12117 (2000).

14.2(h) Explanatory parentheticals

You may include a separate explanatory parenthetical to indicate the significance of the source. Insert one space after the end of the citation and the start of the explanatory parenthetical. Examples of information that might be included are the date of enactment, the date a statute took effect, the date a statute was amended, and a quotation from the statute. For additional information on explanatory parentheticals, consult **Rule 46.**

Examples

35 U.S.C. § 1 (2000) (enacted under the Patent Act of 1952, 66 Stat. 792 (1952)).

17 U.S.C. § 109(a) (2000) (providing that "the owner of a particular copy . . . lawfully made under this title, or any person authorized by such owner, is entitled, without the authority of the copyright owner, to sell or otherwise dispose of the possession of that copy").

14.3 Full Citation, Print Format for Federal Statutes No Longer in Force

Cite statutes no longer in force using **Rule 14.2,** but include a statement that the statute was repealed or superseded, followed by the year in which the statute ceased to be in force.

Example

26 U.S.C. § 1071(a) (repealed 1995).

14.4 Full Citation, Print Format for State Statutes

Each state has at least one code that contains statutes only from that state. The abbreviations and formats for state codes are included in **Appendix 1,** which is arranged alphabetically by state. To the extent consistent with the entries in **Appendix 1,** also follow **Rules 14.2(c), (d), (f), (g),** and **(h).** If a state statute is no longer in force, analogize to **Rule 14.3.**

Examples of state statutes currently in force

Vt. Stat. Ann. tit. 16, § 822(a)(1) (2000 & Supp. 2004).

Fla. Stat. § 608.471 (2004).

Fla. Stat. Ann. § 608.471 (West 2001 & Supp. 2005).

Mich. Comp. Laws § 445.1532 (2004).

215 Ill. Comp. Stat. 5/356m (2003).

Cal. Ins. Code Ann. § 1872.8 (West 1993).

Md. Bus. Reg. Code Ann. § 14-227 (2004).

N.Y. Bus. Corp. Law § 713(a) (McKinney 2003).

Tex. Rev. Civ. Stat. Ann. art. 4413(37) (West Supp. 2004–2005).

14.5   Statutes Available on Electronic Databases

If you wish to cite a state or federal statute that is available on an electronic database, use the regular citation forms in **Rules 14.2** and **14.4**, except in the date parenthetical also include the name of the database provider and the date through which the statute is current in the database.

Examples

Ga. Code Ann. § 7-1-841 (Westlaw current through 2004 1st Spec. Sess.).

Ky. Rev. Stat. Ann. § 15.733 (Lexis current through 2004 Extraordinary Sess.).

14.5(a)

Use the date information provided by the database, which may be a year, an exact date, or a legislative session.

14.5(b)

If **Appendix 1** lists a publisher for the print version of unofficial codes in which the statute appears, put the electronic database name after the publisher's name (if any); otherwise, start the parenthetical with the electronic database name.

Examples

Ohio Rev. Code Ann. § 911.01 (Anderson, findlaw.com current through Nov. 30, 2004).

N.H. Rev. Stat. Ann. § 80:31 (Westlaw current through 2004 Reg. Sess.).

14.5(c)

Within the date parenthetical, abbreviate months, publisher names, and other words that appear in **Appendix 3.**

14.6   Short Citation, Print Format for Federal and State Statutes

If *id.* is appropriate, use *id.* as the preferred short citation format (**Rule 11.3**). In documents with footnotes, if *id.* is not appropriate, use all required components of the full citation, but omit the date. In documents without footnotes, if *id.* is not appropriate, use one of the following short citation formats listed below. In selecting a format, ensure that the short citation will not confuse the reader.

Example (documents with footnotes)

₁₂₁18 U.S.C. § 1965 (2000).

[121] 18 U.S.C. § 1965 (2000).

[122] *Id.* at § 1961.

.   .   .

[126] 18 U.S.C. § 1965.

Examples (document without footnotes)

Full citation (United States Code):   42 U.S.C. § 12101 (2000).
Short citation options: 42 U.S.C. § 12101.
  § 12101.
  Id. at § 12102.
Full citation (named statute):   Administrative Procedure Act § 5(d), 5 U.S.C. § 554(e) (2000).
Short citation options: Administrative Procedure Act § 5(d).
  § 5(d).
  5 U.S.C. § 554(e).
  Id. at § 5(a).
Full citation (state statute):   Okla. Stat. Ann. tit. 21, § 73 (West 2002).
Short citation options: Okla. Stat. Ann. tit. 21, § 73.
  tit. 5, § 6.
  § 6.
  Id. at § 4.

14.7   Full Citation Format for Federal Session Laws Currently in Force

The full citation for federal session laws currently in force contains nine components.

Law abbreviation•No.•Law number•,Pinpoint reference,•Volume number• Stat.•Initial page,•Pinpoint page•(Date).

REFERRING TO STATUTES IN THE TEXT

When referring to a statute in a textual sentence, do not use the citation format. Instead, except for U.S.C., spell out the code name.

Examples

Arizona Revised Statutes Annotated § 13-4304(4)(b) contains a marital exception, under which a spouse must hold the property as separate property to claim innocent owner status.

Delaware Code Annotated title 14, section 1917 concerns the collection and deposit of school taxes.

Title 15 U.S.C. § 53(b) does not authorize the Federal Trade Commission to seek monetary remedies.

If the statute is clearly identified in the sentence, you need not place a citation after the sentence. Also consult **Rule 6.11**, which concerns referring to sections and paragraphs in textual material. Always spell out subsections, such as "chapter" and "title," that cannot be designated with symbols.

Note that including the statute name and number in the text is not always the most effective way to present the legal point to the reader.

Example

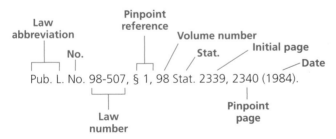

14.7(a) Law abbreviation

Federal laws are either public laws or private laws. The abbreviation for public law is "Pub. L." The abbreviation for private law is "Priv. L." Insert one space after the law abbreviation.

14.7(b) Law number

(1) After the appropriate law abbreviation, include the law number, preceded by the abbreviation "No." and one space.

(2) Current laws are numbered with two parts, such as 107-49. The number 107 represents the number of the Congress that enacted the law (the 107th Congress). The number 49 indicates the chronological sequence of enactment (the 49th law enacted by the 107th Congress).

(3) Insert a comma and one space after the number.

14.7(c) Volume number

After the law number, insert the volume number within Statutes at Large where the cited session law appears. Insert one space after the volume number.

14.7(d) Abbreviation for Statutes at Large

(1) After the volume number, insert "Stat." as the abbreviation for Statutes at Large. Insert one space after the abbreviation.

(2) If the statute is not yet available in Statutes at Large, cite a commercial source, such as United States Code Congressional and Administrative News (U.S.C.C.A.N.) or United States Law Week (U.S.L.W.), or an electronic source, such as LexisNexis, Westlaw, or the Internet. If the volume number of Statutes at Large is available, include that information parenthetically, as shown below.

Example of U.S.C.C.A.N. citation

Pub. L. No. 103-322, § 320935, 1994 U.S.C.C.A.N. (108 Stat.) 2137.

14.7(e) Pages

After "Stat.," insert the page on which the cited law begins. Insert one space after the initial page.

14.7(f) Pinpoint references

When possible, include pinpoint references for both the law number and the Statutes at Large citation. Laws are often divided by section, while Statutes at Large is divided by pages. Consult **Rule 5.2** for additional information on pinpoint references.

119

Example

Pub. L. No. 104-294, § 201, 110 Stat. 3488, 3491 (1996).

14.7(g) Date

After the final page reference, insert the year for the cited volume of Statutes at Large. Enclose the year in parentheses.

14.7(h) Title

You may begin the citation with the title of the act. Present the title in ordinary type. Insert a comma and one space after the title. Use **Rule 3** for capitalization.

Example

Economic Espionage Act of 1996, Pub. L. No. 104-294, § 201, 110 Stat. 3488, 3491 (1996).

14.7(i) Explanatory parenthetical

You may include any parenthetical explanation after the citation that will clarify the reference or otherwise assist readers. Consult **Rule 46** for additional information about explanatory parentheticals.

Examples

Economic Espionage Act of 1996, Pub. L. No. 104-294, § 201, 110 Stat. 3488, 3491 (1996) (amending 18 U.S.C. § 1030(e)(2)).

Pub. L. No. 104-104, § 302, 110 Stat. 56, 118–124 (1996) (to be codified at 47 U.S.C. § 571).

14.8   Full Citation Format for Federal Session Laws No Longer in Force

When citing a session law for a federal statute that is no longer in force, use **Rule 14.7**, but parenthetically add the fact and the date that the statute was repealed or superseded.

Example

Pub. L. No. 67-98, § 219(f), 42 Stat. 227, 247 (1921) (repealed 1939).

14.9   Full Citation Format for State Session Laws

Many states publish their own session laws. The abbreviations and formats for state session laws are included in **Appendix 1**. If a state session law is no longer in force, analogize to **Rule 14.8**.

Examples of state session laws currently in force

1985 N.J. Laws 308.

1993 Tenn. Pub. Acts ch. 534, § 1(c).

14.10   Short Citation Format for Federal and State Session Laws

If *id.* is appropriate, use *id.* as the preferred short citation format. Consult **Rule 11.3** for additional information on *id.* If *id.* is not appropriate, use the following format or analogize to **Rule 14.6**:

Volume number•Session law abbreviation•at•Pinpoint reference.

Examples

Full citation (with title included):	Economic Espionage Act of 1996, Pub. L. No. 104-294, § 201, 110 Stat. 3488, 3491 (1996).
Short citation:	110 Stat. at 3491.
Full citation:	1996 Alaska Sess. Laws 52.
Short citation:	1996 Alaska Sess. Laws at 53.

14.11   Full Citation Format for Federal Slip Laws

14.11(a)

A full citation for a federal slip law contains four components.

Law abbreviation•No.•Law number•(Exact date).

Examples

Public law: Pub. L. No. 107-151 (Mar. 13, 2002).

Private law: Priv. L. No. 104-2 (July 29, 1996).

14.11(b)

When possible, also include a reference to United States Code Congressional and Administrative News, United States Law Week, or an online source, and to the Statutes at Large volume in which the law will appear.

Example

Pub. L. No. 105-304 (Oct. 28, 1998), 1999 U.S.C.C.A.N. (112 Stat.) 2680.

14.12 Full Citation Format for State Slip Laws

Cite state slip laws according to **Rule 14.11,** with the following changes:

(1) Add the state abbreviation to the front of the slip law abbreviation.

(2) Use the numbering format adopted by the particular state.

(3) When possible, include information about how readers might easily access the slip law.

Examples

Ill. Pub. Act No. 91-1003, § 5 (Aug. 23, 2004) (available in Westlaw at 2004 Ill. Legis. Serv. P.A. 91-3).

Ill. Pub. Act No. 91-1003, § 5 (Aug. 23, 2004) (available at Ill. Gen. Assembly, *State of Illinois, Public Acts, 93d General Assembly,* http://www.legis.state.il.us/publicacts/pubact91/acts/91-0003.html (accessed Mar. 23, 2005)).

14.13 Short Citation Format for Federal and State Slip Laws

If *id.* is appropriate, use *id.* as the preferred short citation format. Consult **Rule 11.3** for additional information on *id.* If *id.* is not appropriate, use all required components of the full citation format, but omit the date parenthetical and add a pinpoint reference, when available.

Examples

Full citation: Pub. L. No. 106-4 (Mar. 25, 1999).
Short citation: Pub. L. No. 106-4 at § 2(a).

Full citation: Pub. L. No. 105-304 (Oct. 28, 1998), 1999 U.S.C.C.A.N. (112 Stat.) 2680.
Short citation: Pub. L. No. 105-304 at § 1, 1999 U.S.C.C.A.N. at 2681.

Full citation: Ill. Pub. Act No. 91-1003, § 5 (Aug. 23, 2004) (available in Westlaw at 2004 Ill. Legis. Serv. P.A. 91-3).
Short citation: Ill. Pub. Act No. 91-1003 at § 15(a).

FAST FORMATS

OTHER FEDERAL LEGISLATIVE MATERIALS

Unenacted House bill	H.R. 6, 109th Cong. § 142 (Apr. 18, 2005).
Unenacted Senate resolution	Sen. Res. 283, 108th Cong. (Dec. 9, 2003).
Enacted House simple resolution	H.R. Res. 723, 108th Cong. (2004) (enacted).
Congressional hearing	H.R. Jud. Comm., *The Quality Health-Care Coalition Act of 1998: Hearings on H.R. 4277*, 105th Cong. 82–83 (July 29, 1998).
Congressional report	H.R. Rpt. 107-468 § 2 (May 16, 2002). Sen. Rpt. 107-108, at 18–19 (Dec. 5, 2001).
Congressional debate, permanent edition	116 Cong. Rec. 591 (1970).
Congressional debate, daily edition	148 Cong. Rec. H2634 (daily ed. May 20, 2002).
United States Code Congressional and Administrative News	2004 U.S.C.C.A.N. 668, 678–679.

15.0   OTHER FEDERAL LEGISLATIVE MATERIALS

15.1   Full Citation Format for Unenacted Bills and Resolutions

A full citation to an unenacted bill or resolution contains either five or six components, depending on the date.

Abbreviation for type of bill or resolution●Number of bill or resolution●, Congress number●, Session number [for older bills and resolutions]●Pinpoint reference [if available]●(Exact date).

Example (House Bill)

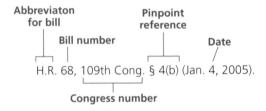

Other examples

House Resolution:	H.R. Res. 126, 109th Cong. (Mar. 1, 2005).
House Concurrent Resolution:	H.R. Con. Res. 55, 107th Cong. (Mar. 7, 2003).
House Joint Resolution:	H.R. Jt. Res. 45, 108th Cong. (Apr. 2, 2003).
Senate Bill:	Sen. 67, 109th Cong. (Jan. 25, 2005).
Senate Resolution:	Sen. Res. 11, 106th Cong. (Jan. 7, 1999).
Senate Concurrent Resolution:	Sen. Con. Res. 72, 108th Cong. (Oct. 3, 2003).
Senate Joint Resolution:	Sen. Jt. Res. 100, 103d Cong. (June 8, 1993).

15.1(a)   Abbreviation for type of bill or resolution

Use the following abbreviations to designate the type of bill or resolution. Insert one space after the last part of the abbreviation.

Type	Abbreviation
House Bill:	H.R.
House Resolution:	H.R. Res.

Type	Abbreviation
House Concurrent Resolution:	H.R. Con. Res.
House Joint Resolution:	H.R. Jt. Res.
Senate Bill:	Sen.
Senate Resolution:	Sen. Res.
Senate Concurrent Resolution:	Sen. Con. Res.
Senate Joint Resolution:	Sen. Jt. Res.

15.1(b) Number

After the abbreviation for the type of bill or resolution, insert the number of the bill or resolution. Insert a comma and one space after the number.

15.1(c) Congress number

(1) After the number of the bill or resolution, designate the Congress in which the bill or resolution was introduced.

(2) To provide this designation, first give the ordinal contraction for the Congress number. Consult **Rule 4.3** for additional information on ordinals. Then insert a space and the abbreviation "Cong." (*examples:* 103d Cong.; 104th Cong.)

(3) If a session number is required, insert a comma and one space after "Cong." If a session number is not required, insert only a space after "Cong."

SIDEBAR 15.1

TYPES OF PROPOSED LAWS

Proposed laws are presented in one of four forms: the bill, the joint resolution, the concurrent resolution, and the simple resolution. The most common form used in both the House of Representatives and the Senate is the bill.

While the same rules, **Rules 15.1** and **15.2,** apply to all types of unenacted bills and resolutions, different rules apply to enacted bills and resolutions:

Rule 15.3:	Enacted bills and joint resolutions
Rules 15.4 and 15.5:	Enacted simple resolutions and concurrent resolutions

15.1(d) Session number

(1) If the bill or resolution was introduced **before** 1881 (for the House) or 1847 (for the Senate), indicate whether the bill was introduced during the first, second, or third session of the particular Congress. For later Congresses, the session can be inferred from the year and thus should not be included.

Example

H.R. Res. 88, 39th Cong., 1st Sess. (Jan. 8, 1866).

(2) Use the ordinal contraction "1st" for first, "2d" for second, and "3d" for third.

(3) Insert one space after the ordinal; then use the abbreviation "Sess." for session. Insert one space after the abbreviation "Sess."

15.1(e) Pinpoint reference

When referring to only part of the bill or resolution, give that subdivision after the Congress or session number. Bills and resolutions typically are divided by sections. For additional information on sections and other subdivisions, consult **Rule 6.** Insert one space after the subdivision information.

Examples

H.R. Res. 282, 106th Cong. § 2 (Jan. 6, 1999).

Sen. 178, 109th Cong. § 3 (Jan. 26, 2005).

15.1(f) Date

Include the exact date for the version of the bill or resolution cited. When it would be helpful to the reader, note the status of the bill or resolution parenthetically.

Examples

H.R. 8336, 95th Cong. 101 (July 14, 1977) (as introduced).

H.R. 8336, 95th Cong. 101 (Sept. 8, 1977) (as reported by House Comm. on Int. & Insular Affairs).

H.R. 8336, 95th Cong. 101 (Feb. 20, 1978) (as passed by House Feb. 14).

15.1(g) Title

You may begin the citation with the title of the bill or resolution. Present the title in ordinary type. Insert a comma and one space after the title. Use **Rule 3** for capitalization.

Example

Graduation for All Act, H.R. 547, 109th Cong. §§ 201–203 (Feb. 2, 2005).

15.1(h) Parenthetical information

You may parenthetically include any explanation after the citation that will clarify the reference or otherwise assist readers. Consult **Rules 15.1(f)** and **46** for additional information about explanatory parentheticals.

Example

H.R. Res. 123, 109th Cong. (Feb. 17, 2005) (resolution, introduced by Rep. Peter T. King, to establish a Select Committee on POW and MIA Affairs).

15.2 Short Citation Format for Unenacted Bills and Resolutions

If *id.* is appropriate, use *id.* as the preferred short citation format. Consult **Rule 11.3** for additional information on *id.* Otherwise, use all required components of the full citation format, but omit the date parenthetical and include the word "at" before any pinpoint reference.

Example

Full citation: H.R. 988, 109th Cong. § 702 (Feb. 17, 2005).
Short citation: H.R. 988, 109th Cong. at §§ 701–703.
***Id.*:**   *Id.* at § 703.

15.3 Enacted Bills and Joint Resolutions

Cite enacted bills and **joint** resolutions as statutes pursuant to **Rule 14**, except when using the bill or joint resolution to document legislative history. In that case, follow **Rule 15.1**.

15.4 Full Citation Format for Enacted Simple and Concurrent Resolutions

15.4(a)

Cite an enacted simple or concurrent resolution as an unenacted bill or resolution under **Rule 15.1**, but use only the year and add the term "enacted" parenthetically.

15.4(b)

When possible, include a parenthetical reference to the Congressional Record (for simple resolutions) or to Statutes at Large (for concurrent resolutions) to assist readers in locating the source. Because only enacted resolutions are printed in Statutes at Large, "(enacted)" may be eliminated as redundant when a Statutes at Large reference is included.

Examples

H.R. Res. 723, 108th Cong. (2004) (enacted).

H.R. Con. Res. 25, 106th Cong. (1999) (enacted).

Sen. Res. 29, 107th Cong. (2001) (enacted).

Sen. Con. Res. 115, 108th Cong. (2005) (enacted).

With reference to Congressional Record (daily edition)

H.R. Res. 188, 109th Cong. (2005) (enacted) (reprinted in 151 Cong. Rec. H1802 (daily ed. Apr. 6, 2005)).

With reference to Statutes at Large

H.R. Con. Res. 464, 107th Cong. (2002) (enacted) (reprinted in 116 Stat. 3150).

15.5   Short Citation Format for Enacted Simple and Concurrent Resolutions

If *id.* is appropriate, use *id.* as the preferred short citation format. Consult **Rule 11.3** for additional information on *id.* Otherwise, use all required components of the full citation format, but omit the date and any reference to the Congressional Record or to Statutes at Large. Insert "at" before the pinpoint reference.

Example

Full citation:	Sen. Con. Res. 8, 109th Cong. § 1 (2005) (enacted) (reprinted in 151 Cong. Rec. S825 (daily ed. Feb. 1, 2005)).
Short citation:	Sen. Con. Res. 8, 109th Cong. at § 1.
***Id.*:**	*Id.* at § 1.

15.6   Proposed House and Senate Amendments

Cite proposed amendments analogously to bills and resolutions under **Rule 15.1.** After the citation, parenthetically note the bill or resolution for which the amendment is proposed.

Examples

H.R. Amend. 280, 109th Cong. (June 15, 2005) (amendment to H.R. 2862).

Sen. Amend. 287, 109th Cong. (Apr. 5, 2005) (amendment to Sen. 600).

15.7   Full Citation Format for Congressional Hearings

A full citation to congressional hearings contains six or seven components, depending on when the hearings were held.

House abbreviation•Name of committee or subcommittee,• *Title and bill number*,•Congress number•, Session number [for older hearings]•Pinpoint reference•(Exact date).

Example

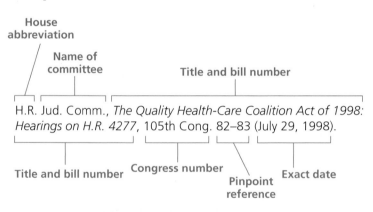

H.R. Jud. Comm., *The Quality Health-Care Coalition Act of 1998: Hearings on H.R. 4277*, 105th Cong. 82–83 (July 29, 1998).

Other examples

Sen. Subcomm. on Commun. of the Comm. on Com., Sci. & Transp., *Broadband Access in Rural America*, 106th Cong. 83–86 (Mar. 29, 2000).

H.R. Comm. on Agric., *Examine New Generation Cooperatives and Strategies to Maximize Farm and Ranch Income*, 108th Cong. 67–186 (Oct. 16, 2003).

15.7(a)   House abbreviation

Begin the citation with the abbreviation "H.R." for House of Representatives or "Sen." for Senate.

15.7(b) Name of committee or subcommittee

(1) After the house abbreviation, provide the abbreviated name of the committee or subcommittee before which the hearings were held. You may omit articles and prepositions not needed for clarity.

(2) If the hearings were before a subcommittee, also indicate the name of the committee.

(3) Present the name in ordinary type and follow **Rule 3** concerning capitalization of titles.

(4) To conserve space, you may abbreviate any parts of the committee or subcommittee name that are listed in **Appendix 3**.

(5) Insert a comma and one space after the name.

15.7(c) Title and bill number

(1) After the committee or subcommittee name, insert the title of the hearing as it appears on the cover of the published hearing.

(2) Do not repeat the name of the committee or subcommittee within the title.

(3) When available, include the bill or resolution number, even if it is not part of the subject matter title.

(4) Present the title and bill number in italics.

(5) Insert a comma and one space after the title.

Examples

H.R. Subcomm. on Telecomm. & Internet of the Comm. of Energy & Com., *Junk Fax Prevention Act of 2004*, 108th Cong. 3–5 (June 15, 2004).

H.R. Comm. of Educ. & Workforce, *H.R. 4283, College Access and Opportunity Act*, 108th Cong. 43 (May 12, 2004).

15.7(d) Congress number

Follow **Rule 15.1(c)**.

15.7(e) Session number

Follow **Rule 15.1(d)**.

15.7(f) Pinpoint reference

Follow **Rule 15.1(e)**.

15.7(g) Date

Provide the exact date of the hearing. Enclose the date in parentheses. Abbreviate months according to **Appendix 3(A)**.

15.7(h) Parenthetical information

You may include any explanation after the citation that will clarify the reference or otherwise assist readers; for example, you might identify the person testifying before the committee. Consult **Rule 46** regarding explanatory parentheticals.

Example

H.R. Subcomm. on Cts., Internet & Intell. Prop. of the Comm. of Jud., *Ninth Circuit Court of Appeals Judgeship and Reorganization Act of 2003*, 108th Cong. 6 (Oct. 21, 2003) (testimony of the Hon. Mary M. Schroeder, Chief Judge of the U.S. Court of Appeals for the Ninth Circuit).

15.8 Short Citation Format for Congressional Hearings

The form of the short citation will vary depending on the type of document you are writing.

15.8(a) Documents without footnotes

If *id.* is appropriate, use *id.* as the preferred short citation format. Consult **Rule 11.3** for additional information on *id.* If *id.* is not appropriate, use the following format:

Committee abbreviation,●Congress number●, Session number [for older hearings]●at●Pinpoint reference.

Example

Full citation: H.R. Subcomm. on Cts., Internet & Intell. Prop. of the Comm. of Jud., *Ninth Circuit Court of Appeals Judgeship and Reorganization Act of 2003*, 108th Cong. 6 (Oct. 21, 2003).

Short citation: H.R. Subcomm. on Cts., Internet & Intell. Prop., 108th Cong. at 6.

15.8(b) Documents with footnotes

If *id.* is appropriate, use *id.* as the preferred short citation format. Consult **Rule 11.3** for additional information on *id.* If *id.* is not appropriate, use the *supra* format that follows. Consult **Rule 11.4** for additional information on *supra*.

Committee abbreviation,●*supra* n. Note number,●at●Pinpoint reference.

Example

---

[19]H.R. Subcomm. on Com. & Admin. L. of the Jud. Comm., *The Bankruptcy Reform Act of 1998—Hearings of H.R. 3150*, 105th Cong. 2 (Mar. 10, 1998).

.   .   .

[25]H.R. Subcomm. on Com. & Admin. L., *supra* n. 19, at 5.

15.9 Full Citation Format for Numbered Congressional Reports, Documents, and Prints

Because numbered reports, documents, and prints are most easily accessed by their number, a full citation will contain four components.

Abbreviation for type of document•Document number•Pinpoint reference• (Exact date).

Example (House Report)

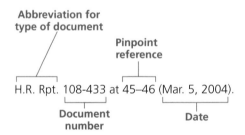

Abbreviation for type of document

Pinpoint reference

H.R. Rpt. 108-433 at 45–46 (Mar. 5, 2004).

Document number

Date

Other examples

House Document:	H.R. Doc. 108-14 (Jan. 7, 2003).
House Committee Print:	H.R. Comm. Print 105-19 app. B (Dec. 10, 1998).
Senate Report:	Sen. Rpt. 106-37 at 9–12 (Mar. 26, 1999).
Senate Executive Report:	Sen. Exec. Rpt. 105-5 pt. 4 (Oct. 30, 1997).
Senate Document:	Sen. Doc. 106-51 at 1 (Apr. 30, 1999).
Senate Committee Print:	Sen. Comm. Print 108-47 (July 2004).

15.9(a) Abbreviation for type of document

Use the following abbreviations to designate the type of report, document, or print. Insert one space after the last part of the abbreviation.

Type	Abbreviation
House Report:	H.R. Rpt.
House Conference Report:	H.R. Conf. Rpt.
House Document:	H.R. Doc.
House Committee Print:	H.R. Comm. Print
Senate Report:	Sen. Rpt.
Senate Conference Report:	Sen. Conf. Rpt.
Senate Executive Report:	Sen. Exec. Rpt.
Senate Document:	Sen. Doc.
Senate Committee Print:	Sen. Comm. Print

15.9(b) Document number

To create the document number, insert the Congress number, a hyphen, and the specific report, document, or print number. Insert one space after the document number.

Example

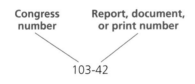

15.9(c) Pinpoint reference

If referring to only part of the report, document, or print, give that subdivision. Use "at" only when referring to one or more pages. For additional information on pinpoint subdivisions, consult **Rule 5.2.** Insert one space after the pinpoint information.

Examples

Sen. Rpt. 107-28 at 16 (June 5, 2001).

H.R. Conf. Rpt. 108-724 pt. 3 (Oct. 4, 2004).

15.9(d) Date

Provide the exact date (month-day-year) on which the report, document, or print was ordered to be printed. Note that, for some documents, only the month and year are available. Abbreviate the month according to **Appendix 3.** Enclose the date in parentheses.

15.9(e) Author and title

You may include the author's name and the document title. Italicize the title. You may abbreviate the name of an institutional author using the terms in **Appendix 3**.

Examples

Sen. Comm. on Env. & Pub. Works, *Children's Environmental Health: What Role for the Federal Government?* Sen. Comm. Print. 107-062 (Nov. 30, 2002).

Charles W. Johnson, *How Our Laws Are Made*, H.R. Doc. 108-93 foreword (rev. & updated June 20, 2003).

15.9(f) Parenthetical information

You may parenthetically include any explanation after the citation that will clarify the reference or otherwise assist readers. Consult **Rule 46** regarding explanatory parentheticals.

Example

Sen. Exec. Rpt. 106-1 (Mar. 24, 1999) (concerning nuclear safety).

15.9(g) References to U.S.C.C.A.N. and Congressional Record

Federal committee reports are selectively published in the United States Code Congressional and Administrative News and the Congressional Record. When possible, include a parenthetical reference to one of these sources, which are often more readily available to most readers than are the congressional reports themselves.

Examples

United States Code Congressional and Administrative News

Sen. Rpt. 109-27 at 27 (July 14, 1987) (reprinted in 1987 U.S.C.C.A.N. 682, 707).

Congressional Record

H.R. Conf. Rpt. 108-779 (Nov. 17, 2004) (reprinted in 150 Cong. Rec. H9895–9959 (daily ed. Nov. 17, 2004)).

15.10   Short Citation Format for Numbered Congressional Reports, Documents, and Prints

If *id.* is appropriate, use *id.* as the preferred short citation format. Consult **Rule 11.3** for additional information on *id.* Otherwise, use all required components of the full citation format, but omit the date.

Example

Full citation:	H.R. Conf. Rpt. 109-123 §§ 2–4 (June 14, 2005).
Short citation:	H.R. Conf. Rpt. 109-123 at § 3.
Id.:	*Id.* at § 4.

15.11   Unnumbered Reports, Documents, and Prints

Cite unnumbered reports, documents, and prints as reports by an institutional author under **Rule 22.1(a), item 3.** Treat the Congress number as part of the author's name. Include the abbreviation for the type of document in the date parenthetical.

Example

Staff of Sen. Comm. on Banking, Hous. & Urb. Affairs, 94th Cong., *Report of the Securities and Exchange Commission on Questionable and Illegal Corporate Payments and Practices* 2–3 (Sen. Comm. Print 1976).

15.12   Full Citation Format for Congressional Debates Occurring after 1873

Cite congressional debates to a compiled source, such as the Congressional Record. The Congressional Record is published daily while either house is in session. This format is known as the "daily edition." In addition, a bound volume of the Congressional Record, called the "permanent edition," is published at the end of each congressional session. The permanent edition is the preferred source for most research. Accordingly, citations to the Congressional Record should be to the bound edition unless the cited material is available only in the daily edition. The daily edition and the permanent edition do not use the same system of pagination.

A full citation to a congressional debate occurring after 1873 contains either four or five components, depending on whether the citation is to the daily edition or the permanent edition of the Congressional Record.

Examples

Permanent edition

Volume number•Cong. Rec.•Pinpoint page•(Date).

| Volume | | Pinpoint | Date |
| number | | page | |

116 Cong. Rec. 591 (1970).

Congressional Record abbreviation

Daily edition

Volume number•Cong. Rec.•Pinpoint page with house designation•(daily ed.•Exact date).

Volume
number

Pinpoint
page   Exact date

151 Cong. Rec. S8988 (daily ed. July 26, 2005).

Congressional Record abbreviation

15.12(a) Volume number

Begin with the volume number of the Congressional Record in which the debate appears. Insert one space after the volume number.

15.12(b) Abbreviation for Congressional Record

After the volume number, insert the abbreviation "Cong. Rec." Insert one space after the abbreviation.

15.12(c) Pages

(1) After "Cong. Rec." insert the page or pages on which the debate appears.

Example (permanent edition)

124 Cong. Rec. 32408–32409 (1978).

(2) When citing the daily edition, follow the format for the permanent edition, but insert "H" before the page number if referring to a House debate and "S" before the page number if referring to a Senate debate.

136

Example

149 Cong. Rec. H9748–9750 (daily ed. Oct. 21, 2003).

(3) Insert one space after the page number.

15.12(d) Edition and date

(1) When citing the permanent edition, include only the year. Enclose the year in parentheses.

(2) When citing the daily edition, enclose the following information in parentheses: (a) the phrase "daily ed." and (b) the exact date (month-day-year) of the Congressional Record cited. Place one space after "daily ed." Abbreviate the month according to **Appendix 3(A)**.

Examples

Permanent edition: 124 Cong. Rec. 32408 (1978).

Daily edition: 150 Cong. Rec. S11653–11660 (daily ed. Nov. 19, 2004).

15.12(e) Parenthetical information

You may include parenthetically any other information that might assist readers, such as the name of the cited speaker. Consult **Rule 46** regarding explanatory parentheticals.

Example

51 Cong. Rec. S546–547 (daily ed. Jan. 26, 2005) (statement of Sen. Jeff Bingaman).

15.13 Short Citation Format for Congressional Debates Occurring after 1873

If *id.* is appropriate, use *id.* as the preferred short citation format. Consult **Rule 11.3** for additional information on *id.* If *id.* is not appropriate, keep all required components, but eliminate the date and insert "at" before the pinpoint page.

Examples

Permanent edition

Full citation: 124 Cong. Rec. 32408 (1978).
Short citation: 124 Cong. Rec. at 32408.
***Id.*:** *Id.* at 32409.

Daily edition

Full citation:	150 Cong. Rec. S11653 (daily ed. Nov. 19, 2004).
Short citation:	150 Cong. Rec. at S11653.
***Id.*:**	*Id.* at S11653.

15.14 Full Citation Format for Congressional Debates through 1873

For debates through 1873, cite the appropriate source listed below.

DATE	CONGRESS	SOURCE	CITATION FORMAT
1789–1824	1st Cong. to 18th Cong., 1st Sess.	Annals of Congress	Volume number● Annals of Cong.● Pinpoint page●(Year). *Example* 18 Annals of Cong. 1766 (1819).
1824–1833	18th Cong., 2d Sess. to 25th Cong., 1st Sess.	Register of Debates	Volume number● Register of Debates● Pinpoint page●(Year). *Example* 11 Register of Debates 130 (1835).
1833–1873	25th Cong., 2d Sess. to 42d Cong., 2d Sess.	Congressional Globe	Cong. Globe,●Congress number●Cong.●, Session number●Sess.● Pinpoint page●(Year). *Example* Cong. Globe, 41st Cong., 1st Sess. 500–501 (1869).

15.15 Short Citation Format for Congressional Debates through 1873

If *id.* is appropriate, use *id.* as the preferred short citation format. Consult **Rule 11.3** for additional information on *id.* If *id.* is not appropriate, use the appropriate short citation format below.

Annals of Congress:	Volume number●Annals of Cong.●at●Pinpoint page.
	Example: 18 Annals of Cong. at 1766.
Register of Debates:	Volume number●Register of Debates●at●Pinpoint page.
	Example: 11 Register of Debates at 130.
Congressional Globe:	Cong. Globe,●Congress number●Cong.●, Session number● Sess.●at●Pinpoint page.
	Example: Cong. Globe, 41st Cong., 1st Sess. at 500.

15.16   Congressional Journals

Both the House of Representatives and the Senate publish their official proceedings in journals. The journals contain motions, actions taken, and roll-call votes but not the text of debates or other proceedings. Journals are published at the end of each session and can be cited using the following formats. *Id.* or the format designated below may be used as the short citation.

Examples

Full citation: H.R. J., 105th Cong., 2d Sess. 2755–2786 (1998).
Short citation: H.R. J., 105th Cong., 2d Sess. at 2757.

Full citation: Sen. J., 1st Cong., 1st Sess. 117 (1789).
Short citation: Sen. J., 1st Cong., 1st Sess. at 117.

15.17   United States Code Congressional and Administrative News

15.17(a)

United States Code Congressional and Administrative News, abbreviated "U.S.C.C.A.N.," is a commercial publication that reprints the text of federal acts. Since 1941, it also has reprinted congressional committee reports on a selective basis.

15.17(b)

When it will assist readers to locate the cited material, include the U.S.C.C.A.N. citation in a parenthetical.

15.17(c)

When citing U.S.C.C.A.N. as part of a full citation, include an opening parenthesis, the phrase "reprinted in," the year of the volume, one space, the abbreviation

"U.S.C.C.A.N.," one space, the page on which the cited source begins, a comma, one space, a pinpoint page reference, and a closing parenthesis.

15.17(d)

When presenting U.S.C.C.A.N. as part of a short citation, include "reprinted in," the year of the volume, one space, the abbreviation "U.S.C.C.A.N.," one space, the word "at," one space, and the pinpoint page within the parentheses.

Example

Full citation: Sen. Rpt. 108-507 at 1 (May 20, 2004) (reprinted in 2004 U.S.C.C.A.N. 726, 726).

Short citation: Sen. Rpt. 108-507 at 1 (reprinted in 2004 U.S.C.C.A.N. at 726).

15.18   Declaration of Independence

Cite the Declaration of Independence as *Declaration of Independence* [¶ 3] (1776). Consult **Rule 6.3** for additional information.

15.19   Other Legislative Materials

To cite legislative materials not specifically addressed in **Rule 15**, analogize to the closest rule above or use the following format. If the suggested format does not work exactly for your source, include as much of the information called for below as possible.

Title,●Document abbreviation,●Congress number●Cong.●Pinpoint reference● (Exact date).

Example

Sen. Calendar, 109th Cong. 34 (July 26, 2005).

FAST FORMATS

OTHER STATE LEGISLATIVE MATERIALS

Consult Appendices 1 and 2 for information specific to the state whose material you are citing.

Unenacted house bill	Mass. H. 3190, 183d Leg., Jt. Sess. 1482 (Mar. 29, 2004).
Unenacted senate bill	Tenn. Sen. Jt. Res. 31, 104th Gen. Assembly (Mar. 17, 2005).
Legislative hearing	Md. Jt. Comm. on Children, Youth & Fams., *Review of Policies and Procedures of Group Homes in Maryland*, 2005 Reg. Sess. (June 21, 2005).
Legislative document	Me. Sen. Doc. 807, 121st Leg., 2d Spec. Sess. (Apr. 15, 2004).
Legislative report	Haw. H. Stand. Comm. Rpt. No. 203, 2005 Leg., Reg. Sess. (2005).
Legislative debate	Tex. Sen., *Debate on Tex. H. 4 on the Floor of the Senate*, 78th Leg., Reg. Sess. (May 16, 2003) (transcript available from Senate Staff Services Office).

16.0 OTHER STATE LEGISLATIVE MATERIALS

16.1 Full Citation Format for State Unenacted Bills, Files, and Resolutions

If the state whose bill, file, or resolution you are citing has a special citation format, use that format. Consult **Appendix 2** to determine whether a particular state has a citation rule for unenacted bills, files, or resolutions. If the state does not have a special format, use the format below.

A full citation to an unenacted bill, file, or resolution may contain up to seven components, depending on the state.

State abbreviation•Abbreviation for type of bill, file, or resolution•Bill, file, or resolution number•, Legislature designation [if available]•, Session designation [if available]•Pinpoint reference [if available]•(Exact date).

Example (Alaska House Bill)

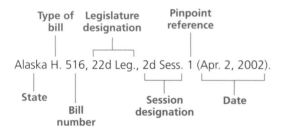

Other examples

Arizona Senate Bill: Ariz. Sen. 1427, 45th Leg., 2d Reg. Sess. (May 15, 2002).

Colorado Senate Joint Resolution: Colo. Sen. Jt. Res. 1027, 63d Gen. Assembly, 2d Reg. Sess. (May 8, 2002).

Georgia House Bill: Ga. H. 410, 146th Gen. Assembly, 2001–2002 (May 10, 2002).

Minnesota House File: Minn. H. File 3731, 82d Reg. Sess. (May 14, 2002).

Nebraska Legislative Resolution: Neb. Leg. Res. 460, 97th Leg., 2d Reg. Sess. (Apr. 19, 2002).

Virginia House Joint Resolution: Va. H. Jt. Res. 782, 2003 Sess. (Jan. 21, 2003).

16.1(a) State abbreviation

Include the state abbreviation as listed in **Appendix 3(B)**. Insert one space after the abbreviation.

16.1(b) State abbreviation for type of bill, file, or resolution

Insert the abbreviation for the type of document cited. Use the abbreviations listed below and in **Appendix 3** to develop the appropriate abbreviation. If a word is not listed below or in **Appendix 3**, spell it out.

Word	Abbreviation
Bill:	[Omit the word "Bill."]
File:	File
Concurrent:	Con.
General:	Gen.
House:	H.
House of Delegates:	H.
House of Representatives:	H.
Joint:	Jt.
Legislative:	Leg.
Resolution:	Res.
Senate:	Sen.

Examples

California Assembly Bill:	Cal. Assembly 1229, 2005–2006 Reg. Sess. 1 (June 14, 2005).
Connecticut Senate Bill:	Conn. Sen. 603, 2002 Reg. Sess. 1–2 (Mar. 11, 2002).
Delaware House Concurrent Resolution:	Del. H. Con. Res. 25, 143d Gen. Assembly (May 11, 2005).

16.1(c) State bill, file, or resolution number

After the abbreviation for the type of bill, file, or resolution, insert the number of the bill, file, or resolution. Insert a comma and one space after the number.

16.1(d) State legislature designation

(1) Identify the legislature in which the bill, file, or resolution was introduced.

(2) Begin with an ordinal contraction (such as 43d) for the legislature or assembly number (**Rule 4.3**). If the state does not number its legislature or assembly, provide any other description used by the state. You may abbreviate any words listed in **Appendix 3** or **Rule 16.1(b)**.

(3) If a session designation is available, add it by inserting a comma and one space after the legislature designation, followed by the session designation. If it is not available, simply insert one space after the legislature designation.

Examples

Iowa H. File 2192, 79th Gen. Assembly, 2d Sess. (May 11, 2002).

Wyo. Sen. 127, 56th Leg. (Feb. 16, 2001).

N.Y. Assembly 7797, 228th Annual Leg. Sess. (May 2, 2005).

16.1(e) State session designation

When available, include the legislative session. Designate the session with an ordinal contraction (such as 1st), an abbreviation for any description used by the state whose legislation is cited (such as "Spec." for Special), and the abbreviation "Sess." for Session. Insert one space after the session designation.

Examples

N.H. H. 1420, 157th Leg., 2d Year (May 16, 2002).

Okla. Sen. 10, 47th Leg., 1st Spec. Sess. (June 16, 1999).

Vt. H. 393, 65th Biennial Sess. (Feb. 26, 1999).

16.1(f) Pinpoint reference

When referring to only part of the bill, file, or resolution, cite that particular subdivision, such as a page or section number. For additional information on sections and other subdivisions, consult **Rules 5, 6,** and **9.** Insert one space after the subdivision information.

16.1(g) Date

If available, include the exact date (month-day-year) on which the bill or resolution was introduced. Abbreviate the month according to **Appendix 3(A).** If the exact date is not available, include at least the year. Enclose the date in parentheses.

16.1(h) Title

You may begin the citation with the title of the bill, file, or resolution. Present the title in ordinary type. Insert a comma and one space after the title. Use **Rule 3** for capitalization.

Example

Regional Transit Authority, La. H. Con. Res. 264, 1999 Reg. Sess. (June 3, 1999).

16.2   Short Citation Format for State Unenacted Bills, Files, and Resolutions

If *id.* is appropriate, use *id.* as the preferred short citation format. Consult **Rule 11.3** for additional information on *id.* Otherwise, use all required components of the full citation format, but omit the date parenthetical and include the word "at" before any pinpoint reference.

Example

Full citation: Conn. Sen. 1359, 1999 Reg. Sess. 2 (Mar. 17, 1999).
Short citation: Conn. Sen. 1359, 1999 Reg. Sess. at 2.
***Id.*:**   *Id.* at 1.

16.3   State Enacted Bills, Files, and Resolutions

Cite enacted bills, files, and resolutions as statutes pursuant to **Rule 14** except when using the bill, file, or resolution to document legislative history. In that case, follow **Rule 16.1**.

16.4   Full Citation Format for State Legislative Hearings

If the state whose legislative hearing you are citing has a special citation format, use that format. Consult **Appendix 2** to determine whether a particular state has a citation rule for legislative hearings. If the state does not have a special format, use the format below.

A full citation to a legislative hearing may contain up to eight components, depending on the state.

State abbreviation•House abbreviation•Name of committee or subcommittee,•*Title and bill number*•, Legislature designation [if available]•, Session designation [if available]•Pinpoint reference [if available]•(Exact date).

Examples

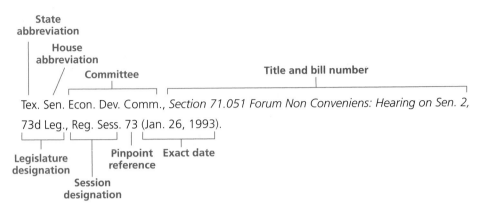

State
abbreviation

House
abbreviation

Committee

Title and bill number

Tex. Sen. Econ. Dev. Comm., *Section 71.051 Forum Non Conveniens: Hearing on Sen. 2,*

73d Leg., Reg. Sess. 73 (Jan. 26, 1993).

Legislature
designation

Pinpoint
reference

Exact date

Session
designation

Cal. Leg. Assembly Comm. on Crim. Justice, *Constitutional Issues Relative to the Death Penalty: Special Hearing on Criminal Justice,* 1977 Reg. Sess. 2–6 (Jan. 24, 1977).

16.4(a) State abbreviation

Include the state abbreviation as listed in **Appendix 3(B).** Insert one space after the abbreviation.

16.4(b) State house abbreviation

Insert the abbreviation "H." for House, House of Representatives, or House of Delegates, or "Sen." for Senate.

16.4(c) Name of state committee or subcommittee

(1) After the house abbreviation, provide the name of the committee before which the hearings were held. You may omit articles and prepositions not needed for clarity.

(2) If the hearings were before a subcommittee, insert a comma and one space after the name of the committee and then include the name of the subcommittee. Insert a comma and one space after the name.

(3) Present the committee and subcommittee names in ordinary type, and follow **Rule 3** concerning capitalization of titles.

(4) To conserve space, you may abbreviate any parts of the committee or subcommittee name that appear in **Appendix 3.**

16.4(d) State title and bill number

(1) After the committee or subcommittee name, insert the title of the hearing as it appears on the cover of the published hearing.

(2) Do not repeat the name of the committee or subcommittee within the title.

(3) When available, include the bill or resolution number, even if it is not part of the subject matter title.

(4) Present the title and bill number in italics. Use **Rule 3** for capitalization.

(5) Insert a comma and one space after the title and bill number.

Example

Cal. Sen. R. Comm., *Hearing on Preschool for All Program, Assembly 712*, 2003–2004 Reg. Sess. (Aug. 31, 2004).

16.4(e) State legislature designation

Follow **Rule 16.1(d)**.

16.4(f) State session designation

Follow **Rule 16.1(e)**.

16.4(g) Pinpoint reference

Follow **Rule 16.1(f)**.

16.4(h) Date

Follow **Rule 16.1(g)**.

16.4(i) Parenthetical information

You may include any parenthetical explanation after the citation that will clarify the reference or otherwise assist readers; for example, you might identify the person testifying before the committee. Consult **Rule 46** regarding explanatory parentheticals. Consult **Rule 15.7(h)** for an analogous example.

16.5   Short Citation Format for State Legislative Hearings

The form of the short citation will vary depending on the type of document you are writing.

16.5(a) Documents without footnotes

If *id.* is appropriate, use *id.* as the preferred short citation format. Consult **Rule 11.3** for additional information on *id.* If *id.* is not appropriate, use the following format:

State abbreviation●House abbreviation●Name of committee or subcommittee,● *Title and bill number*●, at●Pinpoint reference.

Example

Full citation: Tex. H. Jud. Comm., *The Texas Determinate Sentencing Act for Juveniles: Hearings on Tex. H. 682*, 70th Leg., Reg. Sess. 1 (Mar. 2, 1987).

Short citation: Tex. H. Jud. Comm., *The Texas Determinate Sentencing Act for Juveniles: Hearings on Tex. H. 682*, at 1.

16.5(b) Documents with footnotes

If *id.* is appropriate, use *id.* as the preferred short citation format. Consult **Rule 11.3** for additional information on *id.* If *id.* is not appropriate, use the *supra* format that follows. Consult **Rule 11.4** for additional information on *supra*.

Committee abbreviation,● *supra* n. Note number●, at●Pinpoint reference.

Example

---

[3]Tex. H. Jud. Comm., *The Texas Determinate Sentencing Act for Juveniles: Hearings on Tex. H. 682*, 70th Leg., Reg. Sess. 1 (Mar. 2, 1987).

.   .   .

[29]Tex. H. Jud. Comm., *supra* n. 3, at 1.

16.6 Full Citation Format for State Legislative Reports, Documents, and Prints

If the state whose report, document, or print you are citing has a special citation format, use that format. Consult **Appendix 2** to determine whether a particular state has a citation rule for reports, documents, or prints. If the state does not have a special format, use the format listed below.

A full citation to a legislative report, document, or print may contain up to seven components, depending on the state.

State abbreviation●Abbreviation for type of document●Document number,● Legislature designation [if available]●, Session designation [if available]● Pinpoint reference [if available]●(Exact date).

Example (Maine Senate Document)

| State abbreviation | Document number | Session designation | Exact date |

Me. Sen. Doc. 89, 122d Leg., 1st Reg. Sess. 1 (Jan. 11, 2005).

Document abbreviation — Legislature designation — Pinpoint reference

Other example (Hawaii Senate Standing Committee Report)

Haw. Sen. Stand. Comm. Rpt. 502, 22d Leg., Reg. Sess. 1 (2003).

16.6(a) State abbreviation

Include the state abbreviation as listed in **Appendix 3(B).** Insert one space after the abbreviation.

16.6(b) Abbreviation for type of document

Use the following abbreviations, and the abbreviations in **Appendix 3**, to designate the type of report, document, or print you are citing. Spell out words not listed below or in **Appendix 3**. Insert one space after the last part of the abbreviation.

Type	Abbreviation
Committee:	Comm.
Conference:	Conf.
Document:	Doc.
House:	H.
House of Delegates:	H.
House of Representatives:	H.
Joint:	Jt.
Legislature, Legislative:	Leg.
Report:	Rpt.
Senate:	Sen.

16.6(c) Number

After the abbreviation for the type of document, insert the number assigned by the state.

16.6(d) State legislature designation

Follow **Rule 16.1(d)**.

16.6(e) State session designation

Follow **Rule 16.1(e)**.

16.6(f) Pinpoint reference

If referring to only part of the report, document, or print, cite that particular subdivision. For additional information on subdivisions, consult **Rules 5, 6, and 9**. Insert one space after the subdivision information. Consult **Rule 15.9(c)** for analogous examples.

16.6(g) Date

If available, provide the exact date (month-day-year) on which the report, document, or print was ordered to be printed. Abbreviate the month according to **Appendix 3(A)**. Note that, for some documents, only the month and year, or only the year, are available. Enclose the date in parentheses.

16.6(h) Author and title

You may include the author's name and the title. Italicize the title. You may abbreviate the name of an institutional author using the terms in **Appendix 3**. Consult **Rule 15.9(e)** for analogous examples.

16.6(i) Parenthetical information

You may parenthetically include any explanation after the citation that will clarify the reference or otherwise assist readers. Consult **Rule 46** regarding explanatory parentheticals. Consult **Rule 15.9(f)** for an analogous example.

16.7 Short Citation Format for State Legislative Reports, Documents, and Prints

If *id.* is appropriate, use *id.* as the preferred short citation format. Consult **Rule 11.3** for additional information on *id.* Otherwise, use all required components of the full citation format, but omit the legislative designation, session designation, and date. Insert "at" before any pinpoint reference.

Example

Full citation: Me. Sen. Doc. 89, 122d Leg., 1st Reg. Sess. 1 (Jan. 11, 2005).
Short citation: Me. Sen. Doc. 89 at 1.

16.8 Full Citation Format for State Legislative Debates

If the state whose debate you are citing has a special citation format, use that format. Consult **Appendix 2** to determine whether a particular state has a citation rule for legislative debates. If the state does not have a special format, use the format listed below.

A full citation to a legislative debate may contain up to eight components, depending on the state and whether the debate is published.

State abbreviation•House abbreviation•*Description* **or** *published location of debate*•, Legislature designation [if available]•, Session designation [if available]•Pinpoint reference [if available]•(Exact date(s))•(Location for unpublished debates).

Examples

Published

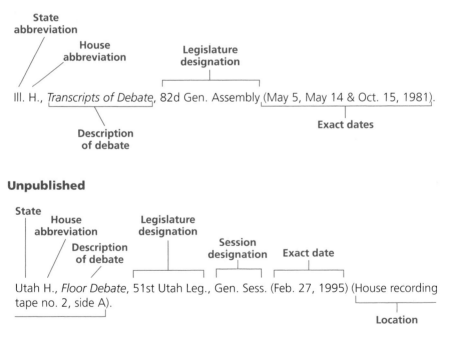

16.8(a) State abbreviation

Include the state abbreviation as listed in **Appendix 3(B).** Insert one space after the abbreviation.

16.8(b) State house abbreviation

Insert the abbreviation "H." for House, House of Representatives, or House of Delegates, or "Sen." for Senate.

16.8(c) Description or published location of debate

(1) If the debate is published, provide the name of the source in which it is contained. Italicize the title. Insert a comma and one space after the title.

(2) If the debate is not published, provide a concise description of the debate. (**Examples:** *Floor Debate, Debate on H. 1731.*)

(3) You may provide the description and the source of publication. If including both, put the description first.

Example

Description   Source of publication

N.Y. Assembly, *Debate on Bill 4843, Record of Proceedings* 474 (Mar. 6, 1995).

16.8(d) State legislature designation

Follow **Rule 16.1(d)**.

16.8(e) State session designation

Follow **Rule 16.1(e)**.

16.8(f) Pinpoint reference

Follow **Rule 16.1(f)**.

16.8(g) Date

If available, provide the exact date (month-day-year) of the debate. Abbreviate months according to **Appendix 3(A)**. If the exact date is not available, provide at least the year. Enclose the date in parentheses.

16.8(h) Location for unpublished debates

If the debate is not published, add a parenthetical indicating where a transcript or audio recording of the debate is located.

Example

Tex. Sen., *Debate on Tex. Sen. 31 on the Floor of the Senate*, 74th Leg., Reg. Sess. 1 (Feb. 1, 1995) (transcript available from Senate Staff Services Office).

16.9   Short Citation Format for State Legislative Debates

If *id.* is appropriate, use *id.* as the preferred short citation format. Consult **Rule 11.3** for additional information on *id.* If *id.* is not appropriate, keep all required components, but eliminate the legislature designation, session designation, location parenthetical, and date. Also insert "at" before any pinpoint reference.

Example

Full citation: Tex. Sen., *Debate on Tex. Sen. 31 on the Floor of the Senate*, 74th Leg., Reg. Sess. 1 (Feb. 1, 1995) (transcript available from Senate Staff Services Office).
Short citation: Tex. Sen., *Debate on Tex. Sen. 31 on the Floor of the Senate* at 1.

16.10   State Legislative Journals

Cite legislative journals using the format provided by the state whose journal you are citing (see **Appendix 2**), or, if not listed in **Appendix 2**, using the following format. *Id.* may be used as the short citation.

State abbreviation•House abbreviation•J.•, Legislature designation [if available]•, Session designation [if available]•Pinpoint reference [if available]•(Date).

Examples

Full citation: Iowa Sen. J., 81st Gen. Assembly, Reg. Sess. 69 (2005).
Short citation: Iowa Sen. J., 81st Gen. Assembly, Reg. Sess. at 69.

Full citation: Haw. H.J., 17th Leg., Reg. Sess. 1467 (1993).
Short citation: Haw. H.J., 17th Leg., Reg. Sess. at 1467.

16.11   Other State Legislative Materials

To cite state legislative materials not specifically addressed in **Rule 16,** analogize to the closest rule above or to **Rule 15,** or use the following format. If the suggested format does not work exactly for your source, include as much of the information called for below as possible.

State abbreviation•House abbreviation [if available]•Document abbreviation•
Title,•Legislature [if available]•, Session [if available]•Pinpoint reference [if
available]•(Date)•(Location information for unpublished material).

Example

Cal. Proposition 58 (2004) (available in Westlaw, Ca-Legis-Old database).

COURT RULES, ETHICS RULES AND OPINIONS, AND JURY INSTRUCTIONS

Federal Rules of Civil Procedure	Fed. R. Civ. P. 30.
Federal Rules of Criminal Procedure	Fed. R. Crim. P. 21(a).
State rules of procedure	Mo. R. Civ. P. 56.01(b)(3).
Federal Rules of Evidence	Fed. R. Evid. 801.
Ethics opinion	ABA Formal Ethics Op. 02-425.
Pattern jury instruction	Neb. Pattern Jury Instr. Civ. vol. 1, 1.43 (2004).

17.0   COURT RULES, ETHICS RULES AND OPINIONS, AND JURY INSTRUCTIONS

17.1   Full Citation Format for Rules Currently in Force

A full citation to a rule currently in force contains two components.

Code abbreviation●Rule number.

Example

Code abbreviation   Rule number

Fed. R. Civ. P. 11.

Other examples

Fed. R. Evid. 401.

Fla. R. Crim. Evid. 3.380.

La. Code Civ. P. Ann. art. 1231.

17.1(a)   Code abbreviation

Begin with the abbreviation for the code that contains the cited rule. To develop this abbreviation, use the abbreviations listed in **Appendix 3**. Follow **Rule 2.2** on spacing. Omit from the abbreviation all prepositions (e.g., "as," "on") and articles (e.g., "the," "an," "a"). Insert one space between the abbreviation and the rule number.

Examples (the symbol ▲ denotes a space)

Fed.▲R.▲Crim.▲P.▲21(a).

Ind.▲Sup.▲Ct.▲Admis.▲&▲Disc.▲R.▲5.

R.I.▲R.▲Evid.▲104(b).

17.1(b)   Rule number

(1)   After the code abbreviation, insert the rule number and any subdivisions. Include the most specific subdivision possible. Consult **Rules 5, 6, and 9** for additional information on subdivisions.

Examples (the symbol ▲ denotes a space)

Mo.▲R.▲Civ.▲P.▲56.01(b)(3).

N.M.▲R.▲Prof.▲Resp.▲16-707.

Iowa▲Code▲Prof.▲Resp.▲DR 2-101(A).

S.C.▲R.▲Civ.▲P.▲45(b)(1).

(2) Insert notes, internal operating procedures (abbreviated "I.O.P."), and similar information after the rule number.

Examples

Fed. R. Evid. 703 advisory comm. nn.

Fed. R. Evid. 1001 hist. n.

11th Cir. R. 34-4, I.O.P. 2(b).

17.2   Full Citation Format for Rules No Longer in Force

If citing a rule no longer in force, such as a rule that has been repealed or superseded, use the citation format for current rules, but, as the date component, include the reason the rule is no longer in force and the year in which it lost effect.

Examples

Tex. R. Civ. Evid. 702 (repealed 1998).

Unif. R. Evid. 9-12 (superseded 1986 by Unif. R. Evid. 201).

17.3   Short Citation Format

When appropriate, use *id.* as a short-form citation for rules, whether current or no longer in force. Consult **Rule 11.3** for additional information on *id.* If *id.* is not appropriate, repeat all the components of the full citation.

Example

Full citation: S.C. R. Civ. P. 45(b)(1).
Short citation: S.C. R. Civ. P. 45(b)(1).

17.4   Full Citation Format for Ethics Opinions

17.4(a)

Cite formal and informal ethics opinions by providing the name of the state or entity that issued the opinion, the type of ethics opinion, and the opinion number. If the date is not evident from the opinion number, also include the year in parentheses. You may abbreviate the name of the state and words in the entity's name that appear in **Appendix 3.**

Examples

ABA Formal Ethics Op. 95-396.

ABA Formal Ethics Op. 432 (2004).

ABA Informal Ethics Op. 430 (2003).

Ariz. Ethics Op. 2002-01.

Colo. B. Assn. Formal Ethics Op. 322 (2001).

Minn. Informal Ethics Op. 3 (1986).

Phila. B. Assn. Ethics Op. 2002-4.

17.4(b)

You may insert a comma after an entity name if not doing would cause confusion or make the citation difficult to read.

Examples

St. B. of Cal. Standing Comm. on Prof. Resp. & Conduct, Formal Ethics Op. 2004-167.

D.C. Bar Leg. Ethics Comm., Ethics Op. 326 (2004).

17.4(c)

When possible, include pinpoint information after the opinion number. Consult **Rules 5, 6, 7,** and **9** for information about various pinpoint references.

Examples

ABA Formal Ethics Op. 96-401 n. 2.

ABA Formal Ethics Op. 92-368 § I(B).

17.4(d)

You may add an italicized title to the beginning of the citation. Use **Rule 3** for capitalization.

Example

Protecting the Confidentiality of Unencrypted E-Mail, ABA Formal Ethics Op. 99-413.

17.4(e)

You may include parenthetical information about print or electronic sources that reprint the rule. See **Rule 46** for additional information on parentheticals.

Examples

N.J. Comm. on Atty. Advert. Op. 27 (reprinted in 9 N.J. Law. 2405 (Dec. 11, 2000)).

Tex. Ethics Op. 533 (2000) (available at 2000 WL 987291).

17.4(f)

If an opinion has been superseded or withdrawn, analogize to **Rule 17.2.** If an opinion has been revised, note that information parenthetically.

Examples

ABA Formal Ethics Op. 320 (1968) (withdrawn in ABA Formal Ethics Op. 00-419).

ABA Formal Ethics Op. 94-386 (revised Oct. 15, 1995).

17.5   Short Citation Format for Ethics Opinions

Use *id.* when appropriate (**Rule 11.3**). If *id.* is not appropriate, repeat all components except any date in a parenthetical. In some instances, the full citation format and the short citation format will be identical.

Examples

Full form: D.C. Bar Leg. Ethics Comm., Ethics Op. 326 (2004).
Short form: D.C. Bar. Leg. Ethics Comm., Ethics Op. 326.

Full form: Ohio Ethics Op. 2000-3.
Short form: Ohio Ethics Op. 2000-3.

17.6   Full Citation Formats for Jury Instructions

17.6(a) Pattern, standard, or approved instructions

A full citation to a pattern, standard, or approved set of jury instructions includes the name of the instructions, the volume if any, the rule or section number, the edition after the first, and the date. You may abbreviate words in the title if they appear in **Appendix 3.**

Examples

Ill. Pattern Jury Instr. Crim. 1.01 (4th ed. 2000).

Ind. Pattern Jury Instr. Civ. vol. 2, 31.03 (2d rev. ed. 2001).

11th Cir. Pattern Jury Instr. § 6 (2000).

17.6(b) Unofficial jury instructions

Cite unofficial jury instructions like a book (**Rule 22**).

Example of full citation

Stephen A. Saltzburg & Harvey S. Perlman, *Federal Criminal Jury Instructions* I-2, 11.01 (2d ed., Michie Co. 1991).

Kevin F. O'Malley et al., *Federal Jury Practice and Instructions* vol. 2, § 23.05 (5th ed., West 2000).

17.7   Short Citation Formats for Jury Instructions

For any type of jury instruction, use *id.* as a short form when appropriate (**Rule 11.3**). For standard, pattern, or approved jury instructions, use the format in **Rule 17.6**, but drop the edition and date. For unofficial jury instructions, use the short citation formats in **Rule 22.2.**

Examples

Pattern instruction:	11th Cir. Pattern Jury Instr. § 6.
Unofficial instruction: **(Document without footnotes)**	Saltzburg & Perlman, *Federal Criminal Jury Instructions* at I-2, 11.01.
(Document with footnotes)	Saltzburg & Perlman, *supra* n. 25, at I-2, 11.01.

FAST FORMATS

LOCAL ORDINANCES

Codified ordinance	Boone Co. Code Ordin. (Ky.) § 91.39 (2003).
Uncodified ordinance	Ft. Lauderdale, Fla., Code Ordin. 12-5 (May 7, 2002).

18.0 | LOCAL ORDINANCES

18.1 Full Citation Format for Codified Ordinances

A full citation to a codified ordinance contains four components.

Abbreviated name of code●(State abbreviation)●Pinpoint reference●(Date).

Example

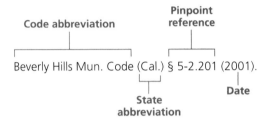

Code abbreviation

Pinpoint reference

Beverly Hills Mun. Code (Cal.) § 5-2.201 (2001).

State abbreviation

Date

18.1(a) Abbreviated name of code

(1) Provide the abbreviated name of the local or municipal code.

(2) Include the political subdivision name, such as a city, even if it is not part of the official title.

(3) Use the abbreviations in **Appendices 1** and **3**, and the spacing conventions in **Rule 2.2**.

(4) Eliminate prepositions, such as "of" or "for," from the abbreviated name.

(5) Insert one space after the last part of the code abbreviation.

Example

Name of code: Municipal Code City of Reno, Nevada.
Citation: Mun. Code Reno (Nev.) § 18.06.445(a) (2003).

Other examples

Austin City Code (Tex.) § 3-1-1 (2001).

Boone Co. Code Ordin. (Ky.) § 91.39 (2003).

Phila. City Code & Home Rule Charter (Pa.) § 16-202 (current through Jan. 2002).

18.1(b) State abbreviation

After the code abbreviation, include the state abbreviation from the list in **Appendix 3(B)**. Enclose the abbreviation in parentheses.

18.1(c) Pinpoint reference

After the state abbreviation, insert the subdivision that contains the specific ordinance cited. Ordinances may be designated by sections, articles, chapters, or other subdivisions. Consult **Rules 5, 6,** and **9** for additional information about subdivisions.

Examples

Glendale Mun. Code (Ariz.) ch. 15 (2001).

Shreveport Code Ordin. (La.) § 24-42 (2000).

18.1(d) Date

After the subdivision, insert the year of the code. If the ordinance is available only online, you may use a "current through" date (see the Philadelphia example in **Rule 18.1(a)**). Enclose the year in parentheses.

SIDEBAR 18.1

LOCATING ORDINANCES ON THE INTERNET

It is often difficult to locate local ordinances in print format. However, the following Web sites provide compilations of ordinances from many local governments. In addition, LexisNexis and Westlaw have limited municipal code databases.

FindLaw's State Resource Index:
http://www.findlaw.com/11stategov/index.html

General Code Advantage:
http://www.generalcode.com/webcode2.html

Municipal Code Corporation:
http://www.municode.com

Seattle Public Library:
http://www.spl.org/default.asp?pageID = collection_municodes

18.2   Full Citation for Uncodified Ordinances

A full citation to an uncodified ordinance contains four components.

Name of political subdivision,●State abbreviation,●Ordinance number or *Name*●(Exact date).

Examples (hypothetical jurisdictions)

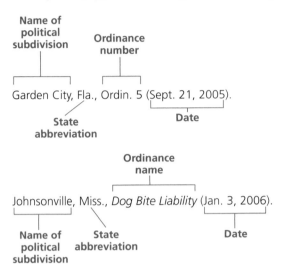

18.2(a) **Name of political subdivision and state abbreviation**

(1) Include the name of the political subdivision and the abbreviated name of the state. Insert a comma and one space between the political subdivision and the state abbreviation.

(2) Do not abbreviate the name of the subdivision unless the name appears in **Appendix 3.**

(3) Use the abbreviations in **Appendix 3(B)** to abbreviate the state name. Insert a comma and one space after the state abbreviation.

18.2(b) **Ordinance number or name**

(1) If providing the ordinance number, use the abbreviation "Ordin."; then insert one space after the ordinance number.

(2) If an ordinance does not have a number, provide the ordinance name in italics. Use **Rule 3** for capitalization.

18.2(c) **Date**

After the ordinance number, give the exact date (month-day-year) on which the ordinance was adopted. Abbreviate the month according to **Appendix 3(A).** Enclose the date in parentheses.

18.3 Short Citation Format for Codified and Uncodified Ordinances

If *id.* is appropriate, use *id.* as the preferred short citation format. Consult **Rule 11.3** for additional information on *id.* If *id.* is not appropriate, use all required components of the full citation format, but omit the state abbreviation for codified ordinances and the date for all ordinances.

Examples

Full citation: Beverly Hills Mun. Code (Cal.) § 5-2.201 (2001).
Short citation: Beverly Hills Mun. Code at § 5-2.201.

Full citation: Johnsonville, Miss., *Dog Bite Liability* (Jan. 3, 2006).
Short citation: Johnsonville, Miss., *Dog Bite Liability*.

FEDERAL ADMINISTRATIVE AND EXECUTIVE MATERIALS

Code of Federal Regulations	31 C.F.R. § 515.329 (2005).
Federal Register	69 Fed. Reg. 55719 (Sept. 16, 2005).
Agency decision	*Appolo Fuels, Inc. v. Off. of Surface Mining Reclamation & Enforcement*, 100 Int. Dec. 63, 65–70 (Dept. Int., Bd. Land App. 1993).
Attorney General opinion	39 Op. Atty. Gen. 509, 514 (1940).
Office of Legal Counsel opinion	17 Op. Off. Leg. Counsel 1, 2–3 (1993).
Executive Order	Exec. Or. 12778, 3 C.F.R. 359, 360 (1992).

19.0 **FEDERAL ADMINISTRATIVE AND EXECUTIVE MATERIALS**

19.1   Full Citation Format for Code of Federal Regulations

Cite final federal administrative rules and regulations to the Code of Federal Regulations, which is abbreviated "C.F.R."

A full citation to the Code of Federal Regulations consists of four components.

Title number•C.F.R.•Pinpoint reference•(Date).

Example

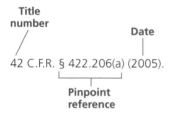

19.1(a) Title number

Insert the title number of the C.F.R. volume that contains the cited subdivision. Insert one space after the title number. Note that the title numbers for C.F.R. do not correspond exactly to the title numbers in the United States Code (U.S.C.).

19.1(b) C.F.R. abbreviation

After the title number, insert "C.F.R." as the abbreviation for Code of Federal Regulations. Insert one space after the abbreviation.

19.1(c) Pinpoint reference

Cite the particular section or other subdivision that contains the referenced rules or regulations. For additional information on subdivisions, consult **Rules 5, 6,** and **9.** Insert one space after the pinpoint reference.

Examples

31 C.F.R. pts. 730–774 (2005).

31 C.F.R. ch. V (2005).

31 C.F.R. § 515.329 (2005).

29 C.F.R. app. § 1630.2(j) (2005).

19.1(d) Date

(1) Current print or official electronic version

When citing the print or the official electronic version of C.F.R., typically include the year of current title; enclose the date in parentheses. The "official" electronic version is found on GPO Access, http://www.gpoaccess.gov/cfr/index.html. See **Sidebar 19.1** for information regarding when each title of C.F.R. is published. Use **Rule 19.1(d)(3)** for historical references.

(2) C.F.R. on unofficial electronic databases

When citing a C.F.R. provision that is available on an unofficial electronic database, such as LexisNexis or Westlaw, include the name of the database provider and the specific date (month-day-year) through which the C.F.R. is current on that database. Use **Appendix 3(A)** to abbreviate the month. Enclose the name of the database provider and the date in parentheses. See **Sidebar 19.1** for additional information about C.F.R. provisions available on LexisNexis and Westlaw.

(3) Historical references

If citing a rule or regulation for a historical purpose, enclose the selected year, not the current year, in parentheses.

Examples

Current print version:	48 C.F.R. § 53.246 (2005).
Current electronic version:	14 C.F.R. § 1201.102 (Westlaw current through July 1, 2005).
	7 C.F.R. § 305.2 (Lexis current through July 13, 2005).
Historical reference:	20 C.F.R. § 404.140 (1998).

19.1(e) Title

If it would assist readers, you may begin the citation with the title of the rule or regulation. Present the title in ordinary type. Insert a comma and one space

SIDEBAR 19.1

DETERMINING THE DATE OF CURRENT C.F.R. VOLUMES

The current Code of Federal Regulations consists of approximately 200 volumes. Although C.F.R. volumes are replaced each year with updated volumes, not all volumes are reprinted simultaneously. Instead, the set is revised in quarters, as follows:

Title numbers	Revision date
1–16	January 1
17–27	April 1
28–41	July 1
42–50	October 1

LexisNexis and Westlaw constantly recodify the C.F.R. to incorporate changes from the Federal Register, just as they constantly recodify federal statutes in U.S.C.S. and U.S.C.A., respectively. Thus, the print version and the electronic version of C.F.R. available on the U.S. Government's Web sites may differ from those on these unofficial databases. Therefore, if you cite a C.F.R. provision from LexisNexis or Westlaw, it is important to convey that information parenthetically, as described in **Rule 19.1(d)(2)**.

after the title. Use **Rule 3** for capitalization. If the title is extremely long, it may be shortened, so long as the reader can easily identify the cited material.

Example

Determination of Endangered or Threatened Status for Four Plants from Southwestern California and Baja California, Mexico, 50 C.F.R. pt. 17 (2005).

19.2   Short Citation Format for Code of Federal Regulations

When appropriate, use *id.* as a short-form citation for rules and regulations in C.F.R. Consult **Rule 11.3** for additional information on *id.* If *id.* is not appropriate, repeat all required components except the date. Insert "at" before the pinpoint reference.

Example

Full citation: 31 C.F.R. § 515.329 (2005).
Short citations: *Id.* at ch. V.
                     31 C.F.R. at § 515.329.

19.3   Full Citation Format for Federal Register

Cite to the Federal Register for any final regulations that are not printed in C.F.R., all proposed federal rules and regulations, and notices. The abbreviation for the Federal Register is "Fed. Reg."

A full citation to the Federal Register contains five components.

Volume number●Fed. Reg.●Initial page●, Pinpoint page●(Exact date).

Example

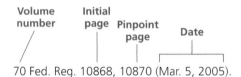

70 Fed. Reg. 10868, 10870 (Mar. 5, 2005).

19.3(a) Volume number

Insert the number of the Federal Register volume that contains the cited material. Insert one space after the volume number.

19.3(b) Federal Register abbreviation

After the volume number, insert "Fed. Reg." as the abbreviation for the Federal Register. Insert one space after the abbreviation.

19.3(c) Pages

Insert the initial page for the rule, regulation, or other material, and, when possible, the pinpoint page. Consult **Rule 5.2** for additional information about pinpoint pages. Separate the initial page from the pinpoint page with a comma and one space.

Examples

70 Fed. Reg. 1506, 1586 (Jan. 7, 2005).

70 Fed. Reg. 4791, 4793–4794 (proposed Jan. 24, 2005).

19.3(d) Date

Because the Federal Register is published daily, include the exact date (month-day-year) of the cited volume. Abbreviate the month according to the list in **Appendix 3(B)**. Enclose the date in parentheses.

When citing a proposed rule or regulation, include that information parenthetically.

Example of proposed regulation

66 Fed. Reg. 307, 307 (proposed Jan. 3, 2001).

19.3(e) Citation to C.F.R.

When the Federal Register indicates that a rule or regulation will appear in the Code of Federal Regulations, provide that information parenthetically, as illustrated below.

Examples

69 Fed. Reg. 75, 839 (Dec. 20, 2004) (to be codified at 31 C.F.R. pt. 10).

70 Fed. Reg. 9013, 9015–9016 (proposed Feb. 24, 2005) (to be codified at 11 C.F.R. § 300.64(a)).

19.3(f) Title

(1) You may begin the citation with the title of the rule or regulation. Present the title in ordinary type. Insert a comma and one space after the title. Use **Rule 3** for capitalization.

Example

September 11th Victim Compensation Fund of 2001, 67 Fed. Reg. 11233 (Mar. 13, 2002).

(2) If the material cited does not have a formal name, you still may include a description for the citation. Present the description in ordinary type, and include a comma and one space before the rest of the citation.

Examples

Notice, 70 Fed. Reg. 1730 (Jan. 10, 2005).

Meeting Notice, 65 Fed. Reg. 70382 (Nov. 22, 2000).

19.4 Short Citation Format for Federal Register

When appropriate, use *id.* as a short-form citation for rules and regulations in the Federal Register Consult **Rule 11.3** for additional information on *id.* If *id.* is not appropriate, repeat all required components except the initial page number and the date. Insert "at" before any pinpoint reference.

Example

Full citation:	70 Fed. Reg. 1506, 1586 (Jan. 7, 2005).
Short citation:	70 Fed. Reg. at 1510.
Id.:	*Id.* at 1550.

19.5   Full Citation Format for Agency Decisions

A full citation to an administrative decision, such as an adjudication or arbitration, typically contains seven components.

Case name,●Volume number●Reporter abbreviation●Initial subdivision●, Pinpoint subdivision●(Agency abbreviation●Date).

Example

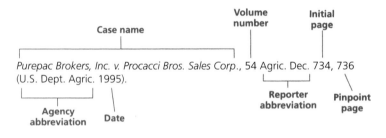

19.5(a)   Case name

Follow **Rule 12.2** for cases.

19.5(b)   Volume number

After the case name, include the volume number of the reporter cited. Insert one space after the volume number.

19.5(c)   Reporter abbreviation

(1)   After the volume number, cite either the official or the unofficial reporter that contains the agency decision.

(2)   **Appendix 8** lists abbreviations for many federal agencies' official reporters. If the reporter you are citing is not listed there, use abbreviations listed in **Appendix 3**.

Examples

Official reporter: *Appolo Fuels, Inc. v. Office of Surface Mining Reclamation & Enforcement*, 100 Int. Dec. 63, 65–70 (Dept. Int., Bd. Land App. 1993).

Unofficial reporter: *REA Express, Inc. v. Bhd. of Ry., Airline & Steamship Clerks*, Lab. L. Rpt. ¶ 10,546 (S.D.N.Y. 1974).

19.5(d) Subdivisions

(1) After the reporter abbreviation, insert the initial subdivision. In bound reports, the initial subdivision will likely be a page number; however, in looseleaf services, the subdivision may be a paragraph or another division (**Rule 28.1(e)**).

(2) If citing a particular part of the decision, insert a comma, one space, and then the pinpoint subdivision. Consult **Rule 5.2** for additonal information on pinpoint references.

(3) Insert one space after the final subdivision.

19.5(e) Agency abbreviation

Include the abbreviation for the agency that rendered the decision. The agency abbreviation appears in the parenthetical that contains the date. Use **Appendix 3** to determine agency abbreviations. After the agency abbreviation, insert one space before the date.

19.5(f) Date

Follow **Rule 12.7**.

19.6   Short Citation Format for Agency Decisions

Follow **Rule 12.21**.

19.7   Full Citation Format for Attorney General Opinions and Justice Department Office of Legal Counsel Opinions

A full citation to an advisory opinion of the Attorney General or Office of Legal Counsel consists of five components.

Volume number•Type of opinion•Initial page•, Pinpoint page•(Date).

Examples

Attorney General

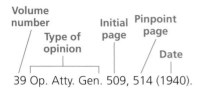

39 Op. Atty. Gen. 509, 514 (1940).

Office of Legal Counsel

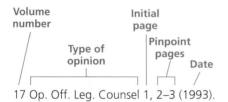

17 Op. Off. Leg. Counsel 1, 2–3 (1993).

19.7(a) Volume number

Insert the volume number of the source that contains the cited opinion. Insert one space after the volume number.

19.7(b) Type of opinion

(1) Start this component with the abbreviation "Op." for opinion. Insert one space after the abbreviation.

(2) If the opinion is from the Attorney General, and thus published in Opinions of the Attorneys General of the United States, insert the abbreviation "Atty. Gen."

SIDEBAR 19.2

PURPOSE OF ATTORNEY GENERAL OPINIONS

Attorney General opinions are somewhat different from other agency decisions. They are written in response to inquiries from federal government officials and are advisory in nature. Thus, they are not binding unless adopted by the requesting office. Today, the Attorney General issues very few formal opinions. Instead, the Justice Department's Office of Legal Counsel tends to issue opinions.

(3) If the opinion is from the Office of Legal Counsel, and thus published in Opinions of the Office of Legal Counsel, insert the abbreviation "Off. Leg. Counsel."

19.7(c) Pages

Insert the initial page on which the cited material begins. To cite a particular part of the opinion, include a pinpoint reference (**Rule 5.2**). Insert a comma and one space between the page references. Insert one space after the final page number.

19.7(d) Date

Include the year of the volume in which the opinion appears. Enclose the year in parentheses.

19.7(e) Title

You may begin the citation with the title of the opinion. Present the title in ordinary type. Insert a comma and one space after the title.

Example

Relative Rank of Navy and Army Officers, 34 Op. Atty. Gen. 521, 523 (1925).

19.8 Short Citation Format for Attorney General Opinions and Justice Department Office of Legal Counsel Opinions

When appropriate, use *id.* as a short-form citation. Consult **Rule 11.3** for additional information on *id.* If *id.* is not appropriate, repeat all required components except the initial page number and the date. Insert "at" before the pinpoint page.

Example

Full citation: 13 Op. Off. Leg. Counsel 370, 371 (1989).
Short citation: 13 Op. Off. Leg. Counsel at 371.

19.9 Full Citation Format for Executive Orders, Proclamations, Determinations, and Reorganization Plans

A full citation to an order, a proclamation, a determination, or a reorganization plan prepared by the President of the United States contains six or seven components.

Document abbreviation●Document number●, Title number●Source abbreviation●Initial subdivision●, Pinpoint subdivision●(Date).

Example

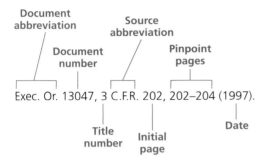

Exec. Or. 13047, 3 C.F.R. 202, 202–204 (1997).

Other examples

Exec. Reorg. Plan 3, 3 C.F.R. 1072 (1970).

Exec. Procl. 6518, 3 C.F.R. 265, 265–267 (1992).

Exec. Determ. 85, 50 Fed. Reg. 7901 (Feb. 16, 1985).

19.9(a) Document abbreviation

(1) Begin with the abbreviation "Exec." for executive.

(2) Then insert the abbreviation for the particular type of document. Use "Or." for order, "Procl." for proclamation, "Determ." for determination, and "Reorg. Plan" for reorganization plan.

19.9(b) Document number

Insert the document number as it appears on the source.

19.9(c) Title number and source abbreviation

(1) Presidential orders, proclamations, and reorganization plans are printed in Title 3 of the Code of Federal Regulations. Thus, insert 3 as the title number, followed by one space and the abbreviation "C.F.R."

(2) If the document is not in the Code of Federal Regulations or has not yet appeared there, cite the appropriate title of the Federal Register.

Examples

Exec. Or. 12834, 3 C.F.R. 580 (1993).

Exec. Procl. 7720, 68 Fed. Reg. 59515 (Oct. 10, 2003).

19.9(d) Subdivisions

Insert the page or other subdivision on which the specific document begins. To refer to material within the document, insert a comma, one space, and the relevant pinpoint citation. Consult **Rules 5, 6,** and **9** for additional information on subdivisions.

Examples

Exec. Or. 12778, 3 C.F.R. 359, 360 (1992).

Exec. Or. 12291, 3 C.F.R. 127, 128, § 2(c) (1981).

Exec. Or. 12435, 3 C.F.R. § 202 (1983).

19.9(e) Date

(1) When citing C.F.R., follow **Rule 19.1(d)**.

(2) When citing Fed. Reg., insert the exact date (month-day-year) of the cited volume. Enclose the date in parentheses.

19.9(f) Title

You may begin the citation with the document title. Present the title in ordinary type and capitalize words according to **Rule 3**. Insert a comma and one space after the title.

Example

Establishing the President's Homeland Security Advisory Council and Senior Advisory Committees for Homeland Security, 67 Fed. Reg. 13241 (Mar. 19, 2002).

19.9(g) Document reprinted in other sources

You may include a citation to another source that contains the cited document, such as United States Code, United States Code Congressional and Administrative News, or Statutes at Large. Include such information in a separate parenthetical that begins "reprinted in."

Examples

Exec. Or. 11246, 3 C.F.R. 167 (1965) (reprinted in 42 U.S.C. § 2000e app. 538–541 (2000)).

Exec. Or. 11785, 3 C.F.R. 874 (1974) (reprinted in 1974 U.S.C.C.A.N. 8277).

Exec. Reorg. Plan 3, 3 C.F.R. 1072 (1970) (reprinted in 84 Stat. 2086 (1970)).

19.10   Short Citation Format for Executive Orders, Proclamations, Determinations, and Reorganization Plans

When appropriate, use *id.* as a short-form citation. Consult **Rule 11.3** for additional information on *id.* If *id.* is not appropriate, repeat all required components, except the initial page number and the date. Insert "at" before the pinpoint page.

Example

Full citation: Exec. Or. 12778, 3 C.F.R. 359, 360 (1992).
Short citation: Exec. Or. 12778, 3 C.F.R. at 360.
Id.:   *Id.* at 359.

19.11   Executive Agreements

Follow **Rule 21** for international treaties.

19.12   Other Presidential Documents

Cite other presidential documents, such as presidential papers and speeches, to one of the following sources, in this order of preference:

• Public Papers of the Presidents
• Weekly Compilation of Presidential Documents
• United States Code Congressional and Administrative News

Examples

Public Papers of the Presidents

Full citation: John F. Kennedy, *Inaugural Address*, 1961 Pub. Papers 1, 1–3.
Short citation: 1961 Pub. Papers at 3.

Weekly Compilation of Presidential Documents

Full citation: William J. Clinton, *Statement on Signing the 1999 Emergency Supplemental Appropriations Act*, 35 Wkly. Comp. Pres. Docs. 961 (May 31, 1999).

Short citation: 35 Wkly. Comp. Pres. Docs. at 962.

United States Code Congressional and Administrative News

Full citation: *Statement of President George Bush upon Signing S. 1745*, 1991 U.S.C.C.A.N. 768, 769.

Short citation: 1991 U.S.C.C.A.N. at 769.

19.13   Patents

19.13(a)   Full Citation Format for Patents

Include "U.S. Patent No.," the patent number (using commas as illustrated below), and the exact date (month-day-year) on which the patent was filed. Use the month abbreviations in **Appendix 3(A)**, and enclose the date in parentheses.

If relevant to the paper you are writing, you may include the patent name (in ordinary type) or the date on which the patent was issued.

If citing a patent application, include "App." before "No." and use the application number instead of the patent number.

To cite a particular part of the patent, insert the pinpoint reference before the date. Consult **Rule 9** for additional information on subdivisions.

Examples

U.S. Patent No. 4,396,601 (filed Sept. 3, 1982).

U.S. Patent No. 6,918,136 fig. 2 (filed Feb. 1, 2001).

U.S. Patent No. 4,396,601 (filed Sept. 3, 1982 & issued Apr. 24, 1984).

U.S. Patent App. No. 20,050,107,339 abstract (filed Sept. 3, 2004).

Service Operations on a Computer System, U.S. Patent No. 6,918,055 (filed Mar. 20, 2002).

19.13(b)   Short Citation Format for Patents

(1)   In citations, to prepare the short form, use the full citation format, but delete the date parenthetical.

Example

Full citation:	U.S. Patent No. 4,396,601 (filed Sept. 3, 1982).
Short citations:	U.S. Patent No. 4,396,601.
	U.S. Patent No. 4,396,601 fig. 1.
Id.:	*Id.*
	Id. at fig. 1.

(2) In textual sentences, the following short form, which includes an apostrophe followed by the last three digits of the patent may be used. Do not use this form if more than one patent would have the same designation.

Example

Full citation:	U.S. Patent No. 4,396,601 (filed Sept. 3, 1982).
Short form in text:	the '601 Patent

19.14   Other Administrative and Executive Materials

To cite federal administrative and executive materials not specifically addressed in **Rule 19**, analogize to the closest rule above or use the following format. If the suggested format does not work exactly for your source, include as much of the information called for below as possible.

Title,●Document abbreviation,●Document number●Source abbreviation●Pinpoint reference●(Agency abbreviation●Date).

Examples

SEC No-Action Letter:	*Sullivan & Cromwell*, SEC No-Action Ltr., 2005 SEC No-Act. LEXIS 612 (June 1, 2005).
Securities Act Release:	Secs. Act Release 2205, Fed. Sec. L. Rep. ¶ 19,116 (SEC Mar. 3, 2005).

SIDEBAR 19.3

CITING TAX MATERIALS

Citation information for commonly used tax materials is contained in **Appendix 7**. For tax materials not contained in **Appendix 7**, consult Gail Levin Richmond, *Federal Tax Research: Guide to Materials and Techniques* (6th ed., Found. Press 2002), or *TaxCite: A Federal Tax Citation and Reference Manual* (ABA Sec. Taxn. 1995).

FAST FORMATS

STATE ADMINISTRATIVE AND EXECUTIVE MATERIALS

**Consult Appendices 1 and 2
for each state's specific citation formats.**

State administrative code	2 Va. Admin. Code 5-150-100 (2005).
State administrative register	29 S.C. Register 14 (May 27, 2005).
State agency decision	*Bass v. Dept. of Lab. & Empl. Sec.*, 7 Fla. Career Servs. Rptr. ¶ 290, at 1063 (Fla. Pub. Empl. Rel. Commn. Oct. 14, 1992).
	Torres v. Manpower, Inc., 2005 Fla. Div. Adm. Hear. LEXIS 966 (June 6, 2005).
State attorney general opinion	Tex. Atty. Gen. Op. GA-0336, 30 Tex. Register 3947 (July 8, 2005).
	Tex. Atty. Gen. Op. GA-0328, 2005 Tex. AG LEXIS (June 8, 2005).
	Tex. Atty. Gen. Op. GA-0328, 2005 WL 1381843 (June 8, 2005).
State executive order	*Establishing the Education Salary Schedule Improvement Committee*, Del. Exec. Or. 50, 1:9 Del. Admin. Register (Mar. 1, 1998).
	Extension of Requirements on Ethics, Financial Controls and Accounting Procedures to the State's Authorities, Agencies and Commissions, N.J. Exec. Or. 41, 37 N.J. Register 2591(a) (July 18, 2005).
	Louisiana's Plan for Access to Mental Health Care, La. Exec. Or. KBB 05-16 § 5 (June 30, 2005) (available at Off. St. Register, http://www.state.la.us/osr/other/2005KBBexo.htm).

| **STATE ADMINISTRATIVE AND EXECUTIVE MATERIALS**

20.1   Full Citation for State Administrative Codes

Each state has its own administrative code, which is the state equivalent of the Code of Federal Regulations. The citation typically includes a title number, the abbreviated name of the code, the pinpoint subdivision, and the year. If citing a current state administrative code provision from LexisNexis or Westlaw, follow **Rule 19.1(d)(2)** for the date parenthetical. The format for each state's code is listed in **Appendix 1**. Follow the format for the particular code you are citing. If necessary, consult **Rule 19.1** for additional guidance.

Examples

Ala. Admin. Code r. 135-X-5-.03 (2005).

Regs. Conn. State Agencies § 3-90-1 (2005).

Ga. Comp. R. & Regs. r. 80-2-8-.04 (Westlaw current through June 30, 2005).

Ohio Admin. Code 109:1-3-01 (2005).

20.2   Short Citation Format for State Administrative Codes

Using the specific state format in **Appendix 1,** analogize to **Rule 19.2** regarding the Code of Federal Regulations.

Examples

Ala. Admin. Code r. 135-X-5-.03.

Regs. Conn. State Agencies § 3-90-1.

20.3   Full Citation Format for State Administrative Registers

Some, but not all, states have administrative registers, which are similar to the Federal Register. Consult **Appendix 1** to determine whether a particular state has an administrative register and, if so, the correct citation format. As with the Federal Register, include the exact date listed on the front cover. If necessary, consult **Rule 19.3** for additional guidance.

Examples

52 D.C. Register 5957 (June 24, 2005).

31 Fla. Admin. Wkly. 2507 (July 8, 2005).

1028 Mass. Register 27 (June 17, 2005).

592 Wis. Admin. Register 11 (June 14, 2005).

20.4 Short Citation Format for State Administrative Registers

Using the specific state format in **Appendix 1**, analogize to **Rule 19.4** regarding the Federal Register.

Examples

1028 Mass. Register at 28.

592 Wis. Admin. Register at 12.

20.5 Full Citation Format for State Agency Decisions

Analogize to **Rule 19.5** and, when necessary, **Rule 12.** Include the state abbreviation before the agency abbreviation. Because these materials are often most easily located in an online or electronic database, you may include that information using the rules in **Part 4** of this book.

Examples

In re Application of S. Cal. Edison Co., 2002 WL 468030 (Cal. Pub. Util. Commn. Mar. 6, 2002).

Hills v. Dept. of Children & Fam. Servs., 2002 WL 845370 (Fla. Div. Admin. Hrgs. May 1, 2002).

20.6 Short Citation Format for State Agency Decisions

Follow **Rule 12.21.**

20.7 Full Citation Format for State Attorney General Opinions

Analogize to **Rule 19.7,** but include the state abbreviation at the beginning of the opinion abbreviation. Because these materials are often most easily located in an online or electronic database, you may include that information using the rules in **Part 4** of this book. You also may include a parallel citation to a state administrative code or register.

Examples

Colo. Atty. Gen. Op. 05-02, 2005 Colo. AG LEXIS 3.

Neb. Op. Atty. Gen. No. 05006, 2005 WL 620437 (Neb. A.G.).

R.I. Atty. Gen. Unofficial Op. PR 02-1, 2002 WL 31115077 (R.I. A.G.).

Tex. Atty. Gen. Op. GA-0336, 30 Tex. Register 3947 (July 8, 2005).

Tex. Atty. Gen. Op. JC-0465 4–5 (Feb. 21, 2002) (available at http://intranet1 .oag.state.tx.us/opinions/jc/JC0465.pdf).

20.8   Short Citation Format for State Attorney General Opinions

Analogize to **Rule 19.8.**

Examples (documents without footnotes)

Neb. Op. Atty. Gen. No. 05006, 2005 WL 620437 at *4.

Tex. Atty. Gen. Op. JC-0465 at 5.

Example (document with footnotes)

---

[17]Tex. Atty. Gen. Op. JC-0465, *supra* n. 4, at 2–3.

20.9   State Executive Materials

Analogize to **Rules 19.9, 19.10,** and **19.12.** Include the state abbreviation as part of the document abbreviation or source abbreviation. Because these materials are often most easily located in an online or electronic database, you may include that information using the rules in **Part 4** of this book. You also may include a parallel citation to a state administrative code or register.

Examples

Connecticut Executive Order

Conn. Exec. Or. 25 (Feb. 8, 2002) (available at http://www.state.ct.us/governor/ executiveorders/no25.htm).

Washington Executive Order

Organ Donation and Other Life-Giving Procedures, Wash. Exec. Or. 02-01 (May 7, 2002) (available at http://www.governor.wa.gov/eo/eo_02-01.htm).

Announcement by Texas Governor, printed in Texas Register

Gov. George W. Bush, *Appointments Made June 9, 1999*, 24 Tex. Register 4637 (June 25, 1999).

20.10 Other State Administrative and Executive Materials

To cite state administrative and executive materials not specifically addressed, analogize to the closest rule above or to **Rule 19,** or use the following format. If the suggested format does not work exactly for your source, include as much of the information called for below as possible.

Title,●Document abbreviation,●Document number●Source abbreviation● Pinpoint reference●(State abbreviation●Agency abbreviation●Exact date).

Examples

Response from California Fair Political Practices Commission

Ginger Osborne, File No. A-03-108, 2003 WL 21436603 at *3 (Cal. Fair Pol. Pracs. Commn. June 11, 2003).

New York State Controller Opinion (analogy to Rule 20.7)

N.Y. St. Controller Op. 01-3, 2001 WL 1178525 at *1.

FAST FORMATS

TREATIES AND CONVENTIONS, INTERNATIONAL SOURCES, AND FOREIGN SOURCES

Treaty	*Treaty of Peace between the Allied and Associated Powers and Austria* pt. XII, art. 372 (Sept. 19, 1919), T.S. No. 8.
Convention	*Convention for the Unification of Certain Rules Relating to International Transportation by Air* (Oct. 12, 1929), 49 Stat. 3000.
United Nations Charter	UN Charter art. 1, ¶ 3.
International Court of Justice Decision	*Fisheries Case (U.K. v. Nor.)*, 1951 I.C.J. 116.

See **Rule 21.5** for examples of selected foreign sources.

21.0   TREATIES AND CONVENTIONS TO WHICH THE UNITED STATES IS A PARTY, INTERNATIONAL SOURCES, AND FOREIGN SOURCES

21.1   Full Citation Format for Treaties and Conventions Currently in Force

A full citation to a treaty, a convention, or an executive agreement to which the United States is a party, and that is currently in force, has four components.

Title●Pinpoint reference●(Exact date)●, Treaty source.

Example

Title

Treaty of Peace between the Allied and Associated Powers and Austria pt. XII, art. 372 (Sept. 10, 1919), T.S. No. 8.

Exact date   Treaty source   Pinpoint reference

21.1(a) Title

(1) For the title, include both a subject matter description and the form of the agreement.

(2) Use the exact subject matter description or title that appears on the title page.

(3) Use the first form description that appears on the title page. Examples of form descriptions include "Treaty," "Convention," "Protocol," and "Agreement."

(4) Present the title in italics. Capitalize words according to **Rule 3**. Insert one space after the title.

21.1(b) Pinpoint reference

When citing only part of an agreement, give the appropriate subdivision or appended document. Use the subdivision abbreviations listed in **Appendix 3(C)**. Consult **Rules 5, 6,** and **9** for additional information on subdivisions.

Examples

Agreement between the Government of the United States of America and the Government of the Republic of Mali for Cooperation in the Globe Program preamble (Nov. 19, 1997), State Dept. No. 98-7.

187

Fisheries North Pacific Memorandum of Understanding between the United States of America and Japan § 5(a) (June 8, 1987), T.I.A.S. No. 11272.

21.1(c) Date

(1) As a general rule, give the exact date (month-day-year) of signing. See **Appendix 3(A)** for abbreviations of months.

(2) If the parties signed on different dates, provide the date on which the last party signed.

(3) If the date of signing is not available, include **one** of the following dates, in this order of preference: the effective date; the date on which ratifications were exchanged between or among the signatories; the date of ratification by the President of the United States; the date of ratification by the Senate; any other date of significance.

(4) When the date of signing is not used, include the significance of the date you are using. If a description is not included within the date parenthetical, readers will assume the date is that of the signing.

(5) Enclose the date in parentheses, and place a comma and one space after the closing parenthesis.

Examples

Date of signing

Convention for the Unification of Certain Rules Relating to International Transportation by Air (Oct. 12, 1929), 49 Stat. 3000.

Other date

Protocol on Environmental Protection to the Antarctic Treaty of 1 December 1959 (entered into force Jan. 14, 1998), 30 I.L.M. 1461.

21.1(d) Treaty source

(1) Which source to cite

After the date, include the citation to **one** source in which the treaty appears. The treaty source cited may be an official source or an unofficial source, including an Internet location.

(2) Bound official or unofficial treaty source citations

For an official or unofficial treaty source citation, include the volume number (if any), the abbreviation for the source, the initial page on which the treaty begins, and any pinpoint pages or other subdivisions (**Rule 5.2**). Abbreviations and citation formats for commonly used treaty sources are listed in **Chart 21.1**.

Examples

Treaty on the Protection of Artistic and Scientific Institutions and Historic Monuments (signed Apr. 13, 1935), 49 Stat. 3267.

Treaty Relating to the Uses of the Waters of the Niagara River (Feb. 27, 1950), 1 U.S.T. 694.

(3)   Internet citation

For treaties that can be easily located on the Internet, the source citation should include the name of the treaty; any pinpoint subdivision, such as a section or article; the date as described in **Rule 21.1(c)**; and the URL (Internet address) of the source.

Example

Inter-American Convention on Letters Rogatory art. 4 (Apr. 15, 1980), http://www.oas .org/En/prog/juridico/english/Treaties/b-36.html.

21.2   Full Citation Format for Treaties and Conventions No Longer in Force

When citing an agreement, or part of an agreement, no longer in force, use the citation format for current agreements, but add a parenthetical that indicates when and why the agreement was terminated or otherwise lost effect.

Example

Convention between the United States of America and Spain Concerning Trade-Marks (terminated Apr. 14, 1903, by treaty of July 3, 1902), 11 Bevans 563.

21.3   Short Citation Format for Treaties and Conventions

21.3(a)

When appropriate, use *id.* as the preferred short citation. Consult **Rule 11.3** for more information on *id.*

21.3(b)

When *id.* is not appropriate, use one of the formats listed below. Be sure to select the format for the type of document you are writing—either one with

CHART 21.1

SELECTED BOUND TREATY SOURCES

(The symbol ▲ denotes a space.)

Treaty Source	Type	Abbreviation and Format
Senate Treaty Documents	Official	Sen.▲Treaty▲Doc.▲No.▲ Treaty number
State Department	Official	State▲Dept.▲No.▲Treaty number
Statutes at Large	Official	Volume number▲Stat.▲Page number
Treaties and Other International Acts Series	Official	T.I.A.S.▲No.▲Treaty number
Treaty Series	Official	T.S.▲No.▲Treaty number
United States Treaties and Other International Agreements	Official	Volume number▲U.S.T.▲ Page number
Senate Executive Documents	Official	S.▲Exec.▲Doc.▲Document number
European Treaty Series	Unofficial	European▲T.S.▲No.▲Treaty number
Hein's United States Treaties and Other International Agreements	Unofficial	Hein's▲T.S.▲No.▲KAV▲ Treaty number
International Legal Materials	Unofficial	Volume number▲I.L.M.▲ Page number
League of Nations Treaty Series	Unofficial	Volume number▲L.N.T.S.▲ Page number
O.A.S. Treaty Series	Unofficial	O.A.S.▲T.S.▲No.▲Treaty number
Pan-American Treaty Series	Unofficial	Volume number▲Pan.-Am. ▲T.S.▲Page number
Parry's Consolidated Treaty Series	Unofficial	Volume number▲Consol.▲ T.S.▲Page number
Tax Treaties	Unofficial	(Cite according to **Rule 28** [looseleafs])
Treaties and Other International Agreements of the United States of America (Charles I. Bevans comp.)	Unofficial	Volume number▲Bevans▲ Page number
United Nations Treaty Series	Unofficial	Volume number▲U.N.T.S.▲ Page number

---

SIDEBAR 21.1

INTERNET ACCESS TO INTERNATIONAL MATERIALS

International materials, including treaties to which the United States is a party, are often difficult to locate. However, more and more international materials may be accessed easily via the Internet. For this reason, an Internet citation may be substituted for a bound treaty source.

---

footnotes or one without footnotes. In documents with footnotes, consult **Rule 11.4** for additional information on "hereinafter" designations.

Examples (the symbol ▲ denotes a space)

**Full citation
(document without footnotes):** *Treaty on the Protection of Artistic and Scientific Institutions and Historic Monuments* (signed Apr. 13, 1935), 49 Stat. 3267.

**Short citation
(document without footnotes):** 49 Stat. at 3268.

**Full citation
(document with footnotes):** *Treaty on the Protection of Artistic and Scientific Institutions and Historic Monuments* (signed Apr. 13, 1935), 49 Stat. 3267 [hereinafter *Protection Treaty*].

**Short citation
(document with footnotes):** *Protection Treaty, supra* n.▲___, at 3268.

21.4 Selected International Law Sources

International legal material comes from intergovernmental organizations—which also are referred to as "public international organizations"—such as the United Nations, and from nongovernmental organizations, which often are referred to as "NGOs." Because the membership of intergovernmental organizations consists of nation-states, these organizations typically are established by treaty. International NGOs usually are formed to advance a common purpose, and may be formed by agreement or charter.

21.4(a) United Nations materials generally

The largest intergovernmental organization is the United Nations, which, as of August 2005, had 191 members. The United Nations was established on June

26, 1945, when 51 states signed the UN Charter. Abbreviate United Nations as "UN," without internal periods.

21.4(b) UN Charter

A full citation to the UN Charter includes the following three components.

UN Charter•Article number•, Paragraph number [if available].

Examples

UN Charter art. 1, ¶ 3.

UN Charter arts. 12(1).

21.4(c) Subsidiary UN organizations

In researching and citing UN materials, writers should distinguish between the UN itself, with its six primary organs, and the larger system of related organizations, programs, funds, commissions, and committees. The primary organs of the UN are the Security Council, the General Assembly, the Secretariat, the International Court of Justice (**Rule 21.4(f)**), the Economic and Social Council, and the Trusteeship Council. In total, the UN has more than one hundred subsidiary and related organizations. No one agency controls all UN information, but publications can be obtained from the UN Web site and the UN Sales Office, from primary organs, and from subsidiary organizations.

Cite all UN materials using the abbreviations for the body in question. Examples of sources appear in subsequent sections.

21.4(d) Sources for UN material

(1) Official records

The main sources of information are Official Records, cited "OR," which contain reports of meetings, supplements, and annexes. The Official Records are the preferred citation for UN materials. The United Nations Dag Hammarskjöld Library has published an online guide, located at http://www.un.org/Depts/dhl/resguide/symbol.htm, to assist writers in understanding the structure of the UN symbols.

Citations to Official Records typically contain three sets of abbreviations:

Symbol for primary organ•Symbol for subsidiary body•Type of document.

Most UN documents contain primary symbols that identify the organ that is either issuing the document or to which the document is directed. The primary symbol will start the citation. Primary symbols include the following:

A   General Assembly
S   Security Council
E   Economic and Social Council
ST   Secretariat

Other significant bodies, while not primary organs of the UN, have their own identifying primary symbol. These include the following:

CRC/C   Committee on the Rights of the Child
DP   UN Development Programme
TD   UN Conference on Trade and Development
UNEP   UN Environment Programme

The second and, when relevant, third, components of a UN citation indicate which subsidiary body of an entity was the author of a document. These symbols include the following:

AC   Ad hoc committee
C   Standing or permanent committee
CN   Commission
CONF   Conference
GC   Governing council
PC   Preparatory committee
SC   Subcommittee
Sub.   Subcommission
WG   Working group

The final component of the citation identifies the nature of the document. Below are several examples.

PET   Petitions
PV   Verbatim records of meetings (*proces-verbaux*)
RES   Resolutions
SR   Summary records of meetings

Use the following format to cite Official Records of meetings of the primary organs or other gatherings.

UN•Organization abbreviation•, Session number [if available] or year since the organization was founded•, Meeting number and pinpoint•, Document number(s)•(Year).

Examples

UN SCOR, 60th year, 5215th mtg. at 3, UN Doc. S/PV.5215 (June 24, 2005).

UN GAOR 3d Comm., 39th Sess., 65th mtg. at 20, UN Doc. A/C.3/39/SR.65 (1984).

(2) UN resolutions and reports

UN resolutions and reports appear as supplements to documents published in the Official Records. For supplements and resolutions, use the following format.

Title [if to a resolution commonly known by its name and noting the author if not otherwise clear from the name]•Resolution or report number•UN•Organization abbreviation•, Session number [if available] or year since the organization was founded•, Document number(s)•(Year).

Examples

Universal Declaration of Human Rights, GA Res. 217(III), UN GAOR, 3d Sess., Supp. No. 13, UN Doc. A/810 (1948).

UN SCOR, 47th Sess., 3116th mtg., UN Doc. S/RES/777 (1992).

Report of the Open-Ended Working Group on the Question of Equitable Representation on and Increase in the Membership of the Security Council and Other Matters Related to the Security Council, UN GAOR, 58th Sess., Supp. No. 48, UN Doc. A/58/47 (2003).

(3) Other UN documents

In addition to the Official Records, the UN and its subsidiary organizations also produce documents. When used in this context, "documents" are texts submitted to a principal organ or a subsidiary organ of the United Nations, usually for internal use in conjunction with pending agenda items. Documents may be produced by mimeograph or word processing. The four general categories of documents are documents for general distribution, documents for limited distribution to depository libraries, restricted documents available to UN staff, and provisional meeting papers. All categories of documents are assigned UN classification numbers. If a document first produced for internal use is later reprinted as an Official Record, cite the Official Record; otherwise, use the following format.

Author or issuing body,•Title•Document number, including pinpoint citation•(Year).

Examples

Statement by the UNEP Governing Council on Sustainable Development, UN Doc. UNEP/GC.15/L.37, Annex II (1989).

Final Act of the United Nations Diplomatic Conference of Plenipotentiaries on the Establishment of an International Criminal Court, UN Doc. A/CONF.183/10, Annex I, Res. E (1998).

(4) Sales publications

Sales publications are materials provided for use or sale to the general public and are not preferred sources. Each sales document has a sales number that identifies the language, year, and category of the sales document. Cite sales documents generally according to the rules for books (**Rule 22**), and include the components listed below.

Author,•*Title*•Pinpoint reference•, UN document number [if available]•, Sales number•(Year).

Example

UN Dept. Econ. & Soc. Affairs, *An Integrated Approach to World Development* 24, E.04.II.A.2 (2004).

21.4(e) League of Nations

The League of Nations was the predecessor organization to the United Nations. It was formed after World War I and disbanded in 1946, although its functions largely ceased after the outbreak of World War II. Like the United Nations, it consisted of the League itself, including the Council, Assembly, and Secretariat, and some official subordinate organizations. In addition, the League authorized the creation of various committees and commissions. Also, as with the United Nations, there were related organizations, such as the Permanent Court of International Justice.

To cite the League Covenant, include the article and, if relevant, paragraph.

Example

League of Nations Covenant art. 11, ¶ 1.

21.4(f) International tribunals

(1) International Court of Justice

Use the following components when citing a decision on the merits from the International Court of Justice in full format.

Case name (First Party v. Second Party),•Reporter year•Reporter abbreviation•Initial page•, Pinpoint page.

Examples

Full citation format

Fisheries Case (U.K. v. Nor.), 1951 I.C.J. 116.

N. Sea Continental Shelf Cases (Ger. v. Den.; Ger. v. Neth.), 1969 I.C.J. 3, 230.

Short citation format (if *id.* is not appropriate)

Fisheries Case, 1951 I.C.J. at 131.

N. Sea Cases, 1969 I.C.J. at 15–21.

(2) Permanent Court of International Justice

Use the following components to cite decisions of the Permanent Court of International Justice in full format.

Case name (First Party v. Second Party),●Reporter Year●Reporter abbreviation ●Series number●, Number and/or page number.

Examples

Full citation format

Case of the S.S. Lotus (Fr. v. Turk.), 1927 P.C.I.J. Ser. A, No. 10, at 18.

Case Concerning the Payment of Various Serb. Loans Issued in Fr. (Fr. v. Serb.), 1929 P.C.I.J. Ser. A, Nos. 20/21, at 41.

Status of E. Carelia, Advisory Op., 1923 P.C.I.J. Ser. B, No. 5.

Short citation format (if *id.* is not appropriate)

S.S. Lotus, 1927 P.C.I.J. at 18.

Serb. Loans, 1929 P.C.I.J. at 41.

(3) Other international tribunals

To cite decisions from other international tribunals, analogize to the examples above; use **Rule 12** on cases for additional guidance.

Examples

International Criminal Tribunal for the Former Yugoslavia

Prosecutor v. Deronjić, Sentencing Judgement, Case No. IT-02-61-S, ¶¶ 5, 18–19, 228 (Intl. Crim. Trib. for the Former Yugo., Tr. Chamber II, Mar. 30, 2004).

Prosecutor v. Deronjić, Judgement on Sentencing Appeal, Case No. IT-02-61-A (Intl. Crim. Trib. for the Former Yugo., App. Chamber, July 20, 2005).

International Criminal Tribunal for Rwanda

Prosecutor v. Rwamakuba, Decision on the Defence Motion Regarding Will-Say Statements, Case No. ICTR-98-44C-T, ¶ 7 (Intl. Trib. Rwanda, Tr. Chamber III, July 14, 2005).

21.5 Selected Foreign Sources

This *Manual* cannot, for space reasons, provide full coverage of foreign sources. The Association of Legal Writing Directors is in the process of completing a companion volume on foreign and international sources that will provide greater detail and coverage. The purpose of this section is to provide general guidance about citing foreign sources and to provide a limited number of examples from selected foreign countries.

21.5(a) General principles

(1) When possible, follow local conventions (such as citation guides for a particular country) for the country within which the source originated. For example, use Canadian conventions when citing a Canadian case.

(2) Include enough information for a law-trained reader to find the cited source. It is always appropriate, and often is helpful to international researchers, to cite an electronic source, such as a Web site.

(3) When citing non-English sources in English-language publications or for English-speaking audiences, include translation information parenthetically, especially for titles, as illustrated in **Rule 22.1(o)** for books.

(4) As explained in **Rule 3.4** with regard to French, German, and Spanish titles, capitalize foreign titles in Roman alphabets as they would be in that particular language.

(5) When presenting material in a foreign language, reproduce all accent and other marks as they appear in the original (for example, école, Fähre, etc.). Most word-processing programs include "multinational" symbols.

(6) It is customary to transliterate sources from countries that do not use the Roman alphabet. "Transliteration" involves converting characters in one alphabet, or phonetic sounds, into another alphabet. Accordingly, material in Arabic, Chinese, Hebrew, Japanese, Korean, Russian, and Ukrainian should be transliterated for English-speaking audiences. As just a few examples, the Library of Congress, the Modern Language Association, and *The Chicago Manual of Style* each have transliteration systems.

21.5(b) Selected foreign materials

Listed below are sample citations from selected foreign countries. Use these examples only as guides; when listed, consult the citation guide for the country.

(1) Australia

Examples

Constitution

Constitution, sec. 51(xxvi).

Statute

Trade Marks Act 1995 (Cth).

Case

Koowarta v. Bjelke-Petersen (1982) 153 CLR 168.

Vakauta v. Kelly (1988) 13 NSWLR 502.

Australian citation guide

Melbourne University Law Review Association, *Australian Guide to Legal Citation*, http://mulr.law.unimelb.edu.au/aglc.asp (2d ed. 2002).

(2) Canada

Examples

Constitutional statutes

Constitution Act, 1867 (U.K.), 30 & 31 Vict., c. 3, *reprinted in* R.S.C. 1985, App. II, No. 5.

Canada Act 1982 (U.K.), 1982, c. 11.

Constitution Act, 1982, being Schedule B to the *Canada Act 1982* (U.K.), 1982, c. 11.

Canadian Charter of Rights and Freedoms, Part I of the *Constitution Act, 1982* (U.K.), being Schedule B to the *Canada Act 1982* (U.K.), 1982, c. 11.

Statutes

Interpretation Act, R.S.C. 1985 c. I-21, s. 5(1).
Access to Education Act, S.B.C. 2001, c. 1.

Cases

L. Socy. Upper Can. v. Skapinker, [1984] 1 S.C.R. 357.

Vaughn v. Can., [2005] 1 S.C.R. 146, 2005 SCC 11. [includes neutral citation]

Wigle v. Allstate Ins. Co. of Can. (1984), 49 O.R. (2d) 101 (H.C.). [semi-official reporter citation]

Canadian citation guide

McGill Law Journal, *Canadian Guide to Uniform Legal Citation* (5th ed., Carswell 2002).

(3) Mexico

Examples

Constitution (Constitución Politica de los Estados Unidos Mexicanos)

Artículo 7 de la Constitución Politica de los Estados Unidos Mexicanos.

Legislation

> ***Example of a citation from the Federal Civil Code (Código Civil Federal):*** C.C.F. art. 997.

> ***Example of a statute:*** Ley Federal del Derecho de Autor, Art. 21.

Case

SJF, 8a, T.I, Segunda Parte, tribunal Colegiado de Circuito, Jun. 1988, p. 451.

Note: It is permissible to include the English translation in a parenthetical that follows the Spanish version.

(4) Russian Federation

Examples

Constitution

Konst. RF art. 125, § 1 (1993) (Russ.).

Statute

Federal Law on Counteracting Extremist Activity, July 25, 2002, No. 114-F2, Sobr. Zakonod, RF, 2002, No. 30, Item 3031.

Cases

Case Concerning the 1995 Federal Law "On Elections of the Deputies of the State Duma," Sobr. Zakonod. RF, (1995), No. 49, Item 4867.

Case Concerning the Constitutionality of Art. 97(5) of the Criminal Procedure Code of the RSFSR, (1996) Vest. Konst. Suda RF, No. 4, p. 2.

In re Barov, Buill. Verkh. Suda RF, 1993, No. 2, Item 15, pp. 3–6.

Note: Transliterate from Cyrillic.

(5) Singapore

Examples

Constitution

Constitution of the Republic of Singapore (1999 Rev. Ed.), art. 58.

Statute

Administration of Muslim Law Act (Cap. 3, 1999 Rev. Ed. Sing.), s. 35(2).

Case

Kok Seng Cheng v. Bukit Timah Turf Club, (1993) 2 Sing. L.R. 388 (C.A.).

Singapore citation guide

Singapore Academy of Law, *The Singapore Academy of Law Style Guide*, http://www.sal.org.sg/Pdf/SALStyleGuide-2004Ed-20050401.pdf (2004 ed., Apr. 2005 consol. reprint).

(6) United Kingdom

Examples

Statutes

Primary legislation: Lunacy Act 1934 s 14(4)(k).
Secondary legislation: Local Authority Precepts Order 1897 SR & O 1897/208.

Cases

Macarthys v. Smith [1981] QB 180 [1981] 1 All ER 111.

Re Bourne [1978] 2 Ch 43 (Ch).

Costello v Chief Constable of Derbyshire Constabulary [2001] EWCA Civ 381, [2001] 1 WLR 1437. [includes neutral citation]

English citation guide

University of Oxford Commonwealth Law Journal, *The Oxford Standard Citation of Legal Authorities*, http://denning.law.ox.ac.uk/published/bigoscola.pdf (2002).

SIDEBAR 21.2

OTHER FOREIGN AND INTERNATIONAL MATERIALS

Citation formats for other foreign and international materials—such as United Nations materials, international law cases, and primary sources from many foreign countries—are presented in *ALWD Citation Manual: International Sources* (Aspen Publishers forthcoming).

BOOKS, TREATISES, AND OTHER NONPERIODIC MATERIALS

Treatise with single author	William L. Burdick, *Handbook of the Law of Real Property* § 56 (West 1914).
Treatise with two authors	Lynn M. LoPucki & Elizabeth Warren, *Secured Credit: A Systems Approach* 700 (4th ed., Aspen Publishers 2002).
Multivolume treatise with three or more authors	Charles Alan Wright, Arthur R. Miller & Mary Kay Kane, *Federal Practice and Procedure* vol. 7A, § 1758, 114–115 (3d ed., West 2005).
Treatise with editor, but no author	*Hart & Wechsler's The Federal Courts and the Federal System* 1256–1323 (Richard H. Fallon et al. eds., 5th ed., Found. Press 2003).
Treatise with author and editor	Arthur L. Corbin, *Corbin on Contracts* vol. 1, § 4.14 (Joseph M. Perillo ed., rev. ed., West 1993).
Treatise with translator	Luigi Miraglia, *Comparative Legal Philosophy* 324 (John Lisle trans., Boston Book Co. 1912).
Collected works of one author	Oliver Wendell Holmes, *Primitive Notions in Modern Law No. II*, in *The Collected Works of Justice Holmes* vol. 3, 21, 22 (Sheldon M. Novick ed., U. Chi. Press 1995).
Collected works of multiple authors	Owen M. Fiss, *Group Rights and the Equal Protection Clause*, in *Law and Philosophy: An Introduction with Readings* 380–381 (Thomas W. Simon ed., McGraw Hill 2001).

22.0 BOOKS, TREATISES, AND OTHER NONPERIODIC MATERIALS

22.1 Full Citation Format

A full citation to a treatise, book, or other nonperiodic work may contain up to eight components.

Author,•*Title*•Pinpoint reference(s)•(Editor [if any]•, Translator [if any]•, Edition [if any]•, Publisher•Date).

Example

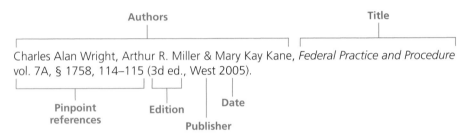

Charles Alan Wright, Arthur R. Miller & Mary Kay Kane, *Federal Practice and Procedure* vol. 7A, § 1758, 114–115 (3d ed., West 2005).

22.1(a) Author's name

(1) Single author

(a) Give the author's full name, exactly as it appears on the front cover or title page.

(b) "Full name" includes designations such as Jr. and III, but does not include degree information, such as J.D., Ph.D., or M.D., or titles of respect, such as "Hon." or "Dr."

Example

Correct: Kelly T. Sayers, Jr.,
Incorrect: Kelly T. Sayers, Jr., J.D.,

(c) The author's name should appear in ordinary type and should be separated from the rest of the citation by a comma and one space.

(2) Multiple authors

(a) Include each author's full name (**item 1 in Rule 22.1(a)**), in the order in which the names appear on the front page or title page.

(b) If the work has **two authors,** separate their names with an ampersand (&).

Example

John Smith & Pamela Johnson,

(c) If the work has **more than two authors,** separate each name from the next with a comma, except for the last two names, which should be separated by an ampersand (&) only.

Example

F. Jason Lee, Dianne M. Robinson & Kathleen Y. Wu,

(d) Alternatively, you may use the phrase "et al." after the first author's name to indicate that the work has **three** or more authors. There is no comma before "et al."

Example

F. Jason Lee et al.,

(e) When citing a single volume of a multivolume work, include only those authors whose names appear on that volume.

(3) Organizational author

(a) If the author is an organization, give the full name of the organization as it appears on the front page or title page. To save space, you may abbreviate any words in the organization name that appear in **Appendix 3 or 5,** and you may omit prepositions that are not necessary for clarity.

Example

ABA Sec. Leg. Educ. & Admis. to the B., *Legal Education and Professional Development—An Educational Continuum, Report of the Task Force on Law Schools and the Profession: Narrowing the Gap* 50–54 (ABA 1992).

(b) If the treatise, book, or document has both a person as author and an organization as author, treat them as multiple authors, and follow **item 2** in **Rule 22.1(a).**

Example

ALWD & Darby Dickerson, *ALWD Citation Manual* 101 (3d ed., Aspen Publishers 2006).

    (c) If a work does not have a listed author, or if the author is unknown, begin the citation with the title.

Example

The Supreme Court and Its Justices ch. 2 (Jesse H. Choper ed., 2d ed., ABA 2000).

22.1(b) Title

(1) Present the title in accordance with **Rule 3** on spelling and capitalization. Do not abbreviate any word in the title unless the word is abbreviated in the cited source. Do not omit prepositions or other words from the title.

(2) You may include a subtitle. If you include the subtitle, insert a colon and one space between the title and subtitle. However, do not insert a colon if the main title ends with a question mark or exclamation point. If the cover or title page of the book does not include punctuation between a title and subtitle, add a colon.

Examples

Catherine A. MacKinnon, *Feminism Unmodified: Discourses on Life and Law* (Harv. U. Press 1988).

Eric Foner, *Who Owns History? Rethinking the Past in a Changing World* (Hill & Wang Publishers 2002).

(3) Typically italicize the title and any subtitle, but do not italicize information that would be italicized in text, such as case names (**Rule 1.6**).

Example of case name within title

James T. Patterson, Brown v. Board of Education: *A Civil Rights Milestone and Its Troubled History* ch. 2 (Oxford U. Press 2001).

(4) In most instances, separate the title from the pinpoint reference by one space.

Example

William L. Burdick, *Handbook of the Law of Real Property* § 56 (West 1914).

(5) If the title ends in a numeral, separate the title from the pinpoint reference by a comma, one space, and the word "at."

Example

Linda Pollock, *Forgotten Children: Parent-Child Relations from 1500 to 1900*, at 30 (Cambridge U. Press 1984).

22.1(c) Pinpoint reference

(1) Include the exact portion of the book, treatise, or document that relates to the stated proposition or contains the quoted passage.

(2) Follow **Rules 5, 6,** and **9** on pages, sections, volumes, and other subdivisions.

(3) Insert one space after the final subdivision.

Examples

Page:	Michael J. Gerhardt, *The Federal Impeachment Process: A Constitutional and Historical Analysis* 20 (2d ed., U. Chi. Press 2000).
Section:	Joshua Dressler, *Understanding Criminal Law* § 10.04[A][1] (3d ed., Lexis 2001).
Section and page:	Charles Alan Wright, Arthur R. Miller & Mary Kay Kane, *Federal Practice and Procedure* vol. 7A, § 1766, 344 (3d ed., West 2005).
Paragraph and page:	Jack B. Weinstein & Margaret A. Berger, *Weinstein's Federal Evidence* vol. 3, ¶ 502.02, 502-5 (Joseph M. McLaughlin ed., 2d ed., Matthew Bender 2005).
Chapter:	Kevin M. Clermont, *Principles of Civil Procedure* ch. 4 (West 2005).

22.1(d) Editor

(1) Include any editor listed on the front cover or title page, even if the work has an author.

Example

Arthur L. Corbin, *Corbin on Contracts* vol. 1, § 4.14 (Joseph M. Perillo ed., rev. ed., West 1993).

(2)   Insert the editor information in the date parenthetical. The editor's name should come before any translator, edition, or publisher information, and before the date.

(3)   Present the editor's full name using the format for authors' names in **Rule 22.1(a)**.

(4)   Insert the abbreviation "ed." for one editor or "eds." for multiple editors. Insert the abbreviation after the last editor's name. Insert a comma and one space after the abbreviation.

Examples

Antitrust Goes Global: What Future for Transatlantic Corporation? 117–118, 134 (Simon J. Evenett, Alexander Lehmann & Benn Steil eds., Brookings Inst. 2000).

Hart & Wechsler's The Federal Courts and the Federal System 1256–1323 (Richard H. Fallon et al. eds., 5th ed., Found. Press 2005).

22.1(e) Translator

(1)   If the book is a translated version of the original, include that information in the citation, even if the book has an author or editor.

Example

Luigi Miraglia, *Comparative Legal Philosophy* 324 (John Lisle trans., Boston Book Co. 1912).

(2)   Include any translator's name in the date parenthetical. The translator's name should come before any edition and publisher information and before the date, but after any editor's name.

Example

The French Institutionalists: Maurice Hauriou, Georges Renard, Joseph T. Delos 93–124 (Albert Broderick ed., Mary Welling trans., Harv. U. Press 1970).

(3)   Present the translator's full name using the format for authors' names in **Rule 22.1(a)**.

(4) Insert the abbreviation "trans." for single or multiple translators. Insert the abbreviation after the last translator's name. Insert a comma and one space after the abbreviation.

Examples

Jean-Francois Lyotard, *The Post-modern Condition: A Report on Knowledge* 53–60 (Geoff Bennington & Brian Massum trans., U. Minn. Press 1984).

The Complete Letters of Sigmund Freud to Wilhelm Fliess, 1887–1904, at 264 (Jeffrey Moussaieff Masson ed. & trans., Belknap Press 1985).

22.1(f) Edition

(1) If the cited work is an edition other than the original or first edition, indicate the edition in the date parenthetical.

(2) Include the edition after any editor or translator information but before the publisher and date.

(3) Typically cite the most current edition that relates to the cited passage or proposition.

(4) Use an ordinal contraction (such as 3d for third) to denote the edition. Consult **Rule 4.3** for more information on ordinals. Also include any other pertinent information about the edition. Abbreviate any words listed in **Appendix 3**. For example, cite a revised edition as "rev. ed."

(5) Insert a comma and one space after the edition.

Examples

Deborah L. Rhode, *Professional Responsibility: Ethics by the Pervasive Method* pt. II (2d ed., Aspen L. & Bus. 1998).

The Changing Constitution ch. 1, 338 (Jeffrey Jowell & Dawn Oliver eds., 3d ed., Clarendon Press 1994).

Other examples

First edition:	(MacMillan 1954).
Second edition:	(2d ed., Aspen Publishers 2006).
Third revised edition:	(3d rev. ed., Little, Brown & Co. 1987).
Fifth abridged edition:	(5th abridged ed., Cambridge U. Press 1947).
Pocket edition:	(pocket ed., West 2003).

22.1(g) Printings of editions

(1) Typically do not include information about a particular printing of an edition.

(2) Include information about the printing only if it differs from other print-ings of that edition in a way that affects the substance of the cited material.

(3) If including information about the printing, insert that information after the edition, and use the year of the printing. Abbreviate printing as "prtg." Use an ordinal contraction, such as "2d," to indicate the number of the printing. Consult **Rule 4.3** for additional information on ordinals.

(4) Insert a comma and one space after the printing information.

Examples

Jonathan Elliot, *The Debates in the Several State Conventions on the Adoption of the Federal Constitution* vol. 1, xv (2d ed., 2d prtg., J.B. Lippincott Co. 1937).

Karl N. Llewellyn, *The Bramble Bush* 68 (3d prtg., Oceana Publications 1969).

22.1(h) Star editions

(1) In a few well-known works, such as William Blackstone's *Commentaries* and certain Greek and Latin works, the page of the original work is indicated by an asterisk (*) in the margins or text of later editions.

(2) If using a source with this "star pagination," you may exclude the pagina-tion in the more current edition and eliminate all information concerning editors, translators, editions, publishers, and dates.

(3) Insert one asterisk (*) before a single page and two asterisks (**) before multiple pages. Do not insert a space after the asterisk.

Examples

William Blackstone, *Commentaries* vol. 4, *292.

William Blackstone, *Commentaries* vol. 1, **50–51.

22.1(i) Publisher

(1) Include the publisher information in the date parenthetical. You may abbreviate any words listed in **Appendices 3** and **5**. You may omit preposi-tions and articles not needed for clarity.

(2) Include the publisher information before the date but after any editor, translator, or edition information.

(3) Insert one space after the publisher's name.

Examples

Daniel R. Cowans, *Bankruptcy Law and Practice* vol. 2, § 4.4 (7th ed., Lexis 1998).

Angela Roddey Holden, *Legal Issues on Pediatrics and Adolescent Medicine* 39 (Yale U. Press 1985).

(4) If the title page identifies two or more publishers—not simply two or more offices or divisions of the same publisher—include all publishers, in the order presented on the title page. Include the year of publication for each, and separate entries with a comma and one space.

Example

H.G. Wells, *The Time Machine* (J.M. Dent 1895, Charles E. Tuttle 1993).

22.1(j) Date

(1) Give the most current date provided on the copyright page or title page of the book, treatise, or document.

(2) The date will come after the editor, translator, edition, and publisher information. Insert a closing parenthesis after the date.

(3) When citing a single volume of a multivolume work, provide the date of the cited volume.

(4) Typically provide only the year of publication. If an exact date will help readers, you may include it. Abbreviate the month in an exact date according to **Appendix 3(A)**.

(5) Consult **Rule 8** to determine whether and how to cite a main volume or supplement.

Examples

Supplement only

Alan Meisel, *The Right to Die* (John Wiley & Sons Supp. 2003).

Main volume and supplement

Charles A. Sullivan et al., *Employment Discrimination* vol. 3, § 10.2.2, 409 (Little, Brown & Co. 1988 & Supp. 1991).

(6) If citing an older work, which is typically defined as one published before 1900, you may cite either the original source or a modern edition. If citing a modern edition, you may include the date of original publication in a separate parenthetical.

Example

Charles Dickens, *Bleak House* (Bantam Classics 1983) (originally published 1853).

(7)   If citing a well-known work that has been republished, you also may include the original date in a separate parenthetical.

Example

Ernest Hemingway, *The Sun Also Rises* (Charles Scribner's Sons 1954) (originally published 1926).

22.1(k) Works in a series

(1)   When citing a work that is part of a series, include the series number and any description in the date parenthetical. If the series includes the name of the publisher, do not repeat the publisher's name.

(2)   Use the lists in **Appendix 3** to abbreviate any information relating to the series. You may omit prepositions that are not necessary for clarity.

(3)   Insert a comma and one space after the series information.

Examples

Child Abuse, Neglect, and the Foster Care System (PLI Course Handbook Series No. 475, 2003).

Bernard Black et al., *Outside Director Liability* 2–4 (Stan. L. Sch. Working Paper No. 250, 2003).

U.S. Gen. Acctg. Off., *Economic Performance: Highlights of a Workshop on Economic Performance Measures* 3 (Pub. No. GAO-05-796SP, 2005).

22.1(l) Collected works of one author

To cite a work by one author that appears in a collection of that author's works, use the following format. Omit any information, such as a translator, that is not relevant to the cited shorter work.

Author's name,•*Title of shorter work,*•in•*Title of larger work* •Initial page or subdivision of shorter work•, Pinpoint subdivision•(Editor [if any]•, Translator [if any]•, Edition [if any]•, Publisher•Date).

Example

Oliver Wendell Holmes, *Primitive Notions in Modern Law No. II*, in *The Collected Works of Justice Holmes* vol. 3, 21, 22 (Sheldon M. Novick ed., U. Chi. Press 1995).

22.1(m) Collected works of several authors

To cite a shorter work within a collection of works by several authors, use the following format. Omit any components, such as a translator, that are not relevant to the cited shorter work. Use this rule to cite introductions, forewords, prefaces, and other similar sections.

Author of shorter work,●*Title of shorter work*,●in●Author of larger work [if any],●*Title of larger work*●Initial page or subdivision of shorter work●, Pinpoint subdivision●(Editor [if any]●, Translator [if any]●, Edition [if any]●, Publisher● Date).

Examples

Bernard Rudden, *Economic Theory v. Property Law: The Numerus Clausus Problem*, in *Oxford Essays in Jurisprudence* 239, 242 (John Eekelaar & John Bell eds., 3d ed., Clarendon Press 1987).

John Foster Dulles, *Introduction*, in Arthur H. Dean, *William Nelson Cromwell 1854–1948: An American Pioneer* i, iii (Ad Press, Ltd. 1957).

22.1(n) The Bible, the Koran, and the Talmud

(1) To cite a biblical reference, use the following format. Do not insert a space before or after the colon. Within the version component, you may abbreviate any word that appears in **Appendix 3**. For a short citation, use *id.* when appropriate. Otherwise, repeat the full citation.

Book name●Chapter:Line●(Version, if relevant).

Examples

John 3:16 (King James).   *Psalms* 147:8–9 (New Intl.).

I *Corinthians* 10:6 (New Am. Stand.).   *Matthew* 5:17.

(2) To cite a passage from the Koran, cite chapter and verse, separated by a colon. You may use the spelling "Koran" or "Qur'an." If relevant, you may cite a particular translation. For a short citation, use *id.* when appropriate. Otherwise, repeat the full citation.

Examples

Koran 2:256.

Qur'an 51:1–10 (Abdullah Yusuf Ali trans.).

(3)   The Talmud consists of the Mishnah and Gemara. The Mishnah is divided into six orders. The Gemara provides a commentary on these codified laws. The Babylonian Talmud and the Jerusalem Talmud use different Gemara. The Babylonian Talmud takes precedence. Typically cite by order or seder, then tractate. It also is acceptable to cite the Talmud like a book.

Example

Babylonian Talmud, Eruvin 13b.

Jerusalem Talmud, Terumot 8:4.

The Babylonian Talmud 50 (Michael L. Rodkinson ed. & trans., 2d ed., Talmud Socy. 1918).

22.1(o)   Books in a foreign language

Cite a book published in a language other than English like any other book. You may need to consult the colophon at the end of the book to retrieve publication information that typically appears on the title or copyright page of English-language books. If it will help readers, provide a translation of the title in square brackets. For capitalization in languages other than English, see **Rule 3.4.**

Examples

Gabriel Garcia Marquez, *El amor en los tiempos del cólera* [*Love in the Time of Cholera*] (Penguin 1996).

Antoine de Saint-Exupéry, *Der Kleine Prinz* [*The Little Prince*] (Harvest Books 2001).

22.2   Short Citation Format for Works Other Than Those in a Collection

22.2(a)   *Id.*

If appropriate, use *id.* as the short citation. For additional information on the use of *id.*, consult **Rule 11.3.** If *id.* is not appropriate, the form of the short citation will vary depending on the type of document you are writing.

22.2(b)   Documents without footnotes

If *id.* is not appropriate, use the following format. You may shorten the title by using "hereinafter," as described in **Rule 11.4(d).**

Author's last name,● *Title*●at●Pinpoint reference.

Example

Full citation: Deborah L. Rhode, *Professional Responsibility: Ethics by the Pervasive Method* pt. II (2d ed., Aspen L. & Bus. 1998) [hereinafter Rhode, *Professional Responsibility*].

Short citation: Rhode, *Professional Responsibility* at pt. II.

22.2(c) Documents with footnotes

If *id.* is not appropriate, use the *supra* format that follows. Consult **Rule 11.4** for additional information on *supra*.

Author's last name,●*supra* n. Note number●, at●Pinpoint reference.

Example

---

[19]Deborah L. Rhode, *Professional Responsibility: Ethics by the Pervasive Method* pt. II (2d ed., Aspen L. & Bus. 1998).

.   .   .

[25]Rhode, *supra* n. 19, at pt. II.

Example of short citation for two authors

Jackson & Murphy, *supra* n. 7, at 299.

Example of short citation for three or more authors

Nance et al., *supra* n. 10, at 21.

22.3   Short Citation Format for Works in a Collection

For items cited under **Rule 22.1(l)** or **22.1(m)**, use the following short citation formats.

22.3(a) Documents without footnotes

(1)   If appropriate, you may use *id.* to refer to the shorter work within the collection. Do not use *id.* to refer to the larger work (**Rule 11.3**). Instead, use the *supra* format to refer to the larger work (**Rule 11.4**).

Example

Full citation: Bernard Rudden, *Economic Theory v. Property Law: The Numerus Clausus Problem*, in *Oxford Essays in Jurisprudence* 239, 242 (John Eekelaar & John Bell eds., 3d ed., Clarendon Press 1987).

Short citation, if referring
to Rudden: *Id.* at 240.

Short citation to another Andrew Ashworth, *Belief, Intent, and Criminal Liability*,
work: in *Oxford Essays in Jurisprudence, supra*, at 2.

Incorrect: Andrew Ashworth, *Belief, Intent, and Criminal Liability*,
in *id.* at 1.

(2) If *id.* is not appropriate for the shorter work, include the author's last name, the main title of the shorter work (but not the subtitle), the word "at," and a pinpoint reference.

Example

Full citation: Bernard Rudden, *Economic Theory v. Property Law: The Numerus Clausus Problem*, in *Oxford Essays in Jurisprudence* 239, 242 (John Eekelaar & John Bell eds., 3d ed., Clarendon Press 1987) [hereinafter *Oxford Essays*].
Short citation: Rudden, *Economic Theory v. Property Law* at 242.

22.3(b) Documents with footnotes

(1) If appropriate, you may use *id.* to refer to the shorter work within the collection. Do not use *id.* to refer to the larger work. Instead, use the *supra* format to refer to the larger work (**Rule 11.4**).

Example

---

³³Bernard Rudden, *Economic Theory v. Property Law: The Numerus Clausus Problem*, in *Oxford Essays in Jurisprudence* 239, 242 (John Eekelaar & John Bell eds., 3d ed., Clarendon Press 1987).

³⁴*Id.* at 243.

³⁵Andrew Ashworth, *Belief, Intent, and Criminal Liability*, in *Oxford Essays in Jurisprudence, supra* n. 33, at 1, 2.

(2) If *id.* is not appropriate for the shorter work, you may use the *supra* format (**Rule 11.4**) to refer to the shorter work. Even under this circumstance, it is still permissible to use *supra* to refer to the larger work.

Last name of author of shorter work,●*supra* n. Note number●, at●Pinpoint reference.

Example

---

[33]Bernard Rudden, *Economic Theory v. Property Law: The Numerus Clausus Problem,* in *Oxford Essays in Jurisprudence* 239, 242 (John Eekelaar & John Bell eds., 3d ed., Clarendon Press 1987).

.   .   .

[39]Rudden, *supra* n. 33, at 242.

[40]Andrew Ashworth, *Belief, Intent, and Criminal Liability,* in *Oxford Essays in Jurisprudence, supra* n. 33, at 2.

LEGAL AND OTHER PERIODICALS

Law review article (consecutively paginated periodical)	Cass R. Sunstein, *Affirmative Action, Caste, and Cultural Comparisons*, 97 Mich. L. Rev. 1311, 1315 (1999).
Law review article (nonconsecutively paginated periodical)	Betsy Brandborg, *Changing Rules of Conduct*, 27 Mont. Law. 6 (Apr. 2002).
Student-written law review article	Pamela M. Dubov, Student Author, *Circumventing the Florida Constitution: Property Taxes and Special Assessments, Today's Illusory Distinction*, 30 Stetson L. Rev. 1469, 1500 (2001).
Symposium	Symposium, *Conceiving a Code for Creation: The Legal Debate Surrounding Human Cloning*, 53 Hastings L.J. 987 (2002).
Newspaper	Matt Richtel, *Suit to Limit Net Access at a Library Is Dismissed*, 149 N.Y. Times G3 (Jan. 21, 1999).
Newsletter	Joseph K. Scully, *Taking the Offensive When Defending a Deposition: Questioning Your Own Witness*, 16 Prod. Liab. (newsltr. of the ABA Sec. Litig.) 13 (Spring 2005).
Electronic journal	Jordan B. Michael, *Automobile Accidents Associated with Cell Phone Use: Can Cell Phone Service Providers Be Held Liable under a Theory of Negligence?* 11 Rich. J.L. & Tech. 2, 6 n. 19 (Winter 2005), http://law.richmond.edu/jolt/v11i2/article5.pdf.

23.1 Full Citation Format

Citations to articles in journals, law reviews, newspapers, newsletters, and other periodicals typically contain seven components.

Author,•*Title*,•Volume number•Periodical abbreviation•Initial page•, Pinpoint page•(Date).

Example

23.1(a) Author's name

(1) Single, multiple, and unknown authors

Follow **Rule 22.1(a)**.

(2) Student authors

If the article was written by a student author, insert "Student Author" after the author's full name. The phrase "Student Author" should be offset with commas. If the name of the student is not listed, begin the citation with "Student Author."

Example

Kathryn J. Ball, Student Author, *Horizontal Equity and the Tax Consequences of Attorney-Client Fee Agreements*, 74 Temp. L. Rev. 387, 407–408 (2001).

When one author is a student but the other is not, include the "Student Author" designation after the student's name.

SIDEBAR 23.1

IDENTIFYING STUDENT AUTHORS

It is sometimes difficult to determine whether an author is a student. Use these guidelines to help identify student authors.

First, student-written articles often are printed at the back of each law review issue.

Second, within a law review, student articles are typically designated as "Notes," "Comments," "Case Comments," or "Recent Developments."

Third, in many law reviews, the names of student authors are given at the end, not the beginning, of the article.

Finally, look for a footnote describing the author's background. An author described as a J.D. candidate is a student.

Example

Kristen David Adams & Josephine Thomas, Student Author,

23.1(b) Title

(1) Present the title, including any subtitle, in accordance with **Rule 3** on spelling and capitalization. Do not abbreviate any word in the title unless the word is abbreviated in the cited source. Do not omit prepositions or other words from the title. For articles written in a language other than English, follow **Rule 22.1(o)**.

Example

Kent D. Syverud, *ADR and the Decline of the American Civil Jury*, 44 UCLA L. Rev. 1935, 1942 (1997).

(2) If the article does not have a specific title, include the designation given the piece by the periodical; for example, "Book Review."

Example

William R. Davis, *Book Review*, 72 Conn. B.J. 407 (Oct. 1998) (reviewing *Connecticut Product Liability Law*).

(3) Italicize the title, but do not italicize matter that would be italicized in text, such as case names and publication names (**Rule 1.6**).

Example

Leslie Friedman Goldstein, *Between the Tiers: The New[est] Equal Protection and* Bush v. Gore, 4 U. Pa. J. Const. L. 372 (2002).

(4) Typically insert a colon and one space between the title and subtitle. Newspapers often insert a semicolon between the title and subtitle; retain the semicolon in this instance. If there is no punctuation between a title and subtitle, add a colon. However, do not insert the colon if the title ends with a question mark or exclamation point. If a title ends with a quotation mark, place the ending punctuation, except the comma that follows the title, inside of the quotation mark. At the end of the complete title, typically insert a comma and one space.

Examples (exceptions to the general rule)

Assaf Hamdani, *Who's Liable for Cyberwrongs?* 87 Cornell L. Rev. 901 (2002).

Eric Lichtblau, *Phone Tape Reveals Flight 11 Attendant Yelled, "Oh My God!"* Star-Ledger (Newark, N.J.) C3 (Sept. 20, 2001).

Neil Gotanda, *A Critique of "Our Constitution Is Color-Blind"*, 44 Stan. L. Rev. 1 (1991).

23.1(c) Volume number

(1) Insert the volume number of the periodical in which the article appears.

Example

Dennis W. Archer, *Diversity and Legal Education*, 37 Ind. L. Rev. 339 (2003).

(2) If a law review does not have a volume, insert the year in place of the volume number. Do not repeat the date at the end of the citation.

Example

Jonathan C. Lipson, *Financing Information Technologies: Fairness and Function*, 2001 Wis. L. Rev. 1067.

(3) If another type of periodical, such as a newspaper, does not have a volume number or if the volume number is not readily available, omit that component. See the examples in **Rule 23.1(d)**. Insert one space after the volume number.

23.1(d) Periodical abbreviation

(1) After the volume number, include the abbreviation for the periodical. Typically omit the words "a," "at," "in," "of," and "the" from the abbreviation. Also omit colons and slashes, and everything following them.

(2) Use **Appendix 5** to determine the appropriate abbreviation for the periodical. If the periodical is not listed in **Appendix 5**, use the abbreviations listed in **Appendix 3**. Insert one space after the periodical abbreviation.

(3) When citing a **newspaper,** if the place of publication is not well known or evident from the periodical's title, include the place of publication immediately after the periodical abbreviation. Enclose the publication information in parentheses, using state abbreviations found in **Appendix 3**. Insert one space after the parenthetical information.

Examples

Michael Vigh, *Trib Suit a Hot Potato for Judges; 2 Have Recused Selves and Others May Follow*, Salt Lake Trib. B2 (July 14, 2002).

Bush to Campaign for Bush, Post & Courier (Charleston, S.C.) B4 (Jan. 15, 2000).

(4) When citing a **newsletter,** you may include the name of the issuing organization. Also, if readers cannot otherwise determine that the publication is a newsletter, you may indicate that fact parenthetically. You may abbreviate any words in the organization's name that appear in **Appendix 3** and omit articles and prepositions not needed for clarity.

Examples

David C. Wilkes, *Negative Job Reference May Now Expose Employers to Title VII Liability*, 22 Litig. News (newsltr. of the ABA Sec. Litig.) 1 (Sept. 1997).

State Court Couldn't Adjudicate Adequacy of Notice, West's Bankr. Newsltr. 2 (May 22, 2002).

23.1(e) Page numbers

(1) After the periodical abbreviation, include the initial page number (the page on which the article starts).

(2) Then, if referring to specific pages within the article, include the relevant pinpoint references. Consult **Rule 5.2** for additional information on pages and pinpoint references. Separate the initial page number from the pinpoint citation with a comma and one space. Insert one space after the final page reference.

23.1(f) Date

(1) Enclose the date in parentheses.

(2) When the issues of a particular periodical are **consecutively paginated,** include only the year of publication. A periodical is consecutively paginated if the first issue in a particular year begins on page 1; the second issue picks up with the numbering where the first issue left off, such as page 307; and so on. Most law reviews and law journals are consecutively paginated. **Appendix 5** distinguishes between consecutively paginated and nonconsecutively paginated journals; a ★ means that the journal is non-consecutively paginated.

Example

Barbara B. Aldave, *Misappropriation: A General Theory of Liability for Trading on Nonpublic Information*, 13 Hofstra L. Rev. 101, 122 (1984).

(3) When the issues of a particular periodical are **not consecutively paginated,** include the exact date as shown on the first page or cover. Use **Appendix 3** to abbreviate months. If the periodical does not contain a date, insert the issue number instead (example: No. 4, 2002). A periodical is nonconsec-utively paginated when each issue begins on page 1: for example, the January issue begins on page 1, the February issue begins on page 1, and so on. Most bar association journals, newspapers, and newsletters are nonconsecutively paginated. A ★ beside the periodical's entry in **Appendix 5** indicates that it is nonconsecutively paginated.

Examples

Steve Seidenberg, *Reporting Errors: Lawyers Need to Consult Federal Law before Ordering Credit Reports for Litigation*, 91 ABA J. 20 (Apr. 2005).

Donna An, *Federal Wetland Grants Program Reaches a Milestone*, 27 Natl. Wetlands Newsltr. 3 (May–June 2005).

Linda Buckley, *A Hole in the Safety Net*, Newsweek 40, 40 (May 13, 2002).

(4) If a law review uses a year as the volume number, do not repeat the date. See the example in **Rule 23.1(c)(2).**

23.1(g) Symposia, colloquia, survey issues, and special issues

When citing an *entire* symposium, colloquium, survey, or special issue, as opposed to a single article within the issue, follow the format in the examples listed below. The page cited is the page on which the symposium begins.

Examples

Symposium, *Issues in Space Law*, 6 Chi. J. Intl. L. 1 (2005).

Special Issue, *Ethical Issues in Representing Older Clients*, 62 Fordham L. Rev. 961 (1994).

23.1(h) Multipart articles

When citing an article that has been published in multiple parts, follow the examples listed below.

Examples

Citing all parts

John P. Dawson, *Negotiorum Gestio: The Altruistic Intermeddler* (pts. 1 & 2), 74 Harv. L. Rev. 817, 74 Harv. L. Rev. 1073 (1961).

Vernon Countryman, *Executory Contracts in Bankruptcy* (pts. 1 & 2), 57 Minn. L. Rev. 439 (1973), 58 Minn. L. Rev. 479 (1974).

Citing one part

Gary Peller, *The Metaphysics of American Law* (pt. 2), 73 Cal. L. Rev. 1152 (1985).

23.1(i) Electronic journals

When citing an article from an electronic journal, that is, from a journal published only on the Internet, use the following format. Consult **Rule 40.1(c)** for information on the Uniform Resource Locator (URL).

Author,•*Title*,•Volume number•Periodical abbreviation•Sequential article number•, Pinpoint paragraph [if available]•(Exact date)•, URL.

Examples

Jordan B. Michael, *Automobile Accidents Associated with Cell Phone Use: Can Cell Phone Service Providers Be Held Liable under a Theory of Negligence?* 11 Rich. J.L. & Tech. 2, 6 n. 19 (Winter 2005), http://law.richmond.edu/jolt/v11i2/article5.pdf.

Rob Frieden, *Regulatory Arbitrage Strategies and Tactics in Telecommunications*, 5 N.C. J.L. & Tech. 227, § 5 n. 10 (2004), http://www.jolt.unc.edu/Vol5_I2/web/Frieden%20v5i2.htm.

23.1(j) Letter to the editor

To cite a letter to the editor, include the author's full name (**Rule 22.1(a)**) followed by "Ltr. to the Ed." Include any title in italics, then insert information about the publication, including the volume (if available), publication abbreviation, section and page number, and exact date.

Examples

Nancy A. Ransom, Ltr. to the Ed., *Better Eating, through Home Ec?* N.Y. Times A22 (Sept. 8, 2003).

Linda Wightman, Ltr. to the Ed., Orlando Sent. G2 (Oct. 5, 2003).

23.1(k) Cartoon or comic strip

To cite a cartoon or comic strip, include the artist's full name (using **Rule 22.1(a)** on authors), the descriptive term "Cartoon" or "Comic Strip" in ordinary type, the title (if available) of the cartoon or comic strip in italics, and information about the publication in which the cartoon or comic strip appears, including the volume (if available), publication abbreviation, section and page number, and exact date.

Examples

Peter Steiner, Cartoon, *On the Internet, Nobody Knows You're a Dog*, 69 New Yorker 61 (July 5, 1993) (available at http://www.epatric.com/funstuff/dog/).

Scott Adams, Comic Strip, *Dilbert*, Bos. Globe D16 (Aug. 15, 2002).

23.1(l) Advertisement

To cite an advertisement, include the name of the product, the company, or the institution that is the subject of the advertisement. Next include the word "Advertisement" in ordinary type. Then insert information about the publication in which the advertisement appears, including the volume (if available), publication abbreviation, section and page number, and exact date.

Examples (hypothetical)

Taryn Rose, Advertisement, Vanity Fair 23 (Sept. 27, 2005).

Southwest Airlines, Advertisement, 12 Travel World 96 (Jan. 17, 2006).

23.2   Short Citation Format

23.2(a) *Id.*

If appropriate, use *id.* as the short citation. For additional information on *id.*, consult **Rule 11.3.** If *id.* is not appropriate, the form of the short citation will vary depending on the type of document you are writing.

23.2(b) Documents without footnotes

If *id.* is not appropriate, use the following format. You may shorten the title by using "hereinafter," as explained in **Rule 11.4(d)**.

Author's last name,●Volume number●Periodical abbreviation●at●Pinpoint reference.

Example

Full citation: L. Ray Patterson, *Legal Ethics and the Lawyer's Duty of Loyalty*, 29 Emory L.J. 909, 915 (1980).

Short citation: Patterson, 29 Emory L.J. at 917–920.

23.2(c) Documents with footnotes

If *id.* is not appropriate, use the *supra* format that follows. Consult **Rule 11.4** for additional information on *supra*.

Author's last name,●*supra* n. Note number●, at●Pinpoint reference.

Example

―――――――――
²L. Ray Patterson, *Legal Ethics and the Lawyer's Duty of Loyalty*, 29 Emory L.J. 909, 915 (1980).

.   .   .

⁴Patterson, *supra* n. 2, at 917–918.

SIDEBAR 23.2

JOURNALS THAT USE LARGE AND SMALL CAPITAL LETTERS

As explained in **Rule 1.1**, some law journals require authors to use large and small capital letters as a typeface convention in footnotes. Although the *ALWD Citation Manual* does not use this typeface, the authors realize that writers may need to use this convention. Below is a short guide about how to use large and small capital letters in footnote citations for *commonly cited* sources.

SIDEBAR 23.2 (CONTINUED)

Statutes and court rules

Use large and small capital letters for the statutory or code abbreviation.

Examples

CAL. PENAL CODE ANN. § 893 (West 2005).

25 ME. REV. STAT. ANN. § 2803-B(1)(K) (2005).

Mo. Rev. Stat. § 115.133 (2004).

UTAH R. CIV. P. 7(b)(2).

Books and treatises

Use large and small capital letters for author names and titles.

Example

ROBERT D. BICKEL & PETER F. LAKE, THE RIGHTS AND RESPONSIBILITIES OF THE MODERN UNIVERSITY: WHO ASSUMES THE RISKS OF COLLEGE LIFE? (Carolina Academic Press 1999).

Law review articles and periodicals

Use large and small capital letters for law review and periodical abbreviations.

Example

Stephen M. Bainbridge, *Why a Board? Group Decisionmaking in Corporate Governance*, 55 VAND. L. REV. 1 (2002).

Restatements and model codes

Use large and small capital letters for titles (Restatements) and title abbreviations (codes).

Examples

RESTATEMENT (THIRD) OF TORTS §§ 3–4 (discussion dft. 1999).

MODEL R. PROF. CONDUCT 2.1 (ABA 2004).

FAST FORMATS

A.L.R. ANNOTATIONS

First Series

P.H. Vartanian, *"Res Ipsa Loquitur" as a Presumption or a Mere Permissible Inference*, 167 A.L.R. 658, 660 (1947).

Second Series

R.D. Hursh, *Propriety and Effect of Jury in Civil Case Taking Depositions to Jury Room*, 57 A.L.R.2d 1011, 1017 (1958).

Third Series

Milton Roberts, *Civil Liability of Physician for Failure to Diagnose or Report Battered Child Syndrome*, 97 A.L.R.3d 338, 339 (1980).

Fourth Series

Sara L. Johnson, *Liability of Employer, Supervisor, or Manager for Intentionally or Recklessly Causing Employee Emotional Distress*, 52 A.L.R.4th 853, 855 (1987).

Fifth Series

Cynthia J. Haycock, *Insurer's Waiver of Defense of Statute of Limitations*, 104 A.L.R.5th 331, 336 (2002).

Sixth Series

George L. Blum, *Criminal Record as Affecting Applicant's Moral Character for Purposes of Admission to the Bar*, 3 A.L.R.6th 49 (2005).

Federal Series

Majorie A. Shields, *Admissibility of Evidence Discovered in Search of Defendant's Property or Residence Authorized by Defendant's Spouse*, 154 A.L.R. Fed. 579, 581 (1999).

Federal Series, Second

Robin Cheryl Miller & Jason Binimow, *Marriage between Persons of Same Sex—United States and Canadian Cases*, 1 A.L.R. Fed. 2d 1 (2005).

Note the space between A.L.R. and Fed.

24.0 | A.L.R. ANNOTATIONS |

24.1   Full Citation Format

A full citation to an A.L.R. (American Law Reports) annotation contains seven components.

Author,● *Title*,●Volume number●A.L.R. series●Initial page●, Pinpoint page● (Date).

Example

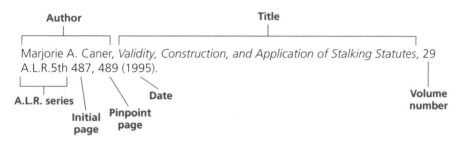

Author

Title

Marjorie A. Caner, *Validity, Construction, and Application of Stalking Statutes*, 29 A.L.R.5th 487, 489 (1995).

A.L.R. series

Initial page

Pinpoint page

Date

Volume number

24.1(a) Author's name

Follow **Rule 22.1(a)** for books.

Examples

Kristine C. Karnezis, *Validity of State Statutory Cap on Punitive Damages*, 103 A.L.R.5th 379, 382 (2002).

Unsigned annotation

Per Diem Compensation of Public Officer, 1 A.L.R. 276, 279 (1919).

24.1(b) Annotation title

Follow **Rule 23.1(b)** for legal periodicals.

24.1(c) Volume number

After the title, give the volume number in which the annotation appears. Insert one space after the volume number.

CHART 24.1

ABBREVIATIONS FOR A.L.R. SERIES

(The symbol ▲ denotes a space.)

First Series (1919–1948)	A.L.R.
Second Series (1948–1965)	A.L.R.2d
Third Series (1965–1980)	A.L.R.3d
Fourth Series (1980–1992)	A.L.R.4th
Fifth Series (1992–2005)	A.L.R.5th
Sixth Series (2005–current date)	A.L.R.6th
Federal Series (1969–2005)	A.L.R.▲Fed.
Federal Series, Second (2005–current date)	A.L.R.▲Fed.▲2d

24.1(d) A.L.R. series

(1) After the volume number, include the A.L.R. series.

(2) The A.L.R. series consists of the abbreviation "A.L.R.," which stands for American Law Reports, and the series number or designation.

(3) Abbreviations for the various A.L.R. series are listed in **Chart 24.1**.

(4) Insert one space after the series.

24.1(e) Page numbers

Follow **Rule 23.1(e)** for legal periodicals.

24.1(f) Date

Include the year in which the A.L.R. volume that contains the cited annotation was published. Enclose the year in parentheses.

24.2 Short Citation Format

Follow **Rule 23.2** for legal periodicals.

Examples

Document without footnotes

Full citation: Deborah F. Buckman, *Reverse Confusion Doctrine under State Trademark Law*, 114 A.L.R.5th 129, 142 (2003).

Short citations: Buckman, 114 A.L.R.5th at 137.
Id. at 141.

Document with footnotes

---

[2]Cara Yates, *Application of State Law to Age Discrimination in Employment*, 51 A.L.R.5th 1, 7 (1997).

[3]*Supra* n. 1 (listing various state statutes concerning age discrimination).

[4]Yates, *supra* n. 2, at 9–12.

LEGAL DICTIONARIES

Legal dictionary	*Black's Law Dictionary* 101 (Bryan A. Garner ed., 8th ed., West 2004).
	James R. Fox, *Dictionary of International and Comparative Law* 56 (Oceana Publications 2003).

25.0 LEGAL DICTIONARIES

25.1 Full Citation Format

Cite a dictionary like a book under **Rule 22.1.** Some dictionaries, however, do not have named authors or editors.

Author [if any],●*Title*●Pinpoint reference●(Editor [if any]●, Edition●, Publisher●Date).

Example

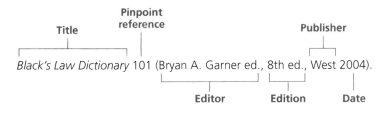

Other examples

Black's Law Dictionary 101 (6th ed., West 1990).

Black's Law Dictionary 240–241 (Bryan A. Garner ed., 2d pocket ed., West 2001).

David Mellinkoff, *Dictionary of American Legal Usage* 56 (West 1992).

Alan Gilpin, *Dictionary of Environmental Law* 42 (John Wiley & Sons 1996).

25.2 Short Citation Format

Follow **Rule 22.2** for books.

Example (document without footnotes)

Full citation: *Black's Law Dictionary* 240–241 (Bryan A. Garner ed., 2d pocket ed., West 2001).

Short citation: *Black's Law Dictionary* at 250.
                     Id. at 255.

25.3 Nonlegal Dictionaries

Cite a nonlegal dictionary like a book under **Rule 22.1.** Follow **Rule 25.2** for short citation formats.

Examples

Merriam-Webster's Collegiate Dictionary 1547 (11th ed., Merriam-Webster 2003).

Oxford English Dictionary vol. 1, 207 (J.A. Simpson & E.S.C. Weiner eds., Oxford U. Press 1989).

LEGAL ENCYCLOPEDIAS

Am. Jur. 2d	67 Am. Jur. 2d *Robbery* § 91 (2003).
C.J.S.	30A C.J.S. *Entertainment and Amusement* § 65(a) (1992).

26.0   LEGAL ENCYCLOPEDIAS

26.1   Full Citation Format

A full citation to a legal encyclopedia consists of six components.

Volume number•Encyclopedia abbreviation• *Title* or *Topic*•§•Section number•(Date).

Example

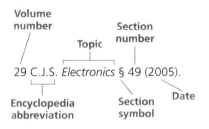

Other examples

76 Am. Jur. 2d *Trusts* §§ 1–4 (2005 & Supp. 2005).

9 Fla. Jur. 2d *Charities* § 36 (2004).

26.1(a)   Volume number

(1)   Start the citation with the number of the encyclopedia volume in which the cited material appears.

(2)   Designate the volume with a numeral and any accompanying letter that appears on the spine or title page. Insert one space after the volume number.

Examples (the symbol ▲ represents a space)

60A▲Am.▲Jur.▲2d▲*Pensions*▲§▲1098▲(2003).

13A▲Cal.▲Jur.▲3d▲*Consumer*▲*and*▲*Borrower*▲*Protection*▲*Law*▲§§▲156–157 ▲(2004).

26.1(b)   Encyclopedia abbreviation

(1)   After the volume number, insert the abbreviated name of the encyclopedia.

(2)   Chart 26.1 lists abbreviations for several legal encyclopedias. If the encyclopedia you are citing is not in this chart, use the abbreviations below and those in **Appendix 3** as guides to formulate an abbreviated title.

CHART 26.1

ENCYCLOPEDIA ABBREVIATIONS

(The symbol ▲ denotes a space.)

Encyclopedia Name	Abbreviation
American Jurisprudence	Am.▲Jur.
American Jurisprudence, Second	Am.▲Jur.▲2d
Corpus Juris	C.J.
Corpus Juris Secundum	C.J.S.
California Jurisprudence, Third	Cal.▲Jur.▲3d
Florida Jurisprudence, Second	Fla.▲Jur.▲2d
Georgia Jurisprudence	Ga.▲Jur.
Illinois Jurisprudence	Ill.▲Jur.
Indiana Law Encyclopedia	Ind.▲L.▲Ency.
Kentucky Jurisprudence	Ky.▲Jur.
West's Maryland Law Encyclopedia	Md.▲L.▲Ency.
Massachusetts Jurisprudence	Mass.▲Jur.
Michigan Civil Jurisprudence	Mich.▲Civ.▲Jur.
New York Jurisprudence, Second	N.Y.▲Jur.▲2d
Ohio Jurisprudence, Third	Ohio▲Jur.▲3d
Pennsylvania Jurisprudence, Second	Pa.▲Jur.▲2d
Pennsylvania Law Encyclopedia	Pa.▲L.▲Ency.
South Carolina Jurisprudence	S.C.▲Jur.
Tennessee Jurisprudence	Tenn.▲Jur.
Texas Jurisprudence, Third	Tex.▲Jur.▲3d
Lexis's Jurisprudence of Virginia and West Virginia	Va.▲&▲W.▲Va.▲Jur.

(3) Include the series number, for any series after the first, in the abbreviation. Present the series as an ordinal contraction (such as 2d). Consult **Rule 4.3** for additional information on ordinals. Insert one space after the encyclopedia abbreviation.

26.1(c) Title or topic

(1) After the encyclopedia abbreviation, include the complete name of the title or topic (in other words, the major subdivision) you are citing. Do not abbreviate words in the title or topic name. You can find the full topic name on the page within the encyclopedia on which the topic begins.

(2) Do not include the name of specific subsections.

(3) Italicize the name of the topic or title. Capitalize words according to **Rule 3.**

(4) Insert one space after the title or topic.

Example

Title:	Robbery
Subsection:	§ 91 Judgment, Sentence, and Punishment
Correct citation:	67 Am. Jur. 2d *Robbery* § 91 (2003).
Incorrect citation:	67 Am. Jur. 2d *Judgment, Sentence, and Punishment* § 91 (2003).

26.1(d) Section symbol

(1) After the title or topic, insert one section symbol (§) to cite one section or two section symbols (§§) to cite multiple sections. Insert one space after the last section symbol.

(2) Consult **Rule 6** for additional information about sections and subdivisions. Consult **Sidebar 6.1** to find out how to physically insert the section symbol.

26.1(e) Section number

(1) After the section symbol, insert the specific section or sections that contain the pertinent information.

(2) Be as specific as possible, and include all relevant subsections.

(3) As noted in **Rule 26.1(c),** do not include the name of the section or subsection in the citation.

(4) Insert one space after the last section number.

Examples

Single section:	44 Fla. Jur. 2d *Real Property Sales and Exchanges* § 39 (2005).
Multiple, consecutive sections:	44 Fla. Jur. 2d *Real Property Sales and Exchanges* §§ 29–30 (2005).
Multiple, consecutive subsections:	11 C.J.S. *Bonds* § 21(a)–(b) (1995).
Multiple, nonconsecutive sections:	64 Cal. Jur. 3d *Wills* §§ 10, 14 (1994).
Multiple, nonconsecutive subsections:	30A C.J.S. *Entertainment and Amusement* § 65(a), (c) (1992).

26.1(f) Date

Use the year in which the particular encyclopedia volume you are using was issued. Enclose the year in parentheses. Consult **Rule 8** regarding when and how to cite a main volume, a supplement, or both.

Examples

Cited material appears only in the main volume

79A C.J.S. *Securities Regulation* § 4 (1995).

Cited material appears only in a supplement

79A C.J.S. *Securities Regulation* § 14 (Supp. 2005).

Cited material appears in both the main volume and a supplement

76 Am. Jur. 2d *Trusts* § 1 (2005 & Supp. 2005).

26.2   Short Citation Format

When appropriate, use *id.* as a short-form citation for legal encyclopedia citations. For additional information on *id.*, consult **Rule 11.3.** Otherwise, repeat all components of the full citation, but omit the date parenthetical.

Example

Full citation: 61 Cal. Jur. 3d *Unfair Competition* § 7 (2003).
Short citation: 61 Cal. Jur. 3d *Unfair Competition* §§ 5–7.
***Id.*:**   *Id.* at § 2.

RESTATEMENTS, MODEL CODES, UNIFORM LAWS, AND SENTENCING GUIDELINES

Restatement (first series)	*Restatement of Security* § 141 (1941).
Restatement (second series)	*Restatement (Second) of Agency* § 27 (1958).
Restatement (third series)	*Restatement (Third) of Suretyship and Guaranty* § 11 (1996).
Restatement (draft)	*Restatement (Third) of Suretyship* § 31 (4th tent. dft. 1995).
Model code	Model Penal Code § 2.02(2)(a)(i) (ALI 1985). Model Penal Code: Sentencing § 6B.04, 184 (ALI prelim. dft. no. 3, 2004).
ABA model ethics codes	Model R. Prof. Conduct 2.1 (ABA 2004). Model Code Prof. Resp. DR 5-105(B) (ABA 1978). Model Code Prof. Resp. EC 7-1 (ABA 1981). Model Code Jud. Conduct canon 3A (ABA 2002).
Uniform law	Unif. Trade Secrets Act § 1(4), 14 U.L.A. 438 (1990).
Sentencing guidelines	*U.S. Sentencing Guidelines Manual* § 4B1.2(a) (2001).

27.0   **RESTATEMENTS, MODEL CODES, UNIFORM LAWS, AND SENTENCING GUIDELINES**

27.1   Full Citation Format for Restatements

A full citation to a Restatement, which is a publication of the American Law Institute, may have three or four components, depending on whether the Restatement is in final or draft form.

Title•Pinpoint reference•(Draft information [if any]•Date).

Example

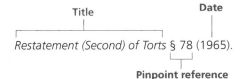

27.1(a)   Title

(1)   Include the title of the Restatement using the following format. Do not abbreviate words in the title.

Restatement•(*Series* [if any])•*Subject matter*

(2)   If the Restatement contains a subtitle, include it as part of the title. Do not abbreviate words in the subtitle. Consult **Rule 22.1(b)(2)** for additional information on formatting subtitles.

Example

Restatement (Third) of Property: Mortgages § 3.1 (1997).

(3)   If the Restatement has a series, include it in a parenthetical after the word "*Restatement.*" Spell out the series number.

Example

Restatement (Second) of Contracts § 90 (1981).

(4)   Italicize the title and any series or subtitle, and use **Rule 3** on capitalization. Insert one space after the title or any subtitle.

SIDEBAR 27.1

SUBJECT MATTERS OF RESTATEMENTS

At this point, available Restatements include Agency, Business Associations, Conflict of Laws, Contracts, Foreign Relations Law of the United States, Judgments, The Law Governing Lawyers, Property, Restitution and Unjust Enrichment, Security, Suretyship and Guaranty, Torts, Trusts, and Unfair Competition.

27.1(b) Pinpoint reference

(1) After the title, include the relevant pinpoint reference. Be as specific as possible, and include all sections, subsections, and other relevant subdivisions, such as comments and illustrations. Consult **Rules 5, 6,** and **9** for additional information about subdivisions.

(2) Abbreviate subdivisions using the lists in **Appendix 3(C)**. Insert one space after the final subdivision.

Examples

Restatement (Second) of Conflict of Laws § 291 cmt. g (1971).

Restatement of Property: Servitudes § 453 illus. 1 (1944).

27.1(c) Draft information

(1) If citing a draft Restatement, indicate in the date parenthetical the type and number of the draft. Insert one space between the draft information and the date. Insert a comma before the date *only* if the draft information ends with a numeral.

(2) If the draft is numbered, present that information as an ordinal contraction (**Rule 4.3**) before the type of draft. If the draft is unnumbered, include only the type of draft. You may abbreviate any words listed in **Appendix 3**.

Examples

**Numbered
official draft:**   *Restatement of Contracts* § 111 (1st off. dft. 1928).

**Numbered
tentative draft:**   *Restatement (Third) of Suretyship* § 31 (4th tent. dft. 1995).

Numbered proposed draft:	*Restatement (Third) of Restitution and Unjust Enrichment* (proposed dft. no. 6, 2004).
Unnumbered discussion draft:	*Restatement (Third) of Torts* §§ 3–4 (discussion dft. 1999).
Unnumbered proposed draft:	*Restatement (Third) of Trusts: Prudent Investor Rule* § 227 (proposed final dft. 1990).

27.1(d) Date

Insert the year of the volume you are citing. Use the date of publication, not the date of adoption. Insert a closing parenthesis after the year.

27.2   Short Citation Format for Restatements

When appropriate, use *id.* as a short-form citation for Restatements. For additional information on *id.*, consult **Rule 11.3.** If *id.* is not appropriate, include all required components except the information in the date parenthetical.

Example

Full citation:	*Restatement (Second) of Contracts* § 90 (1979).
Short citation:	*Restatement (Second) of Contracts* § 90.
***Id.*:**	*Id.* at § 87.

27.3   Model Codes and Acts

27.3(a)

Cite model codes and acts analogously to federal statutes under **Rules 14.2** and **14.6.**

27.3(b)

Abbreviate words in the title of the code or act that appear in **Appendix 3.** You may omit articles and prepositions that are not needed for clarity.

27.3(c)

Include the year of the version that you are citing; before the date, include the organization that promulgated the code or act. Abbreviate the organization's name using **Appendix 3.**

Examples

Full citation:	Model Penal Code § 2.02(2)(a)(i) (ALI 1985).
Short citation options:	Model Penal Code § 2.02(2)(a)(i).
	§ 2.02(a)(i).
	Id. at § 2.02(a)(ii).

Full citation:	Rev. Model Bus. Corp. Act § 15.05(c) (ABA 1984).
Short citation options:	Rev. Model Bus. Corp. Act § 15.05(c).
	§ 15.05(c).
	Id. at § 15.05(a).

Full citation:	Model R. Prof. Conduct 3.1 (ABA 2004).
Short citation options:	Model R. Prof. Conduct 3.3(a).
	Id. at R. 2.1.

27.3(d)

When citing a tentative or proposed draft, provide that information in the date parenthetical; use the year of the draft. Insert a comma before the date *only* if the draft information ends with a numeral.

Examples

Model Code of Pre-arraignment Proc. § SS260.5 (ALI proposed off. dft. 1975).

Model Land Dev. Code app. A (ALI tent. dft. no. 3, 1971).

Model Relocation Act § 10 (Am. Acad. Matrimonial Laws. tent. dft. 1996).

27.3(e)

As with any other source, you may parenthetically note where to locate a particular model code or act online or in a print source (**Rule 38**).

Example

Model Code Jud. Conduct for State A.L.J.s canon 3 (Natl. Conf. A.L.J.s 1999) (available at http://www.naalj.org).

27.4 Uniform Laws

27.4(a)

Cite uniform laws analogously to federal statutes under **Rules 14.2** and **14.6**.

27.4(b)

Abbreviate words in the title of the code or act that appear in **Appendix 3.** You may omit articles and prepositions that are not needed for clarity.

27.4(c)

Whenever possible, include a reference to Uniform Laws Annotated (U.L.A.).

Example

Full citation: Unif. Arb. Act §§ 1–33, 7 U.L.A. 6 (Supp. 2001).
Short citation options: Unif. Arb. Act § 33, 7 U.L.A. 6.
                             Unif. Arb. Act § 33.
                             § 33
                             7 U.L.A. 6.
                             Id. at § 32.

27.4(d)

When a U.L.A. citation is used, include only the date on the copyright page of the U.L.A. main volume or supplement, depending on where the cited information is located (**Rule 8**). If a U.L.A. citation cannot be provided, include the year in which the uniform act was adopted or last amended.

Examples

Unif. Parentage Act § 803(b)(2), 9B U.L.A. 364 (2001).

Unif. Interstate Family Support Act § 205 (amended 1996).

27.4(e)

If a uniform act has been withdrawn, superseded, or amended, include that information parenthetically.

Example

Unif. Sales Act § 17, 1 U.L.A. 309 (1950) (withdrawn 1962).

27.4(f)

If citing a uniform law as adopted by a particular jurisdiction, cite the statute from that jurisdiction using **Rules 14.4** and **14.6,** and **Appendix 1.**

Examples

Del. Stat. Ann. tit. 6, § 2-206 (2000). [Delaware version of UCC § 2-206]

Tex. Bus. & Com. Code Ann. § 2.206 (1994). [Texas version of UCC § 2-206]

N.Y. Code of Prof. Resp. DR 4-101(c)(2) (1999). [New York version of the Model Code of Professional Responsibility DR 4-101(c)(2)]

27.5   Sentencing Guidelines

Cite sentencing guidelines using the following examples. For questions not answered by these examples, analogize to **Rule 22** for books.

Examples

U.S. Sentencing Guidelines Manual § 4B1.2(a) (2004).

U.S. Sentencing Guidelines Manual app. C, at 106–107 (2004).

U.S. Sentencing Guidelines Manual § 1B1.3 cmt. background (2004).

FAST FORMATS

LOOSELEAF SERVICES AND REPORTERS

Case in looseleaf reporter	*Glasow v. DuPont de Nemours & Co.,* 7 Trade Reg. Rep. (CCH) 74,791, 101,998 (N.D. May 17, 2005).
Material in transfer binder	*Copyright.Net Music Publg. v. MP3.Com,* [2002–2003 Transfer Binder] Copy. L. Dec. (CCH) ¶ 28,613, 35,941 (S.D.N.Y. 2003).
Noncase material in looseleaf service	*At-Will Worker Can Bring § 1981 Action, Court Rules,* Fair Empl. (BNA) (July 17, 2003).

28.0 LOOSELEAF SERVICES AND REPORTERS

28.1 Full Citation Format for Cases and Administrative Decisions in Looseleaf Services

A full citation to a case printed in a looseleaf service or reporter is similar to a full citation for a case under **Rule 12.** The typical components are

Case name,•Looseleaf volume•Looseleaf name or abbreviation• (Publisher)•Initial subdivision•, Pinpoint reference•(Court abbreviation• Exact date),•Subsequent history.

Example

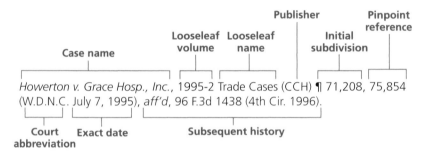

28.1(a) Case name

Follow **Rule 12.2** for cases.

28.1(b) Looseleaf volume

(1) After the case name, present the volume of the looseleaf service in which the case appears. The volume of a looseleaf service may be a number, a year, a descriptive subtitle from the volume's spine, or a combination of these.

Examples (the volume appears in green)

U.S. v. Med. Mut. of Ohio, 1998-1 Trade Cases (CCH) ¶ 50,846, 51,942 (N.D. Ohio Sept. 30, 1998).

Bradley v. U.S., 91-2 U.S. Tax Cases (CCH) ¶ 50332 (2d Cir. June 24, 1991).

(2) When the volume designation, or part thereof, might be confused with the looseleaf abbreviation, enclose the volume in brackets.

Example (the volume appears in green)

N.W. Aerospace Training Corp. v. Commr. of Revenue, [2 Minn.] State Tax Rep. (CCH) ¶ 202-603 (Minn. Tax Ct. Apr. 4, 1995).

(3) If the volume is a transfer binder, the volume designation should also include the years covered by that binder.

Examples (the volume appears in green)

Taft v. Ackermans, [Current Transfer Binder] Fed. Sec. L. Rep. (CCH) 93,245, 96,224 (S.D.N.Y. Apr. 13, 2005).

Fullerton v. State, [1996–2002 Transfer Binder] Blue Sky L. Rep. (CCH) 74,211, 77,954 (Nev. Sept. 19, 2000).

(4) Insert one space after the volume.

28.1(c) Looseleaf abbreviation

Follow **Rule 12.4** concerning reporter abbreviations. Use **Appendix 3** to determine which words in the looseleaf service title may be abbreviated; also use **Rule 4.3** to abbreviate any ordinals, such as 2d for "second," in the title. Insert one space after the name or abbreviation.

Examples (the symbol ▲ denotes a space)

Full name	Abbreviation
Congressional Index	▲Cong.▲Index▲
Employment Safety and Health Guide	▲Empl.▲Safety▲&▲Health▲Guide▲
Federal Rules of Evidence Service Second	▲Fed.▲R.▲Evid.▲Serv.▲2d▲
Federal Tax Coordinator Second	▲Fed.▲Tax▲Coord.▲2d▲

28.1(d) Publisher

(1) Include the name of the looseleaf publisher.

(2) Use the abbreviations in **Chart 28.1**. If the publisher is not listed in **Chart 28.1**, use the abbreviations in **Appendix 3**.

(3) Enclose the publisher name or abbreviation in parentheses. Insert one space after the closing parenthesis.

CHART 28.1

ABBREVIATIONS FOR LOOSELEAF PUBLISHERS

Name	Abbreviation
American Bar Association	ABA
Aspen Publishers	Aspen Publishers
Bureau of National Affairs, Inc.	BNA
Clark Boardman Callaghan	CBC
Commerce Clearing House, Inc.	CCH
Environmental Law Institute	ELI
LexisNexis	Lexis
LRP Publications	LRP
Matthew Bender	Matthew Bender
National Association of College and University Attorneys	NACUA
Pike & Fischer	P & F
Prentice-Hall	PH
Research Institute of America, Inc.	RIA
University Publishing Group	U. Pub. Group
West Group	West

28.1(e) Subdivision information

(1) Looseleafs divided by paragraphs

Insert the paragraph assigned to the cited case. If available, also include a page number as the pinpoint reference.

Example (the symbol ▲ denotes a space)

In re Silicon Graphics, Inc. Secs. Litig., [1997 Transfer Binder] Fed. Sec. L. Rep. (CCH)▲¶▲99,468,▲97,133▲(N.D. Cal. May 23, 1997).

(2) Looseleafs divided by pages

Include the initial page number. Then, if referring to specific pages within the case, include the relevant pinpoint page reference (**Rule 5.2**).

SIDEBAR 28.1

UNDERSTANDING PARAGRAPHS IN LOOSELEAF SERVICES

A "paragraph" in looseleaf terminology is a term of art and usually does not refer to a single block of type. Instead, it can designate any quantity of material and typically spans several pages. In services numbered by paragraphs, each case is typically assigned a single paragraph number. The process of determining the paragraph number to cite can sometimes be confusing, as some pages within the source may contain both a paragraph number and a page number. When a service contains both paragraph and page numbers, the paragraph number is preceded by the paragraph symbol (¶).

Example (the symbol ▲ denotes a space)

In re Savitt/Adler Litig., 26 Media L. Rep. (BNA)▲1882,▲1883▲ (N.D.N.Y. Feb. 5, 1998).

(3) Looseleafs divided by report number

Provide the report number, preceded by the abbreviation "No." When available, also cite a section, paragraph, or page number.

Example (the symbol ▲ denotes a space)

SEC v. Eskind, 29 Sec. Rep. & L. Reg. (BNA)▲No.▲27,▲934▲(N.D. Cal. June 26, 1997).

(4) Other subdivisions

If a looseleaf is divided by some other subdivision, use the subdivisions identified within the source. Analogizing from the above rules for other subdivisions, provide enough information so that readers can locate the cited material. Consult **Rules 5, 6,** and **9** for additional information on subdivisions.

Examples

Section and page

EEOC v. Golden St. Glass Co., Equal Empl. Compl. Man. (CCH) § 615.1, 3202 (C.D. Cal. Mar. 6, 1980).

Decision number

Don Weber II v. Commr., [2004 Transfer Binder] Tax Ct. Rep. (CCH) Dec. 55,588, 4389 (U.S.T.C. Mar. 22, 2004).

28.1(f) Court abbreviation

Follow Rule 12.6 for cases.

28.1(g) Date

Follow Rule 12.7 for cases.

28.1(h) Subsequent history

Present subsequent history information in accordance with **Rules 12.8** and 12.10.

28.1(i) Other information

Follow **Rules 12.9** (prior history) and **12.11** (parenthetical information).

28.2   Short Citation Format for Cases and Administrative Decisions in Looseleaf Services

Follow Rule 12.21 for cases.

Example

Full citation: *Howerton v. Grace Hosp., Inc.*, 1995-2 Trade Cases (CCH) ¶ 71,208 (W.D.N.C. July 7, 1995), *aff'd*, 96 F.3d 1438 (4th Cir. 1996).
Short citation: *Howerton*, 1995-2 Trade Cases ¶ 71,208, 75,856.

28.3   Full Citation Format for Noncase Material in Looseleaf Services

For noncase material within a looseleaf service, follow the rule that covers the particular source, and then add the looseleaf citation.

Examples

Internet Service Provider Not Liable for User's Infringement, 2 Copy. L. (CCH) No. 290, 4 (May 24, 2002).

Industry Canada Issues Final Rules Defining "Secure Electronic Signatures", 10 Elec. Com. & L. Rep. (BNA) No. 9, 194 (Mar. 2, 2005).

House Commerce Committee Plans September Markup of Anti-spam Bill, [2003 Transfer Binder vol. 8, pt. 2] 8 Elec. Com. & L. Rep. (BNA) No. 34, 838 (Sept. 10, 2003).

28.4   Short Citation Format for Noncase Material in Looseleaf Services

The short citation format for noncase material in a looseleaf service should conform to the regular short citation format for the particular source cited. Consult the rule that covers the particular source for additional information.

PRACTITIONER AND COURT DOCUMENTS, TRANSCRIPTS, AND APPELLATE RECORDS

Affidavit	Aff. Kim Faxon ¶¶ 1–3 (Oct. 13, 2004).
Brief	Petr.'s Br. 19 (Apr. 27, 2004).
Court order	Or. Granting Defs.' Mot. S.J. 3–4 (Jan. 20, 2006).
Discovery document	Pl.'s 1st Set Interrogs. Nos. 3, 6, 9 (Oct. 17, 2005).
Pleading	Def.'s 2d Amend. Ans. ¶¶ 5–12 (Apr. 2, 2005).
Hearing transcript	T.R.O. Hrg. Transcr. 9:1 to 12:6 (Sept. 15, 2005).
Appellate record (options)	R. 4. (R. at 4.) R. at 4. [R. 4.] (R. 4.) [R. at 4.]

29.0   PRACTITIONER AND COURT DOCUMENTS, TRANSCRIPTS, AND APPELLATE RECORDS

29.1   Scope of Rule

29.1(a)

This rule applies to material in a case you are litigating. Consult **Rule 12.20** to determine how to cite court documents, transcripts, and records in other cases.

29.1(b)

Practitioner and court documents include, but are not limited to, pleadings, motions and responses, briefs, memoranda of law, discovery and disclosure material, affidavits, declarations, evidence, notices, stipulations, orders, and judgments.

29.2   Full Citation Format for Practitioner and Court Documents

Unless a local court rule requires otherwise (consult **Appendix** 2), there are three components to a full citation for a document that was prepared by attorneys, judges, or other participants in a case you are litigating.

Document name•Pinpoint reference•(Exact date).

Example:

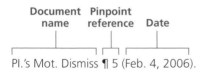

Pl.'s Mot. Dismiss ¶ 5 (Feb. 4, 2006).

29.2(a)   Document name

(1)   Insert the document name as it appears on the face of the document you are citing. Unless the court you are in has a different rule (consult **Appendix** 2), you may abbreviate any word listed in **Appendix** 3, and you may eliminate articles and prepositions in the document name that are not needed for clarity.

(2) Some attorneys prefer to spell out the document name completely the first time it is cited and only then to use abbreviations. This practice is acceptable.

Examples

Document name	Citation
Plaintiff's Complaint paragraph 7	Pl.'s Compl. ¶ 7 (May 1, 2005).
Affidavit of Kim Faxon paragraphs 1–3	Aff. Kim Faxon ¶¶ 1–3 (Oct. 13, 2004).
Defendant's Interrogatory number 2	Def.'s Interrog. No. 2 (Oct. 2, 2005).

29.2(b) Pinpoint reference

After the document name, provide the most specific pinpoint reference possible. Consult **Rule 5.2** for additional information about pinpoint references. Insert one space after the pinpoint reference.

Example

Defs.' 1st Amend. Ans. ¶¶ 1–5 (July 18, 2005).

29.2(c) Date

(1) For material filed with the court, provide the exact date (month-day-year) on which the document was filed. Abbreviate the month according to **Appendix 3(A)**.

(2) For material served on opposing counsel, but not filed with the court, provide the exact date (month-day-year) on which the document was served. Abbreviate the month according to **Appendix 3(A)**. When possible, use the date in the certificate of service.

(3) If the document was not filed or served, provide the exact date (month-day-year) on which it was prepared. Abbreviate the month according to **Appendix 3(A)**.

(4) If you cannot determine the date, enclose the abbreviation "n.d.," for "no date," in the parenthetical.

Example

Aff. Pauline K. Livingston ¶ 2 (n.d.).

29.3 Full Citation Format for Transcripts

Unless a local court rule requires otherwise (consult **Appendix 2**), a full citation to a trial, hearing, or deposition transcript contains three components.

Transcript abbreviation●Pinpoint reference●(Exact date).

Example

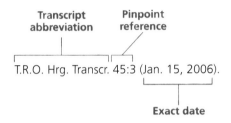

29.3(a) Document name

Use **Rule 29.2(a)**.

29.3(b) Pinpoint reference

(1) Use **Rule 29.2(b)**.

(2) To denote a line number within the transcript, insert the page number, a colon (with no space on either side), and the line number. Thus, 12:3 means that the cited material falls on line 3 of page 12.

Examples

Document and pinpoint reference	Citation
Hearing Transcript at page 4, lines 10 through 12:	Hrg. Transcr. 4:10–12 (Feb. 5, 2006).
Volume 2, Trial Transcript pages 47 through 49:	Tr. Transcr. vol. 2, 47–49 (Mar. 21, 2006).
Deposition of Jackson Foster at page 120, line 17, through page 122, line 3:	Depo. Jackson Foster 120:17–122:3 (Aug. 2, 2005).

or

Depo. Jackson Foster 120:17 to 122:3 (Aug. 2, 2005).

29.3(c) Date

Provide the exact date (month-day-year) or dates on which the proceeding occurred. Abbreviate the month according to **Appendix 3(A)**.

Example

Tr. Transcr. vol. 1, 49–97 (Feb. 4–5, 2006).

29.4 Short Citation Format for Practitioner and Court Documents and for Transcripts

29.4(a)

If *id.* is appropriate, use *id.* as the short citation. Consult **Rule 11.3** for additional information on *id.*

29.4(b)

If *id.* is not appropriate, include all required components, but omit all parts of an individual's name other than the surname; also omit the date parenthetical. For additional information on surnames, see **Rule 12.2(d)**.

Example

Document:	Transcript of the Deposition of Carlton Rhys-Smith (May 23, 2005).
Full citation:	Transcr. Depo. Carlton Rhys-Smith 1:1–5:17 (May 23, 2005).
Short citation:	Transcr. Depo. Rhys-Smith 4:13.

29.5 Full Citation Format for Appellate Records

29.5(a) Options

Unless a local court rule requires otherwise (consult **Appendix 2**), a full citation to an appellate record consists of two components: the abbreviation "R." for "record," and a pinpoint reference. The entire citation may be enclosed in parentheses or brackets. Acceptable formats are listed below. Once you select a format, use it consistently throughout the document.

Formats:	R. 4.	(R. at 4.)
	R. at 4.	[R. 4.]
	(R. 4.)	[R. at 4.]

29.5(b) Line numbers

To denote a line number within the record, insert the page number, a colon (with no space on either side), and the line number. Thus, 12:3 means that the cited material falls on line 3 of page 12.

Example

The Petitioner, Monique Vasquez, worked as a bank teller for seventeen years. (R. 4.) Her primary job duty was to complete customer transactions. (R. 7:12.)

29.6 Short Citation Format for Appellate Records

It is not customary to use *id.* for record citations. Instead, repeat the full citation, as reflected in **Rule 29.5(b)**.

SIDEBAR 29.1

INSERTING DOCUMENT NAMES AND RECORD CITES IN MEMORANDA AND COURT DOCUMENTS

When referring to a court document, practitioner document, transcript, or appellate record in a memorandum, brief, or similar document, you may (a) put the entire citation in bold, (b) enclose the entire name in parentheses, or (c) use both bold and parentheses. Such techniques help readers identify the references quickly.

Example

The company eliminated twenty-seven jobs on January 2, 2005. (**Deposition of Marian Guerrero ¶ 4 (Aug. 19, 2005).**) It then closed the motor parts division on January 30, 2005. (*Id.* at ¶ 5.)

FAST FORMATS

SPEECHES, ADDRESSES, AND OTHER ORAL PRESENTATIONS

Unpublished speech	James B. Comey, Dep. U.S. Atty. Gen., Address, *Health Care Fraud* (ABA, May 13, 2004) (copy on file with *Wake Forest Law Review*).
	Norman Veasey, Speech, *Juxtaposing Best Practices and Delaware Corporate Jurisprudence* (Chi., Ill., May 4, 2004) (copy on file with *The Business Lawyer*, University of Maryland School of Law).
Published speech	Stephen Breyer, Lecture, *Our Democratic Constitution* (N.Y.U. L. Sch., N.Y.C., N.Y., Oct. 22, 2001), in 77 N.Y.U. L. Rev. 245 (2002).

30.0 SPEECHES, ADDRESSES, AND OTHER ORAL PRESENTATIONS

30.1 Full Citation Format for Unpublished Speeches, Addresses, and Other Oral Presentations

A full citation to an unpublished speech, address, or other oral presentation consists of six elements.

Speaker's name,●Type of presentation,●*Subject* or *title of presentation*●(Place of presentation,●Exact date)●(Location).

Example (hypothetical)

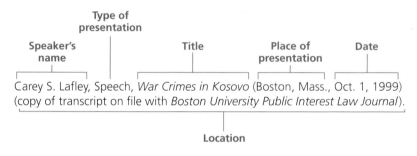

Carey S. Lafley, Speech, *War Crimes in Kosovo* (Boston, Mass., Oct. 1, 1999) (copy of transcript on file with *Boston University Public Interest Law Journal*).

Location

30.1(a) Speaker's name

Give the speaker's full name. Follow **Rule 22.1(a)** for book authors. If the speaker is not generally known, you may include the speaker's title or position after his or her name. You may abbreviate words in the title or position that appear in **Appendix 3**, and you may eliminate articles and prepositions not needed for clarity.

Example

Carl Shapiro, Dep. U.S. Asst. Atty. Gen., Address, *Mergers with Differentiated Products* (ABA, Nov. 9, 1995) (copy on file with *George Mason Law Review*).

30.1(b) Type of presentation

In ordinary type, describe the presentation. Capitalize the initial letter of each word. Examples of types of presentations include Speech, Address, Commencement Address, CLE Presentation, Remarks, and Panel Remarks. Insert a comma and one space after the type of presentation.

259

30.1(c) Subject or title of presentation

(1) If the speech has a formal title, use that title.

(2) If the speech does not have a formal title, provide a concise description of the subject matter.

(3) Present the title or subject in italics, and follow **Rule 3** on capitalization.

(4) Insert one space after the subject or title.

30.1(d) Place of presentation

(1) After the title or subject, insert an opening parenthesis.

(2) Indicate the place where the presentation was given or the organization before whom the presentation was given. The place may be a city and state, school, organization, or meeting name.

(3) You may abbreviate the place using the lists in **Appendix 3** and **Appendix 5**.

(4) Insert a comma and one space after the place of presentation.

Examples

Kay Pasley & Theodore Futris, Presentation, *Annotation of Recent Research Literature: Remarriage and Stepfamilies (1995–1997)* (Stepfamily Assn. of Am. Prof. Training Seminar, Apr. 1998) (copy on file with *William & Mary Journal of Women and the Law*).

Rudolph Berhnhart, Address, *Implementation of the Dayton Accord* (Univ. Conn. Sch. L., Oct. 18, 1996) (copy on file with *Connecticut Journal of International Law*).

30.1(e) Date

If available, provide the exact date (month-day-year) on which the speech or presentation was given. Abbreviate the month according to **Appendix 3(A)**. At a minimum, provide the year. Insert a closing parenthesis after the date.

30.1(f) Information about how to locate source

If the speech was transcribed or recorded, describe in a separate parenthetical where or how readers might obtain a copy. You may abbreviate the name of the organization that maintains the source using the lists in **Appendix 3** and **Appendix 5**.

30.2 Short Citation Format for Unpublished Speeches, Addresses, and Other Oral Presentations

30.2(a) *Id.*

If appropriate, use *id.* as the short citation. For additional information on *id.*, consult **Rule 11.3**. If *id.* is not appropriate, the form of the short citation will vary depending on the type of document you are writing.

30.2(b) Documents without footnotes

If *id.* is not appropriate, use the following format:

Author's last name,●Type of presentation,●*Subject* or *title of presentation.*

Example

Full citation: Carey S. Lafley, Speech, *War Crimes in Kosovo* (Boston, Mass., Oct. 1, 1999) (copy of transcript on file with *Boston University Public Interest Law Journal*).

Short citation: Lafley, Speech, *War Crimes in Kosovo.*

30.2(c) Documents with footnotes

If *id.* is not appropriate, use the *supra* format that follows. Consult **Rule 11.4** for addition information on *supra.*

Author's last name,●*supra* n. Note number.

Example

---

[148]Carey S. Lafley, Speech, *War Crimes in Kosovo* (Boston, Mass., Oct. 1, 1999) (copy on file with *Boston University Public Interest Law Journal*).

.   .   .

[157]Lafley, *supra* n. 148.

30.3 Published Presentations

If the presentation has been published, use the following format:

Speaker's name,●Type of presentation,●*Subject* or *title of presentation*●(Place of presentation,●Exact date)●, in●Citation for source.

Example

Full citation

Derrick A. Bell, Jr., Lecture, *California's Proposition 209: A Temporary Diversion on the Road to Racial Disaster* (Loy. L. Sch., L.A., Cal., Jan. 17, 1997), in 30 Loy. L.A. L. Rev. 1447 (1997).

Short citation (in document without footnotes when *id.* is not appropriate)

Bell, 30 Loy. L.A. L. Rev. at 1460.

Short citation (in document with footnotes when *id.* is not appropriate)

---

[22]Bell, *supra* n. 82, at 1460.

FAST FORMATS

INTERVIEWS

In-person interview	Interview with Regina Ashmon, Sec. Coord., ABA Disp. Res. Sec. (Nov. 18, 2004).
Telephone interview	Telephone Interview with Bruce Walsh, Full Prof. & Assoc. Dept. Head of Ecology & Evolutionary Biology, U. Ariz. (Feb. 11, 2005).
Interview conducted by another	Telephone Interview by M. Celine Cannon with Hon. Mary S. Scriven, U.S. Mag. J., M.D. Fla. (Aug. 1, 2005).

31.0   INTERVIEWS

31.1   Full Citation Format for Interviews Conducted by the Author

A full citation to in-person or telephone interviews you conducted consists of four components.

Designation•Interviewee's name•, Interviewee's title and affiliation•(Exact date).

Example

Interview with Hon. Bruce Loble, Chief Water J. in Bozeman, Mont. (June 4, 1997).

31.1(a)   Designation

(1)   For an in-person interview you conducted, begin "Interview with."

Example

Interview with James F. Flanagan, Oliver Ellsworth Prof. of Fed. Prac., U. of S.C. Sch. L. (Oct. 4, 2004).

(2)   For a telephone interview you conducted, begin "Telephone Interview with."

Example

Telephone Interview with Tammy Wilsker, Equal Just. Works Fellow, U. Miami Children & Youth L. Clinic (May 12, 2004).

31.1(b)   Interviewee's name

Insert the interviewee's full name. Follow **Rule 22.1(a)** for book authors.

31.1(c)   Interviewee's title and affiliation

(1)   In ordinary type, give the interviewee's official title and affiliation. Examples of affiliations include companies, organizations, schools, and government agencies and departments. You may abbreviate any words listed in **Appendix 3**. You may eliminate articles and prepositions not needed for clarity.

(2) If the interviewee does not have a formal title or affiliation, provide a concise description of the person's job, position, or responsibilities. You may abbreviate any words listed in **Appendix 3**.

(3) Follow **Rule 3** concerning capitalization.

(4) Insert one space after the interviewee's title and affiliation or other identification.

31.1(d) Date

Provide the exact date (month-day-year) on which you conducted the interview. Abbreviate the month using **Appendix 3(A)**. Enclose the date in parentheses.

31.1(e) Additional information

You may provide in a parenthetical any additional information that would assist the reader. Examples include an indication about where to obtain the interviewer's notes, a written transcript of the interview, or an audiotape of the interview. If available and relevant to the paper you are writing, you also may include, within the date parenthetical, the place where the interview occurred.

Examples

Interview with Matthieu Reeb, Sec. Gen. Ct. of Arb. for Sport in Lausanne, Switz. (May 25, 2004) (notes on file with Author).

Interview with Joseph Cirincione, Senior Assoc. & Dir., Non-proliferation Project, Carnegie Endowment for Intl. Peace (Nov. 19, 2004) (audio file available at http://www .chicagopublicradio.org/audio_library/wv_ranov04.asp#19 (accessed Jan. 22, 2005)).

Interview with Ann Chaitovitz, Dir. of Sound Recordings, Am. Fedn. of TV & Radio Artists (S.W. Music Conf., Austin, Tex., Mar. 20, 2004).

31.2 Full Citation Format for Interviews Conducted by Another

If you did not personally conduct the interview, use the format above, but change the designation (**Rule 31.1(a)**) to also include the interviewer's full name.

Examples (hypothetical)

Interview by Ebony, Jet & Am. Urban Radio Network with William J. Clinton, Pres. of U.S. (Mar. 27, 1998).

Telephone Interview by M. Celine Cannon with Hon. Mary S. Scriven, U.S. Mag. J., M.D. Fla. (Aug. 1, 2005).

31.3 Short Citation Format

31.3(a) *Id.*

If appropriate, use *id.* as the short citation. For additional information on *id.*, consult **Rule 11.3**. If *id.* is not appropriate, the form of the short citation will vary depending on the type of document you are writing.

31.3(b) Documents without footnotes

If *id.* is not appropriate, use the following format:

Designation, ●Interviewee's full name.

Example

Full citation: Interview with Linda Lee, Supervisory Atty., Fed. Energy Reg. Commn. (July 20, 1998).
Short citation: Interview with Linda Lee.

31.3(c) Documents with footnotes

If *id.* is not appropriate, use the *supra* format that follows. Consult **Rule 11.4** for additional information on *supra*.

Designation,●*supra* n. Note number.

Example

---

[18]Telephone Interview by M. Celine Cannon with Hon. Mary S. Scriven, U.S. Mag. J., M.D. Fla. (Aug. 1, 2005).

.   .   .

[57]Telephone Interview, *supra* n. 18.

FAST FORMATS

LETTERS AND MEMORANDA

Unpublished letter or memorandum	Ltr. from Maryann Jones, Acting Dean, W. St. U. College of L., to Ellen F. Rosenblum, Sec., ABA, *Accreditation* 1 (Aug. 29, 2003) (on reserve with Western State University College of Law, Law Library, Reference Desk).
Published letter or memorandum	Ltr. from William Lloyd Garrison to Rev. Samuel J. May (July 17, 1845), in *The Letters of William Lloyd Garrison* vol. 3, 303 (Walter M. Merrill ed., Harv. U. Press 1974).

32.0   LETTERS AND MEMORANDA

32.1 Full Citation Format for Unpublished Letters and Memoranda

A full citation to a letter or memorandum consists of ten components.

Designation•Author's name•, Author's title and affiliation,•to•Recipient's name•, Recipient's title and affiliation•, *Title* or *Subject*•, Pinpoint reference•(Exact date)•(Location).

Example (memorandum)

Memo. from Robert T. Jackson, Pres., McMillan L. Firm LLP, to Sarah Mayfield, Analyst, PricewaterhouseCoopers, *Valuation of Businesses in Bankruptcy* 4–5 (Dec. 4, 2005) (copy on file with *Howard Law Review*).

32.1(a) Designation

Begin the citation with the phrase "Ltr. from," "Memo. from," or a similar description.

32.1(b) Author's name

Include the author's full name. Follow **Rule 22.1(a)** for books.

32.1(c) Author's title and affiliation

Follow **Rule 31.1(c)** for interviews. Insert a comma, the word "to," and one space after the title and affiliation.

Example

Memo. from William R. Yates, Dep. Exec. Assoc. Commr., U.S. Dept. Homeland Sec., to Reg. Dirs., Dist Dirs., Officers-in-Charge & Serv. Ctr. Dirs., *Addition of Citizen Grandparents and Citizen Legal Guardians as Eligible Applicants Pursuant to INA 322* (Jan. 21, 2003) (available at http://uscis.gov/graphics/lawsregs/handbook/PolMemo91.pdf).

32.1(d) Recipient's name

Insert the recipient's name according to **Rule 31.1(c)** for interviews. For "open letters," use the example below.

Example

Memo. from Robert E. Fabricant, Gen. Counsel, EPA, to Marianne L. Horinko, Acting Adminstr., EPA, *EPA's Authority to Impose Mandatory Controls to Address Global Climate Change under the Clean Air Act* 4–5 (Aug. 28, 2003) (copy on file with *Columbia Law Review*).

Ltr. from Arnold Schwarzenegger, Cal. Gov., to Cal. State Sen., *Senate Bill 1520* (Sept. 29, 2004) (available at http://www.governor.ca.gov/govsite/pdf/press_release/SB_1520_sign.pdf).

Open Ltr. from Gary Francione, Prof., Rutgers Sch. of L., *California Senate Bill 1520* (Oct. 7, 2004) (copy on file with *Animal Law*).

32.1(e) Recipient's title and affiliation

Follow **Rule 31.1(c)** for interviews.

32.1(f) Subject

Provide the title or concisely describe the subject of the letter or memorandum. Present the title or subject in italics.

32.1(g) Pinpoint reference

Include, if possible, the page or other subdivision on which the cited material appears. Consult **Rule 5.2** for additional information on pinpoint citations. Insert one space after the pinpoint reference.

Example (hypothetical)

Ltr. from Stacey J. Straub, Pres., Salmons & Co., to Vincent A. Branton, Atty. at Lockheed Martin, *Security Issues* 1–3 (Jan. 26, 2006) (copy on file with *Stetson Law Review*).

32.1(h) Date

Follow **Rule 31.1(d)** for interviews.

32.1(i) Location

In a separate parenthetical, describe where or how readers might obtain a copy of the letter or memorandum. You may abbreviate the name of the organization that maintains the source using **Appendix 3,** and you may omit prepositions and articles not needed for clarity.

Example

Ltr. from Joe Barton, Chairman, H. Comm. on Energy & Com., to Mark McClellan, Commr., FDA, *Barton, Greenwood Seek Information from FDA on Antidepressants* 1 (Mar. 24, 2004) (available at http://energycommerce.house.gov/108/Letters/03242004_1242.htm).

32.2   Short Citation Format for Unpublished Letters and Memoranda

32.2(a) *Id.*

If appropriate, use *id.* as the short citation. For additional information on *id.*, consult **Rule 11.3.** If *id.* is not appropriate, the form of the short citation will vary depending on the type of document you are writing.

32.2(b) Documents without footnotes

If *id.* is not appropriate, use the following format:

Designation●Author's full name●at●Pinpoint reference.

Example

Full citation: Ltr. from Stacey J. Straub, Pres., Salmons & Co., to Vincent A. Branton, Atty. at Lockheed Martin, *Security Issues* 1–3 (Jan. 26, 2006) (copy on file with *Stetson Law Review*).
Short citation: Ltr. from Stacey J. Straub at 1.

32.2(c) Documents with footnotes

If *id.* is not appropriate, use the *supra* format that follows. Consult **Rule 11.4** for additional information on *supra.*

Designation, ●*supra* n. Note number●, at●Pinpoint reference.

Example

[14]Ltr. from Stacey J. Straub, Pres., Salmons & Co., to Vincent A. Branton, Atty. at Lockheed Martin, *Security Issues* 1–3 (Jan. 26, 2006) (copy on file with *Stetson Law Review).*

·   ·   ·

[17]Ltr., *supra* n. 14, at 2.

32.3   Published Letters and Memoranda

Cite published letters and memoranda according to **Rule 22.1(l)** or **22.1(m)** for collected works.

FAST FORMATS

VIDEO AND VISUAL RECORDINGS AND BROADCASTS

Movie	*To Kill a Mockingbird* (United Artists 1962) (motion picture).
Television show	*Ed*, "Hidden Agendas" (NBC Jan. 20, 2004) (TV series).
Entire television series	*Perry Mason* (CBS 1957–1966) (TV series).
News broadcast	*American Morning* (CNN Dec. 31, 2005) (TV broad.).

<table>
<tr><td>**33.0**</td><td>**VIDEO AND VISUAL RECORDINGS AND BROADCASTS**</td></tr>
</table>

33.1 Full Citation Format

A full citation to a video or visual recording—which would include films, motion pictures, broadcasts, television shows, videotapes, filmstrips, and slide shows—consists of either four or five components, depending on whether the program is nonepisodic (like a movie) or episodic (like a television series). If the program is episodic, the citation will vary depending on whether you are referring to a particular episode or to the series as a whole.

A full citation to a nonepisodic recording or broadcast includes four components.

Title●(Recorder or Producer●Date)●(Type of recording).

Example (nonepisodic)

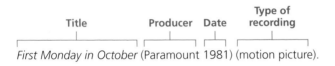

A full citation to an episodic recording or broadcast includes five components.

Title,●"Episode"●(Recorder or Producer●Exact date)●(Type of recording).

Example (episodic—one episode)

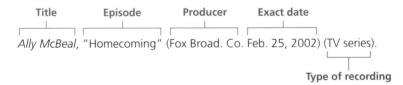

33.1(a) Title

(1) Begin the citation with the title of the recording or broadcast.

(2) Italicize the title. Use **Rule 3** for capitalization.

(3) If the recording or broadcast is episodic, such as a weekly television series or a daily news broadcast, begin with the name of the program, not the name of the episode, even if you intend to cite an episode by name.

273

33.1(b) Episode

(1) If referring to a specific episode, include the episode title after the main title.

Example

CSI: Miami, "Legal" (CBS July 18, 2005) (TV series).

(2) If an episode does not have a title, do not make one up. Include only the program title.

Example

Anderson Cooper 360° (CNN July 29, 2005) (TV broad.).

(3) If an episode does not have a title but you are citing a particular segment of that episode which does have a title, you may include the segment title in place of the episode title.

Example

CBS Evening News with Dan Rather, "Eye on America Series on Health Maintenance Organizations" (CBS July 24–26, 1995) (TV broad.).

(4) Put the episode or segment title in ordinary type, and enclose it in quotation marks. Insert one space after the episode or segment title.

33.1(c) Subdivisions

If the cited source has subdivisions, such as scene numbers from a DVD, you may include that information after the episode information or, if no episode, after the title.

Example

The Castle scene 5 (Miramax Home Ent. 2005) (DVD).

33.1(d) Recorder or producer

(1) After the title, insert an opening parenthesis.

(2) Include the name of the person or company who recorded, broadcasted, or produced the program.

(3) If the recording was not commercially made, include the name of the individual or organization that made the recording.

(4) Use any appropriate abbreviations listed in **Appendix 3** or any common acronyms, such as ABC, CBS, CNN, CSPAN, ESPN, HBO, and NBC.

(5) Insert one space after the recorder or producer name.

Examples

The Paper Chase (Fox Home Ent. 2003) (DVD).

Professionalism for New Lawyers (Prof. Comm. St. B. of Tex. 1995–1996) (videotape).

33.1(e) Date

(1) Nonepisodic recording

(a) For commercial, nonepisodic recordings, include the year in which the recording was released, and then insert a closing parenthesis and one space.

(b) For noncommercial, nonepisodic recordings, include the exact date (month-day-year) on which the recording was made, and then insert a closing parenthesis and one space.

(c) If a recording was originally released on one date and later re-released, you may include information about both releases or just the version cited.

Example (recording re-released in different format)

Reversal of Fortune (Warner 1990) (motion picture) & (Warner Home Video 1990) (videotape movie).

(2) Episodic recordings

(a) To cite a particular episode, include the exact date (month-day-year) on which the recording was broadcast or released. See the example in **item 1** in **Rule 33.1(b)**.

(b) To cite an entire series, include the span of dates during which the show originally aired. If the series is still running, insert "present" after the hyphen or en dash.

Example (entire series)

L.A. Law (NBC 1986–1994) (TV series).

The West Wing (NBC 1999–present) (TV series).

33.1(f) Type of recording

In a separate parenthetical, describe the type or form of the recording. Examples include motion picture, TV series, TV movie, TV broad., videotape, videotape movie, DVD recording, and slide show.

Example

My Cousin Vinny (20th Cent.-Fox 2001) (DVD).

33.1(g) Transcript information

If a transcript of the program is available, you may include the pinpoint reference (**Rule 5.2**) after the title. Also indicate where or how readers might obtain a transcript of the broadcast.

Examples

60 Minutes, "Readin', Writin' & Commercials" 14–15 (CBS Oct. 10, 1993) (TV broad., transcr. available from Burrelle's Info. Servs., vol. XXVI, no. 4).

World News Tonight with Peter Jennings (ABC Aug. 19, 1993) (TV broad., transcr. available in LEXIS, News library, ABCnews file).

World News Tonight with Peter Jennings (ABC Feb. 16, 2005) (TV broad., transcr. available at http://abcnews.go.com/WNT/story?id=506354&page=1).

33.2 Short Citation Format

33.2(a) *Id.*

If appropriate, use *id.* as the short citation. For additional information on *id.*, consult **Rule 11.3**. If *id.* is not appropriate, the form of the short citation will vary depending on the type of document you are writing.

33.2(b) Documents without footnotes

If *id.* is not appropriate, include the title, any subdivision information, and the type of recording.

Example

Full citation: *Trial by Jury* (Warner Bros. 2000) (DVD).
Short citations: *Trial by Jury* (DVD).
                       Trial by Jury scene 10 (DVD).

33.2(c) Documents with footnotes

If *id.* is not appropriate, use the *supra* format that follows. Consult **Rule 11.4** for additional information on *supra*. You may use "hereinafter" to shorten the title.

Title, •*supra* n. Note number.

Example

---

[61]*World News Tonight with Peter Jennings* (ABC June 12, 2002) (TV broad.) [hereinafter *World News*].

.   .   .

[75]*World News, supra* n. 61.

SOUND RECORDINGS

Recording	Nirvana, *Nevermind* (Geffen Recs. 1991) (CD).
Recording in larger collection	Kevin Shields, *City Girl*, in *Lost in Translation* (Emperor Norton 2003) (CD).

34.0 SOUND RECORDINGS

34.1 Full Citation Format for Entire Recordings

A full citation to a sound recording—which includes records, cassette and other tapes, compact discs, digital video discs, and other forms of recorded sound—contains five components. Use **Rule 34.2** to cite a single work within a collection.

Performer or composer,● *Title*● (Recorder●Date)● (Type of recording).

Example

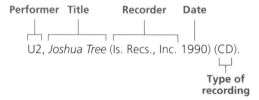

34.1(a) Performer or composer

Provide the performer's or composer's full name. Follow **Rule 22.1(a)** for books.

34.1(b) Title

In italics, present the title, including any subtitle. Insert one space after the title or subtitle.

34.1(c) Recorder

Provide the name of the recording company. Follow **Rule 33.1(c)** for video recordings.

34.1(d) Date

Follow item 1 in **Rule 33.1(d)** for video recordings.

34.1(e) Type of recording

In a separate parenthetical, describe the type or form of the recording. Examples include CD (compact disc), DVD (digital video disc), MD (minidisk), SACD (super audio CD), HD-CD (high definition CD), cassette tape, master tape, 33 rpm L.P., and 45 rpm L.P.

Examples

(Warner Records, Inc. 2006) (DVD).

(Univ. Mich. Sch. L. May 12, 1998) (cassette tape).

34.2 Full Citation Format for a Single Work in a Collection

A full citation for a single work in a collection contains seven components.

Performer or Composer,● *Title of shorter work*●, in● *Title of collection*●(Recorder● Date) (type of recording).

Examples

Joni Mitchell, *Both Sides Now*, in *Love Actually: Original Motion Picture Soundtrack* (J-Recs. 2003) (CD).

Alanis Morissette, *Ironic*, in *Jagged Little Pill* (Maverick/Reprise Recs. 1995) (CD).

34.3 Additional Information

You may add in a parenthetical any information that further describes the recording or that would assist the reader.

Examples

Ray Charles, *Here We Go Again*, in *Genius Loves Company* (Concord Recs. 2004) (CD) (featuring Norah Jones).

Joseph Silverstein, *Vivaldi: The Four Seasons* (Telarc 1990) (CD) (with the Boston Symphony Orchestra, conducted by Seiji Ozawa).

34.4 Short Citation Format for Sound Recordings

Follow **Rule 22.2** for entire works and **Rule 22.3** for single works in a collection.

FAST FORMATS

MICROFORMED MATERIALS

**Microformed materials
(not available in print)**

David M. Bearden, *Defense Cleanup and Environmental Programs: Authorization and Appropriations for FY2001*, at 1–2 (microformed on *Major Studies and Issue Briefs of the Congressional Research Service 2000 Supplement*, No. 00-RL-30554a, U. Publications Am. 2000).

Telegram from Elisha Baxter, Gov. Ark., to Pres. U.S. (Apr. 15, 1874) (microformed on Ltrs. Received by the Dept. Just. from the St. of Ark. 1871–1884, Microfilm Publication M1418, Natl. Archives).

Paul Lucas, *Essays in the Margin of Blackstone's Commentaries* 230–231 (unpublished Ph.D. dissertation, Princeton U. 1962) (microformed on U. Microfilms).

35.0 | MICROFORMED MATERIALS

35.1 Full Citation Format for Microform Collections Containing Material Also Available in Print Format

When a source is available in print format, cite the print version. You may parenthetically add a citation to the microform location. Identify the microform service. You may abbreviate any words in the service name that appear in **Appendix 3**, and you may omit any articles and prepositions not needed for clarity. In addition, if the service assigns a unique identifier to each reproduced document, include that identifier after the service name.

Example

H.R. Subcomm. on Cts. & Intell. Prop. of the Jud. Comm., *Hearings on H.R. 2441* (Feb. 8–9, 1996) (microformed on Cong. Info. Serv. No. 96-H521-18:1).

35.2 Full Citation Format for Microform Collections Containing Material Not Otherwise Available

35.2(a)

When the source is available only in a microform collection, use the normal format for the type of source cited. For example, if citing a letter, use **Rule 32.**

35.2(b)

Then, in a separate parenthetical, insert "microformed on." Also include the organization that issued the microform, the name of the collection (if any), and any unique identifier assigned to the document by the organization. You may abbreviate words in the organization name that appear in **Appendix 3.** You also may omit articles and prepositions in the organization name not needed for clarity.

Examples

Gen. Acctg. Off., *Interstate Child Support: Mothers Report Receiving Less Support from Out-of-State Fathers* (1992) (microformed on U.S. Docs. GA1.13:HRD-92-39FS).

John Pendleton, *Despatch No. 1 to the Sec. of St., Buenos Aires, Sept. 22, 1851* (microfilmed on Despatches from the U.S. Ministers to Argentina, 1817–1906, Micro-copy No. 69, reel 9, Natl. Archives Microfilm Publications).

35.3 Short Citation Format

If *id.* is appropriate, use *id.* as the appropriate short citation. Consult **Rule 11.3** for additional information on *id.* If *id.* is not appropriate, use the short form for the original type of document.

FAST FORMATS

FORTHCOMING WORKS

Forthcoming works	Saikrishna Prakash, *New Light on the Decision of 1789*, 91 Cornell L. Rev. ___ (forthcoming 2006) (copy on file with *Minnesota Law Review*).
	William Domnarski, *The Great Justices, 1941–54: Black, Douglas, Frankfurter, and Jackson in Chambers* (U. Mich. Press forthcoming 2006).

36.0 FORTHCOMING WORKS

36.1 Full Citation Format

If a work has not yet been published but is scheduled for publication, cite the work using the same format that will be used when the work is published, with the following changes.

36.1(a) Unavailable information

If the citation format requires a volume, an initial page number, or other subdivision, and the subdivisions are not yet available, insert three underlined spaces (___) in place of the volume, page number, or subdivision.

36.1(b) Date

Include the term "forthcoming" before the date.

36.1(c) Pinpoint reference and location

If the unpublished manuscript is available, add a parenthetical that provides the pinpoint page—in the unpublished manuscript—on which the cited material can be located. Also describe where or how readers can locate the unpublished manuscript. Abbreviate "manuscript" as "ms."

Examples

Cass R. Sunstein, *Chevron Step Zero*, 92 Va. L. Rev. ___ (forthcoming 2006) (ms. at 10–15, copy on file with Harv. L. Sch. Lib.).

Sean Hagan, *Designing a Legal Framework to Restructure Sovereign Debt*, 36 Geo. J. Intl. L. ___ (forthcoming 2005) (ms. at 11–15, copy on file with Author).

Kim S. Hunt & Michael Connelly, *Advisory Guidelines in the Post-Blakely Era*, 17 Fed. Senten. Rep. ___ (forthcoming 2005) (draft available at http://sentencing.typepad .com/sentencing_law_and_policy/2005/01/in_praise_of_ad.html).

James J. Brudney & Corey Ditslear, *Canons of Construction and the Elusive Quest for Neutral Reasoning*, 58 Vand. L. Rev. ___ (forthcoming 2005) (available in SSRN).

36.1(d) Forthcoming cases

Cite cases that have not yet been reported according to **Rule 12.18.**

36.2 Short Citation Format

If *id.* is appropriate, use it as the preferred short citation. Consult **Rule 11.3** for additional information on *id.* Otherwise, use the short form for the published version of the cited authority. For example, use **Rule 23.2** for legal periodicals.

UNPUBLISHED WORKS AND WORKING PAPERS

Unpublished manuscript	Barry Friedman, *The History of the Countermajoritarian Difficulty, Part Two: Reconstruction's Political Court* 10–12 (unpublished ms., Oct. 25, 2001) (copy on file with Virginia Law Review Association).
Unpublished thesis or dissertation	Beatrice Dong, *An Analysis of the International Hotel Struggle* (unpublished A.B. senior honors thesis, U. Cal., Berkeley, Nov. 22, 1994) (on file with Dept. Ethnic Stud., U. Cal., Berkeley).
	Charles W. Bethany, Jr., *The Guilty Plea Program* 4–7 (unpublished advanced course thesis, J. Advoc. Gen.'s Sch., Apr. 1959) (on file in J. Advoc. Gen.'s Sch. Lib., Charlottesville, Va.).
Working papers	Giancarlo Corsetti et al., *International Lending of Last Resort and Moral Hazard: A Model of IMF's Catalytic Finance* (Natl. Bur. Econ. Research Working Paper No. 10125, Dec. 2003) (available at http://papers.nber.org/papers/w10125.pdf).

37.0   UNPUBLISHED WORKS AND WORKING PAPERS

37.1   Full Citation Format for Unpublished Works

Use this rule for sources, other than cases, that are unpublished and not scheduled for publication. Use **Rule 12.18** for unpublished cases. Use **Rule 36** for works that currently are unpublished but are forthcoming in published format.

A full citation to an unpublished work, such as an unpublished manuscript, thesis, or dissertation, contains six components.

Author's name,●*Title*●Pinpoint reference●(Designation,●Exact date, [if available])●(Location).

Example

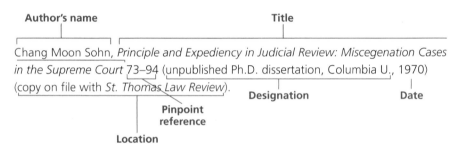

Author's name

Title

Chang Moon Sohn, *Principle and Expediency in Judicial Review: Miscegenation Cases in the Supreme Court* 73–94 (unpublished Ph.D. dissertation, Columbia U., 1970) (copy on file with *St. Thomas Law Review*).

Designation   Date

Pinpoint reference

Location

37.1(a)   Author's name

Insert the author's full name according to **Rule 22.1(a)** for books.

37.1(b)   Title

Insert the title and any subtitle according to **Rule 22.1(b)**.

37.1(c)   Pinpoint reference

Insert the relevant pinpoint reference according to **Rules 5.2** and **22.1(c)**.

37.1(d)   Designation

Insert an opening parenthesis; then describe the cited work. For unpublished manuscripts, insert the phrase "unpublished ms." For a thesis or dissertation, insert "unpublished" and then (1) the degree for which the paper was written, (2) the type of paper, and (3) the school at which the thesis was written. Use any appropriate abbreviations listed in **Appendix 3**. Insert a comma and one space after the designation.

Example

Alexandra Chirinos, *Finding the Balance between Liberty and Security* (unpublished LL.M. thesis, Queen's U., Belfast, Ire., 2004) (copy on file with Harv. L. Sch. Lib.).

37.1(e) Date

If available, provide the exact date (month-day-year) of the unpublished work. If a full date is not available, include as much information as possible. Abbreviate months using **Appendix 3(A)**. Insert a closing parenthesis after the date.

Example

(unpublished LL.M. thesis, Dec. 10, 2002, Yale U. L. Sch.).

37.1(f) Location

In a separate parenthetical, describe where or how readers can obtain a copy of the unpublished work.

Example

Lenda Cook, *Relationships among Learning Style Awareness, Academic Achievement, and Locus-of-Control of Community College Students* 75 (unpublished Ph.D. dissertation, U. Fla., 1989) (on file with Dissertation Abstracts Intl.).

37.2   Short Citation Format for Unpublished Works

Follow **Rule 22.2** for books.

37.3   Working Papers

When citing a working paper, analogize to **Rules 36.1** and **36.2** for other unpublished works, but include the name of the sponsoring organization, the term "Working Paper," and, if available, the working paper number in the parenthetical that also contains the date. You may abbreviate words in the sponsoring organization's name that appear in **Appendix 3(E)**, and you may omit prepositions and articles in the name that are not needed for clarity.

Examples

Bernard Black et al., *Liability Risk for Outside Directors: A Cross-Border Analysis* 3, 16 (U. Tex. L. & Econ. Working Paper No. 27, 2004) (available at http://ssrn.com/abstract=557070).

Roberta S. Karmel, *Should a Duty to the Corporation Be Imposed on Institutional Shareholders?* 24–30 (Brooklyn L. Sch. Pub. L. & Leg. Theory Working Paper Series, Research Paper No. 11, May 2004) (available at http://ssrn.com/abstract=546642).

Geoffrey Stapledon & Jeffrey J. Lawrence, *Do Independent Directors Add Value?* (Working Paper, U. Melbourne, 1999) (copy on file with Author).

Magali Delmas & Yesim Tokat, *Deregulation Process, Governance Structures and Efficiency: The U.S. Electric Utility Sector* (U. Cal. Energy Inst. Working Paper Series, Mar. 2003) (available at http://www.ucei.berkeley.edu/PDF/EPE_004.pdf).

PART 4

ELECTRONIC SOURCES

38.0 **GENERAL INFORMATION ABOUT ONLINE AND ELECTRONIC CITATION FORMATS**

38.1 Source Available in Print and Electronic Formats

38.1(a)

(1) If a source is available in print and electronic formats, typically cite *only* the print source if it is readily available to most readers. Types of material that are readily available in print include most cases, constitutions, statutes, federal administrative materials, and law reviews.

(2) After the print citation, you *may* add a parenthetical with the electronic citation if it will help readers access the source more easily. **Rule 38.1(b)** describes how to format the parenthetical.

Examples

Constitution (Rule 13):	Mo. Const. art. V, § 21 (available at http://www.moga.state.mo.us/const/a05021.htm).
Treatise (Rule 22):	*Wigmore on Evidence* vol. 1, § 21 (Peter Tillers ed., rev. ed., Little, Brown & Co. 1983) (available at http://www.loislaw.com; *select* Treatises, Evidence library).
Traditional Law Review Article (Rule 23):	Patrick Emory Longan, *Judicial Professionalism in a New Era of Judicial Selection*, 56 Mercer L. Rev. 913 (2005) (available at http://www.law.mercer.edu/academics/lawreview/lrissue.cfm?lrissueid=32).

(3) Consult **Rules 12.12** and **12.15** regarding electronic and Internet citations for cases. Consult **Rule 14.5** regarding electronic and online statute citations.

38.1(b)

(1) If the print source either is difficult to locate or is more widely available in electronic format, cite the print source *and* add a parenthetical that cites the electronic version. Hard-to-locate sources include wire service reports, certain government reports, state administrative materials, out-of-state newspapers, and foreign sources.

(2) If a source is available electronically in multiple places, such as Westlaw, LexisNexis, and the Internet, you need cite only one source; you may cite multiple sources if that will help the reader.

(3)   When selecting which electronic source to cite, select the place that the document is the most readily accessible by most readers; thus, a Web-based source might be preferred over a CD-ROM for accessibility. You also should select sources that have high indicia of trustworthiness; thus, a government-sponsored Web site (.gov) might be preferred over some commercial Web sites (.com). See **Sidebar 40.1** for information about different types of Web sites and indicia of reliability.

(4)   Begin the parenthetical containing the electronic citation with a descriptive phrase such as "available in" or "available at." Then include the electronic citation. Use **Rules 39** through **42** to determine how to cite specific electronic sources. When citing a Web site in this context, include only the URL. See **Rule 40.1(d)** for additional information on URLs. When citing other electronic sources, do not repeat information provided in the print citation, such as the date.

Examples

Bill Torpy, *U.S. Opens Trial in Brown's Killing: Two Acquitted in Dekalb Now Face Federal Charges*, Atl. J. & Const. D3 (July 11, 2005) (available at 2005 WLNR 10829748).

Beverly Wang, *For Souter, Seizure Ruling May Hit Home*, Wash. Post A4 (July 25, 2005) (available in Lexis, News library, WPOST file).

U.S. Census Bureau, *Statistical Abstract of the United States* 119 (121st ed. 2001) (available at http://www.census.gov/prod/2002pubs/01statab/stat-ab01.html).

38.2   Source Available Only in Electronic Format

If a source is available or readily accessible only in electronic format, use the electronic format for the specific type of source you are citing. While citation formats for most electronic sources appear in **Rules 39** through **42**, the citation formats for cases that appear only in electronic format are located in **Rules 12.12** and **12.15**, and the citation format for electronic journals is in **Rule 23.1(i)**.

SIDEBAR 38.1

ACCESSING AND PRESERVING ELECTRONIC SOURCES

More and more sources are available in electronic format. Not all attorneys, however, have access to authorities in electronic format. Moreover, the attorneys who do have access may be not able to access those resources at all times. For example, an attorney may be working in a different location, or an electronic resource might be temporarily unavailable because of a power outage or other difficulty. In addition, many resources on the Internet are transient; they might be there one day but gone the next, or the URL (Uniform Resource Locator—or address) might change between the time you cite the source and the time readers attempt to access it.

In light of these concerns, cite a print source whenever possible. In addition, if you are relying on an Internet citation, always print a hard copy for future reference, in case the document is later removed from the place where you located it.

WESTLAW AND LEXISNEXIS

Westlaw citation (with unique identifier)	Dennis Shanahan, *New Asia-Pacific Climate Plan—Bush and Howard Accept Greenhouse Effect Will Make Things Hot*, Australian 1 (July 27, 2005) (available at 2005 WLNR 11691492).
Westlaw citation (without unique identifier)	Tony Mauro, *Is John Roberts the Next Justice? The Two Most Important Attributes for the D.C. Circuit Judge: A Giant Intellect and a Tiny Paper Trail*, 28 Leg. Times 1 (Feb. 21, 2005) (available at WL, 2/21/2005 Legal Times 1).
LexisNexis citation (without unique identifier)	Schuyler M. Moore, *Film-Related Provisions of the 2004 Tax Act* pt. II (ALI-ABA Course of Study Materials, Ent., Arts & Sports L., Course No. SK035, Jan. 2005) (available at Lexis, CLE library, ALLCLE file).

39.0 | WESTLAW AND LEXISNEXIS

39.1 Full Citation Format When a Unique Identifier Is Available

39.1(a)

A unique identifier is a code assigned to a document that will permit you to locate that document on Westlaw or LexisNexis. The identifier typically consists of a year, the database name (typically WL or Lexis), and a document number. Unique identifiers for law reviews and other periodicals often consist of a volume, journal abbreviation, and page. For example, 62 LALR 303 is Westlaw's identifier for the article that starts on page 303 in volume 62 of the *Louisiana Law Review*. It is most common, however, to cite only the print source for a law review (**Rule 38.1(a)**).

39.1(b)

Use the format below for sources, other than cases, statutes, and C.F.R. sections, found on Westlaw and LexisNexis that have unique identifiers. Follow **Rule 12.12** when citing a case available only on Westlaw or LexisNexis. Follow **Rule 14.5** when citing a statute available on Westlaw or LexisNexis.

39.1(c)

Within the regular citation for the source, you may omit an initial page or a pinpoint citation if it is not available on LexisNexis or Westlaw and you are providing a unique identifier.

Regular citation for print source●(available at●Unique identifier).

Example

Citation for print
source (newspaper)

Robert Dodge, *Bush Learning His Economics from Experts,* Dallas Morn. News 1D (June 28, 1999) (available at 1999 WL 4131653).

Unique identifier

39.2 Full Citation Format When a Unique Identifier Is Not Available

If a unique database identifier is not available, use the following formats.

For Lexis: Regular citation for print source●(available at●Lexis●, Library name●, File name).

Example

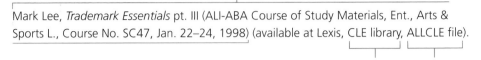

Citation for print source (book)

Mark Lee, *Trademark Essentials* pt. III (ALI-ABA Course of Study Materials, Ent., Arts & Sports L., Course No. SC47, Jan. 22–24, 1998) (available at Lexis, CLE library, ALLCLE file).

Library
name

File
name

Example for source available only online

Associated Press, *Task Force to Study Restoring Voting Rights to Felons* (June 20, 2001) (available at Lexis, Nexis library, AP file).

For Westlaw: Regular citation for print source●(available in●WL●, Database name).

Example

Citation for print source
(state regulation)

Database name

10 Ind. Admin. Code 1.5-4-4 (2005) (available at WL, IN-ADC database).

39.3   Short Citation Format for Westlaw and LexisNexis Citations

39.3(a) *Id.*

If *id.* is appropriate, use *id.* as the preferred short citation format. Consult **Rule 11.3** for additional information on *id.* If *id.* is not appropriate, the short citation format will depend on the type of document you are writing and the type of document you are citing.

39.3(b) Print and electronic version

If the citation contains both a print version and an electronic version, eliminate the electronic version in the short citation.

Example

Full citation (newspaper):   Laura Vanderkam, *If 'Roe' Were Overturned*, USA Today 15A (July 27, 2005) (available at 2005 WLNR 11752503).

Short citation (document without footnotes):	Vanderkam, USA Today at 15A.
Short citation (document with footnotes):	Vanderkam, *supra* n. 117, at 15A.

39.3(c) Only electronic version

If the citation contains only an electronic citation, retain any unique database identifier or database description. Also, if the electronic version contains star paging, you should include that information. Consult **Rule 12.12(b)** for additional information on star paging.

Examples

Full citation (online newsletter):	*Trials of the Rich and Famous*, 17 WL Password (May/June 1997) (available at 1997 WL 343532).
Short citation (document without footnotes):	*Trials of the Rich and Famous*, 1997 WL 343532.
Short citation (document with footnotes):	*Trials of the Rich and Famous*, *supra* n. 3.
Full citation (no unique identifier):	Mark Lee, *Trademark Essentials* pt. III (ALI-ABA Course of Study Materials, Ent., Arts & Sports Law, Course No. SC47, Jan. 22–24, 1998) (available at Lexis, CLE library, ALLCLE file).
Short citation (document without footnotes):	Lee at pt. III (Lexis, CLE library, ALLCLE file).
Short citation (document with footnotes):	Lee, *supra* n. 41, at pts. I–III.

39.4   Compilation of Materials from Electronic Databases

When you compile material by searching an electronic database, include the words "Search of," or another appropriate description, followed by the name of the database searched. You may then describe the search by including search terms used and parts of the database searched. In a parenthetical, provide the exact date (month-day-year) on which the search was performed. Abbreviate the month using **Appendix 3(A)**. In a separate explanatory parenthetical, you may include additional information about the parameters of the search that would help readers find and verify the information.

In addition, you may include compilation information in a textual sentence, as shown in the third example below.

Examples

Search in Westlaw, TP-ALL library, using the search "ludwig or l! w/2 wittgenstein" (Sept. 1, 2004) (yielding 729 results).

Courts regularly cite the works of William Shakespeare. Search of Westlaw, ALLCASES library (Aug. 2, 2005) (searching for the term "Shakespeare" and finding 2,794 cases).

An April 15, 2005, terms and connectors search conducted in the LexisNexis "US & Canadian Law Reviews, Combined" database using the search "elec! /s dereg!" yielded more than nine hundred articles published from April 1, 1985 to April 1, 2005.

WORLD WIDE WEB SITES

Web document with fixed date	FBI, *The Case of the Explosive Shoes and Other Amazing Stories from the FBI Lab*, http://www.fbi.gov/page2/july05/shoebomb071805.htm (July 18, 2005).
Web document with posted updates (breaking news)	CNN, *Reward Offered in Missing Pregnant Woman Case*, http://www.cnn.com/2005/US/07/28/Philadelphia.missing.ap/index.html (posted July 28, 2005, 2:15 p.m. EDT).
"Accessed" document	Workforce Innovation, *Florida's Minimum Wage*, http://www.floridajobs.org/resources/fl_min_wage.html (last accessed July 28, 2005).
Site "last updated"	P.L. Fitzgerald, *Stetson College of Law, Faculty and Courses, International Business Transactions*, http://www.law.stetson.edu/fitz/courses/ibt/ (last updated May 20, 2004).
Web citation using keystroke identifier	Lib. Cong., *THOMAS: A Century of Lawmaking for a New Nation: U.S. Congressional Documents and Debates 1774–1875*, http://thomas.loc.gov/; *select* Historical Documents (last updated May 1, 2003).

40.0 WORLD WIDE WEB SITES

40.1 Full Citation Format

For cases on the World Wide Web, consult **Rule 12.15**. Otherwise, a full citation to a World Wide Web site contains six components.

Author or Owner,● *Title*●Pinpoint reference [if available]●, URL●(Access **or** update information●Exact date).

Example

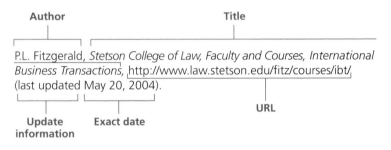

40.1(a) Author's or owner's name

Give the full name of the person or organization that authored the cited material. If an author name is not available, include the full name of the site owner. Follow **Rule 22.1(a)** for author and owner names. If the site does not have an owner or author, start with the title.

Examples

James H. Wyman, *Florida Law Online*, http://www.floridalawonline.net/ (last updated Dec. 5, 2004).

Fed. Jud. Ctr., *History of the Federal Judiciary*, http://www.fjc.gov/history/home.nsf (accessed July 10, 2005).

40.1(b) Title

(1) Always include the main title or top-level heading of the Web site.

(2) If citing a particular section or page of a site, also include that information. Separate the section or page from the main title with a comma and one space. Also separate subsections with a comma and one space.

(3) If you refer to multiple subsections of a site, list the smallest subsection last.

(4) Present the title and any subtitles in italics. Follow **Rule 3** capitalization rules.

(5) Insert a comma and one space after the end of the title or subtitle.

Example

U.S. Govt., *White House, First Lady, Helping America's Youth*, http://www.whitehouse .gov/firstlady/helping-youth.html (accessed July 28, 2005).

40.1(c) Pinpoint reference

(1) Include any subdivision information, such as a section or paragraph number, if it is a fixed feature of the document. A fixed feature is one that does not change when printed on different machines. Do not attempt to make up a "screen number," as the size of screens varies from computer to computer. Insert the pinpoint reference before the URL.

Example

Margie Kelley, *Harvard Law Bulletin, Teaching Lessons: Guided by Their Professors, Students Find HLS a Training Ground for Academic Careers* 2, http://www.law.harvard .edu/alumni/bulletin/2002/summer/feature_4-1.html (Summer 2002).

(2) To help the reader locate material in a long document that does not contain paragraph or section numbers, you may add the name of a section. Insert a comma and one space after the title. Use ordinary type and include the pinpoint reference in quotation marks.

Example

Dan A. Naranjo, *Mediating in a Highly Diverse and Volatile Society*, "Cultural Adaptability," http://www.attorney-mediators.org/diverse.html (2001).

(3) Documents in .pdf format appear in the same format as the original print format. Therefore, page numbers presented in .pdf documents may be used as a pinpoint reference.

Example

Michael Geist, *Fair.com: An Examination of the Allegations of Systemic Unfairness in the ICANN UDRP* 22–23, http://aix1.uottawa.ca/~geist/frameset.html (Aug. 2001).

40.1(d) URL

(1) Electronic address

After the title, insert the URL (Uniform Resource Locator). The URL is the electronic address for the information you are citing.

(2) Contents of URL

The URL consists of several parts. Typically include the entire URL if the address links directly to the cited material.

Parts of URL

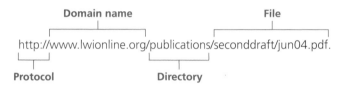

Example

Leg. Writing Inst., *The Second Draft: Bulletin of the Legal Writing Institute*, http://www.lwionline.org/publications/seconddraft/jun04.pdf (June 2004).

(3) Keystroke identifiers

If the URL will not lead the reader directly to the cited material or is very long, or if this method allows the reader to locate the information more easily, include just the protocol, domain name, and directory name. Then, instead of including the names of files and subfiles, identify keystrokes that can lead the user to the particular page you are citing. Sample keystroke identifiers are "select," "path," and "search." Insert a semicolon and one space between the URL and any keystroke information. Use commas to separate different keystroke information. Italicize keystroke identifiers, but not information following keystroke identifiers.

Examples using keystroke identifiers

U.S. Gen. Acctg. Off., *Military Bases: Analysis of DOD's 2005 Selection Process and Recommendations for Base Closures and Realignments*, http://frwebgate.access.gpo .gov/gaoreports/index.html; *path* Legislative branch, *search* 2004 GAO Reports Only (FY04), *search* "military base closures" (July 1, 2005).

Lib. Cong., *THOMAS: To Form a More Perfect Union: The Work of the Continental Congress and the Constitutional Convention*, http://thomas.loc.gov/; *select* Historical Documents (accessed July 4, 2005).

(4) Multiple URLs

If multiple URLs exist for the cited material, include only one in the citation.

(5) Angle brackets

Do not enclose the URL in angle brackets (< >). When the Internet was very new, angle brackets were the common way of signaling the beginning and end of the URL. Now that the Internet has become common, the convention has become one of eliminating brackets, though at times researchers will still see them.

Example

Correct: , http://www.ncsconline.org/
Incorrect: <http://www.ncsconline.org/>

(6) Underlining URL

Typically do not underline the URL. If your computer automatically underlines URLs, change your default settings as described in **Part 1(D)**. However, if you are submitting the document electronically, you may want to keep the hyperlink—which is designated by the underline—working.

(7) Case sensitivity

URLs often are case sensitive; thus, cite all characters as they are presented without changing capitalization or punctuation. When using a word processing program, the safest way to transcribe a URL correctly is to copy it directly from the window of your Internet browser and paste the URL directly into your document.

(8) Breaking across a line

Because URLs can be long, they may not fit onto a single line of text. If you encounter this situation, break the URL at a logical point, preferably after a slash. If necessary, you also may break the URL *before* a period. Never insert a hyphen into a URL, because the hyphen will look like part of the address.

Examples

Preferred breaking point:	http://www.lwionline.org/ publications/seconddraft/jun04.pdf
Alternative breaking point:	http://www.lwionline .org/publications/seconddraft/jun04.pdf
Incorrect breaking points:	http://www.lwionline. org/publications/seconddraft/jun04.pdf
	http://www.lwionline.org/publica- tions/seconddraft/jun04.pdf

(9) Updating URLs

URLs change frequently. Therefore, you should check all URLs cited in your paper immediately before submitting the paper. Law journals should re-check URLs before sending final proofs to the printer. In addition, to avoid the problem of not being able to locate material because the URL has changed or because the document is no longer available online, always print and retain a copy of any online source you cite in a paper (**Sidebar 38.1**).

40.1(e) Date

(1) When possible, provide the exact date (month-day-year) for each World Wide Web citation. Abbreviate months according to **Appendix 3(A)**. If an exact date is not possible, include as specific a date as possible. Enclose the date in parentheses.

(2) Use one of the following date options, which are listed in order of preference.

  (a) The exact date of the document being cited. Use this option for cases, statutes, dated reports, articles, and other information that will not change once posted.

Example

FBI, *The Case of the Explosive Shoes and Other Amazing Stories from the FBI Lab*, http://www.fbi.gov/page2/july05/shoebomb071805.htm (July 18, 2005).

  (b) The exact date of the document being cited, followed by the specific time of the cited posting. Use this option for news articles that are updated over a period of time. Consult **Sidebar 38.1** about printing and retaining a copy of online material that you cite.

Example

CNN, *Reward Offered in Missing Pregnant Woman Case*, http://www.cnn.com/2005/US/07/28/Philadelphia.missing.ap/index.html (posted July 28, 2005, 2:15 p.m. EDT).

(c) **The date on which the site was last updated or modified.** Use the terminology—such as "updated" or "last modified"—that site owner or manager has selected.

Example

Natl. Insts. Health, *Intramural Research, Participation in Clinical Studies*, http://www.niaaa.nih.gov/intramural/web_dicbr_hp/particip.htm (updated Aug. 2002).

(d) **The date on which you accessed the material.** Insert the word "accessed" before the date.

Example

Workforce Innovation, *Florida's Minimum Wage*, http://www.floridajobs.org/resources/fl_min_wage.html (accessed July 28, 2005).

40.2 Short Citation Format

40.2(a) *Id.*

If *id.* is appropriate (**Rule 11.3**), use *id.* as the preferred citation format. It is possible to use *id.* for the same Web site, even if part of the URL has changed.

If *id.* is not appropriate, the short citation will depend on the type of document you are writing.

Example

Full citation: Bully OnLine, *Bullying in School*, http://www.bullyonline.org/schoolbully/school.htm (accessed June 15, 2005).

Short citation (same URL): *Id.*

Short citation (different URL): *Id.* at http://www.bullyonline.org/schoolbully/myths.htm.

40.2(b) Documents without footnotes

If *id.* is not appropriate, include the author's last name or the owner's name, or, if the "hereinafter" format is used (**Rule 11.4(d)**), a partial title. Then add a comma and the word "*supra.*" If needed for clarity, you may also insert a comma after the word "*supra*" and include the URL.

Example

CAR is the airport code for Caribou Municipal Airport in Caribou, Maine. *Airport and City Code Database for 9,000 Airports Worldwide*, http://www.airportcitycodes.com/aaa (accessed Sept. 24, 2000) [hereinafter *Airport Code Database*]. The correct code for Caracas's international airport is CCS, while that for Bogota is BOG. *Id.* The routing slip also lists MIA as the "ABX SORT"—ABX is an abbreviation for Airborne Express. Bezman Depo. at 5. MIA is the airport code for Miami International Airport. *Airport Code Database, supra.*

(*Source:* Adapted from *Mejia v. City of N.Y.*, 119 F. Supp. 2d 232, 250 n. 19 (E.D.N.Y. 2000)).

40.2(c) Documents with footnotes

If *id.* is not appropriate, use a *supra* reference as described in **Rule 11.4.**

Example

---

[263]Rule 10b5-2 went into effect on October 23, 2000. U.S. Secs. Exch. Commn., *Selective Disclosure and Insider Trading, Final Rule*, http:// www.sec.gov/rules/final/33-7881.htm (accessed Feb. 4, 2002) [hereinafter *Final Rule*].

[264]*Id.*

[265]17 C.F.R. § 240.10b5-2 (2002).

[266]*Final Rule, supra* n. 263.

[267]*Id.*

40.3   Weblogs

40.3(a) Full citation format

Analogize to World Wide Web sites in **Rule 40.1** to cite a weblog (or "blog"). Include the full name (if available) of the person who posted the entry (using **Rule 22.1(a)** for author's names), the name of the weblog in ordinary type (words in the name may be abbreviated using **Appendix 3**), the title of the weblog entry in italics, the blog URL, and the exact date the cited entry was posted (month-day-year). Abbreviate the month using **Appendix 3(A).**

Examples

Stephen Bainbridge, ProfessorBainbridge.com, *Delaware's Predictability Redux*, http://www.professorbainbridge.com/2003/10/delawares_predi.html (Oct. 20, 2003).

David, The Blogbook, *Law Review Articles Citing Blogs*, http://blogbook.org/cite/index.html (Feb. 26, 2004).

40.3(b) Short citation format

Use **Rule 40.2** for World Wide Web citations. When citing a different author on a weblog, or when citing a different entry on a weblog, use a full citation format.

FAST FORMATS

ELECTRONIC MAIL

Private e-mail	E-mail from Scott Sternberg, Assoc., Carlton Fields, to Jason Dimitris, State Atty., Dade County, Fla., *Proposed Constitutional Changes* (Oct. 1, 2005, 4:45 p.m. EDT).
E-mail to discussion group	E-mail from Sue Liemer, Dir. Leg. Writing, S. Ill. U. Sch. L., to DIRCON listserv, *Committees* (Feb. 20, 2006) (copy on file with Author).
	E-mail from Jason Jones, Ministry of the Atty. Gen., Ont., to digsig@listserv.temple.edu, *Trade Regulations* (Dec. 15, 2005) (copy on file with *Houston Law Review*).

41.0 ELECTRONIC MAIL

41.1 Full Citation Format for Personal E-mail

41.1(a)

Follow **Rule 32** for unpublished letters and memoranda, but use "E-mail from" as the designation.

41.1(b)

E-mail addresses of the author or recipient are not required but may be included if there is a reason to do so. If you include an e-mail address, insert it after the person's title and affiliation. If you must break an e-mail address, do so at a logical place, such as after a backslash (/) or **before** a period; do not insert a hyphen, as it may be read as part of the address. You may include the exact time of the e-mail after the date.

Example (hypothetical)

E-mail from Jan Levine, Assoc. Prof. & Dir. Research & Writing, Temple U. Sch. L., to Richard K. Neumann, Jr., Prof., Hofstra L. Sch., *ALWD Conference* (June 28, 2005, 3:20 p.m. EDT) (copy on file with Prof. Levine).

Partial example including e-mail address (hypothetical)

E-mail from Darby Dickerson, Dean, Stetson U. College L., darby@law.stetson .edu, to

41.2 Full Citation Format for E-mail Sent to a Discussion Group or Listserv

Follow **Rule 41.1**, but use the discussion group's name or address in place of the recipient's name, title, and affiliation.

Examples (hypothetical)

E-mail from Sue Liemer, Dir. Leg. Writing, S. Ill. U. Sch. L., to DIRCON listserv, *Committees* (Feb. 20, 2006) (copy on file with Author).

E-mail from Jason Jones, Ministry of the Atty. Gen., Ontario, to digsig@listserv.temple .edu, *Trade Regulations* (Dec. 15, 2005) (copy on file with *Houston Law Review*).

41.3 Short Citation Format for E-mail

Follow **Rule 32.2** for unpublished letters and memoranda.

Example

Full citation:	E-mail from Jan Levine, Assoc. Prof. Dir. Research & Writing, Temple U. Sch. L., to Richard K. Neumann, Jr., Prof., Hofstra L. Sch., *ALWD Conference* (June 28, 2005, 3:20 p.m. EDT) (copy on file with Prof. Levine).
Short citation (document without footnotes):	E-mail from Jan Levine.
Short citation (document with footnotes):	E-mail, *supra* n. 14.
	E-mail from Jan Levine, *supra* n. 14.

CD-ROM Material

Privately published	Daniel P. Anderson, *Litigation Ethics* fol. 4 (Sept. 22, 2005) (privately published CD-ROM) (copy available from AAIC Consultants, Inc., St. Petersburg, Fla.).
Commercially published	*The Delaware Law of Corporations and Business Organizations: 2004 Statutory Deskbook with CD-ROM* (R. Franklin Balotti & Jesse A. Finkelstein eds., 3d ed., Aspen Publishers 2004).

42.0   CD-ROM MATERIAL

42.1   Full Citation Format

42.1(a)   Source available in print and on CD-ROM

When the material cited is available in a print format, such as cases and statutes, typically cite the print format.

42.1(b)   Source not in print but contained on privately published CD-ROM

When citing material that a private user has placed on a CD-ROM, follow **Rule 37** for unpublished material. After the date parenthetical, include "(privately published CD-ROM)."

Example (hypothetical)

Daniel P. Anderson, *Litigation Ethics* fol. 4 (Sept. 22, 2005) (privately published CD-ROM) (copy available from AAIC Consultants, Inc., St. Petersburg, Fla.).

42.1(c)   Source not in print but contained on commercially published CD-ROM

When citing material on a commercially published CD-ROM, follow the normal rule for the source cited as closely as possible. For example, cite a book according to **Rule 22.**

(1)   Include the date and, if available, the version used. It is permissible to format the date as "current through" a specific date or to use similar language.

(2)   If the title does not contain the term "CD-ROM," include "(CD-ROM)" at the end of the citation.

Examples

Jane Homeyer & Sarah Mikolajczyk, *Techniques of Crime Scene Investigation: Interactive Training CD-ROM* (CRC Press 2004).

U.S. Bd. Tax App., *Board of Tax Appeals Regulars and Memoranda* (CCH 1998) (CD-ROM).

Law and Employment Library on CD (BNA current through Dec. 31, 2004) (CD-ROM).

The Oxford English Dictionary on CD ROM (2d ed., Oxford U. Press, version 3.0, 2002).

42.2   **Short Citation Format**

Follow the rule for the particular type of source cited. For example, if citing a book on CD-ROM, follow **Rule 22.2** for books.

INCORPORATING CITATIONS

INTO DOCUMENTS

43.0   CITATION PLACEMENT AND USE

43.1   Placement Options

Use the following rules to determine where to place citations within documents.

43.1(a) Citation sentences

When a source relates to the entire textual sentence, include it in a separate citation sentence. Like a textual sentence, a citation sentence begins with a capital letter and ends with a period. Consult **Appendix 6** for a sample memorandum demonstrating the form and placement of citations.

Example (the citation sentence is in green)

"[S]tudents do not shed their rights to freedom of speech or expression at the school house gate." *Tinker v. Des Moines Indep. Community Sch. Dist.*, 393 U.S. 503, 506 (1969).

43.1(b) Citation clauses

When a source relates to only part of a sentence, include it in a citation clause within the textual sentence. Place the citation clause immediately after the text it concerns, and set the clause off with commas. If the citation clause ends a sentence, use a period as the final punctuation.

Examples (the citation clauses are in green)

Although the Fourth Amendment prohibits unreasonable searches, *Elkins v. U.S.*, 364 U.S. 206, 222 (1960), each case must be decided on its own facts and circumstances, *Harris v. U.S.*, 331 U.S. 145, 150 (1947).

Courts have defined the viewpoint variously as that of "an ordinary reader of a particular race," *e.g. Ragin v. N.Y. Times Co.*, 923 F.2d 995, 1000 (2d Cir. 1991), and that of "a reasonable black person," *e.g. Harris v. Intl. Paper Co.*, 765 F. Supp. 1509, 1516 n. 12 (D. Me. 1991).

43.1(c) Embedded citations

(1) A citation may be incorporated into a textual sentence when the authority is mentioned within that sentence. When using this option, do not repeat the citation at the end of the sentence. **Some attorneys do not like embedded citations because they make sentences more difficult to read.** You also may include the case name within the textual sentence and then place the citation—minus the case name—in a subsequent citation sentence.

Example (the embedded citation is in green)

In *International Shoe Co. v. Washington*, 326 U.S. 310, 316 (1945), the Court held that if the defendant was not present in the forum, due process required that he have certain minimum contacts with that forum.

(2) When using an embedded citation, do not use an introductory signal.

(3) Place a comma and one space after the citation.

(4) Do not use embedded citations in the main text of a document with footnotes or endnotes. In such documents, all citations appear in the notes (**Rule 43.1(e)**).

43.1(d) Textual references

You may refer to an authority in the text without using a full-form or short-form citation. A textual reference can be an appropriate way to refer to an authority when it has already been cited once in full citation format nearby or when all the information that typically would be conveyed in a citation is already included in the text.

Example (textual reference is in green)

Federal Rule of Civil Procedure 30(a)(2)(A) presumptively limits each party to ten depositions.

43.1(e) Note reference numbers

(1) Definition

A note reference number is a superscript number within the main text of the document. "Superscript" text appears slightly above regular text; for example:[75]. Each note number will correspond to a footnote in the paper.

Example

The Family and Medical Leave Act grants twelve work weeks of leave during any twelve-month period to any eligible employee who, because of a serious health condition, cannot perform the functions of the position she holds.[1]

---

[1] 29 U.S.C. § 2612 (2000).

(2)   General rules

(a)   Inserting notes. In general, insert a note number for each separate idea in the main text. Also insert a note number immediately after referring to a case in the text for the first time.

Example

In a widely publicized opinion, *Hall v. Clifton Precision*,[65] Judge Gawthrop gained the national spotlight by issuing strict guidelines for deposition conduct.[66]

(b)   Numbering. Typically number the notes consecutively, beginning with the number 1.

(c)   Relation to punctuation. A note reference number should *follow* any punctuation mark.

Examples

Correct: In federal cases, all phases of civil deposition are subject to court control;[61] the court has discretion to issue orders designed to prevent abusive tactics during depositions.[62]

Incorrect: In federal cases, all phases of civil deposition are subject to court control[61]; the court has discretion to issue orders designed to prevent abusive tactics during depositions[62].

(d)   Placement when note concerns entire textual sentence. If a single footnote relates to the entire sentence, place a single note reference number at the end of the sentence.

Example

A serious health condition under the Family and Medical Leave Act includes an illness, an injury, or a condition that requires continuing treatment by a health care provider.[1]

---

[1] 29 U.S.C. § 2611 (2000).

(e)   Placement when note concerns only part of the textual sentence. If the note concerns only a portion of the sentence, place the note reference number within the sentence, next to the portion to which it relates.

Example

Although one court held that an interrogatory with multiple related subparts constituted a single interrogatory,[42] another court held that these subparts constituted multiple interrogatories.[43]

---

[42] *Am. Chiropractic Assn. v. Trigon Healthcare, Inc.*, 2002 WL 1792062, at *2 (W.D. Va. 2002).

[43] *Valdez v. Ford Motor Co.*, 143 F.R.D. 296, 298 (D. Nev. 1991).

SIDEBAR 43.1

USING YOUR WORD PROCESSOR TO FORMAT FOOTNOTES

Most word-processing programs have a footnote and endnote function. If you insert note numbers using this function, the program automatically will superscript the note numbers, place the notes on the appropriate pages, number and renumber notes if you insert or delete other notes, insert separator lines, and adjust the main text. However, without taking several additional steps, the program often will not automatically renumber cross-references to those notes (see **Rule 10** regarding cross-references). Therefore, as a note number changes, always be sure to change all cross-references to that note. As a practical matter, it may be best to draft the paper using only full citations, or short citations other than *id.*, and then substitute short forms and cross-references shortly before completing the paper.

(f) **Multiple notes within a single textual sentence.** Although you may have more than one note within a single sentence, you may not have two consecutive note numbers without any intervening text.

Incorrect example (problem marked in green)

In federal cases, all phases of civil deposition are subject to court control;[61] the court has discretion to issue orders designed to prevent abusive tactics during depositions.[62] [63]

(g) **Note reference numbers within quoted material.** A note reference number generally should not appear within quoted material because the insertion will change the quotation. If you must add a note reference number within a quotation, place the superscript note reference number in brackets (example: [17]).

(h) **Rule 49.3(d)** addresses omitting reference numbers within quoted material.

43.2   Frequency of Citation

43.2(a)

Place a citation immediately after each sentence, or part of a sentence, that contains a statement of legal principle, a reference to or description of a legal authority, an idea, a thought, or an expression borrowed from another source.

43.2(b)

Within a single paragraph of the document you are writing, if you refer to material from the **same** page, section, or other subdivision of the same source, you may place one citation at the end of the material. Do not use this convention if the page, section, or other subdivision of the cited material changes.

Example

A recent Illinois case explains whether a covenant not to compete is ancillary to an otherwise valid agreement. *Smith v. Burkitt*, 795 N.E.2d 385 (Ill. App. 1st Dist. 2003). In September 1999, Billy and Brenda Smith entered into a contract with Fred and Dorothy Burkitt to purchase the Burkitts' business. The contract included a noncompetition agreement. In November 2001, the Smiths sued the Burkitts for conducting business in violation of the noncompetition agreement. *Id.* at 387.

43.3   Number of Sources to Cite

The number of authorities you cite for a particular proposition will depend on the type of document you are writing, the audience for whom you are writing, the number of authorities relative to the topic, and how well established or contested the stated proposition is.

43.3(a) Type of document and audience

(1)   A citation sentence or citation clause that contains multiple authorities for a single proposition is called a "string citation." You will typically have more string citations in a law review article than in a legal memorandum or brief.

(2)   Judges and practitioners who read court documents and legal memoranda typically want to see only those authorities that provide the best and strongest support for the stated proposition. Because they are busy and have limited time to read documents, most do not like to see string citations throughout the paper.

(3)   Scholars and others who read law review articles and similar papers expect to see many more citations in connection with stated propositions because the citations provide the depth of reference necessary to understand and master the selected topic.

43.3(b) Number of relevant authorities

The more authorities that are relevant to a proposition, the more from which you have to choose, and the greater the likelihood that you will want to cite more than one to support or contradict the proposition. In such a case, the "*e.g.*" introductory signal, which can be used alone or combined with another signal, should prove helpful. Consult **Rule 44** for additional information on that signal.

43.3(c) Whether the proposition is established or contested

If a particular proposition is established, it may be sufficient to cite to fewer authorities than if a proposition is contested.

43.4 Guidelines for Determining Which Authorities to Cite in a Legal Memorandum or Court Document

Below are some guidelines to help you determine which and how many authorities to cite to show readers that you have conducted thorough research, while not boring them with too many citations.

43.4(a)

Begin by predicting the amount of citation and explanation interested, but busy, readers would want to see.

43.4(b)

Put yourself in the readers' position. Ask which authorities would be most likely to affect your decision in the matter—whether favorably or unfavorably for your client. Alternatively, ask how angry you would be if you made a decision without knowing about a particular authority. Cite and discuss those authorities. Discard other peripheral sources unless you need them to fill gaps in your argument or analysis.

43.4(c)

If you have several cases you want to cite and discuss, but have limited space, use the following guidelines to decide which cases to include in the paper. These guidelines assume that the cases are all from the jurisdiction whose law controls the outcome of the matter.

(1) Select the case that not only addresses the same legal issue but also is most factually on point.

(2) If the cases are equally good, typically select the case from the highest court.

(3) If the cases are from the same court, select either the most recent case or the landmark case—the case to which all other cases tend to refer.

44.0   SIGNALS

44.1   Purpose of Signals

An introductory signal is a word or term used to inform readers about the type and degree of support or contradiction the cited authority provides for the accompanying text.

44.2   Use of Signals

44.2(a)

Do not use a signal if:

(1)   The cited authority directly supports the stated proposition.

Example

The Family and Medical Leave Act grants twelve work weeks of leave during any twelve-month period to any eligible employee who, because of a serious health condition, cannot perform the functions of the position she holds. 29 U.S.C. § 2612 (2000).

(2)   The cited authority identifies the source of a quotation.

Example

Summary judgment is appropriate "if the pleadings, depositions, answers to interrogatories, and admissions on file, together with the affidavits, show that there is no genuine issue of material fact." Fed. R. Civ. P. 56(c).

(3)   The cited authority merely identifies the authority referred to in the text.

Example

In 2004, the United States decided *Tennessee v. Lane*.[21]

---

[21]541 U.S. 509 (2004).

44.2(b)

If the authority is cited for a reason or purpose not listed in **Rule 44.2(a)**, use the appropriate signal listed in **Rule 44.3**.

44.2(c)

A signal may be used before a full citation or a short citation.

Examples

See Clark v. U.S., 289 U.S. 1, 15 (1933).

See Clark, 289 U.S. at 15.

See id. at 14.

44.3 Categories of Signals

Signals that indicate support

See	Use when the cited authority (a) supports the stated proposition implicitly or (b) contains dicta that support the proposition.
Accord	Use to show that two or more authorities state or support the proposition but the text quotes or refers to only one; the others are then preceded by "*accord.*" Also use to show that the law of one jurisdiction is in accord with that of another jurisdiction.
See also	Use to cite additional material that support the proposition. Support under this signal is not as strong or direct as when no signal or "*see*" is used. "*See also*" may be used when the cited authority supports the point made, but is in some respect distinguishable from previously cited cases.
Cf.	Use when the cited authority supports the stated proposition only by analogy.

Signal that draws a comparison

Compare . . . with	Use to compare authorities or groups of authorities that reach different results concerning the stated proposition.

Signals that indicate contradiction

Contra	Use when the cited authority directly contradicts the stated proposition.
But see	Use when the cited authority (a) contradicts the stated proposition implicitly or (b) contains dicta that contradict the stated proposition.
But cf.	Use when the cited authority contradicts the stated proposition by analogy.

Signal that indicates background material

See generally	Use when the cited authority is presented as helpful background information related to the stated proposition. This signal may be used with primary and secondary authorities.

Signal that indicates an example:

E.g.   Use to reflect that the cited authority is representative of, or merely an example of, many authorities that stand for the same proposition but are not cited. Use alone when the authorities directly support the stated proposition. In other situations, combine with the appropriate signal. Thus:

> *See e.g.*
> *Compare e.g.* . . . *with e.g.*
> *See generally e.g.*

44.4   Signals and Explanatory Parentheticals

When you use a signal, it often helps the reader to include an explanatory parenthetical after the cited source to describe the force or meaning of the authority. For additional information on explanatory parentheticals, consult **Rule 46.**

44.5   Capitalizing Signals

Capitalize the first letter of an introductory signal that begins a citation sentence. Do not capitalize the first letter of an introductory signal that appears within a citation clause or that appears within a citation sentence but does not begin the sentence. Consult **Rule 43.1** for additional information on citation sentences and citation clauses.

Examples

Capitalize the first letter of the signal when it begins a citation sentence.	Freedom to advocate unpopular beliefs in a school setting must be balanced against society's interest in teaching students the boundaries of acceptable behavior. *See Hazelwood Sch. Dist. v. Kuhlmeier*, 484 U.S. 260, 260 (1988) (indicating that a school need not tolerate student speech that is inconsistent with its "basic educational mission").
Do not capitalize the first letter of the signal when it appears within a citation clause.	Freedom to advocate unpopular beliefs in a school setting must be balanced against society's interest in teaching students the boundaries of acceptable behavior. *Bethel Sch. Dist. v. Fraser*, 478 U.S. 675, 681 (1986); *see Hazelwood Sch. Dist. v. Kuhlmeier*, 484 U.S. 260, 260 (1988) (indicating that a school need not tolerate student speech that is inconsistent with its "basic educational mission").

44.6   Placement and Typeface of Signals

44.6(a)

Separate the introductory signal from the rest of the citation with one space. Do not include any punctuation between the signal and the rest of the citation.

44.6(b)

Italicize or underline each introductory signal (**Rule 1**). However, a signal used merely as a verb should not be italicized or underlined.

Example (the signal used as a verb appears in green)

For an article chock-full of examples of unprofessionalism in documents filed with courts, see Judith D. Fischer, *Bareheaded and Barefaced Counsel: Courts React to Unprofessionalism*, 31 Suffolk U. L. Rev. 1 (1997).

44.7   Repeating Signals

When more than one authority provides the same type and degree of support for the textual proposition, do not repeat the signal before each authority. The signal "carries through" until a different signal is used.

Example

Readers will understand that this case takes the *see* signal.

The crime-fraud exception to the attorney-client privilege "acts to ensure that the 'seal of secrecy' does not extend to communications 'made for the purpose of getting advice for the commission of a fraud' or crime." *U.S. v. Zolin*, 491 U.S. 554, 563 (1989) (quoting *O'Rourke v. Darbishire*, [1920] A.C. 581, 604 (P.C.)); *see Clark v. U.S.*, 289 U.S. 1, 15 (1933) (explaining that "[t]he privilege takes flight if the relation is abused"); *In re Grand Jury Matter 91-01386,* 969 F.2d 995, 997 (11th Cir. 1992) (instructing that the attorney-client privilege is, as a matter of law, construed narrowly so as not to exceed means necessary to support the policy it promotes); *see generally* Edna Selan Epstein, *The Attorney-Client Privilege and the Work-Product Doctrine* 251 (3d ed., ABA 1997) (commenting that "[s]ociety . . . has no interest in facilitating the commission of contemplated but not yet committed crimes, torts, or frauds").

44.8   Order of Signals and Punctuation between Different Signals

44.8(a)

When more than one signal is used in a citation sentence or clause, the signals should appear in the order they are listed in **Rule 44.3**. Remember that "no signal" cases come first.

44.8(b)

When *"e.g."* is combined with another signal, such as *see*, the combined signal should appear where the non-*e.g.* signal would normally fall. When *"e.g."* is used alone, it should appear where the "no signal" sources would appear.

44.8(c)

Separate different signals and their accompanying citations with a semicolon and one space.

Examples

Id.; see also Cox v. Shell Oil, 1995 WL 775363, at **6–8 (Tenn. Ch. 1995).

Most service providers will provide user identity information only if a subpoena is issued. *E.g.* AOL Online, *Privacy Policy*, http://www.aol.com/info/p_privacy.adp (accessed July 28, 2005) ("AOL.com may share such information in response to legal process, such as a court order or subpoena, or in special cases such as a physical threat to you or others."); *see generally* Conn, *supra* n. 39, at 164 ("Internet bullying is hard to trace. Internet service providers are not routinely required to identify users of their services.").

See e.g. Smith v. Phillips, 455 U.S. 209, 221 (1982); Ex parte Sanchez, 918 S.W.2d 526, 527 (Tex. Crim. App. 1996); but cf. Stone v. Powell, 428 U.S. 465 (1976) (Fourth Amendment claims not cognizable on federal habeas corpus review).

45.0 ORDER OF CITED AUTHORITIES

45.1 Applicability

Use **Rule 45** to determine how to cite multiple authorities that fall within the same signal. For example, use this rule when you are citing three cases that all implicitly support the textual proposition and all require the *"see"* signal (**Rule 44.3**). Start the ordering process over each time you change signals.

Example (document with footnotes)

Even if the high-ranking official has personal knowledge, courts will examine whether the party seeking the deposition can obtain the same information through another form of discovery, such as interrogatories.[215]

Start a new ordering arrangement when you change signals.

[215]*E.g. Stone City Music v. Thunderbird, Inc.*, 116 F.R.D. 473, 474 (N.D. Miss. 1987); *Buryan v. Max Factor & Co.*, 41 F.R.D. 330, 332 (S.D.N.Y. 1967); *Mulvey v. Chrysler Corp.*, 106 F.R.D. 364 (D.R.I. 1985); *but see Scotch Whiskey Assn. v. Majestic Distilling Co.*, 1988 U.S. Dist. LEXIS 16531 at *15 (D. Md. Nov. 30, 1988) (denying request that interrogatories be served before top official was deposed); *Matarazzi v. H.J. Williams Co.*,1988 U.S. Dist. LEXIS 8706 at *2 (E.D. Pa. Aug. 10, 1988) (denying request for protective order that discovering party had to submit interrogatories before deposing the defendant's CEO).

45.2 Punctuation between Citations

Separate authorities with a semicolon and one space.

45.3 General Ordering Rules

Use these general rules and the specific rules in **Rule 45.4** to determine the order in which authorities should be cited.

45.3(a) Primary versus secondary authorities

Cite primary authority (such as statutes and cases) before secondary authority (such as treatises and legal periodicals).

45.3(b) Authored materials

(1) Order authored material alphabetically by the authors' last names. Integrate student authors with other authors.

(2) When citing multiple pieces by one author, order the material in reverse chronological order.

(3) When citing a document written by more than one author, order by the last name of the first-listed author.

(4) When citing material with an organization as author, alphabetize by the first letter of the first word of the organization's name.

(5) If no author's name is available, order alphabetically by the title, but disregard (but do not omit) the initial "The" in the title for purposes of this rule.

45.3(c) Short-form citations

Place a short-form citation in the same place the full citation for that authority would fall.

45.3(d) Subsequent and prior histories

Ignore subsequent and prior histories when ordering cases. Histories merely "tag along" with the cite for the lower-level case (for subsequent history) or higher-level case (for prior history).

Examples (subsequent history is marked in green)

Dravo Corp. v. Liberty Mut. Ins. Co., 164 F.R.D. 70, 75 (D. Neb. 1995); *Ethicon Endo-Surgery v. U.S. Surgical Corp.*, 160 F.R.D. 98, 99 (S.D. Ohio 1995); *Frazier v. S.E. Pa. Transp. Auth.*, 161 F.R.D. 309, 316 (E.D. Pa. 1995), *aff'd*, 91 F.3d 123 (3d Cir. 1996).

U.S. v. Thomas, 377 F.3d 232, 245 (2d Cir. 2004); *Riddle v. Cockrell*, 288 F.3d 713, 721 (5th Cir. 2002), cert. denied, 537 U.S. 953 (2002); Gantt v. Roe, 389 F.3d 908, 916 (9th Cir. 2004).

45.3(e) State materials

Order state materials of the same type in alphabetical order by state. Thus, a statute from Michigan should be cited before a statute from Montana. A case from Alaska should be cited before a case from California.

45.3(f) Federal courts

(1) For purposes of this rule, treat each United States Court of Appeals as a *separate* court and treat each United States District Court as a *separate* court.

(2) For United States Courts of Appeals, order the courts by ordinal (**Rule 4.3**), with "First" coming before "Second," and so on. Place the D.C. Circuit and the Federal Circuit at the end.

(3) For United States District Courts, order courts first in alphabetical order by state and then in alphabetical order by district. Thus, a case decided by the United States District Court for the Northern District of Alabama would come before a case decided by the United States District Court for the Southern District of Alabama, which in turn would come before a case decided by the United States District Court for the District of Delaware.

45.3(g) Cases from the same jurisdiction

For cases from the same jurisdiction, cite higher courts before lower courts. Thus, a case from the United States Supreme Court would be cited before a case from the United States Court of Appeals for the Seventh Circuit. A Seventh Circuit case would be cited before a case from the United States District Court for the Northern District of Illinois. Similarly, a case from the Alabama Supreme Court would be cited before a case from the Alabama Court of Appeals. Analogize to **Rule 45.3(f)(2)** when ordering state intermediate appellate courts divided by district or division (e.g., Florida's First District Court of Appeal precedes Florida's Fourth District Court of Appeal).

45.3(h) Cases from the same court

For authorities from the same court, place the material in reverse chronological order. Thus, a 2006 case from the United States Supreme Court would be cited before a 2004 case from the United States Supreme Court. Similarly, a 2004 case from the Kentucky Court of Appeals would be cited before a 1999 case from the Kentucky Court of Appeals. A case decided on October 2, 2006 comes before a case decided on October 1, 2006. If cases from the same court were decided on the same date, put the case with the highest initial page number first.

45.3(i) Forthcoming works

Place forthcoming works where they would fall if published. For example, place a forthcoming book in the same place it would be cited had it already been published.

45.3(j) Material available on the Internet

If material is available in both hard copy and on the Internet, use the specific sequencing rule for the hard-copy source. If the material is available only on the Internet, use **Rule 45.4(c)**.

45.4 Specific Order of Authorities

Below are nonexhaustive lists of various primary and secondary sources. Cite sources in the order listed. Sources at the top of the list should be cited before sources lower on the list. If the particular source you are looking for is not listed, select the closest source on the list and interpolate your source's position.

45.4(a) Primary and related sources

(1) **Constitutions** (within each category, cite constitutions from the same jurisdiction in reverse chronological order; cite constitutions in force before repealed versions):

- Federal Constitution;
- State constitutions (alphabetically by state);
- Foreign constitutions (alphabetically by country);
- Foundational documents of the United Nations, the League of Nations, and the European Union, in that order.

(2) **Statutes** (within each category, cite statutes in force before older versions):

- Federal statutes (sequentially by title number, then sequentially by section number);
- State statutes (alphabetically by state; within each state, sequentially by title number, then sequentially by section number);
- Foreign statutes (alphabetically by country; within each country, sequentially by title number, then sequentially by section number).

(3) **Rules of evidence and procedure** (within each category, cite rules in force before older versions):

- Federal rules (alphabetically by code name; within a code, sequentially by rule number);
- State rules (alphabetically by state name; within a state, alphabetically by code name; within a code, sequentially by rule number);
- Foreign rules (alphabetically by country name; within a country, alphabetically by code name; within a code, sequentially by rule number);
- International rules (alphabetically by organization name; within an organization, alphabetically by code name; within a code, sequentially by rule number).

(4) **Treaties and international agreements** (reverse chronological order). See **Rule 45.4(a)(1)** regarding foundational documents of the United Nations, the League of Nations, and the European Union.

(5) **Cases** (including agency decisions):

- Federal (also see **Rule 45.3(f)–(h)**):

  — United States Supreme Court;
  — United States Courts of Appeals (in the following order: First Circuit cases, Second Circuit cases, Third Circuit cases, Fourth Circuit cases, Fifth Circuit cases, Sixth Circuit cases, Seventh Circuit cases, Eighth

Circuit cases, Ninth Circuit cases, Tenth Circuit cases, Eleventh Circuit cases, D.C. Circuit cases, and Federal Circuit cases);
— Emergency Court of Appeals;
— Temporary Emergency Court of Appeals;
— Court of Claims;
— Court of Customs and Patent Appeals;
— Bankruptcy Appellate Panels (use the order above for United States Courts of Appeals);
— United States District Courts (order courts first in alphabetical order by state, then alphabetical order by district; for examples, consult **Rule 45(f)(3)**);
— Judicial Panel on Multidistrict Litigation;
— Court of International Trade (formerly Customs Court);
— District Bankruptcy Courts (order courts first in alphabetical order by state, then alphabetical order by district);
— Railroad Reorganization Court;
— Court of Federal Claims (formerly the trial division for the Court of Claims);
— Court of Appeals for the Armed Forces (formerly the Court of Military Appeals);
— Tax Court (fomerly the Board of Tax Appeals);
— administrative agencies (alphabetically by agency, then reverse chronological order);

• State:

— Courts (consult **Rule 45.3(e)**, **(g)**, and **(h)**);
— Agencies (alphabetically by state; within a state, alphabetically by agency name; within an agency, reverse chronological order);

• Foreign:

— Courts (alphabetically by jurisdiction; within a jurisdiction, highest ranking to lowest ranking; within a court, reverse chronological order);
— Agencies (alphabetically by jurisdiction; within a jurisdiction, alphabetically by agency name; within an agency, reverse chronological order);

• International:

— International Court of Justice;
— Permanent Court of International Justice;
— Other international tribunals and arbitral panels (alphabetically by name).

• Any other cases, followed by any other agency decisions.

(6) **Case-related material** (such as briefs, records, and pleadings). Use the order of courts listed above. For materials from the same case, cite the documents in reverse chronological order.

(7) **Administrative and executive material** (within each category, cite in reverse chronological order; cite material in force before repealed material):

- Federal administrative and executive material:

  — Executive orders and presidential proclamations;
  — Treasury regulations
  — Code of Federal Regulations titles (sequentially by title, then sequentially by chapter, part, or section number);
  — Federal Register (reverse chronological order);
  — Other material (alphabetically by source; reverse chronological order within the same source);

- State administrative and executive material (alphabetically by state);
- Foreign administrative and executive material (alphabetically by country);
- Other administrative and executive material.

(8) **Materials from intergovernmental organizations:**

- Resolutions, decisions, and regulations from the United Nations and League of Nations (General Assembly, then Security Council, then other organs in alphabetical order; within an organ, reverse chronological order);
- Resolutions, decisions, and regulations from other organizations (in alphabetical order by name; within an organization, reverse chronological order).

45.4(b) Legislative material

Within each category, cite in reverse chronological order.

(1) Federal legislative material:

- Bills and resolutions;
- Committee hearings (alphabetically by committee or subcommittee name, and then in reverse chronological order);
- Reports, documents, and committee prints;
- Floor debates;
- Any other material.

(2) State legislative material (alphabetically by state):

- Bills and resolutions;
- Committee hearings (alphabetically by committee or subcommittee name, and then in reverse chronological order);

- Reports, documents, and committee prints;
- Floor debates;
- Any other material.

(3) Other legislative material.

45.4(c) Secondary sources

(1) Restatements, model codes, and uniform laws (in alphabetical order by category);

(2) Books and treatises (in alphabetical order by author's last name (follow Rule 45.3(b)));

(3) Material in law reviews, law journals, or other periodicals (such as newspapers) (in alphabetical order by author's last name (follow **Rule 45.3(b)**));

(4) A.L.R. annotations (in alphabetical order by author's last name (follow Rule 45.3(b)));

(5) Legal encyclopedias (alphabetically by encyclopedia name; then alphabetically by topic or title name);

(6) Legal dictionaries (alphabetically by dictionary name);

(7) Working papers (in alphabetical order by author's last name (follow **Rule** 45.3(b)));

(8) Unpublished material (in alphabetical order by author's last name (follow Rule 45.3(b)));

(9) Electronic sources, including Internet sources (in alphabetical order by author's last name (follow **Rule** 45.3(b)); for Internet sources, consult Rule 45.3(j))); and

(10) Any other secondary source (use general ordering rules).

45.4(d) Internal cross-references

Consult **Rule 10** for information on internal cross-references.

(1) *Supra* references (lower numbers before higher numbers);

(2) *Infra* references (lower numbers before higher numbers).

46.0 EXPLANATORY PARENTHETICALS AND RELATED AUTHORITY

46.1 Using Explanatory Parentheticals

An explanatory parenthetical is a device that can help readers understand the significance of a cited authority.

Example

Very few cases actually proceed to trial. Harry T. Edwards, *Alternative Dispute Resolution: Panacea or Anathema?* 99 Harv. L. Rev. 668, 670 (1986) (reporting that about ninety percent of state and federal cases settle or are dismissed before trial); Marc Galanter & Mia Cahill, *"Most Cases Settle": Judicial Promotion and Regulation of Settlements*, 46 Stan. L. Rev. 1339, 1340 (1994) (noting that approximately two-thirds of federal cases settle before trial).

SIDEBAR 46.1

USING EXPLANATORY PARENTHETICALS EFFECTIVELY

Parentheticals that explain the relevance or significance of the cited authority are used frequently in law review articles and other research papers; they are used less frequently in legal memoranda and court documents. Parentheticals can be valuable because they permit writers to compress information into a small space. However, writers should be wary of overusing parentheticals to explain the substance of cited authorities. As Professor Richard K. Neumann states,

> If the material is complicated and important to the issue, explain it in the text. Use an explanatory parenthetical only for information that is simple and not an important part of your discussion or argument. And resist the temptation to use explanatory parentheticals to avoid the hard work of explaining complicated and important authority.

Richard K. Neumann, Jr., *Legal Reasoning and Legal Writing: Structure, Strategy, and Style* § 20.4, 266 (5th ed., Aspen Publishers 2005).

Using a set of substantive parentheticals after a synthesis can be a useful way to show authority without delving into the facts and holdings of too many cases. Below is a fictional example showing how parentheticals can be used with rule synthesis.

Example

A qualifying expense under the Illinois Family Expense Act includes both household goods and services. *E.g. Carter v. Romano*, 662 N.E.2d 883, 884 (Ill. 2000) (doctor and hospital bills); *Armani v. Gucci*, 893 N.E.2d 99, 101 (Ill. App. 1st Dist. 2005) (clothing); *Crocker v. Hines*, 645 N.E.2d 583, 587 (Ill. App. 1st Dist. 1998) (food); *Broyhill v. Lane*, 559 N.E.2d 32, 33 (Ill. App. 1st Dist. 1992) (furniture).

46.2 Placement of Explanatory Parentheticals

46.2(a)

Place the explanatory parenthetical immediately after the source to which it relates.

Examples

Parenthetical relates to F. Supp. case

Bensusan Rest. Corp. v. King, 937 F. Supp. 295 (S.D.N.Y. 1996) (refusing to exercise personal jurisdiction when the defendant limited its advertising to a local audience), *aff'd*, 126 F.3d 25 (2d Cir. 1997).

Parenthetical relates to F.2d case

Parker v. Bd. of Educ., 237 F. Supp. 222, 228–229 (D. Md. 1965), *aff'd*, 348 F.2d 464 (4th Cir. 1965) (agreeing that a teacher violated school regulations by assigning his class to read *Brave New World*).

46.2(b)

Place a parenthetical that must be included as part of a citation before an explanatory parenthetical.

Example

Fed. R. Civ. P. 30(1) (emphasis added) (also indicating that "[a] party may instruct a deponent not to answer . . . when necessary to preserve a privilege").

46.2(c)

Follow the examples below if an explanatory parenthetical itself requires a parenthetical.

Examples

Byron C. Keeling, *A Prescription for Healing the Crisis in Professionalism: Shifting the Burden of Enforcing Professional Standards of Conduct*, 25 Tex. Tech L. Rev. 31, 38 (1993) (warning that "[u]ntil the profession takes active steps to eliminate [discovery] abuses, the public will continue to hold the legal profession in the same moral contempt that it reserves for used car salesmen" (footnote omitted)).

Inker, *supra* n. 350, at 27 (explaining that "[d]omestic relations litigants may be particularly vulnerable because *a spouse* or former spouse can reveal confidential information that will embarrass or otherwise harm the other spouse" (emphasis added)).

46.3   Formatting Explanatory Parentheticals

Below are several ways to format an explanatory parenthetical. Insert one space before the opening parenthesis of the explanatory parenthetical. If the parenthetical does not contain a complete sentence, do not place final punctuation, such as a period, inside the parenthetical.

Examples

In re Kerr, 548 P.2d 297, 302 (Wash. 1976) (en banc) (finding that an attorney who knowingly participates in subornation of perjury should be disbarred).

Lloyd v. Cessna Aircraft Co., 430 F. Supp. 25, 26 (E.D. Tenn. 1976) (two days' notice unreasonable).

Clark v. U.S., 289 U.S. 1, 15 (1933) ("The privilege takes flight if the relation is abused.").

46.4   Related Authority and Commentary

It sometimes is helpful to cite one authority that in some way relates to another cited authority or provides commentary about the cited authority. In this situation, include the related authority in a parenthetical. Ways to introduce related authority include "reprinted in," "quoted in," "quoting," "cited in," "citing," "construed in," "construing," "reviewed by," "reviewing," "questioned in," "questioning," and "cited with approval in." This list is non-exhaustive; you may use other descriptive words and phrases.

Examples

Report of the White House Task Force on Antitrust Policy (1968) (reprinted in 1 J. Reprints for Antitrust L. & Econ. 631, 637–638 (1969)).

Martinez v. Dretke, 404 F.3d 878, 884 (5th Cir. 2005) (citing 28 U.S.C. § 2254(d)(1)).

Kan. Stat. Ann. § 21-3502(1)(d) (1969) (quoted in *State v. Chaney*, 5 P.3d 492, 495 (Kan. 2000)).

PART

6

QUOTATIONS

47.0 QUOTATIONS

47.1 Using Quotations

Use quotations sparingly and carefully. Use them for statutory language, for other language that must be presented precisely, and for particularly famous, unique, or vivid language. Overquoting may bore readers or may lead them to believe the writer did not understand the material well enough to paraphrase it.

47.2 Accuracy

It is important to present quotations accurately. When presenting a direct quotation, reproduce the wording exactly. Moreover, unless following **Rules 48** and **49** concerning alterations and omissions, do not change spelling, typeface, capitalization, citations, or punctuation within the quoted material.

47.3 Relation to Text

Quotations may be incorporated into the paper in two ways. First, short quotations may be run into the text and designated with double quotation marks (" "). Consult **Rule 47.4** for short quotations. Second, longer quotations, or quotations of verse or poetry, may be set off with a block indent. Consult **Rule 47.5** for longer quotations.

47.4 Short Quotations

47.4(a) General rule

If a quotation is fewer than fifty words or runs fewer than four lines of typed text and is not an epigraph or a quotation of verse or poetry, enclose the quotation in double quotation marks (" "), but do not otherwise set the quotation off from the text.

47.4(b) Citation after quotation: Documents without footnotes and material within footnotes

(1) Generally place the citation after the sentence that contains the quoted material.

Examples

The controlling statute provides that "the trier of facts may find such intention upon consideration of the words, conduct, demeanor, motive, and all other circumstances connected with the act for which the accused is prosecuted." Ga. Code Ann. § 16-2-6 (2004).

Single source quoted within a footnote

[31]Ga. Code Ann. § 16-2-6 (2004). The controlling statute provides that "the trier of facts may find such intention upon consideration of the words, conduct, demeanor, motive, and all other circumstances connected with the act for which the accused is prosecuted." *Id.*

(2) If the sentence contains material from more than one source or from different parts of a single source, use citation clauses as explained in **Rule 43.1(b).**

Example

From 1973 to 1974, the federal judiciary went from requiring merely "a significant correlation to race," *U.S. v. U.S. Steel Corp.*, 371 F. Supp. 1045, 1054 (N.D. Ala. 1973), to "a significant correlation to race and sex," *Wells v. Frontier Airlines*, 381 F. Supp. 818, 821 (N.D. Tex. 1974).

(3) If the source can be identified from material within the sentence, a duplicative citation is not needed.

Example

Under Federal Rule of Civil Procedure 32(d)(3)(B), which concerns depositions, objections must be raised during the deposition—or else be waived—if they concern errors or irregularities "in the manner of taking the deposition," the form of the questions or answers, "the oath or affirmation," or the parties' conduct.

47.4(c) Note reference number after citation: Documents with footnotes

Within the main text, place the note reference number (**Rule 43.1(e)**) immediately after the closing quotation mark. You need not include multiple footnote reference numbers in a single sentence if each quoted phrase in the sentence comes from the same source and pinpoint reference.

Example

The Court concluded that the attorney's deposition conduct was abusive because he "improperly directed the witness not to answer certain questions,"[134] raised improper objections that suggested answers to the deposition, and was "extraordinarily rude, uncivil, and vulgar."[135]

---

[134]*Paramount Commun., Inc. v. QVC Network, Inc.*, 637 A.2d 34, 53 (Del. 1994).

[135]*Id.* at 56.

47.4(d) Punctuation

(1) Place periods and commas inside quotation marks, regardless of whether they are part of the original quotation. An exception to this rule concerns titles of law journal articles that end with a quotation mark (**Rule 23.1(b)(4)**).

Examples

Period

The trial court gave the following instruction on involuntary intoxication: "[I]f because of the influence of alcohol . . . one's mind becomes so impaired as to render him incapable of forming an intent to do the act charged, . . . he would not be criminally responsible for that act." *Blankenship v. Ga.*, 277 S.E.2d 505, 508 (Ga. 1981).

Comma

The controlling statute defines specific intent as "a state of mind which is thought culpable," such as premeditation for first-degree murder. Ga. Code Ann. § 16-2-1 (1996).

(2) Place all other punctuation, such as semicolons and question marks, outside the quotation marks **unless they are part of the original quotation.**

Examples

Semicolon (not part of the quoted material)

The Court held that "an adult child may seek retroactive support up until age [twenty-three]"; "noncustodial parents . . . should not be able to shirk their responsibility as parents simply because the child may not have contacted or found the parent during the child's younger years." *Carnes v. Kemp*, 821 N.E.2d 180, 184 (Ohio 2004).

Question mark (part of the quoted material)

As Judge Posner asked, "What difference does it make whether one thinks that judges found the current doctrines of constitutional law in the Constitution or put them there?" Richard A. Posner, *Overcoming Law* 7 (Harv. U. Press 1995).

(3) Apply these same rules to quotations within quotations, which are discussed in **Rule 47.7.**

Example

"Because the judge was anxious to end the day's proceedings, he was not going to stop the proceedings, no matter how many times counsel asked, 'Judge, might we take a short break?'.'"

47.5 Longer Quotations

47.5(a) General rule

If a quotation contains at least fifty words or exceeds four lines of typed text, or if the material quoted is a verse or poem, present the quotation as a block of type that is single-spaced and indented by one tab on both the right and the left. Do not use quotation marks at the beginning or end of the block quotation. Separate the block quotation from the text below and above with a blank line.

Example

The Constitution provides

> In all criminal prosecutions, the accused shall enjoy the right to a speedy and public trial, by an impartial jury of the State and district wherein the crime shall have been committed, which district shall have been previously ascertained by law, and to be informed of the nature and cause of the accusation; to be confronted with the witnesses against him; to have compulsory process for obtaining witnesses in his favor, and to have the Assistance of Counsel for his defence.

U.S. Const. amend. VI. Many defendants invoke this amendment to obtain counsel.

47.5(b) Quotations within parentheticals

Do not block indent a quotation contained within a parenthetical. For additional information on parentheticals, consult **Rule 46.**

Example

[76]Fla. Stat. § 776.08 (2002) (defining forcible felony as "treason; murder; manslaughter; sexual battery; carjacking; home-invasion robbery; robbery; burglary; arson; kidnapping; aggravated assault; aggravated battery; aggravated stalking; aircraft piracy; unlawful throwing, placing, or discharging of a destructive device or bomb; and any other felony which involves the use or threat of physical force or violence against any individual").

47.5(c) Citations after quotations: Documents without footnotes and material within footnotes

Do not place the citation within the block quotation. Instead, place the citation at the left margin on the next line of text. If you do not want to start a new paragraph after the citation, simply continue the text on the same line as the citation.

Example

---

[8]*Id.* As one commentator observed,

> [T]he law is inherently double-edged: any rule imposed to limit zealous advocacy . . . may be used by an adversary as an offensive weapon. . . . The rules of discovery, for example, initiated to enable one side to find out crucial facts from the other, are used nowadays to delay trial or impose added expense on the other side . . . .

David Luban, *The Adversary System Excuse*, in *The Good Lawyer* 83, 88 (David Luban ed., Rowman & Allanheld 1983).

47.5(d) Placement of note reference number after citation: Documents with footnotes

Place the note reference number at the end of the block quotation.

Example:

As one commentator observed,

> [T]he law is inherently double-edged: any rule imposed to limit zealous advocacy . . . may be used by an adversary as an offensive weapon. . . . The rules of discovery, for example, initiated to enable one side to find out crucial facts from the other, are used nowadays to delay trial or impose added expense on the other side . . . .[13]

---

[13]David Luban, *The Adversary System Excuse*, in *The Good Lawyer* 83, 88 (David Luban ed., Rowman & Allanheld 1983).

47.5(e) Paragraphing within block quotes

(1) Retain the paragraphing from the original source.

(2) If a quotation comes from the beginning of a paragraph, indent a second tab on the left side to reflect the beginning of the paragraph. See the example in **Rule 47.5(a)**.

(3) If the quotation comes from the middle of a paragraph, indent one tab on both the right and the left sides for the block indent, but do not indent further. See the example in **Rule 47.5(c)**.

(4) If a quotation spans multiple paragraphs, reflect the beginning of each new paragraph with a second tab on the left side.

47.6 Epigraphs

47.6(a) Definition

An epigraph is a quotation set at the beginning of a work or chapter.

47.6(b) Format

(1) Format the epigraph as a block quote under **Rule 47.5(a)**.

(2) Do not place an epigraph in quotation marks, regardless of length.

(3) An epigraph may be presented either in ordinary type or in italics.

(4) For documents with footnotes, place the note reference number after the epigraph, and include the complete citation in the corresponding footnote.

Example

It is better to risk saving a guilty man than to condemn an innocent one.[1]

_____

[1]Voltaire, *Zadig* 6 (Viking Press 1978) (1747).

(5) For documents without footnotes, place the completed citation underneath the quotation, flush right. Skip one line between the epigraph and the citation. Single-space the citation if it does not fit on a single line. It is permissible to place an em dash in front of the citation.

Example

It is better to risk saving a guilty man than to condemn an innocent one.

—Voltaire, *Zadig* 6 (Viking Press 1978) (1747).

47.7 Quotations within Quotations

47.7(a) Quotations within short quotations

Designate a quotation within a short quotation with single quotation marks. Follow punctuation conventions in **Rule 47.4(d)**.

Example

The court remarked that under Third Circuit law, a trademark infringement claim arose " 'where the passing off occurs.' " *Zippo Mfg., Inc. v. Zippo Dot Com, Inc.*, 952 F. Supp. 1119, 1127 (W.D. Pa. 1997) (quoting *Cottman Transmission Sys., Inc. v. Martino*, 36 F.3d 291, 294 (3d Cir. 1976)).

47.7(b) Quotations within block quotations

Enclose quoted material within a block quotation in double quotation marks. Enclose quotations within these quotations in single quotation marks. Follow punctuation conventions in **Rule 47.4(d).**

Example

> Unless a proper limitation upon custodial interrogation is achieved—such as these decisions will advance—there can be no assurance that practices of this nature will be eradicated in the foreseeable future. The conclusion of the Wickersham Commission Report, made over 30 years ago, is still pertinent: "To the contention that the third degree is necessary to get the facts, the reporters aptly reply in the language of the present Lord Chancellor of England (Lord Sankey): 'It is not admissible to do a great right by doing a little wrong. . . . It is not sufficient to do justice by obtaining a proper result by irregular or improper means.' "

Miranda v. Ariz., 384 U.S. 436, 447–448 (1966) (quoting 4 Natl. Comm. L. Observance & Enforcement, *Report on Lawlessness in Law Enforcement* 5 (1931)).

47.7(c) Citations for internal quotations

(1) If the source of the internal quotation is cited within the quotation, retain the citation within the quotation, and do not repeat it within the citation for the main quotation.

Example

> Although the Court rejected the position cited in *Hildwin*, it characterized the nature of capital sentencing by quoting *Poland v. Arizona,* 476 U.S. 147, 156 (1986). In that case, the Court described statutory specifications or aggravating circumstances in capital sentences as "standards to guide the . . . choice between the alternative verdicts of death and life imprisonment." *Id.* The Court thus characterized the finding of aggravating facts as a choice between a greater and lesser penalty, not a process of raising the ceiling of the sentencing range available.

Jones v. U.S., 526 U.S. 227, 251 (1999).

(2) If the source of the internal quotation is not cited within the quoted material, include the citation for the internal quotation in a parenthetical that follows the citation for the main quotation.

Example

The Court then reversed, stating: "In this case, . . . petitioner's right to counsel, a 'specific federal right,' is being denied anew." *Burgett v. Tex.,* 389 U.S. 109, 116 (1967) (quoting *Spencer v. Tex.,* 385 U.S. 554, 565 (1966)).

48.0   ALTERING QUOTED MATERIAL

48.1   Altering the Case of a Letter

Within a quotation, when changing a letter from uppercase to lowercase, or vice versa, enclose the altered letter in brackets.

Examples

Original
"The court held . . . ."

Alteration
Moreover, "[t]he court held . . . ."

Original
"In the latter event, the court shall permit the parties or their attorneys to supplement the examination by such further inquiry as it deems appropriate . . . ."

Alteration
"[T]he court shall permit the parties or their attorneys to supplement the examination by such further inquiry as it deems appropriate . . . ."

48.2   Adding, Changing, or Deleting One or More Letters

When adding, changing, or deleting one or more letters from a quoted word, enclose the added, changed, or deleted material in brackets. Alternatively, replace the entire word, as permitted in **Rule 48.4.** Indicate the omission of one or more letters with empty brackets.

Examples

Original	Alteration
state	state[d], stat[ing], state[s] **or** [stated], [stating], [states]
held	h[o]ld **or** [hold]
the employee was	the employee[s were] **or** the [employees were]
the courts indicated	the court[ ] indicated **or** the [court] indicated

48.3   Adding a Footnote within a Block Quotation

As explained in **Rule 47.5(d),** insert a note reference number *at the end* of a block quotation. Although unusual, it is on occasion necessary or desirable to add a note reference number *within* a block quotation. When this situation occurs, enclose the superscripted note reference number in brackets.

Example

> We recognize, as does *Clayton*, that absent a constitutional basis for a challenge,[3] the . . . standing rule, applied to cases of this type,[4] creates a rare situation [where] there is a wrong without a remedy. That is because even though

the citizen taxpayer, who is also a voter, may "throw the rascals out" at the next election, even if such action exacts a measure of retribution it will not restore the looted treasury nor undo the illegally increased tax obligation.[5]

48.4   Substituting or Adding Words

When substituting or adding words to a quotation (often called "interpolation"), enclose those words in brackets. You may add material to clarify an ambiguity, to provide a missing word, or to provide necessary explanations or translations.

Examples

Original
"The court ruled for Mr. Jamison."

"He found it there."

Alteration
"The court ruled for [the defendant]."

"He found it there [by the door]."

48.5   Altering Typeface

48.5(a)

When altering the typeface of quoted material, such as by adding or deleting italics, describe the alteration in a parenthetical that follows the citation.

Examples

Original

We think a "permanent physical occupation" has occurred, for purposes of this rule, where individuals are given a permanent and continuous right to pass to and fro, so that the real property may continuously be traversed, even though no particular individual is permitted to station himself permanently upon the premises.

Nollan v. Cal. Coastal Commn., 483 U.S. 825, 832 (1987).

Alteration

We think a "permanent physical occupation" has occurred, for purposes of this rule, where individuals are given a *permanent and continuous right to pass to and fro*, so that the real property may continuously be traversed, even though no particular individual is permitted to station himself permanently upon the premises.

Nollan v. Cal. Coastal Commn., 483 U.S. 825, 832 (1987) (emphasis added).

48.5(b)

When quoted material contains several instances of emphasis, some of which were included in the original and some of which were added, in a parenthetical at the end of the citation, describe which alterations you made.

Example

In *Shaw v. Reno*,[133] Justice O'Connor, writing for the majority, described the relationship between race and redistricting:

> [R]edistricting differs from other kinds of state decisionmaking in that the legislature always is aware of race when it draws district lines, just as it is *aware* of age, economic status, religious and political persuasion, and a variety of other demographic factors. That sort of race consciousness does not lead *inevitably* to impermissible race discrimination.[134]

---

[133]509 U.S. 630 (1993).

[134]*Id.* at 646 (first emphasis in original, second emphasis added).

48.6 Mistakes within Original Quoted Material

Original material that you desire to quote may contain mistakes, such as spelling, typographical, or grammatical errors. You may retain the mistake, correct the mistake, or indicate that the mistake appeared in the original quoted material. If you wish to correct the mistake, enclose the altered material in brackets as described in **Rule 48.2**. If you wish to retain the mistake but indicate that the mistake appeared in the original (and is thus not attributable to you), use the term "[sic]." Do not clutter quotations from obviously archaic or nonstandard writing with [sic] or alterations.

Examples

Alternative 1: Correcting the mistake

Original	**Alteration**
"The court dismissed there motion."	"The court dismissed [their] motion."
"The court hold that"	"The court h[e]ld that" **or** "The court[s] hold that"

Alternative 2: Using [sic]

Original	**Alteration**
"The court dismissed there motion."	"The court dismissed there [sic] motion."
"The court hold that"	"The court hold [sic] that"

49.0 OMISSIONS WITHIN QUOTED MATERIAL

49.1 General Considerations When Omitting Material within a Quotation

A commonly used writing handbook provides sound advice about omitting material from a quoted passage: "Whenever you wish to omit a word, a phrase, a sentence, or more from a quoted passage, you should be guided by two principles: fairness to the author quoted and the grammatical integrity of your writing." Joseph Gibaldi, *MLA Handbook for Writers of Research Papers* § 3.7.5, 114 (6th ed., Modern Lang. Assn. Am. 2003).

49.2 Indicating Omissions

49.2(a)

Use an ellipsis to indicate the omission of one or more words. An ellipsis consists of three points, or periods, with one space between each (.▲.▲.). (The symbol ▲ represents a space.)

49.2(b)

Typically insert one space before the ellipsis and one space after the ellipsis.

49.2(c)

When quotation marks follow an ellipsis, do not include a space between the last ellipsis point and the closing quotation mark (▲.▲.▲."). (The symbol ▲ represents a space.)

49.3 When to Use an Ellipsis

49.3(a)

Except as noted in **Rule 49.3(b)**, use an ellipsis to designate the omission of one or more words.

49.3(b)

Do not use an ellipsis to denote an omission:

(1) before or after a fragment that is incorporated into the sentence structure;

Example

Correct omission

The Supreme Court held that while "students are entitled to freedom of expression of their views," they may not engage in a type of expression that materially and substantially interferes with schoolwork or discipline.

Incorrect omission

The Supreme Court held that while ". . . students are entitled to freedom of expression of their views, . . ." they may not engage in a type of expression that materially and substantially interferes with schoolwork or discipline.

(2) at the beginning of a quotation (instead, include a bracketed capital letter per **Rules 48.1** and **49.3(c)**);

Example

Complete quotation

"But, in our system, undifferentiated fear or apprehension of disturbance is not enough to overcome the right to freedom of expression." *Tinker v. Des Moines Indep. Community Sch. Dist.*, 393 U.S. 503, 508 (1969).

Correct omission

"[I]n our system, undifferentiated fear or apprehension of disturbance is not enough to overcome the right to freedom of expression." *Tinker v. Des Moines Indep. Community Sch. Dist.*, 393 U.S. 503, 508 (1969).

Incorrect omission

". . . [I]n our system, undifferentiated fear or apprehension of disturbance is not enough to overcome the right to freedom of expression." *Tinker v. Des Moines Indep. Community Sch. Dist.*, 393 U.S. 503, 508 (1969).

(3) at the end of a block quotation that concludes with a complete sentence; or

(4) of a footnote or citation (see **Rule 49.3(d)**).

Example

Complete quotation

"Even electronic surveillance substantially contemporaneous with an individual's arrest could hardly be deemed an 'incident' of that arrest.[20]" *Katz v. U.S.*, 389 U.S. 347, 357 (1967).

Correct omission

"Even electronic surveillance substantially contemporaneous with an individual's arrest could hardly be deemed an 'incident' of that arrest." *Katz v. U.S.*, 389 U.S. 347, 357 (1967) (footnote omitted).

Incorrect omission

"Even electronic surveillance substantially contemporaneous with an individual's arrest could hardly be deemed an 'incident' of that arrest . . . ." *Katz v. U.S.*, 389 U.S. 347, 357 (1967) (footnote omitted).

49.3(c) Quotation as full sentence

When a quotation is used as a full sentence in the text and language beginning the original sentence is omitted, capitalize the first letter in the quotation, and place the altered letter in brackets, as required by **Rule 48.1**.

Example

"[I]n our system, undifferentiated fear or apprehension of disturbance is not enough to overcome the right to freedom of expression." *Tinker v. Des Moines Indep. Community Sch. Dist.*, 393 U.S. 503, 508 (1969).

49.3(d) Omitting footnotes and citations

When omitting a footnote or citation from a quoted passage, indicate the omission in a parenthetical after the citation.

Example

"Even electronic surveillance substantially contemporaneous with an individual's arrest could hardly be deemed an 'incident' of that arrest." *Katz v. U.S.*, 389 U.S. 347, 357 (1967) (footnote omitted).

49.4   How to Use Ellipses

49.4(a) Omission within the quoted passage

When you omit material from the middle of a quoted passage, insert an ellipsis to indicate the omission. Insert one space on either side of the ellipsis.

Example (the symbol ▲ denotes a space)

"The Government concedes▲.▲.▲.▲that appellees' flag burning constituted expressive conduct."

49.4(b) When the end of the quoted sentence is omitted

When the end of a quoted sentence is omitted, insert an ellipsis and the final punctuation. In other words, after the last quoted word, insert a space, then four dots, each with a space in between, then the closing quotation mark, then two spaces before the next sentence.

Example

Original sentence:	We hold today that the Sixth Amendment's right of an accused to confront the witnesses against him is likewise a fundamental right and is made obligatory on the States by the Fourteenth Amendment.
Omissions:	"[T]he Sixth Amendment's right of an accused to confront the witnesses against him is▲.▲.▲.▲a fundamental right▲.▲.▲.▲."▲▲

49.4(c) Matter after a quoted sentence when the quotation continues

When the last word ends the quoted sentence, do not use an ellipsis unless the quotation continues. If the quotation does continue, insert the ellipsis, then the final punctuation. In other words, after the last word, do not include a space, but instead include four dots, each with a space in between, and then insert two spaces before the next sentence. In the example, the ellipsis reflects that one complete sentence has been omitted.

Example (the symbol ▲ denotes a space):

"Certainly the presence of reporters inside the home was not related to the objectives of the authorized intrusion.▲.▲.▲.▲▲The reporters therefore were not present for any reason related to the justification for police entry into the home—the apprehension of Dominic Wilson." *Wilson v. Layne,* 526 U.S. 603, 611 (1999).

49.4(d) Omitting one or more paragraphs

When you omit one or more paragraphs from a quoted passage, indicate that omission by placing the ellipsis on its own line. Center the ellipsis and place five to seven spaces between each ellipsis point.

Example (the symbol ▲ denotes a space):

The Congress shall have Power To lay and collect Taxes, Duties, Imposts and Excises, to pay the Debts and provide for the common Defence and general Welfare of the United States; but all Duties, Imposts and Excises shall be uniform throughout the United States;

To borrow Money on the credit of the United States;

To regulate Commerce with foreign Nations, and among the several States, and with the Indian Tribes;

.▲▲▲▲▲.▲▲▲▲▲.

To make all Laws which shall be necessary and proper for carrying into Execution the foregoing Powers, and all other Powers vested by this Constitution in the Government of the United States, or in any Department or Officer thereof.

U.S. Const. art. I, § 8.

P A R T

APPENDICES

This appendix contains citation information about reporters, statutory compilations, session laws, and administrative compilations and registers for state, territorial, and federal jurisdictions. State information is presented first. The states are arranged in alphabetical order, followed by territorial and federal materials. Information about the Navajo Nation is also included.

Under the "Court System and Reporters" heading, courts within the jurisdiction that have printed reporters are included in hierarchical order. Beside the name of the court, in parentheses, is the proper abbreviation for that court. Consult **Chart 12.7** at http://www.alwd .org for additional information on state intermediate appellate courts. "___" in a court abbreviation means that you must fill in the court division (number, ordinal, letter, etc.). Under the court's name, the most commonly used reporters are listed. This appendix does not contain older, named reporters. If you need that information, consult the most recent edition of Morris L. Cohen et al., *How to Find the Law.* For each reporter, you can determine its proper abbreviation, the dates the reporter has been published, whether it has series and when each series begins and ends, and whether the reporter is official or unofficial.

The "Statutory Compilation" section lists each current code that contains the jurisdiction's statutes. The format of the citation is listed. Moreover, the official code is designated with a star (★). Information printed in green is information that will vary depending on the section you cite.

If the jurisdiction prints its session laws, the abbreviation for the source and the citation format are included.

If the jurisdiction prints an administrative compilation or an administrative register, the abbreviations and citation formats for those sources are listed.

If the jurisdiction has local citation rules or neutral citation rules that must be used when submitting a document to that court, this appendix contains cross-references to **Appendix 2**, which reprints those local rules.

States

Alabama

Court system and reporters:

Alabama Supreme Court (Ala.)

Reporter	Abbreviation	Dates	Status
Alabama Reports	Ala.	1840–1976	Official

Southern Reporter	So.	1887–1941	Unofficial
Second Series	So. 2d	1941–present	Official since 1976
Alabama Reporter (West offprint)	So. 2d	1976–present	Official

**Alabama Court of Civil Appeals (Ala. Civ. App.) and
Alabama Court of Criminal Appeals (Ala. Crim. App.)**

Note: Before 1969, the appellate court was the Alabama Court of Appeals (Ala. App.).

Reporter	Abbreviation	Dates	Status
Alabama Appellate Court Reports	Ala. App.	1910–1976	Official
Southern Reporter	So.	1911–1941	Unofficial
Second Series	So. 2d	1941–present	Official since 1976
Alabama Reporter (West offprint)	So. 2d	1976–present	Official

Statutory compilation:

★Alabama Code	Ala. Code § **section number** (West **Year**)
Michie's Alabama Code	Ala. Code § **section number** (Lexis **Year**)

Session laws:

Acts of Alabama	**Year** Ala. Acts **act number**

Administrative compilation:

Alabama Administrative Code	Ala. Admin. Code r. **rule number** (**Year**)

Administrative register:

Alabama Administrative Monthly	**Volume number** Ala. Admin. Mthly. **page number** (**Month Day, Year**)

Local citation rules?   Yes. See **Appendix 2.**   **Neutral citation rules?**   No.

Alaska

Court system and reporters:

Alaska Supreme Court (Alaska)

Reporter	Abbreviation	Dates	Status
Pacific Reporter			
Second Series	P.2d	1960–2000	Official
Third Series	P.3d	2000–present	Official
Alaska Reporter (West offprint)	P.2d, P.3d	1960–present	Official

Alaska Court of Appeals (Alaska App.)

Reporter	Abbreviation	Dates	Status
Pacific Reporter			
Second Series	P.2d	1980–2000	Official
Third Series	P.3d	2000–present	Official
Alaska Reporter (West offprint)	P.2d, P.3d	1980–present	Official

Statutory compilation:

★Alaska Statutes	Alaska Stat. § **section number** (Lexis **Year**)

Session laws:
Session Laws of Alaska   **Year** Alaska Sess. Laws ch. **chapter number**

Administrative compilation:
Alaska Administrative Code   Alaska Admin. Code tit. **title number,** § **section number** (**Year**)

Administrative register:
Alaska Administrative Journal   **Issue number** Alaska Admin. J. **page number** (**Month Day, Year**)

Local citation rules? No.   **Neutral citation rules?** No.

Arizona

Court system and reporters:

Arizona Supreme Court (Ariz.)

Reporter	Abbreviation	Dates	Status
Arizona Reports	Ariz.	1866–present	Official
Pacific Reporter	P.	1883–1931	Unofficial
Second Series	P.2d	1931–2000	Unofficial
Third Series	P.3d	2000–present	Unofficial

Arizona Court of Appeals (Ariz. App. ___ Div.)

Reporter	Abbreviation	Dates	Status
Arizona Reports	Ariz.	1976–present	Official
Arizona Appeals Reports	Ariz. App.	1965–1976	Official
Pacific Reporter			
Second Series	P.2d	1965–2000	Unofficial
Third Series	P.3d	2000–present	Unofficial

Statutory compilations:
★Arizona Revised Statutes Annotated   Ariz. Rev. Stat. Ann. § **section number** (West **Year**)

Arizona Revised Statutes   Ariz. Rev. Stat. § **section number** (Lexis **Year**)

Session laws:
Session Laws of Arizona   Ariz. Sess. Laws ch. **chapter number** (**Year**) or

                                           Ariz. Sess. Laws § **section number** (**Year**)

Administrative compilation:
Arizona Administrative Code   Ariz. Admin. Code § **section number** (**Year**)

Administrative register:

Arizona Administrative Register	**Volume number** Ariz. Admin. Register **page number** (**Month Day, Year**)

Local citation rules? Yes. See **Appendix 2.**   **Neutral citation rules?** No.

Arkansas

Court system and reporters:

Arkansas Supreme Court (Ark.)

Reporter	Abbreviation	Dates	Status
Arkansas Reports	Ark.	1837–present	Official
South Western Reporter	S.W.	1886–1928	Unofficial
Second Series	S.W.2d	1928–1999	Unofficial
Third Series	S.W.3d	1999–present	Unofficial
Arkansas Cases (West offprint)	S.W., S.W.2d, S.W.3d	1886–present	Unofficial

Arkansas Court of Appeals (Ark. App. Div. ___)

Reporter	Abbreviation	Dates	Status
Arkansas Appellate Reports	Ark. App. (bound with Ark.)	1981–present	Official
Arkansas Reports	Ark.	1979–1981	Official
South Western Reporter			
Second Series	S.W.2d	1979–1999	Unofficial
Third Series	S.W.3d	1999–present	Unofficial
Arkansas Cases (West offprint)	S.W.2d, S.W.3d	1979–present	Unofficial

Statutory compilation:

★Arkansas Code Annotated	Ark. Code Ann. § **section number** (Lexis **Year**)
West's Arkansas Code Annotated	Ark. Code Ann. § **section number** (West **Year**)

Session laws:

Arkansas Acts	**Year** Ark. Acts **law number**

Administrative compilation:

Code of Arkansas Rules	Code Ark. R. **rule number** (Weil **Year**)

Administrative register:

Arkansas Register	**Volume number** Ark. Register **page number** (**Month Year**)

Local citation rules? Yes. See **Appendix 2.**   **Neutral citation rules?** No.

California

Court system and reporters:

California Supreme Court (Cal.)

Reporter	Abbreviation	Dates	Status
California Reports	Cal.	1850–1934	Official

Second Series	Cal. 2d	1934–1969	Official
Third Series	Cal. 3d	1969–1991	Official
Fourth Series	Cal. 4th	1991–present	Official
Pacific Reporter	P.	1883–1931	Unofficial
Second Series	P.2d	1931–2000	Unofficial
Third Series	P.3d	2000–present	Unofficial
West's California Reporter	Cal. Rptr.	1960–1991	Unofficial
Second Series	Cal. Rptr. 2d	1991–2004	Unofficial
Third Series	Cal. Rptr. 3d	2004–present	Unofficial

California Court of Appeal (Cal. App. ___ Dist.)

Note: Before 1966, this court was the California District Court of Appeal (Cal. Dist. App.).

Reporter	Abbreviation	Dates	Status
California Appellate Reports	Cal. App.	1905–1934	Official
Second Series	Cal. App. 2d	1934–1969	Official
Third Series	Cal. App. 3d	1969–1991	Official
Fourth Series	Cal. App. 4th	1991–present	Official
Pacific Reporter	P.	1905–1931	Unofficial
Second Series	P.2d	1931–1959	Unofficial
West's California Reporter	Cal. Rptr.	1960–1991	Unofficial
Second Series	Cal. Rptr. 2d	1991–2004	Unofficial
Third Series	Cal. Rptr. 3d	2004–present	Unofficial

California Superior Court, Appellate Department (Cal. Super. App. Dept.)

Reporter	Abbreviation	Dates	Status
California Appellate Reports Supplement	Cal. App. Supp.	1929–1934	Official
Second Series	Cal. App. Supp. 2d	1934–1969	Official
Third Series	Cal. App. Supp. 3d *(bound with Cal. App. 3d)*	1969–1991	Official
Fourth Series	Cal. App. Supp. 4th *(bound with Cal. App. 4th)*	1991–present	Official
Pacific Reporter	P.	1929–1931	Unofficial
Second Series	P.2d	1931–1959	Unofficial
West's California Reporter	Cal. Rptr.	1960–1991	Unofficial
Second Series	Cal. Rptr. 2d	1991–2004	Unofficial
Third Series	Cal. Rptr. 3d	2004–present	Unofficial

Statutory compilations:

★West's Annotated California Codes

Cal. **Subject abbreviation** Code Ann. § **section number** (West **Year**)

Note: Consult **Appendix 2** for subject abbreviations.

★Deering's Annotated California Code

Cal. **Subject abbreviation** Code Ann. § **section number** (Lexis **Year**)
Note: Consult **Appendix 2** for subject abbreviations.

Session laws:
Statutes of California

Year Cal. Stat. **law number**

Administrative compilation:
Barclay's Official California Code of Regulations

Cal. Code Regs. tit. **title number**, § **section number** (**Year**)

Administrative register:
California Regulatory Notice Register

Register number Cal. Reg. Notice Register § **section number** (**Month Day, Year**)

Local citation rules? Yes. See **Appendix 2.**   **Neutral citation rules?** No.

Colorado

Court system and reporters:

Colorado Supreme Court (Colo.)

Reporter	Abbreviation	Dates	Status
Colorado Reports	Colo.	1864–1980	Official
Pacific Reporter	P.	1883–1931	Unofficial
Second Series	P.2d	1931–2000	Official since 1980
Third Series	P.3d	2000–present	Official
Colorado Reporter (West offprint)	P., P.2d, P.3d	1883–present	Official since 1980

Colorado Court of Appeals (Colo. App.)

Reporter	Abbreviation	Dates	Status
Colorado Court of Appeals Reports	Colo. App.	1891–1905	Official
		1912–1915	Official
		1970–1980	Official
Pacific Reporter	P.	1891–1905	Unofficial
		1912–1915	Unofficial
Second Series	P.2d	1970–2000	Official since 1980
Third Series	P.3d	2000–present	Official
Colorado Reporter (West offprint)	P., P.2d, P.3d	1891–present	Official since 1980

Statutory compilations:
★Colorado Revised Statutes

Colo. Rev. Stat. § **section number** (Lexis **Year**)

West's Colorado Revised Statutes Annotated

Colo. Rev. Stat. Ann. § **section number** (West **Year**)

Session laws:
Session Laws of Colorado

Year Colo. Sess. Laws **law number**

Administrative compilation:
Code of Colorado Regulations

Volume number Colo. Code Regs. **regulation number** (**Year**)

Administrative register:

Colorado Register   Issue number Colo. Register page number (Weil Month Year)

Local citation rules?   Not officially; however, see **Appendix 2** for local practice guides. Neutral citation rules?   Yes. See **Appendix 2.**

Connecticut

Court system and reporters:

Connecticut Supreme Court (Conn.)

Note: Before 1966, this court was the Connecticut Supreme Court of Errors (Conn.).

Reporter	Abbreviation	Dates	Status
Connecticut Reports	Conn.	1814–present	Official
Atlantic Reporter	A.	1885–1938	Unofficial
Second Series	A.2d	1938–present	Unofficial
Connecticut Reporter (West offprint)	A. or A.2d	1885–present	Unofficial

Connecticut Appellate Court (Conn. App.)

Reporter	Abbreviation	Dates	Status
Connecticut Appellate Reports	Conn. App.	1983–present	Official
Atlantic Reporter, Second Series	A.2d	1983–present	Unofficial
Connecticut Reporter (West offprint)	A.2d	1983–present	Unofficial

Connecticut Superior Court (Conn. Super.)

Reporter	Abbreviation	Dates	Status
Connecticut Supplement	Conn. Supp.	1935–present	Official
Atlantic Reporter, Second Series	A.2d	1954–present	Unofficial
Connecticut Reporter (West offprint)	A.2d	1954–present	Unofficial

Connecticut Circuit Court (Conn. Cir.)

Reporter	Abbreviation	Dates	Status
Connecticut Circuit Court Reports	Conn. Cir.	1961–1974	Official
Atlantic Reporter, Second Series	A.2d	1961–1974	Unofficial
Connecticut Reporter (West offprint)	A.2d	1961–1974	Unofficial

Statutory compilations:

  ★General Statutes of Connecticut   Conn. Gen. Stat. § section number (Year)

  Connecticut General Statutes Annotated   Conn. Gen. Stat. Ann. § section number (West Year)

Session laws:

  Connecticut Public and Special Acts   Year Conn. Pub. Act act number

                                       Year Conn. Spec. Act act number

Administrative compilation:

  Regulations of Connecticut State Agencies   Regs. Conn. St. Agencies § section number (Year)

Administrative register:

Connecticut Law Journal	**Volume number** Conn. L.J. **page number** (**Month Day, Year**)
Connecticut Government Register	**Issue number** Conn. Govt. Register **page number** (Weil **Month Year**)

Local citation rules?   Yes. See **Appendix 2.**   **Neutral citation rules?**   No.

Delaware

Court system and reporters:

**Delaware Supreme Court (Del.) and
Delaware Superior Court (Del. Super.)**

> *Note:*   Before 1897, the Delaware Supreme Court was the Delaware High Court of Errors and Appeals (Del.). The Delaware Superior Court was previously the Delaware Superior Court and Orphans' Court (Del. Super.).

Reporter	Abbreviation	Dates	Status
Delaware Reports	Del.	1832–1966	Official
Atlantic Reporter	A.	1885–1938	Unofficial
Second Series	A.2d	1938–present	Official since 1966
Delaware Reporter (West offprint)	A.2d	1966–present	Official

Delaware Court of Chancery (Del. Ch.)

Reporter	Abbreviation	Dates	Status
Delaware Chancery Reports	Del. Ch.	1814–1968	Official
Atlantic Reporter	A.	1885–1938	Unofficial
Second Series	A.2d	1938–present	Official since 1966
Delaware Reporter (West offprint)	A.2d	1966–present	Official since 1966

Delaware Family Court (Del. Fam.)

Reporter	Abbreviation	Dates	Status
Atlantic Reporter, Second Series	A.2d	1977–present	Official

Statutory compilation:
★Delaware Code Annotated   Del. Code Ann. tit. **title number**, § **section number** (Lexis **Year**)

Session laws:
Laws of Delaware   **Volume number** Del. Laws ch. **chapter number** (**Year**)

Administrative compilation:
Code of Delaware Regulations   **Volume number** Del. Code Regs. § **section number** (**Year**)

Administrative register:

Delaware Register of Regulations **Volume number** Del. Register of Regs. **page number** (**Month Day, Year**)

Local citation rules? Yes. See **Appendix 2.** **Neutral citation rules?** No.

District of Columbia

Court system and reporters:

District of Columbia Court of Appeals (D.C.)

Note: Before 1963, the District of Columbia Court of Appeals was the Municipal Court of Appeals (D.C. Mun. App.).

Reporter	Abbreviation	Dates	Status
Atlantic Reporter, Second Series	A.2d	1943–present	Official

Statutory compilation:

★District of Columbia Official Code	D.C. Code § **section number** (West **Year**)
District of Columbia Code Annotated	D.C. Code Ann. § **section number** (Lexis **Year**)

Session laws:

District of Columbia Statutes at Large **Year** D.C. Stat. **law number**

Administrative compilation:

District of Columbia Municipal Regulations D.C. Mun. Regs. tit. **title number**, § **section number** (**Year**)

Administrative register:

District of Columbia Register **Volume number** D.C. Register **page number** (**Month Day, Year**)

Local citation rules? Yes. See **Appendix 2.** **Neutral citation rules?** No.

Florida

Court system and reporters:

Florida Supreme Court (Fla.)

Reporter	Abbreviation	Dates	Status
Florida Reports	Fla.	1846–1948	Official
Southern Reporter	So.	1887–1941	Unofficial
Second Series	So. 2d	1941–present	Official since 1948
Florida Cases (West offprint)	So. 2d	1941–present	Official since 1948

Florida District Court of Appeal (Fla. ⎯ Dist. App.)

Reporter	Abbreviation	Dates	Status
Southern Reporter, Second Series	So. 2d	1957–present	Official
Florida Cases (West offprint)	So. 2d	1957–present	Official

Florida Circuit Court (Fla. ___ Cir.), Florida County Court ([Name of County] Co. Ct.), and other Florida lower courts

Reporter	Abbreviation	Dates	Status
Florida Supplement	Fla. Supp.	1948–1980	Official
Second Series	Fla. Supp. 2d	1980–1992	Official

Statutory compilations:

★Florida Statutes	Fla. Stat. § **section number** (**Year**)
Florida Statutes Annotated	Fla. Stat. Ann. § **section number** (West **Year**)

Session laws:

Laws of Florida	**Year** Fla. Laws ch. **chapter number**
West's Florida Session Law Service	**Year** Fla. Sess. L. Serv. ch. **chapter number** (West)

Administrative compilation:

Florida Administrative Code Annotated	Fla. Admin. Code Ann. r. **rule number** (**Year**)

Administrative register:

Florida Administrative Law Weekly	**Volume number** Fla. Admin. Wkly. **page number** (**Month Day, Year**)

Local citation rules?   Yes. See **Appendix 2.**   Neutral citation rules?   No.

Georgia

Court system and reporters:

Georgia Supreme Court (Ga.)

Reporter	Abbreviation	Dates	Status
Georgia Reports	Ga.	1846–present	Official
South Eastern Reporter	S.E.	1887–1939	Unofficial
Second Series	S.E.2d	1939–present	Unofficial
Georgia Cases (West offprint)	S.E.2d	1939–present	Unofficial

Georgia Court of Appeals (Ga. App.)

Reporter	Abbreviation	Dates	Status
Georgia Appeals Reports	Ga. App.	1907–present	Official
South Eastern Reporter	S.E.	1907–1939	Unofficial
Second Series	S.E.2d	1939–present	Unofficial
Georgia Cases (West offprint)	S.E.2d	1939–present	Unofficial

Statutory compilations:

★Official Code of Georgia Annotated	Ga. Code Ann. § **section number** (**Year**)
West's Georgia Code Annotated	Ga. Code Ann. § **section number** (West **Year**)

Session laws:

Georgia Laws	**Year** Ga. Laws **page number**

Administrative compilation:
Official Compilation of the Rules   Ga. Comp. R. & Regs. r. **rule number** (**Year**)
and Regulations of the State of
Georgia

Administrative register:
Georgia Government Register   **Issue number** Ga. Govt. Register **page number** (Weil
Month Year)

Local citation rules? Yes. See **Appendix 2.**   **Neutral citation rules?** No.

Hawaii

Court system and reporters:

Hawaii Supreme Court (Haw.)

Reporter	Abbreviation	Dates	Status
Hawaii Reports	Haw.	1847–1994	Official
Pacific Reporter			
Second Series	P.2d	1959–2000	Official
Third Series	P.3d	2000–present	Official
West's Hawaii Reports	P.2d, P.3d	1994–present	Official

Hawaii Intermediate Court of Appeals (Haw. App.)

Reporter	Abbreviation	Dates	Status
Hawaii Appellate Reports	Haw. App.	1980–1994	Official
Pacific Reporter			
Second Series	P.2d	1980–2000	Official
Third Series	P.3d	2000–present	Official
West's Hawaii Reports	P.2d, P.3d	1994–present	Official

Statutory compilations:
★Hawaii Revised Statutes   Haw. Rev. Stat. § **section number** (**Year**)
Hawaii Revised Statutes Annotated   Haw. Rev. Stat. Ann. § **section number** (Lexis **Year**)

Session laws:
Session Laws of Hawaii   **Year** Haw. Sess. Laws **act number**

Administrative compilation:
Code of Hawaii Rules   Haw. Admin. R. § **section number** (Weil **Year**)

Administrative register:
Hawaii Government Register   Haw. Govt. Register **page number** (Weil **Month Year**)

Local citation rules? Yes. See **Appendix 2.**   **Neutral citation rules?** No.

Idaho

Court system and reporters:

Idaho Supreme Court (Idaho)

Reporter	Abbreviation	Dates	Status
Idaho Reports	Idaho	1866–present	Official

Pacific Reporter	P.	1883–1931	Unofficial
Second Series	P.2d	1931–2000	Unofficial
Third Series	P.3d	2000–present	Unofficial

Idaho Court of Appeals (Idaho App.)

Reporter	Abbreviation	Dates	Status
Idaho Reports	Idaho	1982–present	Official
Pacific Reporter			
Second Series	P.2d	1982–2000	Unofficial
Third Series	P.3d	2000–present	Unofficial

Statutory compilation:
★Idaho Code Annotated   Idaho Code Ann. § **section number** (Lexis **Year**)

Session laws:
Session Laws of Idaho   **Year** Idaho Sess. Laws ch. **chapter number**

Administrative compilation:
Idaho Administrative Code   Idaho Admin. Code r. **rule number** (**Year**)

Administrative register:
Idaho Administrative Bulletin   Idaho Admin. Bull. **issue number** (**Month Year**)

Local citation rules? No.   **Neutral citation rules?** No.

Illinois

Court system and reporters:

Illinois Supreme Court (Ill.)

Reporter	Abbreviation	Dates	Status
Illinois Reports	Ill.	1819–1954	Official
Second Series	Ill. 2d	1954–present	Official
North Eastern Reporter	N.E.	1885–1936	Unofficial
Second Series	N.E.2d	1936–present	Unofficial
West's Illinois Decisions (offprint)	N.E.2d	1976–present	Unofficial

Illinois Appellate Court (Ill. App. —— Dist.)

Reporter	Abbreviation	Dates	Status
Illinois Appellate Court Reports	Ill. App.	1877–1954	Official
Second Series	Ill. App. 2d	1954–1972	Official
Third Series	Ill. App. 3d	1972–present	Official
North Eastern Reporter, Second Series	N.E.2d	1936–present	Unofficial
West's Illinois Decisions (offprint)	N.E.2d	1976–present	Unofficial

Illinois Court of Claims (Ill. Cl.)

Reporter	Abbreviation	Dates	Status
Illinois Court of Claims Reports	Ill. Cl.	1889–present	Official

Illinois Circuit Court (Ill. Cir.)

Reporter	Abbreviation	Dates	Status
Illinois Circuit Court Reports	Ill. Cir.	1866–1908	Official

Statutory compilations:

★Illinois Compiled Statutes	**Title number** Ill. Comp. Stat. **section number** (**Year**)
West's Smith-Hurd Illinois Compiled Statutes Annotated	**Title number** Ill. Comp. Stat. Ann. **section number** (West **Year**)
★Illinois Compiled Statutes Annotated	**Title number** Ill. Comp. Stat. Ann. **section number** (Lexis **Year**)

Session laws:

Laws of Illinois	**Year** Ill. Laws **page number**

Administrative compilation:

Illinois Administrative Code	Ill. Admin. Code tit. **title number**, pt. **part number** (**Year**)

Administrative register:

Illinois Register	**Volume number** Ill. Register **page number** (**Month Day, Year**)

Local citation rules? Yes. See **Appendix 2.**   **Neutral citation rules?** No.

Indiana

Court system and reporters:

Indiana Supreme Court (Ind.)

Reporter	Abbreviation	Dates	Status
Indiana Reports	Ind.	1848–1981	Official
North Eastern Reporter	N.E.	1885–1936	Unofficial
Second Series	N.E.2d	1936–present	Official since 1981
Indiana Cases (West offprint)	N.E.2d	1936–present	Official since 1981

Indiana Court of Appeals (Ind. App. — Dist.)

Note: Before 1972, this court was known as the Indiana Appellate Court (Ind. App. — Dist.).

Reporter	Abbreviation	Dates	Status
Indiana Court of Appeals Reports	Ind. App.	1890–1979	Official
North Eastern Reporter	N.E.	1890–1936	Unofficial
Second Series	N.E.2d	1936–present	Official since 1979
Indiana Cases (West offprint)	N.E.2d	1936–present	Official since 1979

Statutory compilations:

★Indiana Code	Ind. Code § **section number (Year)**
Burns Indiana Statutes Annotated	Ind. Code Ann. § **section number (Lexis Year)**
West's Annotated Indiana Code	Ind. Code Ann. § **section number (West Year)**

Session laws:

Acts of Indiana	**Year** Ind. Acts **page number**

Administrative compilation:

Indiana Administrative Code	**Title number** Ind. Admin. Code **rule number (Year)**

Administrative register:

Indiana Register	**Volume number** Ind. Register **page number (Month Year)**

Local citation rules?   Yes. See **Appendix 2.**   Neutral citation rules?   No.

Iowa

Court system and reporters:

Iowa Supreme Court (Iowa)

Reporter	Abbreviation	Dates	Status
Iowa Reports	Iowa	1855–1968	Official
North Western Reporter	N.W.	1879–1941	Unofficial
Second Series	N.W.2d	1941–present	Official since 1968

Iowa Court of Appeals (Iowa App.)

Reporter	Abbreviation	Dates	Status
North Western Reporter, Second Series	N.W.2d	1977–present	Official

Statutory compilations:

★Code of Iowa	Iowa Code § **section number (Year)**
West's Iowa Code Annotated	Iowa Code Ann. § **section number (West Year)**

Session laws:

Acts and Joint Resolutions of Iowa	**Year** Iowa Acts **page number**

Administrative compilation:

Iowa Administrative Code	Iowa Admin. Code r. **rule number (Year)**

Administrative register:

Iowa Administrative Bulletin	**Volume number** Iowa Admin. Bull. **page number (Month Day, Year)**

Local citation rules?   Yes. See **Appendix 2.**   Neutral citation rules?   No.

Kansas

Court system and reporters:

Kansas Supreme Court (Kan.)

Reporter	Abbreviation	Dates	Status
Kansas Reports	Kan.	1862–present	Official

Pacific Reporter	P.	1883–1931	Unofficial
Second Series	P.2d	1931–2000	Unofficial
Third Series	P.3d	2000–present	Unofficial
Kansas Cases (West offprint)	P.2d, P.3d	1968–present	Unofficial

Kansas Court of Appeals (Kan. App.)

Reporter	Abbreviation	Dates	Status
Kansas Court of Appeals Reports	Kan. App.	1895–1901	Official
Second Series	Kan. App. 2d	1977–present	Official
Pacific Reporter	P.	1895–1931	Unofficial
Second Series	P.2d	1977–2000	Unofficial
Third Series	P.3d	2000–present	Unofficial
Kansas Cases (West offprint)	P., P.2d, P.3d	1977–present	Unofficial

Statutory compilations:
★Kansas Statutes Annotated   Kan. Stat. Ann. § **section number (Year)**

Vernon's Kansas Statutes Annotated   Kan. **Subject abbreviation** § **section number** (West **Year**)
Note: Consult **Appendix 3(E)** for subject abbreviations.

Session laws:
Session Laws of Kansas   **Year** Kan. Sess. Laws **page number**

Administrative compilation:
Kansas Administrative Regulations   Kan. Admin. Regs. r. **rule number (Year)**

Administrative register:
Kansas Register   **Volume number** Kan. Register **page number (Month Day, Year)**

Local citation rules?   Yes. See **Appendix 2.**   **Neutral citation rules?**   No.

Kentucky

Court system and reporters:

Kentucky Supreme Court (Ky.)

Note: Before 1976, the Kentucky Court of Appeals (Ky.) was the highest state court.

Reporter	Abbreviation	Dates	Status
Kentucky Reports	Ky.	1785–1951	Official
South Western Reporter	S.W.	1886–1928	Unofficial
Second Series	S.W.2d	1928–1999	Official since 1973
Third Series	S.W.3d	1999–present	Official
Kentucky Decisions (West offprint)	S.W., S.W.2d, S.W.3d	1886–present	Official since 1973

Kentucky Court of Appeals (Ky. App.)

Note: Use only for cases after 1975.

Reporter	Abbreviation	Dates	Status
South Western Reporter			
Second Series	S.W.2d	1976–1999	Official
Third Series	S.W.3d	1999–present	Official
Kentucky Decisions (West offprint)	S.W.2d, S.W.3d	1976–present	Official

Statutory compilations:

★Baldwin's Official Edition, Kentucky Revised Statutes Annotated	Ky. Rev. Stat. Ann. § **section number** (West **Year**)
★Kentucky Revised Statutes Annotated	Ky. Rev. Stat. Ann. § **section number** (Lexis **Year**)

Session laws:

Kentucky Acts	**Year** Ky. Acts **page number**

Administrative compilation:

Kentucky Administrative Regulations Service	**Title number** Ky. Admin. Regs. **chapter number**: **regulation number** (**Year**)

Administrative register:

Administrative Register of Kentucky	**Volume number** Ky. Register **page number** (**Month Year**)

Local citation rules?   Yes. See **Appendix 2.**   Neutral citation rules?   No.

Louisiana

Court system and reporters:

Louisiana Supreme Court (La.)

Note: Before 1813, the Louisiana Supreme Court was known as the Superior Court of Louisiana (La.), and the Superior Court of the Territory of Orleans (Orleans).

Reporter	Abbreviation	Dates	Status
Louisiana Reports	La.	1908–1972	Official
Southern Reporter	So.	1887–1941	Unofficial
Second Series	So. 2d	1941–present	Unofficial
Louisiana Cases (West offprint)	So. 2d	1966–present	Unofficial

Louisiana Court of Appeal (La. App. __ Cir.)

Reporter	Abbreviation	Dates	Status
Southern Reporter	So.	1928–1941	Unofficial
Second Series	So. 2d	1941–present	Unofficial
Louisiana Cases (West offprint)	So. 2d	1966–present	Unofficial

Statutory compilations:

★West's Louisiana Statutes
Annotated

La. Stat. Ann. § **section number** (**Year**)

★West's Louisiana Civil Code
Annotated

La. **subject abbreviation** Code Ann. art **article number** (**Year**)
Note: Consult **Appendix 3(E)** for subject abbreviations.

Session laws:

★State of Louisiana: Acts of the
Legislature

Year La. Acts **page number**

West's Louisiana Session Law
Service

Year La. Sess. L. Serv. **page number**

Administrative compilation:

Louisiana Administrative Code

La. Admin. Code tit. **title number**, § **section number** (**Year**)

Weil's Code of Louisiana Rules

La. Code R. tit. **title number**, § **section number** (Weil **Year**)

Administrative register:

Louisiana Register

Volume number La. Register **page number** (**Month Year**)

Local citation rules? Yes. See **Appendix 2.** **Neutral citation rules?** Yes. See **Appendix 2.**

Maine

Court system and reporters:

Maine Supreme Judicial Court (Me.)

Reporter	Abbreviation	Dates	Status
Maine Reports	Me.	1820–1965	Official
Atlantic Reporter	A.	1885–1938	Unofficial
Second Series	A.2d	1938–present	Official since 1966
Maine Reporter (West offprint)	A.2d	1966–present	Official

Statutory compilation:

★Maine Revised Statutes
Annotated

Title number Me. Rev. Stat. Ann. § **section number** (**Year**)

Session laws:

Laws of the State of Maine

Year Me. Laws **page number**

Acts, Resolves and Constitutional
Resolutions of the State of Maine

Year Me. Acts **page number**

Administrative compilation:

Codes of Maine Rules

Code Me. R. **department number bureau number chapter number** (Weil **Year**) (e.g., Code Me. R. 02 02A 110 (Weil 2005))

Administrative register:

Maine Government Register

Issue number Me. Govt. Register **page number** (Weil **Month Year**)

Local citation rules? Yes. See **Appendix 2.**   Neutral citation rules? Yes. See **Appendix 2.**

Maryland

Court system and reporters:

Maryland Court of Appeals (Md.)

Reporter	Abbreviation	Dates	Status
Maryland Reports	Md.	1851–present	Official
Atlantic Reporter	A.	1885–1938	Unofficial
Second Series	A.2d	1938–present	Unofficial
Maryland Reporter (West offprint)	A.2d	1942–present	Unofficial

Maryland Court of Special Appeals (Md. Spec. App.)

Reporter	Abbreviation	Dates	Status
Maryland Appellate Reports	Md. App.	1967–present	Official
Atlantic Reporter, Second Series	A.2d	1967–present	Unofficial
Maryland Reporter (West offprint)	A.2d	1967–present	Unofficial

Statutory compilations:

★Annotated Code of Maryland

Md. **Subject abbreviation** Code Ann. § **section number** (**Year**)
Note: Consult **Appendix 3(E)** for subject abbreviations.

★Annotated Code of Maryland (1957)

Md. Ann. Code Art. **article number**, § **section number** (**Year**)

Session laws:

Laws of Maryland

Year Md. Laws **page number**

Administrative compilation:

Code of Maryland Regulations

Code Md. Regs. **title number. subtitle number. chapter number.regulation** (**Year**)

(e.g., Code Md. Regs. 13A.07.01.03 (2005))

Administrative register:

Maryland Register

Volume Md. Register **page number** (**Month Day, Year**)

Local citation rules?   Yes. See **Appendix 2.**   Neutral citation rules?   No.

Massachusetts

Court system and reporters:

Massachusetts Supreme Judicial Court (Mass.)

Reporter	Abbreviation	Dates	Status
Massachusetts Reports	Mass.	1804–present	Official
North Eastern Reporter	N.E.	1885–1936	Unofficial
Second Series	N.E.2d	1936–present	Unofficial
Massachusetts Decisions (West offprint)	N.E. or N.E.2d	1937–present	Unofficial

Massachusetts Appeals Court (Mass. App.)

Reporter	Abbreviation	Dates	Status
Massachusetts Appeals Court Reports	Mass. App.	1972–present	Official
North Eastern Reporter, Second Series	N.E.2d	1972–present	Unofficial
Massachusetts Decisions (West offprint)	N.E.2d	1972–present	Unofficial

Massachusetts District Court, Appellate Division (Mass. Dist. App. Div.)

Reporter	Abbreviation	Dates	Status
Massachusetts Appellate Division Reports	Mass. App. Div.	1936–1950 / 1980–present	Official / Official
Massachusetts Appellate Decisions	Mass. App. Dec.	1941–1977	Unofficial
Massachusetts Supplement	Mass. Supp.	1980–1983	Unofficial

Massachusetts Superior Court (Mass. Super.)

Reporter	Abbreviation	Dates	Status
Massachusetts Law Reporter	Mass. L. Rptr.	1993–present	Unofficial

Statutory compilations:

★General Laws of the Commonwealth of Massachusetts — Mass. Gen. Laws ch. **chapter number**, § **section number** (**Year**)

Massachusetts General Laws Annotated — Mass. Gen. Laws Ann. ch. **chapter number**, § **section number** (West **Year**)

Annotated Laws of Massachusetts — Mass. Ann. Laws ch. **chapter number**, § **section number** (Lexis **Year**)

Session laws:

Acts and Resolves of Massachusetts — **Year** Mass. Acts **page number**

Administrative compilation:

Code of Massachusetts Regulations — **Three-digit agency number** Code Mass. Regs. **chapter number.section number** (**Year**) (e.g., 106 Code Mass. Regs. 303.510 (2005))

Administrative register:

Massachusetts Register — **Issue number** Mass. Register **page number** (**Month Day, Year**)

Local citation rules? Yes. See **Appendix 2.**   **Neutral citation rules?** No.

Michigan

Court system and reporters:

Michigan Supreme Court (Mich.)

Reporter	Abbreviation	Dates	Status
Michigan Reports	Mich.	1847–present	Official
North Western Reporter	N.W.	1879–1941	Unofficial
Second Series	N.W.2d	1941–present	Unofficial
Michigan Reporter (West offprint)	N.W.2d	1941–present	Unofficial

Michigan Court of Appeals (Mich. App.)

Reporter	Abbreviation	Dates	Status
Michigan Appeals Reports	Mich. App.	1965–present	Official
North Western Reporter, Second Series	N.W.2d	1965–present	Unofficial
Michigan Reporter (West offprint)	N.W.2d	1965–present	Unofficial

Statutory compilations:

★ Michigan Compiled Laws — Mich. Comp. Laws § **section number** (**Year**)

Michigan Compiled Laws Annotated — Mich. Comp. Laws Ann. § **section number** (West **Year**)

Michigan Compiled Laws Service — Mich. Comp. Laws Serv. § **section number** (Lexis **Year**)

Session laws:

Public and Local Acts of the Legislature of the State of Michigan — **Year** Mich. Acts **page number**

Administrative compilation:

Michigan Administrative Code — Mich. Admin. Code r. **rule number** (**Edition number** ed. **Year**)

Administrative register:

Michigan Register — Mich. Register no. **issue number** (**Month Day, Year**)

Local citation rules? Yes. See **Appendix 2.**   **Neutral citation rules?** No.

Minnesota

Court system and reporters:

Minnesota Supreme Court (Minn.)

Reporter	Abbreviation	Dates	Status
Minnesota Reports	Minn.	1851–1977	Official
North Western Reporter	N.W.	1879–1941	Unofficial
Second Series	N.W.2d	1941–present	Official since 1978
Minnesota Reporter (West offprint)	N.W.2d	1978–present	Official

Minnesota Court of Appeals (Minn. App.)

Reporter	Abbreviation	Dates	Status
North Western Reporter, Second Series	N.W.2d	1983–present	Official
Minnesota Reporter (West offprint)	N.W.2d	1983–present	Official

Statutory compilations:

★Minnesota Statutes	Minn. Stat. § **section number** (**Year**)
Minnesota Statutes Annotated	Minn. Stat. Ann. § **section number** (West **Year**)

Session laws:

Laws of Minnesota	**Year** Minn. Laws **page number**
Minnesota Session Law Service	**Year** Minn. Sess. L. Serv. ch. **chapter number** (West)

Administrative compilation:

Minnesota Rules	Minn. R. **chapter number.part number** (**Year**) (e.g., Minn. R. 6800.0600 (2005))

Administrative register:

Minnesota State Register	**Volume number** Minn. Register **page number** (**Month Day, Year**)

Local citation rules? No.   **Neutral citation rules?** No.

Mississippi

Court system and reporters:

Mississippi Supreme Court (Miss.)

Reporter	Abbreviation	Dates	Status
Mississippi Reports	Miss.	1818–1966	Official
Southern Reporter	So.	1887–1941	Unofficial
Second Series	So. 2d	1941–present	Official since 1966
Mississippi Cases (West offprint)	So. 2d	1966–present	Official

Mississippi Court of Appeals (Miss. App.)

Reporter	Abbreviation	Dates	Status
Southern Reporter			
Second Series	So. 2d	1995–present	Official

Statutory compilation:

★Mississippi Code Annotated	Miss. Code Ann. § **section number** (Lexis **Year**)
West's Annotated Mississippi Code	Miss. Code Ann. § **section number** (West **Year**)

Session laws:

General Laws of Mississippi	**Year** Gen. Laws Miss. **page number**

Administrative compilation:

Code of Mississippi Rules	Code Miss. Rules **rule number**

Administrative register:
Mississippi Government Register   Miss. Govt. Register **page number** (Weil **Month Year**)

Local citation rules? Yes. See **Appendix 2.**   **Neutral citation rules?** Yes. See **Appendix 2.**

Missouri

Court system and reporters:

Missouri Supreme Court (Mo.)

Reporter	Abbreviation	Dates	Status
Missouri Reports	Mo.	1821–1956	Official
South Western Reporter	S.W.	1866–1928	Unofficial
Second Series	S.W.2d	1928–1999	Official since 1956
Third Series	S.W.3d	1999–present	Official
Missouri Decisions (West offprint)	S.W., S.W.2d, S.W.3d	1886–present	Official since 1956

Missouri Court of Appeals (Mo. App. —— Dist.)

Reporter	Abbreviation	Dates	Status
Missouri Appeal Reports	Mo. App.	1876–1952	Official
South Western Reporter	S.W.	1902–1928	Unofficial
Second Series	S.W.2d	1928–1999	Official since 1952
Third Series	S.W.3d	1999–present	Official
Missouri Decisions (West offprint)	S.W., S.W.2d, S.W.3d	1902–present	Official since 1952

Statutory compilations:
★Missouri Revised Statutes   Mo. Rev. Stat. § **section number** (**Year**)

Vernon's Annotated Missouri   Mo. Rev. Stat. Ann. § **section number** (West **Year**)
Statutes

Session laws:
Laws of Missouri   **Year** Mo. Laws **page number**

Administrative compilation:
State of Missouri Code of State   Mo. Code Regs. Ann. tit. **title number, division num-**
Regulations Annotated   **ber-chapter number-rule number** (**Year**) (e.g., Mo.
Code Regs. Ann. tit. 3, 40-3-070 (2005))

Administrative register:
Missouri Register   **Volume number** Mo. Register **page number** (**Month
Day, Year**)

Local citation rules? No.   **Neutral citation rules?** No.

Montana

Court system and reporters:

Montana Supreme Court (Mont.)

Reporter	Abbreviation	Dates	Status
Montana Reports	Mont.	1868–present	Official
Pacific Reporter	P.	1883–1931	Unofficial
Second Series	P.2d	1931–2000	Unofficial
Third Series	P.3d	2000–present	Unofficial

Statutory compilation:
  ★Montana Code Annotated   Mont. Code Ann. § **section number** (**Year**)

Session laws:
  Laws of Montana   **Year** Mont. Laws **page number**

Administrative compilation:
  Administrative Rules of Montana   Admin. R. Mont. **title.chapter.rule** (**Year**) (e.g., Admin. R. Mont. 42.22.101 (2005))

Administrative register:
  Montana Administrative Register   **Issue number** Mont. Admin. Register **page number** (**Month Day, Year**)

Local citation rules? No, other than neutral citation rules.
Neutral citation rules? Yes. See **Appendix 2.**

Nebraska

Court system and reporters:

Nebraska Supreme Court (Neb.)

Reporter	Abbreviation	Dates	Status
Nebraska Reports	Neb.	1860–present	Official
North Western Reporter	N.W.	1879–1941	Unofficial
Second Series	N.W.2d	1941–present	Unofficial

Nebraska Court of Appeals (Neb. App.)

Reporter	Abbreviation	Dates	Status
Nebraska Appellate Reports	Neb. App.	1992–present	Official
North Western Reporter, Second Series	N.W.2d	1992–present	Unofficial

Statutory compilations:
  ★Revised Statutes of Nebraska   Neb. Rev. Stat. § **section number** (**Year**)
  Revised Statutes of Nebraska Annotated   Neb. Rev. Stat. Ann. § **section number** (Lexis **Year**)

Session laws:
  Laws of Nebraska   **Year** Neb. Laws **page number**

Administrative compilation:

Nebraska Administrative Rules and Regulations

Title number Neb. Admin. R. & Regs. **chapter number-rule number** (**Year**) (e.g., 15 Neb. Admin. R. & Regs. 2-006.07 (2005))

Administrative register:

Nebraska Government Register

Issue number Neb. Govt. Register **page number** (Weil **Month Year**)

Local citation rules? Yes. See **Appendix 2.**   **Neutral citation rules?** No.

Nevada

Court system and reporters:

Nevada Supreme Court (Nev.)

Reporter	Abbreviation	Dates	Status
Nevada Reports	Nev.	1865–present	Official
Pacific Reporter	P.	1883–1931	Unofficial
Second Series	P.2d	1931–2000	Unofficial
Third Series	P.3d	2000–present	Unofficial

Statutory compilations:

★Nevada Revised Statutes

Nev. Rev. Stat. § **section number** (**Year**)

Nevada Revised Statutes Annotated

Nev. Rev. Stat. Ann. § **section number** (Lexis **Year**)

West's Nevada Revised Statutes Annotated

Nev. Rev. Stat. Ann. § **section number** (West **Year**)

Session laws:

Statutes of Nevada

Year Nev. Stat. **page number**

Administrative compilation:

Nevada Administrative Code

Nev. Admin. Code **chapter.section** (**Year**) (e.g., Nev. Admin. Code 704.689 (2005))

Administrative register:

State of Nevada Register of Administrative Regulations

Nev. Register Admin. Reg. **pinpoint** (**Month Day, Year**)

Local citation rules? Yes. See **Appendix 2.**   **Neutral citation rules?** No.

New Hampshire

Court system and reporters:

New Hampshire Supreme Court (N.H.)

Reporter	Abbreviation	Dates	Status
New Hampshire Reports	N.H.	1816–present	Official
Atlantic Reporter	A.	1885–1938	Unofficial
Second Series	A.2d	1938–present	Unofficial

Statutory compilation:

★ New Hampshire Revised Statutes Annotated N.H. Rev. Stat. Ann. § **section number** (West **Year**)

New Hampshire Revised Statutes Annotated N.H. Rev. Stat. Ann. § **section number** (Lexis **Year**)

Session laws:

Laws of the State of New Hampshire **Year** N.H. Laws **page number**

Administrative compilation:

New Hampshire Code of Administrative Rules Annotated N.H. Admin. R. Ann., **Abbreviated Department Name rule number** (**Year**)

Note: Consult **Appendix 3(E)** for department abbreviations.

Administrative register:

New Hampshire Rulemaking Register **Agency abbreviation chapter**, N.H. Rulemaking Register, vol. **volume number**, no. **issue number** (**Month Day, Year**)

Note: Consult **Appendix 3(E)** for agency abbreviations.

New Hampshire Government Register **Issue number** N.H. Govt. Register **page number** (Weil **Month Year**)

Local citation rules? Yes. See **Appendix 2.** **Neutral citation rules?** No.

New Jersey

Court system and reporters:

New Jersey Supreme Court (N.J.)

Note: Before 1948, this court was called the New Jersey Court of Errors and Appeals (N.J.).

Reporter	Abbreviation	Dates	Status
New Jersey Reports	N.J.	1948–present	Official
New Jersey Law Reports	N.J.L.	1790–1948	Official
New Jersey Equity Reports	N.J. Eq.	1830–1948	Official
New Jersey Miscellaneous Reports	N.J. Misc.	1923–1948	Unofficial
Atlantic Reporter	A.	1885–1938	Unofficial
Second Series	A.2d	1938–present	Unofficial

New Jersey Superior Court Appellate Division (N.J. Super. App. Div.), New Jersey Superior Court Chancery Division (N.J. Super. Ch. Div.), New Jersey Superior Court Law Division (N.J. Super. L. Div.), New Jersey County Courts ([Name of County] County Ct.), and other New Jersey lower courts

Note: Before 1947, the New Jersey Superior Court was called the New Jersey Supreme Court (N.J. Sup. Ct.), New Jersey Court of Chancery (N.J. Ch.) and the New Jersey Prerogative Court (N.J. Prerog.).

Reporter	Abbreviation	Dates	Status
New Jersey Superior Court Reports	N.J. Super.	1948–present	Official
New Jersey Law Reports	N.J.L.	1790–1948	Official
New Jersey Equity Reports	N.J. Eq.	1830–1948	Official
New Jersey Miscellaneous Reports	N.J. Misc.	1923–1948	Unofficial
Atlantic Reporter	A.	1885–1938	Unofficial
Second Series	A.2d	1938–present	Unofficial

New Jersey Tax Court (N.J. Tax)

Reporter	Abbreviation	Dates	Status
New Jersey Tax Court Reports	N.J. Tax	1979–present	Unofficial

Statutory compilation:
★New Jersey Statutes Annotated   N.J. Stat. Ann. § **section number** (West **Year**)
New Jersey Revised Statutes (1937)   N.J. Rev. Stat § **section number** (**Year**)

Session laws:
Laws of New Jersey   **Year** N.J. Laws **page number**
New Jersey Session Law Service   **Year** N.J. Sess. L. Serv. ch. **chapter number** (West)

Administrative compilation:
New Jersey Administrative Code   N.J. Admin. Code **title:chapter-subchapter.section** (**Year**) (e.g., N.J. Admin. Code 3:33-1.1 (2005))

Administrative register:
New Jersey Register   **Volume number** N.J. Register **page number** (**Month Day, Year**)

Local citation rules?   Yes. See **Appendix 2.**   **Neutral citation rules?**   No.

New Mexico

Court system and reporters:

New Mexico Supreme Court (N.M.)

Reporter	Abbreviation	Dates	Status
New Mexico Reports	N.M.	1852–present	Official
Pacific Reporter	P.	1883–1931	Unofficial
Second Series	P.2d	1931–2000	Unofficial
Third Series	P.3d	2000–present	Unofficial

New Mexico Court of Appeals (N.M. App.)

Reporter	Abbreviation	Dates	Status
New Mexico Reports	N.M.	1966–present	Official
Pacific Reporter			
Second Series	P.2d	1966–2000	Unofficial
Third Series	P.3d	2000–present	Unofficial

Statutory compilation:

★New Mexico Statutes	N.M. Stat. § **section number (Year)**
West's New Mexico Statutes Annotated	N.M. Stat. Ann. § **section number** (West **Year**)
Michie's Annotated Statutes of New Mexico	N.M. Stat. Ann. § **section number** (Lexis **Year**)

Session laws:

Laws of New Mexico	**Year** N.M. Laws **page number**

Administrative compilation:

Code of New Mexico Rules	N.M. Code R. § **section number** (Weil **Year**)

Administrative register:

New Mexico Register	N.M. Register **pinpoint (Month Day, Year)**

Local citation rules? Yes. See **Appendix 2.**   Neutral citation rules? Yes. See **Appendix 2.**

New York

Court system and reporters:

New York Court of Appeals (N.Y.)

Note: Before 1846, the highest state courts were the New York Court for the Correction of Errors (N.Y. Errors) and the New York Supreme Court of Judicature (N.Y.). The highest court of equity was the New York Court of Chancery (N.Y. Ch.). Each court had its own reporters, which are not included below.

Reporter	Abbreviation	Dates	Status
New York Reports	N.Y.	1847–1956	Official
Second Series	N.Y.2d	1956–present	Official
North Eastern Reporter	N.E.	1885–1936	Unofficial
Second Series	N.E.2d	1936–present	Unofficial
West's New York Supplement, Second Series	N.Y.S.2d	1956–present	Unofficial

New York Supreme Court, Appellate Division (N.Y. App. Div. __ Dept.), previously Supreme Court, General Term (N.Y. Gen. Term)

Reporter	Abbreviation	Dates	Status
New York Appellate Division Reports	A.D.	1894–1955	Official
Second Series	A.D.2d	1955–2003	Official
Third Series	A.D.3d	2003–present	Official
West's New York Supplement	N.Y.S.	1896–1938	Unofficial
Second Series	N.Y.S.2d	1938–present	Unofficial

Other New York lower courts (e.g., N.Y. App. Term., N.Y. Sup. Ct., N.Y. Ct. Cl., N.Y. Civ. Ct., N.Y. Crim. Ct., N.Y. Fam. Ct.)

Reporter	Abbreviation	Dates	Status
New York Miscellaneous Reports	Misc.	1892–1956	Official
Second Series	Misc. 2d	1956–2003	Official
Third Series	Misc. 3d	2004–present	Official

West's New York Supplement	N.Y.S.	1896–1938	Unofficial
Second Series	N.Y.S.2d	1938–present	Unofficial

Statutory compilations:

★McKinney's Consolidated Laws of New York Annotated (West)
N.Y. **Subject** Law § **section number** (McKinney **Year**)
Note: Consult **Appendix 2** for subject abbreviations.

★Consolidated Laws Service (LexisNexis)
N.Y. **Subject** Law § **section number** (Consol. **Year**)
Note: Consult **Appendix 2** for subject abbreviations.

★Gould's New York Consolidated Laws Unannotated
N.Y. **Subject** Law § **section number** (Gould **Year**)
Note: Consult **Appendix 2** for subject abbreviations.

Session laws:

Laws of New York
Year N.Y. Laws **page number**

McKinney's New York Session Law Service
Year N.Y. Sess. Laws **page number** (McKinney)

Administrative compilation:

Official Compilation of Codes, Rules, and Regulations of the State of New York
Title number N.Y. Comp. Codes, R. & Regs. **chapter number.part number** (**Year**) (e.g., 3 N.Y. Comp. Codes, R. & Regs. 80.3 (2005))

Administrative register:

New York State Register
Volume number N.Y. Register **page number** (**Month Day, Year**)

Local citation rules? Yes. See **Appendix 2.**   **Neutral citation rules?** No.

North Carolina

Court system and reporters:

North Carolina Supreme Court (N.C.)

Reporter	Abbreviation	Dates	Status
North Carolina Reports	N.C.	1778–present	Official
South Eastern Reporter	S.E.	1887–1939	Unofficial
Second Series	S.E.2d	1939–present	Unofficial
North Carolina Reporter (West offprint)	S.E.2d	1939–present	Unofficial

North Carolina Court of Appeals (N.C. App.)

Reporter	Abbreviation	Dates	Status
North Carolina Court of Appeals Reports	N.C. App.	1968–present	Official
South Eastern Reporter, Second Series	S.E.2d	1968–present	Unofficial
North Carolina Reporter (West offprint)	S.E.2d	1968–present	Unofficial

Statutory compilation:

★General Statutes of North Carolina
N.C. Gen. Stat. § **section number** (Lexis **Year**)

| West's North Carolina General Statutes Annotated | N.C. Gen. Stat. Ann. § **section number** (West **Year**) |

Session laws:

| Session Laws of North Carolina | **Year** N.C. Laws **page number** |

Administrative compilation:

| North Carolina Administrative Code | **Title number** N.C. Admin. Code **chapter.subchapter section** (**Year**) (e.g., 17 N.C. Admin. Code 3B.0114 (2005)) |

Administrative register:

| North Carolina Register | **Volume number:issue number** N.C. Register **page number** (**Month Day, Year**) |

Local citation rules?   Yes. See **Appendix 2.**   **Neutral citation rules?**   No.

North Dakota

Court system and reporters:

North Dakota Supreme Court (N.D.)

Reporter	Abbreviation	Dates	Status
North Dakota Reports	N.D.	1890–1953	Official
North Western Reporter	N.W.	1890–1941	Unofficial
Second Series	N.W.2d	1941–present	Official since 1953

North Dakota Court of Appeals (N.D. App.)

Reporter	Abbreviation	Dates	Status
North Western Reporter, Second Series	N.W.2d	1987–present	Official

Statutory compilation:

| ★North Dakota Century Code | N.D. Cent. Code § **section number** (**Year**) |

Session laws:

| Laws of North Dakota | **Year** N.D. Laws **page number** |

Administrative compilation:

| North Dakota Administrative Code | N.D. Admin. Code **title number-article number-chapter number-section number** (**Year**) (e.g., N.D. Admin. Code 92-01-02-20 (2005)) |

Administrative register: None.

Local citation rules?   No, except for neutral citation rules.
Neutral citation rules?   Yes. See **Appendix 2.**

Ohio

Court system and reporters:

Ohio Supreme Court (Ohio)

Reporter	Abbreviation	Dates	Status
Ohio Reports	Ohio	1821–1851	Official
Ohio State Reports	Ohio St.	1852–1964	Official
Second Series	Ohio St. 2d	1964–1982	Official
Third Series	Ohio St. 3d	1982–present	Official
North Eastern Reporter	N.E.	1885–1936	Unofficial
Second Series	N.E.2d	1936–present	Unofficial
Ohio Cases (West offprint)	N.E., N.E.2d	1933–present	Unofficial

Ohio Court of Appeals (Ohio App. — Dist.)

Reporter	Abbreviation	Dates	Status
Ohio Appellate Reports	Ohio App.	1913–1965	Official
Second Series	Ohio App. 2d	1965–1982	Official
Third Series	Ohio App. 3d	1982–present	Official
North Eastern Reporter	N.E.	1927–1936	Unofficial
Second Series	N.E.2d	1936–present	Unofficial
Ohio Cases (West offprint)	N.E.2d	1943–present	Unofficial

Other Ohio lower courts

Reporter	Abbreviation	Dates	Status
Ohio Miscellaneous Reports	Ohio Misc.	1964–1982	Official
Second Series	Ohio Misc. 2d	1982–present	Official
Ohio Opinions	Ohio Op.	1934–1956	Official
Second Series	Ohio Op. 2d	1956–1976	Official
Third Series	Ohio Op. 3d	1976–1982	Official

Statutory compilations:

★Page's Ohio Revised Code Annotated — Ohio Rev. Code Ann. § section number (Lexis Year)

★Baldwin's Ohio Revised Code Annotated — Ohio Rev. Code Ann. § section number (West Year)

Session laws:

State of Ohio: Legislative Acts Passed and Joint Resolutions Adopted — Year Ohio Laws page number

Page's Ohio Legislative Bulletin (Anderson) — Year Ohio Legis. Bull. pinpoint (Lexis)

Baldwin's Ohio Legislative Service (Banks-Baldwin) — Year Ohio Legis. Serv. pinpoint (West)

Administrative compilation:

Ohio Administrative Code — Ohio Admin. Code title number:rule number (Year)
(e.g., Ohio Admin. Code 173:1-102 (2005))

Administrative register:

Ohio Monthly Record   Ohio Mthly. Rec. **page number (Month Year)**

Local citation rules? Some district courts. See **Appendix 2.**   Neutral citation rules? No.

Oklahoma

Court system and reporters:

Oklahoma Supreme Court (Okla.)

Reporter	Abbreviation	Dates	Status
Oklahoma Reports	Okla.	1890–1953	Official
Pacific Reporter	P.	1890–1931	Unofficial
Second Series	P.2d	1931–2000	Official since 1953
Third Series	P.3d	2000–present	Official
Oklahoma Decisions (West offprint)	P.2d, P.3d	1931–present	Official since 1953

Oklahoma Court of Criminal Appeals (Okla. Crim. App.)

Note: Before 1959, this court was called the Oklahoma Criminal Court of Appeals (Okla. Crim. App.).

Reporter	Abbreviation	Dates	Status
Oklahoma Criminal Reports	Okla. Crim.	1908–1953	Official
Pacific Reporter	P.	1908–1931	Unofficial
Second Series	P.2d	1931–2000	Official since 1953
Third Series	P.3d	2000–present	Official
Oklahoma Decisions (West offprint)	P.2d, P.3d	1931–present	Official since 1953

Oklahoma Court of Civil Appeals (Okla. Civ. App.)

Note: The court's name changed in 1996.

Reporter	Abbreviation	Dates	Status
Pacific Reporter			
Second Series	P.2d	1969–2000	Official
Third Series	P.3d	2000–present	Official
Oklahoma Decisions (West offprint)	P.2d, P.3d	1969–present	Official

Oklahoma Court of Appeals of the Indian Territory (Indian Terr.)

Reporter	Abbreviation	Dates	Status
Indian Territory Reports	Indian Terr.	1896–1907	Official
South Western Reporter	S.W.	1896–1907	Unofficial

Statutory compilations: *official* [handwritten]

us code → ★Oklahoma Statutes [handwritten]   Okla. Stat. tit. **title number,** § **section number (Year)**

us code Annotated —Oklahoma Statutes Annotated [handwritten]   Okla. Stat. Ann. tit. **title number,** § **section number** (West **Year)**

           └ Supplement [handwritten]

Session laws:

Oklahoma Session Laws   **Year** Okla. Laws **page number**

Administrative compilation:

Oklahoma Administrative Code   Okla. Admin. Code § **section number (Year)**

a ★ = official version [handwritten]

Administrative register:
Oklahoma Register   **Volume number** Okla. Register **page number (Month Day, Year)**

Local citation rules? Yes. See **Appendix 2.**   Neutral citation rules? Yes. See **Appendix 2.**

Oregon

Court system and reporters:

Oregon Supreme Court (Or.)

Reporter	Abbreviation	Dates	Status
Oregon Reports	Or.	1853–present	Official
Pacific Reporter	P.	1883–1931	Unofficial
Second Series	P.2d	1931–2000	Unofficial
Third Series	P.3d	2000–present	Unofficial
Oregon Decisions (West offprint)	P.2d, P.3d	1967–present	Unofficial

Oregon Court of Appeals (Or. App.)

Reporter	Abbreviation	Dates	Status
Oregon Reports, Court of Appeals	Or. App.	1969–present	Official
Pacific Reporter			
Second Series	P.2d	1969–2000	Unofficial
Third Series	P.3d	2000–present	Unofficial
Oregon Decisions (West offprint)	P.2d, P.3d	1969–present	Unofficial

Oregon Tax Court (Or. Tax)

Reporter	Abbreviation	Dates	Status
Oregon Tax Court Reports	Or. Tax	1962–present	Official

Statutory compilation:
★Oregon Revised Statutes   Or. Rev. Stat. § **section number (Year)**
West's Oregon Revised Statutes   Or. Rev. Stat. Ann. § **section number** (West **Year**)
Annotated

Session laws:
Oregon Laws and Resolutions   **Year** Or. Laws **page number**

Administrative compilation:
Oregon Administrative Rules   Or. Admin. R. **chapter number-rule number (Year)**
Compilation

Administrative register:
Oregon Bulletin   **Volume number** Or. Bull. **page number (Month Year)**

Local citation rules?   Yes. See **Appendix 2.**   Neutral citation rules?   No.

Pennsylvania

Court system and reporters:

Pennsylvania Supreme Court (Pa.)

Reporter	Abbreviation	Dates	Status
Pennsylvania State Reports	Pa.	1845–present	Official

Atlantic Reporter	A.	1885–1938	Unofficial
Second Series	A.2d	1938–present	Unofficial
Pennsylvania Reporter (West offprint)	A.2d	1939–present	Unofficial

Pennsylvania Superior Court (Pa. Super.)

Reporter	Abbreviation	Dates	Status
Pennsylvania Superior Court Reports	Pa. Super.	1895–1997	Official
Atlantic Reporter	A.	1931–1938	Unofficial
Second Series	A.2d	1938–present	Unofficial
Pennsylvania Reporter (West offprint)	A.2d	1939–present	Unofficial

Pennsylvania Commonwealth Court (Pa. Cmmw.)

Reporter	Abbreviation	Dates	Status
Pennsylvania Commonwealth Court Reports	Pa. Cmmw.	1970–1995	Official
Atlantic Reporter, Second Series	A.2d	1970–present	Official since 1995
Pennsylvania Reporter (West offprint)	A.2d	1970–present	Official since 1995

Pennsylvania District and County Courts (Pa. [Name of County or District Court] Ct.)

Reporter	Abbreviation	Dates	Status
Pennsylvania District and County Reports	Pa. D. & C.	1921–1954	Official
Second Series	Pa. D. & C.2d	1955–1977	Official
Third Series	Pa. D. & C.3d	1977–1989	Official
Fourth Series	Pa. D. & C.4th	1990–present	Official

Statutory compilations:
★Pennsylvania Consolidated Statutes — **Title number** Pa. Consol. Stat. Ann. § **section number** (**Year**)

Purdon's Pennsylvania Consolidated Statutes Annotated — **Title number** Pa. Consol. Stat. Ann. § **section number** (West **Year**)

Purdon's Pennsylvania Statutes Annotated — Pa. Stat. Ann. tit. **title number,** § section number (West **Year**)

Session laws:
Laws of Pennsylvania — **Year** Pa. Laws **page number**

Administrative compilation:
Pennsylvania Code — Pa. Code tit. **title number,** § section number (Year)

Administrative register:
Pennsylvania Bulletin — **Volume number** Pa. Bull. **page number** (**Month Day, Year**)

Local citation rules? Yes. See **Appendix 2.**   **Neutral citation rules?** No.

Rhode Island

Court system and reporters:

Rhode Island Supreme Court (R.I.)

Reporter	Abbreviation	Dates	Status
Rhode Island Reports	R.I.	1828–1980	Official
Atlantic Reporter	A.	1885–1938	Unofficial
Second Series	A.2d	1938–present	Official since 1980
Rhode Island Reporter (West offprint)	A.2d	1980–present	Official

Statutory compilation:
★General Laws of Rhode Island   R.I. Gen. Laws § **section number** (**Year**)

Session laws:
Public Laws of Rhode Island   **Year** R.I. Laws **page number**
Acts and Resolves of Rhode Island   **Year** R.I. Acts & Resolves **pinpoint**
and Providence Plantations

Administrative compilation:
Code of Rhode Island Rules   Code R.I. R. r. **rule number** (**Year**)

Administrative register:
Rhode Island Government Register   **Issue number** R.I. Govt. Register **page number** (Weil **Month Year**)

Local citation rules? No.   **Neutral citation rules?** No.

South Carolina

Court system and reporters:

South Carolina Supreme Court (S.C.)

Reporter	Abbreviation	Dates	Status
South Carolina Reports	S.C.	1868–present	Official
South Eastern Reporter	S.E.	1887–1939	Unofficial
Second Series	S.E.2d	1939–present	Unofficial

South Carolina Court of Appeals (S.C. App.)

Reporter	Abbreviation	Dates	Status
South Carolina Reports	S.C.	1983–present	Official
South Eastern Reporter, Second Series	S.E.2d	1983–present	Unofficial

Statutory compilation:
★Code of Laws of South Carolina   S.C. Code Ann. § **section number** (**Year**)
1976 Annotated

Session laws:
Acts and Joint Resolutions of South   **Year** S.C. Acts **page number**
Carolina

Administrative compilation:

Code of Laws of South Carolina 1976 Annotated—Code of Regulations

S.C. Code Regs. **chapter number-rule number (Year)**

Administrative register:

South Carolina State Register

Volume number S.C. Register **page number (Month Year)**

Local citation rules? Yes. See **Appendix 2.**   **Neutral citation rules?** No.

South Dakota

Court system and reporters:

South Dakota Supreme Court (S.D.)

Reporter	Abbreviation	Dates	Status
South Dakota Reports	S.D.	1890–1976	Official
North Western Reporter	N.W.	1890–1941	Unofficial
Second Series	N.W.2d	1941–present	Official since 1976

Statutory compilation:

★South Dakota Codified Laws

S.D. Codified Laws § **section number (Year)**

Session laws:

Laws of South Dakota

Year S.D. Laws **page number**

Administrative compilation:

Administrative Rules of South Dakota

Admin. R. S.D. **title number:article number:chapter number:section number (Year)** (e.g., Admin. R. S.D. 20:51:01:01 (2005))

Administrative register:

South Dakota Register

Volume number S.D. Register **page number (Month Day, Year)**

Local citation rules? Yes. See **Appendix 2.**   **Neutral citation rules?** No.

Tennessee

Court system and reporters:

Tennessee Supreme Court (Tenn.)

Reporter	Abbreviation	Dates	Status
Tennessee Reports	Tenn.	1791–1972	Official
South Western Reporter	S.W.	1886–1928	Unofficial
Second Series	S.W.2d	1928–1999	Official since 1972
Third Series	S.W.3d	1999–present	Official
Tennessee Decisions (West offprint)	S.W., S.W.2d, S.W.3d	1886–present	Official since 1972

Tennessee Court of Appeals (Tenn. App.)

Reporter	Abbreviation	Dates	Status
Tennessee Appeals Reports	Tenn. App.	1925–1971	Official
South Western Reporter			
Second Series	S.W.2d	1932–1999	Official since 1972
Third Series	S.W.3d	1999–present	Official
Tennessee Decisions (West offprint)	S.W.2d, S.W.3d	1932–present	Official since 1972

Tennessee Court of Criminal Appeals (Tenn. Crim. App.)

Reporter	Abbreviation	Dates	Status
Tennessee Criminal Appeals Reports	Tenn. Crim.	1967–1971	Official
South Western Reporter			
Second Series	S.W.2d	1967–1999	Official since 1972
Third Series	S.W.3d	1999–present	Official
Tennessee Decisions (West offprint)	S.W.2d, S.W.3d	1967–present	Official since 1972

Statutory compilation:

★Tennessee Code Annotated   Tenn. Code Ann. § **section number** (Lexis **Year**)

West's Tennessee Code Annotated   Tenn. Code Ann. § **section number** (West **Year**)

Session laws:

Public Acts of the State of Tennessee   **Year** Tenn. Pub. Acts ch. **chapter number**

Private Acts of the State of Tennessee   **Year** Tenn. Priv. Acts ch.**chapter number**

Administrative compilation:

Official Compilation—Rules and Regulations of the State of Tennessee   Tenn. Comp. R. & Regs. **agency control number-division number-chapter number-rule number** (**Year**) (e.g., Tenn. Comp. R. & Regs. 1360-1-1-.02 (2005))

Administrative register:

Tennessee Administrative Register   **Volume number** Tenn. Admin. Register **page number** (**Month Year**)

Local citation rules? Yes. See **Appendix 2.**   **Neutral citation rules?** No.

Texas

Court system and reporters:

Texas Supreme Court (Tex.)

Reporter	Abbreviation	Dates	Status
Texas Reports	Tex.	1846–1963	Official
South Western Reporter	S.W.	1886–1928	Unofficial
Second Series	S.W.2d	1928–1999	Official since 1962
Third Series	S.W.3d	1999–present	Official

| Texas Cases (West offprint) | S.W., S.W.2d, S.W.3d | 1886–present | Official since 1962 |

Texas Court of Criminal Appeals (Tex. Crim. App.)

Note: Before 1891, the Texas Court of Criminal Appeals was the Texas Court of Appeals (Tex. App.).

Reporter	Abbreviation	Dates	Status
Texas Criminal Reports	Tex. Crim.	1892–1962	Official
South Western Reporter	S.W.	1892–1928	Unofficial
Second Series	S.W.2d	1928–1999	Official since 1963
Third Series	S.W.3d	1999–present	Official
Texas Cases (West offprint)	S.W., S.W.2d, S.W.3d	1886–present	Official since 1963

Texas Court of Appeals (Tex. App. ___ Dist.)

Note: Before 1981, the Texas Court of Appeals was the Texas Court of Civil Appeals (Tex. Civ. App.).

Reporter	Abbreviation	Dates	Status
Texas Civil Appeals Reports	Tex. Civ.	1892–1911	Official
South Western Reporter	S.W.	1892–1928	Official since 1911
Second Series	S.W.2d	1928–1999	Official
Third Series	S.W.3d	1999–present	Official
Texas Cases (West offprint)	S.W., S.W.2d, S.W.3d	1892–present	Official

Statutory compilations:

★Vernon's Texas Code Annotated — Tex. **Subject abbreviation** Code Ann. § **section number (Year)**
Note: Consult **Appendix 3(E)** for subject abbreviations.

Vernon's Revised Texas Statutes Annotated — Tex. Rev. Civ. Stat. Ann. art. **article number** (West **Year**)

Session laws:

General and Special Laws of the State of Texas — **Year** Tex. Gen. Laws ch. **chapter number**

Vernon's Texas Session Law Service — **Year** Tex. Sess. L. Serv. **pinpoint**

Administrative compilation:

Official Texas Administrative Code — Tex. Admin. Code tit. **title number**, § **section number (Year)**

Administrative register:

Texas Register — **Volume number** Tex. Register **page number (Month Day, Year)**

Local citation rules? Yes. See **Appendix 2.**   **Neutral citation rules?** No.

Utah

Court system and reporters:

Utah Supreme Court (Utah)

Reporter	Abbreviation	Dates	Status
Utah Reports	Utah	1855–1952	Official
Second Series	Utah 2d	1953–1974	Official
Pacific Reporter	P.	1883–1931	Unofficial
Second Series	P.2d	1931–2000	Official since 1974
Third Series	P.3d	2000–present	Official
Utah Reporter (West offprint)	P.2d, P.3d	1974–present	Official

Utah Court of Appeals (Utah App.)

Reporter	Abbreviation	Dates	Status
Pacific Reporter			
Second Series	P.2d	1987–2000	Official
Third Series	P.3d	2000–present	Official
Utah Reporter (West offprint)	P.2d, P.3d	1987–present	Official

Statutory compilation:

★Utah Code Annotated   Utah Code Ann. § section number (Lexis Year)

West's Utah Code Annotated   Utah Code Ann. § section number (West Year)

Session laws:

Laws of Utah   Year Utah Laws ch. chapter number

Administrative compilation:

Utah Administrative Code   Utah Admin. Code r. rule number (Month Day, Year)

Administrative register:

Utah State Bulletin   Utah Bull. page number (Month Day, Year)

Local citation rules?   See **Appendix 2.**   Neutral citation rules?   No.

Vermont

Court system and reporters:

Vermont Supreme Court (Vt.)

Reporter	Abbreviation	Dates	Status
Vermont Reports	Vt.	1826–present	Official
Atlantic Reporter	A.	1885–1938	Unofficial
Second Series	A.2d	1938–present	Unofficial

Statutory compilation:

★Vermont Statutes Annotated   Vt. Stat. Ann. tit. title number, § section number (Year)

Session laws:

Acts and Resolves of Vermont   Year Vt. Acts & Resolves page number

Administrative compilation:
Code of Vermont Rules

Code Vt. R. nine-digit rule number (Year) (e.g., Code Vt. R. 21 020 032-1 (1999))

Administrative register:
Vermont Government Register

Issue number Vt. Govt. Register page number (Weil Month Year)

Local citation rules? Yes. See **Appendix 2.**   Neutral citation rules? Yes. See **Appendix 2.**

Virginia

Court system and reporters:

Virginia Supreme Court (Va.)

Note: Before 1971, the Virginia Supreme Court was the Virginia Supreme Court of Appeals (Va.).

Reporter	Abbreviation	Dates	Status
Virginia Reports	Va.	1790–present	Official
South Eastern Reporter	S.E.	1887–1939	Unofficial
Second Series	S.E.2d	1939–present	Unofficial

Virginia Court of Appeals (Va. App.)

Reporter	Abbreviation	Dates	Status
Virginia Court of Appeals Reports	Va. App.	1985–present	Official
South Eastern Reporter, Second Series	S.E.2d	1985–present	Unofficial

Virginia Circuit Court (Va. Cir.)

Reporter	Abbreviation	Dates	Status
Virginia Circuit Court Opinions	Va. Cir.	1985–present	Official

Note: Although it began publication in 1985, Virginia Circuit Court Opinions covers cases dating to 1855.

Statutory compilation:
★Code of Virginia Annotated   Va. Code Ann. § section number (Lexis Year)
West's Annotated Code of Virginia   Va. Code Ann. § section number (West Year)

Session laws:
Acts of the General Assembly of the Commonwealth of Virginia

Year Va. Acts ch. chapter number

Administrative compilation:
Virginia Administrative Code

Volume number Va. Admin. Code agency number-chapter number-rule number (Year) (e.g., 21 Va. Admin. Code 5-110-90 (2005))

Administrative register:

Virginia Register of Regulations   **Volume number** Va. Register **page number (Month Day, Year)**

Local citation rules? Yes. See **Appendix 2.**   **Neutral citation rules?** No.

Washington

Court system and reporters:

Washington Supreme Court (Wash.)

Reporter	Abbreviation	Dates	Status
Washington Reports	Wash.	1889–1939	Official
Second Series	Wash. 2d	1939–present	Official
Pacific Reporter	P.	1883–1931	Unofficial
Second Series	P.2d, P.3d	1931–2000	Unofficial
Third Series	P.3d	2000–present	Unofficial

Washington Court of Appeals (Wash. App. Div. ___)

Reporter	Abbreviation	Dates	Status
Washington Appellate Reports	Wash. App.	1969–present	Official
Pacific Reporter			
Second Series	P.2d	1969–2000	Unofficial
Third Series	P.3d	2000–present	Unofficial

Statutory compilations:

★Revised Code of Washington   Wash. Rev. Code § **section number (Year)**

Revised Code of Washington Annotated   Wash. Rev. Code Ann. § **section number** (West **Year**)

Annotated Revised Code of Washington   Wash. Rev. Code Ann. § **section number** (Lexis **Year**)

Session laws:

Laws of Washington   **Year** Wash. Laws **page number**

Washington Legislative Service   **Year** Wash. Legis. Serv. **pinpoint**

Administrative compilation:

Washington Administrative Code   Wash. Admin. Code **title number-chapter number-section number (Year)** (e.g., Wash. Admin. Code 50-24-010 (2005))

Administrative register:

Washington State Register   Wash. Register **issue number-rule filing number (Month Day, Year)**

Local citation rules? Yes. See **Appendix 2.**   **Neutral citation rules?** No.

West Virginia

Court system and reporters:

West Virginia Supreme Court of Appeals (W. Va.)

Reporter	Abbreviation	Dates	Status
West Virginia Reports	W. Va.	1864–present	Official
South Eastern Reporter	S.E.	1887–1939	Unofficial
Second Series	S.E.2d	1939–present	Unofficial

West Virginia Court of Claims (W. Va. Cl.)

Reporter	Abbreviation	Dates	Status
West Virginia Court of Claims Reports	W. Va. Cl.	1942–present	Official

Statutory compilation:

★West Virginia Code	W. Va. Code § **section number** (**Year**)
Michie's West Virginia Code Annotated	W. Va. Code Ann. § **section number** (Lexis **Year**)
West's Annotated Code of West Virginia	W. Va. Code Ann. § **section number** (West **Year**)

Session laws:

Acts of the Legislature of West Virginia	**Year** W. Va. Acts ch. **chapter number**

Administrative compilation:

West Virginia Code of State Rules	W. Va. Code R. § **section number** (**Year**)

Administrative register:

West Virginia State Register	**Volume number** W. Va. Register **page number** (**Month Day, Year**)

Local citation rules? No.   Neutral citation rules? No.

Wisconsin

Court system and reporters:

Wisconsin Supreme Court (Wis.)

Reporter	Abbreviation	Dates	Status
Wisconsin Reports	Wis.	1853–1957	Official
Second Series	Wis. 2d	1957–present	Official
North Western Reporter	N.W.	1879–1941	Unofficial
Second Series	N.W.2d	1941–present	Unofficial
Wisconsin Reporter (West offprint)	N.W.2d	1941–present	Official since 1975

Wisconsin Court of Appeals (Wis. App. Dist. ⎯)

Reporter	Abbreviation	Dates	Status
Wisconsin Reports, Second Series	Wis. 2d	1978–present	Official
North Western Reporter, Second Series	N.W.2d	1978–present	Unofficial
Wisconsin Reporter (West offprint)	N.W.2d	1978–present	Co-official

Statutory compilations:

★Wisconsin Statutes	Wis. Stat. § **section number (Year)**
Wisconsin Statutes Annotated	Wis. Stat. Ann. § **section number** (West **Year**)

Session laws:

Laws of Wisconsin	**Year** Wis. Laws ch. **chapter number**
West's Wisconsin Legislative Service	**Year** Wis. Legis. Serv. **pinpoint** (West)

Administrative compilation:

Wisconsin Administrative Code	Wis. Admin. Code, **Agency abbreviation** § **section number (Year)** *Note:* Consult **Appendix 3** for agency abbreviations.

Administrative register:

Wisconsin Administrative Register	**Issue number** Wis. Admin. Register **page number (Month Day, Year)**

Local citation rules?   Yes. See **Appendix 2.**   **Neutral citation rules?**   No.

Wyoming

Court system and reporters:

Wyoming Supreme Court (Wyo.)

Reporter	Abbreviation	Dates	Status
Wyoming Reports	Wyo.	1870–1959	Official
Pacific Reporter	P.	1883–1931	Unofficial
Second Series	P.2d	1931–2000	Official since 1959
Third Series	P.3d	2000–present	Official
Wyoming Reporter (West offprint)	P.2d, P.3d	1959–present	Official

Statutory compilation:

★Wyoming Statutes Annotated	Wyo. Stat. Ann. § **section number (Year)**

Session laws:

Session Laws of Wyoming	**Year** Wyo. Laws ch. **chapter number**

Administrative compilation:

Weil's Code of Wyoming Rules (unofficial compilation)	Weil's Code Wyo. R. **rule number (Year)**

Administrative register:

Weil's Wyoming Government Register (unofficial compilation)	Wyo. Govt. Register **issue number-page number** (Weil **Month Year**)

Local citation rules?   No.   **Neutral citation rules?**   Yes. See **Appendix 2.**

Territories

American Samoa

Court system and reporters:

High Court of American Samoa (Am. Sam.)

Reporter	Abbreviation	Dates	Status
American Samoa Reports	Am. Sam.	1900–1975	Official
Second Series	Am. Sam. 2d	1983–present	Official

Statutory compilation:
★American Samoa Code Annotated

Title number Am. Sam. Code Ann. § **section number** (**Year**)

Session laws: None.

Administrative compilation:
American Samoa Administrative Code

Am. Sam. Admin. Code **title number.section number** (**Year**) (e.g., Am. Sam. Admin. Code 5.1102 (2005))

Administrative register: None.

Local citation rules? No. Neutral citation rules? No.

Guam

Court system and reporters:

Supreme Court of Guam (Guam)

Reporter	Abbreviation	Dates	Status
Guam Reports	Guam	1955–date	Official

Statutory compilation:
★Guam Code Annotated

Title number Guam Code Ann. § **section number** (**Year**)

Session laws:
Guam Session Laws

Year Guam Sess. Laws **page number**

Administrative compilation:
Administrative Rules and Regulations of the Government of Guam

Guam R. & Regs. tit. **title number**, § **section number** (**Year**)

Administrative register: None.

Local citation rules? No. Neutral citation rules? No.

Navajo Nation

Court system and reporters:

Supreme Court of the Navajo Nation (Navajo)

Note: The Supreme Court of the Navajo Nation was previously known as the Navajo Court of Appeals (Navajo).

Reporter	Abbreviation	Dates	Status
Navajo Reporter	Navajo	1969–present	Official

Navajo District Court (Navajo Dist.)

Reporter	Abbreviation	Dates	Status
Navajo Reporter	Navajo	1969–present	Official

Statutory compilation:
   ★Navajo Nation Code

Navajo Nation Code tit. **title number**, § **section number** (Equity **Year**)

Session laws: None.

Administrative compilation: None.

Administrative register: None.

Local citation rules? No.   **Neutral citation rules?** No.

Northern Mariana Islands

Court system and reporters:

Commonwealth Supreme Court of the Northern Mariana Islands (N. Mar. Is.)

Reporter	Abbreviation	Dates	Status
Northern Mariana Islands Reporter	N. Mar. Is.	1991–present	Official

Commonwealth Superior Court of the Northern Mariana Islands (N. Mar. Is. Super.)

Reporter	Abbreviation	Dates	Status
Northern Mariana Islands Commonwealth Reporter	N. Mar. Cmmw.	1978–present	Official

Statutory compilation:
   ★Northern Mariana Islands Commonwealth Code

Title number N. Mar. Is. Code § **section number** (**Year**)

Session laws: None.

Administrative compilation: None.

Administrative register:
   Northern Mariana Islands Commonwealth Register

N. Mar. Is. Register **page number** (**Month Year**)

Local citation rules? No.   **Neutral citation rules?** No.

Puerto Rico

Court system and reporters:

Puerto Rico Supreme Court (P.R.) (Tribunal Supremo de Puerto Rico)

Reporter	Abbreviation	Dates	Status
Decisiones de Puerto Rico	D.P.R.	1899–present	Official
Puerto Rico Reports	P.R.R.	1899–1972	Official

Official Translations of the Supreme Court of Puerto Rico	P.R. Off. Trans.	1973–present	Official
Avazadas del Colegio de Abogados de Puerto Rico	C.A.	1932–1999	Unofficial
	T.S.P.R.	1999–present	Unofficial
Jurispurdencia del Tribunal Supremo de Puerto Rico	J.T.S.	1973–present	Unofficial

Puerto Rico Circuit Court of Appeals (P.R. Cir.) (Tribunal de Circuito de Apelaciones)

Reporter	Abbreviation	Dates	Status
Decisiones del Tribunal de Circuito de Apelaciones Puerto Rico	T.C.A.	1995–present	Unofficial

Statutory compilation:
 ★Laws of Puerto Rico Annotated (Leyes de Puerto Rico Anotadas) **Title number** Laws P.R. Ann. § **section number (Year)**

Session laws:
 Laws of Puerto Rico (Leyes de Puerto Rico) **Year** Laws P.R. **page number**

Administrative compilation: None.

Administrative register:
 Puerto Rico Register of Regulations (unofficial compilation) **Volume number** P.R. Register **issue number (Month Day, Year)**

Local citation rules? Yes. See **Appendix 2.** **Neutral citation rules?** Yes. See **Appendix 2.**

Virgin Islands

Court system and reporters:

Territorial Court of the Virgin Islands (V.I.)

Reporter	Abbreviation	Dates	Status
Virgin Island Reports	V.I.	1917–present	Official

Statutory compilation:
 ★Virgin Islands Code Annotated V.I. Code Ann. tit. **title number**, § **section number (Year)**

Session laws:
 Session Laws of the Virgin Islands **Year** V.I. Laws **page number**

Administrative compilation:
 Virgin Islands Rules and Regulations V.I. R. & Regs. tit. **title number**, § **section number (Year)**

istrative register:
Virgin Islands Government
Register

Issue Number V.I. Govt. Register **page number** (Weil
Month Year)

Local citation rules? No.   Neutral citation rules? No.

Federal Materials

Court system and reporters:

United States Supreme Court (U.S.)

Reporter	Abbreviation	Dates	Status
United States Reports	U.S.	1789–present	Official
Supreme Court Reporter	S. Ct.	1882–present	Unofficial
United States Supreme Court Reports, Lawyers' Edition	L. Ed.	1879–1956	Unofficial
Second Series	L. Ed. 2d	1956–present	Unofficial
United States Law Week	U.S.L.W.	1933–present	Unofficial

United States Courts of Appeals (e.g., 3d Cir., 11th Cir., D.C. Cir.)

Reporter	Abbreviation	Dates	Status
Federal Reporter	F.	1880–1924	Unofficial
Second Series	F.2d	1924–1993	Unofficial
Third Series	F.3d	1993–present	Unofficial
Federal Appendix	Fed. Appx.	2001–present	Unofficial

Assign #1
#4, 2

More clout

Old Federal Circuit Courts: Consult Rule 12.19.

Temporary Emergency Court of Appeals (created 1971, abolished 1993) (Temp. Emerg. Ct. App.): Cite F. or F.2d.

Emergency Court of Appeals (created 1942, abolished 1961) (Emerg. Ct. App.): Cite F. or F.2d.

Commerce Court (created 1910, abolished 1913) (Com. Ct.): Cite F.

United States Court of Customs and Patent Appeals (previously the Court of Customs Appeals) (Cust. & Pat. App.): Cite F., F.2d, or C.C.P.A.

Court of Customs and Patent Appeals: Cite F., F.2d, or C.C.P.A.

Court of Customs Appeals (Cust. App.): Cite F. or Ct. Cust.

Court of Claims (Ct. Cl.): Cite Ct. Cl., F., F.2d, or F.3d

United States Court of Federal Claims (created 1992) (Fed. Cl.): Cite Fed. Cl.

United States Claims Court (created 1982) (Cl. Ct.): Cite Cl. Ct.

United States Court of International Trade (Intl. Trade): Cite Ct. Intl. Trade.

United States Customs Court (Cust. Ct.): Cite Cust. Ct., F. Supp., F. Supp. 2d, Cust. B. & Dec., or I.T.R.D. (BNA) (in that order of preference).

United States District Courts (e.g., S.D. Cal., W.D.N.Y., D. Mass.)

Reporter	Abbreviation	Dates	Status
Federal Supplement *Trial court*	F. Supp.	1932–1998	Unofficial
Second Series	F. Supp. 2d	1998–present	Unofficial
Federal Rules Decisions	F.R.D.	1938–present	Unofficial
Bankruptcy Reporter	B.R.	1979–present	Unofficial
Federal Reporter	F.	1880–1924	Unofficial
Second Series	F.2d	1924–1932	Unofficial

United States Bankruptcy Courts (e.g., Bankr. S.D.N.Y.)

Reporter	Abbreviation	Dates	Status
Bankruptcy Reporter	B.R.	1979–present	Unofficial

Bankruptcy Appellate Panels (e.g., Bankr. App. 1st Cir.): Cite B.R.

Judicial Panel on Multidistrict Litigation (created 1968) (M.D.L.): Cite F. Supp. or F. Supp. 2d.

Special Court, Regional Rail Reorganization Act (Regl. Rail Reorg.): Cite F. Supp. or F. Supp. 2d.

Tax Court: See Appendix 7.

United States Court of Veterans Claims (Vet. App.): Cite Vet. App.

United States Court of Appeals for the Armed Forces (App. Armed Forces): Cite C.M.A. or M.J.

Statutory compilations:

★United States Code	Title number U.S.C. § section number (Year)
United States Code Annotated	Title number U.S.C.A. § section number (West Year)
United States Code Service	Title number U.S.C.S. § section number (Lexis Year)

Session laws:

United States Statutes at Large	Title number Stat. page number (Year)

Administrative compilation:

Code of Federal Regulations	Volume number C.F.R. subdivision (Year)

Administrative register:

Federal Register	Volume number Fed. Reg. page number (Month Day, Year)

Local citation rules? Some federal courts have local citation rules. See **Appendix 2.**

Neutral citation rules? Some federal courts have or apply neutral citation rules. See **Appendix 2.**

APPENDIX 1A
WEST REGIONAL REPORTER COVERAGE

West Reporter

Coverage

Atlantic Reporter
(A., A.2d)

State appellate court decisions from Connecticut, Delaware, District of Columbia, Maine, Maryland, New Hampshire, New Jersey, Pennsylvania, Rhode Island, and Vermont.

North Eastern Reporter
(N.E., N.E.2d)

State appellate court decisions from Illinois, Indiana, Massachusetts, New York, and Ohio.

North Western Reporter
(N.W., N.W.2d)

State appellate court decisions from Iowa, Michigan, Minnesota, Nebraska, North Dakota, South Dakota, and Wisconsin.

Pacific Reporter
(P., P.2d, P.3d)

State appellate court decisions from Alaska, Arizona, California, Colorado, Hawaii, Idaho, Kansas, Montana, Nevada, New Mexico, Oklahoma, Oregon, Utah, Washington, and Wyoming.

South Eastern Reporter
(S.E., S.E.2d)

State appellate court decisions from Georgia, North Carolina, South Carolina, Virginia, and West Virginia.

South Western Reporter
(S.W., S.W.2d, S.W.3d)

State appellate court decisions from Arkansas, Kentucky, Missouri, Tennessee, Texas, and Indian Territories.

Southern Reporter
(So., So.▲2d)

State appellate court decisions from Alabama, Florida, Louisiana, and Mississippi.

APPENDIX 2
LOCAL COURT CITATION RULES

This appendix contains local citation rules or preferences promulgated by state and federal courts. It also identifies those courts that have adopted a neutral citation format. If a jurisdiction is not listed, it does not currently have formal local rules.

The information in this appendix is current as of July 2005. Check this book's Web site at http://www.alwd.org for regular updates. And always consult your court's rules before submitting a court document.

Use these rules when submitting documents to the listed court. For example, if submitting a document to a Michigan state court, follow the Michigan local rules. Also note that, out of custom rather than rule, some local practitioners use local rules in other documents, such as office memoranda.

State Courts

Alabama

"Citations of authority shall comply with the rules of citation in the latest addition [edition] of either The Bluebook: A Uniform System of Citation or ALWD (Association of Legal Writing Directors) Citation Manual: A Professional System of Citation or shall otherwise comply with the style and form used in opinions of the Supreme Court of Alabama. Citations shall reference the specific page number(s) that relate to the proposition for which the case is cited . . . ." **Ala. R. App. P. 28(a)(10).**

Arizona

"Citation of authorities shall be to the volume and page number of the official reports and also when possible to the unofficial reporters." **Ariz. R. Civ. App. P. 13(a)(6).**

Arkansas

"Citations of decisions of the Court which are officially reported must be from the official reports. All citations of decisions of any court must state the style of the case and the book and page in which the case is found. If the case is also reported by one or more unofficial publishers, these should also be cited, if possible." **Ark. Sup. Ct. R. 4-2(a)(7).**

California

"(c) **Case citation format.** A case citation must include the official report volume and page number and year of decision. No other citations may be required."

"(f) **Use of California Style Manual.** The style used in a memorandum must be that stated in the *California Style Manual* or *The Bluebook: Uniform System of Citation,* at the option of the party filing the document. The same style shall be used consistently throughout the memorandum." **Cal. R. Ct. 313(c) & (g).**

Use the following subject abbreviations when citing the California Code (West or Deering/Lexis). If a term is not listed, spell it out or use the abbreviations in **Appendix 3(E).**

Subject matter	Abbreviation
Business and Professions	Bus. & Prof.
Civil	Civ.
Civil Procedure	Civ. Proc.
Commercial	Com.
Corporations	Corp.
Education	Educ.
Elections	Elec.
Evidence	Evid.
Family	Fam.
Financial	Fin.
Food and Agriculture	Food & Agric.
Government	Govt.
Harbors and Navigation	Harb. & Nav.
Insurance	Ins.
Labor	Lab.
Military and Veterans	Mil. & Vet.
Probate	Prob.
Public Contract	Pub. Cont.
Public Resources	Pub. Res.
Public Utilities	Pub. Util.
Revenue and Taxation	Rev. & Tax.
Streets and Highways	Sts. & High.
Unemployment Insurance	Unemp. Ins.
Vehicle	Veh.
Welfare and Institutions	Welf. & Inst.

Colorado

Although Colorado does not have a statute or court rule addressing local citation forms, the Colorado Supreme Court has developed the internal *Uniform Citation Forms,* which has been incorporated into the Court's manual for its law clerks and is still used to conform citation form in Colorado Supreme Court decisions. In addition, the Colorado Court of Appeals has an internal style sheet. The formats used in both courts are reprinted below.

The following citations are from K.K. Duvivier, *Colorado Citations,* 34 Colo. Law. 39 (2005).

Colorado Court of Appeals Cases (officially published after August 7, 1980, with no available parallel citation)

    All Colorado courts: *Fitzgerald v. Edelen,* 623 P.2d 418 (Colo. App. 1980).

Colorado Statutes

Colorado Supreme Court style: § 18-13-122, C.R.S. (2004)
Colorado Court of Appeals style: § 18-13-122, C.R.S. 2004

Session Laws

Colorado Supreme Court style: Ch. 294, sec. 1, § 18-13-122, 2004 Colo. Sess. Laws 1096–97
Colorado Court of Appeals style: Colo. Sess. Laws 2004, ch. 294, § 18-13-122 at 1096–97

Colorado Regulations

Colorado Supreme Court style: Colorado Court of Appeals: Dep't of Human Services Reg. 16.323, 2C Code Colo. Regs. 503-1

Rules

Colorado Supreme Court and	C.R.C.P. 12(b)	[civil]
Court of Appeals style:	Crim. P. 52	[criminal]
	CRE 611(b)	[evidence]
	C.R.P.P. 2	[probate]
	C.A.R. 58	[appellate]

Neutral Citation Format

In May 1994, the Colorado Supreme Court ordered that its decisions be numbered by paragraph, stating that the paragraph numbers would constitute acceptable pinpoint citations to West's Pacific Reporter page numbers.

Connecticut

"(a) In the table of authorities, citations to state cases shall be to the official reporter first, if available, followed by the regional reporter. Citations to cases from jurisdictions having no official reporter shall identify the court rendering the decision. Citations to opinions of the United States Supreme Court shall be to the United States Reports, if therein; otherwise, such citations shall be to the Supreme Court Reporter, the Lawyer's Edition, or United States Law Week, in that order of preference."

"(b) In the argument portion of a brief, citations to Connecticut cases shall be to the official reporter only. Citations to other state cases may be to either the official reporter or the regional reporter. United States Supreme Court cases should be cited as they appear in the table of authorities."

"(c) If a case is not available in print and is available on an electronic database, such as LEXIS, Westlaw, CaseBase or LOIS, the case shall be cited to that database. In the table of authorities, citations to such cases shall include the case name; docket number; name of the database and, if applicable, numeric identifiers unique to the database; court name; and full date of the disposition of the case. Screen, page or paragraph numbers shall be preceded by an asterisk. In the argument portion of the brief, such cases shall be cited only by name and database. If such a case is published in a print reporter after the filing of the party's brief, but prior to the case on appeal being orally argued or submitted for decision on the record and briefs, the party who cited the unreported case shall, by letter, inform the chief clerk of the print citation of that case." **Conn. R. App. P. 67-11.**

Delaware

"Form of citations. The following shall be the form of citations:

(i) **Reported Opinions.** The style of citation shall be as set forth in THE BLUEBOOK: A UNIFORM SYSTEM OF CITATION, with no reference to State Reporter Systems or other parallel citations. For example:

Melson v. Allman, 244 A.2d 85 (Del. 1968).
Prince v. Bensinger, 244 A.2d 89 (Del. Ch. 1968).
State v. Pennsylvania R.R. Co., 244 A.2d 80 (Del. Super. Ct. 1968).

(ii) **Unreported Opinions.** The style of citation shall be any of the three alternatives set forth below:

LEXIS Citation Form: Fox v. Fox, 1998 Del. LEXIS 179 (Del. Supr.).

   OR

Westlaw Citation Form: Fox v. Fox, 1998 WL 280361 (Del. Supr.).

   OR

Delaware Citation Form: Fox v. Fox, Del. Supr., No. 510, 1997, Berger, J. (May 14, 1998).

(iii) Other Authority. The style of citation to any other type of authority, including but not limited to statutes, books, and articles, shall be as set forth in THE BLUEBOOK: A UNIFORM SYSTEM OF CITATION."

Del. Sup. Ct. R. 14(g); Del. Sup. Ct. R. 93. If relevant, also consult the following local citation rules: **Delaware Superior Court Civil Rule 107(c)(4), Delaware Chancery Court Rule 171(g),** and **Delaware Court Civil Pleas Rule 107(c)(4).**

District of Columbia

"All citations to cases decided by the United States Court of Appeals for the District of Columbia Circuit shall include the volume number and page of both U.S. App. D.C. and the Federal Reporter." **D.C. Super. Ct. Civ. P.R. 12-I(e); D.C. Super. Ct. Small Claims R. 13(a); D.C. Super. Ct. Land. & Ten. R. 13(a); D.C. Super. Ct. Crim. P.R. 47-I(b); D.C. Super. Ct. Dom. Rel. P.R. 7(b); D.C. Super. Ct. Juv. P.R. 47 & 47-I(b); D.C. Super. Ct. Neg. P.R. 43(a); D.C. Super. Ct. Tax P.R. 9(b).**

Florida

"This rule applies to all legal documents, including court opinions. Except for citations to case reporters, all citation forms should be spelled out in full if used as an integral part of a sentence either in the text or in footnotes. Abbreviated forms as shown in this rule should be used if the citation is intended to stand alone either in the text or in footnotes.

"(a) Florida Supreme Court.

    (1) 1846–1886: *Livingston v. L'Engle,* 22 Fla. 427 (1886).

    (2) *Fenelon v. State,* 594 So. 2d 292 (Fla. 1992).

    (3) For recent opinions not yet published in the Southern Reporter, cite to Florida Law Weekly: *Traylor v. State,* 17 Fla. L. Weekly S42 (Fla. Jan. 16, 1992). If not therein, cite to the slip opinion: *Medina v. State* No. SC00-280 (Fla. Mar. 14, 2002).

"(b) Florida District Courts of Appeal.

    (1) *Sotolongo v. State,* 530 So. 2d 514 (Fla. 2d DCA 1988); *Buncayo v. Dribin,* 533 So. 2d 935 (Fla. 3d DCA 1988).

    (2) For recent opinions not yet published in Southern Reporter, cite to Florida Law Weekly: *Myers v. State,* 16 Fla. L. Weekly D1507 (Fla. 4th DCA June 5, 1991). If not therein, cite to the slip opinion: *Fleming v. State,* No. 1D01-2734 (Fla. 1st DCA Mar. 6, 2002).

"(c) Florida Circuit Courts and County Courts.

    (1) *Whidden v. Francis,* 27 Fla. Supp. 80 (Fla. 11th Cir. Ct. 1966).

    (2) *State v. Alvarez,* 42 Fla. Supp. 83 (Fla. Dade Cty. Ct. 1975).

    (3) For opinions not published in Florida Supplement, cite to Florida Law Weekly: *State v. Campeau,* 16 Fla. L. Weekly C65 (Fla. 9th Cir. Ct. Nov. 7, 1990). If not therein, cite to the slip opinion: *State v. Campeau,* No. 90-4363 (Fla. 9th Cir. Ct. Nov. 7, 1990).

"(d) Florida Administrative Agencies. (Cite if not in Southern Reporter.)

    (1) For decisions of the Public Employees Relations Commission: *Indian River Educ. Ass'n v. School Bd.,* 4 F.P.E.R. ¶ 4262 (1978).

    (2) For decisions of the Florida Public Service Commission: I*n re Application of Tampa Elec. Co.,* 81 F.P.S.C. 2:120 (1981).

    (3) For decisions of all other agencies: *Insurance Co. v. Department of Ins.,* 2 F.A.L.R. 648-A (Fla. Dept. of Insurance 1980).

"(e) Florida Constitution. (Year of adoption should be given if necessary to avoid confusion.)

Art. V, § 3(b)(3), Fla. Const.

"(f) Florida Statutes (Official).

§ 350.34, Fla. Stat. (1973).
§ 120.53, Fla. Stat. (Supp. 1974).

"(g) Florida Statutes Annotated. (To be used only for court-adopted rules, or references to other nonstatutory materials that do not appear in an official publication.)

32 Fla. Stat. Ann. 116 (Supp. 1975).

"(h) Florida Laws. (Cite if not in Fla. Stat. or if desired for clarity or adoption reference.)

    (1) After 1956: Ch. 74-177, § 5, at 473, Laws of Fla.

    (2) Before 1957: Ch. 22000, Laws of Fla. (1943).

"(i) Florida Rules.

Fla. R. Civ. P. 1.180.
Fla. R. Jud. Admin. 2.035.
Fla. R. Crim. P. 3.850.
Fla. R. Work. Comp. P. 4.113.

Fla. Prob. R. 5.120.
Fla. R. Traf. Ct. 6.165.
Fla. Sm. Cl. R. 7.070.
Fla. R. Juv. P. 8.070.
Fla. R. App. P. 9.100.
Fla. R. Med. 10.100.
Fla. R. Arb. 11.010.
Fla. Fam. L. R. P. 12.010.
Fla. Admin. Code R. 62D-2.014.
R. Regulating Fla. Bar 4-1.10.
Fla. Bar Found. By-Laws, art. 2.19(b).
Fla. Bar Found. Charter, art. III, § 3.4.
Fla. Bar Integr. R., art XI, § 11.09.
Fla. Jud. Qual. Comm'n R. 9.
Fla. Std. Jury Instr. (Civ.) 6.4(c).
Fla. Std. Jury Instr. (Crim.) 2.03.
Fla. Std. Jury Instr. (Crim.) Robbery.
Fla. Stds. Imposing Law. Sancs. 9.32(a).
Fla. Bar Admiss. R., 3-23.1.

"(j) Florida Attorney General Opinions.

Op. Att'y Gen. Fla. 73-178 (1973).

"(k) United States Supreme Court.

Sansone v. United States, 380 U.S. 343 (1965). (Cite to United States Reports, if published therein; otherwise cite to Supreme Court Reporter, Lawyer's Edition, or United States Law Week, in that order of preference. For opinions not published in these reporters, cite to Florida Law Weekly Federal: *California v. Hodari D.,* 13 Fla. L. Weekly Fed. S249 (U.S. Apr. 23, 1991).

"(l) Federal Courts of Appeals.

Gulf Oil Corp. v. Bivins, 276 F.2d 753 (5th Cir. 1960). For opinions not published in the Federal Reporter, cite to Florida Law Weekly Federal: *Cunningham v. Zant,* 13 Fla. L. Weekly Fed. C591 (11th Cir. March 27, 1991).

"(m) Federal District Courts.

Pugh v. Rainwater, 332 F. Supp. 1107 (S.D. Fla. 1971).

For opinions not published in the Federal Supplement, cite to Florida Law Weekly Federal: *Wasko v. Dugger,* 13 Fla. L. Weekly Fed. D183 (S.D. Fla. Apr. 2, 1991).

"(n) United States Constitution.

Art. IV, § 2, cl. 2, U.S. Const. Amend. V, U.S. Const.

"(o) Other Citations. When referring to specific material within a Florida court's opinion, pinpoint citation to the page of the Southern Reporter where that material occurs is optional, although preferred. All other citations shall be in the form prescribed by the latest edition of The Bluebook: A Uniform System of Citation, The Harvard Law Review Association, Gannett House, Cambridge, MA 02138. Citations not covered in this rule or in The Bluebook shall be in the form prescribed by the Florida Style Manual published by the Florida State University Law Review, Tallahassee, FL 32306.

"(p) Case Names. Case names shall be underscored (or italicized) in text and in footnotes."

Fla. R. App. P. 9.800.

Georgia

"All citations of authority must be full and complete. Georgia citations must include the volume and page number of the official Georgia reporters (Harrison, Darby or Lexis). Cases not yet reported shall be cited by the Supreme Court or Court of Appeals case number and date of decision. The enumeration of errors shall be deemed to include and present for review all judgments necessary for a determination of the errors specified." **Ga. Sup. Ct. R. 22.**

"All citations of cases shall be by name of the case as well as by volume, page and year of the Official Report. Cases not yet reported shall be cited by the Court of Appeals or Supreme Court case number and date of decision." **Ga. Ct. App. R. 24(d).**

> ***Note:*** Many Georgia practitioners abbreviate the Official Code of Georgia Annotated as O.C.G.A.

Hawaii

"A subject index of the matter in the brief with page references and a table of authorities listing the cases, alphabetically arranged, text books, articles, statutes, treatises, regulations, and rules cited, with reference to the pages in the brief where they are cited. Citation to Hawai[]i cases since statehood shall include both the state and regional reporters. Citation to foreign cases may be to only the regional reporters. Where cases are generally available only from electronic databases, citation may be made thereto, provided that the citation contains enough information to identify the database, the court, and the date of the opinion." **Haw. R. App. P. 28(b)(1).**

Idaho

"Citations appearing in opinions shall be in conformity with statutory provision of this state, the rules of this Court and if not therein covered, in conformity with the current edition of 'A Uniform System of Citation,' published and distributed by the Harvard Law Review Association or the 'ALWD (Association of Legal Writing Directors) Citation Manual: A Professional System of Citation.'" **Sup. Ct. Idaho Internal R. 15(e) (amended 2005).**

Illinois

"Citations of cases must be by title, to the page of the volume where the case begins, and to the pages upon which the pertinent matter appears in at least one of the reporters cited. It is not sufficient to use only *supra* or *infra*. Citation of Illinois cases shall be to the official reports, but the citation to the North Eastern Reporter and/or the Illinois Decisions may be added. Quotations may be cited from either the official reports or the North Eastern Reporter or the Illinois Decisions. Citation of cases from other jurisdictions shall include the date and may be to either the official State reports or the National Reporter System, or both. If only the National Reporter System citation is used, the court rendering the decision shall also be identified. Textbook citations shall include the date of publication and the edition. Illinois statutes shall generally be cited to the Illinois Compiled Statutes (ILCS) but citations to the session laws of Illinois shall be made when appropriate. Prior to January 1, 1997, statutory citations may be made to the Illinois Revised Statutes instead of or in addition to the Illinois Compiled Statutes." **Ill. Sup. Ct. R. 6.**

Indiana

"Unless otherwise provided, a current edition of a Uniform System of Citation (Bluebook) shall be followed.

"**A. Citation to Cases.** All Indiana cases shall be cited by giving the title of the case followed by the volume and page of the regional and official reporter (where both exist), the court of disposition, and the year of the opinion, e.g., *Callender v. State*, 193 Ind. 91, 138 N.E. 817 (1922); *Moran v. State*, 644 N.E.2d 536 (Ind. 1994). If the case is not contained in the regional reporter, citation may be made to the official reporter. Where both a regional and official citation exist and pinpoint citations are appropriate, pinpoint citations to one of the reporters shall be provided. Designation of disposition of petitions for transfer shall be included, e.g., *State ex rel. Mass Transp. Auth. of Greater Indianapolis v. Indiana Revenue Bd.*, 144 Ind. App. 63, 242 N.E.2d 642 (1968), *trans. denied by an evenly divided court* 251 Ind. 607, 244 N.E.2d 111 (1969); *Smith v. State*, 717 N.E.2d 127 (Ind. Ct. App. 1999), *trans. denied.*

"**B. Citations to Indiana Statutes, Regulations and Court Rules.** Citation to Indiana statutes, regulations, and court rules shall comply with the following citation format for initial references and subsequent references:

Initial	Subsequent
Ind. Code §34-1-1-1 (20xx)	I.C. §34-1-1-1
Ind. Admin. Code tit. 34, r. 12-5-1 (20xx)	34 IAC 12-5-1
Ind. Trial Rule 56	T.R. 56
Ind. Crim. Rule 4(B)(1)	Crim. R. 4(B)(1)
Ind. Post-Conviction Rule 2(2)(b)	P-C.R. 2(2)(b)
Ind. Appellate Rule 8	App. R. 8
Ind. Original Action Rule 3(A)	Orig. Act. R. 3(A)
Ind. Child Support Rule 2	Child Supp. R. 2
Ind. Child Support Guideline 3(D)	Child Supp. G. 3(D)
Ind. Small Claims Rule 8(A)	S.C.R. 8(A)
Ind. Tax Court Rule 9	Tax Ct. R. 9
Ind. Administrative Rule 7(A)	Admin. R. 7(A)
Ind. Judicial Conduct Canon 2(A)	Jud. Canon 2(A)
Ind. Professional Conduct Rule 6.1	Prof. Cond. R. 6.1
Ind. Alternative Dispute Resolution Rule 2	A.D.R. 2
Ind. Admission and Discipline Rule 23(2)(a)	Admis. Disc. R. 23(2)(a)
Ind. Evidence Rule 301	Evid. R. 301
Ind. Jury Rule 12	J.R. 12"

Ind. R. App. P. 22.

Iowa

"In citing cases the names of parties must be given. In citing Iowa cases, reference must be made to the volume and page where the case may be found in the Iowa Reports, if reported therein, and in the North Western Reporter, if reported therein. In citing cases reference must be made to the court that rendered the opinion and the volume and page where the same may be found in the National Reporter System, if reported therein. E.g., ___ Iowa ___, ___ N.W. ___ (20__); ___ N.W.2d ___ (Iowa 20__); ___ N.W.2d ___ (Iowa Ct. App. 20__); ___ S.W.2d ___ (Mo. Ct. App. 20__); ___ U.S. ___, ___ S.Ct. ___, ___ L. Ed. 2d ___ (20__); ___ F. 2d ___ (___ Cir. 20__); ___ F. Supp. ___ (S.D. Cal. 20__). When quoting from authorities or referring to a specific point within an authority, the specific page or pages quoted or relied upon shall be given in addition to the required page references.

When citing the Iowa Court Rules parties shall use the following:

a. 'Iowa R. Civ. P.'; 'Iowa R. Crim. P.'; 'Iowa R. Evid.'; 'Iowa R. App. P.'; 'Iowa Code of Prof'l Responsibility'; and 'Iowa Code of Judicial Conduct' when citing those rules.

b. 'Iowa Ct. R.' when citing all other rules.

"An unpublished opinion of the Iowa appellate courts or of any other appellate court may be cited in a brief; however, unpublished opinions shall not constitute controlling legal authority. . . . When citing an unpublished appellate opinion, a party shall include, when available, an electronic citation indicating where the opinion may be readily accessed on line.

"When treatises or textbooks are cited, the edition must be designated. In citing authorities other than cases, references shall be made as follows: Codes, to section number; treatises, textbooks and encyclopedias, to section and page; all others, to page or pages. Use of the 'supra' and 'infra' forms of citation is discouraged." **Iowa R. App. P. 6.14(5).**

Kansas

"References to court cases shall be by the official citations followed by any generally recognized reporter system citations." **Kan. Sup. Ct. R. 6.08.**

Kentucky

"All citations of Kentucky Statutes shall be made from the official edition of the Kentucky Revised Statutes and may be abbreviated 'KRS.' The citation of Kentucky cases reported after January 1, 1951, shall be in the following form for decisions of the Supreme Court and its predecessor court: Doe v. Roe, ___ S.W.2d ___ or ___ S.W.3d ___ (Ky. [date]), or for reported decisions of the present Court of Appeals, Doe v. Roe, ___ S.W.2d ___ or ___ S.W.3d ___ (Ky. App. [date]). For cases reported prior thereto both Kentucky Reports and Southwestern citations shall be given." **Ky. R. Civ. P. 76.12(4)(g).**

Louisiana

"A. The following rules of citation of Louisiana appellate court decisions shall apply:

  (1) Opinions and actions issued by the Supreme Court of Louisiana and the Louisiana Courts of Appeal following December 31, 1993 shall be cited according to a uniform public domain citation form with a parallel citation to West's Southern Reporter.

    (a) The uniform public domain citation form shall consist of the case name, docket number excluding letters, court abbreviation, and month, day and year of issue, and be followed by a parallel citation to West's Southern Reporter, e.g.:

    Smith v. Jones, 93-2345 (La. 7/15/94); 650 So.2d 500, or *Smith v. Jones,* 93-2345 (La. App. 1 Cir. 7/15/94); 660 So.2d 400

    (b) If a pinpoint public domain citation is needed, the page number designated by the court shall follow the docket number and be set off with a comma and the abbreviation 'p', and may be followed by a parallel pinpoint citation to West's Southern Reporter, e.g.:

    Smith v. Jones, 94-2345, p. 7 (La. 7/15/94); 650 So.2d 500, 504

  (2) Opinions issued by the Supreme Court of Louisiana for the period between December 31, 1972 and January 1, 1994, and all opinions issued by the Courts of Appeal

417

from the beginning of their inclusion in West's Southern Reporter in 1928 until January 1, 1994, shall be cited according to the form in West's Southern Reporter:

(a) The citation will consist of the case name, Southern Reporter volume number, title abbreviation, page number, court designation, and year, e.g.:

Smith v. Jones, 645 So.2d 321 (La. 1990)

(b) A parallel public domain citation following the same format as that for post-January 1, 1994 opinions may be added after the Southern Reporter citation, but is not required.

(3) Opinions issued by the Supreme Court of Louisiana prior to the discontinuation of the official Louisiana Reports in 1972 and opinions issued by the Courts of Appeal prior to their inclusion in the Southern Reporter in 1928 shall be cited in accordance with pre-1994 practice, as follows:

(a) Cite to Louisiana Reports, Louisiana Annual Reports, Robinson, Martin, Reports of the Louisiana Courts of Appeal, Peltier, Teisser, or McGloin if therein, and to the Southern Reporter or Southern 2d if therein.

(b) A parallel public domain citation following the same format as that for post-January 1, 1994 opinions may be added, but is not required.

"B. These rules shall apply to all published actions of the Supreme Court of Louisiana and the Louisiana Courts of Appeal issued after December 31, 1993. Citation under these rules in court documents shall become mandatory for all documents filed after July 1, 1994."

La. Sup. Ct. Gen. Admin. R. 8.

"Citation of other cases shall be to volume and page of the official reports (and when possible to the unofficial reports). It is recommended that where United States Supreme Court cases are cited, all three reports be cited, e.g., *Miranda v. Arizona,* 384 U.S. 436, 86 S.Ct. 1602, 16 L.Ed.2d 694 (1966)." **La. Unif. R. Ct. App. 2-12.4.**

Notes: (1) A list of commonly used Louisiana abbreviations is contained in Win-Shin S. Chiang, *Louisiana Legal Research* app. M (1990).

(2) Consult *Louisiana Law Review Streamlined Citation Manual,* 50 La. L. Rev. 197 (1989), for additional Louisiana formats.

Neutral Citation Format

See rules above.

Maine

The *Maine Law Review* publishes the *Uniform Maine Citations* (see http://mainelaw.maine.edu/lawreview/muca.html). Consult that source for all rules. Below are citations for commonly cited sources.

Maine cases (issued before January 1, 1997):	*Westman v. Armitage,* 215 A.2d 919 (Me. 1996).
Maine Revised Statutes Annotated:	1 M.R.S.A. § 401 (1989).
Session laws (public laws):	P.L. 1981, ch. 668, § 2.
Legislative bills:	L.D. 2199 (108th Legis. 1978).
Legislative debate:	Legis. Rec. 745 (1943).
Legislative reports:	Report of the Joint Standing Committee on Taxation on the Maine Forestry District Tax 5–6 (1982).

Neutral Citation Format

"1. The *Atlantic Reporter* is the official publication of the Court's opinions commencing January 1, 1966.

"2. Opinions issued on or after January 1, 1966, and before January 1, 1997, shall be cited in the following style:

Westman v. Armitage, 215 A.2d 919 (Me. 1966)

"3. Opinions issued on or after January 1, 1997, shall include the calendar year, the sequential number assigned to the opinion within that calendar year, and shall be cited in the following style:

Smith v. Jones, 1997 ME 7, 685 A.2d 110

"4. The sequential decision number shall be included in each opinion at the time it is made available to the public and the paragraphs in the opinion shall be numbered. The official publication of each opinion issued on or after January 1, 1997 shall include the sequential number in the caption of the opinion and the paragraph numbers assigned by the Court.

"5. Pinpoint citations shall be made by reference to paragraph numbers assigned by the Court in the following style:

Smith v. Jones, 1997 ME 7, ¶ 14, 685 A.2d 110, 115.

"6. Memorandum Decisions and Summary Orders shall not be published in the *Atlantic Reporter* and shall not be cited as precedent for any matter addressed therein."

Or. SJC-216 (Me. Aug. 20, 1996) (also available at http://www.courts.state.me.us/opinions/ supreme/citation.html).

Maryland

"When a reported Maryland case is cited, the citation shall include a reference to the official Report." **Md. R. App. Rev. 8-504(a)(1).**

> *Note:* Cite the Code of Maryland Regulations as COMAR.
> **Example:** COMAR 13A.07.01.03 (2005).

Massachusetts

"Massachusetts Reports between 17 Massachusetts and 97 Massachusetts shall be cited by the name of the reporter. Any other citation shall include, wherever reasonably possible, a reference to any official report of the case or to the official publication containing statutory or similar material. References to decisions and other authorities should include, in addition to the page at which the decision or section begins, a page reference to the particular material therein upon which reliance is placed, and the year of the decision; as, for example: 334 Mass. 593, 597–598 (1956). Quotations of Massachusetts statutory material shall include a citation to either the Acts and Resolves of Massachusetts or to the current edition of the General Laws published pursuant to a resolve of the General Court." **Mass. R. App. P. 16(g);** *see* **Mass. Dist. & Mun. App. Div. R. 16(g).**

Michigan

Citations must conform with the Michigan Uniform System of Citation, which is too lengthy to reprint in this *Manual,* but which does require parallel citations for Michigan cases. The Michigan System is reprinted in the most current version of *Michigan Rules of Court: State* (West) (also available at http://courtofappeals.mijud.net/court/courtrules.htm).

Mississippi

"(2) All Mississippi cases shall be cited to either:

  (i) the Southern Reporter and, in cases decided prior to 1967, the official Mississippi Reports (e.g., Smith v. Jones, 699 So.2d 100 (Miss. 1997)); or

  (ii) for cases decided from and after July 1, 1997, the case numbers as assigned by the Clerk's Office (e.g., Smith v. Jones, 95-KA-01234-SCT (Miss. 1997)).

"(3) Quotations from cases and authorities appearing in the text of the brief shall be cited in one of the following ways:

  (i) preceded or followed by a reference to the book and page in the Southern Reporter and/or the Mississippi Reports where the quotation appears (e.g., Smith v. Jones, 699 So.2d 100, 102 (Miss. 1997)); or

  (ii) in cases decided from and after July 1, 1997, preceded or followed by a reference to the case number assigned by the Clerk's Office and paragraph number where the quotation appears (e.g., Smith v. Jones, 95-KA-01234-SCT (¶1) (Miss. 1997)); or

  (iii) in cases decided from and after July 1, 1997, preceded or followed by a reference to the book and paragraph number in the Southern Reporter where the quotation appears (e.g., Smith v. Jones, 699 So.2d 100 (¶1) (Miss. 1997)); or

  (iv) in cases decided prior to July 1, 1997, preceded or followed by a reference to the case number assigned by the Clerk's Office and paragraph number where the quotation appears when the case is added to the Court's Internet web site in the new format, i.e., with paragraph numbers (e.g., Smith v. Jones, 93-CA-05678-SCT (¶1) (Miss. 1995)); or

  (v) preceded or followed by a parallel citation using both the book citation and the case number citation."

Miss. R. App. P. 28(e).

Neutral Citation Format

"From and after July 1, 1997, the Supreme Court and the Court of Appeals shall assign paragraph numbers to the paragraphs in all published opinions. The paragraph numbers shall begin at the first paragraph of the text of the majority opinion and shall continue sequentially throughout the majority opinion and any concurring or dissenting opinions in the order that the opinions are arranged by the Court." **Miss. R. App. P. 28(e)(1).**

See also the rules above.

Montana

Neutral Citation Format

"In order to facilitate electronic legal research via the Internet; in order to make the opinions and substantive orders issued by this Court more accessible to the print and broadcast media and to members of the public; and in order to more effectively implement the 'Right to Know' provisions of the Constitution of the State of Montana, Article II, Section 9, this Court, pursuant to its authority under Article VII, Section 2(3) of the Constitution of the State of Montana, has determined to make an addition to its current citation format. Accordingly, IT IS ORDERED that, from and after January 1, 1998:

"(1) At the time of issuance, this Court shall assign to all opinions and to those orders designated by this Court for publication (hereinafter referred to as substantive orders), a citation which shall include the calendar year in which the opinion or substantive order is issued followed by the Montana U.S. Postal Code (MT) followed by a consecutive number beginning each year with '1' (for example, 1998 MT 1). This citation shall be known as the public domain or neutral-format citation and shall appear on the title page of each opinion and on the first page of each substantive order issued by this Court. State Reporter Publishing Company and West Group are requested to publish this public domain, neutral-format citation within the heading of each opinion or substantive order published by those companies.

"(2) Beginning with the first paragraph of text, each paragraph in every such opinion and substantive order shall be numbered consecutively beginning with a ¶ symbol followed by an Arabic numeral, flush with the left margin, opposite the first word of the paragraph. Paragraph numbers shall continue consecutively throughout the text of the majority opinion or substantive order and any concurring or dissenting opinions or rationale. Paragraphs within footnotes shall not be numbered nor shall markers, captions, headings or Roman numerals which merely divide opinions or sections thereof. Block-indented single-spaced portions of a paragraph shall not be numbered as a separate paragraph. State Reporter Publishing Company and West Group are requested to publish these paragraph numbers in each opinion or substantive order published by those companies.

"(3) In the case of opinions which are not to be cited as precedent (variously referred to as unpublished, 'noncite,' or memorandum opinions) and in the case of all substantive orders (unless otherwise specifically designated by this Court), the consecutive number in the public domain or neutral-format citation shall be followed by the letter 'N' to indicate that the opinion or substantive order is not to be cited as precedent in any brief, motion or document filed with this Court or elsewhere (for example, 1998 MT 1N). Any 'N' citation, nevertheless, shall be listed along with the result, case title and Supreme Court cause number in the quarterly table of noncitable cases issued by this Court and published by State Reporter Publishing Company and West Group.

"(4) In the case of opinions or substantive orders which are withdrawn or vacated by a subsequent order of this Court, the public domain, neutral-format citation of the withdrawing or vacating order shall be the same as the original public domain, neutral-format citation but followed by a letter 'W' (for example, 1998 MT 1W). An opinion or substantive order issued in place of one withdrawn or vacated shall be assigned the next consecutive number appropriate to the date on which it is issued.

"(5) In the case of opinions or substantive orders which are amended by a subsequent order of this Court, the public domain, neutral-format citation of the amending order shall be the same as the original public domain, neutral-format citation but followed by a letter 'A' (for example, 1998 MT 1A). Amended paragraphs shall contain the same number as the paragraph being amended. Additional paragraphs shall contain the same number as the immediately preceding original paragraph but with the addition of a lower case letter (for example, if two new paragraphs are added following paragraph 13 of the original opinion; the new paragraphs will be numbered ¶ 13a and ¶ 13b). If a paragraph is deleted, the number of the deleted paragraph shall be skipped in the sequence of paragraph numbering in any subsequently published version of the amended opinion of substantive order, provided that at the point where the paragraph was deleted, there shall be a note indicating the deletion of that paragraph.

"(6) The following are examples of proper citations to Montana Supreme Court opinions:

For cases decided before January 1, 1998:
Primary cite:
Roe v. Doe (1997), 284 Mont. 301, 989 P.2d 472.

Primary cite with pinpoint cite:
Roe v. Doe (1997), 284 Mont. 301, 305, 989 P.2d 472, 475.

Pinpoint cite alone:
Roe, 284 Mont. at 305, 989 P.2d at 475.

For cases decided from and after January 1, 1998:
Primary cite:
Doe v. Roe, 1998 MT 12, 286 Mont. 175, 989 P.2d 1312.

Primary cite with pinpoint cite:
Doe v. Roe, 1998 MT 12, ¶¶ 44–45, 286 Mont. 175 ¶¶ 44–45, 989 P.2d 1312, ¶¶ 44–45.

Pinpoint cite:
Doe, ¶¶ 44–45.

"IT IS FURTHER ORDERED that the citation formats adopted herein are in addition to and supplement the current citation formats used by this Court. The Montana Reports is the official reporter of this Court's opinions and this Court will continue to cite to both its official reporter and to the regional, Pacific, reporter in addition to the public domain, neutral-format citation. This Court encourages the adoption and use of these formats in all briefs, memoranda and other documents filed in this Court."

In re Opinion Forms & Citation Standards of the Sup. Ct. of Mont.; & the Adoption of a Form of Public Domain & Neutral-Format Citation (Dec. 16, 1997), http://www.lawlibrary.state.mt.us/dscgi/ds.py/Get/File-4161/order-citation.pdf.

Nebraska

"(4) Every reference to a reported case shall set forth the title thereof, the volume and page where found, the tribunal deciding the case, and the year decided. If the cited opinion is long, it shall also refer to the page where the pertinent portion of the opinion is found. Nebraska cases shall be cited by the Nebraska Reports and/or Nebraska Appellate Reports, but may include citation to such other reports as may contain such cases.

"(5) If a current statute is relied upon, it must be cited from the last published revision or compilation of the statutes, or supplement thereto, if contained therein; if not contained therein, to the session laws wherein contained, or the legislative bill as enacted.

"(6) Citations to textbooks, encyclopedias, and other works shall give the title, edition, year of publication, volume number, section, and page where found." **Neb. Sup. Ct. R. 9(C).**

"Citation to authorities shall conform to generally accepted uniform standards of citation; citation of Nebraska cases shall include the Nebraska Reports or the Nebraska Appellate Reports and North Western Reporter citation." **Neb. Unif. Dist. Ct. R. 5(C).**

Nevada

"Nevada Revised Statutes and its component parts may be cited as follows:

(a) Nevada Revised Statutes: NRS

(b) A title: title 00 of NRS

(c) A chapter: chapter 000 of NRS

(d) A section: NRS 000.000."

Nev. Rev. Stat. § 220.170(4) (2003).

New Hampshire

"Citations to Supreme Court of the United States cases that cannot be made to the official *United States Reports* or to the *Supreme Court Reporter* shall include the month, day, and year of decision or a reference to *United States Law Week.* Citations to other federal decisions not presently reported shall identify the court, docket number, and date.

"Citations to the decisions of this court may be to the *New Hampshire Reports* only. Citations to other State court decisions may either be: (a) to the official report and to the West Reporter system, with the year of decision; or (b) to the West Reporter only, in which case the citation should identify the State court by name or level, and should mention the year of decision." **N.H. Sup. Ct. R. 16(9).**

New Jersey

"New Jersey decisions shall be cited to the official New Jersey reports by volume number but if not officially reported that fact shall be stated and unofficial citation made. All other state court decisions shall be cited to the National Reporter System, if reported therein and, if not, to the official report. In the citation of all cases the court and year shall be indicated in parentheses except that the year alone shall be given in citing the official reports of the United States Supreme Court, the Supreme Court of New Jersey, and the highest court of any other jurisdiction." **N.J. R. App. Prac. 2:6-2(a)(5).**

In addition, practitioners are urged to consult *Manual on Style for Legal Citation in New Jersey,* approved in 1992 and revised in 2004. The *Manual* appears on the Judiciary Web site, at http://www.judiciary.state.nj.us/appdiv/manualonstyle.pdf.

New Mexico

"All New Mexico cases shall be cited from the official reports, with parallel citations if available. As to other authorities, any consistent method or form which adequately identifies the authority may be used." **N.M. R. App. P. 12-213(E).**

Neutral Citation Format

"23-112. Citations for pleadings and other papers.

"A. Applicability. This rule governs the form of citations included in pleadings and papers filed in the courts of this state.

"B. State appellate court citations. For opinions of the New Mexico Supreme Court and New Mexico Court of Appeals, the following is an example of the form of citation: State v. Ray, 2003-NMSC-001, 122 N.M. 23 or State v. Ray, 2003-NMSC-001, 122 N.M. 23, 976 P.2d 54. Use of the vendor neutral citation with citation to both reporters is permitted, but is not required. For opinions not yet published in the reporter system, the vendor neutral citation may be followed by citation to the Bar Bulletin, use the following form of citation: State v. Ray, 2003-NMSC-001, Vol. 26, No. 53, SBB 23. For citations for opinions issued prior to January 1, 1996, follow citation rules in The Bluebook: A Uniform System of Citation (18th Ed. 2005).

"**C.** **Subsequent history.** Effective October, 2003, subsequent history, when cited, shall include the vendor neutral citation for certiorari information, as assigned by the Supreme Court, e.g., State v. Ray, 2003-NMCA-001, {reporter citation}, cert. granted, 2004-NMCERT-003, {reporter citation}. When a vendor neutral citation number is not available, the Supreme Court docket number shall be substituted for the vendor neutral citation, e.g., State v. Ray, 2003-NMCA-001, {reporter citation}, cert. granted, Sup. Ct. No. 28,714, {reporter citation}.

"**D.** **Pinpoint citations.** If a pinpoint citation is used:
   (1) for opinions issued after 1996 that have a paragraph number, the paragraph number shall be used after the vendor neutral citation, e.g., State v. Ray, 2003-NMSC-001, ¶ 2, {reporter citation};
   (2) for opinions issued prior to 1997 or if paragraph numbering is unavailable, the applicable page number of the New Mexico Reports and Pacific Reporter print publication shall be used; A short citation form may be used if it clearly identifies a case that has been cited within the same general textual discussion, e.g., Ray, 2003-NMSC-001, ¶ 2.

"**E.** **Citation to New Mexico statutes.** Citations to section numbers of the New Mexico statutes shall be to the chapter, article and section of the NMSA 1978. The form shall be as follows: 'NMSA 1978, § _____ (year)' or 'NMSA 1978, Section 34-1-1 (1972).' It is unnecessary to include a citation to compilation references such as 'Cum. Supp.' or 'Repl. Pamp.', rather reference shall be made to the date of enactment or amendment, as applicable. This date is the date in the 'History Note' following each statute relied upon in the pleading or paper.

"**F.** **Citation to court rules and uniform jury instructions.** Rules, uniform jury instructions and forms promulgated or approved by the Supreme Court shall be cited to the New Mexico Rules Annotated version by set and rule number. For example: 'Rule 1-001 NMRA' or 'UJI ___ NMRA'. You may also use the citation form approved by the Supreme Court and published in the NMRA. For example, Rule 4A-100 NMRA provides that rules published in set number 4A of the NMRA may be cited as 'Domestic Relations Form 4A-___.' If the rule has been amended since the date the proceedings were filed, it may be necessary to refer to the year of the version of the rule relied upon in the pleading or paper. In such cases the year of the NMRA is added after 'NMRA'.

"**G.** **Administrative code.** If a pleading or paper cites a state agency rule or regulation, the New Mexico Administrative Code shall be cited using Title, Chapter, Part and Subpart, e.g., '1.15.2.1 NMAC'. It may also be necessary to use a year after 'NMAC' to identify the year of the rule applicable to the pending case;

"**H.** Bluebook citations. Except as provided in Paragraphs A through F of this rule, the form of citations as set forth in The Bluebook: A Uniform System of Citation (18th ed. 2005) shall be used for all citation reference for all pleadings and other papers filed in all courts in this state."

N.M. Sup. Ct. Gen. R. 23-112 (effective August 15, 2005).

New York

"Where New York authorities are cited, *New York Official Law Report* citations must be included, if available. Copies of decisions that are not officially published, or are not otherwise available, should be included in the submission in which such decisions are cited." **N.Y. Ct. App. R. 500.1(c).**

"Where New York authorities are cited in any submission, New York Official Law Report citations shall be included, if available." **N.Y. Ct. App. R. 500.1(c).**

"*Citation of Decisions.* New York decisions shall be cited from the official reports, if any. All other decisions shall be cited from the official reports, if any, and also from the National Reporter System, if they are there reported. Decisions not reported officially or in the National Reporter System shall be cited from the most available source." **N.Y. Ct. App. R. 600.10(a)(11).**

"New York decisions shall be cited from the official reports, if any. All other decisions shall be cited from the official reports, if any, and also from the National Reporter System if they are there reported. Decisions not reported officially or in the National Reporter System shall be cited from the most available source." **N.Y.C.P.L.R. 5529(e) (McKinney 2005).**

Additional Information for New York Practitioners

Official Reports Style Manual (N.Y. St. Unified Ct. Sys. 2002) (also known at the *Tanbook*; available at http://www.courts.state.ny.us/reporter/New_Styman.htm)

"The *Tanbook* is designed for anyone who writes to or for a New York State court. Published New York judicial opinions must comply with the *Tanbook*. Adherents should include not only New York State judges and their law clerks and court attorneys but also any advocate who seeks to persuade them by making decision making easier, faster, and more accurate. According to one authority, '[t]he *Official Style Manual* * * * is the citation standard used by judges and * * * is recommended for use by attorneys in briefs and papers submitted to the courts of New York.' (Ellen M. Gibson, New York Legal Research Guide I-170 [2d ed, William S. Hein & Co. 1998].).)" Gerald Lebovits, *New Edition of State's "Tanbook" Implements Extensive Revisions in Quest for Greater Clarity*, 74 N.Y. St. B.J. 8, 8 (Mar.–Apr. 2002).

Subject Abbreviations for Inclusion in State Statutory Citations

Use the following subject abbreviations when citing McKinney's Consolidated Laws of New York Annotated, New York Consolidated Laws Service, or Gould's New York Consolidated Laws. If a term is not listed, spell it out or use the abbreviations in **Appendix 3(E).**

Subject matter	Abbreviation
Abandoned Property	Aband. Prop.
Agricultural Conservation and Adjustment	Agric. Conserv. & Adj.
Agriculture and Markets	Agric. & Mkts.
Alcoholic Beverage Control	Alco. Bev. Cont.
Arts and Cultural Affairs	Arts & Cult. Aff.
Benevolent Orders	Ben. Ord.
Business Corporation	Bus. Corp.
Civil Practice Law and Rules	N.Y.C.P.L.R.
Civil Rights	Civ. Rights
Commerce	Com.
Cooperative Corporations	Coop. Corp.
Correction	Correct.
Criminal Procedure	Crim. Proc.

Subject matter	Abbreviation
Debtor and Creditor	Debt. & Cred.
Domestic Relations	Dom. Rel.
Economic Development	Econ. Dev.
Education	Educ.
Election	Elec.
Eminent Domain Procedure	Em. Dom. Proc.
Employers Liability	Emplrs. Liab.
Environmental Conservation	Envtl. Conserv.
Estates, Powers, and Trusts	Est. Powers & Trusts
Executive	Exec.
General Associations	Gen. Assns.
General Business	Gen. Bus.
General City	Gen. City
General Construction	Gen. Constr.
General Municipal	Gen. Mun.
General Obligations	Gen. Oblig.
Highway	High.
Insurance	Ins.
Judiciary Court Acts	Jud. Ct. Acts
Labor	Lab.
Legislative	Legis.
Limited Liability Company	Ltd. Liab. Co.
Local Finance	Local Fin.
Mental Hygiene	Mental Hyg.
Military	Mil.
Multiple Dwelling	Mult. Dwell.
Multiple Residence	Mult. Resid.
Municipal Home Rule and Statute of Local Governments	Mun. Home Rule
Navigation	Nav.
Not-for-Profit Corporation	Not-for-Profit Corp.
Parks, Recreation and Historic Preservation	Parks Rec. & Hist. Preserv.
Partnership	P'ship.
Personal Property	Pers. Prop.
Private Housing Finance	Priv. Hous. Fin.
Public Authorities	Pub. Auth.
Public Buildings	Pub. Bldgs.
Public Health	Pub. Health
Public Lands	Pub. Lands
Public Officers	Pub. Off.
Public Service	Pub. Serv.
Racing, Pari-Mutuel Wagering and Breeding	Rac. Pari-Mut. Wag. & Breed.
Railroad	R.R.
Rapid Transit	Rapid Trans.

Subject matter	Abbreviation
Real Property	Real Prop.
Real Property Actions and Proceedings	Real Prop. Acts.
Real Property Tax	Real Prop. Tax
Religious Corporation	Relig. Corp.
Retirement and Social Security	Retire. & Soc. Sec.
Rural Electric Cooperative	Rural Elec. Coop.
Social Services	Soc. Serv.
Soil and Water Conservation Districts	Soil & Water Conserv. Dist.
State Administrative Procedures Act	A.P.A.
State Finance	State Fin.
State Printing and Public Documents	State Print. & Pub. Docs.
State Technology	State Tech.
Statutes	Stat.
Surrogate's Court Procedure Act	Surr. Ct. Proc. Act
Transportation	Transp.
Unconsolidated	Unconsol.
Uniform Commercial Code	U.C.C.
Vehicle and Traffic	Veh. & Traf.
Volunteer Ambulance Workers' Benefit	Vol. Ambul. Workers' Ben.
Volunteer Firefighters' Benefit	Vol. Fire. Ben.
Workers' Compensation	Workers' Comp.

North Carolina

"Citations should be made according to *A Uniform System of Citation* (14th ed.)." **N.C. R. App. P. App. B.**

Note: Practitioners are urged to examine current North Carolina Supreme Court opinions for examples of how to cite North Carolina authority. Attorneys submitting briefs in North Carolina appellate courts should (1) include citations to both official and unofficial reporters, if both exist; (2) always quote from official reporters because, in that court's experience, the regional reporters do not always include changes to opinions; and (3) cite to the North Carolina administrative code in the manner specified by that code, not as abbreviated in the Sixteenth Edition.

North Dakota

Neutral Citation Format
"RULE 11.6 MEDIUM-NEUTRAL CASE CITATIONS

"(a) Citations Before January 1, 1997. The initial citation of any published opinion of the Supreme Court released before January 1, 1997, contained in a brief, memorandum, or other document filed with any trial or appellate court and a citation in the table of cases in a brief must include a reference to the volume and page number of the North Western Reporter in which the opinion is published. Subsequent citations within a brief, memorandum, or other document must include the page number and sufficient reference to identify the initial citation.

"(b) **Citations After January 1, 1997.** When available, initial citations must include the volume and initial page number of the North Western Reporter in which the opinion is published. The initial citation of any published opinion of the Supreme Court or Court of Appeals released on or after January 1, 1997, contained in a brief, memorandum, or other document filed with any trial or appellate court and the citation in the table of cases in a brief must also include a reference to the calendar year in which the decision was filed, followed by the court designation of 'ND' for the Supreme Court or 'ND App' for the Court of Appeals followed by a sequential number assigned by the Clerk of the Supreme Court. A paragraph citation should be placed immediately following the sequential number assigned to the case. Subsequent citations within the brief, memorandum or other document must include the paragraph number and sufficient references to identify the initial citation.

"Explanatory Note
"Rule 11.6 was adopted, effective March 5, 1997, subject to comment, to implement the use of medium-neutral case citations in North Dakota.

"For Illustrative Purposes.
Cite to a North Dakota Supreme Court Opinion published prior to January 1, 1997 as follows:

Smith v. Jones, 500 N.W.2d 600, 601 (N.D. 1994).
Smith, 500 N.W.2d at 601.
Id. at 602.
Black v. Black, 79 N.D. 100, 101, 60 N.W.2d 500, 501 (1953).
Black, 79 N.D. at 101, 60 N.W.2d at 501.
Id. at 103, 60 N.W.2d at 502.

Cite to a North Dakota Supreme Court Opinion published after January 1, 1997, as follows:

Before publication in North Western Reporter:

Smith v. Jones, 1997 ND 15.

After publication in North Western Reporter:

Smith v. Jones, 1997 ND 15, 600 N.W.2d 900.

Spot cite to a North Dakota Supreme Court Opinion published after January 1, 1997, as follows:

Before publication in North Western Reporter:

Smith v. Jones, 1997 ND 15, ¶ 21.
Smith, 1997 ND 15, ¶¶ 21–25.
Id. at ¶ 15.

After publication in North Dakota Reporter:

Smith v. Jones, 1997 ND 15, ¶ 21, 600 N.W.2d 900.
Smith, 1997 ND 15, ¶¶ 21–25, 600 N.W.2d 900.
Id. at ¶ 15.

"The use of the ¶ symbol in spot citations is necessary to distinguish paragraph numbers from page numbers. 'N.D.' (with periods) refers to the 'North Dakota Reports,' which were published between 1890 and 1953. 'ND' (without periods) refers to the database containing the electronic version of opinions filed after January 1, 1997. North Dakota Court of Appeals cases filed after January 1, 1997 are to be cited in the same manner as North Dakota Court Supreme Court cases using the database identifier 'ND App' (without periods)." **N.D. R. Ct. 11.6.**

The North Dakota Citation Manual can be found online at http://www.court.state .nd.us/Citation. The rules in are intended as a guide for Supreme Court and Court of Appeals opinions and could be used as a guide for attorneys submitting briefs to North Dakota state courts.

Ohio

"D. Citations
"(1) Published
    "a. All citations to reported Ohio cases in briefs or memoranda shall recite the date, volume and page of the official Ohio report and the parallel citation, where the same exists, to the Northeastern Reporter, e.g., *In Re Doe* 198 Ohio St.3d 309, 2003-Ohio-859,361 N.E.2d 454; *State v. Doe,* 151 Ohio App.3d 353, 2003-Ohio-299, 360 N.E.2d 743.
    "b. All citations to the United States Supreme Court cases in briefs or memoranda shall cite the date, volume and page of the official report and parallel citation to the Supreme Court Reporter, e.g., *Jones v. United States* (1960), 362 U.S. 257, 80 S.Ct. 725.
"(2) Unpublished
    "a. Unpublished opinions and decisions, including judgment entries, may be cited in briefs and memoranda but will not receive recognition unless complete copies thereof are attached to the brief or memorandum in which the citation is made and a full disclosure is made of any disposition by the Supreme Court of any appeal therefrom that has come to the attention of the citing counsel."

Ohio 1st Dist. Ct. App. R. 6(D).

"Case citations and other legal authorities must appear in the text of the argument after the point of law for which the case or legal authority is cited, NOT in a footnote, and must include the volume and page number of the case, and the particular page number where the point of law is found." **Ohio 3d Dist. Ct. App. R. 7(C).**

"Case citations must include volume number, page number, and the particular page numbers relevant to the point of law for which the case is cited. When a case is found in the official reports, the citation shall be to the official volume." **Ohio 9th Dist. Ct. App. R. 7(F).**

"All citations to reported Ohio cases in briefs or memoranda shall recite the date, volume and page of the official Ohio report, (where available), and the Ohio Supreme Court web citation (where available), e.g., *Myocare Nursing Home, Inc. v. Fifth Third Bank,* 98 Ohio St.3d 545, 2003-Ohio-2287; *State v. Watkins,* 99 Ohio St.3d 12, 2003-Ohio-2419; *State v. Schmidt,* 123 Ohio Misc.2d 30, 2002-Ohio-7462. Citations to United States Supreme Court cases shall appear with citations to United States Reports and parallel citations to the United States Supreme Court Reporter, e.g., *Paul v. Davis* (1976), 424 U.S. 693, 96 S.Ct. 1155, rehearing denied (1977), 425 U.S. 985, 96 S.Ct. 2194. Cases that are not cited in an Ohio official reporter and do not appear on the Ohio Supreme Court website shall be cited as follows: *State v. Beagle* (Mar. 1, 1999), Madison App. No. CA98-03-017; *Justice v. Columbus* (Nov. 14, 1991), Franklin App. No. 91AP-675, 1991 WL 244996; *Edinger v. Bd. of Allen Cty. Commrs.* (Apr. 26, 1995), Allen App. No. 1-94-84, 1995 Ohio App.Lexis 1974." **Ohio 12th Dist. Ct. App. R. 11(C).**

Notes: (1)   Practitioners should consult the *Revisions to the Manual of Citations.* The *Manual of Citations* was an interim edition that was published in 1992 by the Reporter's Office of the Ohio Supreme Court. The *Revisions* were published in July 2002 and are available at http://www.sconet.state.oh.us/ROD/pdf/ Rev_Manual_Cit_02.pdf.

        (2)   *Ohio Northern University Law Review* has produced a *Style Manual*—which is designed primarily for internal use—that contains additional information about Ohio sources.

Oklahoma

"The citation to opinions of the Oklahoma Supreme Court and the Oklahoma Court of Civil Appeals shall be in accordance with Rule 1.200(c), (d) and (e). The citation of other authorities shall be to the volume and page of the National Reporter System, if applicable, or to some selected case system, if practical. Where a decision cited in the brief is not included in the National Reporter System a copy may be included in an appendix to the brief. See Rules 1.11(i)(1) and 1.191(d). Citations to decisions of the United States Supreme Court shall be to the official reporter, the United States Reports, and may also include parallel citations to other reporters, or to some selected case system, if practical." **Okla. Sup. Ct. R. 1.11(l).**

Neutral Citation Format: Oklahoma Supreme Court

"(e) **Citation to Designation by Supreme Court and Reporters.** Published opinions of the Oklahoma Supreme Court promulgated after May 1, 1997 shall bear as an official cite the Oklahoma Supreme Court's paragraph citation form in accordance with this Rule. Opinions of the Oklahoma Court of Civil Appeals that are published after May 1, 1997 shall bear as an official citation form the Oklahoma Supreme Court's paragraph citation form in accordance with this Rule. The numbers of the paragraphs are assigned by the Court. The parallel cite to the official reporter is also required.

"The court designation for the Oklahoma Supreme Court is OK when the paragraph citation form is used. The Court designation for the Oklahoma Court of Civil Appeals is 'OK CIV APP' for the purposes the Supreme Court paragraph citation form. The court designation for Court of Appeals of Indian Territory is IT when the paragraph citation form is used to cite opinions of that court.

"Prior to January 1, 1998 citation to opinions of the Oklahoma Supreme Court and Court of Civil Appeals shall include citations to Pacific and Pacific 2d Reporters. Citation to the Supreme Court's paragraph citation is allowed as a parallel cite, but not required. Effective January 1, 1998, citation to opinions of the Oklahoma Supreme Court shall be as follows:

1.   *Oklahoma Supreme Court Opinions Promulgated Prior to May 1, 1997.* Opinions promulgated (filed) prior to May 1, 1997 shall be cited by reference to the Pacific and Pacific 2nd Reporters. Parallel citation to the Supreme Court's official paragraph citation form is strongly encouraged for opinions promulgated prior to May 1, 1997. Parallel citation to Oklahoma Reports is allowed. However, parallel citation to Oklahoma Reports shall not be made when the Supreme Court's official paragraph citation form is used.

Examples of permissible citation form for opinions prior to May 1, 1997:

Skinner v. Braum's Ice Cream Store, 1995 OK 11, 890 P.2d 922.
Skinner v. Braum's Ice Cream Store, 1995 OK 11, ¶ 9, 890 P.2d 922.
Skinner v. Braum's Ice Cream Store, 1995 OK 11, 890 P.2d 922, 925.
Skinner v. Braum's Ice Cream Store, 890 P.2d 922 (Okla. 1995)
Skinner v. Braum's Ice Cream Store, 890 P.2d 922, 925 (Okla. 1995).
Skinner v. Braum's Ice Cream Store, 890 P.2d 922 (Okla. 1995).
Skinner v. Braum's Ice Cream Store, 890 P.2d 922, 925 (Okla. 1995).
Skinner v. Braum's Ice Cream Store, Okl., 890 P.2d 922 (1995).
Skinner v. Braum's Ice Cream Store, Okl., 890 P.2d 922, 925 (1995).

In '*Skinner v. Braum's Ice Cream Store*, 1995 OK 11, ¶ 9, 890 P.2d 922' '1995' refers to the year the opinion was promulgated, 'OK' is the court designation for the Oklahoma Supreme Court, '11' is the number of the opinion in 1995 assigned to that opinion by the Oklahoma Supreme Court, '¶ 9' is paragraph number 9 of the opinion as designated by the Supreme Court, and '890 P.2d 922' is the parallel citation to Pacific 2d Reporter.

2. *Oklahoma Supreme Court Opinions Promulgated After May 1, 1997.* Opinions promulgated (filed) after May 1, 1997 shall be cited by reference to the Supreme Court's official paragraph citation form. Parallel citation to Pacific 2nd and subsequent Pacific Reporters is required. The parallel cite to Pacific 2d Reporter may include a cite to the specific page of that Reporter if a specific paragraph is cited. When the Supreme Court paragraph citation form is used citation to a footnote need not include the paragraph number where the note occurs in the opinion.

Examples of citation form for post-May 1, 1997 opinions using a pre-May 1, 1997 opinion:

Skinner v. Braum's Ice Cream Store, 1995 OK 11, 890 P.2d 922.
Skinner v. Braum's Ice Cream Store, 1995 OK 11, ¶ 9, 890 P.2d 922.
Skinner v. Braum's Ice Cream Store, 1995 OK 11, ¶ 9, 890 P.2d 922, 925.
Skinner v. Braum's Ice Cream Store, 1995 OK 11, n. 10, 890 P.2d 922.

An opinion cited subsequent to issuance of the mandate therein but prior to official publication shall be cited using the following as an example: *Wilkinson v. Dean Witter Reynolds, Inc.*, 1997 OK 20, ___ P.2d ___ (mandate issued April 3, 1997).

In a matter where no mandate issues an opinion may be cited prior to official publication when the time to file a petition for rehearing has lapsed and no petition for rehearing was filed. The following is an example: *Edwards v. Basel Pharmaceuticals*, 1997 OK 22, ___ P.2d ___ (petition for rehearing not filed).

3. *Opinions of the Oklahoma Court of Civil Appeals.* Published opinions of the Oklahoma Court of Civil Appeals promulgated after May 1, 1997 shall be cited by reference to the Supreme Court's official paragraph citation form. Parallel citation to Pacific 2nd Reporters is required. Published opinions prior to May 1, 1997 shall be cited using the Pacific Reporter 2d, and parallel citation to the paragraph citation form is strongly encouraged. Opinions of the Court of Civil Appeals, no matter when published, are subject to the other provisions of Rule 1.200.

4. *Citation to Opinions Supported by Less Than a Majority.* The paragraph citation form is also used to designate material in a published opinion where that opinion is supported by less than a majority of the members of the Supreme Court. When material from such an opinion is cited the name of the author, names of any Justices joining the opinion, and the type of opinion must be designated in the cite. For example, to cite paragraph number nine of the dissenting opinion in *Edwards v. Basel Pharmaceuticals*, 1997 OK

22, ___ P.2d ___ . The correct citation form is: *Edwards v. Basel Pharmaceuticals*, 1997 OK 22, ¶ 9, ___ P.2d ___ (Opala, J., dissenting in part). A footnote of this dissenting opinion is cited thus: *Edwards v. Basel Pharmaceuticals*, 1997 OK 22, n.12, ___ P.2d ___ (Opala, J., dissenting in part). A published opinion, or part thereof, of the Supreme Court has no precedential effect unless a majority of the Court have joined therein.

"(f) **Effective Date.** The policy adopted herein shall be in effect retroactively from and after April 1, 1983. Citation to opinions using the Supreme Court paragraph citation form shall be required after January 1, 1998 in accordance with Rule 1.200(e)." **Okla. Sup. Ct. R. 1.200(e), (f).**

Neutral Citation Format: Oklahoma Court of Criminal Appeals

"C. Argument and Citation of Authorities

"(1) Both parties must provide a brief argument, exhibiting a clear statement of the point of law or fact to be discussed, with a reference to the pages of the record filed and the authorities relied upon in support of each point raised.

"(2) Citation to opinions of the Oklahoma Court of Criminal Appeals shall include citations to Pacific and Pacific 2nd Reporters. Citation to the Court's official paragraph citation form is allowed as a parallel cite, but not required. Effective January 1, 1998, citation to opinions of the Oklahoma Court of Criminal Appeals shall be as follows:

(a) Oklahoma Court of Criminal Appeals Opinions in which mandate has issued prior to January 1, 1954, shall include citations to Pacific and Pacific 2nd Reporters. Parallel citation to Oklahoma Criminal Reports is strongly encouraged. Examples of permissible citation form include:

  (i) *Hunter v. State,* 97 Okl.Cr. 402, 264 P.2d 997 (1953).

  (ii) *Hunter v. State,* 97 Okl.Cr. 402, 264 P.2d 997, 998 (1953).

  (iii) *Hunter v. State,* 97 Okl.Cr. 402, 403, 264 P.2d 997, 998 (1953).

  (iv) *Hunter v. State,* 264 P.2d 997 (Okl.Cr. 1953).

  (v) *Hunter v. State,* 264 P.2d 997, 998 (Okl.Cr. 1953).

(b) Oklahoma Court of Criminal Appeals Opinions in which mandate has issued after January 1, 1954, shall include citations to Pacific and Pacific 2nd Reporters. Parallel citation to the official paragraph citation form of the Oklahoma Court of Criminal Appeals is strongly encouraged. Examples of permissible citation form include:

  (i) *Burns v. State,* 1955 OK CR 46, 282 P.2d 258.

  (ii) *Burns v. State,* 1955 OK CR 46, 282 P.2d 258, 259.

  (iii) *Burns v. State,* 1955 OK CR 46, ¶ 9, 282 P.2d 258, 259.

  (iv) *Burns v. State,* 282 P.2d 258 (Okl.Cr. 1955).

  (v) *Burns v. State,* 282 P.2d 258, 259 (Okl.Cr. 1955).

  In *'Burns v. State,* 1955 OK CR 46, ¶ 9, 282 P.2d 258', '1955' refers to the year the mandate issued, 'OK CR' is the court designation for the Oklahoma Court of Criminal Appeals, '46' is the number of that 1955 opinion assigned by the Court, '¶ 9' is paragraph number 9 of the opinion as designated by the Court, and '282 P.2d 258' is the parallel citation to the Pacific 2nd reporter.

(c) An opinion cited subsequent to issuance of the mandate but prior to official publication shall include citation to the Oklahoma Bar Journal. Parallel citation to the official paragraph citation form of the Oklahoma Court of Criminal Appeals is strongly encouraged. Examples of permissible citation form include:

(i) *Robinson v. State,* 1997 OK CR 24, 68 OBJ 1379.

(ii) *Robinson v. State,* 1997 OK CR 24, 68 OBJ 1379, 1381.

(iii) *Robinson v. State,* 1997 OK CR 24, ¶ 3, 68 OBJ 1379, 1381.

(iv) *Robinson v. State,* 68 OBJ 1379 (Okl.Cr. 1997).

(v) *Robinson v. State,* 68 OBJ 1379, 1381 (Okl.Cr. 1997).

(d) Opinions of the Oklahoma Court of Criminal Appeals issued for publication shall be published on the Court's World Wide Web Site, www.occa.state.ok.us. Such opinions may not be cited as authority in a subsequent appellate opinion nor used as authority by a trial court until the mandate in the matter has issued. After the mandate has issued, the opinion as published on the Web site shall constitute the official paragraph citation form of the Oklahoma Court of Criminal Appeals. *See* Rule 1.0(D) for citation to Rules.

"(3) In all instances, an unpublished opinion is not binding on this Court. However, parties may cite and bring to the Court's attention the unpublished opinions of this Court provided counsel states that no published case would serve as well the purpose for which counsel cites it, and provided further that counsel shall provide opposing counsel and the Court with a copy of the unpublished decision.

"(4) Citation to opinions of the United States Supreme Court shall include each of the following: ___ U.S. ___, ___ S.Ct. ___, ___ L.Ed. ___ (*year*).

"(5) Citation to Oklahoma Uniform Jury Instructions — Criminal (Second) shall be as follows: Instruction No. ___, OUJI-CR(2d); and citation to revised instructions shall be noted with the addition of [Supp. ___ (*year*)].

"(6) Failure to present relevant authority in compliance with these requirements will result in the issue being forfeited on appeal. *See Stafford v. State,* 800 P.2d 738, 741 (Okl.Cr. 1990); *Walton v. State,* 744 P.2d 977, 979 (Okl.Cr. 1987); *S.R.S. v. State,* 728 P.2d 515, 518 (Okl.Cr. 1986)." **Okla. Crim. App. R. 3.5(c).**

Oregon

"In all matters submitted to the circuit courts, Oregon cases must be cited by reference to the Oregon Reports as: *Blank v. Blank,* ___ Or ___ (year) or as *State v. Blank,* ___ Or App ___ (year). Parallel citations may be added." **Or. Unif. Trial Ct. R. 2.010(13).**

"(4) Guidelines for style and conventions in citation of authorities may be found in the Oregon Appellate Courts Style Manual.

"(5) Cases affirmed without opinion by the Court of Appeals should not be cited as authority." **Or. R. App. P. 5.20.**

Note: Copies of the Appellate Courts' Style Manual may be obtained from the Publications Section of the Office of the State Court Administrator, Supreme Court Building, 1163 State Street, Salem, OR 97310; (503) 986-5656.

Pennsylvania

"Citations of uncodified statutes shall make reference to the book and page of the Laws of Pennsylvania (Pamphlet Laws) or other official edition, and also to a standard digest, where the statutes may be found. Citations of provisions of the Pennsylvania Consolidated Statutes may be in the form: '1 Pa.C.S. § 1928 (rule of strict and liberal construction)' and the official codifications of other jurisdictions may be cited similarly. Quotations from authorities or statutes shall also set forth the pages from which they are taken. Opinions of an appellate court of this or another jurisdiction shall be cited from the National Reporter System, if published therein, and to the official reports of Pennsylvania appellate courts, if published therein." **Pa. R. App. P. 2119(b).**

Puerto Rico

"(d) Since unpublished judgments will not be accessible to the public, it will be deemed improper to cite as authority or precedent before any forum a decision of this Court which has not been rendered as an opinion, or has not been published by the Bar Association or the Court itself." **P.R. Sup. Ct. R. 44(d).**

"On October 9, 1997 the Court approved the Rules for the Electronic Distribution of Opinions and other Decisions of the Supreme Court. Pursuant to those rules, the Clerk of this Court has been distributing the opinions of this Court electronically since January of 1997 to all bona fide entities that publish our opinions, including the Bar Association.

"Pursuant to Rule 44(b) of our Rules, which went into effect in May of 1996, and to Rule 4 of the Rules for the Electronic Distribution of Opinions and Other Decisions of the Supreme Court, we authorized the Clerk of this Court to enumerate all decisions to be published.

"The Clerk of this Court has recommended to us, in order to uniform the citations used by the entities which publish our opinions, that we formally adopt a system of citation using the enumeration established by the Clerk.

"Therefore, we officially adopt the abbreviation TSPR to identify the decisions published and distributed electronically starting on January 1998 and until they be published in the official reporter: Decisiones de Puerto Rico (D.P.R.). Once the D.P.R. volume is published, it shall be cited as the final official citation.

"As a result, cases shall be cited as follows: *Velez Miranda* v. *Servicios Legales,* dec. January 21, 1998, 98 TSPR 1. The '98' pertains to the year, the 'TSPR' to Tribunal Supremo de Puerto Rico and the '1' to the number assigned in the Clerk's office.

"We also adopt the abbreviation PRSC ('Puerto Rico Supreme Court') to identify the opinions translated into English, until they are published in the 'Official Translations of the Opinions of the Supreme Court of Puerto Rico'. The citation shall be the same, with the difference that the abbreviation PRSC shall substitute TSPR. In the example above, the citation is '98 PRSC 1'.

"In order to achieve a greater uniformity and efficiency, we urge the publishing entities to use this new system of official citation." **Res. of the P.R. Sup. Ct., June 1, 1999.**

South Carolina

"To provide guidance on citing South Carolina authority, the following forms of citation are given. Once cited in the form given, the authority may thereafter be cited in an abbreviated form. Additional guidance on citation of authority may be found in *A Uniform System of*

Citation published by the Harvard Law Review Association, *A Guide to South Carolina Legal Research and Citation* published by the S.C. Bar C.L.E. Division, or other publications.

"(a) South Carolina Constitution. The South Carolina Constitution should be cited in the following manner: S.C. Const. art. IV, § 4.

"(b) Statutes and Regulations.

(1) Statutes which appear in a hardbound volume of the Code of Laws of South Carolina should be cited in the following form: S.C. Code Ann. § 1-2-345 (1976). Where the statute appears in a replacement hard bound volume, the citation should include the date appearing on the spine of the volume or the copyright date of the volume in the following form: S.C. Code Ann. § 11-35-1210 (1986). Statutes which appear in the supplement to the Code of Laws of South Carolina should be cited in the following form: S.C. Code Ann. § 6-7-890 (Supp. 1988).

(2) Statutes which have not yet been codified should be cited by the number of the Act, and the year and page number where it appears in the South Carolina Acts and Joint Resolutions in the following form: Act No. 100, 1985 S.C. Acts 277.

(3) Regulations which appear in the Code of Laws of South Carolina should be cited in the following manner: 23 S.C. Code Ann. Regs. 19-501 (1976). Regulations which appear in the supplement to the Code of Laws of South Carolina should be cited in the following manner: 24A S.C. Code Ann. Regs. 61-40 (Supp. 1988). The date used in the citation shall be the latest copyright date of the volume or supplement.

"(c) Court Rules. Court rules should be cited by the rule number and the abbreviations shown:

(1) South Carolina Appellate Court Rules: Rule ___, SCACR.

    (a) Rules of Professional Conduct, Rule ___, RPC, Rule 407, SCACR.

    (b) Rules for Lawyer Disciplinary Enforcement, Rule ___, RLDE, Rule 413, SCACR.

    (c) Code of Judicial Conduct, Rule ___, CJC, Rule 501, SCACR.

    (d) Rules for Judicial Disciplinary Enforcement, Rule ___, RJDE, Rule 502, SCACR.

(2) South Carolina Rules of Civil Procedure: Rule ___, SCRCP.

(3) South Carolina Rules of Criminal Procedure: Rule ___, SCRCrimP.

(4) South Carolina Rules of Family Court: Rule ___, SCRFC.

(5) South Carolina Rules of Probate Court: Rule ___, SCRPC.

(6) South Carolina Administrative and Procedural Rules for Magistrates Court: Rule ___, SCRMC.

(7) South Carolina Rules of Evidence: Rule ___, SCRE.

"(d) Appellate Court Decisions.

(1) Published opinions or orders of the Supreme Court or Court of Appeals should be cited in the following manner: *State v. Williams,* 297 S.C. 404, 377 S.E.2d 309 (1989); *Andrews v. Piedmont Air Lines,* 297 S.C. 367, 377 S.E.2d 127 (Ct. App. 1989). If a published opinion does not appear in a reporter, it should be cited in the following manner: *Donahue v. Donahue,* Op. No. 23083 (S.C. Sup. Ct. filed Sept. 25, 1989); *Satcher v. Berry,* Op. No. 1383 (S.C. Ct. App. filed July 31, 1989).

Further, if the opinion has been published in the Advance Sheets published by the Supreme Court, the opinion should be cited in the following manner: *State v. Victor,* Op. No. 23118 (S.C. Sup. Ct. filed Dec. 11, 1989) (Davis Adv. Sh. No. 29 at 5). If a published order does not appear in a reporter, it should be cited by its order number: *State v. Smith,* 89-OR-25 (S.C. Ct. App. dated March 1, 1989), or by reference to the date of the order if no order number has been assigned: *State v. Smith,* S.C. Sup. Ct. Order dated March 1, 1989. Further, if the order has been published on the front of the Advance Sheets the order should be cited in the following manner: *State v. Foster,* S.C. Sup. Ct. Order dated June 9, 1989 (Davis Adv. Sh. No. 14).

(2) Memorandum opinions and unpublished orders have no precedential value and should not be cited except in proceedings in which they are directly involved. Memorandum opinions may be cited in the following form: *Bums v. Burns,* Op. No. 89-MO-110 (S.C. Ct. App. filed July 31, 1989). Unpublished orders may be cited in a similar manner as provided for published orders under Rule 239(d)(1).

(3) The South Carolina Equity Reports, beginning with 1 Desaussure Equity and ending with 14 Richardson Equity should be cited in the following manner: *Taylor v. Taylor,* 4 S.C.Eq. (4 Des.Eq.) 165 (1811).

Reporter	Citation to Be Used
1 Desaussure	1 S.C.Eq. (1 Des.Eq.)
2 Desaussure	2 S.C.Eq. (2 Des.Eq.)
3 Desaussure	3 S.C.Eq. (3 Des.Eq.)
4 Desaussure	4 S.C.Eq. (4 Des.Eq.)
Harper	5 S.C.Eq. (Harp.Eq.)
1 McCord	6 S.C.Eq. (1 McCord Eq.)
2 McCord	7 S.C.Eq. (2 McCord Eq.)
Bailey	8 S.C.Eq. (Bail.Eq.)
Richardson's Cases	9 S.C.Eq. (Rich.Cas.)
1 Hill	10 S.C.Eq. (1 Hill Eq.)
2 Hill	11 S.C.Eq. (2 Hill Eq.)
Riley	12 S.C.Eq. (Ril.Eq.)
Dudley	13 S.C.Eq. (Dud.Eq.)
Rice	14 S.C.Eq. (Rice Eq.)
Cheves	15 S.C.Eq. (Chev.Eq.)
McMullen	16 S.C.Eq. (McMul. Eq.)
Speers	17 S.C.Eq. (Speers Eq.)
1 Richardson	18 S.C.Eq. (I Rich.Eq.)
2 Richardson	19 S.C.Eq. (2 Rich.Eq.)
1 Strobhart	20 S.C.Eq. (I Strob.Eq.)
2 Strobhart	21 S.C.Eq. (2 Strob.Eq.)
3 Strobhart	22 S.C.Eq. (3 Strob.Eq.)
4 Strobhart	23 S.C.Eq. (4 Strob.Eq.)
3 Richardson	24 S.C.Eq. (3 Rich.Eq.)
4 Richardson	25 S.C.Eq. (4 Rich.Eq.)
5 Richardson	26 S.C.Eq. (5 Rich.Eq.)

Reporter	Citation to Be Used
6 Richardson	27 S.C.Eq. (6 Rich.Eq.)
7 Richardson	28 S.C.Eq. (7 Rich.Eq.)
8 Richardson	29 S.C.Eq. (8 Rich.Eq.)
9 Richardson	30 S.C.Eq. (9 Rich.Eq.)
10 Richardson	31 S.C.Eq. (10 Rich.Eq.)
11 Richardson	32 S.C.Eq. (11 Rich.Eq.)
12 Richardson	33 S.C.Eq. (12 Rich.Eq.)
13 Richardson	34 S.C.Eq. (13 Rich.Eq.)
14 Richardson	35 S.C.Eq. (14 Rich.Eq.)

(4) The South Carolina Law Reports beginning with 1 Bay and ending with 15 Richardson should be cited in the following manner: *Roche v. Chaplin*, 17 S.C.L. (1 Bail.) 419 (1830).

Reporter	Citation to Be Used
1 Bay	1 S.C.L. (1 Bay)
2 Bay	2 S.C.L. (2 Bay)
1 Brevard	3 S.C.L. (1 Brev.)
2 Brevard	4 S.C.L. (2 Brev.)
3 Brevard	5 S.C.L. (3 Brev.)
1 Treadway	6 S.C.L. (1 Tread.)
2 Treadway	7 S.C.L. (2 Tread.)
1 Mill (Constitutional)	8 S.C.L. (1 Mill)
2 Mill (Constitutional)	9 S.C.L. (2 Mill)
1 Nott and McCord	10 S.C.L. (1 Nott & McC.)
2 Nott and McCord	11 S.C.L. (2 Nott & McC.)
1 McCord	12 S.C.L. (I McCord)
2 McCord	13 S.C.L. (2 McCord)
3 McCord	14 S.C.L. (3 McCord)
4 McCord	15 S.C.L. (4 McCord)
Harper	16 S.C.L. (Harp.)
1 Bailey	17 S.C.L. (1 Bail.)
2 Bailey	18 S.C.L. (2 Bail.)
1 Hill	19 S.C.L. (1 Hill)
2 Hill	20 S.C.L. (2 Hill)
3 Hill	21 S.C.L. (3 Hill)
Riley	22 S.C.L. (Ril.)
Dudley	23 S.C.L. (Dud.)
Rice	24 S.C.L. (Rice)
Cheves	25 S.C.L. (Chev.)
1 McMullen	26 S.C.L. (1 McMul.)
2 McMullen	27 S.C.L. (2 McMul.)
1 Speers	28 S.C.L. (1 Speers)
2 Speers	29 S.C.L. (2 Speers)
1 Richardson	30 S.C.L. (1 Rich.)

Reporter	Citation to Be Used
2 Richardson	31 S.C.L. (2 Rich.)
1 Strobhart	32 S.C.L. (1 Strob.)
2 Strobhart	33 S.C.L. (2 Strob.)
3 Strobhart	34 S.C.L. (3 Strob.)
4 Strobhart	35 S.C.L. (4 Strob.)
5 Strobhart	36 S.C.L. (5 Strob.)
3 Richardson	37 S.C.L. (3 Rich.)
4 Richardson	38 S.C.L. (4 Rich.)
5 Richardson	39 S.C.L. (5 Rich.)
6 Richardson	40 S.C.L. (6 Rich.)
7 Richardson	41 S.C.L. (7 Rich.)
8 Richardson	42 S.C.L. (8 Rich.)
9 Richardson	43 S.C.L. (9 Rich.)
10 Richardson	44 S.C.L. (10 Rich.)
11 Richardson	45 S.C.L. (11 Rich.)
12 Richardson	46 S.C.L. (12 Rich.)
13 Richardson	47 S.C.L. (13 Rich.)
14 Richardson	48 S.C.L. (14 Rich.)
15 Richardson	49 S.C.L. (15 Rich.)"

S.C. App. Ct. R. 239.

South Dakota

"(1) The initial citation of any published opinion of the Supreme Court released prior to January 1, 1996, in a brief, memorandum, or other document filed with the Court and the citation in the table of cases in a brief shall include a reference to the volume and page number of the South Dakota Reports or North Western Reporter in which the opinion is published. Subsequent citations in the brief, document, or memorandum shall include the page number and sufficient references to identify the initial citation.

"(2) The initial citation of any published opinion of the Supreme Court released on or after January 1, 1996, in a brief, memorandum, or other document filed with the Court and the citation in the table of cases in a brief shall include a reference to the calendar year in which the decision was announced, the Court designation of 'SD,' and a sequential number assigned by the Clerk of the Supreme Court. Citation to specific portions of the opinion shall be made to the paragraph number assigned by the Clerk of the Supreme Court. A paragraph citation should be placed immediately following the sequential number assigned to the case. Subsequent citations within the brief, document, or memorandum shall include the paragraph number and sufficient references to identify the initial citation.

"When available, initial citations shall include the volume and initial page number of the North Western Reporter in which the opinion is published." **S.D. R. App. P. 15-26A-69.1.**

Tennessee

"Citation of cases must be by title, to the page of the volume where the case begins, and to the pages upon which the pertinent matter appears in at least one of the reporters cited. It is not sufficient to use only *supra* or *infra* without referring to the page of the brief at which the complete citation may be found. Citation of Tennessee cases may be to the official or South Western Reporter or both. Citation of cases from other jurisdictions must be to the National Reporter System or both the official state reports and National Reporter System. If only the National Reporter System citation is used, the court rendering the decision must also be identified. All citations to cases shall include the year of decision. Citation of textbooks shall be to the section, if any, and page upon which the pertinent matter appears and shall include the year of publication and edition if not the first edition. Tennessee statutes shall generally be cited to the Tennessee Code Annotated, Official Edition, but citations to the session laws of Tennessee shall be made when appropriate. Citations of supplements to the Tennessee Code Annotated shall so indicate and shall include the year of publication of the supplement." **Tenn. R. App. P. 27(h).**

Texas

"Citations should use jump cites or pinpoint cites and should conform to the most recent editions of HARVARD L. REV., A UNIFORM SYSTEM OF CITATION (the Bluebook), and TEX. L. REV., TEXAS RULES OF FORM (the Greenbook)." **Tex. Loc. R. 4th Ct. App. 8 (2004 update).**

"Proper citation form as outlined in *A Uniform System of Citation* and *Texas Rules of Form* shall be used in all briefs. Petition and certiorari histories shall be included. Specific page citations to relevant holdings and quotations within a case (jump cites) shall be incorporated." **Tex. Loc. R. 8th Ct. App. 38.1(b).**

"In addition to complying with Rules of Appellate Procedure 9 and 38, proper citation form should be observed and subsequent history should be provided. In citing cases, specific page citations should be given to the pages where the relevant holdings or quotations may be found." **Tex. Loc. R. 10th Ct. App. 13(b).**

"This Court requires that citations conform to the current Texas Rules of Form, published by the Texas Law Review. Writ and petition history should always be included. The Court does not require the parallel Texas Report citations." **Tex. Loc. R. 13th Ct. App. 4.**

Note: The *Rules of Form* may be obtained from the *Texas Law Review* Business Office.

Utah

"Effective March 1, 2000, the initial citation of any published opinion of the Utah Supreme Court or the Utah Court of Appeals, released on or after January 1, 1999, in any brief, table of cases in the brief, memorandum, or other document filed in the Utah Supreme Court or the Utah Court of Appeals, shall include the case name, the year the opinion was issued, identification of the court that issued the opinion (UT of Utah Supreme Court and UT App for the Utah Court of Appeals), and the sequential number assigned to the opinion by the respective court. Citation to specific portions of the opinion shall be made by reference to the paragraph numbers assigned by the court. A comma and then a paragraph symbol (¶) should be placed immediately following the sequential number assigned to the case. Subsequent citations within the brief, document, or memorandum should include the paragraph number and sufficient references to identify the initial citation. Initial citations shall also include the volume and initial page number of the Pacific Reporter in which the opinion is published. When an opinion is in slip form awaiting inclusion in a Pacific Reporter volume, the slip opinion form should be used. A pinpoint citation is not required in the parallel citation to the Pacific Reporter since the paragraph numbers assigned by the court are included in the Pacific Reporter version. Likewise, it is not necessary to include the year the case was published since that will be evident from the initial citation.

"Examples of an initial citation to a Utah Supreme Court opinion or a Utah Court of Appeals opinion issued on or after January 1, 1999, using fictitious decisions, would be as follows:

Before publication in Utah Advanced Reports:

Smith v. Jones, 1999 UT 16.
Smith v. Jones, 1999 UT App 16.

Before publication in Pacific Reporter but after publication in Utah Advance Reports:

Smith v. Jones, 1999 UT 16, 380 Utah Adv. Rep. 24.
Smith v. Jones, 1999 UT App 16, 380 Utah Adv. Rep. 24.

After publication in Pacific Reporter:

Smith v. Jones, 1999 UT 16, 998 P.2d 250.
Smith v. Jones, 1999 UT App 16, 998 P.2d 250.

Examples of a pinpoint citation to a Utah Supreme Court opinion or a Utah Court of Appeals opinion issued on or after January 1, 1999, would be as follows:

Before publication in Utah Advance Reports:

Smith v. Jones, 1999 UT 16, ¶21.
Smith v. Jones, 1999 UT App 16, ¶21.
Smith v. Jones, 1999 UT App 16, ¶21-25.

Before publication in Pacific Reporter but after publication in Utah Advance Reports:

Smith v. Jones, 1999 UT 16, ¶21, 380 Utah Adv. Rep. 24.
Smith v. Jones, 1999 UT App 16, ¶21, 380 Utah Adv. Rep. 24.

After publication in Pacific Reporter:

Smith v. Jones, 1999 UT 16, ¶21, 998 P.2d 250.
Smith v. Jones, 1999 UT App 16, ¶21, 998 P.2d 250.

If the immediately preceding authority is a post-January 1, 1999, opinion, cite to the paragraph number:

Id. at ¶15."

Utah Sup. Ct. Stand. Or. 4 (effective Jan. 18, 2000) (available at http://www.utcourts.gov/resources/rules/urap/Supctso.htm#4).

Vermont

"(a) **Form of Opinions.** All opinions issued by the Supreme Court on or after January 1, 2003, will be sequentially numbered within the year of issuance, beginning with the number '1'. Within each opinion, each paragraph will be numbered, beginning with the number '1'. Any official or unofficial publication of an opinion issued after January 1, 2003, must include the sequential number of the opinion in the caption of the opinion and the paragraph numbers in the body of the text.

"(b) **Citation of Vermont Opinions.** The citation of any opinion of the Vermont Supreme Court issued on or after January 1, 2003, must, immediately after the title of the case, indicate the year of issuance in four digits followed by the abbreviation 'VT' and must include the sequential opinion number, followed by citations to the official and unofficial print reporters. Pinpoint citations may be made only by reference to the paragraph numbers in the body of the text. Citations must be made in the following style: *Smith v. Jones*, 2001 VT 1, ¶ 12, 169 Vt. 203, 850 A.2d 421.

"(c) **Citation of Other Opinions.** An opinion of any other court that has been published with sequential and paragraph numbering similar to that required by subdivision (a) of this rule must be cited in a form similar to that provided in subdivision (b)." **Vt. R. App. P. 28.2.**

Virginia

The petition or brief must contain "(1) A subject index and table of citations with cases alphabetically arranged. Citations of Virginia cases shall be to the Virginia Reports and the Southeastern Reporter. Citations of all authorities shall include the year thereof." **Va. Sup. Ct. R. 5:17(c)(1)**; **id. at 5:28(a)**; **Va. Sup. Ct. R. 5A:20(a)** (appellant's brief); **Va. Sup. Ct. R. 5A:21(a)** (appellee's brief).

Washington

"Citations shall conform with the format prescribed by the Reporter of Decisions." **Wash. Ct. R. 14(d).**

Practitioners should consult Washington Court Rules General Appeals GR 14 for the format prescribed by the Reporter of Decisions. Printed below is the "General Principles" section from the Reporter's format.

"1. The Seventeenth Edition of *The Bluebook: A Uniform System of Citation* is the basic citation resource for Washington appellate court opinions except as noted below.

"2. The Practitioners' Notes section of the *Bluebook* (section P at 10–19 on light blue paper) applies specifically to court documents. BLUEBOOK I.1, at 3 and § P at 11. Conflicts between section R of the *Bluebook* (General Rules of Citation and Style at 20–181) and section P of the *Bluebook* are resolved in favor of section P with the exception that for typefaces, a manuscript opinion may follow the rules of section P or section R.

"3. The latest edition of *The Chicago Manual of Style* is the authority for punctuation and style matters not covered by the *Bluebook*.

"4. *Webster's Third New International Dictionary of the English Language* is the authority for spelling, including spacing and hyphens between nouns (e.g., boyfriend, girl friend, day care, baby-sitter). Where two or more spellings are listed, use *Webster's* preferred spelling rather than the variant.

"5. For matters not covered by the *Bluebook*, *The Chicago Manual of Style*, or *Webster's*, the Office of Reporter of Decisions applies formal, traditional, noncolloquial English."

Wisconsin

"An argument, arranged in the order of the statement of issues presented. The argument on each issue must be preceded by a one sentence summary of the argument and is to contain the contention of the appellant, the reasons therefor, with citations to the authorities, statutes and parts of the record relied on as set forth in the Uniform System of Citation and SCR 80.02." **Wis. App. P.R. 809.19(1)(e).**

"(1) The citation of any published opinion of the court of appeals or the supreme court in the table of cases in a brief and the initial citation in a memorandum or other document filed with the court of appeals or the supreme court shall include, in the order set forth, a reference to each of the following:

  (a) the public domain citation, if it exists;

  (b) the volume and page number of the Wisconsin Reports in which the opinion is published;

  (c) the volume and page number of the North Western Reporter in which the opinion is published;

"(2) Subsequent citations shall include at least one of the references in sub. (1) and shall be internally consistent.

"(3) **(a)** Citation to specific portions of an opinion issued or ordered to be published prior to January 1, 2000, shall be by reference to page numbers, in the following form:

  Smith v. Jones, 214 Wis. 2d 408, 412.
  Doe v. Roe, 595 N.W.2d 346, 352.

  (b) Citation to specific portions of an opinion issued on or after January 1, 2000, shall be by reference to paragraph numbers, in the following form:
  Smith v. Jones, 2000 WI 14, ¶ 6
  Smith v. Jones, 214 Wis. 2d 408, ¶ 12
  Doe v. Roe, 2001 WI App 9, ¶ 17
  Doe v. Roe, 595 N.W.2d 346, ¶ 27

  (c) Citation to specific portions of an opinion issued prior to January 1, 2000, and ordered to be published after January 1, 2000, shall be by reference to paragraph numbers if they exist or to page numbers if paragraph numbers do not exist." **Wis. Sup. Ct. R. 80.02.**

Wyoming

Neutral Citation Format
The Supreme Court of Wyoming adopted neutral-format citation formats in October 2000, and the order is available online at http://courts.state.wy.us/universal.htm.

Federal Courts

United States Court of Appeals for the First Circuit

"All citations to State or Commonwealth Courts must include both the official state court citation and the National Reporter System citation when such decisions have been published in both reports; e.g., *Coney v. Commonwealth*, 364 Mass. 137, 301 N.E.2d 450 (1973). Law review or other articles unpublished at the time a brief or memorandum is filed may not be cited therein, except with permission of the court." **1st Cir. R. 32.2.**

United States Court of Appeals for the Third Circuit

"In the argument section of the brief required by F.R.A.P. 28(a)(9), citations to federal opinions that have been reported shall be to the United States Reports, the Federal Reporter, the Federal Supplement or the Federal Rules Decisions, and shall identify the judicial circuit or district, and year of decision. Citations to the United States Supreme Court opinions that have not yet appeared in the official reports may be to the Supreme Court Reporter, the Lawyer's Edition or United States Law Week in that order of preference. Citations to United States Law Week shall include the month, day and year of the decision. Citations to federal decisions that have not been formally reported shall identify the court, docket number and date, and refer to the electronically transmitted decision. Citations to services and topical reports, whether permanent or looseleaf, and to electronic citation systems, shall not be used if the text of the case cited has been reported in the United States Reports, the Federal Reporter, the Federal Supplement, or the Federal Rules Decisions. Citations to state court decisions should include the West Reporter system whenever possible, with an identification of the state court." **3d Cir. R. 28.3(a).**

United States Court of Appeals for the Sixth Circuit

Neutral Citation Format

"The electronic citation will assign a court-generated, vendor neutral, reference number to opinions at the time of their release. The electronic citation is intended to avoid the proliferation of various electronic citations developed by vendors and to provide a common reference for all users of electronic and CD-ROM systems. The electronic citation is considered to be a parallel citation to the opinion in addition to the citation in the published reporter series.

"The court encourages the use of the Sixth Circuit electronic citation by bench and bar when citing cases to or from the Sixth Circuit. While there will be no penalties for not using the electronic citation, the court and the bar will find it easier to retrieve cases from the various electronic publishers when the citation is used." *Sixth Cir. Elec. Op. Distrib. & Citation Policy Changes,* http://www.aallnet.org/committee/citation/rules_6th.html.

United States Court of Appeals for the Seventh Circuit

"Citation to opinions of the Supreme Court of the United States must include the volume and page of the United States Reports, once that citation is available." **7th Cir. R. 28(f).**

United States Court of Appeals for the Eleventh Circuit

"Citations of authority in the brief shall comply with the rules of citation in the latest edition of either the 'Bluebook' (*A Uniform System of Citation*) or the 'ALWD Manual' (*Association of Legal Writing Directors' Citation Manual; A Professional System of Citation*). Citations shall reference the specific page number(s) which relate to the proposition for which the case is cited. For state reported cases the national reporter series should be cross referenced (e.g., Southern Reporter, Southeast Reporter)." **11th Cir. R. 28-1(k).**

United States Court of Appeals for the District of Columbia

"Citations to decisions of this court must be to the Federal Reporter. Dual or parallel citation of cases is not required. Citations of state court decisions included in the National

Reporter System must be to that system in both the text and the table of authorities. Citations to all federal statutes, including those statutes applicable to the District of Columbia, must refer to the current official code or its supplement, or if there is no current official code, to a current unofficial code or its supplement. Citation to the official session laws is not required unless there is no code citation." **D.C. Cir. R. 28(b).**

United States Court of Appeals for the Federal Circuit

"Opinions of this court and its predecessors should be cited as found in the Federal Reporter, and, if reasonably available, the United States Patents Quarterly. Parallel citations to any other reports are discouraged. Examples of acceptable citations are:

Guotos v. United States, 552 F.2d 992 (Ct. Cl. 1976).
In re Sponnable, 405 F.2d 578, 160 USPQ 237 (CCPA 1969).
South Corporation v. United States, 690 F.2d 1368, 215 USPQ 657 (Fed. Cir. 1982) (en banc).
Doe v. Roe, No. 12-345, slip op. (Fed. Cir. Oct. 1, 1982)."

Fed. Cir. R. 28(e).

United States District Court for the Central District of California

"11-3.9.1 Citations.

"11-3.9.1 *Acts of Congress.* All citations to Acts of Congress shall include a parallel citation to the United States Code by title and section.

"11-3.9.2 *Regulations.* All citations to regulations shall include a citation to the Code of Federal Regulations by title and section, and the date of promulgation of the regulation.

"11-3.9.3 *Cases.* Initial citation of any United States Supreme Court case shall include parallel citations to United States Reports, Lawyer's Edition, and Supreme Court Reporter. Federal Reporter, Federal Supplement or Federal Rules Decisions citations shall be used where available. Initial state court citations shall include both the official reports and any regional reporter published by West Publishing Company. California parallel citations may be limited to the official reports and California Reporter." **C.D. Cal. Civ. R. 11-3.**

United States Bankruptcy Court for the Central District of California

"Citations.

"(1) *Acts of Congress.* All citations to Acts of Congress shall include a parallel citation to the United States Code by title and section.

"(2) *Regulations.* All citations to federal regulations shall include a citation to the Code of Federal Regulations by title and section, and the date of promulgation of the regulation.

"(3) *Cases.* Initial citation of any United States Supreme Court cases shall include parallel citations to United States Reports, and Supreme Court Reporter. Federal Reporter, Federal Supplement or Federal Rules Decisions citations shall be used where available. Initial state court citations shall include both the official reports and any regional reporter published by West Publishing Company. California parallel citations may be limited to the official reports and California Reporter. Citation to bankruptcy cases shall be to West's Bankruptcy Reporter, where available. Where a Bankruptcy Reporter citation is not available, the party citing the case must provide the Court with an unmarked copy of the case." **C.D. Cal. Bankr. R. 1002-1(i).**

United States District Court for the Eastern District of California

"Citations of federal cases shall be to the United States Supreme Court Reports, Federal Reports, Federal Supplement, or Federal Rules Decisions, if so reported, and shall indicate the court and year of decision. Citations to federal statutes shall be to the United States Code, if so codified. Citations to federal administrative rules shall be to the Code of Federal Regulations, if so codified, or to the Federal Register, if published therein. Citations of California cases shall be to the official California Reports. Citations of other state cases shall be to the National Reporter System, showing state and year of decision. Other citations may be added. If case, statutory, or regulatory authority is relied upon which has not been reported, published, or codified in any of the foregoing references, a copy of that authority shall be appended to the brief or other document in which it is cited. This requirement shall include, but not be limited to, the Statutes at Large, the Public Laws of the United States, the California Administrative Code, administrative regulations not contained in the Code of Federal Regulations or the Federal Register, and decisions and other matters published in specialized reporter services." **E.D. Cal. R. 5-133(i).**

United States District Court for the Northern District of California

"Unless otherwise directed by the assigned judge, citation to authorities in any paper must include:

"(1) In any citation to Acts of Congress, a parallel citation to the United States Code by title, section, and date;

"(2) In any citation to U.S. regulations, a citation to the Code of Federal Regulations by title and section, and the date of promulgation of the regulation;

"(3) In any citation to a U.S. Supreme Court Case, a citation to United States Reports, Lawyers' Edition, or Supreme Court Reporter must be used. If the case is not yet available in those formats but is available on electronic databases, citation must indicate the database, year and any screen or page numbers, if assigned;

"(4) In any citation to other federal courts, unless an alternate reporting service is widely available, a citation to the Federal Reporter, Federal Supplement or Federal Rules Decisions must be used. If the case is not yet available in those formats but is available on electronic databases, citation must include the database, year and any screen or page numbers if assigned; and

"(5) In any citation to a state court, citations must include either the official reports or any widely available alternate reporting service (e.g., West Publishing). If the case is not yet available in those formats but is available on electronic databases, citation must indicate the database year and any screen or page numbers, if assigned." **N.D. Cal. Civ. R. 3-4(d).**

United States District Court for the Southern District of California

"When citing Acts of Congress or sections of them, counsel shall include the corresponding appropriate United States Code citations. When counsel cite regulations, counsel shall supply the appropriate citations to the Code of Federal Regulations, including code number, page, section, and the date of the regulation's promulgation." **S.D. Cal. Civ. R. 5(l).**

United States District Court for the District of Delaware

"*Form of citations.* Citations will be deemed to be in acceptable form if made in accordance with 'A *Uniform System of Citation*' published and distributed from time to time by the Harvard Law Review Association. State reporter citations may be omitted but citations to the National Reporter System must be included except as to U.S. Supreme Court decisions where the official citation shall be used." **D. Del. R. 7.1.3(5).**

"Citations will be deemed to be in acceptable form if made in accordance with 'A Uniform System of Citation' published and distributed from time to time by the Harvard Law Review Association. State reporter citations may be omitted but citations to the National Reporter System must be included except as to U.S. Supreme Court decisions where the official citation shall be used." **D. Del. R. 7.1.3(F).**

United States District Court for the Northern District of Georgia

"Citations. When Acts of Congress or sections thereof are cited, counsel shall include the corresponding United States Code citation. When citing regulations, counsel shall give all Code of Federal Regulations references and the date of promulgation. All citations shall include the specific page or pages upon which the cited matters appear." **N.D. Ga. R. 5.1(E).**

United States Bankruptcy Court for the Northern District of Georgia

"When Acts of Congress or sections thereof are cited, counsel shall include the corresponding United States Code citation. When citing regulations, counsel shall give all Code of Federal Regulations references and the date of promulgation. All citations shall include the specific page or pages upon which the cited matters appear." **N.D. Ga. Bankr. R. 5000-1(e).**

United States District Courts for the Northern and Southern Districts of Iowa

"All citations to statutes in motions, briefs, pleadings, and other requests for court action must refer to the United States Code or to the appropriate state code and not to a common name or designation for a statutory provision. For example, parties should not cite to the Internal Revenue Code or the Bankruptcy Code, but to the statutory equivalent in the United States Code." **N.D. & S.D. Iowa R. 10.1(d).**

United States District Court for the District of Montana

"(a) All documents filed with the Court shall follow the citation form described in the current edition of the Association of Legal Writing Directors (ALWD) Citation Manual or the most recent edition of The Bluebook. The use of internal citations that refer to a particular page or paragraph of a cited authority is required.

"(b) All citations to federal acts, such as the Miller Act, Federal Employers Liability Act, Indian Child Welfare Act, etc., must be accompanied by a parallel citation to the United States Code, United States Code Service, or United States Code Annotated. Reference to a Code section, without reference to any section within an Act, is acceptable." **D. Mont. R. 10-4.**

United States Bankruptcy Court for the District of Montana

Attorneys must "use a nationally recognized citation form, (i.e., The Harvard Citator or the Association of Legal Writing Directors (ALWD) Citation Manual)." **D. Mont. Bankr. R. 5005-3(a)(7).**

United States District Court for the District of Nevada

"(a) References to an act of Congress shall include the United States Code citation, if available, shall be given. When a federal regulation is cited, the Code of Federal Regulations reference, title, section, page and year shall be given.

"(b) When a Supreme Court decision is cited, the citation of the United States Reports shall be given. When a decision of a court of appeal, a district court, or other federal court has been reported in the Federal Reporter System, that citation shall be given. When a decision of a state appellate court has been reported in West's National Reporter System, that citation shall be given. All citations shall include the specific page(s) upon which the pertinent language appears." **D. Nev. Civ. R. 7-3.**

United States District Court for the Eastern District of North Carolina

"(b) Citation of Published Decisions. Published decisions cited should include parallel citations (except for U.S. Supreme Court cases), the year of the decision, and the court deciding the case. The following are illustrations:

(1) State Court Citation: *Smith v. Jones*, 238 N.C. 162, 77 S.E.2d 701 (1953).

(2) District Court Citation: *Smith v. Jones*, 141 F. Supp. 248 (E.D.N.C. 1956).

(3) Court of Appeals Citation: *Smith v. Jones*, 237 F.2d 597 (4th Cir. 1956).

(4) United States Supreme Court Citation: *Smith v. Jones*, 325 U.S. 196 (1956). United States Supreme Court cases should be cited only to the United States Reports except that if a petition for certiorari or an appeal was filed in the United States Supreme Court, the disposition of the case in that court should always be shown. For example: *Carson v. Warlick*, 238 F.2d 724 (4th Cir. 1956), *cert. denied*, 353 U.S. 910 (1957).

"(c) Citation of Decisions Not Appearing in Certain Published Reports. Decisions published outside the West Federal Reporter System, the official North Carolina reports and the official United States Supreme Court reports (e.g. CCH Tax Reports, Labor Reports, U.S.P.Q., reported decisions of other states or other specialized reporting services) may be cited if the decision is furnished to the court and to opposing parties or their counsel when the memorandum is filed.

"(d) Citation of Unpublished Decisions. Unpublished decisions may be cited only if the unpublished decision is furnished to the court and to opposing parties or their counsel when the memorandum is filed. The unpublished decision of a United States District Court may be considered by this court. The unpublished decision of a United States Circuit Court of Appeals will be given due consideration and weight but will not bind this court. Such unpublished decisions should be cited as follows: *United States v. John Doe*, 5:94-CV-50-F

(E.D.N.C. January 7, 1994) and *United States v. Norman*, No. 74-2398 (4th Cir. June 27, 1975)." **E.D.N.C. Civ. R. 7-2**; *see also* **E.D.N.C. Crim. R. 47-2.**

United States District Court for the Middle District of North Carolina

"Cases cited should include parallel citations, the year of the decision, and the court deciding the case. If a petition for certiorari was filed in the United States Supreme Court, disposition of the case should be shown with three parallel citations [e.g. *Carson v. Warlick*, 238 F.2d 724 (4th Cir. 1956), cert. denied, 353 U.S. 910, 77 S.Ct. 665, 1 L.Ed.2d 664 (1957)]. . . . Decisions published in reports other than the West Federal Reporter System, the official North Carolina reports and the official United States Supreme Court reports (e.g., C.C.H. Reports, Labor Reports, U.S.P.Q., reported decisions of other states or other specialized reporting services) may be cited only if the decision is furnished to the court and to opposing parties or their counsel when the brief is filed." **M.D.N.C. R. 7.2(b) & (d).**

United States District Court for the Southern District of Ohio

"(1)*Statutes and Regulations.* All pleadings, briefs and memoranda containing references to statutes or regulations shall specifically cite the applicable statutes or regulations. United States Statutes should be cited by the United States Code Title and Section number, e.g., 1 U.S.C. Section 1.

"(2) *Preferential Authorities.* In citing authorities, the Court prefers that counsel rely upon cases decided by the Supreme Court of the United States, the United States Court of Appeals for the Sixth Circuit (or, in appropriate cases, the Federal Circuit), the Supreme Court of Ohio, and this Court.

"(3) Supreme Court Citations. Citation to United States Supreme Court decisions should be to the official U.S. Reports if published. Supreme Court Reporter and Lawyer's Edition shall be used where the official U.S. Reports are not yet published. For more recent decisions, United States Law Week, Lexis, or Westlaw citations are acceptable.

"(4) Unreported Opinions. If unreported or unofficially published opinions are cited, copies of the opinions shall be made available upon request by the Court or opposing counsel." **S.D. Ohio Civ. R. 7.2(b).**

United States Bankruptcy Court for the Middle District of Pennsylvania (Northern Tier)

"Briefs shall contain complete citations to all authorities relied upon, including, whenever practicable, citations both to official and unofficial reporters." **Bankr. Prac. Order & Forms, N. Tier, M.D. Pa. ¶ 7070-7** (available at http://www.uslawcenter.com/usmiddle/bpo.htm#_1_57).

United States District Court for the District of South Dakota

"STANDING ORDER IN RE: THE CITATION OF DISTRICT COURT OPINIONS

"After consideration of a proposal for the adoption of an order governing the citation of District Court opinions for the District of South Dakota, it is hereby

"ORDERED that the initial citation of any published opinion of the District Court released prior to October 1, 1996, in a brief, memorandum, or other document filed with the Court and the citation in the table of cases in a brief shall include a reference to the volume and page number of the Federal Supplement in which the opinion is published. Subsequent citations within the brief, document, or memorandum shall include the page number and sufficient references to identify the initial citation.

"IT IS FURTHER ORDERED that the initial citation of any published opinion of the District Court released on or after October 1, 1996, in a brief, memorandum, or other document filed with the Court and the citation in the table of cases in a brief shall include a reference to the calendar year in which the decision was announced, the Court designation of 'DSD' and a sequential number assigned by the District Court. Citation to specific portions of the opinion shall be made to the paragraph number assigned by the District Court. A paragraph citation should be placed immediately following the sequential number assigned to the case. Subsequent citations within the brief, document, or memorandum shall include the paragraph number and sufficient references to identify the initial citation.

"When available, initial citations shall include the volume and initial page number of the Federal Supplement in which the opinion is published.

"IT IS FURTHER ORDERED that this order shall become effective on the 1st day of October, 1996." **Available in WL, Rules-All database.**

United States District Court for the Eastern District of Tennessee

"Citation to decisions of the United States Supreme Court shall include citations to the United States Reports, Supreme Court Reporter, and to the United States Supreme Court Reports, Lawyers' Edition, where such citations exist. For more recent decisions, *United States Law Week* citations or computer assisted legal research citations will be accepted. Citations to any federal court decision or administrative opinion not fully reported in one of the publications of the West Publishing Company, or citations to any decisions of a state court other than Tennessee, shall be accompanied by a copy of the entire text of the decision. Citations to federal statutes shall include at least the title and the section designation as the statute appears in the United States Code. Citations to reported state cases shall include at least the 'official' state reporter citation and the regional reporter when available. The court will NOT consider improperly cited authority." **E.D. Tenn. R. 7.4.**

United States District Court for the Middle District of Tennessee

"(2) Citations to United States Supreme Court decisions shall be to U.S., if therein, otherwise to S.Ct. or L.Ed., in that order of preference. For recent decisions, Westlaw or Lexis citations are acceptable.

"(3) Citations to reported state cases shall include at least the "official" state reporter citation and the regional reporter citation where available. For recent decisions, Westlaw and Lexis citations are acceptable. Any citation to state cases other than Tennessee cases shall be accompanied by a copy of the entire text of the opinion.

"(4) Citations to federal statutes shall include at least the title and section designation as the statute appears in the United States Codes.

"(5) Citations to any federal or state court decisions or administrative opinions not reported in one of the publications of the West Publishing Company shall include Westlaw or Lexis citations and shall be accompanied by a copy of the entire text of the decision." **M.D. Tenn. R. 8(c).**

United States Bankruptcy Court for the Middle District of Tennessee

"(2) Citations to United States Supreme Court decisions shall include 'triple cites' (U.S. Reports, Supreme Court Reporter and Lawyer's Edition) where such citations exist. For more recent decisions, United States Law Week citations are acceptable.

"(3) Citations to reported state cases shall include at least the 'official' state reporter CITATION and the regional reporter CITATION where available. Any citation to state cases other than Tennessee cases shall be accompanied by a copy of the entire text of the opinion.

"(4) Citations to federal statutes shall include at least the title and section designation as the statute appears in the United States Code.

"(5) Citations to any federal court decision or administrative opinion not reported in one of the publications of the West Publishing Company shall be accompanied by a copy of the entire text of the decision." **M.D. Tenn. Bankr. R. 8(c)(2).**

United States District Court for the Eastern District of Washington

"**Washington cases:** cite Washington Reports and year of decision.

"**Federal cases:** For decisions of the United States Supreme Court, cite United States Reports, or if not yet published therein, Supreme Court Reporter, or if not yet published therein, United States Law Week. For all other federal cases, cite Federal Reporter, Federal Supplement, Federal Rules Decisions, or Bankruptcy Reporter including the district or circuit and year of the decision." **E.D. Wash. R. 7.1(g).**

United States Bankruptcy Court for the Eastern District of Washington

"Citations to Washington cases in a memorandum of authorities shall be to the Washington Reports. Citations to cases from other states shall be to the National Reporter System. Citations to federal cases shall be to the United States Reports, Federal Reporter, or Federal Supplement. Citations to bankruptcy cases shall be to West's Bankruptcy Reporter, Collier's Bankruptcy Cases or Bankruptcy Court Decisions." **E.D. Wash. Bankr. R. 9013-1.**

United States Court of Appeals for the Armed Services

"Citations shall conform with the *Uniform System of Citation.*" **U.S. Ct. App. Armed Servs. R. Prac. & Proc. 37(c)(2).**

United States Court of International Trade

For rules of citation for this court, consult Court of International Trade Rule 81 practice comment.

United States Court of Veterans Appeals

"Commonly understood abbreviations may be used." **Vet. App. R. 28(d).**

United States Tax Court

"All citations of case names shall be underscored when typewritten and shall be in italics when printed." **U.S. Tax Ct. R. 23(f).**

Note: Tax practitioners may also want to consult the *Citation and Style Manual* prepared by the United States Department of Justice, Tax Division, and ALWD **Appendix 7.**

Abbreviations are an integral part of legal citation. This appendix contains the following types of abbreviations:

(A) Calendar divisions (months and days);

(B) United States and world geography (states and territories, major United States cities, countries, and regions);

(C) Subdivisions, such as sections and paragraphs;

(D) Publishing terms, such as edition information; and

(E) General abbreviations that can be used whenever a specific rule permits or requires words to be abbreviated.

Three other appendices also contain abbreviations. **Appendix 4** contains abbreviations for various state and federal courts. **Appendix 5** contains abbreviations for legal periodicals. In addition, a few abbreviations are listed in charts within the main text.

To form the plural of a listed abbreviation, simply add "s" to the end, unless the entry indicates otherwise.

A. Calendar Divisions

Month	Abbreviation	Day of the Week	Abbreviation
January	Jan.	Monday	Mon.
February	Feb.	Tuesday	Tues.
March	Mar.	Wednesday	Wed.
April	Apr.	Thursday	Th.
May	May	Friday	Fri.
June	June	Saturday	Sat.
July	July	Sunday	Sun.
August	Aug.		
September	Sept.		
October	Oct.		
November	Nov.		
December	Dec.		

B. United States and World Geography

States and Territories

State or Territory	Abbreviation	State or Territory	Abbreviation
Alabama	Ala.	Montana	Mont.
Alaska	Alaska	Nebraska	Neb.
American Samoa	Am. Sam.	Nevada	Nev.
Arizona	Ariz.	New Hampshire	N.H.
Arkansas	Ark.	New Jersey	N.J.
California	Cal.	New Mexico	N.M.
Canal Zone	C.Z.	New York	N.Y.
Colorado	Colo.	North Carolina	N.C.
Connecticut	Conn.	North Dakota	N.D.
Delaware	Del.	Northern Mariana Islands	N. Mar. Is.
Florida	Fla.	Ohio	Ohio
Georgia	Ga.	Oklahoma	Okla.
Guam	Guam	Oregon	Or.
Hawaii	Haw.	Pennsylvania	Pa.
Idaho	Idaho	Puerto Rico	P.R.
Illinois	Ill.	Rhode Island	R.I.
Indiana	Ind.	South Carolina	S.C.
Iowa	Iowa	South Dakota	S.D.
Kansas	Kan.	Tennessee	Tenn.
Kentucky	Ky.	Texas	Tex.
Louisiana	La.	Utah	Utah
Maine	Me.	Vermont	Vt.
Maryland	Md.	Virgin Islands	V.I.
Massachusetts	Mass.	Virginia	Va.
Michigan	Mich.	Washington (state)	Wash.
Minnesota	Minn.	West Virginia	W. Va.
Mississippi	Miss.	Wisconsin	Wis.
Missouri	Mo.	Wyoming	Wyo.

[handwritten annotation next to Washington: "refer to supreme ct"]

Major United States Cities

City	Abbreviation	City	Abbreviation
Baltimore	Balt.	New York City	N.Y.C.
Boston	Bos.	Philadelphia	Phila.
Chicago	Chi.	Pittsburgh	Pitt.
Detroit	Det.	San Francisco	S.F.
Los Angeles	L.A.	Washington, D.C.	D.C.

Countries and Regions

If a country or region does not appear on this list, spell out the word or words, or abbreviate the words using **Appendix 3(E)**.

Country or Region	Abbreviation	Country or Region	Abbreviation
Afghanistan	Afg.	Algeria	Alg.
Africa	Afr.	America	Am.
Albania	Alb.	[use "U.S." when referring	
Alberta	Alb.	to United States of America]	
[when used with Canada]		Andorra	And.

Country or Region	Abbreviation	Country or Region	Abbreviation
Angola	Angl.	Gambia	Gam.
Antarctica	Ata.	Georgia	Geor.
Antigua and Barbuda	Ant. & Barb.	[Use "Ga." for the U.S.	
Argentina	Arg.	state of Georgia]	
Armenia	Arm.	Germany	Ger.
Australia	Austrl.	Gibraltar	Gib.
Azerbaijan	Azer.	Great Britain	Gr. Brit.
Bahrain	Bhar.	Greenland	Green.
Bangladesh	Bangl.	Grenada	Gren.
Barbados	Barb.	Guadeloupe	Guad.
Belarus	Belr.	Guatemala	Guat.
Belgium	Belg.	Guinea	Gin.
Bermuda	Berm.	Guinea-Bissau	Gin.-Bis.
Bolivia	Bol.	Guyana	Guy.
Bosnia and Herzegovinia	Bosn. & Herz.	Heard & McDonald	H. & McD. Is.
Botswana	Bots.	Islands	
Brazil	Braz.	Holland	Hol.
British Columbia	Brit. Colum.	Honduras	Hond.
Bulgaria	Bulg.	Hong Kong	H.K.
Burkina Faso	Burk. Faso	Hrvatska	Hrv.
Cambodia	Camb.	Hungary	Hun.
Cameroon	Camer.	Iceland	Ice.
Canada	Can.	Indonesia	Indon.
Cayman Islands	Cay. Is.	Ireland	Ir.
Central African Republic	C. Afr. Rep.	Israel	Isr.
Ceskoslovensko	Cesk.	Jamaica	Jam.
Channel Islands	Channel Is.	Jordan	Jor.
China, People's	P.R.C.	Kazakhstan	Kaz.
Republic of		Korea, North	N. Kor.
Christmas Island	Christ. Is.	Korea, South	S. Kor.
Colombia	Colom.	Kyrgyzstan	Kyrg.
Cook Islands	Cook Is.	Labrador	Labr.
Croatia	Croat.	Latvia	Lat.
Czech Republic	Czech Rep.	Lebanon	Leb.
Czechoslovakia	Czech.	Lesotho	Les.
Denmark	Den.	Liechtenstein	Liech.
Djibouti	Djib.	Lithuania	Lith.
Dominican Republic	Dom. Rep.	Luxembourg	Lux.
East Timor	E. Timor	Macedonia	Maced.
Ecuador	Ecu.	Madagascar	Madag.
Egypt	Egy.	Malaysia	Malay.
El Salvador	El. Sal.	Manitoba	Man.
England	Eng.	Marshall Islands	Marshall Is.
Equatorial Guinea	Eq. Guin.	Martinique	Mart.
Eritrea	Eri.	Mayotte	May.
Estonia	Est.	Mexico	Mex.
Ethiopia	Eth.	Micronesia	Micr.
Europe	Eur.	Moldova	Mol.
Falkland Islands	Falk. Is.	Mongolia	Mong.
Finland	Fin.	Montenegro	Monten.
France	Fr.	Morocco	Mor.

Country or Region	Abbreviation	Country or Region	Abbreviation
Mozambique	Mozam.	São Tomé and Príncipe	São Tomé & Príncipe
Myanmar	Myan.		
Namibia	Nam.	Saskatchewan	Sask.
Netherlands	Neth.	Scotland	Scot.
Netherlands Antilles	Neth. Ant.	Serbia	Serb.
New Brunswick	N. Bruns.	Seychelles	Sey.
New Caledonia	N. Caled.	Singapore	Sing.
New Zealand	N.Z.	Slovakia	Slovk.
Newfoundland	Newfl.	Slovenia	Slovn.
Nicaragua	Nicar.	Solomon Islands	Sol. Is.
Northern Ireland	N. Ir.	Somalia	Som.
Norway	Nor.	South Africa	S. Afr.
Nova Scotia	N. Sco.	Soviet Union	U.S.S.R.
Ontario	Ont.	Suriname	Surin.
Pakistan	Pak.	Swaziland	Swaz.
Panama	Pan.	Sweden	Swed.
Papua New Guinea	Papua N. Guin.	Switzerland	Switz.
Paraguay	Parag.	Tajikistan	Taj.
Philippines	Philip.	Tanzania	Tanz.
Pitcairn Island	Pitcairn Is.	Thailand	Thai.
Poland	Pol.	Trinidad and Tobago	Trin. & Tob.
Portugal	Port.	Tunisia	Tun.
Quebec	Que.	Turkey	Turk.
Romania	Rom.	Turkmenistan	Turkm.
Russia	Rus.	Ukraine	Ukr.
Rwanda	Rwa.	United Arab Emirates	U.A.E.
Saint Helena	St. Helena	United Kingdom	U.K.
Saint Kitts and Nevis	St. Kitts & Nevis	Uruguay	Uru.
Saint Lucia	St. Lucia	Uzbekistan	Uzb.
Saint Pierre and Miquelon	St. Pierre & Miquelon	Venezuela	Venz.
Saint Vincent and The Grenadines	St. Vincent	Yugoslavia	Yugo.
		Yukon Territory	Yukon Ter.
		Zimbabwe	Zim.

C. Subdivisions

Subdivision	Abbreviation	Subdivision	Abbreviation
amendment	amend.	folio	fol.
appendix	app.	footnote(s)	n., nn.
article	art.	graphic	gr.
bibliography	bibliog.	historical note(s)	hist. n., hist. nn.
book	bk.	hypothetical	hypo.
chapter	ch.	illustration	illus.
clause	cl.	introduction	intro.
column	col.	line(s)	l., ll.
comment	cmt.	note(s)	n., nn.
division	div.	number	no.
endnote(s)	n., nn.	paragraph(s)	¶, ¶¶
example	ex.	alternative:	para., paras.
figure	fig.	part	pt.

Subdivision	Abbreviation	Subdivision	Abbreviation
record	rec.	subdivision	subdiv.
reference	ref.	subparagraph	subpara.
reporter's note(s)	rptr. n., rptr. nn.	subsection	subsec.
schedule	sched.	supplement	supp.
section(s)	§, §§	table	tbl.
alternative:	sec., secs.	title	tit.
series	ser.	volume	vol.

D. Publishing Terms

Term	Abbreviation	Term	Abbreviation
abridged, abridgement	abr.	no publisher	n.p.
annotated	ann.	old series	o.s.
anonymous	anon.	printing	prtg.
compiled, compiler,		replacement	repl.
compilation	comp.	reprint, reprinted	repr.
copyright	© or copy.	revision, revised	rev.
draft	dft.	special	spec.
edition, editor	ed.	temporary	temp.
manuscript	ms.	tentative	tent.
mimeograph	mimeo.	translator, translated,	
new series	n.s.	translation	trans.
no date	n.d.	unabridged	unabr.
no place	n.p.		

E. General Abbreviations

Use these abbreviations in case names and statutory abbreviations, and in connection with other rules that require or permit abbreviations. To form the plural of a word, simply add "s" to the end unless the word listed indicates otherwise. For example, in "Admission(s)," the "(s)" means that the listed abbreviation is the same for the singular and plural.

Word/Term	Abbreviation	Word/Term	Abbreviation
Academy	Acad.	Alternative Dispute	
Accounting	Acctg.	Resolution	ADR
Acquisition	Acq.	Ambulance	Ambul.
Administrative	Admin.	Amend (ed, ment)	Amend.
Administrative Law	A.L.J.	Americ(a, an)	Am.
Judge		American Bar	
Administrator	Adminstr.	Association	ABA
Administratrix	Admx.	American Law Institute	ALI
Admiralty	Admir.	Amusement	Amuse.
Admission	Admis.	And	&
Advance(d)	Adv.	Annotated	Ann.
Advertising	Advert.	Answer(s)	Ans.
Advoca(te, cy)	Advoc.	Apartment	Apt.
Affidavit	Aff.	App(eal, ellate)	App.
Agricultur(e, al)	Agric.	Arbitrat(or, ion)	Arb.
Air Force	A.F.	Assistant	Asst.
Alcoholic Beverage	Alcoh. Bev.	Associate	Assoc.
Alternative	Alt.	Association	Assn.

457

Word/Term	Abbreviation	Word/Term	Abbreviation
Association of Legal Writing Directors	ALWD	Consolidated	Consol.
Atlantic	A.	Constitution	Const.
Attorney	Atty.	Construction	Constr.
Authority	Auth.	Continental	Contl.
Avenue	Ave.	Continuing Legal Education	CLE
Bankruptcy	Bankr.	Convention	Conv.
Bar	B.	Cooperative	Coop.
Benevolent	Benv.	Coordinator	Coord.
Beverage	Bev.	Copyright	Copy.
Board	Bd.	Corpora(te, tion)	Corp.
Book	Bk.	Correction	Correct.
Boulevard	Blvd.	County	Co.
Brief	Br.	Court	Ct.
Broadcast(ing)	Broad.	Criminal	Crim.
Brother	Bro.	Cumulative	Cum.
Brotherhood	Bhd.	Customs	Cust.
Building	Bldg.	Decision	Dec.
Bulletin	Bull.	Declaration	Decl.
Business	Bus.	Defendant	Def.
Casualty	Cas.	Defense	Def.
Cent(er, re)	Ctr.	Demurrer	Demr.
Central	C.	Department	Dept.
Century	Cent.	Deposition	Depo.
Certiorari	Cert.	Deputy	Dep.
Chancellor	Chan.	Determination	Determ.
Chancery	Ch.	Development	Dev.
Chemical	Chem.	Digest	Dig.
Chief Judge, Chief Justice	C.J.	Director	Dir.
		Disciplin(e, ary)	Disc.
Chronicle	Chron.	Distribut(ive, ion)	Distrib.
Circuit	Cir.	Distributing	Distribg.
Civil	Civ.	District	Dist.
Common, Commerc(e, ial)	Com.	District Attorney	D.A.
		District Court [federal]	D.
Commission	Commn.	Division	Div.
Commissioner	Commr.	Docket	Dkt.
Committee	Comm.	Doctor	Dr.
Commonwealth	Cmmw.	Document	Doc.
Communication(s)	Commun.	Domestic	Dom.
Company	Co.	East(ern)	E.
Comparative	Comp.	Econom(ic, ics, ical, y)	Econ.
Compensation	Compen.	Education(al)	Educ.
Compilation	Comp.	Electr(ical, icity, onic)	Elec.
Complaint, Compliance	Compl.	Emergency	Emerg.
Concurrent	Con.	Eminent Domain	Em. Dom.
Condemnation	Condemn.	Employment	Empl.
Condominium	Condo.	Employment Retirement Income Security Act	ERISA
Conference	Conf.	Encyclopedia	Ency.
Congre(ss, ssional)	Cong.	Engineer(ing)	Engr.
Conservation	Conserv.		

Word/Term	Abbreviation	Word/Term	Abbreviation
Enterprise	Enter.	Institution	Instn.
Entertainment	Ent.	Instruction	Instr.
Environment	Env.	Insurance	Ins.
Environmental	Envtl.	Intellectual	Intell.
Equality	Equal.	Interdisciplinary	Interdisc.
Equipment	Equip.	Interior	Int.
Equit(y, able)	Eq.	Internal Revenue Service	IRS
Esquire	Esq.	International	Intl.
Establishment	Estab.	Interrogatory	Interrog.
Estate	Est.	Intramural	Intra.
Evidence	Evid.	Investment	Inv.
Examination	Exam.	Island(s)	Is.
Examiner	Examr.	Joint	Jt.
Exchange	Exch.	Joint Appendix	Jt. App. or J.A.
Executive	Exec.	Journal	J.
Executrix	Execx.	Judge, Judges	J., JJ.
Exhibit	Ex.	Judge Advocate	
Family	Fam.	General's Corps	JAG
Federal	F. or Fed.	Judgment	Judm.
Federal Savings Bank	F.S.B.	Judicia(l, ry)	Jud.
Federation	Fedn.	Juris Doctor	J.D.
Fidelity	Fid.	Jurisdiction	Jxn.
Financ(e, ial)	Fin.	Jurisprudence	Jur.
Foreign	For.	Justice, Justices	J., JJ.
Fort	Ft.	Justice (other than a	
Foundation	Found.	person)	Just.
Franchis(e, ing)	Fran.	Juvenile	Juv.
Gasoline	Gas.	Labor	Lab.
Gazette	Gaz.	Language	Lang.
General	Gen.	Law	L.
Government	Govt.	Lawyer	Law.
Governmental	Govtl.	Legal	Leg.
Governor	Gov.	Legislat(ure, ive, ion)	Legis.
Guaranty	Guar.	Letter	Ltr.
Headquarters	H.Q.	Liability	Liab.
Hearing	Hrg.	Librarian	Libr.
Highway	Hwy.	Library	Lib.
Honorable	Hon.	Limited	Ltd.
Hospital	Hosp.	Limited Liability	
House	H.	Company	LLC
House of Representatives	H.R.	Limited Liability	
Housing	Hous.	Partnership	LLP
Human Resources	Hum. Res.	Limited Partnership	LP
Immigration	Immig.	Litigat(ion, or)	Litig.
Incorporated	Inc.	Local	Loc.
Indemnity	Indem.	Machine(ry)	Mach.
Independen(t, ce)	Indep.	Magazine	Mag.
Industr(y, ial, ies)	Indus.	Magistrate	Mag.
Information	Info.	Maintenance	Maint.
Injunction	Inj.	Management	Mgt.
Institute	Inst.	Manual	Man.

Word/Term	Abbreviation	Word/Term	Abbreviation
Manufacturer	Mfr.	Petition	Pet.
Manufacturing	Mfg.	Petitioner	Petr.
Maritime	Mar.	Pharmacy;	
Market	Mkt.	Pharmaceutical	Pharm.
Marketing	Mktg.	Philosoph(ical, y)	Phil.
Mechani(cs, cal)	Mech.	Photograph(y)	Photo.
Mediator	Med.	Physician(s)	Phys.
Medic(al, ine)	Med.	Plaintiff	Pl.
Medical Doctor	M.D.	Planning	Plan.
Memorandum	Memo.	Pleading	Pldg.
Memorial	Meml.	Politics	Pol.
Metropolitan	Metro.	Popular	Pop.
Military	Mil.	Practic(al, e)	Prac.
Miscellaneous	Misc.	Practising Law Institute	P.L.I.
Monthly	Mthly.	Practitioner	Pract.
Morning	Morn.	Preliminary	Prelim.
Mortgage	Mortg.	Prepara(tion, tory)	Prep.
Mortgagee	Mtgee.	President(ial)	Pres.
Mortgagor	Mtgor.	Priva(te, cy)	Priv.
Motion	Mot.	Probate	Prob.
Mount(ain)	Mt.	Procedure; Proceeding	P. or Proc.
Municipal	Mun.	Proclamation	Procl.
Mutual	Mut.	Procurement	Procure.
National	Natl.	Product(ion)	Prod.
Natur(e, al)	Nat.	Profess(or, ional)	Prof.
Navigation	Nav.	Professional Association	P.A.
Negligence	Negl.	Professional Corporation	P.C.
Negotiation	Negot.	Property	Prop.
Newsletter	Newsltr.	Protection	Protec.
Newspaper	Newsp.	Psychiatry	Psych.
North(ern)	N.	Psycholog(y, ical)	Psychol.
North America	N.A.	Public	Pub.
Northeast(ern)	N.E.	Publishing	Publg.
Northwest(ern)	N.W.	Quarterly	Q.
Northwestern [Univ.]	Nw.	Railroad	R.R.
Number	No.	Railway	Ry.
Obligation(s)	Oblig.	Record [on appeal]	R.
Occupation(s)	Occ.	Record [other]	Rec.
Offic(e, ial)	Off.	Reference	Ref.
Opinion	Op.	Regional	Regl.
Order	Or.	Regul(ar, ation, atory)	Reg.
Ordinance	Ordin.	Rehabilitation	Rehab.
Organization	Org.	Relations	Rel.
Pacific	P.	Religious	Relig.
Partial Summary		Remed(y, ies)	Rem.
Judgment	P.S.J.	Reorganization	Reorg.
Partnership	Partn.	Report	Rpt. or Rep.
Patent	Pat.	Reporter	Rptr. or Rep.
Pension	Pen.	Representative	Rep.
Performing	Perf.	Reproduct(ion, ive)	Reprod.
Permanent	Perm.	Request	Req.
Perspective	Persp.	Resolution(s)	Res.

Word/Term	Abbreviation	Word/Term	Abbreviation
Respondent	Respt.	Superior	Super.
Responsibility	Resp.	Supplement [N.Y.]	S.
Restaurant	Rest.	Supplement(al) [other]	Supp.
Retirement	Ret.	Supreme [other]	Sup.
Review	Rev.	Supreme Court [U.S.	
Revis(ed, ion)	Rev.	Supreme Court]	S. Ct.
Road	Rd.	Surety	Sur.
Rule(s)	R.	Surroga(te, cy)	Surrog.
Ruling	Rul.	System(s)	Sys.
Saint	St.	Taxation	Taxn.
Savings	Sav.	Technology	Tech.
Schedul(e, ing)	Sched.	Telecommunications	Telecomm.
School	Sch.	Telephone	Tel.
Scien(ce, ces, tific)	Sci.	Television	TV
Secretary	Sec.	Temporary	Temp.
Section [other than a		Temporary Restraining	
subdivision of a		Order	T.R.O.
source]	Sec.	Territorial	Terr.
Security	Sec.	Testimony	Test.
Selective	Sel.	Transcontinental	Transcon.
Senat(e, or)	Sen.	Transcript	Transcr.
Sentencing	Senten.	Transnational	Transnatl.
Service	Serv.	Transportation	Transp.
Session	Sess.	Treasur(er, y)	Treas.
Settlement	Settle.	Trial	Tr.
Shipping	Ship.	Tribun(e, al)	Trib.
Social	Soc.	Unauthorized	Unauth.
Society	Socy.	Unconsolidated	Unconsol.
Solicitor	Sol.	Unemployment	Unempl.
South(ern) [other than		Uniform	Unif.
Southern Reporter]	S.	Uniform Commercial	
South America	S.A.	Code	U.C.C.
Southeast(ern)	S.E.	Uniform Laws Annotated	U.L.A.
Southern Reporter	So.	United Nations	UN
Southwest(ern)	S.W.	United States	U.S.
Southwestern [Univ.]	Sw.	University	U.
Special	Spec.	Urban	Urb.
Standard	Stand.	Utility	Util.
State	St.	Vehicle	Veh.
Statement	State.	Versus, against [in case	
Statute(s)	Stat.	name]	v.
Steamship	S.S.	Veteran	Vet.
Stipulat(e, ion)	Stip.	Vice President	V.P.
Street	St.	Volunteer	Vol.
Studies	Stud.	Weekly	Wkly.
Subcommittee	Subcomm.	West(ern)	W.
Subpoena	Subp.	Yearbook, Year Book	Y.B.
Summary Judgment	S.J.		

APPENDIX 4
COURT ABBREVIATIONS

This appendix contains abbreviations for state and federal courts. If you cannot find an entry for the court you wish to cite, consult **Appendix 3**, which contains general abbreviations. Also, consult **Appendix 1** when using court abbreviations in case citations.

A. State Courts

The listed state courts include each state's court of last resort, any intermediate appellate court, and trial courts of general jurisdiction. It is important to note that some states, such as New York and Pennsylvania, have additional courts. Courts are listed hierarchically, with the highest court in the state appearing first. **For appellate courts, follow Rule 12.6(b) about adding counties, departments, and divisions.**

Court	Abbreviation
Alabama Supreme Court	**Ala.**
Alabama Court of Civil Appeals	**Ala. Civ. App.**
Alabama Court of Criminal Appeals	**Ala. Crim. App.**
Alabama Circuit Court	**Ala. Cir.**
Alaska Supreme Court	**Alaska**
Alaska Court of Appeals	**Alaska App.**
Alaska Superior Court	**Alaska Super.**
Arizona Supreme Court	**Ariz.**
Arizona Court of Appeals	**Ariz. App.**
Arizona Superior Court	**Ariz. Super.**
Arkansas Supreme Court	**Ark.**
Arkansas Court of Appeals	**Ark. App.**
Arkansas Circuit Court	**Ark. Cir.**
Arkansas Chancery Court	**Ark. Ch.**
California Supreme Court	**Cal.**
California Court of Appeal	**Cal. App.**
California Superior Court	**Cal. Super.**
Colorado Supreme Court	**Colo.**
Colorado Court of Appeals	**Colo. App.**
Colorado District Court	**Colo. Dist.**
Connecticut Supreme Court	**Conn.**
Connecticut Appellate Court	**Conn. App.**
Connecticut Superior Court	**Conn. Super.**
Connecticut Circuit Court	**Conn. Cir.**

Court	Abbreviation
Delaware Supreme Court	**Del.**
Delaware Superior Court	**Del. Super.**
Delaware Court of Chancery	**Del. Ch.**
Delaware Family Court	**Del. Fam.**
District of Columbia Court of Appeals	**D.C. App.**
District of Columbia Superior Court	**D.C. Super.**
Florida Supreme Court	**Fla.**
Florida District Court of Appeal	**Fla. Dist. App.**
Florida Circuit Court	**Fla. Cir.**
Georgia Supreme Court	**Ga.**
Georgia Court of Appeals	**Ga. App.**
Georgia Superior Court	**Ga. Super.**
Hawaii Supreme Court	**Haw.**
Hawaii Intermediate Court of Appeals	**Haw. App.**
Hawaii Circuit Court	**Haw. Cir.**
Idaho Supreme Court	**Idaho**
Idaho Court of Appeals	**Idaho App.**
Idaho District Court	**Idaho Dist.**
Illinois Supreme Court	**Ill.**
Illinois Appellate Court	**Ill. App.**
Illinois Circuit Court	**Ill. Cir.**
Indiana Supreme Court	**Ind.**
Indiana Court of Appeals	**Ind. App.**
Indiana Superior Court	**Ind. Super.**
Iowa Supreme Court	**Iowa**
Iowa Court of Appeals	**Iowa App.**
Iowa District Court	**Iowa Dist.**
Kansas Supreme Court	**Kan.**
Kansas Court of Appeals	**Kan. App.**

SIDEBAR A4.1

THE STRUCTURE OF STATE COURT SYSTEMS

For more details about each court—such as the number of judges or justices—and for diagrams of each state's judicial system, consult the most recent annual edition of *Federal-State Court Directory* (Robert S. Want ed., Want Pub. Co.) or of *BNA's Directory of State and Federal Courts, Judges, and Clerks* (Judith A. Miller ed., BNA). In addition, the National Center for State Courts has compiled a list of state and federal court Web sites that can be accessed at http://www.ncsconline.org; *select* Information; *select* Court Web Sites.

Court	Abbreviation
Kansas District Court	**Kan. Dist.**
Kentucky Supreme Court	**Ky.**
Kentucky Court of Appeals	**Ky. App.**
Kentucky Circuit Court	**Ky. Cir.**
Louisiana Supreme Court	**La.**
Louisiana Court of Appeal	**La. App.**
Louisiana District Court	**La. Dist.**
Maine Supreme Judicial Court	**Me.**
Maine Superior Court	**Me. Super.**
Maryland Court of Appeals	**Md.**
Maryland Court of Special Appeals	**Md. Spec. App.**
Maryland Circuit Court	**Md. Cir.**
Massachusetts Supreme Judicial Court	**Mass.**
Massachusetts Appeals Court	**Mass. App.**
Trial Court of the Commonwealth	**Mass. Cmmw.**
Michigan Supreme Court	**Mich.**
Michigan Court of Appeals	**Mich. App.**
Michigan Circuit Court	**Mich. Cir.**
Minnesota Supreme Court	**Minn.**
Minnesota Court of Appeals	**Minn. App.**
Minnesota District Court	**Minn. Dist.**
Mississippi Supreme Court	**Miss.**
Mississippi Court of Appeals	**Miss. App.**
Mississippi Circuit Court	**Miss. Cir.**
Mississippi Chancery Court	**Miss. Ch.**
Missouri Supreme Court	**Mo.**
Missouri Court of Appeals	**Mo. App.**
Missouri Circuit Court	**Mo. Cir.**
Montana Supreme Court	**Mont.**
Montana District Court	**Mont. Dist.**
Nebraska Supreme Court	**Neb.**
Nebraska Court of Appeals	**Neb. App.**
Nebraska District Court	**Neb. Dist.**
Nevada Supreme Court	**Nev.**
Nevada District Court	**Nev. Dist.**
New Hampshire Supreme Court	**N.H.**
New Hampshire Superior Court	**N.H. Super.**
New Jersey Supreme Court	**N.J.**
New Jersey Superior Court, Appellate Division	**N.J. Super. App. Div.**
New Mexico Supreme Court	**N.M.**
New Mexico Court of Appeals	**N.M. App.**
New Mexico District Court	**N.M. Dist.**
New York Court of Appeals	**N.Y.**
New York Supreme Court, Appellate Division	**N.Y. App. Div.**
New York Supreme Court	**N.Y. Sup.**
North Carolina Supreme Court	**N.C.**

Court	Abbreviation
North Carolina Court of Appeals	**N.C. App.**
North Carolina Superior Court	**N.C. Super.**
North Dakota Supreme Court	**N.D.**
North Dakota Court of Appeals	**N.D. App.**

Note: The North Dakota Court of Appeals was a temporary court, effective July 1, 1987 through January 1, 2000.

Court	Abbreviation
North Dakota District Court	**N.D. Dist.**
Ohio Supreme Court	**Ohio**
Ohio Court of Civil Appeals	**Ohio App.**
Ohio Court of Common Pleas	**Ohio Com. Pleas**
Oklahoma Supreme Court	**Okla.**
Oklahoma Court of Criminal Appeals	**Okla. Crim. App.**
Oklahoma Court of Civil Appeals	**Okla. App.**
Oklahoma District Court	**Okla. Dist.**
Oregon Supreme Court	**Or.**
Oregon Court of Appeals	**Or. App.**
Oregon Circuit Court	**Or. Cir.**
Pennsylvania Supreme Court	**Pa.**
Pennsylvania Superior Court	**Pa. Super.**
Pennsylvania Commonwealth Court	**Pa. Cmmw.**
Rhode Island Supreme Court	**R.I.**
Rhode Island Superior Court	**R.I. Super.**
South Carolina Supreme Court	**S.C.**
South Carolina Court of Appeals	**S.C. App.**
South Carolina Circuit Court	**S.C. Cir.**
South Dakota Supreme Court	**S.D.**
South Dakota Circuit Court	**S.D. Cir.**
Tennessee Supreme Court	**Tenn.**
Tennessee Court of Appeals	**Tenn. App.**
Tennessee Court of Criminal Appeals	**Tenn. Crim. App.**
Tennessee Circuit Court	**Tenn. Cir.**
Tennessee Criminal Court	**Tenn. Crim.**
Tennessee Chancery Court	**Tenn. Ch.**
Texas Supreme Court	**Tex.**
Texas Court of Criminal Appeals	**Tex. Crim. App.**
Texas Court of Appeals	**Tex. App.**
Texas District Court	**Tex. Dist.**
Texas Criminal District Court	**Tex. Crim. Dist.**
Utah Supreme Court	**Utah**
Utah Court of Appeals	**Utah App.**
Utah District Court	**Utah Dist.**
Vermont Supreme Court	**Vt.**
Vermont Superior Court	**Vt. Super.**
Vermont District Court	**Vt. Dist.**
Virginia Supreme Court	**Va.**
Virginia Court of Appeals	**Va. App.**
Virginia Circuit Court	**Va. Cir.**

Court	Abbreviation
Washington Supreme Court	**Wash.**
Washington Court of Appeals	**Wash. App.**
Washington Superior Court	**Wash. Super.**
West Virginia Supreme Court of Appeals	**W. Va.**
West Virginia Circuit Court	**W. Va. Cir.**
Wisconsin Supreme Court	**Wis.**
Wisconsin Court of Appeals	**Wis. App.**
Wisconsin Circuit Court	**Wis. Cir.**
Wyoming Supreme Court	**Wyo.**
Wyoming District Court	**Wyo. Dist.**

B. Federal Courts

Court	Abbreviation
United States Supreme Court	**U.S.**

United States Courts of Appeals

Court	Abbreviation
First Circuit	**1st Cir.**
Second Circuit	**2d Cir.**
Third Circuit	**3d Cir.**
Fourth Circuit	**4th Cir.**
Fifth Circuit	**5th Cir.**
Sixth Circuit	**6th Cir.**
Seventh Circuit	**7th Cir.**
Eighth Circuit	**8th Cir.**
Ninth Circuit	**9th Cir.**
Tenth Circuit	**10th Cir.**
Eleventh Circuit	**11th Cir.**
D.C. Circuit	**D.C. Cir.**
Federal Circuit	**Fed. Cir.**

United States District Courts

Court	Abbreviation
Middle District of Alabama	**M.D. Ala.**
Northern District of Alabama	**N.D. Ala.**
Southern District of Alabama	**S.D. Ala.**
District of Alaska	**D. Alaska**
District of Arizona	**D. Ariz.**
Eastern District of Arkansas	**E.D. Ark.**
Western District of Arkansas	**W.D. Ark.**
Central District of California	**C.D. Cal.**
Eastern District of California	**E.D. Cal.**
Northern District of California	**N.D. Cal.**
Southern District of California	**S.D. Cal.**
District of the Canal Zone	**D.C.Z.**

Note: The D.C.Z. ceased to exist on March 31, 1982.

Court	Abbreviation
District of Colorado	**D. Colo.**
District of Connecticut	**D. Conn.**
District of Delaware	**D. Del.**
District of D.C.	**D.D.C.**
Middle District of Florida	**M.D. Fla.**
Northern District of Florida	**N.D. Fla.**
Southern District of Florida	**S.D. Fla.**
Middle District of Georgia	**M.D. Ga.**
Northern District of Georgia	**N.D. Ga.**
Southern District of Georgia	**S.D. Ga.**
District of Guam	**D. Guam**
District of Hawaii	**D. Haw.**
District of Idaho	**D. Idaho**
Central District of Illinois	**C.D. Ill.**
Northern District of Illinois	**N.D. Ill.**
Southern District of Illinois	**S.D. Ill.**
Northern District of Indiana	**N.D. Ind.**
Southern District of Indiana	**S.D. Ind.**
Northern District of Iowa	**N.D. Iowa**
Southern District of Iowa	**S.D. Iowa**
District of Kansas	**D. Kan.**
Eastern District of Kentucky	**E.D. Ky.**
Western District of Kentucky	**W.D. Ky.**
Eastern District of Louisiana	**E.D. La.**
Middle District of Louisiana	**M.D. La.**
Western District of Louisiana	**W.D. La.**
District of Maine	**D. Me.**
District of Maryland	**D. Md.**
District of Massachusetts	**D. Mass.**
Eastern District of Michigan	**E.D. Mich.**
Western District of Michigan	**W.D. Mich.**
District of Minnesota	**D. Minn.**
Northern District of Mississippi	**N.D. Miss.**
Southern District of Mississippi	**S.D. Miss.**
Eastern District of Missouri	**E.D. Mo.**
Western District of Missouri	**W.D. Mo.**
District of Montana	**D. Mont.**
District of Nebraska	**D. Neb.**
District of Nevada	**D. Nev.**
District of New Hampshire	**D.N.H.**
District of New Jersey	**D.N.J.**
District of New Mexico	**D.N.M.**
Eastern District of New York	**E.D.N.Y.**
Northern District of New York	**N.D.N.Y.**
Southern District of New York	**S.D.N.Y.**
Western District of New York	**W.D.N.Y.**
Eastern District of North Carolina	**E.D.N.C.**
Middle District of North Carolina	**M.D.N.C.**
Western District of North Carolina	**W.D.N.C.**
District of North Dakota	**D.N.D.**
District of the Northern Mariana Islands	**D.N. Mar. Is.**

Court	Abbreviation
Northern District of Ohio	**N.D. Ohio**
Southern District of Ohio	**S.D. Ohio**
Eastern District of Oklahoma	**E.D. Okla.**
Northern District of Oklahoma	**N.D. Okla.**
Western District of Oklahoma	**W.D. Okla.**
District of Oregon	**D. Or.**
Eastern District of Pennsylvania	**E.D. Pa.**
Middle District of Pennsylvania	**M.D. Pa.**
Western District of Pennsylvania	**W.D. Pa.**
District of Puerto Rico	**D.P.R.**
District of Rhode Island	**D.R.I.**
District of South Carolina	**D.S.C.**
District of South Dakota	**D.S.D.**
Eastern District of Tennessee	**E.D. Tenn.**
Middle District of Tennessee	**M.D. Tenn.**
Western District of Tennessee	**W.D. Tenn.**
Eastern District of Texas	**E.D. Tex.**
Northern District of Texas	**N.D. Tex.**
Southern District of Texas	**S.D. Tex.**
Western District of Texas	**W.D. Tex.**
District of Utah	**D. Utah**
District of Vermont	**D. Vt.**
Eastern District of Virginia	**E.D. Va.**
Western District of Virginia	**W.D. Va.**
District of the Virgin Islands	**D.V.I.**
Eastern District of Washington	**E.D. Wash.**
Western District of Washington	**W.D. Wash.**
Northern District of West Virginia	**N.D.W. Va.**
Southern District of West Virginia	**S.D.W. Va.**
Eastern District of Wisconsin	**E.D. Wis.**
Western District of Wisconsin	**W.D. Wis.**
District of Wyoming	**D. Wyo.**

SIDEBAR A4.2

DISSECTING A FEDERAL DISTRICT COURT ABBREVIATION

The abbreviation for "District" is "D." Many states have more than one district; these districts are designated by geography. The choices may be Central (C.), Eastern (E.), Middle (M.), Northern (N.), Southern (S.), or Western (W.). To formulate the abbreviation for a United States District Court, put the geographic designation before "D.," and then add the state abbreviation. For state abbreviations, see **Appendix 3(B)**. Consult **Rule 2** for information about how to space the abbreviation.

Military Courts

Court	Abbreviation
United States Court of Appeals for the Armed Forces	**Armed Forces App.**
United States Court of Veterans Appeals	**Vet. App.**
United States Air Force Court of Criminal Appeals	**A.F. Crim. App.**
United States Army Court of Criminal Appeals	**Army Crim. App.**
United States Coast Guard Court of Criminal Appeals	**Coast Guard Crim. App.**
United States Navy-Marine Corps Court of Criminal Appeals	**Navy-Marine Crim. App.**

Bankruptcy Courts

Each United States District Court has a corresponding bankruptcy court. To cite a bankruptcy court, add Bankr. to the district court abbreviation.

Examples

Bankr. N.D. Ala.
Bankr. D. Mass.

Other Federal Courts

Court	Abbreviation
Court of Federal Claims	**Fed. Cl.**
Court of Customs and Patent Appeals	**Cust. & Pat. App.**
Court of Claims	**Ct. Cl.**
Claims Court	**Cl. Ct.**
Court of International Trade	**Ct. Intl. Trade**
Tax Court	**Tax**

Use this appendix to abbreviate the names of periodicals. The citation form for periodicals is addressed in **Rule 23.** Selected periodicals are listed in alphabetical order by the periodical's current name. Prior names are listed immediately below the current name. Use the abbreviation that corresponds to the volume you are citing; do not use the current abbreviation if citing older volumes.

To help you determine how to space each abbreviation, the symbol ▲ has been used to designate a space. Do not include this symbol when you type the abbreviation.

The symbol ★ has been used to indicate whether a periodical is nonconsecutively paginated. Under item 3 in **Rule 23.1(f)**, when the issues of a particular periodical are not consecutively paginated, include the exact date contained on the first page or cover. For consecutively paginated periodicals, include only the year (**item 2 in Rule 23.1(f)**).

Although this list contains many periodicals, the list is not exhaustive. If you cannot locate the name of the periodical you wish to cite in **Appendix 5**, to construct the abbreviation, look up each word in the title in **Appendix 3**; you may also abbreviate any word that appears in another title within **Appendix 5**. If you cannot find an abbreviation for the word in **Appendix 3** or in **Appendix 5**, spell out that word. Remember to use **Rule 2** to properly space your abbreviation. **Finally, omit the words "a," "at," "in," "of," and "the" from a periodical title, unless the reader would not be able to discern the publication name; also omit colons, and everything following them, that may appear within the title.**

Name	Abbreviation
★**ABA Journal**	**ABA▲J.**
Was: American Bar Association Journal (Vol. 1–Vol. 69)	ABA▲J.
Administrative Law Journal of the American University	**Admin.▲L.J.▲Am.▲U.**
Was: Administrative Law Journal (Vol. 1–Vol. 5)	Admin.▲L.J.
Administrative Law Review	**Admin.▲L.▲Rev.**
Was: Administrative Law Bulletin (Vol. 1–Vol. 12)	Admin.▲L.▲Bull.
★**Advocate**	**Advoc.**
Absorbed: ★Idaho State Bar News Bulletin (Mar. 1958)	Idaho▲St.▲B.▲News▲Bull.
African-American Law & Policy Report	**African-Am.▲L.▲&▲Policy▲Rep.**
★**Air and Space Lawyer, The**	**Air▲&▲Space▲Law.**

Name	Abbreviation
Air Force Law Review *Was:* United States Air Force JAG Law Review (Vol. 6, no. 6–Vol. 15, no. 2) *Was:* ★United States Air Force JAG Bulletin (Vol. 1, no. 1–Vol. 6, no. 5)	A.F. ▲L. ▲Rev. U.S.A.F. ▲JAG ▲L. ▲Rev. U.S.A.F. ▲JAG ▲Bull.
Akron Law Review	**Akron ▲L. ▲Rev.**
Akron Tax Journal	**Akron ▲Tax ▲J.**
Alabama Law Review	**Ala. ▲L. ▲Rev.**
★Alabama Lawyer, The	**Ala. ▲Law.**
Alaska Law Review *Was:* UCLA-Alaska Law Review (Vol. 1–Vol. 12) *Was:* Alaska Law Journal	**Alaska ▲L. ▲Rev.** UCLA-Alaska ▲L. ▲Rev. Alaska ▲L.J.
Albany Law Journal of Science & Technology	**Alb. ▲L.J. ▲Sci. ▲& ▲Tech.**
Albany Law Review	**Alb. ▲L. ▲Rev.**
★ALI-ABA Business Law Course Materials Journal *Was:* ★ALI-ABA Course Materials Journal (Vol. 1–Vol. 24, no. 2)	**ALI-ABA ▲Bus. ▲L. ▲Course ▲Materials ▲J.** ALI-ABA ▲Course ▲Materials ▲J.
American Bankruptcy Institute Law Review	**Am. ▲Bankr. ▲Inst. ▲L. ▲Rev.**
American Bankruptcy Law Journal, The *Was:* Journal of the National Conference of Referees in Bankruptcy (Vol. 40–Vol. 44) *Was:* Journal of the National Association of Referees in Bankruptcy (Vol. 1–Vol. 39 and Vol. 45–Vol. 65)	**Am. ▲Bankr. ▲L.J.** J. ▲Natl. ▲Conf. ▲Referees ▲Bankr. J. ▲Natl. ▲Assn. ▲Referees ▲Bankr.
American Bar Association Journal—*see ABA Journal*	
American Bar Foundation Research Journal—*see Law & Social Inquiry: Journal of American Bar Foundation*	
American Business Law Journal *Supersedes:* American Business Law Bulletin, The	**Am. ▲Bus. ▲L.J.** Am. ▲Bus. ▲L. ▲Bull.
American Criminal Law Review *Was:* American Criminal Law Quarterly (Vol. 1–Vol. 9, no. 1)	**Am. ▲Crim. ▲L. ▲Rev.** Am. ▲Crim. ▲L.Q.
American Indian Law Review	**Am. ▲Indian ▲L. ▲Rev.**
American Journal of Comparative Law	**Am. ▲J. ▲Comp. ▲L.**
American Journal of Criminal Law	**Am. ▲J. ▲Crim. ▲L.**
American Journal of Family Law	**Am. ▲J. ▲Fam. ▲L.**
American Journal of International Arbitration	**Am. ▲J. ▲Intl. ▲Arb.**
American Journal of International Law	**Am. ▲J. ▲Intl. ▲L.**

472

Name	Abbreviation
American Journal of Jurisprudence *Was:* Natural Law Forum (Vol. 1–Vol. 13)	**Am.▲ J.▲ Juris.** Nat.▲ L.▲ Forum
American Journal of Law & Medicine	**Am.▲ J.L.▲ &▲ Med.**
American Journal of Legal History	**Am.▲ J.▲ Leg.▲ Hist.**
American Journal of Tax Policy	**Am.▲ J.▲ Tax▲ Policy**
American Journal of Trial Advocacy	**Am.▲ J.▲ Tr.▲ Advoc.**
American Law Register, The—*see University of Pennsylvania Law Review*	
American Lawyer	**Am.▲ Law.**
American Review of International Arbitration, The	**Am.▲ Rev.▲ Intl.▲ Arb.**
American Society of International Law Proceedings	**Am.▲ Socy.▲ Intl.▲ L.▲ Procs.**
American University International Law Review *Was:* American University Journal of International Law and Policy (Vol. 1–Vol. 12, no. 6)	**Am.▲ U.▲ Intl.▲ L.▲ Rev.** Am.▲ U.▲ J.▲ Intl.▲ L.▲ &▲ Policy
American University Journal of Gender, Social Policy & the Law *Was:* American University Journal of Gender and the Law (Vol. 1–Vol. 6, no. 3)	**Am.▲ U.▲ J.▲ Gender▲ Soc.▲ Policy▲ &▲ L.** Am.▲ U.▲ J.▲ Gender▲ &▲ L.
American University Law Review *Was:* American University Intramural Law Review (Vol. 1–Vol. 5)	**Am.▲ U.▲ L.▲ Rev.** Am.▲ U.▲ Intra.▲ L.▲ Rev.
★ **AmLaw Tech**	**AmLaw▲ Tech**
Anglo-American Law Review—*see Common Law World Review*	
Animal Law	**Animal▲ L.**
Annals of Health Law	**Annals▲ Health▲ L.**
Annals of the American Academy of Political and Social Science	**Annals▲ Am.▲ Acad.▲ Pol.▲ &▲ Soc.▲ Sci.**
Annual Institute on Securities Regulation	**Annual▲ Inst.▲ Sec.▲ Reg.**
Annual Review of Banking and Financial Law *Was:* Annual Review of Banking Law (Vol. 1–Vol. 21)	**Annual▲ Rev.▲ Banking▲ &▲ Fin.▲ L.** Annual▲ Rev.▲ Banking▲ L.
Annual Survey of American Law—*see New York University Annual Survey of American Law*	
Annual Survey of International & Comparative Law	**Annual▲ Surv.▲ Intl.▲ &▲ Comp.▲ L.**
Antitrust Bulletin	**Antitrust▲ Bull.**

Name	Abbreviation
★Antitrust Law and Economics Review	Antitrust▲L.▲&▲Econ.▲Rev.
Antitrust Law Journal	Antitrust▲L.J.
Appalachian Journal of Law	Appalachian▲J.L.
★Arizona Attorney *Was:* ★Arizona Bar Journal (1965–June/July 1998) *Was:* ★Arizona Bar Briefs	Ariz.▲Atty. Ariz.▲B.J. Ariz.▲B.▲Brs.
Arizona Journal of International and Comparative Law	Ariz.▲J.▲Intl.▲&▲Comp.▲L.
Arizona Law Review	Ariz.▲L.▲Rev.
Arizona Republic	Ariz.▲Republic
Arizona State Law Journal *Was:* Law and the Social Order (1969–1973)	Ariz.▲St.▲L.J. L.▲&▲Soc.▲Order
★Arkansas Law Notes	Ark.▲L.▲Notes
Arkansas Law Review *Was:* Arkansas Law Review and Bar Association Journal (Vol. 1–Vol. 21) *Was:* Arkansas Law Review (Winter 1946–Spring 1947)	Ark.▲L.▲Rev. Ark.▲L.▲Rev.▲&▲B.▲Assn.▲J. Ark.▲L.▲Rev.
★Arkansas Lawyer	Ark.▲Law.
★Army Lawyer	Army▲Law.
Art and Museum Law Journal	Art▲&▲Museum▲L.J.
Art & the Law—*see Columbia Journal of Law & the Arts, The*	
Asian Law Journal	Asian▲L.J.
Asian Pacific American Law Journal: UCLA School of Law	Asian▲P.▲Am.▲L.J.
Asian-Pacific Law and Policy Journal *Was:* Asian American Pacific Islands Law Journal	Asian-P.▲L.&▲Policy▲J. Asian▲Am.▲P.▲Islands▲L.J.
Association of the Bar of the City of New York, The	Assn.▲B.▲City▲N.Y.
★Atlanta Journal & Constitution	Atlanta▲J.▲&▲Const.
Atomic Energy Law Journal	Atomic▲Energy▲L.J.
Ave Maria Law Review	Ave▲Maria▲L.▲Rev.
★Baltimore Sun	Balt.▲Sun
Banking Law Journal *Absorbed:* Business Law Journal (1932) *Absorbed:* Bankers Magazine	Banking▲L.J. Bus.▲L.J. Bankers▲Mag.
Bankruptcy Developments Journal	Bankr.▲Devs.▲J.

Name	Abbreviation
★**Bar Examiner, The**	**B.▲Examr.**
★**Bar Leader** *Was:* Bar Activities (Vol. 1–Vol. 7, no. 2) *Was:* Bar Keys	**B.▲Leader** B.▲Activities B.▲Keys
Barrister—*see Young Lawyer*	
Barry Law Review	**Barry▲L.▲Rev.**
Baylor Law Review	**Baylor▲L.▲Rev.**
Behavioral Sciences & the Law	**Behav.▲Sci.▲&▲L.**
Bench & Bar *Was*: Kentucky Bench & Bar	**Bench▲&▲B.** Ky.▲Bench▲&▲B.
★**Bench & Bar of Minnesota**	**Bench▲&▲B.▲Minn.**
Benchmark	**Benchmark**
Benefits Law Journal	**Benefits▲L.J.**
Berkeley Journal of Employment and Labor Law *Was:* Industrial Relations Law Journal (Vol. 1–Vol. 13)	**Berkeley▲J.▲Empl.▲&▲Lab.▲L.** Indus.▲Rel.▲L.J.
Berkeley Journal of Health Care Law	**Berkeley▲J.▲Health▲Care▲L.**
Berkeley Journal of International Law *Was:* International Tax & Business Lawyer (Vol. 1–Vol. 13, no. 2)	**Berkeley▲J.▲Intl.▲L.** Intl.▲Tax▲&▲Bus.▲Law.
Berkeley La Raza Law Journal *Was:* La Raza Law Journal (Vol. 1–Vol. 12)	**Berkeley▲La▲Raza▲L.J.** La▲Raza▲L.J.
Berkeley Technology Law Journal *Was:* High Technology Law Journal (Vol. 1–Vol. 10)	**Berkeley▲Tech.▲L.J.** High▲Tech.▲L.J.
Berkeley Women's Law Journal	**Berkeley▲Women's▲L.J.**
★**Beverly Hills Bar Association Journal** *Was:* ★Journal of the Beverly Hills Bar Association (Vol. 1–Vol. 11, no. 3)	**Beverly▲Hills▲B.▲Assn.▲J.** J.▲Beverly▲Hills▲B.▲Assn.
Black Law Journal—*see National Black Law Journal*	
Boalt Journal of Criminal Law *Was:* California Journal of Criminal Law (2000–2004)	**Boalt▲J.▲Crim.▲L.** Cal.▲J.▲Crim.▲L.
★**Boston Bar Journal** *Was:* ★Bar Bulletin (Jan. 1924–Dec. 1956)	**Boston▲B.J.** B.▲Bull.
Boston College Environmental Affairs Law Review *Was:* Environmental Affairs (Vol. 1–Vol. 6)	**B.C.▲Envtl.▲Aff.▲L.▲Rev.** Envtl.▲Aff.
Boston College International and Comparative Law Review *Was:* Boston College International and Comparative Law Journal (Vol. 1–Vol. 2, no. 1)	**B.C.▲Intl.▲&▲Comp.▲L.▲Rev.** B.C.▲Intl.▲&▲Comp.▲L.J.

Name	Abbreviation
Boston College Law Review *Was:* Boston College Industrial and Commercial Law Review (Vol. 1–Vol. 18)	**B.C.▲L.▲Rev.** B.C.▲Indus.▲&▲Com.▲L.▲Rev.
Boston College Third World Law Journal	**B.C.▲Third▲World▲L.J.**
★**Boston Globe**	**Boston▲Globe**
★**Boston Herald**	**Boston▲Herald**
Boston University International Law Journal	**B.U.▲Intl.▲L.J.**
Boston University Journal of Science & Technology Law *Was:* Journal of Science & Technology Law (Vol. 1–Vol. 6)	**B.U.▲J.▲Sci.▲&▲Tech.▲L.** J.▲Sci.▲& ▲Tech.▲L.
Boston University Journal of Tax Law	**B.U.▲J.▲Tax▲L.**
Boston University Law Review	**B.U.▲L.▲Rev.**
Boston University Public Interest Law Journal	**B.U.▲Pub.▲Int.▲L.J.**
Brandeis Law Journal *Was:* Brandeis Journal of Family Law School of Law (Vol. 36, no. 1–Vol. 36, no. 4) *Was:* University of Louisville Journal of Family Law (Vol. 31–Vol. 35) *Was:* Journal of Family Law (Vol. 1–Vol. 30)	**Brandeis▲L.J.** Brandeis▲J.▲Fam.▲L. U.▲Louis.▲J.▲Fam.▲L. J.▲Fam.▲L.
Bridgeport Law Review—*see QLR*	
Brigham Young University Education and Law Journal *Was:* Brigham Young University Journal of Law and Education (Vol. 1)	**BYU▲Educ.▲&▲L.J.** BYU▲J.L.▲&▲Educ.
Brigham Young University Law Review	**BYU▲L.▲Rev.**
Brooklyn Journal of International Law	**Brook.▲J.▲Intl.▲L.**
Brooklyn Law Review	**Brook.▲L.▲Rev.**
Buffalo Criminal Law Review	**Buff.▲Crim.▲L.▲Rev.**
Buffalo Environmental Law Journal	**Buff.▲Envtl.▲L.J.**
Buffalo Human Rights Law Review *Was:* Buffalo Journal of International Law (Vol. 1, no. 1–Vol. 3, no. 2)	**Buff.▲Hum.▲Rights▲L.▲Rev.** Buff.▲J.▲Intl.▲L.
Buffalo Law Review	**Buff.▲L.▲Rev.**
★**Buffalo News**	**Buff.▲News**
Buffalo Public Interest Law Journal: In the Public Interest *Was:* Buffalo Journal of Public Interest Law	**Buff.▲Pub.▲Int.▲L.J.** Buff.▲J.▲Pub.▲Int.▲L.

476

Name	Abbreviation
Buffalo Women's Law Journal	**Buff.▲Women's▲L.J.**
Was: CIRCLES: The Buffalo Women's Journal of Law and Social Policy (Vol. 1–Vol. 6)	CIRCLES
Bulletin of the Copyright Society of the U.S.A.—*see Journal of the Copyright Society of the U.S.A.*	
Business Law Review	**Bus.▲L.▲Rev.**
Business Lawyer	**Bus.▲Law.**
★**Business Week**	**Bus.▲Week**
BYU Journal of Public Law	**BYU▲J.▲Pub.▲L.**
California Bankruptcy Journal	**Cal.▲Bankr.▲J.**
California International Practitioner, The	**Cal.▲Intl.▲Pract.**
California Law Review	**Cal.▲L.▲Rev.**
★**California Lawyer**	**Cal.▲Law.**
Was: ★California State Bar Journal (Vol. 47–Vol. 56)	Cal.▲St.▲B.J.
Was: ★Journal-State Bar of California (Vol. 17, no. 3–Vol. 46)	J.-St.▲B.▲Cal.
Was: ★State Bar Journal of the State Bar of California (Vol. 1–Vol. 17, no. 2)	St.▲B.J.▲St.▲B.▲Cal.
California Regulatory Law Reporter	**Cal.▲Reg.▲L.▲Rep.**
California State Bar Journal	**Cal.▲St.▲B.J.**
California Western International Law Journal	**Cal.▲W.▲Intl.▲L.J.**
California Western Law Review	**Cal.▲W.▲L.▲Rev.**
Campbell Law Review	**Campbell▲L.▲Rev.**
Canada-United States Law Journal	**Can.-U.S.▲L.J.**
Canadian-American Law Journal	**Can.-Am.▲L.J.**
Capital Defense Journal	**Cap.▲Def.▲J.**
Capital University Law Review	**Cap.▲U.▲L.▲Rev.**
Cardozo Arts and Entertainment Law Journal	**Cardozo▲Arts▲&▲Ent.▲L.J.**
Cardozo Journal of International and Comparative Law	**Cardozo▲J.▲Intl.▲&▲Comp.▲L.**
Was: New Europe Law Review (Vol. 1–Vol. 2, no.1)	New▲Europe▲L.▲Rev.
Cardozo Law Review	**Cardozo▲L.▲Rev.**
Cardozo Online Journal of Conflict Resolution	**Cardozo▲Online▲J.▲Conflict▲Res.**
Cardozo Studies in Law and Literature—*see Law & Literature*	
Cardozo Women's Law Journal	**Cardozo▲Women's▲L.J.**
Absorbed: Women's Annotated Legal Bibliography	Women's▲Ann.▲Leg.▲Bibliog.

Name	Abbreviation
★**Case & Comment** *Was:* ★Case and Comment (Vol. 1–Vol. 71, no. 3)	**Case▲&▲Cmt.** Case▲&▲Cmt.
Case Western Reserve Journal of International Law	**Case▲W.▲Res.▲J.▲Intl.▲L.**
Case Western Reserve Law Review *Was:* Western Reserve Law Review (Vol. 1–Vol. 18)	**Case▲W.▲Res.▲L.▲Rev.** W.▲Res.▲L.▲Rev.
Catholic Lawyer—*see Journal of Catholic Legal Studies*	
Catholic University Law Review *Was:* Catholic University of America Law Review, The (Vol. 22–Vol. 23) *Was:* Catholic University Law Review, The (Vol. 20–Vol. 21) *Was:* Catholic University of America Law Review, The (Vol. 1–Vol.19)	**Cath.▲U.▲L.▲Rev.** Cath.▲U.▲Am.▲L.▲Rev. Cath.▲U.▲L.▲Rev. Cath.▲U.▲Am.▲L.▲Rev.
★**CBA Record** *Was:* ★Chicago Bar Record (Vol. 16–Vol. 67, no. 2) *Was:* ★Chicago Bar Association Record, The (Vol. 1–Vol. 15)	**CBA▲Rec.** Chi.▲B.▲Rec. Chi.▲B.▲Assn.▲Rec.
Chapman Law Review	**Chapman▲L.▲Rev.**
Chicago–Kent Journal of Intellectual Property	**Chi–Kent▲J.▲Intell.▲Prop.**
Chicago-Kent Law Review *Was:* Chicago-Kent Review, The (Vol. 1–Vol. 16)	**Chi.-Kent▲L.▲Rev.** Chi.-Kent▲Rev.
★**Chicago Sun Times**	**Chi.▲Sun▲Times**
Chicano-Latino Law Review *Was:* Chicano Law Review (Vol. 1–Vol. 10)	**Chicano-Latino▲L.▲Rev.** Chicano▲L.▲Rev.
★**Children's Legal Rights Journal**	**Children's▲Leg.▲Rights▲J.**
China Law Reporter	**China▲L.▲Rep.**
★**Chronicle of Higher Education**	**Chron.▲Higher▲Educ.**
CIRCLES—*see Buffalo Women's Law Journal*	
Clearinghouse Review	**Clearinghouse▲Rev.**
Cleveland State Law Review *Was:* Cleveland-Marshall Law Review (Vol. 1–Vol. 18, no. 2)	**Clev.▲St.▲L.▲Rev.** Clev.-Marshall▲L.▲Rev.
Clinical Law Review: A Journal of Lawyering and Legal Education	**Clin.▲L.▲Rev.**
Colorado Journal of International Environmental Law and Policy	**Colo.▲J.▲Intl.▲Envtl.▲L.▲&▲Policy**
★**Colorado Lawyer**	**Colo.▲Law.**
Columbia Business Law Review	**Colum.▲Bus.▲L.▲Rev.**

Name	Abbreviation
Columbia Human Rights Law Review	**Colum.▲Hum.▲Rights▲L.▲Rev.**
Was: Columbia Survey of Human Rights Law Review (Vol. 1–Vol. 3)	Colum.▲Surv.▲Hum.▲Rights▲L.▲Rev.
Columbia Journal of Asian Law	**Colum.▲J.▲Asian▲L.**
Was: Journal of Chinese Law (Vol. 1–Vol. 9)	J.▲Chinese▲L.
Columbia Journal of Environmental Law	**Colum.▲J.▲Envtl.▲L.**
Columbia Journal of European Law	**Colum.▲J.▲Eur.▲L.**
Columbia Journal of Gender and Law	**Colum.▲J.▲Gender▲&▲L.**
Columbia Journal of Law and Social Problems	**Colum.▲J.L.▲&▲Soc.▲Probs.**
Columbia Journal of Law & the Arts, The	**Colum.▲J.L.▲&▲Arts**
Was: Columbia-VLA Journal of Law & the Arts (Vol. 1–Vol. 24)	Colum.-VLA▲J.L.▲&▲Arts
Was: Art & the Law (Dec. 1974–1985)	Art▲&▲L.
Columbia Journal of Transnational Law	**Colum.▲J.▲Transnatl.▲L.**
Columbia Law Review	**Colum.▲L.▲Rev.**
Columbia Science and Technology Law Review	**Colum.▲Sci.▲&▲Tech.▲L.▲Rev.**
Columbia-VLA Journal of Law & the Arts—*see Columbia Journal of Law & the Arts, The*	
★**Columbus Dispatch**	**Columbus▲Dispatch**
Commercial Law Journal	**Com.▲L.J.**
Was: Commercial Law League Journal (Vol. 28, no. 9–Vol. 35, no. 7)	Com.▲L.▲League▲J.
Was: Commercial Law League Bulletin (Vol. 27, no. 9–Vol. 28, no. 8)	Com.▲L.▲League▲Bull.
Was: Bulletin of the Commercial Law League of America, The (Vol. 6–Vol. 27, no. 8)	Bull.▲Com.▲L.▲League▲Am.
Was: League Bulletin (Vol. 1–Vol. 5)	League▲Bull.
CommLaw Conspectus: Journal of Communications Law and Policy	**CommLaw**
Common Law World Review	**Com.▲L.▲World▲Rev.**
Was: Anglo-American Law Review (Vol. 1–Vol. 29, no. 4)	Anglo-Am.▲L.▲Rev.
Comparative Juridical Review	**Comp.▲Juridical▲Rev.**
Comparative Labor Law & Policy Journal	**Comp.▲Lab.▲L.▲&▲Policy▲J.**
Was: Comparative Labor Law Journal (Vol. 8–Vol. 18, no. 3)	Comp.▲Lab.▲L.J.
Was: Comparative Labor Law (Vol. 1–Vol. 7)	Comp.▲Lab.▲L.
Compleat Lawyer—*see General Practice, Solo & Small Firm Lawyer*	
Computer/Law Journal—*see John Marshall Journal of Computer & Information Law, The*	

Name	Abbreviation
Computer Lawyer, The	**Computer▲Law.**
Congressional Digest	**Cong.▲Dig.**
★ **Connecticut Bar Journal**	**Conn.▲B.J.**
Connecticut Insurance Law Journal	**Conn.▲Ins.▲L.J.**
Connecticut Journal of International Law	**Conn.▲J.▲Intl.▲L.**
Connecticut Law Review	**Conn.▲L.▲Rev.**
Connecticut Probate Law Journal—*see Quinnipiac Probate Law Journal*	
Constitutional Commentary	**Const.▲Commentary**
★ **Construction Lawyer**	**Constr.▲Law.**
Consumer Finance Law Quarterly Report	**Consumer▲Fin.▲L.Q.▲Rep.**
Was: Personal Finance Law Quarterly Report (Vol. 9, no. 2–Vol. 38, no. 2)	Personal▲Fin.▲L.Q.▲Rep.
Was: Quarterly Report: Conference on Personal Finance Law (Vol. 1, no. 1–Vol. 9, no. 1)	Q.▲Rep.
Contemporary Drug Problems	**Contemp.▲Drug▲Probs.**
Cooley Law Review—*see Thomas M. Cooley Law Review*	
Copyright Law Symposium (American Society of Composers, Authors, & Publishers)	**Copy.▲L.▲Symp.▲(ASCAP)**
Cornell International Law Journal	**Cornell▲Intl.▲L.J.**
Cornell Journal of Law and Public Policy	**Cornell▲J.L.▲&▲Pub.▲Policy**
Cornell Law Review	**Cornell▲L.▲Rev.**
Was: Cornell Law Quarterly (Vol. 1–Vol. 52)	Cornell▲L.Q.
★ **Corporate Counsel**	**Corp.▲Couns.**
Corporate Counsel Review	**Corp.▲Couns.▲Rev.**
★ **Corporate Counsel's Quarterly**	**Corp.▲Couns.▲Q.**
Corporate Governance	**Corp.▲Governance**
Corporate Taxation	**Corp.▲Taxn.**
Was: Journal of Corporate Taxation, The (Vol. 1–Vol. 27)	J.▲Corp.▲Taxn.
★ **Courier-Journal (Louisville, Ky.)**	**Courier-J.▲(Louisville,▲Ky.)**
★ **Court Review**	**Ct.▲Rev.**
Was: Municipal Court Review (Vol. 1–Vol. 9, no. 1)	Mun.▲Ct.▲Rev.
Coverage	**Coverage**
Creighton Law Review	**Creighton▲L.▲Rev.**

Name	Abbreviation
Crime and Justice: Review of Research	**Crime▲&▲Just.**
★**Criminal Justice**	**Crim.▲Just.**
Criminal Justice and Behavior *Supersedes:* Correctional Psychologist (Vol. 1–Vol. 9)	**Crim.▲Just.▲&▲Behav.** Correc.▲Psychol.
★**Criminal Justice Ethics**	**Crim.▲Just.▲Ethics**
Criminal Justice Journal—*see Thomas Jefferson Law Review*	
Criminal Law Bulletin	**Crim.▲L.▲Bull.**
Criminal Law Forum	**Crim.▲L.▲Forum**
Criminology *Was:* ★Criminologica (Vol. 1–Vol. 7)	**Criminology** Criminologica
Cumberland Law Review *Was:* Cumberland-Samford Law Review (Vol. 1–Vol. 5)	**Cumb.▲L.▲Rev.** Cumb.-Samford▲L.▲Rev.
Current Issues in Criminal Justice	**Current▲Issues▲Crim.▲Just.**
★**Currents: International Trade Law Journal**	**Currents**
★**Dallas Morning News**	**Dallas▲Morn.▲News**
D.C. Bar Journal—*see Washington Lawyer, The*	
Defense Counsel Journal *Was:* Insurance Counsel Journal (Vol. 1–Vol. 53)	**Def.▲Couns.▲J.** Ins.▲Couns.▲J.
Defense Law Journal	**Def.▲L.J.**
Delaware Journal of Corporate Law	**Del.▲J.▲Corp.▲L.**
★**Delaware Lawyer**	**Del.▲Law.**
Denver Journal of International Law and Policy	**Denv.▲J.▲Intl.▲L.▲&▲Policy**
★**Denver Post**	**Denv.▲Post.**
Denver University Law Review *Was:* Denver Law Journal (Vol. 43–Vol. 61) *Was:* Denver Law Center Journal (Vol. 40–Vol. 42) *Was:* Dicta (Vol. 6–Vol. 39) *Was:* Denver Bar Association Record, The (Vol. 1–Vol. 5)	**Denv.▲U.▲L.▲Rev.** Denv.▲L.J. Denv.▲L.▲Ctr.▲J. Dicta Denv.▲B.▲Assn.▲Rec.
Department of State Bulletin	**Dept.▲St.▲Bull.**
DePaul Business Law Journal	**DePaul▲Bus.▲L.J.**
DePaul Journal of Health Care Law	**DePaul▲J.▲Health▲Care▲L.**
DePaul Law Review	**DePaul▲L.▲Rev.**
DePaul-LCA Journal of Art and Entertainment Law and Policy	**DePaul-LCA▲J.▲Art▲&▲Ent.▲L.▲&▲Policy**

Name	Abbreviation
Detroit College of Law at Michigan State University Entertainment & Sports Law Journal—*see Entertainment and Sports Lawyer*	
Detroit College of Law at Michigan State University Law Review—*see Michigan State Law Review*	
Detroit College of Law Entertainment & Sports Law Forum—*see Entertainment and Sports Lawyer*	
Detroit College of Law Journal of International Law and Practice—*see Michigan State University DCL Journal of International Law*	
★**Detroit News**	**Det.▲News**
Dickinson Journal of Environmental Law & Policy	**Dick.▲J.▲Envtl.▲L.▲&▲Policy**
Dickinson Journal of International Law—*see Penn State International Law Review*	
Dickinson Law Review *Was:* Forum, The (Vol. 1–Vol. 12)	**Dick.▲L.▲Rev.** Forum
Digest: The National Italian-American Bar Association Law Journal, The	**Digest**
★**Dispute Resolution Journal** *Was:* ★Arbitration Journal (Vol. 1–Vol. 6; n.s. Vol. 1–Vol. 48)	**Dis.▲Res.▲J.** Arb.▲J.
District Lawyer—*see Washington Lawyer, The*	
District of Columbia Law Review—*see University of the District of Columbia Law Review, The*	
Divorce Litigation	**Divorce▲Litig.**
Drake Journal of Agricultural Law	**Drake▲J.▲Agric.▲L.**
Drake Law Review	**Drake▲L.▲Rev.**
Duke Environmental Law & Policy Forum	**Duke▲Envtl.▲L.▲&▲Policy▲Forum**
Duke Journal of Comparative & International Law *Was:* Duke International and Comparative Law Annual (until 1990)	**Duke▲J.▲Comp.▲&▲Intl.▲L.** Duke▲Intl.▲&▲Comp.▲L.▲Annual
Duke Journal of Gender Law & Policy	**Duke▲J.▲Gender▲L.▲&▲Policy**
Duke Law Journal *Was:* Duke Bar Journal (Vol. 1–Vol. 6, no. 2)	**Duke▲L.J.** Duke▲B.J.
Duquesne Business Law Journal	**Duq.▲Bus.▲L.J.**
Duquesne Law Review *Was:* Duquesne University Law Review (Vol. 1–Vol. 6)	**Duq.▲L.▲Rev.** Duq.▲U.▲L.▲Rev.
★**East European Constitutional Review**	**E.▲Eur.▲Const.▲Rev.**

Name	Abbreviation
Ecology Law Quarterly	**Ecol.▲L.Q.**
Elder Law Journal, The	**Elder▲L.J.**

Elder's Advisor: The Journal of Elder Law and Post-Retirement Planning—*see Marquette Elder's Advisors*

Emory International Law Review	**Emory▲Intl.▲L.▲Rev.**

Was: Emory Journal of International Dispute Resolution (Vol. 1–Vol. 3) Emory▲J.▲Intl.▲Dis.▲Res.

Emory Law Journal	**Emory▲L.J.**

Was: Journal of Public Law (Vol. 1–Vol. 22) J.▲Pub.▲L.

Employee Relations Law Journal	**Employee▲Rel.▲L.J.**
Employee Rights and Employment Policy Journal	**Employee▲Rights▲&▲Empl.▲Policy▲J.**
Energy Law Journal	**Energy▲L.J.**

Entertainment & Sports Law Journal—*see University of Miami Entertainment & Sports Law Review*

Entertainment and Sports Lawyer	**Ent.▲&▲Sports▲Law.**

Was: Detroit College of Law at Michigan State University Entertainment & Sports Law Journal (Vol. 2–Vol. 3) Det.▲C.L.▲Mich.▲St.▲ U.▲Ent.▲&▲Sports▲L.J.

Was: Detroit College of Law Entertainment & Sports Law Forum (Vol. 1) Det.▲C.L.▲Ent.▲&▲Sports▲L.▲Forum

Entertainment Law Journal—*see Loyola of Los Angeles Entertainment Law Journal*

Environmental Affairs—*see Boston College Environmental Affairs Law Review*

Environmental Claims Journal	**Envtl.▲Claims▲J.**
Environmental Lawyer, The	**Envtl.▲Law.**

Environmental Perspectives—*see University of Baltimore Journal of Environmental Law*

Environmental Practice News—*see William and Mary Environmental Law and Policy Review*

★**Estate Planning**	**Est.▲Plan.**
Estate Planning Institute	**Est.▲Plan.▲Inst.**
★**Family Advocate**	**Fam.▲Advoc.**

Was: ★Family Law Newsletter, The (Vol. 11–Vol. 18) Fam.▲L.▲Newsltr.
Was: ★Family Lawyer, The (Vol. 1–Vol. 10) Fam.▲Law.

★**Family Court Review: An Interdisciplinary Journal**	**Fam.▲Ct.▲Rev.**

Was: Family and Conciliation Courts Review (Vol. 27, no. 1–Vol. 38, no. 4) Fam.▲&▲Conciliation▲Cts.▲Rev.

Name	Abbreviation
Family Law Quarterly	**Fam.▲L.Q.**
Was: ABA Section of Family Law (1964–1965)	ABA▲Sec.▲Fam.▲L.
Federal Circuit Bar Journal	**Fed.▲Cir.▲B.J.**
Federal Communications Law Journal	**Fed.▲Commun.▲L.J.**
Was: Federal Communications Bar Journal (Vol. 1–Vol. 29)	Fed.▲Commun.▲B.J.
Federal Law Review	**Fed.▲L.▲Rev.**
★**Federal Lawyer, The**	**Fed.▲Law.**
Was: ★Federal Bar & News Journal (Vol. 28–Vol. 41)	Fed.▲B.▲&▲News▲J.
Was: ★Federal Bar News (Vol. 1–Vol. 27)	Fed.▲B.▲News
★**Federal Probation**	**Fed.▲Probation**
Federal Sentencing Reporter	**Fed.▲Senten.▲Rep.**
Was: Federation of Insurance & Corporate Counsel Quarterly (Vol. 36–Vol. 49)	Fedn.▲Ins.▲&▲Corp.▲Couns.▲Q.
Was: ★Federation of Insurance Counsel Quarterly (Vol. 1–Vol. 35)	Fedn.▲Ins.▲Couns.▲Q.
Was: Federation of Insurance & Corporate Quarterly (Vol. 1–Vol. 34)	Fedn.▲Ins.▲&▲Corp.▲Q.
FICC Quarterly	**FICC▲Q.**
FJC Directions	**FJC Directions**
Fletcher Forum of World Affairs, The	**Fletcher▲Forum▲World▲Aff.**
Was: Fletcher Forum, The (Vol. 1–Vol. 12)	Fletcher▲Forum
★**Florida Bar Journal**	**Fla.▲B.J.**
Was: ★Florida Law Journal (Vol. 8–Vol. 27, no. 6)	Fla.▲L.J.
Was: ★Florida State Bar Association Law Journal (Vol. 1–Vol. 8)	Fla.▲St.▲B.▲Assn.▲L.J.
Florida Coastal Law Review	**Fla.▲Coastal▲L.▲Rev.**
Florida Entertainment, Art & Sport Law Journal	**Fla.▲Ent.,▲Art▲&▲Sport▲L.J.**
Florida International University Law Review	**FIU▲L.▲Rev.**
Florida Journal of International Law	**Fla.▲J.▲Intl.▲L**
Was: Florida International Law Journal (Vol. 1–Vol. 5)	Fla.▲Intl.▲L.J.
Florida Law Review	**Fla.▲L.▲Rev.**
Was: University of Florida Law Review (Vol. 1–Vol. 40)	U.▲Fla.▲L.▲Rev.
Florida State Journal of Transnational Law & Policy	**Fla.▲St.▲J.▲Transnatl.▲L.▲&▲Policy**
Florida State University Law Review	**Fla.▲St.▲U.▲L.▲Rev.**
Florida State University Journal of Land Use & Environmental Law	**Fla.▲St.▲U.▲J.▲Land▲Use▲&▲Envtl.▲L.**
Florida Tax Review	**Fla.▲Tax▲Rev.**

Name	Abbreviation
Food and Drug Law Journal	**Food▲&▲Drug▲L.J.**
Was: Food, Drug, Cosmetic Law Journal (Vol. 5–Vol. 46)	Food,▲Drug,▲Cosmetic▲L.J.
Was: Food Drug Cosmetic Law Quarterly (Vol. 1–Vol. 4)	Food▲Drug▲Cosmetic▲L.Q.
★**For the Defense**	**For▲Def.**
Fordham Environmental Law Review	**Fordham▲Envtl.▲L.▲Rev.**
Was: Fordham Environmental Law Journal (Vol. 5–Vol. 14, no. 3)	Fordham▲Envtl.▲L.J.
Was: Fordham Environmental Law Report (Vol. 1–Vol. 4)	Fordham▲Envtl.▲L.▲Rpt.
Fordham Intellectual Property, Media & Entertainment Law Journal	**Fordham▲Intell.▲Prop.,▲Media▲&▲Ent.▲L.J.**
Was: Fordham Entertainment, Media & Intellectual Property Law Forum (Vol. 1–Vol. 3, no. 1)	Fordham▲Ent.,▲Media▲&▲Intell.▲Prop.▲L.▲Forum
Fordham International Law Journal	**Fordham▲Intl.▲L.J.**
Was: Fordham International Law Forum (Vol. 1–Vol. 3)	Fordham▲Intl.▲L.▲Forum
Fordham Law Review	**Fordham▲L.▲Rev.**
Fordham Urban Law Journal	**Fordham▲Urb.▲L.J.**
Forensic Science International	**Forensic▲Sci.▲Intl.**
★**Fort Worth Star-Telegram**	**Ft.▲Worth▲Star-Teleg.**
★**Franchise Law Journal**	**Fran.▲L.J.**
Was: ★Journal of the Forum Committee on Franchising (Vol. 1, no. 4–Vol. 3)	J.▲Forum▲Comm.▲on▲Fran.
Was: ★Newsletter of the Forum Committee on Franchising (Vol. 1, no. 1–Vol. 1, no. 3)	Newsltr.▲Forum▲Comm.▲on▲Fran.
★**General Practice, Solo & Small Firm Lawyer**	**Gen.▲Prac.,▲Solo▲&▲Small▲Firm▲Law.**
Was: ★Compleat Lawyer, The (Vol. 1–Vol. 15, no. 2)	Compleat▲Law.
George Mason Law Review	**Geo.▲Mason▲L.▲Rev.**
Was: George Mason Independent Law Review (1992–Summer 1995)	Geo.▲Mason▲Indep.▲L.▲Rev.
Was: George Mason University Law Review (1981–Summer 1992)	Geo.▲Mason▲U.▲L.▲Rev.
Was: GMU Law Review (Winter 1978–Spring 1980)	GMU▲L.▲Rev.
Was: ISL Law Review (Spring 1976–Winter 1977)	ISL▲L.▲Rev.
George Mason University Civil Rights Law Journal	**Geo.▲Mason▲U.▲Civ.▲Rights▲L.J.**
George Washington Journal of International Law and Economics, The	**Geo.▲Wash.▲J.▲Intl.▲L.▲&▲Econ.**
Was: Journal of International Law and Economics, The (Vol. 5, no. 2–Vol. 15, no. 3)	J.▲Intl.▲L.▲&▲Econ.
Was: Journal of Law and Economic Development, The (Vol. 2, no. 2–Vol. 5, no. 1)	J.L.▲&▲Econ.▲Dev.

Name	Abbreviation
Was: Studies in Law and Economic Development (Apr. 1966–1967)	Stud.▲L.▲&▲Econ.▲Dev.
George Washington Law Review	**Geo.▲Wash.▲L.▲Rev.**
Georgetown Immigration Law Journal	**Geo.▲Immigr.▲L.J.**
Was: ★Georgetown University Law Center Immigration Reporter (Fall 1983–Spring 1985)	Geo.▲U.L.▲Ctr.▲Immig.▲Rep.
Was: ★Immigration Monitoring Report (1981–Spring 1983)	Immig.▲Monitoring▲Rpt.
Georgetown International Environmental Law Review	**Geo.▲Intl.▲Envtl.▲L.▲Rev.**
Georgetown Journal of International Law	**Geo.▲J.▲Intl.▲L.**
Was: Law and Policy in International Business (Winter 1969–Summer 2003)	L.▲&▲Policy▲Intl.▲Bus.
Georgetown Journal of Legal Ethics	**Geo.▲J.▲Leg.▲Ethics**
Georgetown Journal on Poverty Law and Policy	Geo.▲J.▲▲Pov.▲L.▲&▲Policy
Was: Georgetown Journal on Fighting Poverty (Vol. 1–Vol. 5, no. 2)	Geo.▲J.▲Fighting▲Pov.
Georgetown Law Journal	**Geo.▲L.J.**
★Georgia Bar Journal	**Ga.▲B.J.**
Was: Georgia State Bar Journal (Vol. 1–Vol. 31)	Ga.▲St.▲B.J.
Georgia Journal of International & Comparative Law	**Ga.▲J.▲Intl.▲&▲Comp.▲L.**
Georgia Journal of Southern Legal History—*see Journal of Southern Legal History, The*	
Georgia Law Review	**Ga.▲L.▲Rev.**
Georgia State University Law Review	**Ga.▲St.▲U.▲L.▲Rev.**
Glendale Law Review	**Glendale▲L.▲Rev.**
Golden Gate University Law Review	**Golden▲Gate▲U.▲L.▲Rev.**
Was: Golden Gate Law Review (Vol. 1–Vol. 5)	Golden▲Gate▲L.▲Rev.
Gonzaga Law Review	**Gonz.▲L.▲Rev.**
★Government Union Review and Public Policy Digest	**Govt.▲Union▲Rev.▲&▲Pub.▲Policy▲ Dig.**
Graven Images: A Journal of Culture, Law and the Sacred	**Graven▲Images**
★Great Plains Natural Resources Journal	**Great▲Plains▲Nat.▲Resources▲J.**
Was: Greater North Central Natural Resources Journal	Greater▲N.C.▲Nat.▲Resources▲J.
Guild Practitioner	**Guild▲Pract.**
Was: Law in Transition (Vol. 21–Vol. 23)	L.▲Transition
Was: ★Lawyers Guild Review (Vol. 1–Vol. 20)	Laws.▲Guild▲Rev.

Name	Abbreviation

Was: National Lawyer's Guild Quarterly (1937–1940) | Natl.▲Laws.▲Guild▲Q.

Hamline Journal of Public Law and Policy | **Hamline▲J.▲Pub.▲L.▲&▲Policy**
Was: Hamline Journal of Public Law (Vol. 3–Vol. 6) | Hamline▲J.▲Pub.▲L.
Was: Journal of Minnesota Public Law (Vol. 1–Vol. 2) | J.▲Minn.▲Pub.▲L.

Hamline Law Review | **Hamline▲L.▲Rev.**

★Hartford Courant | **Hartford▲Courant**

Harvard Blackletter Law Journal | **Harv.▲Blackltr.▲L.J.**
Was: Harvard Blackletter Journal (Vol. 1–Vol. 10) | Harv.▲Blackltr.▲J.

Harvard Civil Rights-Civil Liberties Law Review | **Har.▲Civ.▲Rights-Civ.▲Libs.▲L.▲Rev.**

Harvard Environmental Law Review | **Harv.▲Envtl.▲L.▲Rev.**

Harvard Human Rights Journal | **Harv.▲Hum.▲Rights▲J.**
Was: Harvard Human Rights Yearbook (Vol. 1–Vol. 2) | Harv.▲Hum.▲Rights▲Y.B.

Harvard International Law Journal | **Harv.▲Intl.▲L.J.**
Was: Harvard International Law Club Journal (Vol. 4–Vol. 7, no. 2) | Harv.▲Intl.▲L.▲Club▲J.
Was: ★Harvard International Law Club Bulletin, The (Vol. 3) | Harv.▲Intl.▲L.▲Club▲Bull.
Was: Bulletin of the Harvard International Law Club (Vol. 1–Vol. 2) | Bull.▲Harv.▲Intl.▲L.▲Club

Harvard Journal of Law and Public Policy | **Harv.▲J.L.▲&▲Pub.▲Policy**

Harvard Journal of Law and Technology | **Harv.▲J.L.▲&▲Tech.**

Harvard Journal on Legislation | **Harv.▲J.▲on▲Legis.**

Harvard Latino Law Review | **Harv.▲Latino▲L.▲Rev.**

Harvard Law Review | **Harv.▲L.▲Rev.**

Harvard Negotiation Law Review | **Harv.▲Negot.▲L.▲Rev.**

Harvard Women's Law Journal | **Harv.▲Women's▲L.J.**

Hastings Business Law Journal | **Hastings▲Bus.▲L.J.**

Hastings Communications and Entertainment Law Journal | **Hastings▲Commun.▲&▲Ent.▲L.J.**
Was: Comm/Ent. (Vol. 1–Vol. 12) | Comm/Ent.

Hastings Constitutional Law Quarterly | **Hastings▲Const.▲L.Q.**

Hastings International and Comparative Law Review | **Hastings▲Intl.▲&▲Comp.▲L.▲Rev.**

Hastings Law Journal | **Hastings▲L.J.**
Was: ★Hastings Journal, The (Vol. 1) | Hastings▲J.

Hastings West-Northwest Journal of Environmental Law and Policy | **Hastings▲W.-N.W.▲J.▲Envtl.▲L.& ▲Policy**

Hastings Women's Law Journal | **Hastings▲Women's▲L.J.**

Name	Abbreviation
★**Hawaii Bar Journal**	**Haw.▲B.J.**
Health Matrix: Journal of Law-Medicine	**Health Matrix**
High Technology Law Journal—*see Berkeley Technology Law Journal*	
Hispanic Law Journal: The University of Texas School of Law—*see Texas Hispanic Journal of Law & Policy: The University of Texas School of Law*	
Hofstra Labor & Employment Law Journal *Was:* Hofstra Labor Law Journal (Vol. 2–Vol. 14) *Was:* Hofstra Labor Law Forum (Vol. 1)	**Hofstra▲Lab.▲&▲Empl.▲L.J.** Hofstra▲Lab.▲L.J. Hofstra▲Lab.▲L.▲Forum
Hofstra Law & Policy Symposium	**Hofstra▲L.▲&▲Policy▲Symp.**
Hofstra Law Review	**Hofstra▲L.▲Rev.**
Hofstra Property Law Journal *Was:* International Property Investment Journal	**Hofsta▲Prop.▲L.J.** Intl.▲Prop.▲Inv.▲J.
Hospital Law—*see Journal of Health Law*	
Houston Business and Tax Law Journal	**Hous.▲Bus.▲&▲Tax▲L.J.**
★**Houston Chronicle**	**Hous.▲Chron.**
Houston Journal of International Law	**Hous.▲J.▲Intl.▲L.**
Houston Law Review	**Hous.▲L.▲Rev.**
Howard Law Journal	**How.▲L.J.**
Howard Scroll: The Social Justice Law Review	**How.▲Scroll**
Human Rights Law Journal *Absorbed:* Human Rights Review (1976–1981)	**Hum.▲Rights▲L.J.** Hum.▲Rights▲Rev.
Human Rights Quarterly *Was:* ★Universal Human Rights (Vol. 1–Vol. 2)	**Hum.▲Rights▲Q.** Universal▲Hum.▲Rights
Hybrid: Journal of Law and Social Change at the University of Pennsylvania—*see Journal of Law and Social Change*	
ICC Practitioner's Journal—*see Journal of Transportation Law, Logistics, and Policy*	
ICSID Review–Foreign Investment Law Journal	**ICSID▲Rev.**
Idaho Law Review	**Idaho▲L.▲Rev.**
IDEA: The Journal of Law and Technology *Was:* IDEA: The PTC Journal of Research and Education (Vol. 16–Vol. 18, no. 1) *Was:* Patent, Trademark, and Copyright Journal of Research and Education, The (Vol. 1–Vol. 8, no. 1)	**IDEA** IDEA Pat., Trade-mark▲&▲Copy.▲J.▲Res.▲& ▲Educ.

Name	Abbreviation
★**Illinois Bar Journal** *Was:* ★Quarterly Bulletin (1912–1931)	**Ill.▲B.J.** Q.▲Bull.
ILSA Journal of International & Comparative Law *Was:* ILSA Journal of International Law (Vol. 11–Vol. 16) *Was:* Association of Student International Law Societies/ASILS International Law Journal (Vol. 1–Vol. 10)	**ILSA▲J.▲Intl.▲&▲Comp.▲L.** ILSA▲J.▲Intl.▲L. ASILS▲Intl.▲L.J.
Immigration Journal	**Immgr.▲J.**
Immigration and Nationality Law Review	**Immgr.▲&▲Nationality▲L.▲Rev.**
Indiana International & Comparative Law Review	**Ind.▲Intl.▲&▲Comp.▲L.▲Rev.**
Indiana Journal of Global Legal Studies	**Ind.▲J.▲Global▲Leg.▲Stud.**
Indiana Law Journal	**Ind.▲L.J.**
Indiana Law Review *Was:* Indiana Legal Forum (Vol. 1–Vol. 5)	**Ind.▲L.▲Rev.** Ind.▲Leg.▲Forum
★**Indianapolis Star**	**Indian.▲Star**
Industrial and Labor Relations Review	**Indus.▲&▲Lab.▲Rel.▲Rev.**
Industrial Law Journal	**Indus.▲L.J.**
Industrial Relations Law Journal—*see Berkeley Journal of Employment and Labor Law*	
Institute on Federal Taxation	**Inst.▲Fed.▲Taxn.**
Insurance Counsel Journal—*see Defense Counsel Journal*	
Intellectual Property & Technology Law Journal *Was:* Journal of Proprietary Rights (Vol. 1–Vol. 13)	**Intell.▲Prop.▲&▲Tech.▲L.J.** J.▲Proprietary▲Rights
Intellectual Property Law Review *Was:* Patent Law Review (Vol. 1–Vol. 9)	**Intell.▲Prop.▲L.▲Rev.** Pat.▲L.▲Rev.
International Journal of Legal Information *Was:* International Journal of Law Libraries (Vol. 1–Vol. 9)	**Intl.▲J.▲Leg.▲Info.** Intl.▲J.L.▲Libs.
International Journal of Marine and Coastal Law, The *Was:* International Journal of Estuarine and Coastal Law (Vol. 1–Vol. 7)	**Intl.▲J.▲Marine▲&▲Coastal▲L.** Intl.▲J.▲Estuarine▲&▲Coastal▲L.
International Journal of Refugee Law	**Intl.▲J.▲Refugee▲L.**
International Law and Management Review	**Intl.▲L.▲& Mgt.▲Rev.**
International Lawyer *Was:* ABA Section of International and Comparative Law Bulletin (1957–1966)	**Intl.▲Law.** ABA▲Sec.▲Intl.▲&▲Comp.▲L.▲Bull.

Name	Abbreviation
★**International Legal Perspectives** (nonconsecutively paginated in 2004)	**Intl.▲Leg.▲Persps.**
International Property Investment Journal—*see Hofstra Property Law Journal*	
International Quarterly	**Intl.▲Q.**
International Review of Law and Economics	**Intl.▲Rev.▲L.▲&▲Econ.**
International Review of Law, Computers & Technology	**Intl.▲Rev.▲L.,▲Computers▲&▲Tech.**
★**International Tax Journal, The**	**Intl.▲Tax▲J.**
International Trade Law Journal, The—*see Maryland Journal of International Law and Trade*	
Iowa Law Review *Was:* Iowa Law Bulletin (Vol. 1–Vol. 10)	**Iowa▲L.▲Rev.** Iowa▲L.▲Bull.
I/S: A Journal of Law and Policy for the Information Society	**I/S**
Issues in Law & Medicine	**Issues▲L.▲&▲Med.**
JAG Journal, The—*see Naval Law Review*	
Jewish Lawyer, The	**Jewish▲Law.**
John Marshall Journal of Computer & Information Law, The *Was:* Computer/Law Journal (Vol. 1–Vol. 12, no. 2) *Was*: Software Law Journal (Vol. 1–Vol. 6, no. 2)	**John▲Marshall▲J.▲Computer▲&▲Info.▲L.** Computer/L.J. Software▲L.J.
John Marshall Law Review, The *Was:* John Marshall Journal of Practice and Procedure, The (Vol. 1–Vol.12) *Was:* John Marshall Law Quarterly, The (Dec. 1935–June 1943)	**John▲Marshall▲L.▲Rev.** John▲Marshall▲J.▲Prac.▲&▲P. John▲Marshall▲L.Q.
Journal of Accountancy	**J.▲Accountancy**
Journal of Affordable Housing & Community Development Law *Was:* ABA Journal of Affordable Housing & Community Development Law (Vol. 1–Vol. 3)	**J.▲Afford.▲Hous.▲&▲Community▲Dev.▲L.** ABA▲J.▲Afford.▲Hous.▲Community▲Dev.▲L.
Journal of Air Law and Commerce *Was:* Journal of Air Law (Vol. 1–Vol. 9)	**J.▲Air▲L.▲&▲Com.** J.▲Air.▲L.
Journal of Art and Entertainment Law	**J.▲Art▲&▲Ent.▲L.**
Journal of Arts Management, Law and Society *Was:* ★Journal of Arts Management and Law (Vol. 12–Vol. 21) *Was:* Performing Arts Review (Vol. 1–Vol. 11)	**J.▲Arts▲Mgt.,▲L.▲&▲Socy.** J.▲Arts▲Mgt.▲&▲L. Perf.▲Arts▲Rev.
Journal of Bankruptcy Law and Practice	**J.▲Bankr.▲L.▲&▲Prac.**

Name	Abbreviation
Journal of BioLaw and Business, The	**J.▲BioLaw▲&▲Bus.**
Journal of Business Law	**J.▲Bus.▲L.**
Journal of Catholic Legal Studies *Was:* Catholic Lawyer (Vol. 1–Vol. 43, no. 2)	**J.▲Cath.▲Leg.▲Stud.** Cath.▲Law.
Journal of Chinese Law—*see Columbia Journal of Asian Law*	
Journal of Church and State	**J.▲Church▲&▲St.**
Journal of Collective Negotiations in the Public Sector	**J.▲Collective▲Negots.▲Pub.▲Sector**
Journal of College and University Law, The *Supersedes:* College Counsel (Vol. 1–Vol. 6)	**J.C.▲&▲U.L.** C.▲Coun.
Journal of Constitutional Law	**J.▲Const.▲L.**
Journal of Contemporary Health Law and Policy	**J.▲Contemp.▲Health▲L.▲&▲Policy**
Journal of Contemporary Law	**J.▲Contemp.▲L.**
Journal of Contemporary Legal Issues, The	**J.▲Contemp.▲Leg.▲Issues**
Journal of Corporate Taxation, The—*see Corporate Taxation*	
Journal of Corporation Law	**J.▲Corp.▲L.**
Journal of Criminal Justice	**J.▲Crim.▲Just.**
Journal of Criminal Law and Criminology, The *Was:* Journal of Criminal Law, Criminology & Police Science (Vol. 42–Vol. 63) *Was:* Journal of Criminal Law and Criminology (Vol. 22–Vol. 41) *Was:* Journal of the American Institute of Criminal Law and Criminology (Vol. 1–Vol. 21) *Absorbed:* American Journal of Police Science	**J.▲Crim.▲L.▲&▲Criminology** J.▲Crim.▲L.,▲Criminology▲&▲Police▲Sci. J.▲Crim.▲L.▲&▲Criminology J.▲Am.▲Inst.▲Crim.▲L.▲&▲Criminology Am.▲J.▲Pol.▲Sci.
Journal of Dispute Resolution *Was:* Missouri Journal of Dispute Resolution (1984–1987)	**J.▲Dis.▲Res.** Mo.▲J.▲Dis.▲Res.
Journal of Energy Law & Policy—*see Journal of Land, Resources, & Environmental Law*	
Journal of Energy, Natural Resources & Environmental Law—*see Journal of Land, Resources, & Environmental Law*	
Journal of Environmental Law and Litigation	**J.▲Envtl.▲L.▲&▲Litig.**
Journal of Family Law—*see Brandeis Law Journal*	

Name	Abbreviation
Journal of Health Care Law & Policy, The	**J.▲Health▲Care▲L.▲&▲Policy**
Was: Maryland Journal of Contemporary Legal Issues (1990–1997)	Md.▲J.▲Contemp.▲Leg.▲Issues
Was: Maryland Law Forum (1978–1989)	Md.▲L.▲Forum
Was: University of Maryland Law Forum, The (1970–1978)	U.▲Md.▲L.▲Forum
Journal of Health Law	**J.▲Health▲L.**
Was: Journal of Health and Hospital Law (Vol. 21–Vol. 31, no. 2)	J.▲Health▲&▲Hosp.▲L.
Was: Hospital Law (Vol. 1–Vol. 20)	Hosp.▲L.
Journal of Health, Politics, Policy and Law	**J.▲Health,▲Pol.,▲Policy▲&▲L.**
Journal of Individual Employment Rights	**J.▲Ind.▲Empl.▲Rights**
Journal of Intellectual Property, The	**J.▲Intell.▲Prop.**
Journal of Intellectual Property Law, The	**J.▲Intell.▲Prop.▲L.**
Journal of International Aging Law and Policy	**J.▲Intl.▲Aging▲L.▲&▲Pol.**
Journal of International Legal Studies	**J.▲Intl.▲Leg.▲Stud.**
Journal of Juvenile & Family Courts—*see Juvenile & Family Court Journal*	
Journal of Juvenile Law	**J.▲Juv.▲L.**
Journal of Land, Resources, & Environmental Law	**J.▲Land,▲Resources,▲&▲Envtl.▲L.**
Was: Journal of Energy, Natural Resources & Environmental Law (Vol. 11–Vol. 16)	J.▲Energy,▲Nat.▲Res.▲&▲Envtl.▲L.
Was: Journal of Energy Law & Policy, The (Vol. 1–Vol. 10)	J.▲Energy▲L.▲&▲Policy
Journal of Land Use and Environmental Law	**J.▲Land▲Use▲&▲Envtl.▲L.**
Journal of Law and Commerce	**J.L.▲&▲Com.**
Journal of Law and Economics	**J.L.▲&▲Econs.**
Journal of Law & Education	**J.L.▲&▲Educ.**
Journal of Law and Family Studies	**J.L.▲&▲Fam.▲Stud.**
Journal of Law and Health	**J.L.▲&▲Health**
Journal of Law and Policy	**J.L.▲&▲Policy**
Journal of Law and Politics	**J.L.▲&▲Pol.**
Journal of Law and Religion, The	**J.L.▲&▲Religion**
Journal of Law and Social Change	**J.L.▲&▲Soc.▲Change**
Was: Hybrid: Journal of Law and Social Change at the University of Pennsylvania (Vol. 1 –Vol. 5)	Hybrid
Journal of Law, Economics & Organization, The	**J.L.,▲Econ.,▲&▲Org.**
Journal of Law, Economics and Policy	**J.L.▲Econ.▲&▲Policy**

Name	Abbreviation
Journal of Law, Medicine & Ethics, The	**J.L., Med. & Ethics**
Was: ★Law, Medicine & Health Care (Vol. 9, no. 4–Vol. 20)	L., Med. & Health Care
Was: ★Medicolegal News (Vol. 1–Vol. 9, no. 3)	Medicolegal News
Absorbed: ★Nursing Law & Ethics	Nursing L. & Ethics
Journal of Law Reform—*see University of Michigan Journal of Law Reform*	
Journal of Legal Economics	**J. Leg. Econ.**
Journal of Legal Education	**J. Leg. Educ.**
Journal of Legal Medicine, The	**J. Leg. Med.**
Journal of Legal Studies	**J. Leg. Stud.**
Journal of Legal Studies Education	**J. Leg. Stud. Educ.**
Journal of Legal Studies/The United States Air Force Academy	**J. Leg. Stud./U.S. A.F. Academy**
Journal of Legislation	**J. Legis.**
Was: Notre Dame Journal of Legislation (Vol. 1–Vol. 2)	Notre Dame J. Legis.
Journal of Maritime Law and Commerce	**J. Mar. L. & Com.**
Journal of Medicine and Law	**J. Med. & L.**
Journal of Mineral Law & Policy—*see Journal of Natural Resources & Environmental Law*	
Journal of National Security Law, The	**J. Natl. Sec. L.**
Journal of National Security Law and Policy	**J. Natl. Sec. L. & Policy**
Journal of Natural Resources & Environmental Law	**J. Nat. Resources & Envtl. L.**
Was: Journal of Mineral Law & Policy (Vol. 1–Vol. 7)	J. Min. L. & Policy
Journal of Online Law	**J. Online L.**
Journal of Pension Planning & Compliance	**J. Pension Plan. & Compl.**
Was: Pension and Profit-Sharing Tax Journal (Vol. 1–Vol. 3)	Pension & Profit-Sharing Tax J.
Journal of Pharmacy & Law	**J. Pharm. & L.**
Journal of Products and Toxics Liability	**J. Prods. & Toxics Liab.**
Was: Journal of Products Liability (Vol. 1–Vol. 14)	J. Prods. Liab.
Journal of Psychiatry & Law, The	**J. Psych. & L.**
Journal of Public Law—*see Emory Law Journal*	
Journal of Real Estate Taxation	**J. Real Est. Taxn.**
Journal of S Corporation Taxation, The	**J. S Corp. Taxn.**
Journal of Science & Technology Law – *see Boston University Journal of Science & Technology Law*	

Name	Abbreviation
Journal of Small and Emerging Business Law, The	**J.▲Small▲&▲Emerging▲Bus.▲L.**
Journal of Southern Legal History, The *Was:* Georgia Journal of Southern Legal History (Vol. 1–Vol. 2)	**J.▲S.▲Leg.▲Hist.** Ga.▲J.▲S.▲Leg.▲Hist.
Journal of Space Law	**J.▲S. ▲L.**
★**Journal of State Taxation**	**J.▲St.▲Taxn.**
Journal of Supreme Court History *Was:* Supreme Court Historical Society Yearbook—Supreme Court Historical Society (1976–1989)	**J.▲S.▲Ct.▲Hist.** S.▲Ct.▲Hist.▲Socy.▲Y.B.
Journal of Taxation of Investments	**J.▲Taxn.▲Inv.**
Journal of the American Academy of Matrimonial Lawyers	**J.▲Am.▲Acad.▲Matrimonial▲Laws.**
Journal of the American Academy of Psychiatry and the Law, The *Was:* Bulletin of the American Academy of Psychiatry and the Law, The (Vol. 1–Vol. 25)	**J.▲Am.▲Acad.▲Psych.▲&▲L.** Bull.▲Am.▲Acad.▲Psych.▲&▲L.
Journal of the American Judicature Society—*see Judicature*	
Journal of the American Medical Association	**JAMA**
Journal of the Association of Legal Writing Directors	**J. ALWD**
Journal of the Copyright Society of the U.S.A. *Was:* Bulletin of the Copyright Society of the U.S.A. (Vol. 1–Vol. 29, no. 1)	**J.▲Copy.▲Socy.** Bull.▲Copy.▲Socy.
★**Journal of the Kansas Bar Association, The** *Was:* ★Journal of the Bar Association of the State of Kansas, The (Vol. 1–Vol. 32) *Absorbed:* ★Kansas Barletter	**J.▲Kan.▲B.▲Assn.** J.B.▲Assn.▲St.▲Kan. Kan.▲Barltr.
Journal of the Legal Profession, The	**J.▲Leg.▲Prof.**
Journal of the Missouri Bar *Was:* Missouri Bar Journal (1930–1944)	**J.▲Mo.▲B.** Mo.▲B.J.
Journal of the National Association of Administrative Law Judges	**J.▲Natl.▲Assn.▲Admin.▲L.▲Judges**
Journal of the National Association of Referees in Bankruptcy—*see American Bankruptcy Law Journal*	
Journal of the National Conference of Referees in Bankruptcy—*see American Bankruptcy Law Journal*	
Journal of the Patent and Trademark Office Society *Was:* Journal of the Patent Office Society (Vol. 1–Vol. 66)	**J.▲Pat.▲&▲Trademark▲Off.▲Socy.** J.▲Pat.▲Off.▲Socy.

Name	Abbreviation
Journal of the Suffolk Academy of Law	**J.▲Suffolk▲Acad.▲L.**
Journal of Transnational Law and Policy	**J.▲Transnatl.▲L.▲&▲Policy**
Journal of Transportation Law, Logistics, and Policy	**J.▲Transp.▲L.,▲Logistics▲&▲Policy**
Was: Transportation Practitioners Journal (Vol. 52–Vol. 61)	Transp.▲Practs.▲J.
Was: ICC's Practitioner's Journal (Vol. 1–Vol. 51)	ICC's▲Practs.▲J.
Was: ★Bulletin of the Association of Practitioners before the Interstate Commerce Commission (1931–1933)	Bull.▲Assn.▲Practs.▲before▲ICC

Journal of Urban Law—*see University of Detroit Mercy Law Review*

★Judges Journal	**Judges▲J.**
Was: ★Trial Judges' Journal (Vol. 1–Vol. 10, no. 1)	Tr.▲Judges'▲J.
★Judicature	**Judicature**
Was: ★Journal of the American Judicature Society (Vol. 1–Vol. 49)	J.▲Am.▲Judicature▲Socy.
Jurimetrics	**Jurimetrics**
Jurist: Studies in Church Law and Ministry, The	**Jurist**
★Justice System Journal, The	**Just.▲Sys.▲J.**
★Juvenile & Family Court Journal	**Juv.▲&▲Fam.▲Ct.▲J.**
Was: ★Journal of Juvenile & Family Courts (Vol. 1–Vol. 29, no. 1)	J.▲Juv.▲&▲Fam.▲Cts.
★Kansas City Star	**Kan.▲City▲Star**
★Kansas Journal of Law and Public Policy	**Kan.▲J.L▲&▲Pub.▲Policy**

Kentucky Bench & Bar—*see Bench & Bar*

Kentucky Law Journal	**Ky.▲L.J.**

La Raza Law Journal—*see Berkeley La Raza Law Journal*

Labor Law Journal	**Lab.▲L.J.**
Labor Lawyer, The	**Lab.▲Law.**

Land and Water Law Review—*see Wyoming Law Review*

Law and Contemporary Problems	**L.▲&▲Contemp.▲Probs.**
Law and History Review	**L.▲&▲Hist.▲Rev.**
Law and Human Behavior	**L.▲&▲Hum.▲Behav.**
Law and Inequality: A Journal of Theory and Practice	**L.▲&▲Inequal.**
Law & Literature	**L.▲&▲Lit.**

Name	Abbreviation
Was: Cardozo Studies in Law and Literature (Vol. 1–Vol. 13)	Cardozo▲Stud.▲L.▲&▲Lit.
Law and Philosophy	**L.▲&▲Phil.**
Law and Policy	**L.▲&▲Policy**
Was: Law and Policy Quarterly (Vol. 1–Vol. 5)	L.▲&▲Policy▲Q.
Law and Policy in International Business—*see Georgetown Journal of International Law*	
Law & Psychology Review	**L.▲&▲Psychol.▲Rev.**
Law and Sexuality	**L.▲&▲Sexuality**
Law & Social Inquiry: Journal of American Bar Foundation	**L.▲&▲Soc.▲Inquiry**
Was: American Bar Foundation Research Journal (Vol. 1–Vol. 12)	Am.▲B.▲Found.▲Res.▲J.
Law and Society Review	**L.▲&▲Socy.▲Rev.**
Supersedes: Law & Society Association Newsletter	L.▲&▲Socy.▲Assn.▲Newsltr.
Law Library Journal	**L.▲Lib.▲J.**
Absorbed: Law Library News (Sept. 1937)	L.▲Lib.▲News
Law, Medicine & Health Care—*see Journal of Law, Medicine & Ethics, The*	
★**Law Office and Computing**	**L.▲Off.▲&▲Computing**
★**Law Practice**	**L.▲Prac.**
Was: ★Law Practice Management (Vol. 16–Vol. 29)	L.▲Prac.▲Mgt.
Was: ★Legal Economics (Vol. 1–Vol. 15)	Leg.▲Econ.
★**Law School Record, The**	**L.▲Sch.▲Rec.**
★**Law/Technology**	**L./Tech.**
Was: Law and Computer Technology (Vol. 1–Vol. 13, no. 1/2)	L.▲&▲Computer▲Tech.
Lawyer of the Americas—*see University of Miami Inter-American Law Review, The*	
★**Lawyers Weekly U.S.A.**	**Laws.▲Wkly.▲USA**
★**Legal Management**	**Leg.▲Mgt.**
Was: ★Legal Administrator (Vol. 1–Vol. 7)	Leg.▲Adminstr.
Legal Medicine	**Leg.▲Med.**
Was: Legal Medicine Annual (1972–1975)	Leg.▲Med.▲Annual
★**Legal Reference Services Quarterly**	**Leg.▲Ref.▲Servs.▲Q.**
Legal Studies	**Leg.▲Stud.**
Was: Journal of the Society of Public Teachers of Law (1924–1938; n.s. Vol. 1 (1947–1951)–Vol. 15 (Mar. 1980))	J.▲Socy.▲Pub.▲Teachers▲L.

Name	Abbreviation
Legal Studies Forum	**Leg.▲Stud.▲Forum**
Was: American Legal Studies Association: ALSA Forum (Vol. 2–Vol. 8)	ALSA▲Forum
Was: ★Newsletter (American Legal Studies Association) (Vol. 1)	ALSA▲Newsltr.
Legal Theory	**Leg.▲Theory**
Legal Writing: The Journal of the Legal Writing Institute	**Leg.▲Writing**
Legislative Studies Quarterly	**Legis.▲Stud.▲Q.**
Lewis and Clark Law Review	**Lewis▲&▲Clark▲L.▲Rev.**
Liberty, Life and Family: An Interdisciplinary Journal of Common Concerns	**Liberty,▲Life▲&▲Fam.**
★**Lincoln Law Review**	**Lincoln▲L.▲Rev.**
★**Litigation**	**Litig.**
★**Los Angeles Lawyer**	**L.A.▲Law.**
★**Los Angeles Times**	**L.A.▲Times**
★**Louisiana Bar Journal**	**La.▲B.J.**
Louisiana Law Review	**La.▲L.▲Rev.**
Loyola Consumer Law Review	**Loy.▲Consumer▲L.▲Rev.**
Was: Loyola Consumer Law Reporter (Vol. 1–Vol. 9)	Loy.▲Consumer▲L.▲Rep.
★**Loyola Intellectual Property & High Technology Law Quarterly**	**Loy.▲Intell.▲Prop.▲&▲High▲Tech.▲L.Q.**
Loyola Law Review	**Loy.▲L.▲Rev.**
Loyola of Los Angeles Entertainment Law Journal	**Loy.▲L.A.▲Ent.▲L.J.**
Was: Loyola Entertainment Law Journal (Vol. 2–Vol. 11)	Loy.▲Ent.▲L.J.
Was: Entertainment Law Journal (Vol. 1)	Ent.▲L.J.
Loyola of Los Angeles International and Comparative Law Review	**Loy.▲L.A.▲Intl.▲&▲Comp.▲L.▲Rev.**
Was: Loyola of Los Angeles International and Comparative Law Journal (Vol. 4–Vol. 21, no. 4)	Loy.▲L.A.▲Intl.▲&▲Comp.▲L.J.
Loyola of Los Angeles Law Review	**Loy.▲L.A.▲L.▲Rev.**
Was: Loyola University of Los Angeles Law Review (Vol. 1–Vol. 4)	Loy.▲U.▲L.A.▲L.▲Rev.
Loyola Poverty Law Journal	**Loy.▲Poverty▲L.J.**
Loyola University of Chicago Law Journal	**Loy.▲U.▲Chi.▲L.J.**
Maine Bar Journal	**Me.▲B.J.**
Was: Bar Bulletin (1983–1985)	B.▲Bull.
Was: ★Maine Bar Bulletin (1967–1982)	Me.▲B.▲Bull.
Maine Law Review	**Me.▲L.▲Rev.**
Absorbed: Portland University Law Review	Portland▲U.▲L.▲Rev.

Name	Abbreviation
Major Tax Planning	Maj.▲Tax▲Plan.
Margins/University of Maryland Journal of Race, Religion, Gender and Class	Margins
Marquette Elder's Advisor *Was:* Elder's Advisor: The Journal of Elder Law and Post-Retirement Planning (Vol. 1–Vol. 4)	Marq.▲Elder's▲Advisor Elder's▲Advisor
Marquette Intellectual Property Law Review	Marq.▲Intell.▲Prop.▲L.▲Rev.
Marquette Law Review	Marq.▲L.▲Rev.
Marquette Sports Law Review *Was:* Marquette Sports Law Journal (Vol. 1, no. 1–Vol. 10, no. 2)	Marq.▲Sports▲L.▲Rev. Marq.▲Sports▲L.J.
★**Maryland Bar Journal**	Md.▲B.J.
Maryland Journal of Contemporary Legal Issues—*see Journal of Health Care Law & Policy, The*	
Maryland Journal of International Law and Trade *Was:* International Trade Law Journal, The (Vol. 1–Vol. 7)	Md.▲J.▲Intl.▲L.▲&▲Trade Intl.▲Trade▲L.J.
Maryland Law Forum—*see Journal of Health Care Law & Policy, The*	
Maryland Law Review	Md.▲L.▲Rev.
Massachusetts Law Review *Was:* Massachusetts Law Quarterly (Vol. 1–Vol. 62)	Mass.▲L.▲Rev. Mass.▲L.Q.
McGeorge Law Review *Was:* Pacific Law Journal (Vol. 1–Vol. 28)	McGeorge▲L.▲Rev. P.▲L.J.
Media Law & Policy	Media▲L.▲&▲Policy
Medical Trial Technique Quarterly Annual	Med.▲Tr.▲Technique▲Q.▲Annual
Medicolegal News—*see Journal of Law, Medicine & Ethics, The*	
Memphis State University Law Review—*see University of Memphis Law Review*	
Mental & Physical Disability Law Reporter	Mental▲&▲Physical▲Disability▲L.▲Rptr.
Mercer Law Review	Mercer▲L.▲Rev.
Miami Law Quarterly—*see University of Miami Law Review*	
★**Michigan Bar Journal** *Was:* ★Journal/State Bar of Michigan (Vol. 55, no. 3–Vol. 57) *Was:* ★Michigan State Bar Journal (Vol. 1–Vol. 55, no. 2)	Mich.▲B.J. J./St.▲B.▲Mich. Mich.▲St.▲B.J.

Name	Abbreviation
Michigan Business Law Journal	**Mich. Bus. L.J.**
Michigan Journal of Gender & Law	**Mich. J. Gender & L.**
Michigan Journal of International Law	**Mich. J. Intl. L.**
Michigan Journal of Race & Law	**Mich. J. Race & L.**
Michigan Law & Policy Review	**Mich. L. & Policy Rev.**
Michigan Law Journal	**Mich. L.J.**
Michigan Law Review	**Mich. L. Rev.**
Michigan State Law Review	**Mich. St. L. Rev.**
Was: Michigan State DCL Law Review (Summer 2003–Fall 2003)	Mich. St. DCL L. Rev.
Was: Law Review of Michigan State University Detroit College of Law, The (Spring 1999–Spring 2003)	L. Rev. Mich. St. U. Det. C.L.
Was: Detroit College of Law at Michigan State University Law Review (1995; no. 3–1998)	Det. C.L. Mich. St. U. L. Rev.
Was: Detroit College of Law Review (1975–1995)	Det. C.L. Rev.
Michigan State University–DCL Journal of International Law	**Mich. St. U. DCL J. Intl. L.**
Was: Detroit College of Law Journal of International Law and Practice (Vol. 1–Vol. 7)	Det. C. L.J. Intl. L. & Prac.
Michigan Tax Lawyer	**Mich. Tax Law.**
Michigan Telecommunications & Technology Law Review	**Mich. Telecommun. & Tech. L. Rev.**
Military Law Review	**Mil. L. Rev.**
★**Milwaukee Journal & Sentinel**	**Milw. J. & Sent.**
Minnesota Journal of Global Trade	**Minn. J. Global Trade**
Minnesota Law Review	**Minn. L. Rev.**
Mississippi College Law Review	**Miss. C. L. Rev.**
Mississippi Law Journal	**Miss. L.J.**
Missouri Environmental Law and Policy Review	**Mo. Envtl. L. & Policy Rev.**
Missouri Journal of Dispute Resolution—*see Journal of Dispute Resolution*	
Missouri Law Review	**Mo. L. Rev.**
Montana Law Review	**Mont. L. Rev.**
MSL Law Review: A Journal for Practitioners and Judges	**MSL L. Rev.**
National Black Law Journal	**Natl. Black L.J.**
Was: Black Law Journal (Vol. 1–Vol. 9)	Black L.J.
★**National Law Journal**	**Natl. L.J.**

Name	Abbreviation
National Tax Journal	**Natl.▲Tax▲J.**
Natural Law Forum—*see American Journal of Jurisprudence*	
★**Natural Resources & Environment** *Was:* Natural Resources Lawyer (1968–1985)	**Nat.▲Res.▲&▲Env.** Nat.▲Res.▲Law.
Natural Resources Journal	**Nat.▲Resources▲J.**
Naval Law Review *Was:* JAG Journal, The (Vol. 1–Vol. 33)	**Naval▲L.▲Rev.** JAG▲J.
Nebraska Law Review *Was:* Nebraska Law Bulletin (Vol. 1–Vol. 19)	**Neb.▲L.▲Rev.** Neb.▲L.▲Bull.
Negotiation Journal	**Negot.▲J.**
★**Nevada Lawyer** *Was:* ★Inter Alia Journal of the State Bar of Nevada (Apr. 1973–Oct. 1992) *Was:* ★Nevada State Bar Journal (Jan. 1936–Jan. 1973)	**Nev.▲Law.** Inter▲Alia▲J.▲St.▲B.▲Nev. Nev.▲St.▲B.J.
New England International and Comparative Law Annual	**New▲Eng.▲Intl.▲&▲Comp.▲L.▲Annual**
New England Journal of Medicine	**New▲Eng.▲J.▲Med.**
New England Journal on Criminal and Civil Confinement *Was:* New England Journal on Prison Law (Vol. 1–Vol. 8)	**New▲Eng.▲J.▲on▲Crim.▲&▲Civ.▲Confinement** New▲Eng.▲J.▲on▲Prison▲L.
New England Law Review *Was:* Portia Law Journal (Vol. 1–Vol. 4, no. 1)	**New▲Eng.▲L.▲Rev.** Portia▲L.J.
★**New Hampshire Bar Journal**	**N.H.▲B.J.**
★**New Jersey Lawyer**	**N.J.▲Law.**
New Mexico Law Review	**N.M.▲L.▲Rev.**
★**New Orleans Times-Picayune**	**N.O.▲Times-Picayune**
New York City Law Review	**N.Y.C.▲L.▲Rev.**
New York International Law Review	**N.Y.▲Intl.▲L.▲Rev.**
New York Law School Journal of Human Rights *Was:* New York Law School Human Rights Annual (Vol. 1–Vol. 4)	**N.Y.▲L.▲Sch.▲J.▲Hum.▲Rights** N.Y.▲L.▲Sch.▲Hum.▲Rights▲Annual
New York Law School Journal of International and Comparative Law *Absorbed:* New York Law School Law Review *Was:* Journal of International and Comparative Law/New York Law School (Vol. 3)	**N.Y.▲L.▲Sch.▲J.▲Intl.▲&▲Comp.▲L.** J.▲Intl.▲&▲Comp.▲L.

Name	Abbreviation
Was: New York Law School Journal of International and Comparative Law (Vol. 1–Vol. 2)	N.Y.▲L.▲Sch.▲J.▲Intl.▲&▲Comp.▲L.
Was: New York Law School International Law Society Journal (Vol. 1)	N.Y.▲L.▲Sch.▲Intl.▲L.▲Soc.▲J.
New York Law School Law Review	**N.Y.▲L.▲Sch.▲L.▲Rev.**
Was: New York Law Forum (Vol. 1–Vol. 21)	N.Y.▲L.▲Forum
★**New York State Bar Journal**	**N.Y.▲St.▲B.J.**
★**New York Times**	**N.Y.▲Times**
New York University Annual Survey of American Law	**N.Y.▲U.▲Annual▲Survey▲Am.▲L.**
Was: Annual Survey of American Law (Vol. 1–Vol. 21)	Annual▲Survey▲Am.▲L.
New York University Environmental Law Journal	**N.Y.U.▲Envtl.▲L.J.**
New York University Journal of International Law and Politics	**N.Y.U.▲J.▲Intl.▲L.▲&▲Pol.**
New York University Journal of Legislation and Public Policy	**N.Y.U.▲J.▲Legis.▲&▲Pub.▲Policy**
New York University Law Review	**N.Y.U.▲L.▲Rev.**
Was: New York University Law Quarterly Review (Vol. 7–Vol. 24)	N.Y.U.▲L.Q.▲Rev.
Was: New York University Law Review (Vol. 2–Vol. 6)	N.Y.U.▲L.▲Rev.
Was: Annual Review of the Law School of New York University (Vol. 1)	Annual▲Rev.▲L.▲Sch.▲N.Y.U.
New York University Review of Law and Social Change	**N.Y.U.▲Rev.▲L.▲&▲Soc.▲Change**
News Media and the Law, The	**News▲Media▲&▲L.**
Supersedes: Press Censorship Newsletter (1973–1976)	Press▲Censorship▲Newsltr.
NEXUS: A Journal of Opinion	**NEXUS**
North Carolina Central Law Journal	**N.C.C.▲L.J.**
North Carolina Journal of International Law and Commercial Regulation	**N.C.▲J.▲Intl.▲L.▲&▲Com.▲Reg.**
Was: Journal of International Law and Commercial Regulation (Vol. 1)	J.▲Intl.▲L.▲&▲Com.▲Reg.
North Carolina Law Review	**N.C.▲L.▲Rev.**
North Dakota Law Review	**N.D.▲L.▲Rev.**
Was: North Dakota Bar Briefs: Journal of the State Bar Association (Vol. 24–Vol. 26)	N.D.▲B.▲Brs.
Was: Bar Briefs (Vol. 1–Vol. 24)	B.▲Brs.
Northern Illinois University Law Review	**N.▲Ill.▲U.▲L.▲Rev.**
Was: Lewis University Law Review	Lewis▲U.▲L.▲Rev.
Northern Kentucky Law Review	**N.▲Ky.▲L.▲Rev.**
Was: Northern Kentucky State Law Forum (Vol. 1–Vol. 3, no. 1)	N.▲Ky.▲St.▲L.▲Forum

Name	Abbreviation
Northwestern Journal of International Law and Business	**Nw.▲J.▲Intl.▲L.▲&▲Bus.**
Northwestern University Law Review	**Nw.▲U.▲L.▲Rev.**
Was: Illinois Law Review/Northwestern University (Vol. 33, no. 5–Vol. 46)	Ill.▲L.▲Rev.▲Nw.▲U.
Was: Illinois Law Review of Northwestern University (Vol. 31, no. 8–Vol. 33, no. 4)	Ill.▲L.▲Rev.▲Nw.▲U.
Was: Illinois Law Review/Northwestern University (Vol. 1–Vol. 31, no. 7)	Ill.▲L.▲Rev.▲Nw.▲U.
Absorbed: Illinois Law Quarterly (Dec. 1921–June 1924)	Ill.▲L.Q.
Notre Dame Journal of Law, Ethics & Public Policy	**Notre▲Dame▲J.L.,▲Ethics▲&▲Pub.▲Policy**
Notre Dame Journal of Legislation—*see Journal of Legislation*	
Notre Dame Law Review	**Notre▲Dame▲L.▲Rev.**
Was: Notre Dame Lawyer (Vol. 1–Vol. 57)	Notre▲Dame▲Law.
Nova Law Review	**Nova▲L.▲Rev.**
Was: Nova Law Journal (Vol. 1–Vol. 10)	Nova▲L.J.
NU Forum: A Cooperative Law Journal of Northeastern University School of Law	**NU▲Forum**
Nursing Law & Ethics—*see Journal of Law, Medicine & Ethics, The*	
Ocean and Coastal Law Journal	**Ocean▲&▲Coastal▲L.J.**
Was: Territorial Sea Journal	Territorial▲Sea▲J.
Ocean Development and International Law	**Ocean▲Dev.▲&▲Intl.▲L.**
Was: ★Ocean Development and International Law Journal (Vol. 1, no. 1–Vol. 1, no. 2)	Ocean▲Dev.▲&▲Intl.▲L.J.
Ohio Northern University Law Review	**Ohio▲N.U.▲L.▲Rev.**
Ohio State Journal on Dispute Resolution	**Ohio▲St.▲J.▲on▲Dis.▲Res.**
Ohio State Law Journal	**Ohio▲St.▲L.J.**
Oil & Gas Tax Quarterly	**Oil▲&▲Gas▲Tax▲Q.**
Oklahoma City University Law Review	**Okla.▲City▲U.▲L.▲Rev.**
Oklahoma Law Review	**Okla.▲L.▲Rev.**
★Orange County Register	**Orange▲Co.▲Register**
Oregon Law Review	**Or.▲L.▲Rev.**
★Orlando Sentinel	**Orlando▲Sent.**
Pace Environmental Law Review	**Pace▲Envtl.▲L.▲Rev.**

Name	Abbreviation
Pace International Law Review	**Pace▲Intl.▲L.▲Rev.**
Was: Pace Yearbook of International Law (Vol. 1–Vol. 4)	Pace▲Y.B.▲Intl.▲L.
Pace Law Review	**Pace▲L.▲Rev.**
Pacific Rim Law & Policy Journal	**P.▲Rim▲L.▲&▲Policy▲J.**
PAR: Public Administration Review	**PAR**
Patent Law Annual	**Pat.▲L.▲Annual**
Was: Patent Law Developments (1964–1965)	Pat.▲L.▲Devs.
Was: Patent Procurement and Exploitation (1963)	Pat.▲Procur.▲&▲Exploitation

Patent Law Review—*see Intellectual Property Law Review*

Patent, Trademark, and Copyright Journal of Research and Education—*see IDEA: The Journal of Law and Technology*

Penn State Environmental Law Review	**Penn▲St.▲Envtl.▲L.▲Rev.**
Penn State International Law Review	**Penn▲St.▲Intl.▲L.▲Rev.**
Was: Dickinson Journal of International Law (Vol. 2, no. 2–Vol. 19)	Dick.▲J.▲Intl.▲L.
Was: Dickinson International Law Annual (Vol. 1–Vol. 2, no. 1)	Dick.▲Intl.▲L.▲Annual
Pennsylvania Bar Association Quarterly	**Pa.▲B.▲Assn.▲Q.**

Pension and Profit-Sharing Tax Journal—*see Journal of Pension Planning & Compliance*

Pepperdine Law Review	**Pepp.▲L.▲Rev.**

Performing Arts Review—*see Journal of Arts Management, Law and Society*

Personal Finance Law Quarterly Report—*see Consumer Finance Law Quarterly Report*

Perspectives	**Persps.**
★**Philadelphia Inquirer**	**Phila.▲Inquirer**
★**Pittsburgh Post-Gazette**	**Pitt.▲Post-Gaz.**
★**Plain Dealer (Cleveland, Ohio)**	**Plain▲Dealer▲(Cleveland, Ohio)**
★**Portland Oregonian**	**Port.▲Oregonian**
Potomac Law Review	**Potomac▲L.▲Rev.**
★**Practical Lawyer**	**Prac.▲Law.**
★**Practical Litigator, The**	**Prac.▲Litig.**
★**Practical Real Estate Lawyer, The**	**Prac.▲Real▲Est.▲Law.**
★**Practical Tax Lawyer, The**	**Prac.▲Tax.▲Law.**

Name	Abbreviation
Practical Tax Strategies	Prac.▲Tax▲Strategies
★Preventive Law Reporter *Was:* ★Preventive Law Newsletter	Preventive▲L.▲Rep. Preventive▲L.▲Newsltr.
Preview of United States Supreme Court Cases	Preview▲U.S.▲S.▲Ct.▲Cases
★Probate & Property	Prob.▲&▲Prop.
Probate Law Journal	Prob.▲L.J.
★Professional Lawyer, The	Prof.▲Law.
★Prosecutor, Journal of the National District Attorneys Association, The *(nonconsecutively paginated starting with Vol. 16)* *Was:* NDAA: Journal of the National District Attorneys Association (Vol. 1–Vol. 3, no. 3)	Prosecutor NDAA▲J.
Prospectus—*see University of Michigan Journal of Law Reform*	
Public Contract Law Journal	Pub.▲Contract▲L.J.
★Public Interest Law Reporter	Pub.▲Interest▲L.▲Rptr.
Public Interest Law Review, The	Pub.▲Interest▲L.▲Rev.
Public Land & Resources Law Review *Was:* Public Land Law Review (Vol. 1–Vol. 16)	Pub.▲Land▲&▲Res.▲L.▲Rev. Pub.▲Land▲L.▲Rev.
Publishing, Entertainment, Advertising and Allied Fields Law Quarterly	Publg.,▲Ent.,▲Advert.▲& ▲Allied▲Fields▲L.Q.
QLR *Was:* Bridgeport Law Review (Vol. 12, no. 2–Vol. 13) *Was:* University of Bridgeport Law Review (Vol. 1–Vol. 12, no. 1)	QLR Bridgeport▲L.▲Rev. U.▲Bridgeport▲L.▲Rev.
★Quarterly/Christian Legal Society *Was:* ★Christian Legal Society Quarterly (Vol. 1)	Q./CLS Christian▲Leg.▲Socy.▲Q.
Quinnipiac Health Law Journal	Quinnipiac▲Health▲L.J.
Quinnipiac Probate Law Journal *Was:* Connecticut Probate Law Journal (Vol. 1–Vol. 10)	Quinnipiac▲Prob.▲L.J. Conn.▲Prob.▲L.J.
Race and Ethnic Ancestry Law Journal—*see Washington and Lee Journal of Civil Rights and Social Justice*	
Real Estate Law Journal	Real▲Est.▲L.J.
Real Property, Probate and Trust Journal	Real▲Prop.,▲Prob.▲&▲Trust▲J.
Regent University Law Review	Regent▲U.▲L.▲Rev.
★Res Gestae	Res▲Gestae
Research in Law and Economics	Res.▲L.▲&▲Econs.

Name	Abbreviation
Restitution Law Review	Restitution▲L.▲Rev.
Review of Litigation	Rev.▲Litig.
Review of Securities & Commodities Regulation	Rev.▲Secs.▲&▲Commodities▲Reg.
Revista de Derecho Puertorriqueno	Rev.▲de▲D.P.
Revista Juridica de la Universidad de Puerto Rico	Rev.▲Juridica▲U.P.R.
Revista Juridica de la Universidad Interamericana de Puerto Rico	Rev.▲Juridica▲U.▲Inter.▲P.R.
★Rhode Island Bar Journal	R.I.▲B.J.
Richmond Journal of Global Law and Business	Rich.▲J.▲Global▲L.▲&▲Bus.
Richmond Journal of Law & Technology	Rich.▲J.L.▲&▲Tech.
Risk: Health, Safety, & Environment *Was:* Risk: Issues in Health & Safety (Vol. 1–Vol. 4)	Risk Risk
Rocky Mountain Law Review/University of Colorado—*see University of Colorado Law Review*	
★Rocky Mountain News	Rocky▲Mt.▲News
Roger Williams University Law Review	Roger▲Williams▲U.▲L.▲Rev.
Rutgers Computer and Technology Law Journal *Was:* Rutgers Journal of Computers, Technology, and the Law (Vol. 7–Vol. 8, no. 1) *Was:* Rutgers Journal of Computers and the Law (Vol. 1–Vol. 6)	Rutgers▲Computer▲&▲Tech.▲L.J. Rutgers▲J.▲Computers,▲Tech.,▲&▲L. Rutgers▲J.▲Computers▲&▲L.
Rutgers Conflict Resolution Law Journal	Rutgers▲Conflict▲Res.▲L.J.
Rutgers Law Journal *Was:* Rutgers-Camden Law Journal (Vol. 1–Vol. 11)	Rutgers▲L.J. Rutgers-Camden▲L.J.
Rutgers Law Review *Was:* Rutgers University Law Review (Vol. 1–Vol. 2)	Rutgers▲L.▲Rev. Rutgers▲U.▲L.▲Rev.
Rutgers Race & the Law Review	Rutgers▲Race▲&▲L.▲Rev.
★Sacramento Bee *Also see "St."*	Sacramento▲Bee
Saint Louis University Law Journal	St.▲Louis▲U.▲L.J.
Saint Louis University Public Law Review *Was:* Public Law Forum (Vol. 1–Vol. 5)	St.▲Louis▲U.▲Pub.▲L.▲Rev. Pub. L. Forum
Saint Louis-Warsaw Transatlantic Law Journal	St.▲Louis-Warsaw▲Transatl.▲L.J.
★San Antonio Express-News	San▲Antonio▲Exp.-News
San Diego Justice Journal—*see Thomas Jefferson Law Review*	
San Diego Law Review	S.D.▲L.▲Rev.

Name	Abbreviation
★San Diego Union-Tribune	S.D.▲Union-Trib.
San Fernando Valley Law Review	San▲Fernando▲Valley▲L.▲Rev.
★San Francisco Attorney	S.F.▲Atty.
★San Francisco Chronicle	S.F.▲Chron.
Santa Clara Computer & High Technology Law Journal	Santa▲Clara▲Computer▲& ▲High▲Tech.▲L.J.
Santa Clara Law Review *Was:* Santa Clara Lawyer (Vol. 1–Vol. 15)	Santa▲Clara▲L.▲Rev. Santa▲Clara▲Law.
★School Law Bulletin	Sch.▲L.▲Bull.
Scribes Journal of Legal Writing, The	Scribes▲J.▲Leg.▲Writing
★Scrivener	Scrivener
★Search and Seizure Law Report	Search▲&▲Seizure▲L.▲Rpt.
Seattle University Law Review *Was:* University of Puget Sound Law Review (Vol. 1–Vol. 17)	Seattle▲U.▲L.▲Rev. U.▲Puget▲Sound▲L.▲Rev.
Securities and Federal Corporate Law Report	Secs.▲&▲Fed.▲Corp.▲L.▲Rpt.
Securities Law Review	Secs.▲L.▲Rev.
Securities Regulation Law Journal	Secs.▲Reg.▲L.J.
Seton Hall Circuit Review	Seton▲Hall▲Cir.▲Rev.
Seton Hall Constitutional Law Journal	Seton▲Hall▲Const.▲L.J.
Seton Hall Journal of Sports and Entertainment Law *Was:* Seton Hall Journal of Sport Law	Seton▲Hall▲J.▲Sports▲&▲Enter.▲L. Seton▲Hall▲J.▲Sport▲L.
Seton Hall Law Review *Was:* Seton Hall Law Journal (1968–1969)	Seton▲Hall▲L.▲Rev. Seton▲Hall▲L.J.
Seton Hall Legislative Journal	Seton▲Hall▲Legis.▲J.
SMU Law Review *Was:* Southwestern Law Journal (1948–Spring 1992) *Was:* Texas Law and Legislation (1947)	S.M.U.▲L.▲Rev. Sw.▲L.J. Tex.▲L.▲&▲Legis.
Social Responsibility: Business, Journalism, Law, Medicine *Was:* Social Responsibility: Journalism, Law, Medicine (Vol. 1–Vol. 9)	Soc.▲Resp. Soc.▲Resp.
Software Law Journal—*see John Marshall Journal of Computer & Information Law, The*	
South Carolina Environmental Law Journal—*see Southeastern Environmental Law Journal*	

Name	Abbreviation
South Carolina Journal of International Law and Business	S.C.▲J.▲Intl.▲L.▲&▲Bus.
South Carolina Law Review	S.C.▲L.▲Rev.
Was: South Carolina Law Quarterly, The (Vol. 1–Vol. 14)	S.C.▲L.Q.
★**South Carolina Lawyer**	S.C.▲Law.
South Dakota Law Review	S.D.▲L.▲Rev.
South Texas Law Review	S.▲Tex.▲L.▲Rev.
Was: South Texas Law Journal (Vol. 1–Vol. 26)	S.▲Tex.▲L.J.
Southeastern Environmental Law Journal	S.E.▲Envtl.▲L.J.
Was: South Carolina Environmental Law Journal (Vol. 1–Vol. 10)	S.C.▲Envtl.▲L.J.
Southern California Interdisciplinary Law Journal	S.▲Cal.▲Interdisc.▲L.J.
Southern California Law Review	S.▲Cal.▲L.▲Rev.
Southern California Review of Law and Women's Studies	S.▲Cal.▲Rev.▲L.▲&▲Women's▲Stud.
Southern Illinois University Law Journal	S.▲Ill.▲U.▲L.J.
Southern Law Quarterly—*see Tulane Law Review*	
Southern University Law Review	S.U.▲L.▲Rev.
Southwestern Journal of Law and Trade in the Americas	Sw.▲J.L.▲&▲Trade▲Ams.
Southwestern Law Journal—*see SMU Law Review*	
Southwestern Legal Foundation Institute on Oil and Gas Law and Taxation	Sw.▲Leg.▲Found.▲Inst.▲on▲Oil▲&▲Gas▲L.▲&▲Taxn.
Southwestern University Law Review	Sw.▲U.▲L.▲Rev.
Sports Lawyers Journal, The	Sports▲Laws.▲J.
Also see "Saint"	
St. John's Journal of Legal Commentary	St.▲John's▲J.▲Leg.▲Comment.
St. John's Law Review	St.▲John's▲L.▲Rev.
St. Louis Law Review—*see Washington University Law Quarterly*	
★**St. Louis Post-Dispatch**	St.▲Louis▲Post-Dispatch
St. Mary's Law Journal	St.▲Mary's▲L.J.
Was: St. Mary's Law Review (Vol. 1–Vol. 24)	St.▲Mary's▲L.▲Rev.
★**St. Petersburg Times**	St.▲Pete.▲Times
St. Thomas Law Review	St.▲Thomas▲L.▲Rev.
Was: St. Thomas Law Forum/Saint Thomas University, School of Law (Vol. 1–Vol. 3)	St.▲Thomas▲L.▲Forum

Name	Abbreviation
Stanford Environmental Law Journal *Was:* Stanford Environmental Law Annual (Vol. 1–Vol. 5)	**Stan.▲Envtl.▲L.J.** Stan.▲Envtl.▲L.▲Annual
Stanford Journal of Civil Rights and Civil Liberties	**Stan.▲J.▲Civ.▲Rights▲&▲Civ.▲Liberties**
Stanford Journal of International Law *Was:* Stanford Journal of International Studies (Vol. 3–Vol. 15)	**Stan.▲J.▲Intl.▲L.** Stan.▲J.▲Intl.▲Stud.
Stanford Journal of Law, Business & Finance	**Stan.▲J.L.,▲Bus.▲&▲Fin.**
Stanford Law & Policy Review	**Stan.▲L.▲&▲Policy▲Rev.**
Stanford Law Review *(Volumes 5–8 are nonconsecutively paginated)*	**Stan.▲L.▲Rev.**
★**Star-Ledger▲(Newark, N.J.)**	**Star-Ledger▲(Newark,▲N.J.)**
★**Star Tribune (Minneapolis)**	**Star▲Trib.▲(Minneapolis,▲Minn.)**
Stetson Law Review	**Stetson▲L.▲Rev.**
★**Student Lawyer** *Was:* ★Student Lawyer Journal (Dec. 1967–June 1972) *Was:* ★Student Lawyer of the American Bar Association (Sept. 1967–Nov. 1967) *Was:* ★Student Lawyer Journal of the American Law Student Association (Oct. 1955–Aug. 1967)	**Student▲Law.** Student▲Law.▲J. Student▲Law.▲ABA Student▲Law.▲J.▲Am.▲L.▲Student▲Assn.
Studies in Law, Politics, and Society *Was:* Research in Law, Deviance and Social Control (Vol. 4–Vol. 9) *Was:* Research in Law and Sociology (Vol. 1–Vol. 3)	**Stud.▲L.,▲Pol.,▲&▲Socy.** Res.▲L.,▲Deviance▲&▲Soc.▲Control Res.▲L.▲&▲Sociology
Suffolk Transnational Law Review *Was:* Suffolk Transnational Law Journal (Vol. 1–Vol. 15)	**Suffolk▲Transnatl.▲L.▲Rev.** Suffolk▲Transnatl.▲L.J.
Suffolk University Law Review	**Suffolk▲U.▲L.▲Rev.**
★**Sun-Sentinel (Ft. Lauderdale, Fla.)**	**Sun-Sent.▲(Ft.▲Lauderdale,▲Fla.)**
Supreme Court Economic Review	**S.▲Ct.▲Econ.▲Rev.**
Supreme Court Historical Society—*see Journal of Supreme Court History*	
Supreme Court Review	**S.▲Ct.▲Rev.**
Syracuse Journal of International Law and Commerce	**Syracuse▲J.▲Intl.▲L.▲&▲Com.**
Syracuse Journal of Legislation & Policy	**Syracuse▲J.▲Legis.▲&▲Policy**
Syracuse Science and Technology Law Reporter *Was:* Syracuse Law and Technology Journal (2000–2004)	**Syracuse▲Sci.▲&▲Tech.▲L.▲Rptr.** Syracuse▲L.▲Tech.▲J.
Syracuse Law Review	**Syracuse▲L.▲Rev.**

Name	Abbreviation
Tax Adviser	Tax▲Adviser
Tax Executive	Tax▲Exec.
Tax Law Review	Tax▲L.▲Rev.
Tax Lawyer *Was:* Bulletin of the Section of Taxation, American Bar Association (Vol. 1–Vol. 20, no. 4)	Tax▲Law. Bull.▲Sec.▲Taxn.
Tax Management Estates, Gifts and Trusts Journal *Was:* ★Estates, Gifts and Trusts Journal, The (July/Aug. 1976–Nov./Dec. 1983)	Tax▲Mgt.▲Ests.,▲Gifts ▲&▲Trusts ▲J. Ests.,▲Gifts▲&▲Trusts▲J.
★Tax Management Memorandum	Tax.▲Mgt.▲Memo.
Tax Management Real Estate Journal	Tax▲Mgt.▲Real▲Est.▲J.
Tax Notes	Tax▲Notes
Tax Notes International	Tax▲Notes▲Intl.
Taxation for Lawyers	Taxn.▲for▲Laws.
★Taxes: The Tax Magazine	Taxes
Temple Environmental Law & Technology Journal	Temp.▲Envtl.▲L.▲&▲Tech.▲J.
Temple International and Comparative Law Journal	Temp.▲Intl.▲&▲Comp.▲L.J.
Temple Law Review *Was:* Temple Law Quarterly (Vol. 19, no. 3–Vol. 60) *Was:* Temple University Law Quarterly (Vol. 13–Vol. 19, no. 2) *Was:* Temple Law Quarterly (Vol. 1–Vol. 12)	Temp.▲L.▲Rev. Temp.▲L.Q. Temp.▲U.▲L.Q. Temp.▲L.Q.
Temple Political and Civil Rights Law Review	Temp.▲Pol.▲&▲Civ.▲Rights▲L.▲Rev.
★Tennessee Bar Journal	Tenn.▲B.J.
Tennessee Law Review	Tenn.▲L.▲Rev.
Texas Bar Journal	Tex.▲B.J.
Texas Hispanic Journal of Law & Policy: The University of Texas School of Law *Was:* Hispanic Law Journal: The University of Texas School of Law (Vol. 1–Vol. 3)	Tex.▲Hispanic▲J.L.▲&▲Policy Hispanic▲L.J.
Texas Intellectual Property Law Journal	Tex.▲Intell.▲Prop.▲L.J.
Texas International Law Journal *Was:* Texas International Law Forum (Vol. 1, no. 2–Vol. 6, no. 2) *Was:* Journal of the University of Texas International Law Society, The (Jan. 1965)	Tex.▲Intl.▲L.J. Tex.▲Intl.▲L.▲Forum J.▲U.▲Tex.▲Intl.▲L.▲Socy.
Texas Journal of Women and the Law	Tex.▲J.▲Women▲&▲L.
Texas Law Review	Tex.▲L.▲Rev.

Name	Abbreviation
Texas Review of Law and Politics	**Tex.▲Rev.▲L.▲&▲Pol.**
Texas Southern University Law Review—*see Thurgood Marshall Law Review*	
Texas Tech Journal of Texas Administrative Law	**Tex.▲Tech▲J.▲Tex.▲Admin.▲L.**
Texas Tech Law Review	**Tex.▲Tech▲L.▲Rev.**
Texas Wesleyan Law Review	**Tex.▲Wes.▲L.▲Rev.**
The Scholar: St. Mary's Law Review on Minority Issues	**Scholar**
Thomas Jefferson Law Review	**Thomas▲Jefferson▲L.▲Rev.**
Was: San Diego Justice Journal (Winter 1993–Summer 1995)	San▲Diego▲Just.▲J.
Was: Criminal Justice Journal (1976–1992)	Crim.▲Just.▲J.
Thomas M. Cooley Journal of Practical and Clinical Law	**Thomas▲M.▲Cooley▲J.▲Prac.▲&▲Clin.▲L.**
Thomas M. Cooley Law Review	**Thomas▲M.▲Cooley▲L.▲Rev.**
Was: Cooley Law Review (Vol. 1–Vol. 7)	Cooley▲L.▲Rev.
Thurgood Marshall Law Review	**Thurgood▲Marshall▲L.▲Rev.**
Was: Texas Southern University Law Review (Vol. 2–Vol. 6)	Tex.▲S.U.▲L.▲Rev.
Toledo Journal of Great Lakes' Law, Science & Policy, The	**Toledo▲J.▲Great▲Lakes'▲L.,▲Sci.▲&▲Policy**
Tort Trial and Insurance Practice Law Journal	**Tort▲Tr.▲&▲Ins.▲Prac.▲L.J.**
Was: Tort & Insurance Law Journal (Vol. 1–Vol. 37)	Tort▲&▲Ins.▲L.J.
Touro Environmental Law Journal	**Touro▲Envtl.▲L.J.**
Touro International Law Review	**Touro▲Intl.▲L.▲Rev.**
Was: Touro Journal of Transnational Law (Vol. 1–Vol. 4)	Touro▲J.▲Transnatl.▲L.
Touro Law Review	**Touro▲L.▲Rev.**
Trademark Reporter, The	**Trademark▲Rep.**
Absorbed: Bulletin of the United States Trademark Association (Before 1911)	Bull.▲U.S.▲Trademark▲Assn.
Transnational Law & Contemporary Problems	**Transnatl.▲L.▲&▲Contemp.▲Probs.**
Transnational Lawyer, The	**Transnatl.▲Law.**
Transportation Law Journal	**Transp.▲L.J.**
Transportation Practitioners Journal—*see Journal of Transportation Law, Logistics, and Policy*	
★Trauma	**Trauma**
★Trial	**Tr.**
Trial Advocate Quarterly	**Tr.▲Advoc.▲Q.**

Name	Abbreviation
Trial Lawyer, The	**Tr.▲Law.**
Was: Trial Diplomacy Journal (Spring 1978–May/June 1998)	Tr.▲Dipl.▲J.
Trial Lawyer's Guide, The	**Tr.▲Laws.▲Guide**
★Trial Lawyers Quarterly	**Tr.▲Laws.▲Q.**
(nonconsecutively paginated since Volume 118)	
Trusts & Estates	**Trusts▲&▲Ests.**
Was: Trust Companies (Vol. 1–Vol. 67)	Trust▲Cos.
Tulane Environmental Law Journal	**Tul.▲Envtl.▲L.J.**
Tulane European and Civil Law Forum	**Tul.▲Eur.▲&▲Civ.▲L.▲Forum**
Was: ★Tulane Civil Law Forum	Tul.▲Civ.▲L.▲Forum
Ceased with Volumes 6/7, issued 1991–1992 (**Note:** Suspended 1977–1987)	
Tulane Journal of International and Comparative Law	**Tul.▲J.▲Intl.▲&▲Comp.▲L.**
Tulane Law Review	**Tul.▲L.▲Rev.**
Was: Southern Law Quarterly (Vol. 1–Vol. 3)	S.▲L.Q.
Tulane Maritime Law Journal	**Tul.▲Mar.▲L.J.**
Was: Maritime Lawyer, The (Vol. 1–Vol. 11)	Mar.▲Law.
Tulsa Journal of Comparative & International Law	**Tul.▲J.▲Comp.▲&▲Intl.▲L.**
Tulsa Law Review	**Tulsa▲L.▲Rev.**
Was: Tulsa Law Journal (Vol. 1–Vol. 34)	Tulsa▲L.J.
U.C. Davis Journal of International Law and Policy	**U.C.▲Davis▲J.▲Intl.▲L.▲&▲Policy**
UCLA-Alaska Law Review—*see Alaska Law Review*	
UCLA Bulletin of Law and Technology	**UCLA▲Bull.▲L.▲&▲Tech.**
UCLA Entertainment Law Review	**UCLA▲Ent.▲L.▲Rev.**
UCLA Journal of Environmental Law & Policy	**UCLA▲J.▲Envtl.▲L.▲&▲Policy**
UCLA Journal of International Law and Foreign Affairs	**UCLA▲J.▲Intl.▲L.▲&▲For.▲Affairs**
UCLA Law Review	**UCLA▲L.▲Rev.**
UCLA Pacific Basin Law Journal	**UCLA▲P.▲Basin▲L.J.**
UCLA Women's Law Journal	**UCLA▲Women's▲L.J.**
UMKC Law Review	**UMKC▲L.▲Rev.**
Was: University of Missouri at Kansas City Law Review (Vol. 32–Vol. 34)	U.▲Mo.▲Kan.▲City▲L.▲Rev.
Was: University of Kansas City Law Review: A Journal of the University of Kansas City (Vol. 7–Vol. 31)	U.▲Kan.▲City▲L.▲Rev.
Was: Kansas City Law Review (Vol. 1–Vol. 6)	Kan.▲City▲L.▲Rev.

Name	Abbreviation
Unbound: Harvard Journal of the Legal Left	**Unbound**
Uniform Commercial Code Law Journal	**U.C.C.▲L.J.**
Uniform Commercial Code Reporter-Digest	**U.C.C.▲Rptr.-Dig.**
United States Air Force Academy Journal of Legal Studies	**U.S.A.F.▲Acad.▲J.▲Leg.▲Stud.**
United States Air Force JAG Law Review—*see Air Force Law Review*	
United States-Mexico Law Journal	**U.S.-Mex.▲L.J.**
University of Arkansas at Little Rock Law Review *Was:* University of Arkansas at Little Rock Law Journal (1978–1998)	**UALR▲L.▲Rev.** UALR▲L.J.
University of Baltimore Intellectual Property Law Journal	**U.▲Balt.▲Intell.▲Prop.▲L.J.**
University of Baltimore Journal of Environmental Law *Was:* Environmental Perspectives	**U.▲Balt.▲J.▲Envtl.▲L.** Envtl.▲Persps.
University of Baltimore Law Forum	**U.▲Balt.▲L.▲Forum**
University of Baltimore Law Review	**U.▲Balt.▲L.▲Rev.**
University of Bridgeport Law Review—*see QLR*	
University of California at Davis Law Review	**U.▲Cal.▲Davis▲L.▲Rev.**
University of Chicago Legal Forum	**U.▲Chi.▲Leg.▲Forum**
University of Chicago Law Review	**U.▲Chi.▲L.▲Rev.**
University of Chicago Law School Roundtable, The	**U.▲Chi.▲L.▲Sch.▲Roundtable**
University of Cincinnati Law Review	**U.▲Cin.▲L.▲Rev.**
University of Colorado Law Review *Was:* Rocky Mountain Law Review/University of Colorado (Vol. 1–Vol. 34)	**U.▲Colo.▲L.▲Rev.** Rocky▲Mt.▲L.▲Rev.
University of Dayton Law Review *Was:* University of Dayton Intramural Law Review (1976)	**U.▲Dayton▲L.▲Rev.** U.▲Dayton▲Intra.▲L.▲Rev.
University of Denver Water Law Review	**U.▲Denver▲Water▲L.▲Rev.**
University of Detroit Mercy Law Review *Was:* University of Detroit Law Review (Vol. 62–Vol. 68) *Was:* University of Detroit Journal of Urban Law (Vol. 54–Vol. 61) *Was:* Journal of Urban Law (Vol. 44–Vol. 53) *Was:* University of Detroit Law Journal (Vol. 1–Vol. 43)	**U.▲Det.▲Mercy▲L.▲Rev.** U.▲Det.▲L.▲Rev. U.▲Det.▲J.▲Urb.▲L. J.▲Urb.▲L. U.▲Det.▲L.J.

Name	Abbreviation
University of Florida Journal of Law and Public Policy	**U.▲Fla.▲J.L.▲&▲Pub.▲Policy**
University of Hawaii Law Review	**U.▲Haw.▲L.▲Rev.**
University of Illinois Journal of Law, Technology and Policy	**U.▲Ill.▲J.L.▲Tech.▲&▲Policy**
University of Illinois Law Review	**U.▲Ill.▲L.▲Rev.**
Was: University of Illinois Law Forum (1949–1980)	U.▲Ill.▲L.▲Forum
University of Kansas Law Review	**U.▲Kan.▲L.▲Rev.**
University of Louisville Journal of Family Law—*see* Brandeis Law Journal	
University of Memphis Law Review	**U.▲Mem.▲L.▲Rev.**
Was: Memphis State University Law Review (Vol. 1–Vol. 24)	Mem.▲St.▲U.▲L.▲Rev.
University of Miami Business Law Review	**U.▲Miami▲Bus.▲L.▲Rev.**
University of Miami Entertainment & Sports Law Review	**U.▲Miami▲Ent.▲&▲Sports▲L.▲Rev.**
Was: Entertainment & Sports Law Journal (Vol. 1–Vol. 5)	Ent.▲&▲Sports▲L.J.
University of Miami Inter-American Law Review, The	**U.▲Miami▲Inter-Am.▲L.▲Rev.**
Was: Lawyer of the Americas (Vol. 1–Vol. 15)	Law.▲Ams.
University of Miami International and Comparative Law Review	**U.▲Miami▲Intl.▲&▲Comp.▲L.▲Rev.**
Was: University of Miami Yearbook of International Law (Vol. 1–Vol. 6)	U.▲Miami▲Y.B.▲Intl.▲L.
University of Miami Law Review	**U.▲Miami▲L.▲Rev.**
Was: Miami Law Quarterly (Vol. 1–Vol. 11)	Miami▲L.Q.
University of Michigan Journal of Law Reform	**U.▲Mich.▲J.L.▲Reform**
Was: Journal of Law Reform (Vol. 4–Vol. 5)	J.L.▲Reform
Was: Prospectus (Vol. 1–Vol. 3)	Prospectus
University of Pennsylvania Journal of Constitutional Law	**U.▲Pa.▲J.▲Const.▲L.**
University of Pennsylvania Journal of International Economic Law	**U.▲Pa.▲J.▲Intl.▲Econ.▲L.**
Was: University of Pennsylvania Journal of International Business Law (Vol. 1–Vol. 16)	U.▲Pa.▲J.▲Intl.▲Bus.▲L.
University of Pennsylvania Journal of Labor and Employment Law	**U.▲Pa.▲J.▲Lab.▲&▲Empl.▲L.**
University of Pennsylvania Law Review	**U.▲Pa.▲L.▲Rev.**
Was: University of Pennsylvania Law Review and American Law Register (Vol. 56–Vol. 93)	U.▲Pa.▲L.▲Rev.▲&▲Am.▲L.▲Register
Was: American Law Register, The (Vol. 46–Vol. 55)	Am.▲L.▲Register

Name	Abbreviation
Was: American Law Register and Review, The (Vol. 40–Vol. 45)	Am.▲L.▲Register▲&▲Rev.
Was: American Law Register, The (Vol. 1–Vol. 39)	Am.▲L.▲Register
University of Pittsburgh Law Review	**U.▲Pitt.▲L.▲Rev.**
University of Puget Sound Law Review—*see Seattle University Law Review*	
University of Richmond Law Review	**U.▲Rich.▲L.▲Rev.**
Was: University of Richmond Law Notes (Vol. 1–Vol. 2)	U.▲Rich.▲L.▲Notes
University of Saint Thomas Law Journal	**U.▲St.▲Thomas▲L.J.**
University of San Francisco Law Review	**U.S.F.▲L.▲Rev.**
University of San Francisco Maritime Law Journal	**U.S.F.▲Mar.▲L.J.**
University of the District of Columbia Law Review, The	**U.D.C.▲L.▲Rev.**
Was: District of Columbia Law Review (Vol. 1–Vol. 3)	D.C.▲L.▲Rev.
University of Toledo Law Review	**U.▲Toledo▲L.▲Rev.**
Was: University of Toledo Intramural Law Review (Vol. 1)	U.▲Toledo▲Intra.▲L.▲Rev.
University of Washington Law Review—*see Washington Law Review*	
Urban Law Annual—*see Washington University Journal of Law & Policy*	
Urban Lawyer, The	**Urb.▲Law.**
★USA Today	**USA▲Today**
★Utah Bar Journal	**Utah▲B.J.**
Utah Law Review	**Utah▲L.▲Rev.**
UWLA Law Review: University of West Los Angeles School of Law	**UWLA▲L.▲Rev.**
Was: University of West Los Angeles Law Review (Vol. 1–Vol. 13)	U.W.L.A.▲L.▲Rev.
Valparaiso University Law Review	**Val.▲U.▲L.▲Rev.**
Vanderbilt Journal of Entertainment Law & Practice	**Vand.▲J.▲Ent.▲L.▲&▲Prac.**
Vanderbilt Journal of Transnational Law	**Vand.▲J.▲Transnatl.▲L.**
Vanderbilt Law Review	**Vand.▲L.▲Rev.**
★VBA News Journal	**VBA▲News▲J.**
Was: ★Virginia Bar Association Journal (Jan. 1975–Spring 1998)	Va.▲B.▲Assn.▲J.
Vermont Law Review	**Vt.▲L.▲Rev.**

Name	Abbreviation
Villanova Environmental Law Journal	**Vill.▲Envtl.▲L.J.**
Villanova Information Law Chronicle, The	**Vill.▲Info.▲L.▲Chron.**
Villanova Journal of Law and Investment Management	**Vill.▲J.L.▲&▲Inv.▲Mgt.**
Villanova Law Review	**Vill.▲L.▲Rev.**
Villanova Sports & Entertainment Law Journal	**Vill.▲Sports▲&▲Ent.▲L.J.**
Was: Villanova Sports & Entertainment Law Forum (Vol. 1–Vol. 2)	Vill.▲Sports▲&▲Ent.▲L.▲Forum
Virginia Environmental Law Journal	**Va.▲Envtl.▲L.J.**
Was: Virginia Journal of Natural Resources Law (Vol. 1–Vol. 8, no. 1)	Va.▲J.▲Nat.▲Resources▲L.
Virginia Journal of International Law	**Va.▲J.▲Intl.▲L.**
Was: Journal of the John Bassett Moore Society of International Law (Vol. 1–Vol. 2)	J.▲John▲Bassett▲Moore▲Socy.▲Intl.▲L.
Virginia Journal of Law and Technology	**Va.▲J.L.▲&▲Tech.**
Virginia Journal of Social Policy & the Law, The	**Va.▲J.▲Soc.▲Policy▲&▲L.**
Virginia Law Review	**Va.▲L.▲Rev.**
Virginia Sports and Entertainment Law Journal	**Va.▲Sports▲&▲Enter.▲L.J.**
Was: Virginia Journal of Sports and the Law (Vol. 1–Vol. 3, no. 1)	Va.▲J.▲Sports▲&▲L.
Virginia Tax Review	**Va.▲Tax▲Rev.**
Wake Forest Law Review	**Wake▲Forest▲L.▲Rev.**
★**Wall Street Journal**	**Wall▲St.▲J.**
Washburn Law Journal	**Washburn▲L.J.**
Washington and Lee Journal of Civil Rights and Social Justice	**Wash.▲&▲Lee▲J.▲Civ.▲Rights▲&▲Soc.▲Just.**
Was: Washington and Lee Race and Ethnic Ancestry Law Journal (2000–2004)	Wash.▲&▲Lee▲Race▲&▲Ethnic▲Ancestry▲L.J.
Was: Race and Ethnic Ancestry Law Journal (1998–1999)	Race▲&▲Ethnic▲Ancestry▲L.J.
Was: Race Ethnic Law Digest (1995–1997)	Race▲Ethnic▲L.▲Dig.
Washington and Lee Law Review	**Wash.▲&▲Lee▲L.▲Rev.**
Washington Law Review	**Wash.▲L.▲Rev.**
Was: University of Washington Law Review (Vol. 41, no. 2–Vol. 42)	U.▲Wash.▲L.▲Rev.
★**Washington Lawyer, The**	**Wash.▲Law.**
Was: ★District Lawyer (1976–July/Aug. 1985)	Dist.▲Law.
Was: ★D.C. Bar Journal (Nov. 1966–1973)	D.C.▲B.J.
Was: ★Journal of the Bar Association of the District of Columbia (1934–Oct. 1966)	J.B.▲Assn.▲D.C.
★**Washington Monthly**	**Wash.▲Mthly.**

Name	Abbreviation
★**Washington Post**	**Wash.▲Post**
★**Washington State Bar News**	**Wash.▲St.▲B.▲News**
Washington University Journal of Law & Policy	**Wash.▲U.▲J.L.▲&▲Policy**
Was: Washington University Journal of Urban and Contemporary Law (Vol. 1–Vol. 55 (1999))	Wash.▲U.▲J.▲Urb.▲&▲Contemp.▲L.
Was: Urban Law Annual (Vol. 1 (1968)–Vol. 23 (1982))	Urban▲L.▲Annual
Washington University Law Quarterly	**Wash.▲U.▲L.Q.**
Was: St. Louis Law Review (Vol. 1–Vol. 21)	St.▲Louis▲L.▲Rev.
Wayne Law Review	**Wayne▲L.▲Rev.**
West Virginia Law Review	**W.▲Va.▲L.▲Rev.**
Was: West Virginia Law Quarterly and the Bar (Vol. 25–Vol. 51)	W.▲Va.▲L.Q.▲&▲B.
Was: ★Bar, The (Vol. 3–Vol. 24)	B.▲(W.▲Va.)
Was: West Va. Bar, The (Vol. 1–Vol. 2)	W.▲Va.▲B.
Was: West Virginia Bar, The (1894–1895)	W.▲Va.▲B.
Western Legal History	**W.▲Leg.▲Hist.**
Western New England Law Review	**W.▲New▲Eng.▲L.▲Rev.**
Western Reserve Law Review—*see Case Western Reserve Law Review*	
Western State University Law Review	**W.▲St.▲U.▲L.▲Rev.**
Was: Western State Law Review (Vol. 1, no. 2–Vol. 2, no. 1)	W.▲St.▲L.▲Rev.
Was: Law Review (Anaheim) (Vol. 1, no. 1)	Anaheim▲L.▲Rev.
Whittier Journal of Child & Family Advocacy	**Whittier▲J.▲Child▲&▲Fam.▲Advoc.**
Whittier Law Review	**Whittier▲L.▲Rev.**
Widener Law Journal	**Widener▲L.J.**
Was: Widener Journal of Public Law	Widener▲J.▲Pub.▲L.
Widener Law Review	**Widener▲L.▲Rev.**
Was: Widener Law Symposium Journal (Vol. 1, no. 1–Vol. 9, no. 2)	Widener▲L.▲Symposium▲J.
Willamette Journal of International Law & Dispute Resolution	**Willamette▲J.▲Intl.▲L.▲&▲Dis.▲Res.**
Was: Willamette Bulletin of International Law & Policy (Vol. 1–Vol. 4)	Willamette▲Bull.▲Intl.▲L.▲&▲Policy
Willamette Law Review	**Willamette▲L.▲Rev.**
Was: Willamette Law Journal (Vol. 1–Vol. 14)	Willamette▲L.J.
William & Mary Bill of Rights Journal	**Wm.▲&▲Mary▲Bill▲Rights▲J.**
William and Mary Environmental Law and Policy Review	**Wm.▲&▲Mary▲Envtl.▲L.▲&▲Policy▲Rev.**
Was: William and Mary Journal of Environmental Law (Vol. 15–Vol. 18)	Wm.▲&▲Mary▲J.▲Envtl.▲L.
Was: ★Environmental Practice News (Vol. 1–Vol. 14)	Envtl.▲Prac.▲News

Name	Abbreviation
William & Mary Journal of Women and the Law	**Wm.▲&▲Mary▲J.▲Women▲L.**
William and Mary Law Review	**Wm.▲&▲Mary▲L.▲Rev.**
Was: William and Mary Review of Virginia Law (Vol. 1–Vol. 2)	Wm.▲&▲Mary▲Rev.▲Va.▲L.
William Mitchell Law Review	**Wm.▲Mitchell▲L.▲Rev.**
Wisconsin Environmental Law Journal	**Wis.▲Envtl.▲L.J.**
Wisconsin International Law Journal	**Wis.▲Intl.▲L.J.**
Wisconsin Law Review	**Wis.▲L.▲Rev.**
★**Wisconsin Lawyer, The**	**Wis.▲Law.**
Was: ★Wisconsin Bar Bulletin, The (Vol. 22–Vol. 61)	Wis.▲B.▲Bull.
Was: Bulletin of the Wisconsin Bar Association (Vol. 21, no. 3–Vol. 21, no. 4)	Bull.▲Wis.▲B.▲Assn.
Was: Bulletin of the State Bar Association of Wisconsin (Vol. 1–Vol. 21, no. 2)	Bull.▲St.▲B.▲Assn.▲Wis.
Wisconsin Women's Law Journal	**Wis.▲Women's▲L.J.**
Women & Criminal Justice	**Women▲&▲Crim.▲Just.**
★**Women's Rights Law Reporter**	**Women's▲Rights▲L.▲Rep.**
(nonconsecutively paginated since Volume 3)	
Wyoming Law Journal—*see Wyoming Law Review*	
Wyoming Law Review	**Wyo.▲L.▲Rev.**
Was: Land and Water Law Review (1966–2000)	Land▲&▲Water▲L.▲Rev.
Absorbed: Wyoming Law Journal (Dec. 1946–Fall 1965)	Wyo.▲L.J.
Yale Human Rights & Development Law Journal	**Yale▲Hum.▲Rights▲&▲Dev.▲L.J.**
Yale Journal of International Law	**Yale▲J.▲Intl.▲L.**
Was: Yale Journal of World Public Order, The (Vol. 7–Vol. 9)	Yale▲J.▲World▲Pub.▲Or.
Was: Yale Studies in World Public Order, The (Vol. 1–Vol. 6)	Yale▲Stud.▲World▲Pub.▲Or.
Yale Journal of Law and Feminism	**Yale▲J.L.▲&▲Feminism**
Yale Journal of Law and Liberation	**Yale▲J.L.▲&▲Liberation**
Yale Journal of Law and the Humanities	**Yale▲J.L.▲&▲Humanities**
Yale Journal on Regulation	**Yale▲J.▲on▲Reg.**
Yale Law & Policy Review	**Yale▲L.▲&▲Policy▲Rev.**
Yale Law Journal	**Yale▲L.J.**
★**Young Lawyer**	**Young▲Law.**
Was: ★Barrister (Feb. 1974–Fall 1996)	Barrister
Zoning and Planning Law Report	**Zoning▲&▲Plan.▲L.▲Rep.**

Below is a *condensed* student-written office memorandum that demonstrates how citations will look in a document. Because underlining is an acceptable way to denote italics, and some law professors require students to underline citations, that typeface has been used throughout this memo. Italics also would be acceptable.

MEMORANDUM

TO: Kelly Foster

FROM: Jeffrey P. Rosato

DATE: October 25, 2005

RE: Julia Bergan: Analysis of Credible Threat Element of the Colorado
             Harassment by Stalking Statute (our file 05/1278)

Issue

Under the Colorado harassment by stalking statute, did Patrick Bergan make a credible threat with the intent to annoy, harass, or alarm his estranged wife, Julia Bergan, when she received faxes originating from his place of business that contained statements such as "Do you think anyone would notice if you disappeared?"

Brief Answer

Yes. Patrick Bergan made a credible threat against Julia Bergan. Mrs. Bergan received a fax that originated from her ex-husband's workplace; it was signed with the initial "P," the same as Mr. Bergan's first initial; and the fax alluded to her possible disappearance. This fax, combined with the fact that others spotted his car outside her new residence, would be sufficient to meet the "credible threat" prong of the Colorado harassment statute.

Facts

Our client, Julia Bergan, has accused her estranged husband, Patrick Bergan, of stalking her. On August 24, 2005, Julia and Patrick Bergan were legally separated pending a divorce that will be final in a few weeks. Mrs. Bergan alleged that, over a five-year period, Patrick Bergan abused her emotionally and verbally, but not physically. Mrs. Bergan's family and friends witnessed the alleged abuse.

After the separation, Mrs. Bergan moved thirty-five miles away to her sister and brother-in-law's home. Over a six-month period, Mrs. Bergan and her sister saw Patrick Bergan's vehicle parked across the street from their residence almost daily. On several occasions, neighbors saw a man who fit Mr. Bergan's description in the driver's seat watching Mrs. Bergan's house with binoculars.

Mrs. Bergan has also received several faxes sent from Mr. Bergan's place of employment. These faxes were unsigned. One fax stated:

> I am watching you. I know your every move and am one step behind you all the way. I will never leave you alone. If I can't have you, no one can. Do you think anyone would notice if you disappeared? Neither the judge, nor your family can protect you. I'll be seeing you. Forever, *P.*

After she received this fax, Mrs. Bergan called the police, who then arrested Patrick Bergan for stalking.

Discussion

The Colorado harassment by stalking statute provides that

> [a] person commits stalking if . . . such person knowingly: (I) Makes a credible threat to another person and, in connection with such threat, repeatedly follows, approaches, contacts, or places under surveillance that person . . . ; or (II) Makes a credible threat to another person and, in connection with such threat, repeatedly makes any form of communication with that person . . . regardless of whether a conversation ensues . . . .

Colo. Rev. Stat. § 18-9-111(4)(b) (Lexis 2004). Therefore, Patrick Bergan can be convicted of harassment by stalking if he (a) made an explicit credible threat against Julia Bergan with (b) the intent to harass, annoy, or alarm her. As requested, the memorandum will focus solely on credible threat.

"'Credible threat' means a threat or physical action that would cause a reasonable person to be in fear for the person's life or safety or the safety of his or her immediate family." Id. at § 4(c)(II); see generally People v. Baer, 973 P.2d 1225, 1228–1230, 1234 (Colo. 1999) (analyzing the credible threat portion of the statute and holding that the element is constitutional and not void for vagueness). In addition, the Colorado Supreme Court has defined "threat" as "a statement of purpose or intent to cause injury or harm to the person, property or rights of another." People v. Hines, 780 P.2d 556, 559 (Colo. 1989).

Colorado requires that stalkers make an explicit threat against their victims. See Jennifer L. Bradfield, Anti-Stalking Laws: Do They Adequately Protect Stalking Victims? 21 Harv. Women's L.J. 229, 249 (1998). Thus, "[a] stalker can engage in conduct that he knows will terrify his victim and which he intends to be a threat, such as repeatedly watching and following her, but without an explicit threat, his conduct remains lawful." Id. The "credible threat" need not be separate from the harassing conduct, and it need not be verbal. People v. Cross, 114 P.3d 1, 5 (Colo. App. Div. V 2004) (defendant stared at and watched the victim at her workplace for hours each day over a several-week period, even though the victim changed her schedule; the defendant also appeared at the victim's church and stared at her), cert. granted in part, 2005 WL 1323263 (Colo. June 6, 2005).

People v. Czemerynski, 786 P.2d 1100 (Colo. 1990), contains an example of a statement that constitutes an explicit credible threat under the Colorado harassment statute. In Czemerynski, the defendant made sexually explicit phone calls and said to a girl, "[I]f you don't help me, I'm around the corner and I know where you live and I am going to get you." Id. at 1103. The defendant did not always request sex, but most conversations contained vague threats to "get" the victim. Id. The court found that such communications met the harassment statute's credible threat requirement because the calls were "intended to harass or threaten bodily injury." Id. at 1110. Thus, in Czemerynski, the threat was a stated intent to actually harm and not merely to frighten the victim. Id.; see D.L.D. v. State, 815 So. 2d 746, 747 (Fla. 5th Dist. App. 2002) (holding that the defendant's statement that he would "get" the victim satisfied Florida's statute).

Courts in some jurisdictions have ruled that the circumstances behind the alleged threat must be considered to determine its alleged credibility. E.g. People v. Falck, 60 Cal. Rptr. 2d 624 (App. 1st Dist. 1997). In Falck, the court examined the entire factual context, including surrounding events and the alleged effect the threats had on the listener. Id. at 626. Because the alleged threats caused the recipient to change her phone number, the Falck court considered the threat more credible. Id. Most courts, however, do not require ability or actual intent to carry out the alleged threats. E.g. Smith v. State, 532 So. 2d 50, 52 (Fla. 2d Dist. App. 1988) (ruling that the defendant's claim that his threatening letters were a hoax was irrelevant); State v. Lasley, 130 S.W.3d 15, 17 (Mo. App. E. Dist. 2004) (finding that the tone of the defendant's denial that he intended to kill the victim lent credence that he made a credible threat).

Based on the definitions, the Czemerynski case, and cases from other jurisdictions, the faxes do constitute a credible threat. Statements such as "I know your every move and am one step behind you all the way," "Do you think anyone would notice if you disappeared?," and "If I can't have you, no one can," are explicit credible threats. Further, when the underlying circumstances of the bad marriage and the prior history of verbal abuse are combined with this language, the threat becomes even more credible. Thus, given the harshness of the language and the abuse Mrs. Bergan suffered during the marriage, she was reasonable to fear for her physical safety from Patrick Bergan.

Conclusion

The facts and law show that Mr. Bergan did make a credible threat against Julia Bergan. The language of the faxes Mr. Bergan allegedly sent her contained statements that are explicit threats to Mrs. Bergan. Because courts have considered factors outside of the threats, the Bergans' failed marriage and Mr. Bergan's long history of verbal abuse toward Mrs. Bergan also make the threat more credible. Accordingly, it is likely that Mr. Bergan will be convicted of harassment by stalking.

This appendix is limited to statutory, judicial, and administrative sources. Cite tax treaties and secondary sources relating to taxation—such as treatises, books, legal periodicals, and looseleaf services—using the general rules for those sources in the *Manual*.

This appendix is divided into the following sections:

A. Statutory Compilations
B. Courts and Reporters
  1. Trial Courts Where Federal Tax Cases Are Heard
  2. Appellate Courts for Federal Tax Cases
  3. Unreported Opinions
C. Administrative Materials
  1. Administrative Announcements
  2. I.R.S. Compilations
  3. Officially Published I.R.S. Pronouncements
  4. Publicly Released I.R.S. Pronouncements
  5. Taxpayer Forms and Publications

A. Statutory Compilations

Although the Internal Revenue Code is located in Title 26 of the United States Code, tax courts and practitioners typically cite the separate Internal Revenue Code (I.R.C.).

When citing material within the Internal Revenue Code, include the abbreviation "I.R.C.," a section symbol followed by one space, and the section number; and enclose the date in parentheses. See **Sidebar A7-1** for additional information on the date. Practitioners sometimes do not include the year if citing the current version of the I.R.C.; however, a date is encouraged.

If citing an unofficial version of I.R.C., such as the I.R.C. that appears within the United States Code Annotated or the United States Code Service, include the publisher's name before the date.

If citing a portion of the I.R.C. that no longer is in effect, follow **Rule 14.3**, except enclose in a separate parenthetical the year of the version of the I.R.C. under which the section was promulgated. For additional information on citing federal statutes, consult **Rule 14**.

Examples

Official version: I.R.C. § 165(g) (2000).
Unofficial version: I.R.C. § 212 (West 2004).
Repealed section: I.R.C. § 275(c) (1939) (repealed 1954).

VERSIONS OF THE INTERNAL REVENUE CODE

The current Internal Revenue Code (I.R.C.) was enacted in 1986 and applies to transactions occurring after October 22, 1986. Other versions since 1900 were the I.R.C. of 1939 (which applies to most transactions that occurred between January 1, 1939 until August 16, 1954), and the I.R.C. of 1954 (which applied to income tax transactions that occurred on or after January 1, 1954, to estate tax matters that occurred after August 16, 1954, and to gift tax transactions that occurred on or after January 1, 1955; it applied until the 1986 I.R.C. was enacted).

B. Tax Courts and Reporters

1. Trial Courts Where Federal Tax Cases Are Heard

United States District Courts

The official reporters are the Federal Reporter (F., F.2d) through 1931 and the Federal Supplement (F. Supp., F. Supp. 2d) after 1931. Cite the official reporter when available. See **Rule 12.6(a)** for proper citation format.

Unofficial reports are American Federal Tax Reports (A.F.T.R., A.F.T.R.2d) and United States Tax Cases (U.S.T.C.). Cite A.F.T.R. cases by initial and pinpoint page numbers (**Rule 5**); cite U.S.T.C. cases by paragraph number and pinpoint page number. Consult **Rule 12.21** for short citation formats.

Examples of unofficial reporter citations

Estate of Smith v. U.S., 93 A.F.T.R.2d 2004-556 (S.D. Tex. 2004), *aff'd*, 94 A.F.T.R.2d 2004-5501 (5th Cir. 2004).

U.S. v. Luongo, 2000-1 U.S.T.C. ¶ 50,416 at 84,318 (N.D. Tex. 2000).

Bell A. Corp. v. U.S., 99-1 U.S.T.C. ¶ 50,119 at 87,041 (E.D. Pa. 1998), *aff'd*, 224 F.3d 200 (3d Cir. 2000).

United States Tax Court (1942 to present)

The official reporter, United States Tax Court Reports (T.C.), publishes regular decisions that generally concern novel and important tax issues. From 1942–1968, the court was called the Tax Court of the United States and the reporter was titled Tax Court of the United States Reports (T.C.). Cite the official reporter when possible.

Follow the guidelines in **Rule 12.1** regarding case citations: provide the italicized case name, the volume number, the reporter abbreviation, the initial page, the pinpoint page, and the year enclosed in parentheses. If the pinpoint page is not yet available, include number information as illustrated in the 2005 example. Consult **Rule 12.21** for short citation formats.

Examples   *Robinette v. Commr.*, 123 T.C. 85 (2004).
Smith v. Commr., 124 T.C. No. 3 (2005).

Tax Court **regular decisions** also are available in the following unofficial reporters. Use the examples below to develop citations. Regarding the date, material in looseleaf reporters typically requires an exact date; material in bound volumes requires only a year. Consult **Rule 28** for additional information on citing looseleaf reporters.

Tax Court Reporter (Tax Ct. Rep. (CCH))

Examples

Citation to looseleaf material: *Landry v. Commr.*, [Current Regular Decisions] Tax Ct. Rep. (CCH) Dec. 54,224 (Jan. 30, 2001).

Citation to transfer binder: *Suzy's Zoo v. Commr.*, [2000 Transfer Binder] Tax Ct. Rep. (CCH) Dec. 53,701 at 3911 (Jan. 6, 2000).

Tax Court Reported Decisions (Tax Ct. Dec. (RIA)), after April 15, 1991. The RIA volume and paragraph numbers correspond to the volume in which the case appears or will appear in the United States Tax Court Reports.

Examples

Citation to looseleaf material: *Katz v. Commr.*, 116 Tax. Ct. Rep. Dec. (RIA) ¶ 116.2 at 116-5 (Jan. 2, 1997).

Citation to bound material: *Suzy's Zoo v. Commr.*, 114 Tax Ct. Rep. Dec. (RIA) ¶ 114.1 (Jan. 6, 2000).

Tax Court Reported Decisions (Tax Ct. Dec. (PH)), before April 15, 1991. *Note:* The 1990–1991 volume was published by Maxwell Macmillan (MM); use the same citation format, but use (MM) in place of (PH).

Example   *Commr. v. Todd*, 89 Tax Ct. Dec. (PH) ¶ 89.63 (Oct. 26, 1987).

Tax Court Memorandum Decisions (T.C.M.) are Tax Court opinions that typically concern fact-based cases with well-settled legal issues. Unofficial versions are published by CCH, PH (before April 15, 1991), and RIA (after April 15, 1991). *Note:* The 1990–1991 volume was published by Maxwell Macmillan (MM); use the same citation format, but use (MM) in place of (PH).

Examples

CCH looseleaf version:	*Braden v. Commr.*, [Current Memo Decisions] Tax Ct. Rep. (CCH) Dec. 54,283(M) at 1383 (Mar. 22, 2001).
CCH bound version:	*Seagate Tech., Inc. v. Commr.*, 80 T.C.M. (CCH) 912, 913–914 (2000).
RIA looseleaf version:	*Bello v. Commr.*, 2001 T.C.M. (RIA) ¶ 2001-395 at 2001-401 (Mar. 9, 2001). *Peterson v. Commr.*, 97 T.C.M. (R.I.A.) ¶ 97,018 (Jan. 8, 1997).
RIA bound version:	*Sidell v. Commr.*, 99 T.C.M. (RIA) ¶ 99,301 at 99-1929.
PH looseleaf version:	*Noonan v. Commr.*, T.C.M. (PH) ¶ 86,449 (Sept. 17, 1996).
PH bound version:	*Young v. Commr.*, 48 T.C.M. (PH) ¶ 79,242 at 79,923 to 79,925 (1979).

Tax Court Summary Opinions (T.C. Summ. Op.) are from the small case division; the taxpayer can elect this division for controversies of $50,000 or less. These decisions cannot be used as precedent or appealed. Provide a parallel citation to an electronic database, Web site, or looseleaf service.

Example   *Wentland v. Commr.*, T.C. Summ. Op. 2004-134 (Sept. 27, 2004), 2004 Tax Ct. Summary LEXIS 81.

Board of Tax Appeals (1924–1942)

The Board of Tax Appeals was the original Tax Court and is the predecessor to the United States Tax Court. The official reporter is United States Board of Tax Appeals Reports (B.T.A.). Consult **Rule 12.21** for short citation formats.

Examples   *Am. Cigar Co. v. Commr.*, 21 B.T.A. 464 (1930).

                    Standard Oil Co. v. Commr., 43 B.T.A. 973, 998 (1941), *aff'd*, 129 F.2d 363 (7th Cir. 1942).

The unofficial Board of Tax Appeals Memorandum Decisions (B.T.A. Memo. Dec.) was published by Prentice-Hall (PH) from 1928–1942. Commerce Clearing House also published an unofficial reporter titled Board of Tax Appeals Service (B.T.A. Serv. (CCH)).

Example   *Kilpatrick's Estate v. Commr.*, 11 B.T.A. Memo. Dec. (PH) ¶ 42,335 (1942).

United States Court of Federal Claims (Oct. 29, 1992 to present)

The official reporter is the Federal Claims Reporter (Fed. Cl.). Unofficial reporters for the court are American Federal Tax Reports (A.F.T.R., A.F.T.R.2d) and United States Tax Cases

SIDEBAR A7.2

CASE NAMES IN OLDER TAX AUTHORITIES

Some older tax authorities use the administrative style of the case—the plaintiff's full name in place of the adversarial case name. In these situations, it is preferable to convert the case name to an adversarial style, such as the hypothetical *Plaintiff v. Commr.*

(U.S.T.C.), examples of which appear above under United States District Courts. Cite the official reporter when possible. Consult **Rule 12.21** for short citation formats.

Examples

Official version: *Honeywell, Inc. v. U.S.*, 64 Fed. Cl. 188, 195 (2005).

Unofficial version: *BP Exploration & Oil, Inc. v. U.S.*, 2000-1 U.S.T.C. ¶ 50,460 at 84,493 (Fed. Cl. 2000).

United States Claims Court (1982–Oct. 28, 1992)

The United States Claims Court is the predecessor to the United States Court of Federal Claims. The official reporter is the United States Claims Court Reporter (Cl. Ct.). Unofficial reporters for the court are American Federal Tax Reports (A.F.T.R., A.F.T.R.2d) and United States Tax Cases (U.S.T.C.), examples of which appear above under United States District Courts. Cite the official reporter when possible. Consult **Rule 12.21** for short citation formats.

Examples

Official version: *Shook v. U.S.*, 26 Cl. Ct. 1477 (1992).

Unofficial version: *Kircher v. U.S.*, 61 A.F.T.R.2d 88-1182, 88-1183 (Cl. Ct. 1988).

Court of Claims (1856–1982)

This court of original jurisdiction preceded the United States Claims Court. The official reporter for the Court of Claims is Court of Claims Reports (Ct. Cl.). These cases also can be found in the appropriate Federal Reporter (F., F.2d) or Federal Supplement (F. Supp.). The unofficial reporter is the United States Tax Cases (U.S.T.C.), an example of which is reprinted under United States District Courts above. Cite the official reporter when possible. Consult **Rule 12.21** for short citation formats.

Examples

Official version: *McCann v. U.S.*, 202 Ct. Cl. 611 (1981).

Unofficial version: *A.P. Green Export Co. v. U.S.*, 6 A.F.T.R.2d 5951, 5955 (Ct. Cl. 1960).

2. Appellate Courts for Federal Tax Cases

Decisions of United States District Courts and the United States Tax Court are appealed to the appropriate U.S. Court of Appeal—which cases are reported in the Federal Reporter (F., F.2d, F.3d)—and ultimately to the United States Supreme Court (U.S.). See **Rule 12.1** for information about how to cite these cases. In addition, both circuit courts of appeal and U.S. Supreme Court cases are unofficially reported by American Federal Tax Reports (A.F.T.R., A.F.T.R.2d) and United States Tax Cases (U.S.T.C.). United States Supreme Court cases are also published by the I.R.S. in its semiannual Cumulative Bulletin (C.B.) and its weekly Internal Revenue Bulletin (I.R.B.), which are described below in **7, Part C.** Cite the official reporter when possible. Consult **Rule 12.21** for short citation formats.

Examples of unofficial reporter citations

Grogan v. Garner, 70 A.F.T.R.2d 92-5639, 92-5640 (U.S. 1991).

Crisp v. U.S., 2002-2 U.S.T.C. ¶ 50,765 at 85,791 (9th Cir. 2000).

Venture Funding, Ltd. v. Commr., 99-2 U.S.T.C. ¶ 50,972 (6th Cir. 1999).

3. Unreported Opinions

Slip opinions: To cite unreported opinions available only in a separately paginated slip opinion, refer to **Rules 12.18** and **12.21(e).**

Electronic Databases: Use **Rule 38** to cite a case that is unreported but available on an electronic database like LexisNexis or Westlaw.

C. Administrative Materials

1. Administrative Announcements

Treasury Regulations (Treas. Reg.): Include the source abbreviation, section symbol followed by one space, and a section number; enclose the year of promulgation in parentheses.

The numbering scheme for final Treasury Regulations has three parts: the first number, which precedes the decimal point, represents the type of tax—for example: "1" for income tax regulations (see **Sidebar A7-3** for additional information)—the second number, which follows the decimal point, corresponds to the Internal Revenue Code section; and the third number, which follows a hyphen, corresponds to the order of codification. Treasury Regulations also may be cited to title 26 of the Code of Federal Regulations, which is discussed in **Rule 19.1.**

Examples   Treas. Reg. § 1.263(a)-4 (2004).

26 C.F.R. § 1.701-1 (2005).

Proposed Treasury Regulations (Prop. Treas. Reg.): Add "Prop." to the designation for Treasury Regulations; whenever possible, provide a parallel citation to the Federal Register, which is discussed in **Rule 19.3.** Use an exact date for proposed regulations.

Example   Prop. Treas. Reg. § 1.494-36, 70 Fed. Reg. 43811 (July 29, 2005).

Temporary Treasury Regulations (Treas. Reg.): Cite like a final Treasury Regulation, but include a "T" after the section number (but before any subsection); whenever possible, provide a parallel citation to the Federal Register, which is discussed in **Rule 19.3.**

Example   Treas. Reg. § 1.409(p)-1T (issued July 18, 2003).

2. I.R.S. Compilations

Cumulative Bulletin (C.B): The Cumulative Bulletin is published semiannually and serves as a compilation of Internal Revenue Bulletins, which are described below. The Cumulative Bulletin also contains notices of disbarment of individuals practicing before the I.R.S., as well as listings of I.R.S. acquiescence or nonacquiescence to court decisions. Additional volumes are published in years when major tax legislation is passed. **When choosing between I.R.B. and C.B., cite C.B. when possible.**

SIDEBAR A7.3

CATEGORIES OF TAX REGULATIONS

Below are the following categories of Treasury Regulations under the I.R.C. of 1986:

Income tax regulations	1.xxx
Practice before the I.R.S.	10.xxx
Disbarments and suspensions	19.xxx
Estate tax regulations	20.xxx
Gift tax regulations	25.xxx
Generation-skipping transfer tax	26.xxx
Employment tax regulations	31.xxx through 35.xxx
Contract Coverage of Employees of Foreign Subsidiaries	36.xxx
Manufacturers and Retailers Excise Tax	48.xxx
Excise taxes (miscellaneous)	51.xxx through 56.xxx
Alcohol, tobacco, and other excise taxes	156.xxx
Procedure and Administration	301.xxx
Disposition of Seized Personal Property	403.xxx
I.R.S. procedural rules	601.xxx

From **1919–1921,** citations to C.B. are to the volume number and also include the source abbreviation, an initial page number, a pinpoint page number when appropriate, and the year enclosed in parentheses.

Example 1 C.B. 25 (1919).

From **1921–1936,** citations to C.B. are to the volume and part. Also include the source abbreviation, initial page number, pinpoint page number when appropriate, and the year enclosed in parentheses.

Example 6-1 C.B. 13 (1927).

Since 1937, Cumulative Bulletins have been numbered by year and volume, separated by a hyphen. Internal Revenue Bulletins 1 through 26 are republished in the first Cumulative Bulletin (Vol. 1) each year, and Internal Revenue Bulletins 26 through 52 are republished in the second Cumulative Bulletin (Vol. 2) each year. Also include the source abbreviation, initial page number, and pinpoint page number when appropriate.

Example 2003-1 C.B. 599.

Internal Revenue Bulletin (I.R.B.): The Internal Revenue Bulletin is published weekly by the I.R.S. and contains I.R.S. pronouncements such as Revenue Rulings, Revenue Procedures, Treasury Decisions, Notices, and Announcements. It is the advance sheet for the Cumulative Bulletin. It is numbered sequentially by year and week of issue, separated by a hyphen. Also include the source abbreviation, initial page number, and pinpoint page number when appropriate.

Example 2004-6 I.R.B. 1.

Sources Not Yet Published in C.B. or I.R.B.: If a source will be published in C.B. or I.R.B., but has not yet been so published, it is appropriate to cite to an electronic database, a Web site, or another commonly available source, such as a major tax looseleaf service.

Example 2005-9 I.R.B. 630, 2005 IRB LEXIS 68.

3. Officially Published I.R.S. Pronouncements (in alphabetical order)

Announcements (I.R.S. Ann.): Cite by year and sequential and number of issue, separated by a hyphen. Provide a parallel citation to the Cumulative Bulletin (C.B.) or the Internal Revenue Bulletin (I.R.B.). It is appropriate to include an italicized title before the citation.

Examples I.R.S. Ann. 2004-54, 2004-1 C.B. 1061.

I.R.S. Ann. 2005-50, 2005-30 I.R.B. 152.

Mutual Agreement on U.K. Pension Arrangements, I.R.S. Ann. 2005-30, 2005-18 I.R.B. 988.

Acquiescence: The I.R.S. reviews tax decisions made by the courts and issues its own opinion in the Cumulative Bulletin (C.B.) and Internal Revenue Bulletin (I.R.B.) about whether it agrees with the decision. The opinion is published as either an acquiescence (*acq.,*), which means that the I.R.S. will not contest the point in later cases; a nonacquiescence (*nonacq.,*), which means that the I.R.S. will not appeal but will not follow the decision with other taxpayers; or an acquiescence in result (*acq. in result,*), in which the I.R.S. agrees with the result of the decision, but disagrees with one or more stated reasons.

Examples *Lemmen v. Commr.*, 77 T.C. 1326, 1348 (1981), *acq.*, 1983-1 C.B. 1.

Dean v. Commr., 35 T.C. 1083 (1961), *nonacq.*, 1973-2 C.B. 4.

Golden Belt Tel. Assn., Inc. v. Commr., 108 T.C. 498 (1997), *acq. in result in part*, 1998-18 I.R.B. 4 (May 4, 1998).

Delegation Orders (Deleg. Or. or D.O.): Cite by order number and, when available, revision number (Rev.). Provide a parallel citation to the Cumulative Bulletin (C.B.), the Internal Revenue Bulletin (I.R.B.), or the Federal Register (Fed. Reg.). Federal Register citations are discussed in **Rule 19.3.**

Examples Deleg. Order No. 42 (Rev. 12), 1979-2 C.B. 482.

D.O. No. 5 (Rev. 18), 2000-51 I.R.B. 587.

D.O. No. 97 (Rev. 19), 47 Fed. Reg. 19842 (May 7, 1982).

Executive Orders (I.R.S. Exec. Or. or I.R.S. E.O.): Cite by number and provide a parallel citation to the Cumulative Bulletin (C.B.) or the Internal Revenue Bulletin (I.R.B.).

Examples I.R.S. Exec. Or. 12,477, 1991-1 C.B. 31.

I.R.S. E.O. 12,403, 1983-12 I.R.B. 17.

Notices (I.R.S. Notice): Cite by year and sequential number of issue, separated by a hyphen. Provide a parallel citation to the Cumulative Bulletin (C.B.) or the Internal Revenue Bulletin (I.R.B.). It is appropriate to include an italicized title before the citation.

Examples I.R.S. Notice 99-7, 1999-1 C.B. 351.

I.R.S. Notice 2004-78, 2004-48 I.R.B. 879.

Weighted Average Interest Rate Update, I.R.S. Notice 99-7, 1999-1 C.B. 351.

Revenue Procedures (Rev. Proc.): Cite by year and sequential number of issue, separated by a hyphen. Provide a parallel citation to the Cumulative Bulletin (C.B.) or the Internal Revenue Bulletin (I.R.B.).

Examples Rev. Proc. 99-25, 1999-1 C.B. 1117.

Rev. Proc. 2005-38, 2005-28 I.R.B. 81.

Revenue Rulings (Rev. Rul.): Cite by year and sequential number of issue, separated by a hyphen. Provide a parallel citation to the Cumulative Bulletin (C.B.) or the Internal Revenue Bulletin (I.R.B.). Before 1953, rulings had different designations depending on the type of tax involved, for example, I.T. for income tax rulings and E.T. for employment tax rulings. An example of this early citation form appears below.

Examples   Rev. Rul. 2004-52, 2004-1 C.B. 973.

Rev. Rul. 99-56, 1999-1 C.B. 676, *revoking* Rev. Rul. 66-9, 1966-1 C.B. 39.

Rev. Rul. 2005-46, 2005-30 I.R.B. 120.

I.T. 3278, 1939-1 C.B. 76.

Treasury Decisions (T.D.): Proposed and final treasury regulations pertaining to tax matters are issued by the Secretary of Treasury as Treasury Decisions (T.D.). Proposed regulations are identified by a REG prefix followed by a project number. Provide a parallel citation to the weekly Internal Revenue Bulletin (I.R.B.), the semiannual Cumulative Bulletin (C.B.), Treasury Decisions under Internal Revenue Laws (Treas. Dec. Int. Rev.), or the Federal Register (Fed. Reg.). Treasury Decisions are codified in, and may be cited to, Title 26 of the Code of Federal Regulations (C.F.R.).

Examples   REG-255786-97, 1997-11 I.R.B. 19.

T.D. 9154, 2004-40 I.R.B. 560.

T.D. 8346, 1991-1 C.B. 150, 151.

T.D. 4723, 34 Treas. Dec. Int. Rev. 4 (1937).

Treasury Department Directives (Treas. Dept. Directive or T.D.D.): Cite by number and provide a parallel citation to the Cumulative Bulletin (C.B.) or the Internal Revenue Bulletin (I.R.B.).

Examples   T.D.D. 15-42, 1995-2 C.B. 459.

Treas. Dept. Directive 15-42, 1995-41 I.R.B. 32.

Treasury Department Orders (Treas. Dept. Or. or T.D.O.): Cite by order number and prove a parallel citation to the Cumulative Bulletin (C.B.) or the Internal Revenue Bulletin (I.R.B.).

Examples   T.D.O. No. 150-02, 1994-1 C.B. 721.

Treas. Dept. Or. No. 150-01, 1995-44 I.R.B. 23.

Other sources: For other officially published sources, include the type of document and document number. Also provide a parallel citation to the Cumulative Bulletin (C.B.) or the Internal Revenue Bulletin (I.R.B.). Analogize to the most similar source listed above.

Example for a Treasury Department Circular

Treas. Dept. Circular No. 848 (Rev. 2), 1958-2 C.B. 1086.

Example for a Mimeograph

Mim. 6583, 1951-1 C.B. 97.

4. Publicly Released I.R.S. Pronouncements (listed alphabetically)

Actions on Decisions (Action on Decision or A.O.D.): Cite by year and three-digit sequential order of issuance, separated by a hyphen; enclose the exact date of issue in parentheses. It is appropriate to provide a parallel citation to an electronic database, Web site, or looseleaf service. It is also appropriate to cite an action on decision as subsequent history to a court decision (**Rules 12.8** and **12.10**).

Examples   A.O.D. 84-022 (Feb. 2, 1984).

Action on Decision 2005-01 (June 7, 2005), 2005 WL 1331108.

A.O.D. 2000-008 (Oct. 30, 2000), 2000 AOD LEXIS 8.

Action on Decision 2000-20, Daily Tax Rep. (BNA) L3 (Apr. 28, 2000).

Keller v. Commr., 79 T.C. 7 (1982), Action on Decision 84-037 (Apr. 23, 1984).

Chief Counsel Advice Memoranda (Chief Couns. Advice or C.C.A.): Cite by year followed by a hyphen, week of issue followed by a hyphen, and three-digit sequential number of issue; enclose the exact date of issue in parentheses. It is appropriate to provide a parallel citation to an electronic database, Web site, or looseleaf service.

Examples   Chief Couns. Advice 2005-29-007 (June 7, 2005).

C.C.A. 2001-19-054 (May 11, 2001), 2001 WL 499979.

C.C.A. 2001-17-034 (Apr. 27, 2001), 2001 IRS CCA LEXIS 23.

SIDEBAR A7.4

DOCUMENT NUMBERS BEFORE AND AFTER 2000

Before 2000, many tax sources are numbered using **two** initial digits, such as 87- or 99-. After 2000, many tax sources are numbered using **four** digits, such as 2000- or 2001-.

Chief Counsel Memoranda (Chief Couns. Mem. or C.C.M.): Cite these memoranda using the examples for General Counsel Memoranda below.

Chief Counsel Notices (Chief Couns. Notice or C.C.N.): Cite by number and enclose the exact date of issue in parentheses. The current numbering system consists of the letters CC followed by a hyphen, the fiscal year followed by a hyphen, and the three-digit sequential number of the notice. The numbering was different before fiscal year 2001, and is illustrated below. It is appropriate to provide a parallel citation to an electronic database, Web site, or looseleaf service.

Examples   Chief Couns. Notice CC-2001-001 (Dec. 19, 2000), 2000 IRS Chief Counsel Notice LEXIS 53.

C.C.N. CC-2002-021 (Mar. 15, 2002), 2002 IRS Chief Counsel Notice LEXIS 5.

Collection, Bankruptcy, and Summonses Bulletins (C.B.S.): Cite by year followed by a hyphen, week of issue followed by a hyphen, and a three-digit sequential identifier number. Alternatively, C.B.S. may be cited by bulletin number. If citing by bulletin number, enclose the date of issue in parentheses. It is appropriate to provide a parallel citation to an electronic database, Web site, or looseleaf service. C.B.S. started in July 2000 with No. 478; before this time they were referred to as General Litigation Bulletins (see below). C.B.S. was discontinued in January 2002.

Examples   C.B.S. 2001-17-035, 2001 WL 429799 (IRS LB).

C.B.S. No. 480 (Sept. 2000).

C.B.S. No. 483 (Jan. 2001), *available at* http://www.irs.gov/news/efoia/ccbull.html.

Criminal Tax Bulletin (Crim. Tax Bull. or C.T.B.): Cite by year followed by a hyphen, the week of issue followed by a hyphen, and the three-digit sequential identifier number. It is appropriate to provide a parallel citation to an electronic database, Web site, or looseleaf service.

Examples   C.T.B. 2000-07-033, 2001 WL 128984.

Crim. Tax Bull. 2000-07-002, 1999 IRS CTB LEXIS 1.

Disclosure Litigation Bulletin (Disclosure Litig. Bull. or D.L.B.): Cite by year and number, separated by a hyphen; enclose the month and year of issue in parentheses. It is appropriate to provide a parallel citation to an electronic database, Web site, or looseleaf service.

Examples   D.L.B. No. 97-3 (July 1997), 1997 IRS DLB LEXIS 3.

Disclosure Litig. Bull. No. 2000-3, *available at* http://www.irs.gov/news/efoia/ccbull.html.

Field Service Advice (Field Service Advice or F.S.A.): Cite by year followed by a hyphen, week of issue followed by a hyphen, and three-digit sequential number of issue; enclose the exact date of issue in parentheses. It is appropriate to provide a parallel citation to an electronic database, Web site, or looseleaf service.

Examples   Field Service Advice 2001-19-001 (May 11, 2001).

F.S.A. 2004-09-001 (Feb. 27, 2004), 2004 WL 363847.

F.S.A. 2002-38-045 (Sept. 20, 2002), 2002 FSA LEXIS 74.

General Counsel Memoranda (Gen. Couns. Mem. or G.C.M.): These memoranda are numbered sequentially but without reference to the year of issue; enclose the exact date of issue in parentheses. It is appropriate to provide a parallel citation to an electronic database, Web site, or looseleaf service.

Examples   Gen. Couns. Mem. 39,892 (Nov. 26, 2002), 2002 IRS GCM LEXIS 1

G.C.M. 39,719 (Mar. 30, 1988), 1988 WL 567295.

General Litigation Bulletin (Gen. Litig. Bull. or G.L.B.): Cite by sequential number and enclose the date in parentheses. It is appropriate to provide a parallel citation to an electronic database, Web site, or looseleaf service. These bulletins end in July 2000 with No. 477; they are now called Collection, Bankruptcy, and Summonses Bulletins (see above).

Examples   G.L.B. No. 458 (Nov. 1998).

Gen. Litig. Bull. No. 463 (July 23, 1999), 1999 GLB LEXIS 6.

Information Letters (Info. Ltr.): Include the year and sequential number of issue, separated by a hyphen; enclose the exact date of issue in parentheses. It is appropriate to provide a parallel citation to an electronic database, Web site, or looseleaf service.

Example   Info. Ltr. 2005-0063 (June 30, 2005), 2005 WL 1564559.

Internal Revenue Manual (I.R.M.): The I.R.M. is cited in decimal format. The first digit is the part number, the second number is the chapter number, the third number is the section number, and the fourth number is the subsection number. Sub-subsections are set off by an additional decimal. If citing the official version published by the I.R.S., enclose the year of issue in parentheses. If citing an unofficial version, include the publisher and the year of publication. Use **Rule 42** to cite a CD-ROM version; use **Rule 35** to cite a microfiche version.

Examples   I.R.M. 5.7.5 (1996) (CD-ROM).

I.R.M. 5.7.5.4 (RIA 2001).

I.R.M. 3.0.167 (LEXIS current through June 7, 2005).

I.R.M. 9.2.1, *available at* http://www.irs.treasury.gov/prod/bus_info/ tax_prof/irm-part/part09/36231.htm (accessed May 22, 2005).

Litigation Guideline Memoranda (Litig. Guide. Mem. or L.G.M.): Cite by tax litigation (TL) or general litigation (GL) designation and by number, separated by a hyphen; enclose the exact date in parentheses. It is appropriate to provide a parallel citation to an electronic database, Web site, or looseleaf service.

Examples   L.G.M. TL-104 (Sept. 18, 1998).

Litig. Guide. Mem. GL-36 (Apr. 24, 1998), 1998 WL 1757110.

Litig. Guide. Mem. TL-82 (Jan. 5, 1990), 1990 IRS LGM LEXIS 32.

News Releases (I.R.S. News Rel.): Cite by year and sequential release number, separated by a hyphen; enclose the exact date in parentheses. It is appropriate to include the title of the release in italics and to provide a parallel citation to an electronic database, Web site, or looseleaf service. Before 1976, news releases were called Technical Information Releases (see below).

Examples   I.R.S. News Rel. 2005-76 (July 25, 2005).

E-Filing Running at Record Pace, I.R.S. News Rel. 2005-21 (Mar. 2, 2005), 2005 WL 475112.

Private Letter Rulings (Priv. Ltr. Rul. or P.L.R.): Cite by year followed by a hyphen, the week of release followed by a hyphen, and the three-digit sequential item number for the week; enclose the exact date of issue in parentheses. It is appropriate to provide a parallel citation to an electronic database, Web site, or looseleaf service.

Examples   Priv. Ltr. Rul. 90-31-022 (May 7, 1990).

Priv. Ltr. Rul. 2005-29-001 (July 22, 2005), 2005 WL 1707488.

P.L.R. 2002-38-051 (June 28, 2002), 2002 PLR LEXIS 853.

Service Center Advice (Serv. Center Advice or S.C.A.): Cite by year followed by a hyphen, the week of release followed by a hyphen, and the three-digit item number for the week; enclose the exact date of issue in parentheses. It is appropriate to provide a parallel citation to an electronic database, Web site, or looseleaf service.

Examples   Serv. Center Advice 2001-14-033 (Apr. 6, 2001).

S.C.A. 2005-04-033 (Jan. 28, 2005), 2005 WL 190327.

S.C.A. 2002-39-029 (Aug. 23, 2002), 2002 SCA LEXIS 18.

Serv. Center Advice 2001-19-013, *available at* http://www.irs.gov/news/efoia/sca.html.

Tax Litigation Bulletin (Tax Litig. Bull. or T.L.B.): Cite by year and number, separated by a hyphen; enclose the exact date of issue in parentheses. It is appropriate to provide a parallel citation to an electronic database, Web site, or looseleaf service.

Examples   Tax Litig. Bull. No. 96-5 (Mar. 21, 1996).

T.L.B. 92-11 (Nov. 1992), 1992 IRS TLB LEXIS 23.

Technical Advice Memoranda (Tech. Adv. Mem. or T.A.M.): Cite by year followed by a hyphen, the week of release followed by a hyphen, and the three-digit sequential item number for the week; enclose the exact date of issue in parentheses. It is appropriate to provide a parallel citation to an electronic database, Web site, or looseleaf service.

Examples   Tech. Adv. Mem. 87-14-008 (Dec. 17, 1986).

T.A.M. 2005-28-026 (July 15, 2005), 2005 WL 1657282.

Technical Information Releases (Tech. Info. Rel. or T.I.R.): See News Releases above for additional information.

Example   T.I.R. 55-109, 1955-1 C.B. 139.

Technical Memoranda (Tech. Mem. or T.M.): No numbering system is used for these memoranda, so they should be cited by their Westlaw or LexisNexis unique identifier. If available, enclose the exact date of issue in parentheses.

Examples   2002 TM LEXIS 11 (June 25, 2002).

Tech. Mem., 1980 WL 140722.

Written Determinations (Written Determ.): Cite by year followed by a hyphen, week of issue followed by a hyphen, and three-digit sequential order of issue; enclose the exact date of issue in parentheses. It is appropriate to provide a parallel citation to an electronic database, Web site, or looseleaf service.

Example   Written Determ. 2001-20-028 (May 18, 2001), *available at* http://www.irs.gov/news/efoia/determine.html.

Other sources: For other publicly released I.R.S. pronouncements, cite the type of document, using any abbreviations above or in **Appendix 3,** and the number used on the face of the document. When possible, enclose the exact date in parentheses and provide a parallel citation to an electronic or commonly available source.

5. Taxpayer Forms and Publications

Taxpayer Forms (I.R.S. Form): Cite by number. For forms that are issued or revised annually, enclose the year in parentheses. For forms that are not issued or revised annually, enclose the date of last revision in parentheses, preceded by the term "last rev." It is appropriate to include an italicized title before the citation.

Examples   I.R.S. Form 1040 (2006).

I.R.S. Form 1040 sched. R (2006).

I.R.S. Form 1001 (last rev. July 1998).

Cancellation of Debt Statement, IRS Form 1099-C (2005).

Taxpayer Publications (I.R.S. Pub.): Cite by italicized title, I.R.S. publication number, pinpoint page if available, and year. It is appropriate to provide a parallel citation to an electronic database, Web site, or looseleaf service.

Examples   *Tax Guide for Individuals*, I.R.S. Pub. No. 17, at 31 (1998).

Business Expenses, I.R.S. Pub. 535 (2000), 2000 WL 1742834.

CHART A7.1

ABBREVIATIONS FOR LESS FREQUENTLY CITED TAX MATERIALS

Alcohol Tax Unit	A.T.
Appeals and Review Memoranda	A.R.M., App. & Rev. Mem.
Capital Stock Tax Rulings	C.S.T.
Estate Tax Rulings	E.T.
Excess Profits Tax Council Ruling	E.P.C.
General Counsel Orders	G.C.O., Gen. Couns. Or.
Income Tax Unit Rulings	I.T.
Law Opinions	L.O., Law Op.
Mimeographs	Mim.
Reorganization Orders	R.O., Reorg. Or.
Sales Tax Rulings	S.T.
Social Security Tax Rulings	S.S.T.
Treasury Department Circular	D.C., Treas. Dept. Circular

APPENDIX 8
SELECTED OFFICIAL FEDERAL ADMINISTRATIVE PUBLICATIONS

This appendix lists major official federal administrative publications and their abbreviations. For a comprehensive Web site that contains many federal agency decisions, visit Washburn University School of Law, *WashLaw Collection of Agency Decisions,* http://www.washlaw.edu/doclaw/executive5m.html#arms.

Publication	Dates	Abbreviation
Administrative Decisions under Immigration and Nationality Laws	1940–present	I. & N. Dec.
Agriculture Decisions	1942–present	Agric. Dec.
Atomic Energy Commission Reports	1956–1975	A.E.C.
Civil Aeronautics Board Reports	1940–1984	C.A.B.
Copyright Decisions	1909–1985	Copy. Dec.
Cumulative Bulletin	1919–present	C.B.
Customs Bulletin and Decisions	1967–present	Cust. Bull. & Dec.
Decisions and Orders of the National Labor Relations Board	1935–present	N.L.R.B.
Decisions of the Commissioner of Patents	1869–1968	Dec. Commr. Pats.
Decisions of the Comptroller General	1921–1994	Comptr. Gen.
Decisions of the Department of the Interior	1930–present	Interior Dec.
Decisions of the Employees' Compensation Appeals Board	1947–present	Empl. Comp. App. Bd.
Decisions of the Federal Labor Relations Authority	1979–present	F.L.R.A.
Decisions of the United States Merit Systems Protection Board	1979–present	Merit Sys. Dec.
Determinations of the National Mediation Board	1934–present	Natl. Med. Bd.
Equal Opportunity Employment Commission Decisions	1984–present	E.E.O.C. Dec.
Federal Communications Commission Record	1986–present	F.C.C. Rec.
Federal Energy Guidelines	1977–present	F.E.R.C.
Federal Mine Safety and Health Review Commission	1979–present	F.M.S.H.R.C.
Federal Power Commission Reports	1931–1977	F.P.C.

Publication	Dates	Abbreviation
Federal Reserve Bulletin	1915–present	Fed. Res. Bull.
Federal Trade Commission Decisions	1915–present	F.T.C.
Food and Drug Administration Enforcement Reports	1990–present	F.D.A. Enforc. Rpts.
Interstate Commerce Commission Reports	1887–1995	I.C.C., I.C.C.2d
National Transportation Safety Board Decisions	1967–1977	N.T.S.B.
Nuclear Regulatory Commission Issuances	1975–present	N.R.C.
Occupational Safety and Health Administration and Occupational Safety and Health Review	1971–present	O.S.H.A.
Official Gazette of the United States Patent Office	1892–present	Off. Gaz. Pat. Off.
Securities and Exchange Commission Decisions and Reports	1934–present	SEC
Social Security Rulings, Cumulative Edition	1960–present	S.S.R.

INDEX

Unless otherwise noted, references are to rule numbers.